TEMPLE RESTORATION IN EARLY ACHAEMENID JUDAH

SUPPLEMENTS

TO THE

JOURNAL FOR THE STUDY
OF JUDAISM

Editor

JOHN J. COLLINS

Divinity School, Yale University

Associate Editor

FLORENTINO GARCÍA MARTÍNEZ

Qumran Institute, University of Groningen

Advisory Board

P.ALEXANDER – J. DUHAIME – A. HILHORST
M.A. KNIBB – J.T.A.G.M. VAN RUITEN – J. SIEVERS
G. STEMBERGER – J. TROMP – A.S. VAN DER WOUDE

VOLUME 65

TEMPLE RESTORATION
IN
EARLY ACHAEMENID JUDAH

BY

PETER ROSS BEDFORD

BRILL
LEIDEN · BOSTON · KÖLN
2001

This book is printed on acid-free paper.

Library of Congress Cataloging-in Publication data

DS
109.3
.B43
2001

Bedford, Peter Ross, 1957-
 Temple restoration in early Achaemenid Judah / by Peter Ross Bedford.
  p.   cm. — (Supplements to the journal for the study of Judaism,
  ISSN 1384-2161 ; v. 65)
 Includes bibliographical references and index.
 ISBN 9004115099 (cloth : alk. paper)
  1. Temple of Jerusalem (Jerusalem)—History. 2. Jews—History—568
B.C.-70 A.D. 3. Achaemenid dynasty, 559-330 B.C. 4. Bible. O.T. Ezra
I-VI—History of Biblical events. I. Title. II. Series.

DS109.3 .B43   2000
956.94'42—dc21
                                                        00–050734
                                                             CIP

Die Deutsche Bibliothek – CIP-Einheitsaufnahme

Bedford, Peter Ross:
Temple restoration in early Achaemenid Judah / by Peter Ross Bedford.
 – Leiden ; Boston; Köln : Brill, 2000
   (Supplements to the journal for the study of judaism ; Vol. 65)
   ISBN 90–04–11509–9

ISSN   1384-2161
ISBN   90 04 11509 9

For Kerry Maree,

my love

CONTENTS

ACKNOWLEDGMENTS ix

ABBREVIATIONS xi

I. INTRODUCTION 1

The Jerusalem Temple of Yahweh in Achaemenid
  Judah: Issues, Sources and Recent Interpretations 1
  Issues 1
  Sources and Recent Interpretations 7
Scope of the Present Study 27

II. LIVING WITHOUT THE JERUSALEM TEMPLE—
  IN JUDAH AND BABYLONIA 41

Judean Communities in Judah and Babylonia 42
Restoration Hopes and the Reformulation of
  Royal-State Ideology 63

III. REBUILDING THE JERUSALEM TEMPLE OF
  YAHWEH IN ACHAEMENID JUDAH I:
  THE REIGN OF CYRUS II 85

The Ezra Narrative 87
The Cyrus Edicts 111
  The Hebrew Edict 114
  The Aramaic Edict 129
The Policy of Cyrus 132
Between Cyrus and Darius: Explaining the Delay
  in Rebuilding 157
Summary 180

IV. REBUILDING THE JERUSALEM TEMPLE OF
    YAHWEH IN ACHAEMENID JUDAH II: THE
    REIGN OF DARIUS I 183

    Temple Rebuilding as an Achaemenid Persian
      Initiative 185
        The Meyerses 185
        J. P. Weinberg 207
    Temple Rebuilding as a Judean Initiative 230
        Temple Rebuilding as an Act of Judean
          Rebellion 230
        Ideology for Temple Rebuilding 237
            Haggai 238
            Zechariah 254
        Temple Rebuilding as an Act of Political
          Legitimation and Social Integration 264
            Haggai and Zechariah as "Millenarian"
              Prophets 264
            The Timing of the Rebuilding and the
              Identity of the Supporters of the
              Rebuilding 270
            The Participation of Zerubbabel and Joshua
              in the Temple Rebuilding 292
        Summary 298

V. CONCLUSION 301

BIBLIOGRAPHY 311

INDEX OF MODERN AUTHORS 347

INDEX OF BIBLICAL REFERENCES 353

INDEX OF OTHER ANCIENT SOURCES 367

ACKNOWLEDGMENTS

This volume is a slightly revised, and at a few points expanded, version of a Ph.D. dissertation accepted by the Department of Near Eastern Languages and Civilizations, The University of Chicago, in February 1992. The dissertation was supervised by the late Gösta W. Ahlström, with Dennis G. Pardee and Matthew W. Stolper serving on the committee. It was written at Chicago's Oriental Institute in fulfilment of the requirements for the History of Ancient Syria-Palestine programme established by Gösta Ahlström. This programme reflected Ahlström's commitment to studying the history of ancient Israel and Judah as part of Syro-Palestinian history and, more broadly, as a branch of ancient Near Eastern history. Ahlström's reputation for an independent, critical cast of mind was well deserved and he stimulated generations of students. I am grateful to have been one of those students. There are many arguments in the following pages he vigorously debated with me, and I know we would have greatly enjoyed continuing the discussion had it not unfortunately been cut short. I hope that in any case he might have detected his influence on this study and not have been displeased.

At the Oriental Institute I was fortunate to have studied not only with Professors Ahlström, Pardee and Stolper, but also with Lawrence E. Stager, Walter Farber, Robert Biggs, J. A. Brinkman, Martha Roth, Sam Wolfe, McGuire Gibson, Gene Gragg, Richard Beal, and Mario Liverani. For comments on the dissertation I am grateful to Diana V. Edelman, John J. Collins and, especially, Matthew Stolper for a particularly close reading. I was able to discuss some of the points raised here with Sara Japhet and Israel Eph'al during the 1993–94 academic year when I was a Golda Meir Postdoctoral Fellow at the Institute of Jewish Studies, The Hebrew University of Jerusalem. I want to thank both of them for their hospitality, collegiality and encouragement, especially Sara Japhet who acted as my sponsor for the fellowship. My thanks also to the Australian Friends of the Hebrew University for their financial support of the fellowship programme. It goes without saying that none of those named above is necessarily in agreement with the arguments presented here; indeed, I expect there is much at which they are likely to demur.

I have been able to take account of only a portion of the burgeoning secondary literature published in the past few years on the Achaemenid Persian empire, Achaemenid Judah, and Judaism in the Persian period. Despite the delay in its appearance, I was persuaded by John Collins and Ed Conrad that the study still had something to contribute to current discussions. Were it not for them the manuscript would still be languishing in my desk draw. They of course should not be held responsible for shortcomings in the final product. I owe a further debt of gratitude to John Collins for accepting the work for publication in this series and for sage editorial advice during its preparation.

I would also like to thank my friends in Chicago for their support over many years of graduate school (and after): Joe Manning, the Manning family, Steven N. Sachman and the Sachman family, Walter and Gertrud Farber. In Australia, my teachers in Semitic Studies at Sydney University, Alan D. Crown and the late W. J. (Bill) Jobling, gave every encouragement. My parents and my wife's parents offered loving support and, at times, much needed financial assistance. Kerry Maree, my wife, put her own career on hold for a number of years and permitted social and family dislocation in order to facilitate my studies. Her graciousness and long-suffering in the face of personal adversity, while living in a foreign country no less, is testament to the quality of her character. I consider myself most fortunate that she shares her life with me.

P. R. Bedford
Perth, Western Australia
March, 2000

ABBREVIATIONS

AASOR	Annual of the American Schools of Oriental Research
AB	Anchor Bible
ABR	*Australian Biblical Review*
AcIr	Acta Iranica
AcAnt	*Acta antiqua*
AfO	*Achiv für Orientforschung*
AGAJU	Arbeiten zur Geschichte des antiken Judentums und des Urchristentums
AJSL	*American Journal of Semitic Languages and Literature*
AnBi	Analecta biblica
ANET	*Ancient Near Eastern Texts* (3rd ed.; ed. J. B. Pritchard; Princeton: Princeton University Press, 1969)
AOAT	Alter Orient und Altes Testament
AP	A. Cowley, *Aramaic Papyri of the Fifth Century B.C.* (Oxford: Clarendon, 1923)
ASOR	American Schools of Oriental Research
ATD	Das Alte Testament Deutsch
AUSS	*Andrews University Seminary Studies*
BA	*Biblical Archaeologist*
BASOR	*Bulletin of the American Schools of Oriental Research*
BBB	Bonner Biblischer Beiträge
BEATAJ	Beiträge zur Erforschung des Alten Testaments und des antiken Judentums
BETL	Bibliotheca ephemeridum theologicarum lovaniensium
BHS	*Biblia hebraica stuttgartensia*
BKAT	Biblischer Kommentar. Altes Testament
BiOr	*Bibliotheca orientalis*
BSOAS	*Bulletin of the School of Oriental and African Studies*
BWANT	Beiträge zur Wissenschaft vom Alten und Neuen Testament
BZ	*Biblische Zeitschrift*
BZAW	Beihefte zur *Zeitschrift für die alttestamentlichen Wissenschaft*
CAD	*The Assyrian Dictionary of the Oriental Institute of the University of Chicago*
CAH	*Cambridge Ancient History*

CHJ	*Cambridge History of Judaism* (3 vols.; ed. W. D. Davies, L. Finkelstein et al.; Cambridge: Cambridge University Press, 1984–99)
CBQ	*Catholic Biblical Quarterly*
CRAIBL	*Comptes rendus de l'Académie des inscriptions et belles-lettres*
CR:BS	*Currents in Research: Biblical Studies*
ConBOT	Coniectanea Biblica. Old Testament Series
EPROER	Études preliminaires au religions orientales dans l'empire romain
EThL	*Ephemerides theologicae lovanienses*
FRLANT	Forschungen zur Religion und Literatur des Alten und Neuen Testaments
HAT	Handbuch zum Alten Testament
HSM	Harvard Semitic Monographs
HUCA	*Hebrew Union College Annual*
ICC	International Critical Commentary
IEJ	*Israel Exploration Journal*
JA	*Journal asiatique*
JANES	*Journal of the Ancient Near Eastern Society of Columbia University*
JAOS	*Journal of the American Oriental Society*
JBL	*Journal of Biblical Literature*
JEA	*Journal of Egyptian Archaeology*
JESHO	*Journal of the Economic and Social History of the Orient*
JNES	*Journal of Near Eastern Studies*
JNSL	*Journal of Northwest Semitic Languages*
JSJ	*Journal for the Study of Judaism in the Persian, Hellenistic and Roman Period*
JSOT	*Journal for the Study of the Old Testament*
JSOTSup	*Journal for the Study of the Old Testament* Supplement Series
JSS	*Journal of Semitic Studies*
JTS	*Journal of Theological Studies*
KAI	*Kanaanäische und aramäische Inschriften* (3 vols.; 2d ed.; ed. H. Donner and W. Röllig; Wiesbaden: Harrassowitz, 1969–73)
KAT	Kommentar zum Alten Testament
NCB	New Century Bible Commentary
NICOT	New International Commentary on the Old Testament
NS	New Series
OBO	Orbis Biblicus et Orientalis
OLA	Orientalia Lovaniensia Analecta

OLP	*Orientalia lovaniensia periodica*
OLZ	*Orientalische Literaturzeitung*
Or	*Orientalia*
OTL	Old Testament Library
OTS	Oudtestamentische Studiën
PEQ	*Palestine Exploration Quarterly*
RA	*Revue d'assyriologie et d'archéologie orientale*
RB	*Revue biblique*
SBLDS	Society of Biblical Literature Dissertation Series
SBLMS	Society of Biblical Literature Monograph Series
SJLA	Studies in Judaism in Late Antiquity
SJOT	*Scandinavian Journal of the Old Testament*
SEÅ	*Svensk Exegetisk Årsbok*
TLZ	*Theologische Literaturzeitung*
Transeu	*Transeuphratène*
TWAT	*Theologisches Wörterbuch zum Alten Testament* (ed. G. J. Botterweck and H. Ringgren; Stuttgart: Kohlhammer, 1970–)
TynB	*Tyndale Bulletin*
VAB	Vorderasiatische Bibliothek
VT	*Vetus Testamentum*
VTSup	*Vetus Testamentum*, Supplements
WdO	*Die Welt des Orients*
WMANT	Wissenschaftliche Monographien zum Alten und Neuen Testament
ZA	*Zeitschrift für Assyriologie*
ZABR	*Zeitschrift für altorientalische und biblische Rechtsgeschichte*
ZAW	*Zeitschrift für die alttestamentlichen Wissenschaft*
ZDPV	*Zeitschrift des Deutschen Palästina-Vereins*
ZThK	*Zeitschrift für Theologie und Kirche*

CHAPTER ONE

INTRODUCTION

The Jerusalem Temple of Yahweh in Achaemenid Judah:
Issues, Sources and Recent Interpretations

Issues

The invasion of Judah in 588–587 was the second undertaken by Nebuchadrezzar to quash Judean rebellion since Jehoiakim of Judah had become a Babylonian vassal around 604/3.[1] It effectively eradicated the kingdom of Judah. Jerusalem, the capital city, was captured and at least partially destroyed. Zedekiah, a member of the Judean royal house whom Nebuchadrezzar had installed as king after the first Babylonian invasion in 597, was blinded and carried off to Babylon, together with the sacred temple vessels. Certain Judean notables were taken for summary trial and execution, while the remainder of the inhabitants of Jerusalem, as well as other segments of the population (priests, royal advisors and officials, aristocrats, craftsmen), were deported to Babylonia (II Ki 24:20b–25:24). The kingship was dissolved and Judah absorbed into the Babylonian provincial system. A governor, a Judean named Gedaliah, was appointed with his seat of government moved from Jerusalem to Mizpah.[2]

---

[1] All dates are B.C.E.

[2] On the last years of the kingdom of Judah (609–587/6), see A. Malamat, "The Twilight of Judah: In the Egyptian-Babylonian Maelstrom," in *Congress Volume: Edinburgh 1974* (ed. J. A. Emerton; VTSup 28; Leiden: E. J. Brill, 1975) 123–45; idem, "The Last Years of the Kingdom of Judah," in *The Age of the Monarchies: Political History* (ed. A. Malamat; World History of the Jewish People First Series: Ancient Times 4/1; Jerusalem: Massada, 1979) 205–22; B. Oded, "Judah and the Exile. §5 The last days of Judah and the destruction of Jerusalem (609–586 B.C.E.)," in *Israelite and Judean History* (ed. J. H. Hayes and J. M. Miller; OTL; London: SCM, 1977) 469–76; G. W. Ahlström, *The History of Ancient Palestine from the Palaeolithic Period to Alexander's Conquest* (with a contribution by G. O. Rollefson; ed. D. Edelman; JSOTSup 146; Sheffield: JSOT Press, 1993) 781–803. The date of the destruction of Jerusalem remains disputed; see the discussion in H. Cazelles, "587 ou 586," in *The Word of the Lord Shall Go Forth* (ed. C. L. Meyers and M. O'Connor; Winona Lake, IN: Eisenbrauns/ASOR, 1983) 427–35; J. Hughes, *Secrets of the Times: Myth and History in Biblical Chronology* (JSOTSup 66; Sheffield: Sheffield Academic Press,

Judah's experience was by no means unique. During the early to mid-first millennium all the independent Syro-Palestinian states suffered political extinction at the hands of either Assyria (which extended its hegemony over the whole region during the early ninth to late seventh centuries, incorporating the Syrian kingdoms, the northern Phoenician cities, Israel and the southern Palestinian coast into its provincial system) or Babylonia (which in the early sixth century expanded the provincial system inherited from Assyria to include the southern Palestinian states and Tyre).[3] Sections of the population of these states were deported and, in the Assyrian period at least, replaced by peoples from other areas of the empire.[4] Among the Syro-Palestinian states Judah proves to be of particular interest since extant texts afford some insight into indigenous reactions to the loss of statehood and exile, as well as revealing something of the territory's continued existence within the Babylonian and, later, Achaemenid Persian provincial administrative systems.

A significant development in Judah under the Achaemenid Persian administration was the reconstruction of the temple of Yahweh in Jerusalem. It is notable because this temple formerly had been the preeminent national shrine in the kingdom of Judah.[5] Built and main-

---

1990) 229–32. Both Cazelles and Hughes argue for 587 as the date for the destruction of Jerusalem and this is adopted in the present study. In support of the 586 date, see G. Galil, "The Babylonian Calendar and the Chronology of the Last Kings of Judah," *Biblica* 72 (1991) 367–78.

[3] On Assyrian involvement in Syria-Palestine, see J. D. Hawkins, "The Neo-Hittite States in Syria and Anatolia," in *CAH* (2d ed.; ed. J. Boardman et al.; Cambridge: Cambridge University Press, 1970–) 3/1. 388–435 (with bibliography); J. M. Miller and J. H. Hayes, *A History of Ancient Israel and Judah* (Philadelphia: Westminster Press, 1986) 314–76; Ahlström, *History of Ancient Palestine*, 601–753. On the Babylonian period, see the articles cited in note 2 above and also E. F. Weidner, "Jojachin, König von Juda, in babylonischen Keilinschrifttexten," in *Mélanges Syriens offerts à M. René Dussaud* (2 vols.; Bibliothèque archéologie et histoire 30/1–2; Paris: Guethner, 1939) 2. 923–35; J. Lindsay, "The Babylonian Kings and Edom, 605–550 B.C.," *PEQ* 108 (1976) 23–39; Ahlström, *History of Ancient Palestine*, 781–811; A. Lemaire, "Les transformations politiques et culturelles de la Transjordanie au VIe siècle av. J.-C.," *Transeu* 8 (1994) 9–27; H. J. Katzenstein, *The History of Tyre. From the Beginning of the Second Millennium B.C.E. until the Fall of the Neo-Babylonian Empire in 538 B.C.E.* (2d ed.; Beer Sheva: Ben-Gurion University of the Negev, 1997) 295–347.

[4] For Assyrian deportation practices, see B. Oded, *Mass Deportation and Deportees in the Neo-Assyrian Empire* (Wiesbaden: Reichert, 1979). The Babylonians do not appear to have resettled Palestine with peoples from elsewhere in the empire.

[5] Judah is emphasized here for although this temple probably served for a time as the national shrine of the united kingdom of Israel under Solomon and, briefly, Rehoboam, for the most part it functioned within the kingdom of Judah. On the architecture of the temple, our understanding of which is derived from I Ki 6;

tained by Judean kings, it had been a monarchical institution which served both to legitimate the political order and as an arm of state administration.[6] Judean royal-state ideology had averred that Jerusalem was the divinely chosen abode of Yahweh on earth. Situated on the acropolis of Jerusalem, beside the king's own residence, the temple was the national deity's "palace" from which he ruled over the people and territory of Judah. It symbolized the deity's presence in the state, ensuring divine management of the political order and the population's well-being. Since Yahweh's kingship over Judah was predicated on his position as creator and sustainer of the cosmos and the lord of all gods, the temple was also the symbol of Yahweh's cosmic kingship.[7] His kingship brought order to the cosmos; an order

7:13–22 (cf. II Chrons 3; Ezek 40:48–41:15a) and parallels with Semitic temples, see the extensive discussion in the first volume of Th. A. Busink, *Der Tempel von Jerusalem von Salomo bis Herodes. Eine archälogisch-historische Studie unter Berücksichtigung des westsemitischen Tempelbaus* (2 vols.; Nederlands Instituut voor het Nabije Oosten/Studia Francisci Scholten Memoriae Dicta 3; Leiden: E. J. Brill, 1970–80).

[6] J. M. Lundquist, "The Legitimating Role of the Temple in the Origin of the State," in *Society of Biblical Literature 1982 Seminar Papers* (ed. K. H. Richards; Chico, CA: Scholars Press/The Society of Biblical Literature, 1982) 271–97; G. W. Ahlström, *Royal Administration and National Religion in Ancient Palestine* (Studies in the History of the Ancient Near East 1; Leiden: E. J. Brill, 1982).

[7] On temple ideology, see M. Metzger, "Himmlische und irdische Wohnstatt Jahwehs," *Ugarit-Forschungen* 2 (1970) 139–58, especially pp. 141–44; R. J. Clifford, *The Cosmic Mountain in Canaan and the Old Testament* (HSM 4; Cambridge, MA: Harvard University Press, 1972) 131–81; G. W. Ahlström, "Heaven on Earth—at Hazor and Arad," in *Religious Syncretism in Antiquity* (ed. B. A. Pierson; Missoula, MT: Scholars Press, 1975) 67–83; J. Lundquist, "The Common Temple Ideology of the Ancient Near East," in *The Temple in Antiquity: Ancient Records and Modern Perspectives* (ed. T. G. Madsen; Religious Studies Center Monograph Series 9; Provo: Brigham Young University Press, 1984) 53–76; T. N. D. Mettinger, "YHWH Sabaoth—The Heavenly King on the Cherubim Throne," in *Studies in the Period of David and Solomon and Other Studies* (ed. T. Ishida; Winona Lake, IN: Eisenbrauns, 1982) 109–38; O. Keel, *The Symbolism of the Biblical World: Ancient Near Eastern Iconography and the Book of Psalms* (trans. T. J. Hallett; New York: Crossroad, 1985) 113–20, 171–76; E. Bloch-Smith, "'Who is the King of Glory?' Solomon's Temple and its Symbolism," in *Scripture and Other Artifacts: Essays on the Bible and Archaeology in Honor of Philip J. King* (ed. M. D. Coogan, J. C. Exum and L. E. Stager; Louisville: Westminster/John Knox Press, 1994), 18–33.

The kingship of Yahweh and the establishment of his throne in Zion (Jerusalem) are described in Judean cultic poetry largely in mythic or cosmological terms. The major sources are the *Yahweh mālak* Psalms (the so-called "enthronement" Psalms; Pss 29, 47, 93, 96–99), which extol Yahweh's kingship, and the Psalms of Zion which place emphasis on Zion/Jerusalem as the place from which Yahweh rules (Pss 46, 48, 76). While these traditions can be distinguished, it is clear that they are closely related. There are many references to Yahweh as king and to his presence in Zion elsewhere in the Psalms and prophetic traditions; see, for example, on Yahweh as king, Pss 10:16, 68:25; 74:12–17; 84:9–12, 19; 104:1–9; 146:10;

channelled into the world through the human king who was divinely
charged and equipped for the task.[8] David and his lineage had been
chosen by Yahweh for kingship. The royal house was supported by
divine promises of protection and blessing.[9]

149:2; Is 6:5; 24:23; 33:22, Jer 8:19; Mic 4:7; Zeph 3:15. On Zion as Yahweh's
dwelling place see, for example, Pss 50:2; 65:2; 68:17; 84:8; 132:13–14; 133:3;
146:10; Is 6:1; 24:23; Jer 8:19; 17:12; Mic 4:7; Zeph 3:14–15. For an overview of
these themes, see E. Otto, "צִיּוֹן," *TWAT* 6. 1012–19 (with an exhaustive bibliography
assembled on pp. 994–1005); K. Seybold, "מֶלֶךְ," *TWAT* 4. 947–56 (with bibliography).

Whatever the origins of these traditions (some, for example, B. C. Ollenburger,
Zion. The City of the Great King: A Theological Symbol of the Jerusalem Cult [JSOTSup
41; Sheffield: Sheffield Academic, 1987] 39–41, understand the kingship of Yahweh,
at least, to belong to pre-monarchical Israelite traditions; others, such as H. Schmid,
"Jahweh und die Kulttraditionen von Jerusalem," *ZAW* 26 [1955] 168–98; F. Stoltz,
*Struckturen und Figuren von Jerusalem. Studien zur altorientalishen, vor- und frühisraelitischen
Religion* [BZAW 118; Berlin: de Gruyter, 1970], understand them to have been
adopted from Jerusalemite/Canaanite religion in the early monarchical period; still
others, such as J. J. M. Roberts, "The Davidic Origin of the Zion Tradition," *JBL*
92 [1973] 329–44, see them as belonging to the early monarchical period but to
represent a mixed tradition, not purely Jerusalemite/Canaanite) they came to serve
monarchical interests and to legitimate the state.

[8] On the anointing of the king, the royal charisma, and the king's divine son-
ship, see I. Engnell, *Studies in Divine Kingship in the Ancient Near East* (2d ed.; Oxford:
Blackwell, 1967); T. N. D. Mettinger, *King and Messiah: The Civil and Sacral Legitimation
of the Israelite Kings* (ConBOT 8; Lund: Gleerup, 1976) 185–275. On the king's
divinely given wisdom, see H. Ringgren, *Word and Wisdom: Studies in the Hypostatization
of Divine Qualities and Functions in the Ancient Near East* (Lund: Gleerup, 1947);
L. Kalugila, *The Wise King: Studies in Royal Wisdom as Divine Revelation in the Old
Testament and Its Environment* (ConBOT 15; Lund: Gleerup, 1980). On the sacral
character of Judean kingship, as distinct from the idea of the king as divine, see
A. R. Johnson, *Sacral Kingship in Ancient Israel* (2d ed.; Cardiff: University of Wales
Press, 1967); J. H. Eaton, "The Psalms and Israelite Worship," in *Tradition and
Interpretation: Essays by the Members of the Society for Old Testament Study* (ed. G. W.
Anderson; Oxford: Clarendon, 1979) 238–73.

The basic sources for the ideology of Judean kingship are the Royal psalms: Pss
2, 18, 20, 21, 45, 72, 89, 101, 110, 132, 144, to which can be added certain sections of the Deuteronomistic History (for example, I Sam 8–10, 16; II Sam 5–7,
24; I Ki 1–2).

[9] On the election of David and the originally unconditional nature of the covenant
made with him, see M. Weinfeld, "The Covenant of Grant in the Old Testament
and in the Ancient Near East," *JAOS* 90 (1970) 184–96; T. Ishida, *The Royal Dynasty
of Ancient Israel* (BZAW 142; Berlin: de Gruyter, 1977) 99–117, cf. L. Perlitt,
Bundestheologie im Alten Testament (WMANT 36; Neukirchen-Vluyn: Neukirchener
Verlag) 47–53, who contends that the covenant aspect of the Davidic tradition post-
dates the united monarchy.

On the melding of the kingship of Yahweh, Zion ideology, and the election of
David into the royal-state ideology, see O. H. Steck, *Friedensvorstellung im alten Jerusalem;
Psalmen, Jesaja, Deuterojesaja* (Theologischen Studien 111; Zurich: Theologischer, 1972)
5–51; J. Bright, *Covenant and Promise: The Prophetic Understanding of the Future in Pre-
Exilic Israel* (Philadelphia: Westminster, 1976) 49–77; Ishida, *Royal Dynasties*, 81–117,

The formation and continuation of the state was thus not due to human endeavour but to the divine will.[10] Kingship, the constitutive institution of the state, was a divine creation patterned after and expressing the role of the national deity as king over the cosmos and other gods. The earthly king, as the divine king's representative, established the divinely constituted order through, first, the enactment of divinely revealed laws and the exercise of justice, and second, the construction of the temple for the national deity and the performance therein of the proper rituals by the king himself and by cultic personnel.[11] Funding for the temple building and maintenance, as

143–50; J. J. M. Roberts, "Zion in the Theology of the Davidic-Solomonic Empire," in *Studies in the Period of David and Solomon and Other Essays*, 93–108. On the place of the temple in royal-state ideology, see N. Poulssen, *König und Tempel im Glaubenszeugnis des Alten Testaments* (Stuttgarter Biblische Monographien 3; Stuttgart: Katholisches Bibelwerk, 1967) 11–86.

While it is possible that the Davidic tradition was traditio-historically unrelated to the Zion/*Yahweh mālak* tradition(s) as Ollenburger (*Zion*, 59–66) points out, that they can somehow be separated from state ideology during the monarchical period is highly improbable, even though the human king barely figures in the *Yahweh mālak* psalms and Zion psalms. The Zion ideology, for example, could not have come to prominence in Israel/Judah before David's capture of Jerusalem (Zion) and his bringing the Ark of the Covenant there (II Sam 6). That is, this ideology is dependent on the monarchy for its status. Similarly, while Yahweh could possibly have been viewed as a "king" in the pre-monarchical period, once the terrestrial institution was established under the deity's auspices it must have remained closely linked with and have accentuated the deity's kingship.

[10] For the biblical tradition which portrays Yahweh as reluctant to establish a monarchical state, see below pp. 67–70.

[11] On the king's concern for law and justice, see K. Whitelam, *The Just King: Monarchical Judicial Authority in Ancient Israel* (JSOTSup 12; Sheffield: JSOT, 1979), cf. for Mesopotamia, G. Ries, *Prolog und Epilog in Gesetzen des Altertums* (Münchener Beiträge zur Papyrusforschung und Antiken Rechtsgeschichte 76; Munich: C. H. Beck, 1983) 40–74.

For the king as a temple builder, see A. S. Kapelrud, "Temple Building, A Task for Gods and Kings," *Or* NS 32 (1963) 56–62. On the king's priestly role in the cult in offering sacrifices see II Sam 6:13, 17–18; 24:25; I Ki 3:4, 15; 8:5, 62–64; 9:25; II Ki 16:12–15. The rituals in which the king was involved have been the subject of protracted debate. It is supposed that he must have participated in a New Year Festival which reaffirmed both the national deity's and his own kingship; on this see S. Mowinckel, *Psalmenstudien II.* (Videnskapsselskapets skrifter II. Hist.-filosof. klasse 1921, 4, 6; 1922, 1–2; 1923, 3; 1924, 1; Kristiania: Dybwad, 1921–24) 2 (1921) *Das Thronbesteigungsfest Jahwäs und der Ursprung der Eschatologie*; J. C. De Moor, *New Year with Canaanites and Israelites* (2 vols.; Kamper Cahiers 21–22; Kampen: Kok, 1972); J. H. Eaton, *Kingship in the Psalms* (2d ed.; The Biblical Seminar; Sheffield: JSOT Press, 1986); T. N. D. Mettinger, *The Dethronement of Sabaoth: Studies in the Shem and Kabod Theologies* (ConBOT 18; Lund: Gleerup, 1982) 67–72. There is little unambiguous evidence in the biblical texts for this festival and its existence has been questioned by many. For a summary of the arguments in the debate concerning this festival, see Ollenburger, *Zion*, 24–33; K. van der Toorn, "The Babylonian

well as emoluments for cultic personnel, came from the royal-national treasury (a role taken over by the temple upon its completion) (I Ki 5:15–32; 7:51; 9:10–14, 25; II Ki 12:1–17) and were doubtless augmented by voluntary and *ex voto* offerings. The king oversaw and directed the cult, appointing the major cultic functionaries (such as the head priest—II Sam 8:17–18; 20:25; I Ki 2:26–27, 35) who, together with other cultic personnel, served as government administrators both in Jerusalem and in various state shrines scattered throughout the country.[12] The temple personnel were thus state employees who were the beneficiaries of royal patronage.

The Jerusalem temple of Yahweh operated in the Persian period in a context quite unlike that of the monarchical period when it served the ideological and administrative needs of the kingdom of Judah. Given that there was no longer a Judean state or indigenous king, why was this temple needed? What was its ideological significance to be now that Judah was but a sub-province of the Achaemenid Persian empire, and what temple ideology would legitimate its rebuilding? Since the rebuilt temple could no longer serve an independent nation-state, what polity would it serve? What was the temple's function in Achaemenid Judah and in what ways did this differ from its function in the monarchical period? Further, without an indigenous king to support and direct the cult, how and under whose authority should the temple operate and be organized? From where would it derive financial support? Since the exiled Judeans, as well as some among those who had remained in Judah, had maintained the worship of Yahweh for almost seventy years (587–520) without the Jerusalem temple, the question of *when* the temple was to be rebuilt

New Year Festival: New Insights from the Cuneiform Texts and their Bearing on Old Testament Study," in *Congress Volume: Leuven, 1989* (ed. J. A. Emerton; VTSup 42; Leiden/New York/Cologne: E. J. Brill, 1991) 331–44. On this festival in Babylonia see also J. Black, "The New Year Ceremonies in Ancient Babylon: 'Taking Bel by the Hand' and a Cultic Picnic," *Religion* 11 (1981) 39–54; B. Pongratz-Leisten, *ina šulmi īrub. Die kulttopographische und ideologische Programmatik der akītu-Prozession in Babylonien und Assyrien im 1. Jahrtausend v. Chr.* (Baghdader Forschungen 16; Mainz am Rhein: P. von Zabern, 1994).

[12] Ahlström, *Royal Administration*, 44–74. On the Jerusalem temple serving as both a royal chapel and national shrine, see Busink, *Tempel von Jerusalem*, 1. 618–46. On the king as chief administrator of the cult see II Ki 12:5–9; 16:10–18; 22:3–7; 23. On the funding of the cult and royal supervision thereof, see V. Hurowitz, "Another Fiscal Practice in the Ancient Near East. 2 Kings 12:5–17 and a Letter to Esarhaddon (LAS 277)," *JNES* 45 (1986) 289–94.

also arises. When was this temple needed? Political change had an impact not only on the role of former state institutions and the ideology that underpinned them but also on how Judean society was structured. It is within this new structuring that a role for the temple must be sought. A related issue here is the development of Judean identity in this new political context. How did Judeans view themselves as a social entity now that they were no longer a monarchical state? These questions are to be directed to the Judean community which undertook the rebuilding. Investigation of them should illuminate the continuity and change in the function and symbolic significance of this former monarchical institution, symbol of Yahweh as king of the state, in the radically changed social and political circumstances of provincial Achaemenid Judah.

Questions regarding the purpose and timing of the temple rebuilding, its ongoing function and organization, and the social organization of Judah must also have been addressed by Judah's Achaemenid overlords. What view did the Achaemenid Persian administration have of the rebuilding of the former national shrine of Judah? As its rebuilding would certainly not have been held to constitute the restoration of the kingdom of Judah, for what purpose would they have permitted the rebuilding? Did the rebuilding and/or timing of the rebuilding and the function of the temple owe anything to Achaemenid Persian policy? What was the relationship of the Jerusalem cultic personnel to secular Achaemenid Persian administrative officials? What authority did Achaemenid Persian officials have over the function and organization of the temple?

Sources and Recent Interpretations

The study of these questions falls under the general heading of the social history of Achaemenid Judah. The basic source for the study of these questions is the corpus of Judean literary texts from the Persian period included in the Old Testament/Hebrew Bible. While scholarly opinion differs as to which texts belong to this corpus, the broadest consensus accepts Haggai, Zechariah 1–8, Isaiah 55–66, Joel, Malachi, I and II Chronicles, and Ezra-Nehemiah.[13] Although

---

[13] On the provenance of these texts and their dating to the Persian period, see the relevant sections of R. Pfeiffer, *Introduction to the Old Testament* (rev. ed.; New York: Harper, 1948); O. Eissfeldt, *The Old Testament: An Introduction* (trans. P. R. Ackroyd; Oxford: Blackwell, 1965), G. Fohrer, *Introduction to the Old Testament* (trans.

these texts differ as to genre, date, purpose, and authorship, a review of their contents reveals that they share a desire to vindicate the Jerusalem cult of Yahweh and emphasize its centrality in the life of the Judean community. Various other biblical texts, or portions thereof, have been reckoned among the corpus of Judean literary texts of the Persian period, reflecting the recent trend toward understanding the Babylonian and Achaemenid periods as the creative highpoint of Judean literary activity.[14] The most discussed text in this regard is the Pentateuch. A growing number of scholars understand the J (Yahwist) narrative strand of the Pentateuch, alongside the P (Priestly) legal-narrative strand, to be a product of the late Neo-Babylonian or Achaemenid Persian periods rather than the period of the united monarchy.[15] Other texts, such as Ruth, Nahum,

D. E. Green; Nashville/New York: Abingdon, 1968); O. Kaiser, *Introduction to the Old Testament* (trans. J. Sturdy; Minneapolis: Augsburg, 1975); N. K. Gottwald, *The Hebrew Bible: A Socio-Literary Introduction* (Philadelphia: Fortress, 1985); J. A. Soggin, *Introduction to the Old Testament* (3d ed.; trans. J. Bowden; London: SCM, 1989).

[14] See, for example, R. W. Klein, *Israel in Exile: A Theological Interpretation* (Overtures to Biblical Theology; Philadelphia: Fortress Press, 1979); P. R. Davies, *In Search of Ancient Israel* (JSOTSup 148; Sheffield: JSOT Press, 1992); E. Ben Zvi, "The Urban Centre of Jerusalem and the Development of the Literature of the Hebrew Bible," in *Urbanism in Antiquity: From Mesopotamia to Crete* (eds. W. E. Aufrecht, N. A. Mirau, and S. W. Guley; JSOTSup 244; Sheffield: Sheffield Academic Press, 1997) 194–207; N. P. Lemche, "The Old Testament—a Hellenistic Book," *SJOT* 7 (1993): 163–93; T. M. Bolin, "When the End is the Beginning: The Persian Period and the Origins of the Biblical Tradition," *SJOT* 10 (1996) 3–15.

[15] So, T. L. Thompson, *The History of the Patriarchal Narrative: The Quest for the Historical Abraham* (BZAW 133; Berlin: de Gruyter, 1974); J. van Seters, *Abraham in History and Tradition* (New Haven/London: Yale University Press, 1975); H. Vörlander, *Die Entstehungszeit des jehowistischen Geschichtswerkes* (Europäischen Hochschulschriften 109; Frankfurt am Main: Lang, 1978); K. W. Whitelam, "Israel's Traditions of Origin: Reclaiming the Land," *JSOT* 44 (1989) 19–42; C. Levin, *Der Jahwist* (FRLANT 157; Göttingen: Vandenhoeck & Ruprecht, 1993).
Pentateuchal studies continue to be in a state of flux. Only a few aspects of this ever more complex debate need be broached here. The date of the Priestly source (P), which is commonly thought to reflect the views of the priestly élite exiled in Babylonia, has been given a Palestinian provenance and dated to the late monarchical period (specifically, the reign of Hezekiah) by, for example, Y. Kaufmann, *The Religion of Israel from Its Beginnings to the Babylonian Exile* (trans. and abridged by M. Greenberg; Chicago: University of Chicago Press, 1960) 175–200; M. Haran, *Temple and Temple Service in Ancient Israel: An Inquiry into the Character of Cult Phenomena and the Historical Setting of the Priestly School* (Oxford: Clarendon, 1978) 141: "I am prepared to suppose that the ideal conception which formed the basis of Hezekiah's reform was that which found its literary expression in P"; idem, "Behind the Scenes of History: Determining the Date of the Priestly Source," *JBL* 100 (1981) 321–33. A. Hurvitz, *A Linguistic Study of the Relationship between the Priestly Source and the Book of Ezekiel: A New Approach to an Old Problem* (Cahiers de la Revue Biblique 20; Paris:

Zechariah 9–14, Job, Ecclesiastes, Proverbs 1–9, Song of Songs, Jonah, Lamentations, and certain Psalms have also been dated to the Achaemenid Persian period.[16] There is nothing approaching a

---

Gabalda, 1982), holds on linguistic grounds that P predates Ezekiel and is thus pre-exilic, although he realizes that "those who date Ezekiel—or certain parts thereof—to the post-exilic period can claim, for instance, that although P is relatively earlier than Ez[ekiel] . . . there is still room to push it deep into the exilic period (as is commonly accepted)" (p. 152); idem, "Dating the Priestly Source in Light of the Historical Study of Biblical Hebrew. A Century after Wellhausen," *ZAW* 100 (1988) 88–100. Supporting Hurvitz's pre-exilic dating is G. Rendsburg, "Late Biblical Hebrew and the Date of P," *JANES* 12 (1980) 65–80. For an another view of the linguistic evidence for the dating of P, see R. Polzin, *Late Biblical Hebrew: Toward a Typology of Biblical Hebrew Prose* (HSM 12; Missoula, MT: Scholars Press, 1976), who dates P to the early exilic period, but distinguishes it from Late Biblical Hebrew. For a summary of the arguments in favour of a pre-exilic date for P, see Z. Zevit, "Converging Lines of Evidence Bearing on the Date of P," *ZAW* 94 (1982) 481–511; cf. J. Blenkinsopp, "An Assessment of the Alleged Pre-Exilic Date of the Priestly Material in the Pentateuch," *ZAW* 108 (1996) 495–518.

More commonly P is given a Babylonian provenance and dated to the exilic period, although its authority may not have been widely accepted until later in the Persian period, so A. S. Kapelrud, "The Date of the Priestly Code," *Annual of the Swedish Theological Institute* 3 (1964) 58–64, who dates P's completion to before 550. Others date its completion to around the time of Ezra, so J. G. Vink, "The Date and Origin of the Priestly Code in the Old Testament," *OTS* 16 (1969) 1–144. For a history of scholarship on the identification, character, and dating of P, see Eissfeldt, *Introduction*, 164–66, 204–08; R. J. Thompson, *Moses and the Law in a Century of Criticism since Graf* (VTSup 19; Leiden: E. J. Brill, 1970); and see below chapter 2, nn. 22–28.

Others question that P existed as a separate text, contending that it is rather a priestly editorial revision of an existing narrative (JE); so, for example, R. Rendtorff, *Das überlieferungsgeschichtliche Problem des Pentateuch* (BZAW 147; Berlin: W. de Gruyter, 1977) 141–42. Rendtorff, among others, has questioned the validity of source criticism for the study of the Pentateuch. He notes that ". . . wir kaum zuverlässige Kriterien für die Datierung der pentateuchischen Literatur besitzen. Jede Datierung der Pentateuch 'quellen' beruht auf rein hypothetischen Annahmen, die letzten Endes nur durch den Konsens der Forscher Bestand haben" (p. 169) (English trans.: R. Rendtorff, *The Problem of the Process of Transmission in the Pentateuch* [trans. J. J. Scullion; JSOTSup 89; Sheffield: JSOT Press, 1990] 201–02). For a critical appraisal of the history of scholarship on the formation of the Pentateuch, including recent critiques of source criticism, see R. N. Whybray, *The Making of the Pentateuch: A Methodological Study* (JSOTSup 53; Sheffield: Sheffield Academic Press, 1987). Also reviewing recent currents in pentateuchal scholarship, and sympathetic to a traditional source critical approach, is E. W. Nicholson, *The Pentateuch in the Twentieth Century: The Legacy of Julius Wellhausen* (Oxford: Clarendon, 1998).

[16] On the dating of many of these texts to the Persian period, see G. Wanke, "Prophecy and Psalms in the Persian Period," in *CHJ*, 1. 162–88; H. Gese, "Wisdom Literature in the Persian Period," in *CHJ*, 1. 189–218; M. Smith, "Jewish Religious Life in The Persian Period," in *CHJ*, 1. 244. On Psalms, see R. J. Tournay, *Voir et entendre dieu avec les Psaumes ou la liturgie prophétique du second temple à Jerusalem* (Cahiers de la Revue Biblique 24; Paris: Gabalda, 1988). On Proverbs, see C. V. Camp, *Wisdom and the Feminine in the Book of Proverbs* (Bible and Literature Series 11; Sheffield: Almond,

consensus on the dating of these texts, however. Problematic also
are those sources supposedly embedded in earlier works (such as Is
24–27), as well as editorial work on earlier texts, for example, sections of Isaiah 1–39, Ezekiel, and Jeremiah.[17] It is widely accepted
that the canonical biblical texts were given their final form in the
Persian and Hellenistic periods, but the attempt to detect redactional
influence in the texts in the hope of supplementing the available evidence for Achaemenid Judah has largely proven to be a subjective
affair. The texts one includes in the corpus of Judean literary texts
of the Persian period obviously affect one's reconstruction of the
period, but an agreed method for identifying such texts has not been
arrived at.[18]

   Since literary texts are the basic sources for the study of Achaemenid
Judean society, questions arise regarding their value for writing social
history and how they can be properly used. Much of the recent
research on the social history of Achaemenid Judah has read the
biblical texts from the Persian period within one of two interpretive
schemas. Both schemas attempt to delineate the character of Judean
social and political organization in this post-monarchical setting. In

---

1985) 227–91. On Zechariah 9–14, see D. L. Petersen, *Zechariah 9–14 and Malachi:
A Commentary* (OTL; Louisville: Westminster/John Knox, 1995) 3–6; C. L. Meyers
and E. M. Meyers, *Zechariah 9–14* (AB 25C; New York: Doubleday, 1993) 26–27.
On Jonah, see J. M. Sasson, *Jonah* (AB 24B; New York: Doubleday, 1990) 26–28.
   [17] See, for example, W. Zimmerli, *Ezekiel* (2 vols.; trans. J. D. Martin; Hermeneia;
Philadelphia: Fortress, 1979–83) 1. 68–74; R. P. Carroll, *Jeremiah. A Commentary*
(OTL; London: SCM, 1986); M. A. Sweeny, *Isaiah 1–4 and the Post-Exilic Understanding
of the Isaianic Tradition* (BZAW 171; Berlin/New York: de Gruyter, 1988); B. Gosse,
*Isaïe 13, 1–14, 23 dans la tradition littéraire du livre d'Isaïe et dans la tradition des oracles
contre les nations* (OBO 78; Fribourg: Universitätsverlag/Göttingen: Vandenhoeck &
Ruprecht, 1988).
   [18] Other evidence, in the form of archaeological remains and epigraphic evidence, sheds little light on the function of the Jerusalem temple. Since the Persian
period temple has not been excavated our knowledge of the form of the structure
is also derived from the biblical texts, on which see Busink, *Tempel von Jerusalem*, 2.
810–41. For the epigraphic evidence, see A. Lemaire, "Les inscriptions palestiniennes d'époque perse: un bilan provisoire," *Transeu* 1 (1989) 87–105. The archaeological evidence is summarised in E. Stern, *The Material Culture of the Land of the
Bible in the Persian Period 538–332 B.C.E.* (Warminster: Aris and Phillips/Jerusalem:
Israel Exploration Society, 1982); H. Weippert, *Palästina in vorhellenistische Zeit* (Handbuch
der Archäologie, Vorderasien 2/1; Munich: Beck, 1988) 682–728, which includes
an appendix by Leo Mildenberg on the YHD coins on pp. 719–28; C. E. Carter,
"A Social and Demographic Study of Post-Exilic Judah" (Ph.D. dissertation Duke
University, 1992; Ann Arbor: University Microfilms International) 93–165.

both schemas the Jerusalem temple figures prominently as a central socio-political and religious institution.[19]

The first schema interprets the texts in terms of a conflict theme; social and political life in Achaemenid Judah being marked by social conflict. All variants of this paradigm are ultimately indebted to Ezra-Nehemiah where social conflict is the theme around which the historical narrative develops. This schema not only establishes the context out of which the biblical texts from this period arose but also frames the relationship of the relevant texts to each other.

The nature of the conflict and the identity of the protagonists involved differ in various accounts. For some the conflict is fundamentally between the Judeans repatriated from Babylonia in the early Achaemenid Persian period and those whom they found living in Judah and its environs at their return. This conflict is explicitly mentioned in Ezr 3–4, and Ezra-Nehemiah gives this interpretation its narrative structure. In Ezra-Nehemiah the returnees are portrayed as constituting a "cultic community" or "theocracy" whose character was marked by observance of the Torah under the supervision of the priests of the Jerusalem cult of Yahweh. Concern for the Jerusalem cult of Yahweh was paramount.[20] It was demanded of the

---

[19] For a review of some of the literature on the social history of Achaemenid Judah, see W. Schottroff, "Zur Sozialgeschichte Israels in der Perserzeit," *Verkündigen und Forschung* 27 (1982) 59–68; L. L. Grabbe, *Judaism from Cyrus to Hadrian* (2 vols.; Minneapolis: Fortress, 1992) 1. 27–145.

[20] The term "theocracy" was coined by Josephus (*Contra Apionem*, ii. 165), on which see Y. Amir, "θεωκρατία as a Concept of Political Philosophy: Josephus' Presentation of Moses' *Politeia*," *Scripta Classica Israelica* 8–9 (1985–88) 83–105. Ezr-Neh give this group a number of names, most commonly: (ה)גולה "(the) exile" and compounds such as בני הגולה "sons of the exile"; קהל "community" and compounds, such as קהל ישראל; קהל הגולה "Israel". On these and other names, see H. C. M. Vogt, *Studie zur nachexilischen Gemeinde in Esra-Nehemia* (Werl: Dietrich-Coelde, 1966) 22–99; S. Stiegler, *Die nachexilische JHWH-Gemeinde in Jerusalem. Ein Beitrag zu einer alttestamentlichen Ekklesiologie* (BEATAJ 34; Franfurt am Main: Lang, 1994) 105–35. On this group's appropriation of the name "Israel", see G. W. Ahlström, *Who were the Israelites?* (Winona Lake, IN: Eisenbrauns, 1986) 101–118. On this group see further, O. Plöger, *Theocracy and Eschatology* (2d ed.; trans. S. Rudman; Oxford: Blackwell, 1968); W. Rudolph, *Chronikbücher* (HAT 21; Tübingen: J. C. B. Mohr [Paul Siebeck], 1955) xviii–xxiv; idem, "Problems of the Books of Chronicles," *VT* 4 (1954) 401–9 (which reproduces parts of the introduction to his commentary on Chronicles); O. H. Steck, "Das Problem theologischer Strömungen in nachexilischer Zeit," *Evangelische Theologie* 28 (1968) 445–58. For a nuanced approach the development of the notion that "exilic Israel = Israel", see E. Ben Zvi, "Inclusion and Exclusion from Israel as Conveyed by the use of the Term 'Israel' in Post-Monarchical Biblical Texts," in *The Pitcher is Broken: Memorial Essays for Gösta W. Ahlström* (ed. S. W. Holloway and L. K. Handy; JSOTSup 190; Sheffield: Sheffield Academic Press, 1995) 95–149.

returnees that they separate themselves from those who did not go
into exile. This was necessary since, as a cultic community, they had
to separate themselves from the impurity which was inherent in outsiders.[21] The exclusion covered outsiders' participation in the Jerusalem
cult of Yahweh and intermarriage. Ezra-Nehemiah holds that only
those who went into exile were the people of Yahweh, that is, the
descendants of the kingdom of Judah. To them alone had the
Achaemenid Persians given permission to rebuild the Jerusalem temple and they alone had the right to worship there (Ezr 4:3; Neh
13:4–9). They also had to avoid intermarriage in order to preserve
the "holy seed" (Ezr 9:2). They thus formed a distinct community
in Judah. Certain persons who had not been exiled approached the
leaders of the repatriated Judeans claiming to be Yahwists, but this
claim was rejected according to Ezr 4:1–5 on the basis that these
people were self-confessed foreigners. This rejection led to conflict
between the returnees and those in the land (Ezr 4; Neh 1:19–20,
3:33–4:17, 6:1–19). It also led to conflict within the community of
repatriated Judeans since some did not hold to a separatist line, an
attitude reflected in some of its members marrying these outsiders
(Ezr 9; Neh 13:13–27).

In this interpretation of the conflict the repatriates' antagonists
("the people[s] of the land[s]"—Ezr 3:3; 4:4) are understood by some
to be the Judeans who never went into exile.[22] Others identify them
with the inhabitants of Samaria (who are not to be confused, as they
still sometimes are, with the later Samaritans whose schism with

---

[21] Ezr 9:1–3, 11–15 cf. 4:1–3, but note Ezr 6:21 cf. Neh 10:29 where outsiders
can join the cultic community if they "separate themselves from the impurity of
the surrounding peoples". Also, cf. I and II Chrons which is thought by some to
accept Samarians into the Judean cultic community.

[22] So, Vogt, *Studie*; M. Smith, *Palestinian Parties and Politics that Shaped the Old
Testament* (New York: Columbia University Press, 1971; reprint, with minor corrections, London: SCM, 1987) 75–146; W. Th. In der Smitten, "Historische Probleme
zum Kyrosedikt und zum Jerusalemer Tempelbau von 515," *Persica* 6 (1972–74)
167–68, 172–75; Miller and Hayes, *History of Ancient Israel and Judah*, 458–59;
M. Barker, *The Older Testament: The Survival of Themes from the Royal Cult in Sectarian
Judaism and Early Christianity* (London: SPCK, 1987) 185–87; D. L. Smith, *Religion
of the Landless: The Social Context of the Babylonian Exile* (Bloomington, IN: Meyer-Stone,
1989) 179–200; J. Blenkinsopp, "A Jewish Sect of the Persian Period," *CBQ* 52
(1990) 5–20 (esp. 18–19); R. P. Carroll, "The Myth of the Empty Land," *Semeia*
59 (1992) 79–93 (esp. 84–85); J. L. Berquist, *Judaism in Persia's Shadow: A Social and
Historical Approach* (Minneapolis: Fortress Press, 1995) 26–29, 74–79.

Judaism came in the Hellenistic period at the earliest).[23] The distinction between these two variations is (i) the location of the opponents—in Judah versus in Samaria, and (ii) the ethnic-national identity of the opponents—Judeans versus foreigners. Another common view considers the opponents to be an alliance or amalgam of non-exiled Judeans and Samarians.[24] The date of the conflict between the repatriates and the "people of the land" also varies. Many date it, following Ezr 1–3, to the initial return under Cyrus (538), while others, who understand the repatriation to have taken place in the reign of

---

[23] So, for example, J. W. Rothstein, *Judean und Samaritaner* (BWANT 3; Leipzig: Hinrichs, 1908); M. Gaster, *The Samaritans: Their History, Doctrines and Literature* (London: Oxford University Press, 1925) 20–24; H. H. Rowley, "The Samaritan Schism in Legend and History," in *Israel's Prophetic Heritage: Studies in Honor of James Muilenburg* (ed. B. W. Anderson and W. Harrelson; New York: Harper, 1962) 215; R. S. Foster, *The Restoration of Israel* (London: Darton, Longman and Todd, 1970) 108–111; H. Donner, *Geschichte des Volkes Israel und seiner Nachbarn in Grundzügen* (2 vols.; ATD Ergänzungsreihe Band 4/1–2; Göttingen: Vandenhoeck & Ruprecht, 1985–6) 2. 414–15; C. L. Meyers and E. M. Meyers, *Haggai, Zechariah 1–8* (AB 25B; Garden City, NY: Doubleday, 1987) xxxiv; H. W. Wolff, *Haggai: A Commentary* (trans. M. Kohl; Minneapolis: Ausburg, 1988) 92–3, who all term these antagonists "Samaritans" (although they variously understand them to be descendants of those who lived in the northern kingdom [Israel] and/or descendants of foreigners settled in Israel by the Assyrians). This is a misnomer since it is now generally accepted that the Samaritan schism did not take place until the Hellenistic period; see J. D. Purvis, *The Samaritan Pentateuch and the Origin of the Samaritan Sect* (HSM 2; Cambridge, MA: Harvard University Press, 1968); R. J. Coggins, *Samaritans and Jews: The Origins of Samaritanism Reconsidered* (Growing Points in Theology; Atlanta: John Knox, 1975), cf. A. D. Crown, "Redating the Schism between Judeans and the Samaritans," *Jewish Quarterly Review* 82 (1991) 17–50, who dates the real break between the communities as late as the third century C.E. F. Dexinger, "Limits of Tolerance in Judaism: The Samaritan Example," in *Jewish and Christian Self-Definition* (3 vols.; ed. E. P. Sanders with A. I. Baumgarten and A. Mendelson; Philadelphia: Fortress, 1981) 2. 92–6, drawing on Bickerman's distinction between proto-Samaritans, who were the descendants of Israelites not exiled by the Assyrians, and Samarians, the syncretistic foreign imports (Ezr 4:4, 9–10), contends the conflict in the Persian period was with the latter; similarly, O. Margalith, "The Political Background of Zerubbabel's Mission and the Samaritan Schism," *VT* 41 (1991) 312–23; Z. Zevit, "The Gerizim-Samarian Community in and between Texts and Times: An Experimental Study," in *The Quest for Context and Meaning: Studies in Biblical Intertextuality in Honor of James A. Sanders* (ed. C. A. Evans and S. Talmon; Biblical Interpretation Series 28; Leiden/New York/Cologne: E. J. Brill, 1997) 564–66.

[24] So, for example, W. O. E. Oesterley and T. H. Robinson, *A History of Israel* (2 vols.; Oxford: Clarendon, 1932) 2. 86; J. Bright, *A History of Israel* (3rd ed.; OTL; Philadelphia: Westminster Press, 1981) 365–66; S. Talmon, "The Emergence of Jewish Sectarianism in the Early Second Temple Period," in *Ancient Israelite Religion. Essays in Honor of Frank Moore Cross* (ed. P. D. Miller, P. D. Hanson, and S. D. McBride; Philadelphia: Fortress, 1987) 587–616 (a slightly different version is published in S. Talmon, *King, Cult and Calendar in Ancient Israel* [Jerusalem: Magnus, 1986] 165–201; Ahlström, *History of Ancient Palestine*, 844–45.

Cambyses or Darius I, date it to the temple rebuilding under Darius
I (520).[25]

Another understanding of the social conflict in Achaemenid Judah
focuses on differing views of the nature of the restoration of Judah.
There were two groups with competing notions of how Judean society was to be ordered and the kingship of Yahweh find expression.
One group, commonly termed "eschatologists", was animated by
nationalist sentiment and stood heir to the royal ideology of the
Judean court.[26] The dissolution of the kingdom of Judah had called
into question the twin pillars of Judean state ideology, namely, the
divine election of Zion (Jerusalem) as Yahweh's earthly abode, and
the divine election of David and his dynasty. Despite the punishment meted out to Judah, Jerusalem, and the House of David, divine
election was held to be immutable. There thus developed an expectation of Yahweh's activity on behalf of Judah to restore her fortunes. Emphasis is placed on those prophetic texts which envisage
Judah's future to lie in the restoration of the state and the renewal
of its monarchical institutions under an indigenous (Davidic) king.
The temple was once again to be the throne of Yahweh from where
he would rule through his viceroy, the king. This coming kingdom
would be greater than any before with its rule extending over the
peoples of the earth, giving new expression to Yahweh's sovereignty
and power.[27] The Persian period texts thought to have been written

---

[25] On dating the conflict to the repatriation under Cyrus see, for example, Bright,
History of Israel, 365–66; Berquist, *Judaism in Persia's Shadow*, 26–29. On dating the
origin of the conflict to the reign of Darius I, see In der Smitten, "Historische
Probleme," 167–68, 171–75; Miller and Hayes, *History of Ancient Israel and Judah*,
458–59; Donner, *Geschichte des Volkes Israel*, 2. 414–15; Ahlström, *History of Ancient
Palestine*, 844–45. Others consider that the conflict developed later, with the arrival
of Ezra and Nehemiah on their reforming missions. On Nehemiah's mission as the
catalyst for the division, see H. G. Kippenberg, *Garizim und Synagogue. Traditionsgeschichtliche
Untersuchungen zur samaritanische Religion der aramäische Period* (Religionsgeschichtliche
Versuche und Vorarbeiten 30; Berlin/New York: de Gruyter, 1971) 38–41, and cf.
Neh 13:28; Josephus, *Antiquities*, xi. 8.

[26] For a summary of this ideology, see Bright, *Covenant and Promise*, 49–77.

[27] See, for example, Is 9:5–6 (Eng. vv. 6–7); 11:1–5; Jer 23:5–6; 30:8–9; 33:14–26;
Ezek 29:21; 34:23–24; 37:24–25; Amos 9:11–12; Mic 5:1–3 (Eng. vv. 2–4). The
expectation in other prophetic texts focuses on the temple rather than the Davidic
dynasty (Is 2:2–4 = Mic 4:1–4; Ezek 40–48), or has no place for the dynasty (Is
55:1–5).
Whether this expectation should be termed "eschatological" depends on one's
understanding of the term. Those who understand it in the literal sense of a vision
of the end of time or "the last things" would deny its appropriateness here; so, for
example, S. Mowinckel, *He That Cometh* (trans. G. W. Anderson; Nashville: Abingdon,
1955) 153–54; J. P. M. van der Ploeg, "Eschatology in the Old Testament," OTS

by this group are Haggai, Zechariah 1–8, and, in the opinion of some, the first edition of the books of Chronicles, since these texts are interpreted as portraying the rebuilding of the Jerusalem temple as heralding the restoration of the kingdom of Judah.[28]

---

17 (1972) 89–99; G. W. Ahlström, *Joel and the Temple Cult of Jerusalem* (VTSup 21; Leiden: E. J. Brill, 1971) 89. Those who use the term in the sense that the divine activity to change the current wretched circumstances into a marvelous new age simply lies in the future would accept its use here; so, T. C. Vriesen, "Prophecy and Eschatology," in *Congress Volume: Copenhagen 1953* (VTSup 1; Leiden: E. J. Brill, 1953) 199–229; Bright, *Covenant and Promise*, 15–24.

Temple rebuilding in this context has been understood by a number of scholars to denote Judean rebellion against Achaemenid Persian control since it reaffirms both the kingship of Yahweh and indigenous Judean kingship. This hope for the restoration of the monarchy, even though it is cast in idealistic terms, should be distinguished from "Messianism" which developed only in the late Hellenistic and Roman Periods. On the development of the expectation of the restoration of the monarchy and state in response to their dissolution in 587 see the classic study of Mowinckel, *He That Cometh*, 125–154, and the biblical references cited there, and also see J. Becker, *Messianic Expectation in the Old Testament* (trans. D. E. Green; Philadelphia: Fortress, 1980) 54–63; A. Laato, *Josiah and David Redivivus: The Historical Josiah and the Messianic Expectations of Exilic and Postexilic Times* (ConBOT 33; Stockholm: Almqvist & Wiksell, 1992), who deems expectations for a renewal of the monarchy to have originated in the reign of Josiah. In Persian period Judah this expectation is placed in the context of social tension or conflict with opposing views by, for example, U. Kellermann, *Nehemiah. Quellen, Überlieferung und Geschichte* (BZAW 102; Berlin: Töpelmann, 1967) 173–91; W. Th. In der Smitten, "Nehemias Parteigänger," *BiOr* 29 (1972) 155–57; idem, "Historische Probleme," 167–78; idem, *Gottesherrschaft und Gemeinde. Beobachtungen an Frühformen eines jüdischen Nationalismus in der Spätzeit des Alten Testaments* (Europäische Hochschulschriften 23/42; Frankfurt am Main: Lang, 1974) 5–63; idem, "Erwägungen zu Nehemias Davidszität," *JSJ* 5 (1975) 41–8; Becker, *Messianic Expectation*, 48–67.

It should be pointed out that there are many divergent views on the nature and content of the eschatology of exilic and post-exilic biblical texts. An expectation of the restoration of the monarchy and state appears in these texts (on which, in addition to the above works, see H. Ringgren, *The Messiah in the Old Testament* [Studies in Biblical Theology 18; London: SCM, 1956]; M. Rehm, *Der königlishe Messias im Licht der Immanuel-Weissagungen des Buches Jesaja* [Kevelaer: Butzon and Berker, 1968]; J. Coppens, *Le messianisme royal* [LeDiv 54; Paris: Editions du Cerf, 1968]; U. Kellerman, *Messias und Gesetz. Grundlinien einer alttestamentlicher Heilserwartung. Einer traditionsgeschichtliche Einführung* [Biblische Studien 61; Neukirchen-Vluyn: Neukirchener Verlag, 1971]; A. Laato, *A Star is Rising: The Historical Development of the Old Testament Royal Ideology and the Rise of the Jewish Messianic Expectations* [University of South Florida International Studies in Formative Christianity and Judaism 5; Atlanta: Scholars Press, 1997]). It is hardly the dominant theme, however, unless, like Mowinckel, one makes all the various elements in these texts' eschatology contingent on the establishment of the new monarch. This topic, and the secondary literature discussing it, is too vast to be dealt with here. On these other elements, see S. Herrmann, *Die prophetischen Heilserwartungen im Alten Testament. Ursprung und Gestaltwandel* (BWANT 85; Stuttgart: Kohlhammer, 1965); D. E. Gowan, *Eschatology in the Old Textament* (Philadelphia: Fortress, 1986).

[28] On a first edition of Chronicles, see D. N. Freedman, "The Chronicler's Purpose," *CBQ* 23 (1961) 436–42; F. M. Cross, "A Reconstruction of the Judean

The competing group, termed "theocratists", eschewed eschatological expectation, at least with regard to the restoration of the
indigenous monarchy. For the "theocratists", who understood the
repatriates as constituting a cultic community, there was no place
for, nor indeed need for, the monarchy in a community governed
by priests. No new kingdom was awaited. Indeed, how could it be
expected when they saw their own community as the fulfilment of
the divine plan? As Plöger puts it:

> Can a theocracy, which regards itself not as a specially exalted nation
> alongside other nations but as a divine creation, incommensurable in
> terms of this world, a theocracy, in fact, which interprets its existence
> as the fulfilment of definite promises which Yahweh had once announced
> by the mouth of the prophets, take seriously an historical eschatology,
> according to which substantially more would be given to it than it
> already possessed? It can, of course, make use of older eschatological
> ideas to illustrate its present situation; but it can hardly endow them
> with historical influence, at any rate not in comparison with the prin-
> ciples, delivered to it at its foundation, which determine its present
> existence.[29]

For the "theocratists" the rule of Yahweh over his people was
expressed through the divine presence in the cult; it did not require
any eschatological activity on Yahweh's part to actualize his sovereignty or devotion to his chosen people.[30] The theocratists were thus

---

Restoration," *JBL* 94 (1975) 4–18; J. D. Newsome, "Toward a New Understanding
of the Chronicler and His Purpose," *JBL* 94 (1975) 201–17, who all contend that
the first edition of Chronicles was written to legitimate the Jerusalem temple reconstruction under Zerubbabel. For a critique of this position, see H. G. M. Williamson,
"Eschatology in Chronicles," *TynB* 29 (1979) 120–33. The majority of scholars who
hold to the existence of parties ascribe Chronicles to the opposition "theocratist" party.

[29] Plöger, *Theocracy and Eschatology*, 109. Plöger's interest is in understanding the
rise of apocalyptic eschatology in the context of a struggle between the theocratists
and those were heirs to the prophetic eschatology at the time of the Maccabean
rebellion. He sees the tension between these two groups going back at least into
the fifth century, but it need not have issued in outward division before the Maccabean
period. On the "theocratists", see further Rudolph, *Chronikbücher*, xxiii–xxiv; idem,
"Problems of the Books of Chronicles," 401–9; Steck, "Das Problem theologischer
Strömungen," 445–58; J. Blenkinsopp, "Interpretation and the Tendency to
Sectarianism: An Aspect of Second Temple History," in *Jewish and Christian Self-
Definition*, 2. 4–13.

[30] There is considerable debate concerning whether or not the theocrat position could admit an eschatological component, and if so, what it was. Becker,
Messianic Expectation, for example, disagrees that the theocratists lacked an eschatology. He identifies three distinctive traits of this group: (i) "renunciation of the con-
crete monarchy in favor of . . . the direct kingship of God" (p. 48); (ii) "the transfer

content to collaborate with the Persians and supported the political status quo since they believed that the current political order had been instituted by Yahweh, as evidenced by the Achaemenid Persians' supposed benevolence towards the Jerusalem cult of Yahweh (Ezr 1, 7). Thus for the theocratists the Jerusalem temple did not symbolize the restitution of the state of Judah, but rather it functioned solely as the cultic centre for the worship of Yahweh. The texts thought to present this perspective are the Priestly narrative in the Pentateuch (P), Ezra, Nehemiah, and Chronicles.

Paul D. Hanson also understands the "theocratists" (Hanson prefers the term "hierocratic party") and "eschatologists" (Hanson names them "visionaries") to be embroiled in conflict in this period, but he contends that the latter party eschewed the restoration of the monarchy and state. Rather than expecting Yahweh's rule to be expressed in an earthly king, they looked to Yahweh himself ruling.[31] This

---

of earthly powers to foreign rulers" (pp. 52–53); (iii) "the collectivizing transfer of the idea of king to the nation" (pp. 68–70). According to Becker, certain texts, notably Deutero-Isaiah, await the future fulfilment of these notions. That is, they are eschatological expectations. The problem with Becker's analysis is that he forces Deutero-Isaiah into the theocratist camp on the basis of Is 55:1–5, which falls under his third trait above, and on the basis of Deutero-Isaiah's emphasis on the direct kingship of God (his second trait). The "eschatology" of Deutero-Isaiah is, in my view, too complex to permit this. Becker's interpretation of Deutero-Isaiah can be compared with that of P. D. Hanson, *The Dawn of Apocaylptic: The Historical and Sociological Roots of Jewish Apocalyptic Eschatology* (rev. ed.; Philadelphia: Fortress, 1979), who places this text in the "eschatologist" camp. On the issue of the existence and nature of an eschatology in so-called "theocratic" texts, see R. Mosis, *Untersuchungen zur Theologie des chronistischen Geschichtswerkes* (Freiburger Theologische Studien 92; Freiburg: Herder, 1973); Hanson, *Dawn of Apocalyptic*, 209–79; Williamson, "Eschatology in Chronicles," 115–54.

This raises one of the problems with the "parties" approach to the analysis the Judean literary texts of the Babylonian and Persian periods (for example, "theocratists" versus "eschatologists"), namely, that it tends to be reductionist. When only two parties are envisaged all the texts are ascribed to one party or the other. Expanding the number of parties does not solve the problem since the history of the relationships between these groups is often difficult to substantiate (see, for example, the table in In der Smitten, *Gottesherrschaft und Gemeinde*, 100–101. While he does not attempt to ascribe texts to the seven groups there listed, his historical reconstruction falters in the attempt to justify the existence of these groups or to account for the relationships between them). Another issue is how early one should see the development of these parties. By including Deutero-Isaiah in his analysis Becker places their formation in the Babylonian period. Plöger, in comparison, considers the theocratists to be a phenomenon of the Persian and Hellenistic periods.

[31] Hanson, *Dawn of Apocalyptic*, 32–208. Hanson's interpretation of the conflict in this period has little place for the restoration of the monarchy. This may be due to his purpose to establish a social context for the rise of apocalyptic eschatology.

expectation is not apolitical since, in common with the above interpretation, the revelation of Yahweh's kingship will bring all the
nations and peoples of the earth under the sway of Yahweh in Zion
(Jerusalem). According to Hanson, this group consisted of Levites
who did not go into exile, together with some returnees who stood
in the tradition of Deutero-Isaiah in rejecting the restoration of the
monarchy. They claimed the legitimate priesthood but were disenfranchised from the Jerusalem cult by the repatriated Zadokite priests
(Hanson's "theocratists") who, also claiming the legitimate priesthood,
gained the support of the Persian government because of their col-
laborationist policy.[32] Trito-Isaiah (Is 56–66) is the fundamental text
from the visionary group which Hanson uses to plot the developments
in the relationship between the two groups. Hanson's "visionaries"
were against the rebuilding of the temple since they envisaged the
restoration of Judah to be a miraculous, divine undertaking, not done
with human hands. Having lost the struggle for the control of the
cult, the visionaries withdrew from it. Their hopes for divine vindica-
tion in the context of their disenfranchisement gave rise to apocalyptic

This eschatology embraced "a cosmic vision of Yahweh's sovereignty" (p. 11) which
had abandoned the emphasis of the earlier prophetic eschatology on the historical,
temporal fulfilment of the expectation of Yahweh's activity in favour of a fulfilment
which transcended the historico-temporal plane. Hanson understands its origins, and
its earliest literary expression, to lie in the period of the temple reconstruction under
Zerubbabel. Plöger, who is also interested to account for the rise of apocalyptic
eschatology in his *Theocracy and Eschatology*, sees its literary expression to arise later
in the Persian period; certainly not before the missions of Ezra and Nehemiah.
Hanson's "visionaries" (Plöger terms them "eschatologists") are indebted to the ideas
of Deutero-Isaiah (Is 40–55) who has no place for the monarchy in his restoration
hopes. According to Is 55:1–5 the divine promises once given to the Davidic dynasty
are to be democratized. Hanson has no comment on those texts which are commonly considered to reflect a hope for the restoration of the monarchy (see n. 27
above). Hanson's definition of the visionaries shares important features in common
with Becker's definition (*Messianic Expectation*) of the theocratists. Both include (i) the
direct kingship of God to the exclusion of an indigenous monarchy; (ii) the passing of kingship to the nation as a whole. Note the role played by Deutero-Isaiah
in their respective schemes. For Hanson it is the forerunner of the visionary party,
while for Becker is reflects theocratic ideals. The opposite is the case with Haggai
and Zechariah 1–8 since Hanson understands them as belonging to the "theocratist"
group, while Becker understands them as reflecting the "restorative monarchist"
position. Similarly, Hanson understands Ezra and Nehemiah as belonging to the
theocratists, albeit as moderates (p. 270), while Kellermann (*Nehemia*, 179–89) numbers them among the eschatologists, understanding Nehemiah's wall rebuilding to be
a claim to kingship.
[32] For his treatment of the "theocratists", see Hanson, *Dawn of Apocalyptic*, 209–79.

eschatology. Hanson thus places Haggai and Zechariah 1–8 in the hierocratic group because of their focus on temple rebuilding.[33]

The protagonists in the "eschatologist"/"theocratist" division have been variously understood. Some identify them as different groups within the Judean repatriates, this conflict being basically confined to the repatriates. Others understand this conflict to be between the repatriates ("theocratists") and "the people of the land".[34] Many commentators thus attempt to integrate both areas of conflict noted above (namely, conflict between the repatriates and "the people of the land", and conflict over expectations for the restoration of Judah) since they are not necessarily mutually exclusive interpretations and both appear to have support in the texts.

Morton Smith offers a different interpretation of the social conflict in Achaemenid Judah. It was between those who sought to worship Yahweh as strict monotheists (the "Yahweh-alone" party) and those who held that other gods could be worshipped alongside Yahweh (the "syncretist" party). This interpretation also incorporates aspects of the division between the repatriates and those who had remained in Judah since the "Yahweh-alone" group was substantially comprised of the repatriates. The "syncretists" were largely those who had remained in the land together with some repatriated priests. Smith interprets the history of Achaemenid Judah from this standpoint. The two parties struggled for control of the Jerusalem cult. Power moved back and forth between the two parties throughout this period depending on who could gain the support of the

---

[33] Hanson has restated his interpretation of this conflict in "Israelite Religion in the Early Postexilic Period," in *Ancient Israelite Religion*, 485–508; idem, *A People Called: The Growth of Community in the Bible* (San Francisco: Harper and Row, 1987), 215–311. Also developing similar themes to Hanson and Plöger is D. L. Petersen, *Late Israelite Prophecy: Studies in Deutero-Canonical Literature and in Chronicles* (SBLMS 23; Missoula, MT: Scholars Press, 1977) who argues:

> that there was an essential bifurcation within post-exilic Israelite society, an ideological split which is represented, on the one hand, by the Chronicler's history, a work written and redacted by the Levitical members of the Jerusalemite hierocracy, and on the other hand, by the deutero-prophetic corpus . . . literature composed by traditionalists who preserved and added to the oracles and narratives of Israel's classical prophets. (p. 97)

[34] For the former view, see Hanson, *Dawn of Apocalyptic*; Blenkinsopp, "Interpretation and the Tendency to Sectarianism," 8–13. For the latter view, see In der Smitten, "Historische Probleme," 167–74. Hanson does not attempt to absorb the returnees vs. the Samarians debate into his interpretation. He understands Ezr 4:1–5 as referring to the hierocratic party's rejection of the visionaries (*Dawn of Apocalyptic*, 243).

Achaemenid Persian administration. The Judean literary texts of the
Persian period are all generated by the "Yahweh-alone" party. The
only understanding of the "syncretist" party one can now obtain is
through the filter of the texts of the finally victorious "Yahweh-alone"
party since they were responsible for the formation of the canon.[35]

The above conflicts were not confined to the Persian period but
had roots in the Neo-Babylonian period, if not earlier. So, for example, the origin of the division between the repatriates and those who
stayed in the land has been thought to lie in the competing claims
of each community to be the locus of Yahweh's saving plan in the
aftermath of the dissolution of the kingdom of Judah. Those in
Babylonia contended that far from being abandoned by Yahweh
they were a remnant saved by him who were being chastised and
purified by their humiliating experience. Yahweh was soon expected
to restore their fortunes by returning them to their homeland.[36] Not
surprisingly, those who remained in Judah adopted a diametrically
opposed position. Yahweh had expelled the exiles as a means of
extirpating the source of corruption in the society. His interest was
in those who remained in his land—Judah. Those banished to foreign parts now lay outside Yahweh's salvation.[37] Regarding the devel-

---

[35] Smith, *Palestinian Parties*, 75–146; idem, "Palestinian Judaism in the Persian
Period," in *The Greeks and the Persians from the 6th to 4th Centuries* (ed. H. Bengston;
Delacorte World History 5; New York: Delacorte,1968) 381–401; idem, "Jewish
Religious Life," 243–76. Similarly, B. Lang, *Monotheism and the Prophetic Minority: An
Essay in Biblical History and Sociology* (The Social World of Biblical Antiquity 1;
Sheffield: Almond, 1983) 13–56, 138–56.

[36] This view is thought to be reflected in the oracles of salvation in Ezekiel,
Jeremiah and Deutero-Isaiah, which are directed to the Babylonian exiles. Yahweh
had abandoned Jerusalem and Judah but not forsaken the exiles (regarding the 597
deportation: Jer 23:1–8, 24:1–10, 29:11–14, 32:27–41; Ezek 10:1–22, 11:14–21;
regarding the 587 deportation: Is 41:8–16). The curse under which the land of
Judah currently lay was to be lifted when Yahweh returned to Jerusalem, bringing
the exiles with him. The use of the second Exodus motif shows that the writers'
interest is in those who had left the land, not those who remained there (Jer
16:14–15; 23:7–8; Ezek 20:33–44; Is 40:3–5, 9–11; 41:17–20; 43:16–21).

[37] So Ezek 11:15 and 33:23–29 which refer to such attitudes expressed in reac-
tion to the 597 deportation. According to R. P. Carroll, *From Chaos to Covenant:
Prophecy in the Book of Jeremiah* (New York: Crossroad, 1981) 236–48; C. R. Seitz,
"The Crisis of Interpretation over the Meaning and Purpose of the Exile. A
Redactional Study of Jeremiah xxi–xliii," *VT* 35 (1985) 78–98 (especially pp. 92–95).
That such views were also current after the deportation of 587 can be reasonably
inferred from the contention in the Deuteronomic History and the Deuteronomistic
redaction of Jeremiah that the land of Judah was vacant after Gedaliah's death (II
Ki 25:25–26; Jer 42:7–22, 43:5–7, 44:2, 22). One function of such a blatantly false

opment of the theocratist-eschatologist division, Hanson proposes that certain biblical texts can be arranged to give an outline of the history of the struggle between these two groups, beginning in the Babylonian exile with two competing programmes of restoration envisaged in Ezekiel 40–48 (hierocratic) and Deutero-Isaiah (visionary) around which the parties formed, going through the period of the ascendancy of the hierocratic party and the disenfranchisement of the visionary group in the early Persian period, and concluding with a more conciliatory position of the hierocrats to the visionaries (Chronicler).[38] Morton Smith understands the conflict between the "Yahweh-alone" and "syncretist" groups to have existed throughout the monarchical period and on into the Persian period.[39] All the above interpretations understand their perceived conflict to have continued into the Hellenistic and Roman periods.[40] "Conflict" is thus an organizing principle for Judean social history from at least the Babylonian through to the Roman period.

It is noteworthy that while there is little agreement as to the nature of the social conflict in Achaemenid Judah or the definition of the groups involved, there is a general consensus that the Jerusalem cult of Yahweh figured prominently in the struggles; its cultic personnel are always protagonists, while the cult itself is often the focus of the conflict. The various factions were supposedly struggling for control over, or at least participation in, this cult in order to realize their

assertion was to disarm the claim by the Judeans who were not deported that they, and not the exiles, were the locus of divine salvation since they inhabited Yahweh's land. The land of Judah played such an important role in Babylonian exilic restoration hopes that those who remained in it would have had to be conceded favoured status in Yahweh's eyes. Since in the ideology of the Deuteronomist no one was in the land, the exiles' own status could be unchallenged. Further, the land had to be devoid of people since after the "sins" committed there it stood in need of a cleansing Sabbath—70 years (Jer 25:11, 29:10 cf. II Chrons 36:21). On this view, see also Carroll, "Myth of the Empty Land," 79–93. For a response to the contention that the exile served as the background to social division in Achaemenid Judah, see below pp. 54–61.

[38] Hanson, *Dawn of Apocalyptic*, passim.

[39] Smith, *Palestinian Parties*, 11–42, 62–74.

[40] Many see the roots of the Jewish sectarianism of the Hellenistic and Roman periods to lie in these social conflicts or divisions of the Persian period; so, for example, Plöger, *Theocracy*; H. Mantel, "The Dichotomy of Judaism during the Second Temple," *HUCA* 44 (1973) 55–87; In der Smitten, *Gottesherrschaft und Gemeinde*; Talmon, "Emergence"; R. P. Carroll, "Israel, History of (Post-Monarchic Period)," in *The Anchor Bible Dictionary* (6 vols.; ed. D. N. Freedman; New York: Doubleday, 1992) 3. 573–76.

own vision of its function in the divine economy.[41] This religious motivation was closely aligned with a political agenda. It is commonly assumed that with the loss of indigenous kingship the priesthood acquired some of the authority that formerly belonged to the king. Priests became the leaders of the people and enjoyed wider powers than they had had during the monarchical period in both sacral and secular domains.[42] This development in their role and status is traced to the Babylonian exile where, together with "the elders of Judah/Israel" (Ezek 8:1; 14:1; 20:1, 3 cf. Jer 29:1), they directed

---

[41] A thread running through many forms of this conflict schema is the notion of competing claims by priestly houses (Zadokites and Levites) to be the legitimate cultic personnel to serve at the restored Jerusalem temple. Each house sought to exclude the other, or at least to limit its rights. The Zadokites, the former incumbents of the monarchical period Jerusalem temple, are held to have been the victorious party. The Levites are generally considered to be priests who officiated at local shrines in monarchical Judah, many of whom were forced to abandon their local cultic activities and move to Jerusalem in the so-called "Deuteronomic Reform" of Josiah (c. 622). This policy was opposed by the Levites since their status and role in the Jerusalem cult was lower than the Zadokite priests who had officiated there at least from the time of David. It is supposed that there was significant tension between the Levites one the one hand, and the Zadokites and Judean government on the other. This tension then carried over into the Babylonian and Persian periods. On the history of the conflict between these priestly groups, see A. Cody, *A History of Old Testament Priesthood* (AnBi 35; Rome: Pontifical Biblical Institute, 1969) 125–74; A. H. J. Gunneweg, *Leviten und Priester. Hauptlinien der Traditionsbildung und Geschichte des israelitische-jüdischen Kultpersonels* (FRLANT 89; Göttingen: Vandenhoeck and Ruprecht, 1965) 117–218; H. Gese, *Der Verfassungsentwurf des Ezechiel (Kap. 40–48) traditionsgeschichtlich untersucht* (Beiträge zur Historischen Theologie 25; Tübingen: Mohr-Siebeck, 1957); E. Auerbach, "Der Aufsteig der Priesterschaft zur Macht im Alten Israel," in *Congress Volume: Bonn 1960* (VTSup 9; Leiden: E. J. Brill, 1962) 236–49; Hanson, *Dawn of Apocalyptic,* 220–28. E. Rivkin, *The Shaping of Jewish History: A Radical New Interpretation* (New York: Scribner's, 1971) 21–41; idem, "Aaron," in *The Interpreter's Dictionary of the Bible: Supplementary Volume* (ed. K. Crim et al.; Nashville: Abingdon, 1976) 1–3, who sees in this period the rise of the Aaronide priesthood at the expense of the Levites. On the relationship between Aaronites and Zadokites in the post-monarchical period, see also J. Blenkinsopp, "The Judean Priesthood during the Neo-Babylonian and Achaemenid Periods: A Hypothetical Reconstruction," *CBQ* 60 (1998) 25–43.

[42] "Wellhausen assumed, as did practically all Old Testament scholars, that the priesthood occupied the vacuum created by the collapse of the monarchy" (J. Blenkinsopp, *Prophecy and Canon: A Contribution to the Study of Jewish Origins* [University of Notre Dame Center for the Study of Judaism and Christianity in Antiquity; Notre Dame/London: University of Notre Dame Press, 1977] 19, and see also p. 74). On the rise of the authority of the priesthood and the priestly interpretation of the history and identity of Israel during the early Babylonian exilic period, see B. W. Anderson, *Understanding the Old Testament* (4th ed.; Englewood Cliffs, NJ: Prentice-Hall, 1986) 449–66; Smith, *Religion of the Landless,* 139–51; Blenkinsopp, "Judean Priesthood," 25–43.

the life of the Judean exiles. When numbers of exiled Judeans were repatriated in the early Achaemenid Persian period, those priests who returned maintained their role as leaders among them. Their position and authority were enhanced by the reconstruction of the Jerusalem temple of Yahweh and the revival of the cult there since it was the premier Yahwistic shrine. It is thought that this temple became the central institution in Judean society, certainly among the repatriated Judeans and perhaps also for the sub-province of Judah. As a consequence, its cultic officials were a dominant social and political force in the community, a role which, in some interpretations, was at least sanctioned, if not fostered, by the Achaemenid Persians. By gaining acceptance into or political dominance over the Jerusalem priesthood, or by supplanting it, one would obtain access to the authority inherent in its position. The conflicts in this period, however they be discerned, are thus seen to relate to the acquisition or use of political and social authority which was vested in the temple cult and its personnel.[43] In short, therefore, temple rebuilding and participation in the temple cult was about political power.

---

[43] On the cult as the centre of the struggle, see Hanson, *Dawn of Apocalyptic*, passim, but explicitly on pp. 96–100, 209–79; idem, *A People Called*, 215–311, according to whom the "visionaries" (Hanson's term for the eschatologist group) supposedly lost interest in the struggle for the temporal cult once it was clear that they could not gain control of it; Smith, *Palestinian Parties*, 75–146; Rivkin, *Shaping of Jewish History*, 21–43. On the social and political importance of the Jerusalem cult of Yahweh and its personnel, see Hanson, *Dawn of Apocalyptic*, 226–28; Smith, *Palestinian Parties*, 80–84, 102, 115–20; Cody, *Priesthood*, 174–92; Rivkin, *Jewish History*, 21–43. Even those works which do not emphasize the notion of conflict in this period (for example, J. Wellhausen, *Prolegomena to the History of Israel. With a Reprint of the Article, Israel, from the Encyclopaedia Britannica* [with a preface by W. Robertson Smith; trans. J. S. Black and A. Menzies; Edinburgh: Black, 1885; repr., New York: Meridian, 1957]; E. Meyer, *Die Entstehung des Judentums. Eine historische Untersuchung* [Halle: Niemeyer, 1896]) subscribe to the political and social importance of the Jerusalem cult of Yahweh.

The importance of the Jerusalem cult to the community of the repatriates is also assumed by the standard histories of Judah in this period, such as Bright, *History of Israel*, 360–412; Foster, *Restoration*; W. S. McCullough, *The History and Literature of the Palestinian Jews from Cyrus to Herod, 550 B.C. to 4 B.C.* (Toronto/Buffalo: University of Toronto Press, 1975) 17–80; S. Herrmann, *A History of Israel in Old Testament Times*, (2d ed., rev. and enlarged; trans. J. Bowden; Philadelphia: Fortress, 1981) 298–338; Donner, *Geschichte des Volkes Israel*, 2. 405–39, but these works make no attempt to understand its place in Judean society. Following Ezra-Nehemiah, they emphasize the role of the "great men", that is, the leading characters in this "history", namely, Sheshbazzar, Zerubbabel, Ezra, and Nehemiah. M. Noth, *The History of Israel*, (2d ed.; trans. P. R. Ackroyd; Edinburgh: Black, 1960) 314–16, 337–45, differs in that he follows the historiography of the last century (for example, Wellhausen and Kuenen) in at least trying to define a role for the cult.

The second main interpretive schema for the Persian period biblical texts uses extra-biblical data to discern patterns of social and political organization in the Achaemenid Persian empire. These patterns then serve as the context in which to interpret the limited information in the biblical texts on these matters regarding Achaemenid Judah. Since Judah formed part of the Achaemenid Persian empire the Judean literary texts should, to some extent at least, reflect issues and patterns of provincial organization evidenced elsewhere in the empire. The extra-biblical materials, for their part, not only raise issues hitherto unexplored, they also illuminate the topics explicitly raised in the biblical texts, such as social conflict, temple rebuilding, and the role of the cult in society.

Although discussion of the socio-economic and administrative functions of the temple is disadvantaged by the lack of legal and administrative documents from Achaemenid Judah,[44] a number of studies have focused on the socio-economic and administrative roles of the

Mantel, "Dichotomy," 55–87, differs from the prevalent trend which understands the temple to be at the centre of the repatriates' ("sons of the golah") existence by contending that they were instead focused on the Torah and that the mission of Ezra was to establish them as a semi-autonomous community within Judah.

[44] In contrast to, for example, texts from the Neo-Babylonian and Persian periods from the Eanna temple in Uruk and the Ebabbar temple in Sippar, studies on which have been conducted by D. Cocquerillat, *Palmeraies et cultures de l'Eanna d'Uruk (559–520)* (Ausgrabungen der Deutschen Forschungsgemeinschaft in Uruk-Warka 8; Berlin: Mann, 1968) (with bibliography on p. 13 n. 13); idem, "Compléments aux 'Palmeraies et cultures de l'Eanna d'Uruk'," (I–III) *RA* 75 (1981) 151–69; *RA* 78 (1984) 49–70, 143–67; idem, "Recherches sur le verger du temple campagnard de l'Akitu (KIRI₆ ḫallat)," *WdO* 7 (1973) 96–134; H. M. Kümmel, *Familie, Beruf und Amt in spätbabylonischen Uruk: Prosopographische Untersuchungen zu Berufsgruppen des 6. Jahrhunderts v. Chr. in Uruk* (Abhandlung der Deutschen Orient-Geschellschaft 20; Berlin: Mann, 1979); F. Joannès, *Textes économiques de la Babylonie récente* (Recherche sur les Civilisations 5; Paris: Éditions Recherche sur les Civilisations, 1982) 111–260; M. A. Dandamaev, *Slavery in Babylonia: From Nabopolassar to Alexander the Great (626–331 B.C.)* (rev. ed.; trans. V. A. Powell; ed. M. A. Powell with D. B. Weisberg co-editor; De Kalb, IL: Northern Illinios Univerity Press, 1984) 469–557; M. Jursa, *Die Landwirtschaft in Sippar in neubabylonischer Zeit* (*AfO* Beiheft 25; Vienna: Institut für Orientalistik der Universität Wien, 1995); idem, *Der Tempelzehnt in Babylonien: vom siebenten bis zum dritten Jahrhundert v. Chr.* (AOAT 254; Münster: Ugarit-Verlag, 1998); A. C. V. M. Bongenaar, *The Neo-Babylonian Ebabbar Temple at Sippar: Its Administration and its Prosopography* (Uitgaven van het Nederlands Historisch-Archaelogisch Instituut te Istanbul 80; Leiden: Nederlands Historisch-Archaelogisch Instituut te Istanbul, 1997).

There are no temple archives extant from Egypt in this period, but some of the functions of the temples and their personnel can be inferred from donation texts, private texts, and the petition of Petiese (Papyrus Rylands IX). See, for example, D. Meeks, "Les donations aux temples dans l'Égypte du Iᵉʳ millénaire avant J.-C.," in *State and Temple Economy in the Ancient Near East* (2 vols.; ed. E. Lipiński; OLA 6; Leuven: Departement Oriëntalistiek, 1979) 2. 605–87; G. A. Wainwright, "Studies

Jerusalem temple using this approach. These roles stand in close connection with the social and political organization of Achaemenid Judah. Joel P. Weinberg, for example, has developed a theory concerning the socio-economic role of the Jerusalem temple in Judah suggested by comparative data drawn from other temples in the Achaemenid Persian empire. The Jerusalem temple was rebuilt as the economic and administrative centre of Judah as part of an Achaemenid Persian administrative policy which sought to establish a Bürger-Tempel-Gemeinde type of polity within Judah. Especially favoured by this policy was a community composed largely, although not exclusively, of those Judeans who were repatriated from Babylonia. This community was granted special semi-autonomous status and certain socio-economic advantages within the sub-province of Judah by virtue of its relationship to the temple. The temple's role as an economic and administrative centre is thought to reflect Achaemenid Persian policy regarding indigenous temples throughout the empire.[45] The conflict theme, exemplified in the economic and social division between those who were connected with the temple and those who were not, also plays an important role in Weinberg's understanding of Achaemenid Judean society.

Although not sharing Weinberg's distinctive understanding of the character of Achaemenid Judean social organization, others have also drawn on supposed Achaemenid Persian policy concerning the function of indigenous temples in the empire to contend that the importance of the Jerusalem temple lay in its function as an economic institution and its role in the political and social organization of the sub-province of Judah.[46] In one study, Carol and Eric Meyers's major

---

in the Petition of Peteêsi," *Bulletin of the John Rylands Library* 28 (1944) 228–71; E. Bresciani, "La satrapia d'Egitto," *Studi classici ed orientali* 7 (1958) 174–76.

[45] See, for example, J. P. Weinberg, *The Citizen-Temple Community* (trans. D. L. Smith Christopher; JSOTSup 151; Sheffield: Sheffield Academic Press, 1992); idem, *Der Chronist in seiner Mitwelt* (BZAW 239; Berlin/New York: W. de Gruyter, 1996). For a fuller bibliography, see below chapter 4 n. 58.

[46] On the rebuilding of the temple specifically, see C. L. Meyers and E. M. Meyers, *Haggai, Zechariah 1–8* (AB 25B; Garden City, NY: Doubleday, 1987) xxix–xl. Aspects of the place of Achaemenid provincial administrative policy in the social, religious, and political affairs of Judah are also addressed in Grabbe, *Judaism from Cyrus to Hadrian*, 1. 73–145; S. S. Tuell, *The Law of the Temple in Ezekiel 40–48* (HSM 49; Atlanta: Scholars Press, 1992); Berquist, *Judaism in Persia's Shadow*; J. Blenkinsopp, *A History of Prophecy in Israel* (Rev. ed.; Louisville: Westminster John Knox Press, 1996) 194–226; P. Frei and K. Koch, *Reichsidee und Reichsorganisation im Perserriech* (2d ed.; OBO 55; Göttingen: Vandenhoeck & Ruprecht, 1996) 7–131.

commentary on Haggai and Zechariah 1–8, this supposed Achaemenid
Persian policy is used to account for the temple rebuilding and the
status of temple personnel in Judean political affairs. Social division,
in this case between the Judeans and the Samaritans (sic), also figures
in their portrait of Achaemenid Judean society. Studies using this
second interpretive schema which comment upon the timing of the
temple rebuilding agree that it was due to a specific Achaemenid
Persian policy initiative.

These two interpretive schemas (social conflict, and the use of
comparative data on temples and social organization) overlap in
many respects, each recognizing and finding a place for the emphases
of the other. They share the desire to relate the Jerusalem temple
of Yahweh to the social, economic and administrative organization of
Achaemenid Judah and affirm the importance of this temple in
Achaemenid Judean society, both for Judean religion and in the
socio-political realm. The schemas address, either directly or indirectly, many of the questions raised above on pp. 6f. regarding the
purpose for and timing of the temple rebuilding, the political and
social context of the rebuilding, and the function of the temple in
Achaemenid Judean society. They both affirm that social conflict
dominated the social and political landscape of Achaemenid Judah
and that this served as the context for the temple rebuilding, although
there is a diversity of opinion regarding the exact character of this
conflict and the identity of the protagonists. The social conflict is
understood to reflect a struggle to define Judean identity, social organization, and the character of Judean religion in the aftermath of the
loss of indigenous kingship and statehood. A major outcome of the
temple rebuilding was that division in the society was entrenched
through granting certain groups (notably, those Judeans repatriated
from Babylonia) socio-economic and/or political power thus disenfranchising other groups (non-repatriates and/or "eschatologists"
and/or Levites and/or Samarians), and that the undertaking was an
expression of a specific Achaemenid Persian administrative policy
which gave political power to cultic officials and others participating in the temple cult. The various studies outlined above differ in
their understanding of the polity which the temple served; be it a
"cultic community", the "theocratists", the "hierocrats", the repatriates, a renewed kingdom of Judah, a Bürger-Tempel-Gemeinde, or
the sub-province of Judah. This reflects the diversity of opinion
regarding the form of polity or social identity Judeans had adopted

in the post-monarchical period and how it related to the Achaemenid Persian administration of Judah. It also accounts for the differing conceptions of the function of the Jerusalem temple of Yahweh in Achaemenid Judah exhibited in these works.

Scope of the Present Study

Like the studies outlined above, the present study attempts to address the issues of the purpose and timing of the rebuilding of the Jerusalem temple, the social and political context in which the rebuilding was undertaken, and the place of the temple in the development of a new Judean polity in the aftermath of the dissolution of the kingdom. While many of the above studies trace developments in the relationship of the temple to both Judean society and the imperial administration throughout the Neo-Babylonian and Achaemenid Persian periods and often into the Hellenistic and Roman periods, the present study is limited to the Neo-Babylonian and early Achaemenid Persian periods. In part this is due to the problem of dating the biblical sources necessary to undertake a larger diachronic study. More important perhaps is the fact that too little attention has been given to addressing the peculiar problems of the early Achaemenid Persian period, that is, the period of the reconstruction of the Jerusalem temple.

The present study also differs from the major interpretive schemas by questioning certain contentions they articulate, namely, that social conflict, in the various ways it is understood in the schemas, serves as the context in which the rebuilding of the Jerusalem temple is to be understood; that temple rebuilding entrenched social division between those participating in the temple cult and those who were excluded from it; that the temple accorded a particular segment of the Judean population, commonly identified with the Judeans repatriated from Babylonia, socio-economic and political power in Judah; and that the temple rebuilding was an expression of a specific Achaemenid Persian administrative policy effected for indigenous cults throughout the empire for the purpose of re-establishing indigenous polities in their homelands. Discussion of these topics naturally leads to a consideration of other closely allied matters identified in the schemas, namely, the timing of the rebuilding, the polity which the rebuilt temple served, and how it was possible to rebuild this

former monarchical shrine when Judah was no longer an independent kingdom and lacked an indigenous king.

To argue against the central contentions of the schemas is not to
deny the existence of social division in early Achaemenid Judean
society, even regarding the rebuilding of the Jerusalem temple, since
it is a truism that diversity of opinion and a measure of conflict are
endemic to all societies. Under question in the present study is the
contention that the Jerusalem temple in the early Achaemenid Persian
period was at the centre of a struggle among competing groups for
socio-economic and political power and for the authority to define
Judean identity, the limits of Judean society (that is, who was a
Judean and who was not), and the character of Judean religion.
Early Achaemenid Judean society is specified here as it is possible
that later in the history of Achaemenid Judah, notably with the missions of Nehemiah and Ezra to Judah from the mid-fifth century,
participation in the temple cult became the focus of social division
in Achaemenid Judah, perhaps as a result of the action of the
Achaemenid Persian administration (Ezr 7, 9; Neh 13). This, however, is a distinct area for discussion which must be distinguished
from the period of the temple rebuilding. One of the flaws in many
of the studies briefly outlined above is that such a distinction is not
observed, with the result that many of the issues characteristic of
later Achaemenid Judean society are improperly imported into the
early period. Further, in regard to the contentions of the schemas,
it is not denied that the Achaemenid Persian administration was in
some way involved with the temple rebuilding. The contention being
questioned is that the undertaking was an expression of an explicit
Achaemenid Persian administrative *policy* which sought to establish
indigenous temples as economic and administrative centres of local
polities and which concomitantly gave political power to cultic officials
and others connected with these shrines.

The main sources for the period of the temple rebuilding are Ezra
1–6, the narrative history of the rebuilding covering the period
538–516, and the prophetical texts Haggai and Zechariah 1–8, recounting aspects of the rebuilding undertaken in the reign of Darius
I (520–519).[47] The biblical literary texts from the Achaemenid Persian

---

[47] While accepting that Is 60–62 and 66:1–4 might be dated to around the time
of the temple rebuilding, I differ from Hanson (*Dawn of Apocalyptic; People Called,*

period, including the above texts, are, however, highly tendentious works whose value for reconstructing the history of Achaemenid Judah is severely limited.[48] It is recognized by most commentators

---

253–68) and others (such as P. A. Smith, *Rhetoric and Redaction in Trito-Isaiah: The Structure, Growth, and Authorship of Isaiah 56–66* [VTSup 62; Leiden/New York/Cologne: E. J. Brill, 1995]) who view Trito-Isaiah (Is 56–66) as almost completely a product of the early Persian period. While Zech 9–14 may well be a product of the Persian period, I do not consider any part of it to be relevant to the temple rebuilding. With Trito-Isaiah, Malachi and Jonah, it should be dated to a time after the rebuilding. I have also excluded the Priestly source from considerations regarding the temple rebuilding since I take it to be a product of the later Persian period (see discussion of dating in n. 15 above, and chapter 2 nn. 22–27, 49).

[48] This case is put most pointedly by D. J. A. Clines, "The Nehemiah Memoir: The Perils of Autobiography," in *What Does Eve Do to Help? and Other Readerly Questions to the Old Testament* (JSOTSup 44; Sheffield: Sheffield Academic, 1990) 124–64, specifically regarding the Nehemiah Memoir; G. Garbini, *History and Ideology in Ancient Israel* (trans. J. Bowden; New York: Crossroad, 1988) 151–69, on the narrative concerning the mission of Ezra, and see also his review of the scholarly study of Israelite and Judean history on pp. 1–21. Their approach can be compared with H. G. M. Williamson, *Ezra, Nehemiah* (Word Biblical Commentary 16; Waco, TX: Word, 1985), who is generally very supportive of the historical veracity of Ezra-Nehemiah.

There has been an extended debate in biblical studies, mirroring that in historical, literary, and anthropological studies, regarding what literary texts are evidence for and how they should be properly interpreted. Recourse to so-called "external evidence", such as archaeology, extra-biblical literary and non-literary texts, and comparative sociological and anthropological data, has not resolved the debate but has merely moved it to other areas; for example, the value of and means of interpreting archaeological evidence, and the proper use of comparative data. Compare, for example, on the use of comparative anthropological data to illuminate the character of Israelite prophecy, R. P. Carroll, "Prophecy and Society," in *The World of Ancient Israel: Sociological, Anthropological and Political Perspectives* (ed. R. E. Clements; Cambridge: Cambridge University Press, 1989) 203–25, with R. R. Wilson, *Prophecy and Society in Ancient Israel* (Philadelphia: Fortress, 1980). This is not to say that comparative anthropological data is never useful in interpreting ancient texts, only that its use is attended by difficult methodological problems, which Carroll well highlights. Carroll has himself attempted to apply certain insights from social psychology to the study of Israelite prophecy in *When Prophecy Failed: Cognitive Dissonance in the Prophetic Traditions of the Old Testament* (New York: Seabury, 1979).

A growing number of studies investigate the biblical texts not as historical sources but as literature. This trend has not come about in response to the claims of critical historians that the texts must be read as something other than "history". Rather, the vast majority of these studies reflect dissatisfaction with the historical-critical reading of the Bible which is quite rightly considered to atomize the text. That is, it is dissatisfaction with the older literary (basically, source) criticism that has spawned these new literary studies. The scholars undertaking these studies, who are trained in modern literary theory, can be divided into two groups. The first read the text as an integrated whole, without consideration of its historical development. It is thus the final, canonical form of the text with which they deal. Examples of this approach are R. Alter, *The Art of Biblical Narrative* (New York: Basic Books, 1981); M. Sternberg, *The Poetics of Biblical Narrative: Ideological Literature and the Drama of Reading* (Bloomington: Indiana University Press, 1985); R. Polzin, *Samuel and the*

that the biblical texts were generated by and reflect the opinions of
certain élites and small groups in society whose interest was in the
Jerusalem temple and its cult. It is not possible on the basis of these
sources either to write a history of the Jerusalem cult in the Achaemenid
Persian period or to reconstruct Achaemenid Judean society with
any assurance. The schemas also recognize the tendentiousness of
the biblical texts but, as summarized above, they all accept the claim
of Ezra-Nehemiah, the biblical narrative history of Achaemenid Judah,
that social division centred on participation in the temple cult was
the characteristic feature of Achaemenid Judean society from its
beginning, this understanding commonly being developed in terms
of a specific Achaemenid Persian administrative policy which made
the Jerusalem temple the economic and/or administrative hub of
Achaemenid Judah. However, as will be more fully argued in chapter 3, the account of the temple rebuilding in Ezra 1–6 anachronistically imports the concerns of a later age into its account of the
early Achaemenid period; views which reflect the author's understanding of the character of Achaemenid Judean society current in
his own day. The portrait of Achaemenid Judean society given in
Ezra-Nehemiah underlies the schemas' interpretation of the entire
corpus of biblical texts ascribed to Achaemenid Persian period. Since
it is assumed that social division and the economic/administrative
role of the temple formed the social context in which the texts were
written and which indeed occasioned the texts, proponents of the
schemas promote the value of the biblical texts as historical sources
on exactly these matters. The texts are held to be windows through

Deuteronomist: a Literary Study of the Deuteronomistic History (San Francisco: Harper and
Row, 1989). For studies of Ezra-Nehemiah using this approach, see T. C. Eskenazi,
In an Age of Prose. A Literary Approach to Ezra-Nehemiah (SBLMS 36; Atlanta: Scholars
Press, 1988); idem, "The Structure of Ezra-Nehemiah and the Integrity of the Book,"
JBL 107 (1988) 641–56. The second group recognize that the texts developed over
a long period and so attention must be paid to their historical development and
the possible historical contexts in which they were written. As literary works, these
texts tell us more about the time in which they were written than about the epoch
of which they purport to speak. An example of this approach is D. Damrosch, *The
Narrative Covenant: Transformations of Genre in the Growth of Biblical Literature* (San Francisco:
Harper and Row, 1987). Historians have a good deal in common with literary crit-
ics of the latter kind. On the problems attending the interpretation of ancient lit-
erary/historical texts see also M. Liverani, "Memorandum on the Approach to
Historiographic Texts," *Or* NS 42 (1973) 178–94; N. P. Lemche, *Early Israel:
Anthropological and Historical Studies on the Israelite Society before the Monarchy* (VTSup 37;
Leiden: E. J. Brill, 1985) 377–85.

which to view these dominant concerns and through which their development in the history of Achaemenid Judah can be traced. What one can see through these windows is thought to be brought into sharper focus through the use of extra-biblical material or comparative sociological data. To peer through the windows supposedly offered by these texts is not to behold "history", however, particularly when they are interpreted in terms of concerns peculiar to Ezra-Nehemiah. The texts may contain valuable, accurate historical information about this period, but it is often difficult to identify such material in its present literary context. To read these texts is foremost to behold the world as constructed by the authors/editors; to see the issues they considered to be important, and behind those issues the historical conditions that produced them as understood by the authors/editors. In adopting from Ezra-Nehemiah the notions of social division and the economic/administrative centrality of the temple as their organizing principles, the schemas inevitably reproduce in their portrayal of Achaemenid Judean society this text's tendentious view of the character and historical development of the society. This is not to say, however, that Ezra-Nehemiah's emphasis on social division and the centrality of the temple should be dismissed by students of Achaemenid Judean society. Rather than understand these emphases as an accurate, historical representation, they should be read as expressions of their author's/editor's peculiar understanding of Achaemenid Judean society and should be interpreted in light of the time in which the text was written. As a literary work Ezra-Nehemiah has its own tendentious concerns which demand analysis. Thus its concerns should be used neither to define the study of the role of the temple in early Achaemenid Judean society nor to establish the context in which to interpret other texts from this period.

It is clearly an assumption on the part of the proponents of the schemas that Ezra-Nehemiah reflects the issues that dominated early Achaemenid Judean society or establishes the context in which the biblical texts from this period should be read. It is interesting that proponents of the schemas, while recognizing that the biblical texts were written to serve the tendentious interests of their authors in the presumed conflict, do not question that the conflict theme and the emphasis on the economic and administrative roles of the temple which they identify in these texts may also be tendentious. The present study rejects the attempt to use the central contentions of the schemas, drawn from Ezra-Nehemiah, as the framework in which

to interpret the Persian period biblical texts and as the key issues
by which the workings of early Achaemenid Judean society can be
unlocked. It will be argued that neither social conflict nor a specific
Achaemenid Persian administrative policy is the context in which to
understand the purpose and timing of the rebuilding of the Jerusalem
temple of Yahweh. Further, while it is admitted that the temple
rebuilding project was highly significant to Judeans when it was
undertaken, it will be argued that this was not due to its putative
role as an administrative or economic centre.

Having criticized the schemas for too readily adopting the perspective of Ezra-Nehemiah and having claimed that the biblical texts
will not permit the writing of a history of Achaemenid Judah, the
question arises as to the value of these texts for the study of early
Achaemenid Judah. An important consideration is the dating of the
texts. Unlike Ezra 1:1–4:5, for example, which will be shown to be
a late, tendentious text with no first-hand knowledge of the early
years of Achaemenid Persian rule, the prophetical texts Haggai and
Zechariah 1–8 have been generally accepted by scholars as substantially belonging to the commencement of the temple rebuilding
in the reign of Darius I.[49] This does not, of course, remove the problem of the tendentiousness of these texts, but it does give us access
to views of the purpose and timing of the rebuilding, as well as
understandings of the Judean polity, that were current in the Judean
community when the temple was rebuilt rather than introducing the
anachronistic views of later texts (Ezr 1–6). For these texts the issues
facing the community rebuilding the temple are not cast in terms
of social conflict and Achaemenid Persian administrative policy but
are rather understood in the context of theological (ideological) concerns which arose in the aftermath of the dissolution of the kingdom of Judah and destruction of the Jerusalem temple: Does the

---

[49] See the entries in Haggai and Zechariah 1–8 in the major Introductions cited
in n. 13 above and see also the major commentaries of W. Rudolph, *Haggai—
Sacharja 1–8—Sacharja 9–14—Maleachi* (KAT 13/4; Gütersloh: Mohn, 1976) 21–23,
61–63; D. L. Petersen, *Haggai and Zechariah 1–8: A Commentary* (OTL; Philadelphia:
Westminster, 1984) 19–39, 109–25; Wolff, *Haggai*, 15–20; Meyers and Meyers,
Haggai, Zechariah 1–8, xl–xliv; and studies such as K.-M. Beyse, *Serubbabel und die
Königserwartungen der Propheten Haggai und Sacharja. Eine historische und traditionsgeschicht-
liche Untersuchung* (Arbeiten zur Theologie 1/48; Stuttgart: Calwer, 1972); S. Japhet,
"The Temple in the Restoration Period: Reality and Ideology," *Union Seminary Quar-
terly Review* 44 (1991) 199–200; J. E. Tollington, *Tradition and Innovation in Haggai and
Zechariah 1–8* (JSOTSup 150; Sheffield: Sheffield Academic Press, 1993) 19–47.

deity want the temple to be rebuilt and how does one determine this? When should the temple be rebuilt? Why should it be rebuilt when Judah neither has an indigenous king nor is it an independent state? What ideology could be used to legitimate the temple rebuilding in these circumstances? Who may legitimately rebuild the temple? One focus of this study is the investigation and elucidation of these prophetical texts' understanding of the social context of the rebuilding over against the contention that social division defined the character of early Achaemenid Judean society. Rather than impose an interpretative schema on these prophetical texts drawn from Ezra-Nehemiah, by which means they are made to reflect the central concerns of that schema, the texts should be investigated for their own understanding of the social context of the rebuilding. The use of external evidence, drawn from supposed Achaemenid Persian provincial policy, to establish the social context of the rebuilding is of course to be welcomed, but at exactly what points it is relevant needs to be determined.

The study of these issues from the perspective of Haggai and Zechariah 1–8 may, however, be viewed by some with more suspicion than that accorded the schemas since at least the latter seek to understand the temple rebuilding in terms of the changing political and social circumstances in Achaemenid Judah. But to use these texts is not to substitute theology for politics, rather it is to emphasize the point that in the ancient world the two were inseparable. Political and social developments influenced ideology and hence ideology can be used to help to understand the character of political and social change, albeit from a particular perspective.[50] Some exemplars of the schemas emphasize political and social circumstances over ideological concerns or introduce later ideological concerns into the period of the temple rebuilding, and thus skew the picture. If the present study places the emphasis on ideology it is in part to redress the imbalance, but it is also to bring out insights into contemporary Judeans' understanding of early Achaemenid Judean society that would otherwise be neglected.

---

[50] J. Z. Smith, "The Influence of Symbols on Social Change: A Place on Which to Stand," in *Map is Not Territory: Studies in the History of Religion* (SJLA 23; Leiden: E. J. Brill, 1978) 143–46.

While it is impossible to tell how representative these prophets' views are, they remain our only contemporary sources for the study of these basic ideological issues. In using these prophetical texts' understanding of the temple rebuilding it is recognized that these views reflect the tendentious perspectives of the authors. These prophets' concerns should not be considered idiosyncratic, however. Since the Jerusalem temple of Yahweh was the former national shrine of the kingdom of Judah which legitimated the state and the royal Judean house and which was abandoned by the deity to permit the destruction of the state, it cannot be doubted that these ideological issues needed to be addressed before the temple could be rebuilt. The significance of these prophets and their responses to these issues must have been considerable since their preaching issued in the Judeans actually rebuilding the temple.[51] The texts do not necessarily exhaust the historical reasons why the temple was rebuilt, and the present study offers an interpretation of the social context for the participation of Judeans, Zerubbabel and Joshua in the rebuilding and for the working out of these ideological concerns. These texts nevertheless give insight into how certain Judeans contemporary with the temple rebuilding understood the purpose of the undertaking and how they sought to legitimate it. They are sources for *conceptions* of the purpose of rebuilding the Jerusalem temple of Yahweh in early Achaemenid Judean society, the nature of the society, and the relationship of the temple to the community in the changed political and social circumstances of early Achaemenid Judah. Matters of note to the authors at the time of writing regarding social organization, the nature of the Judean polity, and Judean identity lie behind these conceptions.

---

[51] It must be admitted, however, that it is an assumption, based on Ezr 4:24–5:2 and the date formulae in Haggai and Zechariah 1–8, that these prophets prompted the Judeans to rebuild the temple. Similarly, there is no external evidence to support the contention that the Jerusalem temple was rebuilt in the early years of the reign of Darius I. Recently, L. Dequeker has argued that the rebuilding of the Jerusalem temple was undertaken in the reign of Darius II, not Darius I; see L. Dequeker, "Darius the Persian and the Reconstruction of the Jewish Temple in Jerusalem (Ezra 4, 23)," in *Ritual and Sacrifice in the Ancient Near East* (ed. J. Quaegebeur; OLA 55; Leuven: Peeters, 1993) 67–92; idem, "Nehemiah and the Restoration of the Temple after Exile," in *Deuteronomy and Deuteronomic Literature: Festschrift C. H. W. Brekelmans* (BETL 133; Leuven: Peeters/Leuven University Press, 1997) 547–67. The present study accepts the traditional dating of the temple rebuilding to the reign of Darius I.

The present study is structured in the following manner. Chapter 2 briefly reviews the evidence for the Judean communities in Judah and Babylonia in the aftermath of the dissolution of the kingdom of Judah. As the summary of the schemas given above showed, the period between the first Babylonian deportation from Jerusalem in 597 and the repatriation of exiled Judeans in the first decade(s) of Achaemenid Persian rule is considered by many to be the nascency of the social division of which we read in Ezra-Nehemiah. It is generally agreed that this period witnessed among the Judean communities in Judah and Babylonia the reformulation of Judean identity and social organization. The community of exiles in Babylonia is often thought to have reformulated Judean identity to exclude those who had remained in Judah and this reformulation served as the basis for the repatriates' exclusion of "the people of the land" on their return to their homeland. The division between "eschatologists" and "theocratists" identified by some commentators is also thought to have developed among the repatriates on the basis of conflicting ideas of the nature of the restoration of Judah adumbrated by prophets and others in the Babylonian exilic community. The evidence for the social organization of Judean communities in both Judah and Babylonia is shown to be scant, and evidence in support of the notion of separatism is questionable. The contention that the dissolution of the kingdom of Judah and the exile led to the reformulation of Judean identity as a "cultic community" (which on repatriation was centred on the temple), the repudiation of the non-exiles, and social division over the nature of the restoration, is rejected. These considerations therefore undermine claims that the rebuilding of the Jerusalem temple was undertaken in the context of or as an expression of some form of social conflict among Judeans. What is evidenced in texts attributed to Judeans in Babylonia are concerns for restoration, the legitimation of Yahweh's sovereignty, and the reworking of the monarchical royal-state ideology, all a result of the dissolution of the kingdom of Judah. The return of Yahweh to Jerusalem and, concomitantly, the Jerusalem temple of Yahweh feature in prophetic hopes for restoration (notably, in Deutero-Isaiah and Ezekiel 40–48). While these expectations differ in many respects, from which it is improper to conclude that they represent different "parties", they exhibit many features in continuity with the monarchical period ideology of Judean identity and share a common conception of the restoration of Judah in terms of historical recurrence. The period of

divine ire will pass and Yahweh will return to Jerusalem, restoring
the fortunes of Judah and her people, thus displaying Yahweh's sovereignty over the nations and the affairs of his people. This expectation of the restoration of Judah and the possibility of framing
restoration hopes, specifically for the present study the rebuilding of
the Jerusalem temple, in terms of a reworked monarchical period
royal-state ideology can be identified also in the preaching of Haggai
and Zechariah who support the temple's reconstruction in the first
years of the reign of Darius I.

Before turning to a discussion of Haggai, Zechariah and the temple rebuilding in the reign of Darius however, attention must be
given to a prior attempt to rebuild the Jerusalem temple in the reign
of Cyrus the Great. Chapter 3 addresses this supposed rebuilding
attempt, the source for which is Ezr 1:1–4:5. The importance of this
discussion lies in the fact that Ezr 1:1–4:5 offers an understanding
of the social context of the temple rebuilding, the place of the temple in the development of a new Judean polity, the purpose and
timing of the rebuilding of the Jerusalem temple, and the role of
the Achaemenid Persian administration in the undertaking. The evidence for this attempt to rebuild having taken place and the reasons posited for its failure are discussed, as are the concepts of Judean
identity and polity reflected in this text. Ezra 1:1–4:5 places social
division and the centrality of the temple for Judeans at the very
beginning of the Achaemenid Persian period when the exiles were
supposedly repatriated in the first years of the reign of Cyrus. There
is a discussion of the historical value of this narrative where it is
argued that it is a late, tendentious text which has little first-hand
knowledge the period it recounts. It places into the early period of
the restoration anachronistic concerns which reflect the author's
understanding of the character of Achaemenid Judean society current in his own day. Attempts to buttress the historical veracity of
Ezr 1:1–4:5 through the contention that the rebuilding attempt reflects
an Achaemenid Persian administrative policy are investigated and
found wanting, although it is most likely that the undertaking was
explicitly sanctioned by the administration. Ezr 1:1–4:5 is thus an
unreliable historical source for establishing the character and concerns of early Achaemenid Judean society and hence its understanding
of that society cannot serve as the framework in which to read the
other sources of early Achaemenid Judean history, namely, Ezr 5–6
(an Aramaic narrative on the rebuilding in the reign of Darius I),

Haggai and Zechariah 1–8. This is further borne out by a discussion of sections of Haggai and Zechariah 1–8 which display a completely different view of the Judeans' commitment to the temple rebuilding and the reasons for it not being built in the reign of Cyrus based on their understanding of the divinely propitious "time" to rebuild the temple.

Chapter 4 addresses the second, successful rebuilding attempt in the reign of Darius I. Arguments propounded in the schemas regarding the social context of this rebuilding are evaluated, including the proposition that the temple was rebuilt on the initiative of the Achaemenid Persian administration as a means of establishing the temple as the economic or administrative centre of Achaemenid Judah. Having discussed and rejected the claims that the temple was rebuilt as part of an Achaemenid Persian administrative policy and/or in order to institutionalize the separation between the repatriates and "the people of the land", attention is turned to positing an alternative understanding of the purpose of the rebuilding of the Jerusalem temple in the new political context of Achaemenid Judah and the social context in which it was undertaken.

It will be argued that Haggai and Zechariah 1–8, prophetical texts dated to the time of the temple rebuilding, in contradistinction to the arguments put forward in the schemas, understand the temple to have been rebuilt as a means of social integration, not in order to entrench social division. In the aftermath of the dissolution of the state and the repatriation of Judeans exiled to Babylonia, temple rebuilding afforded a way of reintegrating the two communities by means of a return to a state of normality under the sovereign rule of Yahweh and his chosen leaders. The symbolic significance of the temple and the ideology underpinning the temple rebuilding are particularly pertinent in this regard since they were drawn from traditions common to both groups. By participating in rebuilding the temple, an activity which both prophets proclaimed as ushering in a new age of Yahweh's kingship, the two groups could become one in a new community. The character of this new polity is not closely defined, however, but it is the expectation of these prophets that Judah would eventually return to the status of a monarchical state.

It is further argued that the impetus for the temple rebuilding came not from Judeans repatriated with Zerubbabel and Joshua c. 520 or from the Achaemenid Persian bureaucracy, although the latter established a favourable context for Judeans to undertake the

work themselves. Judeans already living in their homeland when
Zerubbabel, Joshua and others returned supplied the impetus for the
temple rebuilding. Included among these Judeans are those who
never went into exile. Temple rebuilding was thus undertaken by
both repatriates and non-repatriates, which belies the claim that division between these two groups was the social context of the rebuilding.
The social and political reasons why Zerubbabel and Joshua decided
to participate in the rebuilding are also briefly outlined; this again
being related to social integration and also to political legitimation.

The relationship of the Achaemenid Persian administration to the
temple rebuilding and its impact on temple ideology must also be
considered. Judah was no longer an independent kingdom with an
indigenous king but was a sub-province of the Achaemenid Persian
empire presided over by a Governor appointed by the Achaemenid
Persian bureaucracy (at what stage Judah obtained the status of sub-
province with its own Governor is still a debated point, but the present study accepts that at the time of the temple rebuilding in the
reign of Darius I Judah had its own Governor). Institutions in society, such as the temple, served the interests of the empire. For the
rebuilding of this former national shrine not to be construed as an
act of Judean rebellion, it must have been sanctioned by the Achaemenid Persian administration. Judeans faced the problem of developing a new temple ideology to justify and legitimate the rebuilding
of the temple, one that took into account the new political and social
structures obtaining in Achaemenid Judah, since the old monarchical ideology of the temple was inappropriate to justify the temple's
rebuilding in the Persian period. (Such an ideology would have been
unacceptable to the Achaemenid Persian administration). As the building of temples in the ancient Near East was a significant act symbolically, socially, and politically, the problem of developing an ideology
to justify and legitimate the rebuilding of the Jerusalem temple in
Achaemenid Judah was one that had to have been addressed by
Judeans. The temple ideology in Haggai and Zechariah 1–8 can be
understood as an attempt to remain in continuity with monarchical
period ideas of the temple while reworking these traditions for a
changed political context. The role of Zerubbabel both as the legitimate temple rebuilder in the eyes of the Judeans and as the Judean
governor (פחה *peḥāh*) appointed by the Achaemenid Persian administration is central in understanding how the rebuilding could pro-

ceed in a manner which was ideologically acceptable to Judeans and politically acceptable to the Achaemenid Persians.

Although the bulk of the present study focuses on the rebuilding of the Jerusalem temple, since it was the initial undertaking and raises the main issues addressed by Judeans and their Achaemenid Persian overlords, this is not to assume that the function of the temple in Achaemenid Judean society necessarily remained static; that is, that the purpose for which it was reconstructed remained its ongoing purpose. The purpose for its rebuilding must nevertheless bear some relationship to its ongoing function. To establish, if possible, why and when both Judeans and the Achaemenid Persian administration wanted this former national shrine rebuilt is a necessary first step to understanding any changing role for the temple.

CHAPTER TWO

LIVING WITHOUT THE JERUSALEM TEMPLE—IN JUDAH AND BABYLONIA

This chapter seeks to do two things. First, since social conflict figures prominently in numerous studies of early Achaemenid Judean society as the context in which to understand the rebuilding of the Jerusalem temple, section one discusses the putative background to such conflict in the period immediately after the dissolution of the kingdom of Judah. The evidence for the social organization and reformulation of Judean identity among the communities in Judah and Babylonia is briefly reviewed. It is argued that there is insufficient evidence to support the claim that the Judean exiles in Babylonia defined themselves as a "cultic community" and that they considered themselves to be the sole survivors of and successors to the kingdom of Judah to the exclusion of Judeans who had remained in their homeland.

Second, in order for the Jerusalem temple to be rebuilt in the changed social and political context of Achaemenid Judah, a temple ideology needed to be developed which would maintain continuity with the monarchical period ideology yet not be a challenge to Achaemenid Persian sovereignty over Judah. Section two of this chapter briefly explores changes to the monarchical period royal-state ideology (of which temple ideology was a part) in texts attributed to Judeans exiled in Babylonia. Of particular interest is the reworking of the relationship between the temple, Davidic kingship and the concept of the kingship of Yahweh. Both Deutero-Isaiah and Ezekiel 40–48 envisage the restoration of Israel to include the rebuilding of the Jerusalem temple as the symbol of Yahweh's kingship but adapt the role of the indigenous monarch in the temple rebuilding. This serves as the backdrop for understanding the relationship between indigenous kingship and temple rebuilding in Haggai and Zechariah 1–8, a topic to be addressed in chapter 4.

JUDEAN COMMUNITIES IN JUDAH AND BABYLONIA

The demise of the kingdom of Judah deeply affected Judean social
and political consciousness. Judeans were bereft of statehood, kingship and, for those forced to leave Judah, their homeland. The temple of Yahweh in Jerusalem was ruined and the capital city destroyed
(Ps 74:1–7; Ps 79:1; Is 64:9–10 [Eng. vv. 10–11]; Lam 2; II Ki
25:8–17). The deportation (II Ki 25:8–21; Jer 39:8–10; 52:12–30) or
flight (Jer 43:4–7; II Ki 25:26) of many politically and economically
prominent members of Judah led to the creation of communities of
Judeans living in exile in Babylonia, Elam, and Egypt, as well as living in Judah.[1] Scholarly attention has focused on the two major con-
centrations of Judeans—in Judah and in Babylonia. It must be said
at the outset that the period between the dissolution of the state
(587) and the repatriation of the exiled Judeans (under Cyrus and/or
Cambyses/Darius—538–522) remains something of a dark age for
Jewish history. This has not prevented a number of scholars from
delineating the nature of Judean society and religion in the aftermath of the destruction of the state, especially regarding those exiled
in Babylonia.

---

[1] On the communities in Judah and Babylonia see below. Regarding Elam,
specifically Susa (Neh 1:1; Esth 2:5, 4:16), there are questions concerning the value
of the book of Esther for establishing the role of Jews in Achaemenid Susa; see
C. A. Moore, "Archaeology and the Book of Esther," *BA* 38 (1975) 62–79, cf.
R. Gordis, "Religion, Wisdom and History in the Book of Esther—A New Solution
to an ancient Crux," *JBL* 100 (1981) 359–88; W. H. Shea, "Esther and History,"
AUSS 14 (1976) 227–46.
   In respect of Egypt, according to Jer 44:1 there were Judeans living "in the land
of Egypt with homes in Migdol, Tahpanhes [both on the north-eastern border of
Egypt], Noph [Memphis in Middle Egypt] and the land of Pathros [Upper Egypt]".
There was also a Jewish military colony at Elephantine (Yeb) in Upper Egypt which
was formed before the Judean exile. On this community, see B. Porten, *Archives from
Elephantine: The Life of an Ancient Jewish Military Colony* (Berkeley/Los Angeles: University
of California Press, 1968), and see pp. 8–16 for a history of Judean settlement in
Egypt; idem, "The Jews in Egypt," in *CHJ*, 1. 372–400. On the worship of Yahweh
at Elephantine, where a Yahwistic shrine was built and offerings, including animal
sacrifices, made (AP 30:21, 25; cf. AP 32:9 and AP 33:10–11 disallowing the con-
tinued sacrifice of animals), see A. Vincent, *La religion des judéo-araméens d'Elephantine*
(Paris: Geuthner, 1937); Porten, *Archives from Elephantine*, 103–86; Smith, "Jewish
Religious Life," 223–33; P. R. Bedford, "Jews at Elephantine," *Australian Journal of
Jewish Studies* 13 (1999) 6–23. This temple was already built when Cambyses entered
Egypt (AP 30:13). There were other deities besides Yahweh worshipped by the
Elephantine Jews, however Porten minimizes these Jews' religious syncretism.

Little is known about Judah after the dissolution of the state.[2] While the claim that the land of Judah was devoid of inhabitants is certainly incorrect, the extent of the Judean deportation is difficult to assess. The available archaeological evidence points to widespread deurbanization, but this should not necessarily be construed as reflecting mass deportation rather than ruralization.[3] The numbers of deportees cited in the biblical texts, while contradictory, show that a sizable proportion of the population must have remained in Judah and sought to resume normal life.[4] Although the biblical texts speak

[2] For an general overview of the evidence regarding Judah in the exilic period, see E. Janssen, *Juda in der Exilzeit. Ein Beitrag zur Frage der Entstehung des Judentums* (FRLANT 69; Göttingen: Vandenhoeck & Ruprecht, 1956) 39–56; P. R. Ackroyd, *Exile and Restoration: A Study of Hebrew Thought of the Sixth Century B.C.* (OTL; London: SCM, 1968) 20–31; H. Kreissig, *Die sozialökonomische Situation in Juda zur Achämenidenzeit* (Schriften zur Geschichte und Kultur des Alten Orients 7; Berlin: Akademie, 1973) 20–34; H. M. Barstad, "On the History and Archaeology of Judah during the Exilic Period. A Reminder," *OLP* 19 (1988) 25–36; idem, *The Myth of the Empty Land: A Study of the History and Archaeology of Judah During the "Exilic" Period* (Symbolae Osloenses Fasciculi suppletorii 28; Oslo: Scandinavian University Press, 1996).

[3] The available evidence points to the continued settlement of Benjamin and areas of the northern Judean hill country, but the specific dating of the latter settlements remains unclear. Benjamin appears to have escaped much of the destruction surrounding Nebuchadrezzar's invasion of 588–87 and enjoyed some prosperity in the ensuing period as evinced at Tell el-Ful, Bethel, Tell en-Naṣbeh, Gibeon, and, perhaps, Moṣah. On these sites see the summary in Stern, *Material Culture*, 31–35. As Stern notes (pp. 34–35), Moṣah has yet to be excavated, but the unpublished survey by A. Leon found a large amount of Persian period pottery at the site. On Moṣah see also N. Avigad, "Two Hebrew Inscriptions on Wine Jars," *IEJ* 22 (1972) 7–9; J. Zorn, J. Yellin and J. Hayes, "The *m(w)ṣh* Stamp Impressions and the Neo-Babylonian Period," *IEJ* 44 (1994) 161–83. A. Malamat, "The Last Wars of the Kingdom of Judah," *JNES* 9 (1950) 226–27, accounts for this lack of destruction by postulating that the Benjaminites surrendered their territory to the Babylonians. In Judah the urban sites (such as Jerusalem, Tell ed Duweir [= Lachish? cf. Jer 34:7], Tell Zakariya (Azekah), Eglon, Tell Beth Mirsim, Beth Zur, Ramat Rahel, Beth-Shemesh, Arad, Ein Gedi [see Jer 34:7; 44:2]) were destroyed in Nebuchadrezzar's invasion in 588–87. How the countryside and villages were affected is unclear since the necessary survey work has yet to be completed. For a summary of the archaeological evidence, see Janssen, *Juda in der Exilzeit*, 24–56; S. S. Weinberg, "Post-Exilic Palestine. An Archaeological Report," *Proceedings of the Israel Academy of Sciences and Humanities* 4/5 (1969) 78–97; Carter, "Social and Demographic Study," 93–166; idem, "The Province of Yehud in the Post-Exilic Period: Soundings in Site Distribution and Demography," in *Second Temple Studies: 2. Temple and Community in the Persian Period* (ed. T. C. Eskenazi and K. H. Richards; JSOTSup 175; Sheffield: JSOT Press, 1994) 106–45; Barstad, *Myth of the Empty Land*, 47–60.

[4] Although many have proffered population estimates for Judah in this period, there is scant evidence available. J. P. Weinberg's estimate ("Demographische Notizen zur Geschichte der nachexilischen Gemeinde in Juda," *Klio* 54 [1972] 45–50) of the population of monarchical period Judah (8th–6th centuries) at 200,000–250,000

of only the "poor of the land" (דלת הארץ) remaining after 587, one
should not thereby conclude that all who remained were of lowly
station. Literate Judeans who remained in the land were probably
responsible for a number of the texts ascribed to the post-destruc-
tion period,[5] and it is reasonable to assume that Gedaliah had a
number of pro-Babylonian colleagues who were people of note (Jer
42:8). Even after the assassination of Gedaliah (II Ki 25:25) and subsequent flight or deportation of certain groups in 582, the district
would still have had a sizeable population.[6]

---

is generally considered to be too high. M. Broshi and I. Finkelstein, "The Population
of Palestine in Iron Azge II," *BASOR* 287 (1992) 47–60, estimate the population of
Iron II Palestine to be c. 400,000, with c. 132,000 living in Judea (including the
Shephelah). The relevant biblical texts (Jer 52:15–16, 28–30; II Ki 24:8–16, 25:8–27)
are confused as to the number of exiles and the relationship between the first deportation of 597 and that of 587. According to Jer 52:28, 3,023 Judeans were deported
in the Babylonian invasion of 597, while II Ki 24:14 claims that 10,000 persons,
"all Jerusalem", were deported (though cf. II Ki 24:16 where a figure of 8,000 [oth-
ers?] is mentioned). For the deportation of 587, one can compare Jer 52:29, which
has 832 persons deported "from Jerusalem" with II Ki 25:8–12, which presumes
mass deportation from Judah as a whole. With regard to the scholarly discussion
one can compare, for example, Janssen (*Juda in der Exilzeit*, 28–36), who considers
that 4,600 persons were exiled, with A. Malamat ("Last Wars," 223), who contends
that about 10,000 men, "about thirty thousand people, most of them from Jerusalem,
and the others from the Shephelah and the Negev (cf. Jer. 13:18–19)", were exiled.
K. Galling (*Studien zur Geschichte Israels im persischen Zeitalter* [Tübingen: J. C. B. Mohr
(Paul Siebeck), 1964] 51–52) puts the number exiled at no more than twenty thousand persons. According to II Ki 24:12–16; Jer 24:1, 27:20, 29:1–2, the ruling class,
soldiers and tradesmen were deported. Even after the number of those killed in the
wars is reckoned in, those who remained in Judah—"the poor of the land" (II Ki
25:12 cf. 24:14; Jer 39:10, 52:15f.)—must account for the vast majority of the population. Carter, "Province of Yehud," argues that the population of Achaemenid
Judah ranged between 11,000 and 17,000, and that the area of the sub-province
is much smaller than is usually recognized. Carter is followed by Meyers and Meyers,
Zechariah 9–14, 22–26.
    [5] Janssen, *Juda in der Exilzeit*, sees Lamentations, Is 21, the Deuteronomistic
History, Obadiah, and Pss 44, 74, 89, 102 being written in Judah. The date and
provenance of the Deuteronomistic History in particular is still under debate. H. M.
Barstad has argued for a Judean provenance for Deutero-Isaiah in *A Way in the
Wilderness: The "Second Exodus" in the Message of Second Isaiah* (JSS Monograph 12;
Manchester: University of Manchester, 1989); idem, *The Babylonian Captivity of the
Book of Isaiah: "Exilic" Judah and the Provenance of Isaiah 40–55* (Oslo: Novus: Instituttet
for sammenlignende kulturforskining, 1997).
    [6] A further deportation of 745 inhabitants from Jerusalem took place in 582,
Nebuchadrezzar's twenty-third year (Jer 52:30). This should be seen as a response
to the assassination of Gedaliah by Judean nationalists (II Ki 25:25; Jer 41:1–3).
On dating this event to c. 582, see Oesterley and Robinson, *History of Israel*, 1. 442–43;
P. R. Ackroyd, *Israel Under Babylon and Persia* (New Clarendon Bible; Oxford: Oxford
University Press, 1970) 36–37. This deportation coincides, according to Josephus,
Antiquities, x. 181ff., with Nebuchadrezzar's subjugation of the Ammonites and

Beyond fleeting insights into the political and social confusion in Judean life during Gedaliah's brief tenure as governor, little is known about this territory over the next fifty years. Economic conditions were difficult immediately after the 588–87 invasion, but they may have slowly ameliorated through the Babylonians permitting those who remained in Judah to work the former royal estates and the land abandoned by the deportees.[7] The area of Judah was greatly reduced with the Negev and southern Judah lost to Edomite encroachments. This territory may have been formally ceded to Edom by the Babylonians.[8] If Judah had not been subsumed within the neighbouring district of Samaria immediately, it probably had been by 582, and remained so for the duration of the Babylonian administration.[9]

Moabites who up until that time had enjoyed a certain amount of independence within the empire. On Transjordan under the Babylonians, see Lemaire, "Les transformations politiques et culturelles," 9–27.

[7] So Jer 39:10 cf. Jer 52:16; II Ki 25:12 (and cf. Ezek 11:15 which refers to the 597 deportation). J. N. Graham, "Vinedressers and Ploughmen," *BA* 47 (1984) 55–58, contends that the Babylonians instituted "a state-managed economic plan" in which they pressed the Judeans into forced labour on the land left abandoned. Gedaliah's role as governor was to oversee this programme.

[8] A. Alt, "Judas Gaue unter Josiah," in *Kleine Schriften zur Geschicte des Volkes Israels* (3 vols; Munich: Beck, 1953–59) 2. 280–81, and Noth, *History*, 283, think that the Negev had been detached from Judah as early as 597 (cf. Jer 13:19). On Edomite incursions, which started as early as the eighth century, see J. M. Myers, "Edom and Judah in the Sixth–Fifth Centuries B.C.," in *Near Eastern Studies in Honor of William Foxwell Albright* (ed. H. Goedicke; Baltimore: The Johns Hopkins University Press, 1971) 377–92; I. Beit-Arieh, "New Data on the Relationship between Judah and Edom toward the End of the Iron Age," in *Recent Excavations in Israel: Studies in Iron Age Archaeology* (ed. S. Gitin and W. G. Dever. AASOR 49; Winona Lake, IN: Eisenbrauns for ASOR, 1989) 125–31; although cf. J. R. Bartlett, "Edom and the Fall of Jerusalem, 587 B.C.," *PEQ* 114 (1982) 17–18, who does not accept that Edomites were involved in the fall of Jerusalem or that they encroached onto Judean territory. There was also increased Phoenician and Greek influence in the region, on which see H.-P. Müller, "Phönizien und Juda in exilisch-nachexilischer Zeit," *WdO* 6 (1971) 189–204; Smith, *Palestinian Parties*, 43–61; J. Elayi, "Studies in Phoenician Geography during the Persian Period," *JNES* 41 (1983) 83–110; S. Mittmann, "Die Küste Palastinas bei Herodot," *ZDPV* 99 (1983) 130–140. The borders of Judah after 587 are difficult to establish as the earliest information available refers to the time of Nehemiah (c. 445) and may not reflect conditions prior to then. On the borders in Nehemiah's time, see M. Avi-Yonah, *The Holy Land. From the Persian to Arab Conquest (536 B.C.–A.D. 640): A Historical Geography* (Text Revisions and Toponymic Index by A. F. Rainey; Grand Rapids: Baker, 1977) 14–23. On the political geography of the southern Levant in the Persian period, see A. Lemaire, "Populations et territoires de la Palestine à l'époque perse," *Transeu* 3 (1990) 31–74 (on Judah see esp. pp. 36–45), and for a recent attempt to define the borders of Judah more narrowly than is commonly done, see Carter, "Social and Demographic Study," 53–92.

[9] One point in favour of Judah having been subsumed within Samaria is that its borders in Nehemiah's time were different from those at the end of the monarchy.

Jer 41:5 attests that cultic life continued in Jerusalem on the site
of the ruined temple of Yahweh, at least during the time of Gedaliah,
but neither the nature of cultic activity undertaken there nor its duration can be established.[10] The book of Lamentations has been thought
by some to have been read in Jerusalem at an annual cultic ceremony for the destruction of the temple.[11]

There is also scant information regarding the social organization
and religious life of those Judeans exiled to Babylonia.[12] It appears
that Babylonian policy was to settle deported ethnic minorities in
their own communities.[13] The biblical texts mention a number of
locations where Judean communities were founded, namely, Tel Abib
(Ezek 3:15), Casiphia (Ezr 8:17), and, perhaps, Tel Melah, Tel
Harsha, Cherub, Addan/Addon, and Immer (Ezr 2:59 // Neh 7:61).
Only the location of Tel Abib, "beside the river Chebar", is possibly

---

These new borders could have been drawn up after a period as an enclave in
Samaria. Had Judah immediately been placed within Samaria, Gedaliah would have
served under its district governor. On the relationship between Samaria and Judah
in this period, see A. Alt, "Die Rolle Samarias bei der Entstehung des Judentums,"
in *Kleine Schriften*, 2. 316–37; S. McEvenue, "The Political Structure in Judah from
Cyrus to Nehemiah," *CBQ* 43 (1981) 353–64, who view Judah as under the jurisdiction of Samaria until the time of Nehemiah; E. Stern, "The Province of Yehud:
the Vision and the Reality," *The Jerusalem Cathedra* 1 (1981) 9–21, who is in general agreement, except that for a time under Zerubbabel Judah was independent.
I consider it likely, however, that Judah was an autonomous sub-province under its
own governor from the time of Sheshbazzar; on which see below chapter 3 n. 4,
chapter 4 n. 7.

[10] For a discussion of the nature of the cultic activity and the cultic officials
involved, see D. R. Jones, "The Cessation of Sacrifice after the Destruction of the
Temple in 586 B.C.," *JTS* NS 14 (1963) 12–31, who contends that only cereal
offerings were made; N. Allen, "The Identity of the Jerusalem Priesthood during
the Exile," *Heythrop Journal* 23 (1982) 259–69, sees continued cultic activity under
certain Levites who were not exiled; J. Blenkinsopp, "Judean Priesthood," 25–43,
argues for a shift of cultic activity to Mizpah, followed by Bethel after the attempted
coup d'état of Ishmael.

[11] H.-J. Kraus, *Klagelieder (Threni)* (BKAT 20; Neukirchen: Kries Moers, 1956)
10–13.

[12] These were deportees from the Babylonian invasions of 597, 588/7 and 582.
For a summary of the available evidence regarding their life in Babylonia, see
Ackroyd, *Exile and Restoration*, 31–38; E. J. Bickerman, "The Diaspora: The Babylonian
Captivity," in *CHJ*, 1. 342–58. Weidner, "Jojachin, König von Juda," 923–28, attests
that Jehoiachin received rations from the Babylonian court. How this text relates
to II Ki 25: 27–30, a passage concerning the imprisonment of Jehoiachin in Babylonia
and his later release, is unclear.

[13] I. Eph'al, "The Western Minorities in Babylonia in the 6th–5th Centuries B.C.:
Maintenance and Cohesion," *Or* NS 47 (1978) 74–90; M. A. Dandamayev, "Aliens
and the Community in Babylonia in the 6th–5th Centuries B.C.," *Recueils de la
Société Jean Bodin* 41 (1983) 133–45.

known. This "river" has been identified with an irrigation canal of the Euphrates, the *nār kabāri*, which flowed through Nippur.[14] The Murašû archive from Nippur attests a Judean presence there in the second half of the fifth century. The Judeans mentioned in these texts were largely tenant farmers, though some are known to be rent collectors and minor officials.[15] Individuals were integrated into Babylonian economic structures, such as the *ḫaṭru*, and it has been suggested that the Judeans who formed distinct communities may have had limited self-determination under the authority of their own elders (Ezek 8:1; 14:1; 20:1, 3; Jer 29:1) and assemblies.[16] Other ethnic

---

[14] H. V. Hilprecht and A. T. Clay, *Business Documents of Murashû Sons of Nippur* (The Babylonian Expedition of the University of Pennsylvania, Series A: Cuneiform Texts 9; Philadelphia: Department of Archaeology and Palaeontology of the University of Pennsylvania, 1898) 28. For references in cuneiform sources to this canal, see R. Zadok, *Répertoire géographie des textes cunéiformes. Band 8: Geographical Names according to New- and Late-Babylonian Texts* (Beihefte zum Tübinger Atlas des vorderen Orients Reihe B 7/8; Wiesbaden: Reichert, 1985) 373 s.v. Nar-Kabāru; idem, "The Nippur Region during the Late Assyrian, Chaldean and Achaemenid Periods, chiefly according to written sources," *Israel Oriental Studies* 8 (1978) 287.

New evidence for Judean communities in Babylonia can be found in two cuneiform legal texts recently published in F. Joannès and A. Lemaire, "Trois tablettes cunéiformes à onomastique ouest-sémitique," *Transeu* 17 (1999) 17–30. One text, dated to 498 (24th year of Darius I), contains twelve Hebrew names and was written in Al-Yahudu (URU *ia-a-ḫu-du*) "city/town of Judah", which the editors locate near Sippar. The second text, written at Alu Bit-Našar (URU É *na-šar*) near Borsippa in 532 (7th year of Cyrus), contains probably a half-dozen Hebrew names, but most interestingly designates one of them, Abda-Yahu, as [lú]*dēkû*, an official responsible for collecting taxes (cf. *CAD* vol. 3, s.v. *dēkû* "summoner [for taxes and corvée work]"). As the editors note (p. 30), "Il est, de toute manière, important de remarquer que dès le règne de Cyrus on trouve dans l'administration officielle une personne clairement juive d'après son onomastique."

[15] For the identification of Judeans on the basis of onomastica, see R. Zadok, *The Jews in Babylonia during the Chaldean and Achaemenian Periods* (Haifa: University of Haifa, 1979), 1–34. Zadok (pp. 51–52) also gives a list of settlements in the region of Nippur where Judeans lived. At a number of these locations they were settled beside other foreign ethnic groups. On Judeans at Nippur, see M. D. Coogan, "Life in the Diaspora: Jews at Nippur in the Fifth Century B.C.," *BA* 37 (1974) 6–12; R. Zadok, *Jews in Babylonia*; G. Wallis, "Jüdische Bürger in Babylonien während der Achämeniden-Zeit," *Persica* 9 (1980) 129–86; E. J. Bickerman, "The Generation of Ezra and Nehemiah," in *Studies in Jewish and Christian History*, (3 vols.; AGAJU 9; Leiden: E. J. Brill, 1976–86) 3. 299–326; idem, "Diaspora," 346–48. On the significance of the Murašû archive in general, see M. W. Stolper, *Entrepreneurs and Empire. The Murašû Archive, the Murašû Firm, and Persian Rule in Babylonia* (Uitgaven van het Nederlands Historisch-Archaelogisch Instituut te Istanbul 54; Leiden: Nederlands Historisch-Archaelogisch Instituut te Istanbul, 1985); cf. G. van Driel, "The Murašûs in Context," *JESHO* 32 (1989) 203–29.

[16] See Zadok, *Jews in Babylonia*, 44–81, for members of *ḫaṭru* organizations. Some ethnic minorities appear to have formed their own *ḫaṭru*s; see Stolper, *Murašû*, 72–79.

minorities are known to have been so organized.[17] While it is plausible that certain groups of exiled Judeans lived in distinct communities, the Murašû texts yield no direct information regarding the social organization, authority structures, or religious practices of the Judeans.[18]

Of doubtless concern to many Judean exiles was the maintenance of their identity. With the loss of statehood and kingship it is often claimed that the identity of the Babylonian Judean community was defined by the exiled priesthood and founded on the priestly Torah. The separation of the community from things foreign (most notably, women and gods) was supposedly one aspect of this. Increased prominence is thought to have been given to circumcision and to the observance of the Sabbath and other holy days as a means of maintaining group identity.[19] The loss of the temple is thought to have

---

[17] M. A. Dandamayev, "Aliens and the Community in Babylonia," 133–45; idem, "The Neo-Babylonian Elders," in *Societies and Languages of the Ancient Near East. Studies in Honour of I. M. Diakonoff* (ed. M. A. Dandamayev et al.; Warminster: Aris and Phillips, 1982) 31; I. Eph'al, "On the Political and Social Organization of the Jews in Babylonian Exile," in *XXI. Deutscher Orientalistentag. Vorträge* (ed. F. Steppat; Zeitschrift der Deutschen Morgenländischen Gesellschaft Supplement 5; Wiesbaden: Steiner, 1983) 106–12; M. Heltzer, "The Story of Suzanna and the Self-Government of the Jewish Community in Achaemenid Babylonia," *Annali dell'Institute Orientale di Napoli* 41 (1981) 35–39; Smith, *Religion of the Landless*, 94–107, on elders and the development of בתי אבות as a form of exilic social organization. On other West Semites in Babylonia, see M. D. Coogan, *West Semitic Personal Names in the Murašû Documents* (HSM 7; Missoula, MT: Scholars Press, 1976); R. Zadok, *On West Semites in Babylonia during the Chaldean and Achaemenian Periods* (Jerusalem: Wanaarta, 1977); idem, "Phoenicians, Philistines, and Moabites in Mesopotamia," *BASOR* 230 (1978) 57–65. Elias Bickerman has suggested that the social position and organization of such groups may be similar to the *politeumata* of Hellenistic Greek cities ("The Edict of Cyrus in Ezra 1," in *Studies in Jewish and Christian History*, 1. 89), but the available information is too limited to determine the correctness of this suggestion.

[18] Bickerman, "Generation," 319–26, sees a return to traditional Judean (Yahwistic) names in the Murašû texts as reflecting a revival in the worship of Yahweh among the descendants of the Judean exiles. It is questionable, however, that such a conclusion should be drawn from this onomastic evidence alone.

[19] So, for example, W. E. O. Oesterley and T. H. Robinson, *Hebrew Religion: Its Origin and Development* (2d ed., rev. and enlarged; New York: Macmillan, 1937) 286–87; H.-J. Kraus, *Worship in Israel: A Cultic History of the Old Testament* (trans. G. Buswell; Richmond: John Knox, 1966) 87–88; N. Wyatt, "Symbols of Exile," *SEÅ* 55 (1990) 41–48; K. Grünwaldt, *Exil und Identität. Beschneidung, Passa und Sabbat in der Priesterschrift* (BBB 85; Frankfurt am Main: Anton Hain, 1992); Albertz, *History of Israelite Religion*, 2. 407–11. On circumcision, see also R. de Vaux, *Ancient Israel: Its Life and Institutions* (trans. J. McHugh; London: Darton, Longman and Todd, 1961) 46–48. However, the evidence cited for the rise or increased importance of either Sabbath observance or circumcision in this period is not unequivocal. On the Sabbath, see also N.-E. A. Andreasen, *The Old Testament Sabbath: A Tradition*

led to the rise of prayer in the place of sacrifice, although it is unlikely that the meeting of Judeans for prayer (and, supposedly, Torah study) is the origin of what is later known as the synagogue.[20] The development of this new mode of identity for the Babylonian Judean communities is held to be the basis of the social division in Achaemenid Judah between the repatriates and the Judeans who had remained in their homeland. The non-repatriates were not familiar with the repatriates' authority structures, sacred texts, and practices. This, coupled with the concept that Yahweh had rejected all those who had not gone into exile, demanded that the non-repatriates be viewed as something other than "Judeans".[21]

The priestly Torah has been commonly understood to be the charter of the Babylonian Judean communities. It articulates a polity and manner of life for Judeans apart from kingship, temple, and homeland. In Leviticus-Numbers, quintessential priestly texts, Judeans are

---

Historical Investigation (SBLDS 7; Missoula, MT: Society for Biblical Literature, 1972) 235–54; G. Robinson, *The Origin and Development of the Old Testament Sabbath: A Comprehensive Exegetical Approach* (Beiträge zur biblischen Exegeses und Theologie 21; Frankfort am Main: Lang, 1988) 247–72. Both Sabbath observance and circumcision could have been practiced in the Judean homeland as well as in the Babylonian diaspora. Even if their practice came to be more prominent in the diaspora, it remains unclear how it spread and over what period of time its prominence developed (before 538?, 522?, 445?). A. Lemaire, "Le sabbat à l'époque royale israélite," *RB* 80 (1983) 182–84, followed by E. Nodet, *A Search for the Origins of Judaism: From Joshua to the Mishnah* (trans. E. Crowley; JSOTSup 248; Sheffield: Sheffield Academic Press, 1997) 119–20, would see the institution of a weekly Sabbath observance as no earlier than Nehemiah.

[20] On prayer replacing sacrifice, see J. D. Levenson, "From Temple to Synagogue: 1 Kings 8," in *Traditions in Transformation. Turning Points in Biblical Faith* (ed. B. Halpern and J. D. Levenson; Winona Lake, IN: Eisenbrauns, 1981) 143–66. On Ptolemaic Egypt as the location of the origin of the synagogue, see J. G. Griffiths, "Egypt and the Rise of the Synagogue," *JTS* NS 38 (1987) 1–15; L. L. Grabbe, "Synagogues in Pre-70 Palestine," *JTS* NS 39 (1988) 401–10.

The existence of a Jewish temple in Babylonia has been suggested on the basis of biblical references to "the place" (Heb. מקום) in Casiphia (Ezr 8:17) and "sanctuary" (Heb. מקדש; Ezek 11:16), the former with the technical sense of "holy place", "shrine" (so, L. E. Browne, "A Jewish Sanctuary in Babylonia," *JTS* OS 17 [1916] 400–1; J. H. Chong, "Were there Yahwistic Sanctuaries in Babylon?" *Asia Journal of Theology* 10 [1996] 198–217). Judean cultic personnel were certainly exiled, but there are elements in Israelite and Judean traditions which hold that it was impossible to worship Yahweh outside his territory. See, for example, I Sam 26:19; II Ki 5:17 where the Aramean general Naᶜaman takes sacks of Israelite soil with him to Damascus in order to worship Yahweh there; see also Ps 137. Whether or not the Deuteronomic prohibition against having sanctuaries other than the Jerusalem temple influenced these exiles is unknown.

[21] On the rejection of those who had not gone into exile by those who had, see chapter 1 n. 37.

conceived of as the people of Yahweh who constitute a cultic community living outside the land of Judah under the authority of the
priesthood and Torah. These texts have been thought to reflect
priestly conceptions of the social organization and authority structures of the Judeans in Babylonian exile and later, after their repatriation, in Achaemenid Judah. This community has been variously
termed a "theocracy", "hagiocracy", and "hierocracy". The exiled
priests are thought to have been integral to these developments since
they supposedly filled some of the power vacuum in the community
created by the loss of kingship, perhaps by virtue of their former
role in the national cult of Yahweh in Jerusalem.

The prominence supposedly accorded the priestly Torah (P, or
perhaps only the Holiness Code—Lev 17–26 [H])[22] has been held
to attest the increased importance of the priesthood since much of
this Torah is cultic law applied to the daily life of the ordinary person (for example, purity laws, marriage laws, cultic feasts) and in its
world-view the cult and the preservation of its holiness are the preeminent concerns of the community.[23] In this vision of the community priests are indispensable. Their authority rests in their knowledge
and control of divine revelation as embodied in the Torah and in
their specialist role in offering sacrifices at the altar. Since the cult

---

[22] Even defining the extent of this Torah is problematic. There is no unanimity
regarding what the priestly Torah consisted of in this period. Indeed, P and H
have been interpreted as reflecting two distinct priestly schools rather than as texts
from a single source; see I. Knohl, "The Priestly Torah versus the Holiness School:
Sabbath and the Festivals," *HUCA* 58 (1987) 65–117; idem, *The Sanctuary of Silence:
The Priestly Torah and the Holiness School* (Minneapolis: Fortress Press, 1995). Knohl
dates both P and H to the monarchical period. Also contending for a monarchical period date for H is J. Joosten, *People and Land in the Holiness Code: An Exegetical
Study of the Ideational Framework of the Law in Leviticus 17–26* (VTSup 67; Leiden/New
York/Cologne: E. J. Brill, 1996).
[23] On the role of the priestly Torah in the exilic community see, for example,
A. Lods, *The Prophets and the Rise of Judaism* (trans. S. H. Hooke; New York: Dutton,
1937) 251–64; R. H. Pfeiffer, *Religion in the Old Testament: The History of a Spiritual
Triumph* (New York: Harper and Brothers, 1961) 175–79; J. M. Myers, *The World
of the Restoration* (Background to the Bible Series; Englewood Cliffs, NJ: Prentice-
Hall, 1968) 15–20; Ackroyd, *Exile and Restoration*, 84–91; R. W. Klein, *Israel in Exile:
A Theological Interpretation* (Overtures to Biblical Theology; Philadelphia: Fortress, 1979)
125–48; Anderson, *Understanding the Old Testament*, 451–66; Smith, *Religion of the
Landless*, 139–51. The book of Ezekiel is widely held to reflect views similar to the
Holiness Code (Lev 17–26) and thus the existence of a priestly Torah; see the above
works and also G. Fohrer, *Die Hauptprobleme des Buches Ezechiel* (BZAW 72; Berlin:
Töpelmann, 1952) 144–48; and on the relationship between P and Ezekiel, see
Blenkinsopp, *Prophecy and Canon*, 69–73.

of Yahweh was of great significance to the priesthood, by dint of their authority over the community it must have been made central to the life of the community once they were repatriated.

Even if one allows a leadership role for priests in Babylonia and, after the repatriation, in Judah, over whom and in what areas they exercised authority remain undefined. The circumstances in which the priestly laws could have been implemented also remain unclear. Closely related to this issue is the question of when this Torah was written or compiled. P and H have been dated anywhere from the reign of Hezekiah to the reign of Artaxerxes II.[24] Although these texts, or early editions of them, may have had long-standing authority within sections of the priesthood, the majority of scholars would not date this Torah's enactment in the community before the fall of the kingdom of Judah. As to the context in which it came into force in the community, some relate it to the Babylonian exile where there was a need to define the distinctive features of Judaism in a pagan environment,[25] others to Darius's supposed codification of the indigenous laws of his subject peoples (and then, it is assumed, making them the civil law),[26] still others relate it to the mission of Ezra who in the reign of Artaxerxes II (?) comes with "the law of God" (Ezr 7:10 cf. 7:25) that is to be implemented in Abar Nahara.[27] However,

---

[24] On the spectrum of dates for P see chapter 1 n. 15 above. On the date of H, which is commonly ascribed to the Babylonian exile, see Eissfeldt, *Introduction*, 236–39; cf. Knohl, *Sanctuary of Silence*, 199–224, for a monarchical period dating. Lods, *The Prophets and the Rise of Judaism*, 266, understands the repatriates to be "permeated with the spirit of Ezekiel and the Holiness Code". They formed a "little colony of ritualists grouped together in the province of Judah" (p. 267). Those who had remained in Judah had been living under the Deuteronomistic law (p. 265).

[25] See the works cited in n. 23 and also Kapelrud, "Date of the Priestly Code," 58–64; D. N. Freedman, "The Earliest Bible," *Michigan Quarterly Review* 22 (1983) 167–75, who understands the Pentateuch and Former Prophets to have been edited and prepared in exile; Smith, *Religion of the Landless*, 139–53. Smith also emphasizes the position of elders in the leadership of the exilic community (pp. 94–99) but does not explain the relationship between the roles of elder and priest.

[26] On dating the Torah's enactment to Darius I see, for example, M. Noth, *A History of Pentateuchal Traditions* (trans. B. W. Anderson; Englewood Cliffs, NJ: Prentice-Hall, 1972) 243; idem, *Exodus: A Commentary* (trans. J. Bowden; OTL; Philadelphia: Westminster, 1962) 17, who is followed by R. E. Clements, *God and Temple* (Oxford: Blackwell, 1965) 111, in dating P to c. 515, that is, to the completion of the temple. See, similarly, Meyers and Meyers, *Haggai, Zechariah 1–8*, 380. In support of this is cited the codification of Egyptian cultic laws of the House of Life by Udjahorresne in 519 at the behest of Darius I, on which see below, pp. 197–201.

[27] This view was current in earlier critical literature, for example, A. Kuenen, *The History of Israel to the Fall of the Jewish State* (3 vols.; trans. A. H. May; London/

there are no means at our disposal to test these claims regarding
either the date of the enactment of the priestly Torah or the supposed increased authority of the priesthood on the basis of the enactment of the priestly Torah in either Babylonia or Achaemenid Judah.
In any case, much of the material in this code (including H) is

Edinburgh: Williams and Norgate, 1874–75; original Dutch edition published in
1869–70) 2. 231; Meyer, *Entstehung*, 206–08. For a history of scholarship on the
identification, character, and dating of P, see Thompson, *Moses and the Law*. Vink,
"The Date and Origin of the Priestly Code in the Old Testament," 1–144, is a
relatively recent attempt to identify Ezra's law book with P. Wellhausen, *Prolegomena
to the History of Israel*, 404–46, understood the Deuteronomic law to be in effect
until Ezra enacted his law, namely, the Pentateuch (including, of course, P), cf.
S. Mowinckel, *Studien zu dem Buche Ezra-Nehemia* (3 vols. Skrifter utgitt av det Norske
Videnskaps-akademi i Oslo. II. Hist.-filos. klasse. Ny serie 3, 5, 7; Oslo: Universitetsforlaget, 1964–65) 3. 124–41, who understands Ezra's laws to be the Pentateuch in penultimate form; J. M. Myers, *Ezra-Nehemiah* (AB 14; New York: Doubleday,
1965) lix; F. M. Cross, *Cannanite Myth and Hebrew Epic* (Cambridge, MA: Harvard
University Press, 1974) 324. J. Blenkinsopp, "The Mission of Udjahorresnet and
those of Ezra and Nehemiah," *JBL* 106 (1987) 409–21, sees the activity of Ezra
and Nehemiah as similar to that of Udjahorresne in Egypt (during the reigns of
Cambyses and Darius I) in codifying local laws. That is, the codification of the
Jewish law took place in the reign of Artaxerxes II who supposedly continued the
policy of Darius.
   If these cultic stipulations were formulated in Babylonia after the initial return
(538), then much of Ezra's law may have been new to the Jerusalem priesthood.
It would also show that the real authority over the Jerusalem cult lay with Babylonian
Jewry, not the Jerusalem priesthood. It is doubtful, however, that Ezra's law was,
in fact, P or any large portion of it, let alone the Pentateuch. For an overview of
opinions as to the identity of Ezra's law book, see C. Houtman, "Ezra and the
Law: Observations on the Supposed Relationship between Ezra and the Pentateuch,"
OTS 21 (1981) 91–115. He concludes that "the law book which the books of Ezra
and Nehemiah suppose cannot be identified with the Pentateuch or any part of it"
(p. 111). He considers the law book to be another legal document which had many
laws in common with the Pentateuch, but which also contained "commandments
which differ in some degree from the commandments in the Pentateuch and moreover prescriptions which are not known from the Pentateuch" (p. 109). U. Kellermann,
"Erwägungen zum Ezragesetz," *ZAW* 80 (1968) 373–85, and Williamson, *Ezra,
Nehemiah*, 104–05, understand the law to be Deuteronomy; cf. K. Koch, *Die Priesterschrift
von Exod. xxv bis Lev. xvi* (FRLANT 71; Göttingen: Vandenhoeck & Ruprecht, 1959).
J. Blenkinsopp, *Ezra-Nehemiah* (OTL; Philadelphia: Westminster Press, 1988) 155,
contends that "Ezra's law *as understood by the redactor* refers basically to Deuteronomic
law supplemented by ritual legislation in the Pentateuchal corpora conventionally
designated P and H." [author's emphasis]
   To complicate matters further, some hold that Ezra and his mission are literary
fiction. Among the recent exponents of this view are Garbini, *History and Ideology in
Ancient Israel*, 151–69, where the history of scholarship on this view is also briefly
recounted; cf. L. L. Grabbe, "What was Ezra's Mission?" in *Second Temple Studies:
2*, 286–99, who, while deeply suspicious of the historical veracity of the narrative,
is somewhat more circumspect in his conclusions.

utopian. It would have been possible only for certain sections of it to have been implemented.[28]

To illuminate the life of the Judean exiles in Babylonia, Daniel Smith has made judicious use of comparative sociological data regarding the mechanisms of group maintenance of modern exiled peoples.[29] Some similarities in this regard between the Judean and modern exiles should be expected. Smith draws attention to four areas: first, structural adaptation (that is, changes in social organization), in which he sees the development of the בית אבות as the basic form of group organization and the rise of elders to positions of leadership within this structure. Both of these innovations were carried into Judah with the repatriation of the exiles; second, the rise of new leadership, markedly in the struggle between prophets with differing perspectives on the exiles' attitude to living in exile (he cites the example of Jeremiah and Hananiah—Jer 27–29); third, ritual means of group maintenance, such as concerns with the ritual purity of the exiles as reflected in the Levitical food laws and the separation from foreigners, particularly the prohibition on intermarriage; fourth, folklore, particularly the use of the "hero" as a model of behaviour in exile as exemplified in the books of Daniel and Esther, the Joseph story (Gen 27–45), and the so-called Suffering Servant of Deutero-Isaiah.[30] These mechanisms of social adaptation, leading to the development of group identity, were unique to those who were in exile and explain why the repatriates sought to separate themselves from those they found living in their homeland at their return.[31] Smith's work is helpful for identifying issues that the Judean exiles should have faced and as a paradigm for dating and interpreting texts from this period. It must still be recognized that the evidence for the Judean exiles is scant and the dating of the biblical texts problematic.[32]

---

[28] On utopian aspects, see Haran, *Temple and Temple Service in Ancient Israel*, 10–11, 129–31. On the partial realization of P's programme in the Persian period, see M. Haran, "Priests and Priesthood," in *Encyclopaedia Judaica* (16 vols.; Jerusalem: Keter, 1971) 13. 1085. However, why should one expect P to be any more important, or likely to be implemented, than Ezek 40–48 which is admitted to be a highly idiosyncratic text (even within priestly circles; that is, when compared with P) whose notions were never realized?

[29] Smith, *Religion of the Landless*, 49–90.

[30] Ibid., 93–178.

[31] Ibid., 179–200.

[32] The only insight Ezekiel 1–39 gives us into the life of the exiles (those exiled

The insights of the comparative data, while suggestive, cannot substitute for the paucity of evidence or the uncertainties regarding the date of the biblical texts upon which the reconstruction relies. There are also certain problems raised by Smith's analysis which are not addressed by him. For example, what was the relationship between the elders as leaders in the exilic community and the priests who were responsible for the ritual purity of the community? Was one group dominant over the other? Did they have conflicting understandings of the character of the community? It is possible that these two groups of community leaders operated in concert, but Smith offers no portrait of the community which integrates the two groups or which delineates their nature and the relationship between their respective realms of authority.

Although the sources may not permit the identification of the mechanisms by which the Judean exiles in Babylonia maintained their identity, it is arguable that the experience of exile itself marked a line of division between those Judeans who had been exiled and those who had not. If the exiles viewed themselves as the remnant of Judah to the exclusion of other communities of Judeans in Judah and Egypt which they believed to be cut off from Yahweh, this could have given the exiles an identity which led them to repudiate those Judeans whom they found living in the homeland when they were repatriated.

While pre-exilic prophets had spoken of a remnant of the population being saved from the Yahweh's judgement on the kingdoms of Israel and Judah,[33] the designation of *the exiles* as "the remnant" occurs infrequently in exilic prophecy. Is 46:3 is an indisputable example, but here "remnant" should not be understood as a technical term denoting the Babylonian exiles as the sole survivors of the kingdom of Judah since it is clear from Is 43:47, Is 44:25 and Is 49:12–13 that there were exiles elsewhere who could expect to

---

in 597) is that they had "elders" and that there were house meetings to listen to the prophet; see Ezek 8:1; 14:1; 20:1, 3; cf. Jer 29:1.

[33] See, for example, Am 3:12; 5:15; 9:8–10; Is 4:2–3 (although this text may be post-exilic); 6:13; 7:3; 10:20–21; 11:11; 37:4, 32; Mic 4:7; 5:2, 6–7 (Eng. vv. 3, 7–8); Zeph 2:7, 9; 3:12. On the concept of the remnant in pre-exilic prophecy, see G. F. Hasel, *The Remnant: The History and Theology of the Remnant Idea from Genesis to Isaiah* (2d ed.; Andrews University Monograph Studies in Religion 5; Berrien Springs, MI: Andrews University, 1974) 216–348; J. Hausmann, *Israels Rest. Studien zum Selbstverstandnis der nachexilischen Gemeinde* (BWANT 124; Stuttgart: Kohlhammer, 1987) 139–97. There are four roots used in the Hebrew Bible to express the idea of the remnant: שאר; פלט; שרד; יתר.

be restored to their homeland by Yahweh.[34] "Remnant" can be used of any group which survives a disaster (see, for example, II Ki 19:4; Jer 52:15; Ezek 17:21; 25:16; Is 45:20). Neither Jeremiah nor Ezekiel use "remnant" to denote the exiles in Babylonia. Jeremiah uses "remnant of Jerusalem" to refer to those remaining after the 597 deportation (Jer 24:8). This use of "remnant" also occurs in Ezekiel 1–39 (Ezek 5:10; 9:8; 11:13). In Jeremiah, "remnant of Judah" denotes the Judeans who had left their country at the fall of the kingdom but who returned under Gedaliah (Jer 40:11, 15). It is further used in Jeremiah in reference to the Judeans who fled to Egypt after the assassination of Gedaliah (Jer 42:2, 15, 19; 43:5; 44:12, 14, 18, 28). "Remnant" gains currency as a designation for the Babylonian exiles only in Persian period biblical texts. It appears in Haggai and Zechariah (Hag 1:12, 14; 2:2; Zech 8:6, 11–12), but the referent for the term is unclear, and in Haggai at least may refer to both the repatriates and those who had remained in the homeland.[35] It is only in Ezra that the notion of the Babylonian exiles as the sole group of survivors of the kingdom of Judah is introduced (see Ezr 9 where "remnant" refers to those repatriated from Babylonia).[36]

---

[34] See Hausmann, *Israels Rest*, 76–78, who also emphasizes that "remnant" in this text should not be construed in exclusive terms. In discussing the definition of "Israel" in Deutero-Isaiah, H. G. M. Williamson, "The Concept of Israel in Transition," in *The World of Ancient Israel: Sociological, Anthropological and Political Perspectives* (ed. R. E. Clements; Cambridge: Cambridge University Press, 1989) 148, notes that "Deutero-Isaiah's narrowing of the concept of Israel . . . was far from exclusive; its purpose was a purified Israel which should lead to the restoration not only of empirical Israel but in some sense the nations too". Against those arguing for division between the repatriates and those who had remained in the homeland, Williamson suggests that "though no longer a sovereign state, 'Israel' may still have been kept sufficiently alive in the memory and in literature to embrace communities which had been geographically divided". (pp. 152–53)

[35] See the discussion in Hausmann, *Israels Rest*, 36–49, who notes differences between Haggai and Zech 1–8 in the conception of "remnant". In Zech it is more likely to refer to the exiles/repatriates, but even here is does not carry the theological (ideological) sense of exclusiveness. W. A. M. Beuken, *Haggai—Sacharja 1–8. Studien zur Überlieferungsgeschichte der frühnachexilischen Prophetie* (Studia Semitica Neerlandica 10; Assen: Van Gorcum, 1967) 29–31, and R. A. Mason, "The 'Editorial Framework' of the Book of Haggai," *VT* 27 (1977) 417–18, view these references to be from the hand of a later redactor; cf. the analysis of the editorial framework in M. H. Floyd, "The Nature of Narrative and the Evidence for Redaction in Haggai," *VT* 45 (1995) 470–90.

[36] On reviewing the exilic period texts relevant to the notion of "remnant" (Deutero-Isaiah, Ezekiel, Jeremiah, Obadiah, Deuteronomistic History, Leviticus), Hausmann, *Israels Rest*, 137, concludes:

Jer 24 would appear to lend credence to the view that the exiles (in this case those deported in 597) had obtained divine favour to the exclusion of the Judeans who had remained in the land.[37] The exiles are allegorized as "good figs", those remaining in Judah are "bad figs". The former will be watched over by Yahweh and will be brought back to their land while the latter will be banished from the land. Ackroyd is correct, however, in emphasizing the *ad hoc* character of this pronouncement. It was "directed to a particular situation in which it was necessary to indicate that the exiles were not automatically to be regarded as condemned and the community in Jerusalem and Judah as vindicated" (see, for example, Ezek 11:14–21).[38] It reinforces the fact that far from obtaining some privileged status, those who escaped the first deportation continue to remain under the judgement of Yahweh, as the events of 588–87 confirmed. Since Jer 24 is a reaction to social tensions specifically arising from the 597 deportation, to interpret this text as a blanket endorsement of the Babylonian Judean community to the exclusion of other communities of Judeans is to read into it concerns that were evidenced only in the later Achaemenid Persian period. Similarly, the divine abandonment motif in Ezek 9–11 should not be construed as legitimating the exiles and disenfranchising those who stayed in Judah. Its function is to legitimate the prophetic claim that Yahweh has handed over Jerusalem and Judah to destruction. In Ezek 11:14–21, those who remained in Judah after the 597 deportation said of the exiles: "You have been sent away from Yahweh; it is to us that the land was given as our domain". The prophet Ezekiel's reaction to this is not a rejection of those who articulated this sentiment, rather he claims that they have misinterpreted the plan of Yahweh. He affirms that the land vacated by those who were deported still belongs to them and that they will return to their holdings in the future.

So scheint sich immer mehr herauszuschälen, daß die theologisch qualifizierte Rede vom Rest ihre eigentliche Entfaltung erst nach dem Exil erfahren hat und nur wenig Belege in die Zeit davor zu daterien sind.
For her treatment of "remnant" in Ezr-Neh, see Hausmann, *Israels Rest*, 23–36.

[37] Similarly, Jer 29:16–20, although this passage is absent from the LXX of Jeremiah. For a defence of the attribution of Jer 24 to Jeremiah, see W. L. Holladay, *Jeremiah* (2 vols.; Hermeneia; Philadelphia: Fortress, 1986–89) 1. 655–57. Jer 24 has undergone later redaction as is shown by the reference to "those living in the land of Egypt" (Jer 24:8). The community referred to are those who went to Egypt after the death of Gedaliah.

[38] Ackroyd, *Exile and Restoration*, 55.

The attempt of those who remained in the land to exclude the exiles; that is, to claim that the exiles have been rejected by Yahweh since they have been cast out of the land of Yahweh, is discounted by the prophet. A similar affirmation of the exiles is displayed in Jeremiah's purchase of a field (Jer 32) since it expresses confidence that the exiles will return to their own holdings rather than have these holdings appropriated by those who remained in the land. Again, after the 587 deportation, those who remained in the land claimed: "Abraham was alone when he was given possession of this land. Now we are many and we hold the country as our domain" (Ezek 33:24). Ezekiel responds by prophesying that those left in Judah can expect further judgement from the hand of Yahweh—they will die by the sword and plague or be devoured by wild animals (Ezek 33:25–29). In short, those remaining in Judah cannot claim their position to be a sign of divine favour. There is no "special" community which Yahweh has spared.

R. P. Carroll argues that Jer 40–44 has been redacted to show that it was only among the Babylonian exiles that there was any hope for the future of Judah.[39] Those who had remained in Judah after 587 had forfeited any claim to divine preference by disobeying the prophetic word in going to Egypt after the assassination of Gedaliah (Jer 42–44). This Egyptian exilic community is denounced. Judah is left desolate and devoid of population; there thus being no Judean community to lay claim to being the nucleus of a future, divinely reinvigorated nation based on inhabiting Yahweh's land. The contention of Jer 40–44 and of the Deuteronomistic History that the land of Judah was devoid of population following the death of Gedaliah (Jer 42:7–22; 43:5; 44:2, 22; II Ki 25:25–26) need not, however, be interpreted as legitimating the claims of the Babylonian

---

[39] Carroll, *From Chaos to Covenant*, 235–48; idem, "The Myth of the Empty Land," 81–83. On the problem of competing claims to divine preference by different groups of Judeans in the complex redactional history of Jeremiah, a work which contains elements from both Judah and Babylonia, from both the Babylonian and Persian periods, see further P. R. Ackroyd, "Historians and Prophets," *SEÅ* 33 (1968) 37–54; G. Wanke, *Untersuchungen zur sogenannten Baruchschrift* (BZAW 122; Berlin: W. de Gruyter, 1971) 91–133; K.-F. Pohlmann, *Studien zum Jeremiabuch. Ein Beitrag zur Frage nach der Entstehung des Jeremiabuches* (FRLANT 118; Göttingen: Vandenhoeck & Ruprecht, 1978). I agree with Carroll, "Empty Land," 79–93, that the "exile" and "empty land" are ideological constructions, but I gauge their significance to have developed much later in the Persian period than Carroll does, interpreting them as a response to the continued existence of the diaspora after the temple had been completed.

exiles to be the locus of divine salvation to the exclusion of all other
communities of Judeans (in Judah and Egypt).[40] While the claim that
the land of Judah was empty is false, the function of that claim was
to place everyone under divine judgement for disobedience to the
prophetic word of Yahweh. Hope was given to those who remained
in Judah after the dissolution of the kingdom (Jer 42:7–13), but now
all Judeans, both those who had already been exiled and those about
to go to Egypt, are consigned to divine punishment. No-one was to
escape the punishment of Yahweh since no-one heeded the prophetic
word. The ideology underpinning Jer 40–44 and the Deuteronomistic
History is the legitimation of the prophets who proclaimed the judgement of Yahweh on the nation and the castigation of the *whole* nation
for its disobedience; including the disobedience of those who remained
in the land after 587 and who were offered yet another opportunity
to heed the word of Yahweh. Similar views concerning prophecy
and disobedience are expressed elsewhere in Jeremiah and in Ezekiel
1–39. Jer 15:1–9; 25:1–13; Ezek 5:7–17; 9:8–11; 11:1–13 emphasize
the destruction or exile of all Judeans. Despite the prophetic warnings of imminent destruction at the hand of Yahweh the Judeans
are portrayed as impervious to the word of Yahweh. The people are
bent on their own destruction.

This understanding of prophecy and disobedience permeates the
Deuteronomistic History, particularly the history of the divided monarchy (I Ki 12–II Ki 25).[41] The prophetic word of judgement occasioned by cultic infractions and/or inattention to the warnings of
prophets is always fulfilled. The perpetrators are always punished.[42]
The kings and peoples of Israel and Judah are invariably portrayed

---

[40] Against, also, the contention of Seitz, "Crisis of Interpretation," 92–95.

[41] An earlier example of this theme in the Deuteronomistic History is Yahweh's
rejection of Saul as king of Israel via the prophetic intermediary Samuel because
of Saul's disobedience to the orders of Yahweh (I Sam 15:10–23). This prophetic
word is fulfilled in the divine favour passing from Saul to David and culminates in
Saul's death (I Sam 16–31).

[42] Manasseh caused the Deuteronomistic Historian problems since he was not
punished for his cultic infractions in his lifetime. The Deuteronomistic Historian
responds by making Manasseh's actions the cause of the later destruction of the
kingdom of Judah (II Ki 21:10–15 cf. Jer 15:4). On the reign of Manasseh and his
treatment by the Deuteronomistic Historian, see Ahlström, *Royal Administration*, 75–81.

The responsibility of kings, leaders and the people for forcing Yahweh to bring
about their destruction is a recurring theme in the pre-exilic prophets (see, for example, Jer 2; 4–6; 9; 25:1–13; Ezek 6–11; 16; 19–23) as well as in the Deuteronomistic
History. A similar theme is played out regarding the demise of the northern kingdom of Israel (for example, Am 2–6; Hos 4–13; II Ki 17).

as inveterate in their disloyalty to Yahweh, which makes it hardly surprising that they do not heed Yahweh's prophets. The prophetic condemnation of the kings of Israel and Judah for introducing non-Yahwistic cults is a common theme, as is the condemnation of Israel for neither worshipping at Jerusalem nor acknowledging the sovereignty of the Davidic House (see, for example, I Ki 16:1–7; I Ki 17–18; I Ki 20:35–43; I Ki 22:1–38; II Ki 9–10; II Ki 17:5–23; II Ki 21:1–18; II Ki 23:31–25:20). Particularly significant is II Ki 21:10–15 where in the reign of Manasseh, over fifty years before the first Babylonian deportation, prophets proclaim the destruction of Judah and Jerusalem.

Judah is devoid of people because the ideology demands that it be, not because Jer 40–44 and the Deuteronomistic History sought to grant divine favour to the Babylonian exiles to the exclusion of all other groups of Judeans. Ideologically it was impossible for anyone to have remained in the land since invariably no-one heeded the prophetic word of Yahweh. The fact that many Judeans, arguably the majority, remained in Judah is not a problem for these writers since they are committed to the notion of the fulfilment of prophecy and the disobedience of all. They want to show the irresistible character of divine judgement delivered by the "legitimate" prophets of Yahweh and how that judgement was faithfully executed. No attack is directed against those who did remain in Judah since this writer holds that by definition there cannot be anyone left there.

It is true, however, that the Babylonian exiles might draw the conclusion that they were divinely favoured and those in the land rejected, since there should be no "Judeans" remaining there, but it is not explicit in these texts. It is only in the book of Ezra that the empty land motif is used to disarm any claim by those Judeans who did not go into exile that they were part of Yahweh's people and participants in the restoration of Israel. The Deuteronomistic History does not, however, extol the exiles as the future for Israel/Judah, indeed it says nothing of what the future will hold. Prophetic hopes for restoration in Jeremiah, Ezekiel 1–39, and Deutero-Isaiah display no repudiation of any of the communities of Judeans. The prophetic texts are united in their vision that *all* Israel will be restored to its homeland.[43] The fact that in Ezek 1–39 and Deutero-Isaiah

---

[43] See, for example, Jer 3:18; 23:3–8; Jer 30–31; 44:28; Ezek 28:24–26; 37:15–28; Is 49:12–13 (cf. Is 11:10–16, another post-587 oracle of salvation. Other relevant

"Israel" is used as a name for the exiles does not necessarily mean
that these prophets were excluding non-exiles.[44] There is no castigation of the non-exiles in these texts. It is undeniable, however,
that the Judean exiles in Babylonia are the focus of much prophetic
reflection on the restoration.[45] Again, this is not to disparage the
Judean community which remained in the land but is rather to give
meaning to the experience of the exiles. If in the mind of the prophets
there was no differentiation between these two communities regarding Yahweh's judgement on them and his coming restoration of
them, then how could the exiles account for the fact that they had
been deported from their homeland while others had not? In slightly
differing ways these prophets explain that the deportation and subsequent repatriation of Judeans was in order to display the sovereignty and holiness of Yahweh.[46] The Babylonian exiles are a "special"

---

texts are Hos 2:2; Mic 2:12; Zeph 3:18–20). The inclusive character of certain of
these pronouncements is such that the exiles from the former northern kingdom of
Israel are to share in the restoration. Other prophetical texts include the nations
in the restoration (see, for example, Is 2:2–4 // Mic 4:1–4; Is 11:10; 14:1–2;
19:16–25; 25:6–8; 45:14, 22–24; 55:4–5; 60:1–3; 66:18–21; Jer 3:17; 12:15–16;
16:19–21; Zeph 3:9–10; Jonah; Zech 8:20–23; Pss 22:27–29; 86:9–10; 87) On
restoration themes in the major prophets, see B. W. Anderson, "Exodus Typology
in Second Isaiah," in *Israel's Prophetic Heritage*, 177–95; W. Zimmerli, "Le nouvel
'exode' dans le message des deux grands prophètes de l'exil," in *Maqqél shâqédh, la
branche d'amandier. Hommage à Wilhelm Fischer* (Montpellier: Causse, Graille, Castelnau,
1960) 216–27, German translation: "Der 'neue Exodus' in der Verkündigung der
beiden grossen Exilpropheten," in *Gottes Offenbarung. Gesammelte Aufsätze zum Alten
Testament* (Theologische Bücherei 19; Munich: Kaiser, 1963) 192–204; Herrmann,
Die prophetischen Heilserwartungen; D. Baltzer, *Ezechiel und Deuterojesaja. Berührungen in der
Heilswartungen der beiden großen Exilspropheten* (BZAW 121; Berlin/New York: W. de
Gruyter, 1971); D. C. Greenwood, "On the Jewish Hope for a Restored Northern
Kingdom," *ZAW* 88 (1976) 376–85; T. M. Raitt, *A Theology of Exile: Judgment/Deliverance
in Jeremiah and Ezekiel* (Philadelphia: Fortress, 1977) 128–222.

[44] On "Israel" in Ezekiel, see W. Zimmerli, "Israel im Buch Ezechiel," *VT* 8
(1958) 75–90; idem, *Ezekiel* (2 vols.; trans. J. D. Martin; Hermeneia; Philadelphia:
Fortress, 1979–83) 2. 563–65. On "Israel" in Ezekiel and Deutero-Isaiah, see
Williamson, "Concept of Israel in Transition," 143–47.

[45] In addition to the references cited in n. 43 above see Jer 33; Ezek 11:16–21;
Deutero-Isaiah and texts exhibiting the second Exodus motif (Jer 16:14–15; 23:7–8;
Ezek 20:33–44; Is 40:3–5, 9–11; 41:17–20; 43:16–21).

[46] In Ezekiel and Deutero-Isaiah Yahweh acts so that "they (Israel) will learn
that I am Yahweh" (for example, Ezek 12:15, 20; 13:14, 21, 23; 16:62; 20:44;
22:16; 28:26; Is 41:20; 49:23), and his acts are "for the sake of my name" (for
example, Ezek 20:9, 14, 22, 44; 36:22; Is 48:11). In Deutero-Isaiah Yahweh acts
to show himself to be Israel's redeemer (for example, Is 40:10–11; 41:14, 17–20;
42:10–17; 43:11; 44:6, 24; 45:15; 49:36) and "the Holy One" (for example, Is 40:25;
41:14, 16; 43:1–7, 14, 16–21; 49:7).

community, not in that they are the sole locus of divine salvation
but in that they are a public display to both all Israel and the nations
that Yahweh is the preeminent deity (for Deutero-Isaiah, indeed the
only deity).[47] The extraordinary suffering of the exiles, when compared with those who remained in Judah, is offset by their role as
symbols of Yahweh's power to save his people. In Deutero-Isaiah in
particular the exiles are given the privilege of being led back to their
homeland by Yahweh himself, just as Israel at its origins had been
led by Yahweh from Egypt to the promised land. Yahweh will return
to his land and to Jerusalem, his city, only with the exiles in train.
This will amaze Israel and the nations. The restoration of Israel cannot begin, much less be complete, without the exiles' return. Just as
their deportation was a precursor to the judgement of all Israel, so
their repatriation is a precursor to the restoration of all Israel. It is
perhaps in the light of the Babylonian exiles' need to explain their
historical experience compared to that of the Judeans who remained
in the land that the passage regarding the Suffering Servant in Is
52:13–53:12 should be interpreted. Here, more punishment is exacted
of the exiles, especially their children born in exile, because they
suffered exile on behalf of all Israel.[48]

Attempts to find in exilic period texts the roots of a division
between the Babylonian exiles and those who remained in Judah,
which supposedly later manifested itself at the repatriation of the
exiles, must be judged to be unsuccessful. The other putative basis
for division between the repatriates and those they found living in
the land of Judah at their return, namely, that the communities of
Judeans exiled in Babylonia reformulated and maintained their identity by forming a cultic community under the leadership of exiled

---

[47] See, for example, Ezek 36:23; 37:28; Is 40:12–26; 41:1–7, 21–29; 43:8–13;
44:6–8, 24–28; 45:9–13, 20–25; 46:1–47:15.

[48] The interpretation of Is 52:13–53:12 has vexed scholars for generations. To
defend the interpretation suggested in passing here would demand a sizeable monograph. I believe that this passage is an attempt to address the problem of individual responsibility which is handled in a different manner in Ezek 18 and Ezek
33:10–20. For the Babylonian exiles the questions are: Why have we suffered more
than other Judeans? Why do our children suffer for sins committed by us? Recent
studies on Is 52:13–53:12 which include substantial bibliographic material are
D. J. A. Clines, *I, He, We, and They: A Literary Approach to Isaiah 53* (JSOTSup 1;
Sheffield: JSOT, 1976); T. N. D. Mettinger, *A Farewell to the Servant Songs: A Critical
Examination of an Exegetical Axiom* (Lund: Gleerup, 1983); A. Laato, *The Servant of
YHWH and Cyrus: A Reinterpretation of the Exilic Messianic Programme in Isaiah 40–55*
(ConBOT 35; Stockholm: Almqvist and Wiksell, 1992).

priests and characterized by attention to the precepts of the priestly
Torah, including separation from foreigners, is found wanting since
there is a clear lack of evidence from which one can draw conclusions as to their social organization, their means of maintaining group
identity, and their religious practices. This common assumption should
be viewed as an attempt by scholars to bridge the chasm between
the dissolution of the kingdom of Judah and the repatriation of exiles
in the Persian period by reading back into this period the attitudes
and patterns of social organization evidenced in much later texts. It
is only in Ezra-Nehemiah that the community of repatriated Judeans
is shown to be living under the Torah and to be keeping separate
from their neighbours. Since it is believed that such attitudes should
not have appeared fully grown, they must therefore have been developed among the exiles in Babylonia. In this way the portrait of community life presented in Ezra-Nehemiah can be accounted for, standing
in continuity with the exilic period. This further assumes that Ezra-
Nehemiah offers an accurate portrait of the social organization and
concerns of the Babylonian Judeans who were repatriated to their
homeland; a matter to be addressed, specifically regarding Ezr 1:1–4:5,
in chapter 3. These texts themselves show, however, that the people were not following the precepts of the cultic community. Certain
priests, whom one would expect to be most scrupulous regarding
cultic purity, intermarried with Samarians and "the peoples of the
lands" (Ezr 9:1; Neh 13:28), as did other repatriates (Ezr 9:1; Neh
13:23–27). Further, the repatriates do not appear to be familiar with
the Torah Ezra espouses (Neh 8:7, 13). Since the people had to be
instructed in this Torah it is to be concluded that it was new to
them. It should rather be acknowledged that while Judeans exiled
in Babylonia may have sought to reformulate their identity and developed mechanisms to maintain it, the evidence is too meager to draw
any firm conclusions on either of these matters. As mentioned above,
the Murašû texts offer no help regarding either the mechanisms of
group maintenance or the extent to which, if at all, the exiled Judeans
regarded Babylonians and other non-Judeans as a threat to their
identity.

There is one conclusion to be drawn from this discussion of the
sparse evidence for the communities of Judeans in both Judah and
Babylonia that is of note for the present study. As outlined in chapter 1, it is the contention of many scholars that the social division
in early Achaemenid Judah, whether it be between the repatriates

and those whom they found dwelling in their homeland at their return or between factions within the repatriates, turns on the repatriates, or at least a section of them, seeing themselves as a "cultic community" or "theocracy" under priestly leadership. This cultic community separated itself from "the people of the land" and/or rejected those repatriates (and others) who held out eschatological views of the restoration. The existence of this exilic cultic community is questionable and remains to be proved. This being so, it calls into question the very basis upon which the supposed social conflicts rest.

RESTORATION HOPES AND THE REFORMULATION OF ROYAL-STATE IDEOLOGY

One important insight we gain into the Babylonian Judean communities from the literary texts ascribed to them is their reaction to the royal-state ideology which had defined their relationship to Yahweh, their national deity, and which had underpinned their worship of Yahweh in the monarchical period. These texts, while not informing us as to the structure of Babylonian Judean society or the ritual means by which it retained its identity, reflect a desire to preserve the worship of Yahweh in the aftermath of the loss of king, state and national cult. Certain of these texts attempt to maintain faith in Yahweh by explaining why the events of 597–87 happened (II Kings; Ezek 1–39; Deuteronomistic recension of Jeremiah), while other texts focus on the future of the exiles' relationship with their deity and their hopes for restoration (for example, Ezek 40–48; Deutero-Isaiah).[49]

---

[49] For an introduction to the theology of these texts, see Ackroyd, *Exile and Restoration*, 50–137; Klein, *Israel in Exile.* I subscribe to the Babylonian provenance of Deutero-Isaiah, in concert with the majority scholarly opinion. The priestly texts of the Pentateuch, despite their late date, also display a concern to understand the nature of the community and the worship of Yahweh apart from a king and state.

The priestly material in the Pentateuch (understood by many scholars to be a document—P; but see the discussion in chapter 1 n. 15, and above nn. 22–28) has been omitted from the present discussion since it is quite uncertain as to (i) whether or not P existed as a distinct text; (ii) what its date is (it is probably to be dated to the late Persian period; on problems of dating see, again, chapter 1 n. 15; chapter 2 nn. 22–27) and thus whether or not it addresses problems of the exilic period and the restoration; (iii) whether or not P offers an ideology for the reconstruction of the Jerusalem temple.

This reformulation of the royal-state ideology and the connection of the Jerusalem temple of Yahweh with it grew out of the need to meet the challenge that the events of 587 presented to Yahweh's authority and credibility. The dissolution of the kingdom of Judah raised questions about the authority of Yahweh, its national deity. The event demanded explication if the worship of Yahweh was not to go the way of the kingdom over which he had ruled. Yahweh was preserved from charges of delinquency or impotence by the interpretation of Babylonian hegemony and the subsequent deportations as reflecting the activity of Yahweh in judging his people, rather than reflecting his inability to protect them. The dissolution of the state and concomitant exile were held to have been inflicted on the nation by Yahweh himself; justifiable punishments occasioned by offences committed against the deity by Judean kings and people. Yahweh was thus not considered to be a passive spectator in the demise of the state; rather, he is portrayed as orchestrating events and using the Babylonian armies for his own ends. So although Babylonian, and earlier Assyrian, monarchs may have interpreted their domination of Judah as a testament to the authority of their respective deities over Yahweh, certain Judeans countered that Yahweh himself controlled these historical events.[50] In this way Yahweh's sov-

---

Regarding the last point, P obviously exhibits a tradition of building a sanctuary for Yahweh (Ex 25–31, 35–40). The majority of commentators consider it to share in common with Ezek 40–48 and Ezr 1–6 the notion of "Israel" as a worshipping community gathered around the shrine of Yahweh which has no need for an indigenous king. In the priestly material, however, the people are in the wilderness, not Jerusalem or Judah, and the shrine is not the Jerusalem temple but rather the mobile Tent of Meeting. It is unclear, therefore, that the building of the tabernacle in Exodus in fact prefigures or refers to the reconstruction of the Jerusalem temple. On P as text from the exilic period portraying the restoration of Israel after the dissolution of the state, see Clements, *God and Temple*, 109–22; E. Zenger, *Gottes Bogen in den Wolken. Untersuchungen zu Komposition und Theologie der priesterschriftlichen Urgeschichte* (Stuttgarter Bibelstudien 112; Stuttgart: Katholisches Bibelwerk, 1983) 45–49. Other commentators read P quite differently. T. E. Fretheim, "The Priestly Document: Anti-Temple?" *VT* 18 (1968) 313–29, thinks that P is against the reconstruction of a permanent shrine (that is, the Jerusalem temple), preferring the movable tabernacle. Another interpretation of P holds that in its earliest edition (Pg) it held a monarchical conception of Israel; that is, Yahweh was to restore the kingship; see W. Gross, "Israel's Hope for the Renewal of the State," *JNSL* 14 (1988) 101–33.

[50] See, for example, Lam 1:18–20; 2:1–8, 17; 3:42; Ezek 6:1–7:14; Jer 1:13–19; 4:5–5:17; 9:9–21; II Ki 24:1–4. All these passages may come from the hand of the Deuteronomist. For the notion that Yahweh controls foreign kings and their armies which he uses to punish Israel and Judah, see also Is 5:26–30; Jer 5:15–17; 6:1, 22–30; 27:1–22.

ereignty was protected in the face of events that could be construed as manifesting his impotence.

This device of placing responsibility for political (or natural) catastrophes on the people and their leaders in order to maintain the authority of the deity over events has a distinguished pedigree. It is used in Sumerian literature to account for the destruction of Agade.[51] In Assyrian literature it is used to justify the destruction of Assyria's enemies or recalcitrant vassals. These enemies had brought down the divine wrath on their own heads by oath breaking or by some cultic infraction. The Assyrian king thus justly acted as the agent of divine recompense.[52] In all these the punishment meted out is just;

---

[51] J. S. Cooper, *The Curse of Agade* (The Johns Hopkins Near Eastern Studies; Baltimore/London: The Johns Hopkins University Press, 1983). The Sumerian city laments (over Ur, Sumer and Ur, Nippur, and Eridu, on which see M. W. Green, "Eridu in Sumerian Literature" [Unpublished Ph.D., University of Chicago, 1975] 277–325) offer no explanation for the destruction of the respective cities; that is, it is not accorded to sins committed by the city's king or inhabitants. On the possibility that this notion nevertheless underlay the gods' abandonment of at least Ur, see P. Michalowski, *The Lamentation over the Destruction of Sumer and Ur* (Mesopotamian Civilizations 1; Winona Lake, IN: Eisenbrauns, 1989) 8–9.

[52] So, for example, the Middle-Assyrian Tukulti-Ninurta Epic in which Tukulti-Ninurta's attack on Kastiliaš is so justified; see P. B. Machinist, "The Epic of Tukulti-Ninurta: A Study in Middle Assyrian Literature" (Ph.D. Dissertation, Yale University, 1978; Ann Arbor: University Microfilms International), I B 32'–47' (pp. 62–65), III A/E 25'–61' (pp. 92–99); idem, "Literature as Politics: The Tukulti-Ninurta Epic and the Bible," *CBQ* 38 (1976) 462–64. Esarhaddon uses it to justify the destruction of Babylon by his father Sennacherib, see R. Borger, *Die Inschriften Asarhaddons, Königs von Assyrien* (*AfO* Beiheft 9; Graz: Weidner, 1956), 12–14, episodes 2–5, for discussion of which see J. A. Brinkman, "Through a Glass Darkly: Esarhaddon's Retrospects on the Downfall of Babylon," *JAOS* 103 (1983) 35–42. For its use in Neo-Assyrian royal inscriptions as a legitimation for Assyrian actions against vassals, see M. Cogan, *Imperialism and Religion: Assyria, Judah and Israel in the Eighth and Seventh Centuries B.C.E.* (SBLMS 19; Missoula, MT: Scholars Press, 1974) 9–21; F. M. Fales, "The Enemy in Assyrian Royal Inscriptions: 'The Moral Judgement'," in *Mesopotamien und seine Nachbarn. Politische und kulturelle Wechselbeziehungen im Alten Vorderasien vom 4. bis 1. Jahrtausend v. Chr.* (2 vols.; ed. H.-J. Nissen and J. Renger; Berliner Beiträge zum Vorderen Orient 1/1–2; Berlin: Reimer, 1982) 2. 425–35. Also cf. Weidner Chronicle in A. K. Grayson, *Assyrian and Babylonian Chronicles* (Texts from Cuneiform Sources 5; Locust Valley, NY: Augustin, 1975) 43–45, 145–51; "Nabonidus' Rise to Power" in *ANET*, 308–11. The Mesha Stele (KAI 181) lines 4–5 also display a similar notion. On these texts see also B. Albrektson, *History and the Gods: An Essay on the Idea of Historical Events as Divine Manifestations in the Ancient Near East and in Israel* (ConBOT 1; Lund: Gleerup, 1967) 98–114, where a number of Hittite parallels are further adduced. The destruction of Babylon in the Erra epic resulted from a struggle between gods rather than from divine displeasure with the inhabitants of the city, so J. Bottéro, *Mythes et rites de Babylone* (Preface by M. Fleury; Bibothèque de l'École des Hautes Études IVe Section: Sciences Historiques et Philologiques 328; Geneva: Slatkine/Paris: Champion, 1985) 262–71.

permitted and overseen by the gods. This aspect is reinforced by the gods' abandonment of their shrines as a necessary prelude to the destruction of the city and/or state.

Such explanations in defence of Yahweh were not satisfying to everyone. Deutero-Isaiah, for example, addresses deep scepticism on the part of a number of the Judeans exiled in Babylonia regarding the sovereignty of Yahweh and the necessity of worshipping him given the events of the 587 and the subsequent experiences of the exiles.[53] Jer 44:16–19 indicates that some Judeans who fled to Egypt held "the Queen of Heaven", not Yahweh, to be the deity responsible for Judah's demise (probably acting with the permission of Yahweh, the national deity). The "sin" thought to have brought about the disaster was inattention to that deity's cult. It is not surprising that an affront to a locally worshipped deity other than Yahweh was considered to have precipitated the Babylonian invasions since it is incontrovertible that gods other than Yahweh were worshipped in Judah and that they also formed part of the state religion.[54] The canonical biblical texts, however, not only discount the power of other gods over both Israel's and Judah's fortunes but also account for the dissolution of these states in terms of Yahweh's anger being incited by the worship of these other gods.[55]

Yahweh's freedom to abandon his city and king, handing them over to the power of a foreign nation as just punishment, was a

---

[53] See, for example, the prophecies against idolatry—Is 40:12–31, 44:6–23, 46:1–13—which presume that numbers of Judean exiles considered the power of Bel (Marduk) to be greater than that of Yahweh. On these prophecies, see R. J. Clifford, "The Function of Idol Passages in Second Isaiah," *CBQ* 42 (1980) 450–64; A. Wilson, *The Nations in Deutero-Isaiah: A Study on Composition and Structure* (Ancient Near Eastern Texts and Studies 1; Lewiston/Queenston: Mellen, 1986) 129–92. We can but assume that some (many?) exiles would have been integrated into Babylonian society and adopted the worship of local deities, despite the likelihood that the exiled Judeans lived together in their own communities.

[54] On the role of non-Yahwistic cults in the national religion of Judah, see G. W. Ahlström, *Aspects of Syncretism in Israelite Religion* (Horae Soederblomianae V; Lund: Gleerup, 1963); idem, *Royal Administration*, 65–81; idem, *An Archaeological Picture of Iron Age Religions in Palestine* (Studia orientalia 55.3; Helsinki: Societas Orientalis Fennica, 1984); S. M. Olyan, *Asherah and the Cult of Yahweh in Israel* (SBLMS 34; Atlanta: Scholars Press, 1988); O. Keel and C. Uehlinger, *Gods, Goddesses, and Images of God in Ancient Israel* (trans. T. H. Trapp; Minneapolis: Fortress, 1998) 177–372.

[55] See, for example, Ezek 8; 16; 20; 22; Jer 2:14–25; 7:16–20; 7:29–8:3; 44; II Ki 21. In light of these texts it is interesting that Ps 44:18–20 (Eng. 17–19), if it is in fact to be dated to the exilic period, claims that Judeans had not worshipped other gods and hence the Psalmist cannot understand why destruction had come upon the nation.

direct challenge to the royal-Zion ideology which claimed that Yahweh had enthroned himself on the cherubim of the Ark in the sanctuary of the Jerusalem temple, assuring the divine protection of Jerusalem and its king. Since kingship and temple were held to be divinely instituted and sustained, the corollary was that they would endure forever. Such sentiments are expressed in the Zion Psalms and in the original divine promise to David.[56] According to a number of scholars, already in the monarchical period there were voices critical of this royal-state ideology and its use of the divine presence in Jerusalem as an unconditional guarantee for the continuance of the state. Certain of the writing prophets have been commonly cast in this role. They have been characterized as upholders of older, premonarchical traditions against the newly instituted monarchical ideas. Perhaps they were heirs to the anti-monarchical tradition reflected in Judges 6–9, I Samuel 8 and 10:17–24, or to the Sinai covenant traditions which constitute Yahweh's relationship with Israel without the mediation of a king.[57]

---

[56] On the inviolability of Zion theme, see J. H. Hayes, "The Tradition of Zion's Inviolability," *JBL* 82 (1963) 419–26. On the promise to David, see above chapter 1 n. 9.

[57] On the origin of the anti-monarchical tradition, see F. Crüsemann, *Der Widerstand gegen das Königtum. Die antiköniglichen Texte des Alten Testamentes und der Kampf um den frühen israelitischen Staat* (WMANT 49; Neukirchen-Vluyn: Neukirchener Verlag, 1978), who understands the tradition to have arisen under Solomon as a response to the social and economic burden of kingship. On prophetic criticism of the monarchy, see R. Hentschke, *Die Stellung der vorexilischen Schriftpropheten zum Kultus* (BZAW 75; Berlin: Töpelmann,1957) 20–46. On the Sinai covenant tradition as the basis for the prophets' criticism of the monarchy, see L. Rost, "Sinaibund und Davidsbund," *TLZ* 72 (1947) 129–34; M. Sekine, "Davidsbund und Sinaibund bei Jeremiah," *VT* 9 (1959) 47–57; Bright, *History*, 293, 325; idem *Covenant and Promise*, 87–94, 101–3, 144; cf. K. Seybold, *Das davidischen Königtum im Zeugnis der Propheten* (FRLANT 107; Göttingen: Vandenhoeck & Ruprecht, 1972), who sees continuity between the Sinai covenant and the covenant with David; similarly, J. D. Levenson, *Sinai and Zion: An Entry into the Jewish Bible* (New Voices in Biblical Studies; Minneapolis: Winston Press, 1985). The date of the Sinai covenant tradition is difficult to establish, however. For the return to the classic critical position, dating it to the eighth century at the earliest, see Perlitt, *Bundestheologie*; E. W. Nicholson, *God and His People: Covenant and Theology in the Old Testament* (Oxford: Clarendon, 1986).

For anti-Zion polemic see Micah 3:9–12; Is 29:1–10, Jer 7:1–15; 26:1–19, on which see M. Schmidt, *Prophet und Tempel. Eine Studie zum Problem der Gottesnähe im Alten Testament* (Zürich: Evangelischer, 1948) 59–60, 91–108; Bright, *Covenant and Promise*, 104–05, 116–19, 163–65, 172. Other prophetic texts affirm the Zion ideology, for example, Is 6; 38. On the Zion ideology in Isaiah 1–39, see Schmidt, *Prophet und Tempel*, 32–54; G. von Rad, *Old Testament Theology* (2 vols.; trans. D. M. G. Stalker; New York: Harper and Row, 1962–65) 2. 155–69; H. Wildberger, *Jesaja* (3 vols.; BKAT 10/1–3; Neukirchen-Vluyn: Neukirchener Verlag, 1972–82) 3. 1596–1606.

Other texts ostensibly from the monarchical period have also been recognized as adopting a similar perspective. The most notable are Deuteronomy and the Deuteronomistic History which are widely held to represent the so-called Deuteronomic reform movement. This movement sought to reorient royal-state ideology by reformulating the nature of both the divine presence in the Jerusalem temple and the covenant with David.[58] Rather than understanding Yahweh Sabaoth as enthroned on the cherubim in the temple (a theology of immanence), it was Yahweh's "name" that had been placed there (theology of transcendence).[59] The promises to David, rather than being unconditional, were in fact conditional on his descendants' obedience to divine instruction, their keeping the population obedient to it, and on their devotion to Yahweh alone.[60] The Deuteronomistic Historian cites failure to conform to these divine demands as the reason for all manner of difficulties faced by the kings and for the demise of both Israel and Judah. The importance of this movement is heightened by those who claim that reforms were undertaken in Judah in the reigns of both Hezekiah and Josiah to make royal-state ideology and practices conform to these perspectives (II Ki 18:1–8; 22:1–23:27).[61] However, since these reforms were overturned by later

[58] On the Deuteronomistic movement, see Poulssen, *König und Tempel*, 87–141; Clements, *God and Temple*, 88–99; M. Weinfeld, *Deuteronomy and the Deuteronomic School* (Oxford: Clarendon, 1972).

[59] On the Deuteronomistic "name theology", see Weinfeld, *Deuteronomic School*, 192–94; Mettinger, *Dethronement of Sabaoth*, 38–66; M. Keller, *Untersuchungen zur deuteronomisch-deuteronomischen Namenstheologie* (BBB 105; Weinheim: Beltz Athenäum, 1996), who emphasizes the elaboration of this understanding in the exilic period.

[60] On the Davidic covenant becoming conditional, see Mettinger, *King and Messiah*, 275–78, cf. Cross, *Canaanite Myth and Hebrew Epic*, 229–87. Although Deuteronomy and the Deuteronomistic History circumscribe the rights and position of the king, they are generally considered not to be anti-monarchical. On the latter text, see G. E. Gerbrandt, *Kingship According to the Deuteronomistic History* (SBLDS 87; Atlanta: Scholars Press, 1986). See, however, Barker, *The Older Testament*, 145–48, who notes Deuteronomy's democratization of royal ideology. Some roles are given to the people (they, not the king, are chosen; the people, not the king, are the sons of God), others to Moses (he is the lawgiver, judge, political and military leader). Barker dates this to the post-monarchical period. On the change in the view of Israel from a state to a community in the post-monarchical period as reflected in Deuteronomy, see also U. Rüterswörden, *Von der politischen Gemeindschaft zur Gemeinde. Studien zu Dt 16,18–18,22* (BBB 65; Frankfurt am Main: Athenäum, 1987). Ps 89, which on the basis of vv. 39–53 (Eng. vv. 38–51) is arguably post-587 in date, still holds to the unconditional character of the promise to David (vv. 29–38 [Eng. vv. 28–37]). This view may also underlie the renewal of the House of David evidenced in certain prophetical texts.

[61] Mettinger, *Dethronement of Sabaoth*, 67–77.

Judean monarchs, Yahweh consigned the kingdom to destruction.

Such distancing of the divine presence in the Jerusalem temple from royal-state ideology is seen also in the temple sermons in Jeremiah 7 and 26, which have been recognized as reflecting the hand of the Deuteronomist.[62] Ezekiel also eschews the royal-state ideology of the divine presence by developing a theology of the presence of Yahweh's "glory" (כבוד) in the temple in the place of the enthronement of Yahweh. Similarities between Ezekiel's theology on this point and P have been noted.[63]

It is, however, difficult to determine just how much of this alternative to the royal-state ideology of kingship and temple belongs to the monarchical period. The texts have been redacted after the loss of statehood and so many may present a reinterpretation of the events with the aid of hindsight. The Deuteronomistic History in particular is recognized as having been redacted in the Babylonian exile, but its basic orientation has been seen by many to have been established in the monarchical period. Others question that this text's views owe much at all to the monarchical period, preferring to see its outlook as being a reaction to and product of the dissolution of the state.[64] In the latter case the reforms of Hezekiah and Josiah are but literary constructs.[65] Jeremiah's temple sermons can also be similarly explained.

It is possible that there was questioning of the royal-state ideology during the monarchical period, but how significant or influential it may have been is difficult to ascertain. The extant texts give a biased view of the importance of their own ideas in the interpretation of

---

[62] Carroll, *From Chaos to Covenant*, 85–95.

[63] Mettinger, *Dethronement of Sabaoth*, 80–115. On these theologies of Yahweh's presence, see S. Terrien, *The Elusive Presence: Toward a New Biblical Theology* (Religious Studies Perspectives 26; New York: Harper and Row, 1978) 197–213; T. N. D. Mettinger, "The Name and the Glory: The Zion-Sabaoth Theology and its Exilic Successors," *JNSL* 24 (1998) 1–24.

[64] For the voluminous literature on the date and redaction history of the Deuteronomistic history see, most recently, M. A. O'Brien, *The Deuteronomistic History Hypothesis: A Reassessment* (OBO 92; Freiberg: Universitätsverlag/Göttingen: Vandenhoeck & Ruprecht, 1989), who has a critical survey of the major approaches on pp. 3–23; T. Römer and A. de Pury, "L'historiographie deutéronomiste (HD). Histoire de la recherche et enjeux du débat," in *Israël construit son histoire: L'historiographie deutéronomiste à la lumière de recherches récentes* (ed. A. de Pury, T. Römer and J.-D. Macchi; Le Monde de la Bible 34; Geneva: Labor et Fides, 1996) 9–120.

[65] H.-D. Hoffmann, *Reform und Reformen. Untersuchungen zu einen Grundthema der deuteronomistischen Geschichtschreibung* (Abhandlung zur Theologie des Alten und Neuen Testaments 66; Zurich: Theologischer Verlag, 1980).

Judean and Israelite history. Critiques may have been made only by
prophets and others on the periphery of society rather than such
views being fostered within the royal court.[66] Perhaps critical perspectives developed only after the first deportation in 597. In any
case, it is questionable that any king would support a reform such
as that envisaged in Deuteronomy or the Deuteronomistic History
since both texts seek to limit his authority, to question his unique
relationship with the national deity, and to undermine the symbolism of the Jerusalem temple as the throne of the national deity.

Regardless of how early one places the revision of the royal-state
ideology and the role of the Jerusalem temple in it, it is undeniable
that by the end of the Judean monarchy ideas about Judean kingship and the Jerusalem temple were undergoing reformulation in
order to preserve the sovereignty of Yahweh from being debased by
these institutions' demise. The defence of Yahweh's sovereignty was
naturally predicated on the assumption that despite the loss of kingship, temple and land, the exiles were still to consider themselves as
the people of Yahweh; that is, that Yahweh was still their deity.
Continued allegiance to Yahweh therefore demanded not only an
explanation of the recent events but also what future Yahweh had
planned for his faithful worshippers. As both a corollary to and a
buttress for the attempts to defend Yahweh's sovereignty after the
dissolution of the state prophetical texts declare that Yahweh would
restore the fortunes of the exiles by returning them, along with himself, to Jerusalem.

It was commonly understood in ancient Western Asia that disasters justly meted out by the god(s) would last for a divinely appointed
period. In due time the deity's anger would relent and he would
return to his shrine, reversing the misfortunes his people had endured.[67]
This period may be announced by the deity or remain a secret. The
understanding of history underpinning this view is recurrence. "Historical recurrence" has usually been associated with the "myth and
ritual" school of biblical interpretation, but this is only one exem-

---

[66] On peripheral prophets, see Wilson, *Prophecy and Society in Ancient Israel*, especially pp. 38–39, 69–83. On the Deuteronomistic tradition as peripheral in Judean
society, see A. D. H. Mayes, *The Story of Israel between Settlement and Exile: A Redactional
Study of the Deuteronomistic History* (London: SCM, 1983) 137–39.
[67] For examples of ancient Near Eastern texts exhibiting these features, see the
texts cited in chapter 3 nn. 192–95.

plar of the view that history is to be understood as the repetition or recurrence of standard patterns or events. What is in view in the present context is not a cultic reenactment of annual rites (a cyclical view of history) but rather the restoration of conditions that existed before the deity brought destruction on his people. The end of the deity's ire brought about the return of the deity to his city and the restoration of his cult, city and people to normality.[68]

That Judeans shared this understanding of history is displayed in biblical texts from the post-monarchical period in a number of ways. Both the Deuteronomistic History and the Books of Chronicles understand Israelite and Judean history to undulate between periods of faithfulness to Yahweh and apostasy, giving rise to periods of fortune and misfortune respectively. As noted above, such a view explains and legitimates Israel's and Judah's historical experience. But this is historiography, and it aims to explain the past. What of Judeans' future after the catastrophe of 587? Here ideas of historical recurrence are evidenced also. First, there is the concern of certain Psalmists to determine the duration of Yahweh's anger against Judah and Judeans. They ask "how long?" before Yahweh will restore their fortunes (Pss 74: 9–11; 79:5; 80:5 [Eng. v. 4] cf. Lam 5:20, 22), the expectation being that the divine punishment would last a defined, but as yet unknown, period and that it would be followed by Yahweh's return. Other texts, such as Jer 25:11–12, 29:10, give the duration of the divine anger as seventy years, after which time there will be a restoration.[69]

---

[68] I owe the idea of historical recurrence to G. W. Trompf, *The Idea of Historical Recurrence in Western Thought: From Antiquity to the Reformation* (Berkeley: University of California Press, 1979). He summarises different forms of historical recurrence on pp. 1–3. Little work has been done on this notion of recurrence in ancient Near Eastern literature since it became generally assumed that both biblical and Near Eastern historiography have a linear view of history. Trompf briefly discusses the notion of historical recurrence in biblical and Near Eastern historiography on pp. 116–20, 156–64. The former body of texts is more extensively dealt with in G. W. Trompf, "Notions of Historical Recurrence in Classical Hebrew Historiography," in *Studies in the Historical Books of the Old Testament* (ed. J. A. Emerton; VTSup 30; Leiden: E. J. Brill, 1979) 213–29. On historical recurrence in ancient Near Eastern historiography, see H. G. Güterbock, "Die historische Tradition und ihre literarische Gestaltung bei Babyloniern und Hethitern bis 1200 (pt. 1)," *ZA* 42 (NS 8) (1934) 13–22; E. A. Speiser, "Ancient Mesopotamia," in *The Idea of History in the Ancient Near East* (ed. R. C. Dentan; New Haven: Yale University Press, 1955) 55–60.

[69] On the problem of determining the duration of the divine anger, see below pp. 164–68.

Second, there are prophetical texts which: (a) view the fall of Babylon as marking the end of Yahweh's ire and as thus introducing the return to normality. Yahweh himself was to ensure Babylon's destruction (thus repaying the Babylonians for their destruction of Judah) and repatriate the exiles (thus reversing the deportation undertaken by the Babylonians) (Deutero-Isaiah; Jer 50–51). In addition, Yahweh himself was to lead the exiles home in his train as he returned to Jerusalem from his self-imposed exile (thus reversing the original abandonment). In Jerusalem a new temple was to be rebuilt and an age of divine blessing ushered in (particularly, Deutero-Isaiah);[70] (b) include the re-establishment of the Davidic monarchy as part of the restoration (Is 8:23–9:6; 11:1–9; 32:1–8; Jer 23:1–8; 33:14–26; Ezek 17:22–24; 34:23–31; 37:21–28; Am 9:11–15; Hos 3:5; Mic 5:1–5 [Eng. vv. 2–6]). Many of these texts are difficult to date securely but they appear to range from the exilic period to well into the Achaemenid Persian period. The theme of historical recurrence is thus understood to demand a return to the conditions that existed before the dissolution of the kingdom. In these texts the distancing of Yahweh from the royal-state ideology was only a temporary measure to help explain the events of 587. The prophets sometimes claim that in the restoration Yahweh will add safeguards, such as establishing a "new covenant" (Jer 31:23–34; Ezek 37:26), to ensure that divine abandonment and the destruction of the nation would never happen again. These hopes for restoration, although cast in idealistic terms, should be distinguished from "Messianic" eschatological views which developed only in the late Hellenistic and Roman Periods. The reinstitution of kingship is not seen to usher in the end of history nor does it instigate an idyllic final age of the rule of Yahweh.[71] The emphasis in these texts is on a return to the

---

[70] The "new Exodus" theme (Is 40:3ff.; 41:17–20; 43:16–21; Jer 16:14–15; 23:7–8) is an excellent example of the notion of historical recurrence. The return of exiles (both Judean and Israelite) to the homeland appears in a number of other texts, for example, Is 11:12; Mic 2:12, 4:6; Jer 23:3, 30:11, 50:19; Ezek 11:17, 39:27. On the theme of the return of exiles, see J. Lust, "'Gathering and Return' in Jeremiah and Ezekiel," in *Le livre de Jérémie: le prophète et son milieu, les oracles et le transmission* (ed. P.-M. Bogaert; BETL 54; Leuven: Leuven University Press/Peeters, 1981) 119–42; G. Widengren, "Yahweh's Gathering of the Dispersed," in *In the Shelter of Elyon: Essays on Ancient Palestinian Life and Literature in Honor of G. W. Ahlström* (ed. W. B. Barrick and J. R. Spencer; JSOTSup 31; Sheffield: JSOT Press, 1984) 227–45.

[71] On the concept of "eschatology" and the development of the expectation of

conditions which mark the normal state of affairs and which bring the cosmos back into order, most notably, the presence of Yahweh in Jerusalem (which presumes a rebuilt temple) and the people of Yahweh dwelling in their land.

The return to normalcy that attends this notion of historical recurrence is significant not only for Judean sensibilities about "order", but also for Yahweh's sovereignty and Judean identity. The effectiveness of claiming that the punishment of Judah reflected Yahweh's sovereignty (rather than Marduk's) much depended on Yahweh's ability to meet his responsibilities at the other end of the historical equation: restoration when the divine ire abated. If Yahweh were unable to restore Judah, perhaps he was not responsible for its demise; in fact, he may show himself to be a rather ineffectual provincial deity. Restoration, or the return to normalcy, was needed to "prove" that Yahweh was indeed in control of historical events and Judeans' fate, and had always been. A Judean identity fashioned around the continued worship of Yahweh, in the diaspora and in the homeland, depended on evidence of both the continued interest of that deity in his people and the deity's ability to act on his people's behalf. The return of Yahweh to Jerusalem, the repatriation of displaced Judeans, the restoration of cultic normalcy, and divinely instituted political leadership were such indicators.

The idea of historical recurrence does not demand, however, that the coming restoration be simply the past revisited, although there are important symbols drawn from the monarchical ideology which must be re-established for order to be restored. The major prophets of the Babylonian exile, Deutero-Isaiah (Is 40–55) and Ezekiel (Ezek 40–48), share in common an emphasis on the restoration of Jerusalem/ Zion and Judah based on the establishment of Yahweh's presence in his city.[72] Their paramount concern, which is quite understandable

---

the restoration of the monarchy, see the discussion in chapter 1 n. 27. On the development of messianism only in the Hasmonean and Roman periods, see J. J. Collins, *The Scepter and the Star: The Messiahs of the Dead Sea Scrolls and Other Ancient Literature* (The Anchor Bible Reference Library; New York: Doubleday, 1995).

[72] On Deutero-Isaiah, see T. N. D. Mettinger, "In Search of the Hidden Structure: YHWH as King in Isaiah 40–55," *SEÅ* 51–52 (1986–87) 148–57 (revised version in *Writing and Reading the Scroll of Isaiah: Studies of an Interpretive Tradition* [2 vols.; ed. C. C. Broyles and C. A. Evans; VTSup 70, 71; Leiden: E. J. Brill, 1997] 1. 143–54); Wilson, *Nations in Deutero-Isaiah*; C. Stuhlmueller, *Creative Redemption in Deutero-Isaiah* (AnBi 43; Rome: Biblical Institute Press, 1970); idem, "Yahweh-King and Deutero-Isaiah," *Biblical Research* 15 (1970) 32–45; Laato, *The Servant of YHWH and Cyrus.*

given the dissolution of the kingdom of Judah and the destruction
of the Jerusalem temple of Yahweh, is the affirmation of the kingship of Yahweh. This is expounded using the monarchical Zion ideology, but neither prophet ties this ideology to the Davidic monarchy
nor to the monarchical state in the manner of the royal-Zion ideology of the monarchical period. There is a longstanding debate as
to whether these prophets' visions of the restoration have any place
for the king or monarchical state. The debate has centred on the
meaning of the term נָשִׂיא in Ezek 40–48 and on the mention of
David in Is 55:1–5. The human ruler (king or נָשִׂיא) is much more
prominent in Ezek 40–48 in comparison with Deutero-Isaiah where
apart from Is 55:1–5 Israelite kingship is not mentioned.[73] This problem does not need to be resolved here. It suffices to say that the
perspective of these texts regarding the restoration differs from texts
which envisage the re-establishment of the Davidic monarchy. The
monarchical period ideology of the divine presence on Zion/Jerusalem
has been retained in Deutero-Isaiah and Ezekiel 40–48 but it is also
reworked in these prophets' visions of the restoration. The restoration of Judah in which the Jerusalem temple of Yahweh is severed
from its links with the monarchical period conceptions of kingship

---

On Ezekiel 40–48, see W. Zimmerli, "Plannungen für Wiederaufbau nach der
Katastrophe von 587," *VT* 18 (1968) 229–55; idem, *Ezekiel*, 2. 325–553; J. D.
Levenson, *Theology of the Programme of Restoration of Ezekiel 40–48* (HSM 10; Missoula,
MT: Scholars Press, 1976); M. Haran, "The Law-Code of Ezekiel xl–xlviii and Its
Relation to the Priestly School," *HUCA* 50 (1979) 45–71; M. Greenberg, "The
Design and Themes of Ezekiel's Program of Restoration," *Interpretation* 38 (1984)
181–208; S. Niditch, "Ezekiel 40–48 in a Visionary Context," *CBQ* 48 (1986)
208–24; R. Klein, *Ezekiel: The Prophet and His Message* (Studies on Personalities in
the Old Testament; Columbia, South Carolina: University of South Carolina, 1988)
169–92; Tuell, *Law of the Temple in Ezekiel 40–48*; I. M. Duguid, *Ezekiel and the
Leaders of Israel* (SVT 56; Leiden: E. J. Brill, 1994); K. R. Stevenson, *Vision of
Transformation: The Territorial Rhetoric of Ezekiel 40–48* (SBLDS 154; Atlanta: Scholars
Press, 1996).
    [73] In Ezek 34:24; 37:25 the new David is called נָשִׂיא (Jer 30:21 also uses נָשִׂיא
as the title of the future leader of the restored community). The נָשִׂיא in Ezek 40–48
may therefore be identified as the new David, although this is not explicitly done
in the text. Levenson, *Theology of the Programme of Restoration*, 143, understands the
Davidic נָשִׂיא to be no more than a liturgical figurehead. On Is 55:1–5, which rein-
terprets the covenant with David, establishing it with all Yahweh's people, see
O. Eissfeldt, "The Promises of Grace to David In Isaiah 55:1–5," in *Israel's Prophetic
Heritage*, 196–207. For a list of interpretations of Is 55:3, see Coppens, *Le messianisme royal*, 100. J. H. Eaton, *Festal Drama in Deutero-Isaiah* (London: SPCK, 1979),
argues that Deutero-Isaiah draws on the liturgy of the monarchical period Autumn
festival at Jerusalem and that consequently the whole text presumes the re-establishment of Judean kingship. This view has not found much acceptance, however.

and the state is an important development given that the temple was reconstructed when Judah was a district under Achaemenid Persian administration and did not have an indigenous king. By disengaging the temple from the earlier monarchical ideology these prophets nevertheless understand the symbolic significance of the Jerusalem temple in nationalistic terms. Indeed, since this temple is the earthly abode of the god of Israel, it would be impossible to understand its significance in any other terms.

In Deutero-Isaiah, Yahweh is about to display his divine sovereignty by once again acting on the world political stage, this time in order to reverse or end the chastisement of his people, the exiles, (40:1–2) and to punish the Babylonians who perpetrated the destruction of Judah (41:11–12; 43:14–15; 47:1–15). Yahweh is to return to Jerusalem, taking his people with him (40:3–5, 9–11; 41:17–20; 42:10–17; 43:16–21). Judah and Jerusalem are to be restored by divine action (49:7–26; 51:3; 51:17–52:2; 52:7–12; 54:1–3; 54:11–17).[74] Cyrus is given a high profile in these chapters for his role in fulfilling Yahweh's plans regarding his people (41:1–7, 25–29; 44:24–45:13; 46:8–13; 48:12–16). In his capacity as the Creator of the Earth and humanity, Yahweh commissioned Cyrus for world conquest (41:2–4; 45:1–3, 11–13; 48:12–16). Yahweh's goal in this was the repatriation of the exiled Judeans and the rebuilding of Jerusalem with Yahweh's temple therein (44:24–28; 45:4–6, 13; 46:10b–13). Thus, Yahweh claims responsibility for Cyrus's military success and for Cyrus's actions on behalf of the Judean exiles and the land of Judah. Since these events were ostensibly announced before the fact, their accomplishment manifests Yahweh's sovereignty, bringing him glory and honour (41:25–27; 45:5–6; 46:8–10; 48:14, 16). Yahweh's march to Zion, while overtly expressing the Exodus motif, also has connections to the monarchical *Yahweh mālak*-Zion ideology. Yahweh is the divine warrior marching to his temple mount the successful resolution of the *Chaoskampf* (51:9–10). The restoration of Jerusalem/Zion (they are equated in 40:9, 41:27, 52:1) is envisaged in terms of Yahweh, the Creator, recreating the land of Judah and the city of Jerusalem, motifs related to the mythology of divine kingship.[75] As in the Zion psalms, Jerusalem is to be the garden of God (51:3) whose divine inhabitant ensures its protection (54:14).

---

[74] Jer 50–51 exhibits a number of similar features; see Carroll, *Jeremiah*, 814–56.
[75] See Stuhlmueller, *Creative Redemption*, 74–98.

In this context the significance of rebuilding the temple has two
aspects. First, it is one of the signs of Yahweh's sovereignty since it
displays his control of Cyrus's actions and of historical events. Second,
although in the oracles recounting the nature of the restoration prominence is given to the city itself (Jerusalem/Zion) as the symbol of
Yahweh's presence and focus of restoration/re-creating, the city's
significance lies in the fact that it is the locus of the temple. The
temple is mentioned in Deutero-Isaiah only in 44:28, within an oracle
regarding Cyrus in which Yahweh states that he will have Cyrus lay
the foundation of the temple and restore Jerusalem. The rebuilding
of the temple is nevertheless implicit in Yahweh's return to and restoration of Jerusalem/Zion since the divine presence demands a temple
and a cult. In this regard note 52:11 where the exiles returning to
Jerusalem take the cultic vessels with them. This presumes there will
be a renewed cult. The city is the site of pilgrimage for the exiles
and later the nations precisely because Yahweh will "reside" there.

Deutero-Isaiah's emphasis on the universal sovereignty of Yahweh,
which is evidenced in his creation of the world (40:15–26), in his
returning the exiles to their homeland (40:1–11; 43:1–21), in his election of Cyrus to conquer all before him (45:1–6), and in the worship of Yahweh by all the nations (45:14–15, 20–25; 49:6; 55:4–5),
is a nationalistic sentiment, even though a restored monarchical state
does not feature.[76] For Deutero-Isaiah to view Cyrus as the instrument of Yahweh does not conflict with the prophet's nationalist sentiments since he stands heir to a prophetic tradition which sees
Yahweh using foreign kings to perform the divine will with regard
to the kingdoms of Israel and Judah. Cyrus is not the king of Judah
but rather a monarch who has been given the task of temple rebuilding.[77] A legitimate temple builder (that is, a king) was needed, and

---

[76] See N. H. Snaith, "Isaiah 40–55. A Study of the Teaching of the Second
Isaiah and its Consequences," in *Studies on the Second Part of the Book of Isaiah* (VTSup
14; Leiden: Brill, 1967) 139–264. Others have considered the worship of Yahweh
by the nations to represent a new theological emphasis—universalism—which rejected
or transcended nationalism; see Wilson, *Nations in Deutero-Isaiah*, 1–10, for a brief
survey of the discussion. See also the balanced appraisal of D. W. Van Winkle,
"The Relationship of the Nations to Yahweh and to Israel in Isaiah xl–lv," *VT* 35
(1985) 446–58, who notes that "salvation of the nations does not preclude their
submission to Israel" (p. 457). The peoples of the earth coming to Jerusalem to
worship Yahweh, the god of Israel/Judah, must reflect nationalist sentiment.

[77] A number of these oracles speak of Cyrus in terms of a divinely elected king.
It is not David redivivus who was called to perform the will of Yahweh, but the

Yahweh rejecting the notion of reconstituting the indigenous monarchy for this role, had decided to use Cyrus. While some of the prophet's audience thought it preposterous that Yahweh should use Cyrus, the prophet himself is unperturbed since, as Creator, Yahweh's actions are above question (45:9–13). Yahweh's choice of Cyrus as his agent is related to the prophet's understanding of the coming restoration. It is not envisaged as the resuscitation of the state of Judah. With no Davidide to perform those tasks typically assigned to the king by the deity, such as temple (re)building and restoration of the city, Yahweh raises up a royal person whom he appoints for these tasks.

The rebuilt temple on Zion will be the throne of the divine king Yahweh, borrowing language from the monarchical Jerusalem cult, but Yahweh does not rule over a monarchical state. He rules over all peoples and nations, and all of them will come to acknowledge him. Implicit in the rule of Yahweh from Zion is the overthrow of all temporal powers, including the Persian empire. The acceptance of Cyrus is in order to finally transcend his authority and bring in a new age of the rule of Yahweh. Deutero-Isaiah can conceive of rebuilding the Jerusalem temple without reconstituting the kingdom of Judah because the political reality will in fact transcend that. That is, it is a larger, not smaller, view of the people of Judah and their role on the world stage. The conclusion to be drawn is that the present political order is sanctioned by Yahweh, but only for a time. It is a means to a greater end—the revelation and recognition of the sovereignty of Yahweh.

Deutero-Isaiah thus displays that some among the exiled Judeans considered the rebuilding of the Jerusalem temple to manifest the sovereignty of Yahweh without the need for a Davidic monarch or a monarchical state, while including a role for the Persian king Cyrus, in the short term at least. The prophet develops his view of the temple within a teleological framework which permits him to recast the role of both the temple and the foreign monarch. The Jerusalem

---

foreign king, Cyrus. Yahweh calls him (41:25; 46:11; 48:15 cf. 45:13; 41:2); bestows royal titles upon him (shepherd—44:28, anointed—45:1, beloved—48:14); leads him victoriously into battle (41:2–5; 45:1–3; 45:13); and instructs him as to the care of his people and sanctuary (44:26b–28; 45:4–6; 45:13). Although Cyrus certainly is a king, he is not, however, the exiled Judeans' king. The title "king" is used of Yahweh only (42:21; 43:15; 44:6; 52:7); he is their king (see Becker, *Messianic Expectation*, 52–53).

temple will not signify the reconstitution of the state nor will it be
the throne of Yahweh as the head of the kingdom of Judah. Yahweh's
sovereignty is to be expressed in a new way without a monarchical
state, yet Yahweh will be king over all the earth.

Ezekiel 40–48, like Deutero-Isaiah, rejects the idea of the re-establishment of an indigenous monarchy along the lines of the earlier
kingdoms of Israel and Judah but, in comparison with Deutero-
Isaiah, has a very strong territorial emphasis. The nationalistic under-
pinnings of the restoration envisaged in Ezekiel 40–48 have largely
gone unrecognized, particularly since the political leader of the restored
community, the נשׂיא, is now not understood to be a messianic figure.
Nevertheless, the tribal allotments outlined in Ezek 47:13–48:29 take
in all of the territory which was imagined as formerly belonging to
the united kingdom of Israel (cf. I Ki 5:1 [Eng. 4:21]). This emphasis on the re-establishment of the territory of Israel is clearly a nationalist sentiment. Jerusalem/Zion is again to serve as the capital of
Israel. Zion as Yahweh's abode and cosmic mountain/centre also
reflects nationalist concerns.

Ezekiel 40–48 envisages a reconstructed Jerusalem temple which
stands at the centre of a restored Jerusalem. The reader is not told
how the temple came to be built. There is no mention of a royal
temple builder. The presence (כבוד "glory") of Yahweh having returned
to the temple (43:1–6; 48:35), thus redressing the divine abandonment in Ezek 8–11, ushers in a new age in which the evils of the
past will not be repeated (43:7–12). Motifs from the Zion theology
are reworked, taking up such elements as the temple built on the
mountain of God from whence flows the river of life (43:1–6; 47:1–12).
The temple is not set in the context of royal-state ideology since the
nation will not be a monarchical state. The people and territory will
be organized as a temple state under the leadership of an appointed
נשׂיא who is stripped of the absolute royal authority once enjoyed by
the kings of Judah. His title itself reflects something of the change
in his status. The prophet thus maintains some continuity with the
monarchy while reinterpreting its place and status within the new
divine polity. The temple figures prominently in the text, with the
layout of the temple buildings and furniture elaborately described
(40–42; 43:13–17). Regulations for the cultus, which include defining
of the role of the נשׂיא therein, also feature in the text (45:13–46:24).
The reconstituted state is divided into equal allotments for each of
the twelve tribes with land also apportioned to Yahweh, the נשׂיא,

the priests, and the Levites (45:1–8; 47:13–48:29). In this way Ezekiel envisions the restoration of all Israel (that is, the Israel prior to the division of the kingdoms), and the boundaries of the land (47:13–23) contain much of the territory supposedly occupied by the Davidic-Solomonic empire. At the centre of this restored polity is the Jerusalem temple.

Both these prophets conceive of the Jerusalem temple as an institution functioning apart from the previously known monarchical state. While a king may be needed to build it (Deutero-Isaiah; Is 44:28) or a pseudo-monarchical figure needed to oversee it (Ezek 40–48), its *raison d'être* is not to legitimate a king and state or to function within a state administration, unlike the first temple. The rebuilt temple legitimates Yahweh and, in the aftermath of the dissolution of the state and exile, vindicates his actions and sovereignty. The monarchical Zion ideology still informs these prophets' understanding of the temple, but it has been reworked to suit their respective visions of the new polity. These prophets' rejection of the restoration as a return to the monarchical period can be compared with the prophetical texts noted earlier which specifically mention the reinstitution of the Davidic monarchy. While the various texts are all informed by the notion of historical recurrence, and all agree that the restoration must include the return of Yahweh to Jerusalem (and hence to a rebuilt temple) and the repatriation of the exiles, it is clear that there were differing opinions as to what form the restoration polity would take. As was noted in chapter 1, these differing opinions are considered by some to reflect the existence of parties, each vying to implement its vision of the restored polity. It is true to say that different understandings of the nature the Judean community, its future and purpose for existence are reflected in the literary texts from this period. This is not equivalent, however, to asserting the existence of parties struggling for control of the society. The detection of a new line of thought in a text, or the development of ideas known from texts of an earlier period, does not necessarily denote the generation of a new party or realm of struggle—the two are not coincident.[78] Indeed, the discovery and interpretation of such lines of thought, especially in the prophetic material,

---

[78] This is also the case for supposed insertions in and redactions of Ezekiel 40–48. It has been argued that there is a נשיא stratum and a Zadokite stratum within Ezek

is often a quite subjective affair. Invariably, such "parties", once "identified", are placed in elaborate social and historical contexts and usually given a formative role in the development of second-temple Judaism and/or a central position in the socio-political affairs of this period. It must be added further that not all religious ideologies and parties (if they formed such) necessarily found political expression. They may well have influenced those with political power, but not directly entered the political struggle themselves.[79] Parties can arise out of and respond to social cleavages and tensions, but the available evidence is insufficient to draw conclusions as to the status, authority or function in society of the supposed parties. None of these texts (that is, those envisaging the re-establishment of the Davidic monarchy; Deutero-Isaiah; Ezekiel 40–48) is programmatic, despite claims to the contrary regarding Deutero-Isaiah and Ezekiel 40–48 at least, since they do not articulate realistic, achievable goals and the means to attain them. For example, the apportionment of equal lots to the tribes of Israel in Ezekiel 40–48 (47:14; 48:1–29), and Yahweh ruling over the people directly, without an intermediary, in Deutero-Isaiah, are examples of utopian features of the restoration that could never be instituted. Further, it is noteworthy that Yahweh is consistently the instigator and primary actor in the restoration, not the people. This is not a programme that the people have to bring about. These texts' utopian visions of the restoration of Judah pay scant attention to the practical considerations attending temple rebuilding.[80] Rather than offering a programme to be imple-

---

40–48; so, for example, Gese, *Der Verfassungsentwurf des Ezechiel (Kap. 40–48)*, who is followed by many commentators. These strata need not reflect social division, however, and it is worthwhile pointing out that the existence of such strata is itself questionable; see, Greenberg, "Design and Themes of Ezekiel's Program"; R. K. Duke, "Punishment or Restoration? Another Look at the Levites in Ezekiel 44.6–16," *JSOT* 40 (1988) 61–81; Duguid, *Ezekiel and the Leaders of Israel*, 27–31, 87–90.

[79] As Albertz, *History of Israelite Religion*, 2. 436, comments on the vision of restoration in Ezek 40–48: "And the amazing thing about this new order is that the marked emphasis on the temple at the expense of the monarchy and the capital was not matched by any political claim to power on the part of the priesthood". I also view the texts that look forward to the restoration of the indigenous, Davidic monarchy as simply another take on the form of restoration that was expected. They are not programmatic texts, rather they are expressions of hope for the future.

[80] Tuell, *Law of the Temple*, contends that Ezek 40–48 depicts "an actual society, centered on a state-supported Temple in which secular leadership played an important role" (p. 176), and that what we learn of this society accords with Achaemenid Persian treatment of the cults of subjugated peoples. However, as will be argued

mented, they should be viewed as expressions of hope for restoration. In discussing the notion of the mission to the Gentiles in Is 40–66, J. Blenkinsopp writes:

> To speak of a Gentile mission does not, of course, mean that we are dealing with actual proposals and strategies. What these texts express are attitudes, even dreams and fantasies, entertained by one segment of post-exilic Judaism. That such attitudes can be self-deceptive, self-serving and self-defeating goes without saying. But it is also true to our experience to affirm that projections of a possible future, especially when emitted with the passion and power of conviction often attested in these chapters, can actually create a future, even if the reality is never quite the same as the projection.[81]

I concur with this sentiment and believe it serves well as a general reading strategy for Deutero-Isaiah and Ezekiel 40–48. The significance of "attitudes, even dreams and fantasies" lies in their witness to the expectation of restoration and return to normalcy marked by Yahweh in Jerusalem, the people of Yahweh in their land, and the manifestation of Yahweh's sovereignty.

Attempts to relate the restoration visions of these texts to developments in Achaemenid Judah falter not only on the assumption that they represent "parties", but also on the inability to resolve the social and historical contexts in which to interpret the "parties". For example, Hanson, who attempts to integrate the restoration visions of Deutero-Isaiah and Ezekiel 40–48 with the Judean restoration in the early Achaemenid Persian period, contends that Ezekiel 40–48 was no political threat to Achaemenid Persian control of Judah since

---

in chapters 3 and 4, it is problematic to relate the rebuilding and function of the Jerusalem temple to Achaemenid Persian administrative policy and practices. Greenberg, "Design and Themes of Ezekiel's Program", 208, considers Ezek 40–48 to be much more than "mere announcements of restoration" since the prophet "composed an ideal revision of the institutions of the new Israel that would ensure the permanence of that restoration". But he has to admit that "wherever Ezekiel's program can be checked against subsequent events it proves to have had no effect". Stevenson, *Vision of Transformation*, emphasizes that Ezek 40–48 is a response to the threat of assimilation in Babylonia, so that its primary concern was to encourage the Judean exiles rather than to offer a blueprint for restoration. She notes, "the rhetorical purpose of the book was to give hope to the community in exile. It does this by creating a vision of a restructured society, a society centered around the temple of YHWH, a society at home in its own land, a society with YHWH in its midst". (p. 163)

[81] J. Blenkinsopp, "Second Isaiah—Prophet of Universalism," *JSOT* 41 (1988) 98–99.

its programmatic description of Judah as a temple state could be
realized under the Achaemenids. The supporters of this perspective,
the repatriated Zadokite priests, were thus pro-Persian because the
Achaemenids supposedly patronized this form of the social and political organization of Judah. The Zadokites thus came to political
ascendancy. Deutero-Isaiah's eschatological vision of the Yahweh's
sovereignty over the nations of the earth, with Judah/Israel as his
chosen people, could not, however, be made compatible with the
continued submission of the Judeans to Achaemenid Persian rule and
so those who adopted this perspective were politically disenfranchised.
In regard to distinctions between Deutero-Isaiah and Ezekiel 40–48,
Hanson sees Deutero-Isaiah and his followers as expecting Yahweh
to build the temple himself and bring in the new age without human
effort, while Ezekiel 40–48 gives a role in building the temple and
establishing the theocratic state (under the נשׂיא) to the people.[82]

The texts actually argue the other way around. Deutero-Isaiah has
Yahweh using a human king, Cyrus, to rebuild, while Ezekiel 40–48
makes no mention of how the temple gets built; it is just there in
Jerusalem. Further, neither Deutero-Isaiah nor Ezekiel 40–48 would
have proven acceptable to the Achaemenids as an ideology supporting the reconstruction of the Jerusalem temple. Deutero-Isaiah
envisions Yahweh transcending the authority of the Achaemenids,
giving the Judeans a privileged place on the world stage, while Ezekiel
40–48 demands that the restored community reappropriate all the
idealized territorial holdings of the former united kingdom of Israel.

Four points can be made from this brief examination of the impact
of the dissolution of the kingdom of Judah on royal-state ideology
and restoration hopes in Babylonian Judean texts. First, restoration
hopes (whether they restate or rework the royal-state ideology) do
not exhibit the notion of Israel as constituting a "cultic community"
under priestly leadership. Ezekiel 40–48 comes closest in this regard
but it still displays strong influence of the royal-state ideology. Further,
there is no hint of the rejection of those Judeans who remained in
their homeland or who were exiled to places other than Babylonia.
All texts have an inclusivist purview, often including foreign nations
in their visions of the restoration. Second, there is a clear expectation of the return of Yahweh to Jerusalem and the re-establishment

---

[82] Hanson, *Dawn of Apocalyptic*, 32–279.

of Zion as the throne of Yahweh. This will reverse the misfortune of 587, return Judah to normality, and reaffirm the sovereign kingship of Yahweh. Third, concomitant with the preceding point, there was interest in the rebuilding of the Jerusalem temple since this was the traditional earthly abode of Yahweh. Fourth, Deutero-Isaiah and Ezekiel 40–48 rework the monarchical royal-state ideology so that while the temple's link to the kingship of Yahweh was maintained, it no longer served to legitimate the monarchical polity and political structures as it had done when it was originally built. This can be compared with those texts which look forward to the re-establishment of Davidic kingship which, while they do not mention the rebuilding of the temple, must understand the temple to legitimate indigenous kingship.

Ezra 1–6, the narrative history of the rebuilding of the temple in the reigns of Cyrus II and Darius I, shares in common with Deutero-Isaiah and Ezekiel 40–48 the notion that Yahweh had rejected the re-establishment of the indigenous monarchy. While these prophets looked forward to the future restoration, Ezra 1–6 understands the community of the repatriates to be the fulfilment of those restoration hopes; although the character of the restoration it propounds is vastly different from both Deutero-Isaiah and Ezekiel 40–48. In Ezra 1–6, no demands are made of Judah's Achaemenid Persian overlords beyond that they grant permission for the temple to be rebuilt and permit the Judeans freedom to worship Yahweh without interference from outsiders. With Ezekiel 40–48, Ezr 1–6 views the restored community as gathered around the temple in Jerusalem, but it lacks Ezekiel's nationalist territorial concerns. This narrative displays a pro-Persian proclivity whereby the Achaemenid Persian administration is accepted as the divinely appointed administrators of the territory of Judah rather than as a temporary rule which Yahweh will transcend, as Deutero-Isaiah avers. The rebuilding of the temple was undertaken with the sanction, indeed encouragement and financial support, of the Persians. Since Ezra 1–6 has shaped the discussion of the historical events surrounding the rebuilding, the Judean ideology of temple reconstruction, and the place of Achaemenid administrative policy in the rebuilding, it is to a consideration of this narrative that attention is now turned.

CHAPTER THREE

REBUILDING THE JERUSALEM TEMPLE OF YAHWEH IN ACHAEMENID JUDAH I: THE REIGN OF CYRUS II

In the previous chapter it was argued that for the period immediately after the demise of the kingdom of Judah it is currently impossible to determine the social organization of the communities of Judeans in Babylonia and Judah, their religious practices, or the ritual means by which they maintained their identity. On the basis of the available evidence the contention that the Judean exiles formed a "cultic community" devoted to the Torah, living under the authority of the priesthood and separating themselves from outsiders (both foreigners and those Judeans who had remained in the land) cannot be sustained. It was noted that a number of texts written in the Babylonian Judean community sought to defend Yahweh in the face of the dissolution of the state and exile in an attempt to justify the continued worship of Yahweh by the exiles (II Ki; Ezek 1–39; Deuteronomistic revision of Jeremiah; Deutero-Isaiah), while the prophetical texts Ezekiel 40–48 and Deutero-Isaiah proclaimed the expected restoration of the Jerusalem temple of Yahweh and the repatriation of the Judean exiles to their homeland. These texts were not exclusivist in outlook, and although nationalistic in tenor the expectations they expressed were couched in non-monarchical terms. For these prophets the future of Yahweh's people was not simply to be the monarchical period revisited. The traditional state ideology of the election of David and Zion/Jerusalem was reworked so as to sever the latter from the former in order to develop new possibilities for a Judean polity.

The reconstruction of the temple is portrayed as being fundamental to the reconstitution of the Judean people in their homeland since the temple denoted the renewal of the presence of Yahweh with them in the aftermath of the dissolution of the state and the deportation. It was held to reverse the divine abandonment, exile and humiliation of 587. It is not surprising, therefore, that certain Persian period biblical texts, notably Ezra 1–6, Haggai and Zechariah 1–8, focus on the rebuilding of Jerusalem temple of Yahweh. According

to Ezra 1–6 there were two attempts by the Judeans to rebuild the
Jerusalem temple. The first, unsuccessful, attempt was in the first
years of the reign of Cyrus the Great and is recounted in Ezr 1:1–4:5.
The second attempt, which resulted in the reconstruction of the temple, commenced in the second year of Darius I (Ezr 4:24; Hag 1:1,
1:15b–2:1a, 2:10; Zech 1:1, 7).

The present chapter investigates the attempt to rebuild the temple of Yahweh in the reign of Cyrus. The initial issues for consideration are the character of the Ezra narrative and its historical value
for establishing the social context in which the rebuilding was undertaken. Ezr 1:1–4:5 contends that the impetus for the rebuilding came
from an edict issued by Cyrus repatriating the Judeans exiled in
Babylonia and granting them permission to rebuild. Although the
repatriates were committed to the task of rebuilding the temple, their
efforts came to little as their work was stopped by "the people(s) of
the land(s)"; that is, peoples whom the repatriates found in Judah
and its environs at their return and whom they considered to be
foreigners earlier imported into the region. These people hampered
the repatriates' attempt to rebuild the temple because their claim to
be Yahwists, which issued in their offer to participate in the rebuilding, was rejected by the repatriates who saw themselves as the only
legitimate Yahwists (and hence the only legitimate temple rebuilders).
Temple rebuilding was thus the centre of social conflict in Achaemenid
Judah between repatriates and non-repatriates. This portrayal of
events in the reign of Cyrus is rejected as being a late, tendentious
account which reflects social tensions current at the time the text
was written, probably in the fourth century or later.

The next two sections of this chapter review the debate surrounding
the veracity of the two Cyrus edicts included in Ezra 1–6 and the
role of the Achaemenid Persian administration in the temple rebuilding, exemplified by a supposed policy of Cyrus pertaining to indigenous cults within the empire. The claim of many commentators is
that even if Ezr 1:1–4:5 is tendentious, on the basis of the Cyrus
edicts it can be affirmed that there was a sizeable repatriation of
Babylonian exiles in the reign of Cyrus and that this repatriation
was for the purpose of rebuilding the temple. In support of this claim
it is argued that the Cyrus edicts conform to a general empire-wide
policy of Cyrus in repatriating exiled peoples and encouraging the
re-establishment of local cults. In response, it is argued that although

Cyrus may have granted permission to rebuild the Jerusalem temple of Yahweh, the Hebrew edict (Ezr 1:2–4) is unlikely to be a decree issued by the Achaemenid Persian bureaucracy because of its distinctive vocabulary and the number of anachronistic features it exhibits. Further, it cannot be shown that Cyrus implemented an empire-wide policy of repatriations or that he consistently supported re-establishing local cults. The Aramaic edict of Cyrus (Ezr 6:2c–5) is more likely to contain original elements, but it is notable that this text does not speak of the mass repatriation of the Babylonian exiles (it mentions only the return of the temple vessels under a delegation led by Sheshbazzar), nor does it authorize the exiles alone to undertake the rebuilding.

If it is granted that Cyrus did issue a decree granting permission for Judeans to rebuild their temple, why was this decree not fulfilled? Since the explanation offered in Ezr 1:1–4:5 must be rejected, the final section of this chapter investigates alternative explanations and argues from a study of Hag 1:2–11 and Zech 1:12–17 that the Judeans, both those who had remained in the land after 587 and those who had been repatriated, had not made a concerted effort to rebuild the Jerusalem temple because of ideological problems they had with the undertaking. Social conflict was not, therefore, the reason for the delay in rebuilding after the edict of Cyrus had been issued. Contrary to Ezr 1:1–4:5, and in contrast to what one might have deduced from Deutero-Isaiah and Ezekiel 40–48, those repatriated proved to be ambivalent about the rebuilding of the temple. This was an attitude they shared with those Judeans who had remained in the homeland. Haggai and Zechariah offer insight into the purpose of the temple rebuilding, the ideology underpinning the rebuilding in the new social and political setting of Achaemenid Judah, the determination of the timing of the rebuilding, and the community that undertook the rebuilding; all matters to be taken up in the following chapter.

THE EZRA NARRATIVE

The attempted rebuilding of the Jerusalem temple in the reign of Cyrus is recounted in Ezr 1:1–4:5 and Ezr 5:13–16. These passages form part of a larger narrative, Ezra 1–6, which is the primary narrative history of the rebuilding of the temple.[1] It covers the period from "the first year of Cyrus, King of Persia" (Ezr 1:1), which is identified with his first year of rule over the former Babylonian empire (539–8), to the completion of the Jerusalem temple of Yahweh in "the sixth year of the reign of King Darius (I)" (Ezr 6:15; that is, 515). As it now stands, this narrative has three sections: Repatriation of exiled Judeans and first rebuilding attempt in the reign of Cyrus (Ezr 1:1–3:13); hiatus in the rebuilding due to the intervention of hostile neighbours (Ezr 4:1–24); successful second rebuilding attempt in the reign of Darius (Ezr 5:1–6:22). A notable feature of the narrative is that two sections (Ezr 1:1–4:7; 6:19–22) are written in Hebrew, while the rest (Ezr 4:8–6:18), enclosed in the Hebrew narrative, is written in Aramaic. The Aramaic section is thus considered to have been a separate narrative originally.[2]

---

[1] Ezr 1–6 is universally recognized as being a discrete section of Ezr-Neh. There are other accounts of the rebuilding of the temple in I Esdras (Esdras α in LXX = 3 Esdras in Vulgate) and Josephus (*Antiquities*, xi. 1–119). Josephus depends on I Esdras for his account of the post-exilic period; see H. Bloch, *Die Quellen des Flavius Josephus in seiner Archäologie* (Leipzig: Teubner, 1879); J. M. Myers, *I and II Esdras* (AB 42; Garden City, NY: Doubleday, 1974) 8–15; S. J. D. Cohen, *Josephus in Galilee and Rome: His Vita and Development as a Historian* (Columbia Studies in the Classical Tradition; Leiden: Brill, 1979) 42–43.
There are scholars who accord I Esdras priority over canonical Ezra (for example, Mowinckel, *Studien zu dem Buche Ezra-Nehemia*, 1. 24–45; K.-F. Pohlman, *Studien zum dritten Esra. Ein Beitrag zur Frage nach dem ursprünglichen Schluß des chronistischen Geschichtswerkes* [FRLANT 104; Göttingen: Vandenhoeck & Ruprecht, 1970] 57–64; D. Böhler, *Die heilige Stadt in Esdras A und Esra-Nehemia. Zwei Konzeptionen der Wiederherstellung Israels* [OBO 158; Freiburg: Universitätsverlag/Göttingen: Vandenhoeck & Ruprecht, 1997]), although the vast majority of scholars affirm the priority of canonical Ezra (so, for example, H. G. M. Williamson, *Israel in the Books of Chronicles* [Cambridge: Cambridge University Press, 1977] 12–36; R. Hanhart, "Zu Text und Textgeschichte des ersten Esrabuches," in *Proceedings of the Sixth World Congress of Jewish Studies* [ed. A. Shinan; Jerusalem: World Union of Jewish Studies, 1977] 201–12). On the relationship of I Esdras to Ezra-Nehemiah, see also Eissfeldt, *Introduction*, 575; Myers, *I and II Esdras*, 5–6; Pohlmann, *Studien*, 307–8; Eskenazi, *In An Age of Prose*, 155–74; A. Schenker, "La rélation d'Esdras A au texte massorétique d'Esdras-Néhémie," in *Tradition of the Text: Studies Offered to Dominique Barthélemy in Celebration of his 70th Birthday* (ed. G. J. Nelson and S. Pisano; OBO 109; Freiburg: Universitätsverlag/Göttingen: Vandenhoeck & Ruprecht, 1991) 218–48, cf. H. G. M. Williamson, "The Problem with 1 Esdras," in *After the Exile: Essays in Honour of Rex Mason* (ed. J. Barton and D. J. Reimer; Macon, GA: Mercer University Press, 1996) 201–16, esp. 211–213.
[2] The sources from which Ezr 1–6 is constructed are still a matter of debate. W. Rudolph, *Esra und Nehemia samt 3. Esra* (HAT 20; Tübingen: J. C. B. Mohr [Paul Siebeck], 1949) xxiii, represents the widely held view that the author had at his disposal the list of temple vessels (Ezr 1:8–11a), a list of returnees (Ezr 2; borrowed and adapted from Neh 7), and an Aramaic narrative of the temple rebuilding under Darius with later complaints of those living in Samaria directed to

The legitimacy of the temple rebuilding and of the repatriated Judeans to undertake the task are central concerns of these chapters. These concerns are immediately introduced in Ezr 1:1–11. Verses 2–4 are ostensibly an edict of Cyrus II issued soon after his coming to power in Babylon as a result of his recognition that the God of Israel was responsible for his victory (cf. Is 41:1–7; 44:28; 45:1–6). The edict deals with the reconstruction of "the temple of Yahweh, the God of Israel . . . in Jerusalem" (v. 3). Although addressed generally to those "among you of all his [Yahweh's] people" (v. 3),[3] the edict is nevertheless understood by the author/editor to pertain to the *exiled* Judeans and to be a repatriation order for them since v. 11 names Babylon as the place of departure for those taking advantage of the edict.

Thus interpreted, the edict legitimizes the repatriated Judeans' measures to rebuild the temple; a point of contention throughout chapters 3–6. It recognizes that it is they who stand in continuity with monarchical Judah as evidenced by the consignment of the temple vessels confiscated by Nebuchadrezzar to Sheshbazzar, who is the leader of the repatriation (vv. 7–8), for return to Jerusalem.[4]

Achaemenid kings, specifically concerning the Judeans rebuilding the wall of Jerusalem (Ezr 4:8–6:18). H. G. M. Williamson, "The Composition of Ezra i–vi," *JTS* NS 34 (1983) 1–30, sees the sources as being: the Cyrus edict (Ezr 1:2–4), the list of the temple vessels, and the correspondence in Aramaic. He holds that the rest of the Aramaic section was written by the same author as the Hebrew narrative. A. H. J. Gunneweg, "Die aramäische und die hebräische Erzählung über die nachexilische Restauration—ein Vergleich," *ZAW* 94 (1982) 299–302, understands the Hebrew and Aramaic narratives to be separate traditions, since they reflect different themes. P. R. Ackroyd, "Historical Problems of the Early Achaemenian Period," *Orient* 20 (1984) 1–15, identifies three distinct traditions regarding the restoration: Ezr 1, Ezr 3:2–13, and Ezr 5–6, which the author has integrated into a continuous narrative. On the structure of Ezr 1–6, see also Eskenazi, *In An Age of Prose*, 42–60; B. Halpern, "A Historiographic Commentary on Ezra 1–6: Achronological Narrative and Dual Chronology in Israelite Historiography," in *The Hebrew Bible and Its Interpreters* (ed. W. H. Propp, B. Halpern, and D. N. Freedman; Winona Lake, IN: Eisenbrauns, 1990) 81–142.

[3] Since the edict is sent throughout the empire (Ezr 1:1) the "you" appears to denote all the inhabitants of the empire.

[4] P. R. Ackroyd, "The Temple Vessels: A Continuity Theme," in *Studies in the Religion of Ancient Israel* (VTSup 23; Leiden: Brill, 1972) 177–79. It has long been supposed that the Sheshbazzar mentioned here is none other than "Shenazzar the son of Jehoiachin" of I Chron 3:18, the contention being that the "politically astute" Cyrus would have appointed a Davidide as governor over Judah (so, Meyer, *Entstehung*, 76–77. The view still has wide currency; see, for example, Cross, "Reconstruction of the Judean Restoration," 15; Bright, *History*, 361–62). The names, however, are linguistically distinct (P.-R. Berger, "Zu den Namen ששבצר und שנאצר," *ZAW* 83

Continuity of the restoration cult with that of monarchical Judah is also highlighted by the construction of the temple "on its site" (Ezr 2:68) and the altar "in its place" (Ezr 3:3). The legitimacy of the restoration cult is further established by virtue of the genealogical continuity of the cultic personnel (Ezr 1:5, 2:36). Certain persons who could not prove their priestly ancestry were excluded from the priesthood (Ezr 2:60–63). Also, the preparations for the rebuilding parallel those of the first temple (Ezr 3:7),[5] and the feasts and sacrifices of the first temple were reinstituted soon after the return (Ezr 3:4–6).

According to Ezr 1:2–3, the repatriation was for the explicit purpose of rebuilding the Jerusalem temple. The names of those who returned at this time, "each to his own town" (Ezr 2:1, 70; 3:1), are listed in Ezr 2. According to Ezr 3, soon after their arrival in Judah

---

[1971]: 98–100; P. E. Dion, "ששבצר and שנאצר," *ZAW* 95 [1983]: 111–12). Sheshbazzar lacks a patronymic, which has been interpreted as denoting that his father was unknown to the author of the narrative and that Sheshbazzar was a Babylonian official appointed by Cyrus, and not a Jew (so, A. C. Welch, *Post-Exilic Judaism* [Edinburgh/London: Blackwood, 1935] 98–99). M. Noth contends (*History*, 309) that it is unclear as to why Cyrus would appoint a Babylonian rather than a Persian to such a position. In light of this, Noth considers it likely that Sheshbazzar was a deported Judean who had a Babylonian name (cf. Zerubbabel).

The character of Sheshbazzar's office is debated. The titles given him in Ezra are not very informative. In Ezr 1:8 he is called נשיא ליהודה, while in Ezr 5:14 (one of the Aramaic letters) he is termed פחה. The latter term has led a number of commentators to assume that Sheshbazzar must have been appointed governor of Judah which was at this time removed from the jurisdiction of Samaria, so N. Avigad. *Bullae and Seals from a Post-Exilic Judean Archive* (Qedem 4; Jerusalem: Hebrew University) 35; S. Japhet, "Sheshbazzar and Zerubbabel. Against the Background the Historical and Religious Tendencies of Ezra-Nehemiah," *ZAW* 94 (1982) 80, 98 (who thinks that נשיא was an attempt to offer a Hebrew equivalent for Aramaic פחה); Williamson, *Ezra, Nehemiah*, 17–19 (who links the title נשיא to the 'prince' in Ezek 40–48); Meyers and Meyers, *Haggai, Zechariah 1–8*, 13–16; H. G. M. Williamson, "The Governors of Judah Under the Persians," *TynB* 39 (1988): 59–82. An earlier scholarly tradition, which still has many adherents, considers Zerubbabel or Nehemiah to be the first governor of Achaemenid Judah. It is true that פחה need not refer to the office of district governor since it is used of various appointments of widely differing function and status within the Achaemenid Persian administration. It could thus be used of Sheshbazzar in Ezr 5:14 with reference to his task in leading the repatriates and returning the temple vessels. He would still have been subject to the governor of Samaria; see Alt, "Die Rolle Samarias," 333–37 (cf. Smith, *Palestinian Parties*, 147–53); Galling, *Studien*, 81–82; F. C. Fensham, "Peḥâ in the Old Testament and the Ancient Near East," *Die Oud Testamentiese Werkgemeenskap in Suid-Afrika* 19 (1976): 47; McEvenue, "Political Structure in Judah," 353–64.

   [5] Wood from Sidonians/Tyrians—I Ki 5:15ff. (Eng. vv. 1ff.) cf. II Chrons 1:18ff. (Eng. 2:1ff.); I Chrons 22:4. Sacrifices—I Chrons 23:31; II Chron 2:4 (Eng. v. 3); 8:13; 31:3. Masons—II Ki 22:3ff. // II Chrons 34:8ff.; I Chrons 22:2, 15.

the repatriates gathered in Jerusalem and now under the supervision of Zerubbabel and Joshua they "set up the altar on its original site" (Ezr 3:3), the foundation of the temple having not yet been laid (Ezr 3:6).[6] Funds were outlaid to retain craftsmen and to obtain materials for the rebuilding of the temple (Ezr 3:7). Then, in "the second year after their arrival at the house of God in Jerusalem, in the second month . . ." (Ezr 3:8) a start was made on the rebuilding by relaying the foundation of the temple (Ezr 3:8ff.).

Since the repatriates were single-minded in their aim to rebuild the temple, and since they had both ample funds for the undertaking (Ezr 1:6; 2:68–69) and strong support from the Persian government (Ezr 1), explaining why the rebuilding was not completed by those who returned in the reign of Cyrus but rather delayed until the reign of Darius I is a major concern of Ezra 1–4. It attributes the delay in rebuilding to obstructions raised by "the people of the land" whose offer of aid in the rebuilding project was rejected by the repatriates.[7] This incident is recounted in Ezr 4:1–5—

---

[6] Ezr 3:1 states that it was "in the seventh month" that the repatriates erected the altar. Whether this was the seventh month of the first, second or third year of Cyrus is unclear. In any case, this chronological referent is taken from Neh 7:72b (Eng. v. 73b) where it refers to a completely different epoch. On this further, see below.

[7] There is a group of related terms in Ezr-Neh used for "the people of the land":

עם־הארץ   Ezr 4:4
עמי הארץ   Ezr 10:2, 11; Neh 9:24; 10:31–32
יושבי הארץ   Neh 9:24
גויי־הארץ   Ezr 6:21

עמי הארצות   Ezr 3:3; 9:1–2, 11; Neh 9:30, 10:29 (cf. מלכי הארצות Ezr 9:7)

Note that all these references occur in Ezra and the portions of Nehemiah outside the "Nehemiah Memoir" (the Nehemiah Memoir consists of Neh 1–7, parts of Neh 12:27–43, and Neh 13:4–31 and is viewed as an independent source. There is extensive debate concerning the nature of this source and its relationship to the rest of Ezr-Neh. On this source see, in addition to the major commentaries and Introductions, Mowinckel, *Studien zu dem Buche Esra-Nehemia*, vol. 2; Kellerman, *Nehemia*; Clines, "Nehemiah Memoir," 124–64; J. Blenkinsopp, "The Nehemiah Autobiographical Memoir," in *Language, Theology and the Bible: Essays in Honour of James Barr* [ed. S. E. Balentine and J. Barton; Oxford: Clarendon, 1994] 199–212).

"The people of the land" and related terms have various meanings in the biblical texts of different periods; see E. W. Nicholson, "The Meaning of the Expression עם הארץ in the Old Testament," *JSS* 10 (1965) 59–66; A. H. J. Gunneweg, "עם הארץ—A Semantic Revolution," *ZAW* 95 (1983) 437–40. In Ezr-Neh these terms are not used to identify a particular political entity (for example, the inhabitants of Samaria), nor a particular group, such as "Samaritans" or the nobles of Samaria (contra Alt, "Die Rolle Samarias," 322; E. Würthwein, *Der 'amm ha'arez im Alten Testament* [Stuttgart: Kohlhammer, 1936], 57–64; Vogt, *Studie*, 152–54). The terms

1) When the enemies of Judah and Benjamin heard that the exiles
were building a temple for Yahweh, God of Israel, 2) they came to
Zerubbabel and the heads of families and said to them, "Let us build
with you, for we worship the same God as you, and we have been
sacrificing to him[8] since the time of Esarhaddon, king of Assyria, who
brought us here". 3) But Zerubbabel, Joshua, and the rest of the heads
of families of Israel replied, "You have nothing in common with us
to permit you to build a house for our God; rather we alone will build
(it) for Yahweh, God of Israel, as King Cyrus, king of Persia, has commanded us". 4) Then the people of the land discouraged the people
of Judah and made them afraid to build. 5) They bribed counselors
to oppose them in order to frustrate their purpose all the days of
Cyrus, king of Persia, until the reign of Darius, king of Persia.

Those outside the community of repatriated Judeans were excluded
from participation in the rebuilding because they were considered
to be "foreigners". According to Ezr 4:1–3, 9–10, they were self-
confessedly so. They were originally inhabitants of foreign lands who
were imported into the region by foreign kings. No mention is made
of those Judeans who remained in the land since for the author of
this narrative there were none. They may be in view in Ezr 3:3,
where they too are unacceptable to the repatriates, but most commentators consider Ezr 3:3 ("the peoples of the lands") to relate to the
same group as that mentioned in Ezr 4:4 ("the people of the land").

Despite their claims to the contrary in Ezr 4:2, the neighbouring
peoples were not legitimate worshippers of Yahweh nor, in the opinion of the author, were they included in Cyrus's edict. This had

---

are used of any people whom the author wishes to discredit, either in Samaria or
in Judah. They are derogatory terms emphasizing that the group so designated was
found in the territory or neighbourhood of Judah when the exiles returned and
thus are not members of the group of repatriated Judeans ("the golah", "sons of
the golah" in Ezr; see Vogt, *Studie*, 22–42). "The people of the land" are thus not
a single, homogenous group in Ezr-Neh.

That the basic reason for the exclusion of "the people of the land" in Ezr-Neh
(with the exception of Ezr 6:21 and Neh 10:29 [Eng. v. 28]) was ethnic is clear
from the use of this term alongside ethnic designations (Ezr 9:1; 10:2, 10–11, 14,
17–18; Neh 9:24 cf. Ezr 4:2, 4). To be sure, some (much?) of this ethnic differentiation
was fictionalized, for the descendants of the inhabitants of Judah who had remained
in the land were ethnically the same as the repatriated Judeans. One should expect
some admixture of those Judeans who were not exiled with neighbouring peoples
as the latter encroached on the territory of the former kingdom of Judah; see
Ahlström, *Who were the Israelites?*, 104–08.

[8] Reading Qere (וְלוֹ), which is supported by a number of the ancient versions.
MT has וְלֹא. The claim that they had not been sacrificing to Yahweh would make
little sense in the present context.

been issued to the Judeans (that is, for this author, those in exile in Babylonia), and since only the repatriates were the remnant of the kingdom of Judah, there being no Judeans left in the land, they alone could build.[9] The temple to be rebuilt was Yahweh's legitimate temple (legitimated by the Persians and by the continuity of the returnees and their cultic officials with monarchical Judah). To include "foreign" neighbours in the rebuilding project would be to legitimate them as true worshippers of Yahweh and to include them among his people. It would be improper to do so, therefore they must be excluded. In any case they reveal themselves to be "the enemies of Judah and Benjamin" (Ezr 4:1) by gaining an injunction against the temple rebuilding, claiming that the repatriates were attempting to rebel (Ezr 4).[10] Construction of the temple recommenced in the second year of Darius I and continued through an investigation by Tattenai, the provincial satrap, in which a check was made of records to verify the Judeans' permission to rebuild the temple. The rebuilding was completed in the sixth year of Darius I (Ezr 5–6).

Ezr 1–6 sets forth a clear conception of both the purpose of the rebuilding of the Jerusalem temple and the community that undertook the work. The rebuilding was undertaken in two stages, the first in the reign of Cyrus, which was halted by the intervention of "the people of the land" (Ezr 1:1–4:24); the second in the reign of Darius (Ezr 5:1–6:18). The temple was rebuilt because Yahweh's ire against his people, exemplified in the dissolution of the kingdom of Judah and concomitant exile of the kingdom's inhabitants, had now abated. The reference to the prophecy of Jeremiah (Ezr 1:1) refers to this prophet's announcement that the exile would last only seventy years (Jer 25:11–12; 29:10 cf. II Chrons 36:21).[11] The author/editor

---

[9] On יחד in Ezr 4:3 meaning "alone", see M. D. Goldman, "Misunderstood Polaric Meaning of a Word," *ABR* 1 (1951) 61–63; J. C. de Moor, "Lexical Remarks Concerning YAḤAD and YAḤDAW," *VT* 7 (1957) 350–55.

[10] Ezr 4:6–23 speaks of such complaints being lodged against the repatriates in the reigns of Xerxes and Artaxerxes, but no further information regarding the incidents is given. On the chronological displacement of this narrative, see below p. 105.

[11] The use of עור "to stir up" in Ezr 1:1, which is similarly used of Yahweh's action towards Cyrus in Deutro-Isaiah (Is 41:25; 45:13), has led a number of commentators to consider that the prophecy in question concerns Yahweh's rousing the spirit of Cyrus to issue a proclamation (Ezr 1:1), and that the author thus has erroneously attributed to Jeremiah the prophecy of Deutero-Isaiah. Williamson, *Ezra,*

of the Ezra narrative sees behind the proclamation of Cyrus the hand of Yahweh acting to realize this prophetic word. The repatriates do not seek to reconstitute the kingdom of Judah, nor do they define their identity in terms of kingship and statehood. Rather, they are a cultic community who are recalled to their homeland to return their cultic life to normality, and the cultic community is the polity the rebuilt temple was to serve. The rebuilding is a legitimate undertaking since their deity had demanded that the temple be rebuilt and an earthly king (Cyrus, later Darius) had been commissioned to oversee the work. In this regard Ezr 1–6 does not differ from Deutero-Isaiah in the way the temple rebuilding is legitimated. Unlike Deutero-Isaiah, however, Ezr 1–6 gives little attention to the temple rebuilding as a symbol of Yahweh's kingship or to the underlying political significance of the act. The only concession to this ideology is the mention that Yahweh stands behind Cyrus's decision to permit the repatriation and rebuilding. The community undertaking the rebuilding is identified with those Judeans repatriated from Babylonia, seeing that all whom they find living in Judah and its environs at their return were "foreigners", and hence not Judeans. As a community devoted to the Jerusalem temple cult and living in obedience to the prescripts of the Torah, they had to separate themselves from foreigners (Ezr 3:1–6; 4:1–5). The delay in the rebuilding was due to the intervention of these hostile foreigners.

There are many features of this narrative that are problematical, however, and which raise questions regarding this narrative's historical veracity. Did the repatriates form a "cultic community" in Judah, given that there is no evidence to support the contention that Judeans in Babylonia formed such a social organization? Why is there no mention of the Judeans who had remained in their homeland after 587? Why are Zerubbabel and Joshua said to have laid the temple's foundation in the reign of Cyrus in Ezr 3:8–9 while in Ezr 5:14–16 Sheshbazzar is credited with the same? Why do the biblical texts attributed to the prophets Haggai and Zechariah, who

---

Nehemiah, 9–10, proposes that the author has in mind here Jer 50–51 which foretells the downfall of Babylon and which uses the verb עוּר to describe Yahweh's action in rousing a destroyer against Babylon (Jer 51:1), who is identified as "the king (so LXX; MT: kings) of the Medes" (Jer 51:11). He contends that "because of the catchword עִיר ("stir up") and the explicit reference to Cyrus, [the author] would have expected his readers to interpret the negative prophecy in Jer 51 in the light of the positive statements of Is 41, 44, and 45".

in Ezr 5:1 stir the people up to rebuild in the reign of Darius, display no knowledge of the rebuilding attempt in the reign of Cyrus and have Zerubbabel and Joshua laying the foundation of the temple in the reign of Darius I (Ezr 3:8–9 cf. Hag 2:18; Zech 4:8–9)? Was the funding for the temple to come from the Judeans (Ezr 1:5–6; 2:68; 3:7) or the Achaemenid Persian government (Ezr 6:5, 8–9)? Why are the letters cited in Ezr 4:6–24 showing that "the people of the land" thwarted the repatriates' rebuilding attempt statedly from the reign of Artaxerxes (I?), not from the reign of Cyrus? Why do these letters refer to the rebuilding of the wall of Jerusalem, not the temple rebuilding? What is the relationship of the Hebrew narrative which recounts the rebuilding attempt under Cyrus (Ezr 1:1–4:5) with the Aramaic narrative (Ezr 4:6–6:18) which recounts (i) complaints of neighbouring peoples against the repatriates and (ii) the temple rebuilding under Darius?

Since our concern is with the temple rebuilding that supposedly took place in the reign of Cyrus, the problem of the foundation laying is most germane.[12] There are two separate issues involved. First, in Ezra 1–6 the foundation laying in the reign of Cyrus is attributed to both Zerubbabel (Ezr 3:8–13; the Hebrew narrative) and Sheshbazzar (Ezr 5:16; the Aramaic narrative). Second, there is the tension between Haggai/Zechariah 1–8, on the one hand, and Ezr 3 and Ezr 5, on the other hand, over when the temple foundation was laid. Each knows of only one foundation laying—Ezra in the reign of Cyrus (Ezr 3:10–12; Ezr 5:13–16); Haggai and Zechariah 1–8 in the reign of Darius (they make no mention of any earlier foundation laying; cf. Ezr 5–6, recounting the rebuilding in the reign of Darius, which makes no mention of a foundation laying at that time). Resolution of this second issue is important since if there was no temple foundation laying in the reign of Cyrus then it raises a question mark over the historical veracity of the Ezra Hebrew narrative and its explanation of the delay in the rebuilding due to social conflict.

There have been four main responses to the issue of when the temple foundation was laid. The first three attempt to harmonize

---

[12] Ezr 3:1–6 mentions an altar dedication on the temple site soon after the repatriates return, but this is quite distinct from an attempt to rebuild the temple (Ezr 3:8–4:5).

the various accounts in different ways, while the fourth rejects attempts at harmonizing the sources.[13] The first approach contends that there were two foundation layings, one in the reign of Cyrus, as recounted in Ezr 3:7–12, and a second in the reign of Darius, as Haggai and Zechariah 1–8 aver. Thus Ezr 3 and Haggai/Zechariah 1–8 are not in tension.[14] Ezr 5:13–16 can be harmonized with the other accounts by identifying Sheshbazzar with Zerubbabel.[15] The problem with this solution is that it is in accord with none of the texts since they all affirm but *one* foundation laying. Further, for reasons noted below, it is doubtful that two foundation layings would have taken place, especially when Zerubbabel is held to be responsible for both.

The second approach to this question argues that there were no foundation layings. The discrepancy between Haggai/Zechariah 1–8 and Ezr 3:7–12; 5:13–16 over when the temple foundation was laid is resolved by the claim that these references do not actually speak of foundation laying, but only of repair work. A start was made at

---

[13] Discussion of the first two approaches substantially reproduces P. R. Bedford, "Discerning the Time: Haggai, Zechariah and the 'Delay' in the Rebuilding of the Jerusalem Temple," in *The Pitcher is Broken* (ed. S. W. Holloway and L. K. Handy) 89–92.

[14] So, for example, J. S. Wright, *The Building of the Second Temple* (London: Tyndale, 1958) 17, and more recently, F. C. Fensham, *The Books of Ezra and Nehemiah* (NICOT; Grand Rapids: Eerdmans, 1982) 61–62, who thinks that the foundation had been laid in 537 (Ezr 3:10), but when building recommenced in the first years of Darius, after a hiatus of some eighteen years, the foundation was dilapidated and hence had to be re-laid. C. G. Tuland, "'uššayyāʾ and ʾuššarnâ. A Clarification of Terms, Date, and Text," *JNES* 17 (1958) 274–75, also holds that there were two foundation layings, the first to be dated to 530/29; that is, towards the end of Cyrus's reign.

[15] Josephus, *Antiquities*, xi. 11–13, implicitly identifies Sheshbazzar with Zerubbabel. Some moderns identify them also, so A. van Hoonacker, *Zorobabel et la second temple* (Gent/Leipzig: Engelcke, 1892) 42–46; idem, "Notes sur l'histoire de la restauration juive," *RB* 10 (1901) 7–10; J. Lust, "The Identification of Zerubbabel with Sheshbazzar," *EThL* 63 (1987) 90–95; M. Sæbø, "The Relation of Sheshbazzar to Zerubbabel—Reconsidered," *SEÅ* 54 (1989) 168–77. Most commentators consider Sheshbazzar and Zerubbabel to be distinct individuals and that the author/editor understood them as such; so, most recently, Japhet, "Sheshbazzar and Zerubbabel," *ZAW* 94 (1982) 66–98 (especially p. 91) and *ZAW* 95 (1983) 218–29; Williamson, *Ezra, Nehemiah*, 17–18. Rudolph, *Esra und Nehemiah*, 18, holds that Sheshbazzar and Zerubbabel were distinct individuals historically, but the author of Ezr 1–6 understands them to be one and the same person. Y. Kaufmann, *History of the Religion of Israel IV: From the Babylonian Captivity to the End of Prophecy* (trans. C. W. Efroymson; New York: Ktav, 1977) 194, assumes Sheshbazzar and Zerubbabel were distinct individuals, but Ezr attributed the work to Sheshbazzar as leader of the repatriates (Ezr 1:8), although in reality Zerubbabel, Sheshbazzar's contemporary (Ezr 2:2) and subordinate, undertook the task (Ezr 3:7–12).

repairing the temple in the reign of Cyrus and after the intervention of "the people of the land" construction was recommenced only
in the reign of Darius (Hag 2:15–19). Thus there were not two temple foundation layings but rather two separate beginnings were made
to repair the temple.[16]

These arguments are unconvincing, however, since they cannot
satisfy the claims of the relevant texts. The reference to the rebuilding under Cyrus in the Aramaic narrative (Ezr 5:13–16) credits
Sheshbazzar with setting the אֻשַּׁיָּא in place (Ezr 5:16); the אֻשַּׁיָּא being
the foundation of the temple.[17] That the temple foundation re-laying specifically is in view in Ezr 3:7–13 (attributed to Zerubbabel
and Joshua) can be shown by the author's use of features in common with the description of the first temple foundation laying in II
Chrons 3–5. Particularly notable is the use of the hophal of יסד in
Ezr 3:11 and II Chrons 3:3. The latter verse clearly refers to the
foundation laying of the first temple since a description of the dimensions of the building immediately follows, which are marked out by
the foundations. הוּסַד cannot mean anything other than "cause to
be founded" in this context. In Ezr 3:11, those who had seen the
first temple are moved to tears when the new foundations are set
in place (עַל הוּסַד בֵּית־יְהוָה) since they recognize that this building
will not be on the grand scale of its predecessor.[18] "Repair work" is
therefore not in view here, but rather the foundations themselves.
Also, II Chrons 5:11–14 recounts a religious celebration which shares
many elements with Ezr 3:10–12, and which was held at the completion of the first temple. Ezr 3:10–12 should thus be related to a

---

[16] So, F. I. Andersen, "Who Built the Second Temple?" *ABR* 6 (1958) 10–22;
A. Gelston, "The Foundations of the Second Temple," *VT* 16 (1966) 232–35, who
argue that יסד (Ezr 3:10) need not specifically refer to foundation laying but can
have a much broader sense of "repair, restore, rebuild". They also claim that the
temple foundations would not have been destroyed by Nebuchadrezzar, so there
would be no need to re-lay them, only to clear the debris and repair (יסד) them;
cf. II Chron 24:27. Ezr 5:16, however, says that Sheshbazzar יְהַב אֻשַּׁיָּא דִי־בֵית אֱלָהָא
which Gelston suggests means the (re-)setting of the original foundations, which
could be subsumed under the work described by יסד in Ezr 3:10. D. J. A. Clines,
Ezra, Nehemiah, Esther (NCB; Grand Rapids: Eerdmans, 1984) 88–89, considers אֻשַּׁיָּא
to be the temple platform, not the foundations.
[17] See Tuland, "'uššayyā' and 'uššarnâ," 69–71, for אֻשַּׁיָּא meaning "foundation".
[18] Cf. the Aramaic edict of Cyrus (Ezr 6:2c–5) which gives the dimensions of the
new temple. These dimensions can be compared with those given for the first temple in II Chrons 3:3–8. On the syntactical problems in Ezr 3:12 regarding בְּיָסְדוֹ זֶה
הַבַּיִת, which has to denote the second temple, see M. Fishbane, *Biblical Interpretation
in Ancient Israel* (Oxford: Clarendon, 1985) 51–55.

foundation laying or temple dedication ceremony, not simply to the clearing away of debris on the temple site or the renovation of its superstructure. Zechariah 1–8 incorporates a foundation-laying ritual which affirms the contention that Zerubbabel was actually re-laying the temple's foundation.[19] Since he would not have re-laid the temple foundation twice, once in the reign of Cyrus (Ezr 3:7–10) and a second time in the reign of Darius I (Hag 2:18; Zech 4:9), the Ezra 3 narrative actually relates to the rebuilding in the time of Darius I, but has been read back into the reign of Cyrus.[20] Indeed, Haggai and Zechariah are not simply ignorant of any foundation laying before their day. Rather, as Haggai puts it, before construction began in the second year of Darius "not one stone [of the temple] was set on another" (Hag 2:15); that is, against the contention that repairs were undertaken in the reign of Cyrus, no work whatsoever had been carried out on the temple. Haggai and Zechariah apparently know nothing of the edict of Cyrus nor of any rebuilding attempt prior to that undertaken under Darius I, thus pointing to the fact that there was but one rebuilding, and that in the second year of Darius.[21]

A third interpretation of the texts dealing with the laying of the temple foundations seeks to preserve the veracity of Ezra's Hebrew narrative while acknowledging that there was only one foundation laying by Zerubbabel in the reign of Darius. S. Talmon, followed by H. G. M. Williamson, has offered an interpretation of Ezr 3:1–4:5, the narrative of the foundation laying, whereby this passage is understood to be not an account of a rebuilding attempt in the reign of

---

[19] On the connection of Zech 1–6, particularly Zech 4:6b–10a with the Mesopotamian *kalû* ritual, see A. Petitjean, "La mission de Zorubabel et la reconstruction du temple," *EThL* 42 (1966) 40–71; E. Lipiński, "Recherches sur le livre de Zacharie," *VT* 20 (1970) 30–33; D. Petersen, "Zerubbabel and Jerusalem Temple Reconstruction," *CBQ* 36 (1974) 366–72; idem, *Haggai and Zechariah 1–8*, 240–44; B. Halpern, "The Ritual Background of Zechariah's Temple Song," *CBQ* 40 (1978) 167–90; A. Laato, "Zachariah 4,6b–10a and the Akkadian Royal Building Inscriptions," *ZAW* 106 (1994) 53–69.
[20] On Ezr 3 recounting events in the reign of Darius I note, for example, Hag 2:3 and Ezr 3:12, which both mention the sullenness exhibited at the laying of the foundation of the new temple by those who had known the monarchical period temple.
[21] Andersen, "Second Temple," 22–27, interprets חרב in Hag 1:4, 9 as meaning "deserted" rather than "in ruins" since in his understanding of the events surrounding the rebuilding there had been rebuilding work undertaken before Haggai's day. This view cannot satisfactorily interpret Hag 1:2 or 2:18, however.

Cyrus, but rather an account in Hebrew of the rebuilding undertaken by Zerubbabel and Joshua in the reign of Darius I which should be read in tandem with the account given in Aramaic in Ezr 5–6.[22] It thus also presents no conflict with Haggai and Zechariah 1–8.

Talmon and Williamson have analyzed Ezr 3:1–4:5 so: Ezr 3:1–6 recounts an altar dedication in the reign of Cyrus; Ezr 3:7–4:3 refers to the rebuilding of the temple undertaken in the reign of Darius I; Ezr 4:4–5 is a "summary notation" which harks back to Ezr 3:3 and to the intervention of hostile neighbours in the reign of Cyrus which prevented the commencement of rebuilding, while it also anticipates Ezr 5:1 and the rebuilding undertaken in the reign of Darius I. According to Talmon, rather than offering a parallel account to that given in Ezr 3:7–4:3, Ezr 5–6 continues the same narrative of the rebuilding undertaken in the reign of Darius. Williamson differs from this, holding that, with regard to Ezr 3:7–4:3, "much of [the author's] account here is thus parallel with chaps. 5–6".[23] The only overlap Talmon allows is Ezr 3:8–9 // Ezr 5:1–2. In this analysis, Ezr 4:6–24 is a digression (Williamson) or is topically associated with Ezr 4:1–5 (Talmon) to show how the hostile neighbours identified in Ezr 4:1–5 continued to harass the repatriates' attempts to re-establish themselves.[24] Ezr 4:24 then resumes the story at the point left off in Ezr 4:4–5.

This interpretation of Ezr 1:1–4:5 thus attempts to give historical credence to the repatriates' interest in restoring the Jerusalem cult; it explains why no rebuilding was immediately undertaken; and it accounts for the absence of any mention of an earlier rebuilding in Haggai and Zechariah 1–8. As Ezr 3:7–4:3 recounts the commencement of rebuilding in the reign of Darius I, it can be related quite well to the account given in Haggai and Zechariah 1–8, except that certain idealizations have been made in the interests of the theme of the continuity of the repatriates with monarchical Judah. The incident recorded in Ezr 4:1–3 can be interpreted either as being reflected in Hag 2:10–19 (Talmon), or as the background to Tattenai's investigation (Ezr 5–6) (Williamson).

---

[22] S. Talmon, "Ezra and Nehemiah (Books and Men)," in *The Interpreter's Dictionary of the Bible: Supplementary Volume*, 322–24; Williamson, *Ezra, Nehemiah*, 43–45.

[23] Williamson, *Ezra, Nehemiah*, 45.

[24] Williamson, *Ezra, Nehemiah*, 57; Talmon, "Ezra and Nehemiah," 323.

There are, however, a number of reasons for rejecting this interpretation.[25] First, there is no reason to believe that Ezr 3:7 introduces a new section in the narrative, moving from the reign of Cyrus (Ezr 3:1–6) to the reign of Darius (Ezr 3:7–4:3). The natural reading of this verse is as a direct continuation of Ezr 3:6. It is in Ezr 3:8 that we are taken further along in time to "the second year after their arrival at the house of God in Jerusalem, in the second month . . ." This, however, belongs to the reign of Cyrus, not to the reign of Darius. It continues the narrative begun in Ezr 2:68, which commences with the arrival of the returnees in Jerusalem. Note the use of a similar formula in 3:8 to that used in 2:68:

2:68   בבואם לבית יהוה אשר בירושלם

3:8   ובשנה השנית לבואם אל־בית האלהים לירושלם

Thus the events of 3:8ff. are dated some two years after 2:68. Also, Ezr 3:1 continues directly from 2:70:

2:70   Concerning priests et al. . . .
        וישבו . . . בעריהם וכל־ישראל בעריהם

3:1   . . . העם ויגע החדש השביעי ובני ישראל בערים ויאספו

Ezr 2:68–4:5 thus forms a single, unified section. Its structure is as follows:—

2:68–70 Arrival of the returnees "at the temple of Yahweh in Jerusalem". They disperse to settle "in their own towns".
3:1–7 "When the seventh month came" the returnees gather in Jerusalem. An altar is erected and the sacrificial cult reinstituted. Craftsmen are retained and raw materials obtained for the temple.
3:8–13 "In the second year after their arrival at the house of God in Jerusalem, in the second month . . ." temple rebuilding commences and the foundation is laid.
4:1–5 "the enemies of Judah and Benjamin" offer their help for the rebuilding but it is rejected. They then take steps to have the rebuilding stopped. It is stopped "until the reign of Darius, king of Persia".

---

[25] See also the discussion in Halpern, "Historiographic Commentary on Ezra 1–6," 104–11.

All these events ostensibly took place in the first years of the restoration, in the reign of Cyrus.[26]

Williamson's proposal to read Ezr 3:8 as referring to the reign of Darius because it was at this time that the repatriates "turned their attention in earnest to the work of rebuilding"[27] must be rejected as this verse simply resumes Ezr 2:68 and should be seen as a continuation of the same programme. Historically it may well be correct that rebuilding took place only in the reign of Darius, but this is not the perspective of the author/editor of Ezr 1:1–4:5. As Ezr 2:68 makes clear, in the context of Ezr 1–2, the return from exile was in order to undertake the task of temple rebuilding immediately.

Second, as Ezr 2:68–70 clearly has rebuilding the temple in view, Talmon feels compelled to place it after Ezr 3:6, making it the initial step in the rebuilding undertaken in the reign of Darius.[28] Williamson does not displace Ezr 2:68–70 but together with Talmon he recognizes that Ezr 2:68 is an addition by the editor of Ezr 1–6 (cf. Neh 7:69–72 [Eng. vv. 70–73] from which Ezr 2:68–70 is drawn).[29] Granting this, it seems most likely that Ezr 2:68 has a tendentious purpose and that this continues throughout Ezr 2:68–4:5. There is no need to unravel this narrative either to determine what historical kernel underlies it or to defend its historical veracity. The author writes a straightforward narrative of what he believes to have occurred in the first few years after the return from exile. It should not be manipulated to harmonize with other, divergent sources but rather should be understood in terms of the purpose and ideology of the author/editor.

Third, Ezr 3:3 contains no hint of an explanation as to why the rebuilding did not commence. Rather it informs us that from the beginning the returnees perceived some animosity towards them from "the people of the land". At the time they erected the altar the returnees already felt afraid of these people. Ezr 3:3 foreshadows Ezr 4:1–5, a problem which arose almost two years later in this chronology.

Fourth, in light of the studies by May and Koch on the term "the

---

[26] See, similarly, Japhet, "Temple in the Restoration Period," 201–03; Halpern, "Historiographic Commentary on Ezra 1–6," 111 (table, summarizing his earlier discussion).

[27] Williamson, *Ezra, Nehemiah*, 47.

[28] Talmon, "Ezra and Nehemiah," 323.

[29] Williamson, *Ezra, Nehemiah*, 29–30.

people of the land" in Haggai, Hag 2:10–19 does not relate to Ezr
4:1–3 as Talmon has proposed.[30] Haggai does not know of any contention between the returnees and "the people of the land" at the
time of rebuilding in the reign of Darius.[31] Williamson's submission,
following Rudolph, that Ezr 4:1–3 is the background for Tattenai's
enquiry in Ezr 5–6 is possible, although no further mention of the
complaints of "the people of the land" is made in these chapters. It
may be more likely, especially in the light of Haggai and Zechariah
1–8 which cite no such complaints, that Tattenai conducted his
enquiry because permission to rebuild the temple had been forgot-
ten due to the long delay in rebuilding.

   The fourth response to the question of the date of the foundation
laying rejects all attempts to harmonize Ezr 3 with Haggai and
Zechariah 1–8 and rejects the contention of Ezr 3:1–4:5, adopted
in the above three views, that rebuilding work in the reign of Cyrus
was stopped by the intervention of hostile neighbours. Rather, the
prophetical accounts of the rebuilding are accorded historical veracity while the Ezra account of the rebuilding under Cyrus is dismissed
as tendentious and ahistorical. There was thus only one foundation
laying, and that in the reign of Darius I. This approach makes best
sense of the evidence and is adopted here.[32]

   Ezr 1:1–4:5 (that is, the Hebrew narrative) has traditionally been
seen to be the work of the Chronicler, the name given to the author
of the long narrative history of Israel and Judah (with an emphasis
on the latter for the monarchical and post-monarchical periods) which
comprises the canonical books of Chronicles, Ezra, and Nehemiah.[33]

---

[30] H. G. May, "'This people' and 'this nation' in Haggai," *VT* 18 (1965) 190–97;
K. Koch, "Haggais unreines Volk," *ZAW* 79 (1967) 52–66. See further, Coggins,
Samaritans and Jews, 46–54; Hausmann, *Israels Rest*, 41–42.
[31] Smith, *Religion of the Landless*, 179–88, has attempted to rehabilitate the thesis
that conflict between the repatriates and another group is reflected in Hag 2:10–19.
On this see also below pp. 279–82.
[32] Japhet, "Temple in the Restoration Period", also recognizes the tendentiousness of Ezr 1–6 and holds to one foundation laying. However, she accepts (pp.
222–24) the claim of Ezr 5:16 that Sheshbazzar laid the temple's foundations in
the reign of Cyrus and that Zechariah attributes this to Zerubbabel due to the
prophet's conflating all the significant events of rebuilding into his own time, since
it was only now that Yahweh had decisively moved to have the temple rebuilt. For
Zechariah, Zerubbabel is not the literal foundation-layer; he is the temple rebuilder
under whom the work of foundation laying is subsumed.
[33] See the relevant sections of the Introductions by Eissfeldt, Sellin-Fohrer, and
Pfeiffer. S. R. Driver, *An Introduction to the Literature of the Old Testament* (rev. ed.; New

While estimates of the Chronicler's historical worth vary, it is generally agreed that Ezr 3:1–4:5 is at best a tendentious account of rebuilding undertaken in the reign of Cyrus, either based on sources

York: Scribner's, 1913) 546–47, lists the features of the Chronicler's hand in Ezr 3:1–4:5. The Aramaic narrative is often held to be an independent source which the Chronicler has incorporated into the Ezra-Nehemiah narrative.

Dates for the Chronicler vary, but c. 400 is commonly accepted as the period in which this history found its current form. The Chronicler's purpose is perceived to be (i) the legitimation of the House of David, the Jerusalem cult of Yahweh, and the descendants of that nation—the Judeans repatriated from Babylonian exile; (ii) the condemnation of the kingdom of Israel for its rejection of the kingship of David and the Jerusalem cult of Yahweh and the repudiation of those living in the territory of the former kingdom of Israel who continue not to worship Yahweh in Jerusalem but who nevertheless consider themselves to be Yahwists. On the date, purpose and historiographic method of the Chronicler, see G. von Rad, *Das Geschichtsbild des chronistischen Werkes* (Stuttgart: Kohlhammer, 1930); Ruldolph, *Chronikbücher*, xiii–xxiv; idem, "Problems in the Books of Chronicles," 404, 408; J. M. Myers, *I Chronicles* (AB 12; Garden City, NY: Doubleday, 1965) xxxii–xl; T. Willi, *Die Chronik als Auslegung* (FRLANT 106; Göttingen: Vandenhoeck and Ruprecht, 1972); P. Welten, *Geschichte und Geschichtsdarstellung in der Chronikbüchen* (WMANT 42; Neukirchen-Vluyn: Neukirchener Verlag, 1973); Mosis, *Untersuchungen*; P. R. Ackroyd, "The Theology of the Chronicler," *Lexington Theological Quarterly* 8 (1973) 110–16. Freedman, "Chronicler's Purpose," 436–42, and Cross, "Reconstruction of the Judean Restoration," 4–18, hold that one edition of the Chronicler's work (which Cross defines as I Chrons 10–II Chrons 34 plus the *Vorlage* of I Esdras [= II Chrons 34:1–Ezr 3:3]; Freedman includes up to Ezr 4:5) was written to legitimate the Jerusalem temple reconstruction under Zerubbabel in the reign of Darius.

The last three decades has witnessed a debate regarding the extent of the Chronicler's work. S. Japhet ("The Supposed Common Authorship of Chronicles and Ezra-Nehemiah Investigated Anew," *VT* 18 [1968] 330–71) arguing on linguistic grounds, and H. G. M. Williamson (*Israel in the Books of Chronicles*) arguing on the basis of a study of the Greek versions, vocabulary and style, and ideology of the works, have contended that Chronicles and Ezra-Nehemiah come from different authors. The linguistic evidence does, however, lend itself to divergent interpretations; see Polzin, *Late Biblical Hebrew*, cf. M. A. Thronveit, "Linguistic Analysis and the Question of Authorship in Chronicles, Ezra and Nehemiah," *VT* 32 (1982) 201–16; D. Talshir, "A Reinterpretation of the Linguistic Relationship between Chronicles and Ezra-Nehemiah," *VT* 38 (1988) 165–93. Japhet has restated her position, drawing on more than linguistic evidence, in S. Japhet, "The Relationship between Chronicles and Ezra-Nehemiah," in *Congress Volume: Leuven, 1989*, 293–313. Others concurring with Japhet and Williamson include, Eskenazi, *In an Age of Prose*; S. Talmon, "Esra und Nehemiah: Historiographie oder Theologie?" in *Ernten, was man sät. Festschrift für Klaus Koch zu seinem 65. Geburtstag* (ed. D. R. Daniels et al.; Neukirchen-Vluyn: Neukirchener Verlag, 1991) 329–56; I. Kalimi, "Die Abfassungszeit der Chronik—Forschungsstand und Perspektiven," *ZAW* 105 (1993) 222–33. Continuing to attribute Ezra-Nehemiah to the Chronicler are, among others, Blenkinsopp, *Ezra, Nehemiah*, 47–54; K.-F. Pohlmann, "Zur Frage von Korrespondenzen und Divergenzen zwischen den Chronikbüchern und dem Esra/Nehemia-Buch," in *Congress Volume: Leuven, 1989*, 314–30.

Those who presume that Chronicles has a different author from Ezra-Nehemiah discern a different attitude in Chronicles from Ezra-Nehemiah, seeing in these texts available to him (such as the Aramaic narrative of the rebuilding) or simply as a fictional account.[34]

This view holds that in blaming "the people of the land" for the delay in temple rebuilding (Ezr 3–4) the author was reading back into the early years of the restoration a dispute current when the narrative was written, that is, in the fourth century, between certain Judeans who worshipped at Jerusalem and the Samarians.[35] The nar-

---

examples of both the hard-line exclusivists (Ezr-Neh) and a later, more moderate, conciliatory position toward the Samarians (Chrons). But Chrons offers conciliation on its own terms, namely, recognition of Jerusalem temple as the sole place to worship Yahweh and, hence, submission to the Jerusalem priesthood and their cultic law; see S. Japhet, *The Ideology of the Books of Chronicles and Its Place in Biblical Thought* (trans. A. Barber; BEATAJ 9; Frankfort am Main: Lang, 1989); R. Braun, "The Message of Chronicles: Rally 'Round the Temple," *Concordia Theological Monthly* 42 (1971) 502–14; idem, "A Reconsideration of the Chronicler's Attitude toward the North," *JBL* 96 (1977) 59–62; idem, "Chronicles, Ezra and Nehemiah: Theology and Literary History," in *Studies in the Historical Books of the Old Testament* (ed. J. A. Emerton) 52–64; Newsome, "Toward a New Understanding," 201–17 (who also holds to Freedman's view that one edition of Chrons was written to legitimate the temple rebuilding); Williamson, *Israel in the Books of Chronicles*. For a brief review of the work of Japhet, Braun, and Williamson on the extent and purpose of the Chronicler's work, see P. Abadie, "Ancien Testament III. Où en est aujourd'hui la recherche sur l'historiographie du Chroniste?" *Transeu* 1 (1989) 170–76. For an overview of the main lines of research on Chronicles in the 1980s and early 1990s, see J. W. Kleinig, "Recent Research in Chronicles," *CR:BS* 2 (1994) 43–76.

A recent development among some who reject the notion of "the Chronicler" is a recognition that Ezra and Nehemiah each display fundamentally different concerns, which may point to different authors; see J. C. VanderKam, "Ezra-Nehemiah or Ezra and Nehemiah?" in *Priests, Prophets and Scribes: Essays on the Formation and Heritage of Second Temple Judaism in Honour of Joseph Blenkinsopp* (ed. E. Ulrich et al.; JSOTSup 149; Sheffield: JSOT Press, 1992) 55–75; D. Kraemer, "On the Relationship of the Books of Ezra and Nehemiah," *JSOT* 59 (1993) 73–92.

The present study has retained "the Chronicler" nomenclature, although for the arguments presented here it is not strictly relevant whether Ezr 1–6 was written/edited by the Chronicler or was authored/edited separately. The dating of Ezr 1–6 would still be well after the events it recounts.

[34] On the Hebrew account as a parallel to that given in the Aramaic text see Eissfeldt, *Introduction*, 543. On the narrative as a fiction of the author (identified as the Chronicler), see Pfeiffer, *Introduction*, 821.

[35] It is likely that Samarians, rather than Samaritans, are the antagonists in view here, especially if one accepts that the Hebrew narrative is part of the Chronicler's history. This would date this text to c. 400 and thus before the Samaritan schism (on dating the Samaritan schism, see above chapter 1 n. 23). Williamson, who argues that Ezr 1–6 is not from the hand of the Chronicler, dates the narrative to the early Hellenistic period and thus proposes that the Samaritans are the antagonists; see Williamson, "Composition of Ezra i–vi," 1–30, where he contends that Ezr 1–6 is based on reliable sources, but that the text itself is written "early in the Hellenistic period . . . intended in part as counter propaganda to the building at this time of the first Samaritan temple on Mount Gerizim" (p. 29). In either case, how-

rative thus not only accounts for the delay in the temple rebuilding but also shows that these Judeans' current antagonists have always been against the Jerusalem temple. These emphases are marked in the Hebrew narrative (Ezr 1:1–4:5). The Aramaic narrative (Ezr 4:6–6:18), in comparison, mentions no reason for the delay in the temple rebuilding. By placing the Samarian opposition to the wall rebuilding in the reigns of Xerxes and Artaxerxes at the head of this section (Ezr 4:8–24), out of chronological order but juxtaposed to the interference in the temple rebuilding by "the people of the land" (Ezr 4:1–5), the author/editor gathered at one place (Ezr 3–4) the material relating to local opposition to the repatriates and managed to fill the chronological gap between the rebuilding attempt under Cyrus and that undertaken in the reign of Darius. The author/editor thus interprets Tattenai's investigation of the temple rebuilding in the reign of Darius as having been precipitated by the complaints of the Samarians/"the people of the land".[36] It is important to note that Ezr 5–6 mentions neither the opposition of Samarians/"the peoples of the land" to the temple rebuilding project nor the legal injunction against the rebuilding handed down in the reign of Cyrus (Ezr 4:5).[37] We are not informed how the Judeans overturned the injunction in order to obtain permission to rebuild the temple. Actually, in Ezr 5–6, the Judeans, Tattenai, and Darius know nothing of this injunction. Had it been executed one would expect, in the light of Ezr 3–4, that the Samarians would have brought it to

---

ever, Ezr 3–4 should not be read as a historical account of why the temple was not rebuilt in the reign of Cyrus.

[36] Ezr 4:24, an editorial gloss which links Ezr 4 and 5, is clear evidence of this. Ezr 4:8–23 was probably at the end of the Aramaic narrative and was purposely moved to its present position by the author/editor of Ezr 1–6, rather than the Aramaic narrative itself having confused chronology; see Rudolph, *Esra und Nehemia*, 40; Halpern, "Historiographic Commentary on Ezra 1–6," 108–09, 112. Editorial work on the Aramaic material is also detectable in the reference to Artaxerxes in Ezr 6:14. Williamson, "Composition of Ezra i–vi," 16–18, cites Ezr 4:24 and Ezr 6:14 as evidence that the editor of Ezr 1–6 could write Aramaic and thus could have written the whole Aramaic section. Some consider Ezr 6:16–18 to come from a later hand as it reflects the Chronicler's characteristic interests in cultic matters, so A. H. J. Gunneweg, *Esra* (KAT 19/1; Gütersloh: Mohn, 1985) 113–15. On II Ki 17:24–41, the Deuteronomistic Historian's account of the foreign origin of the Samarians (cf. Ezr 4:1–5), as a tendentious account, see S. Talmon, "Polemics and Apology in Biblical Historiography—2 Kings 17:24–41," in *The Creation of Sacred Literature: Composition and Redaction of the Biblical Text* (ed. R. E. Friedman; Berkeley: University of California Press, 1981) 57–68.

[37] So, also, Japhet, "Temple in the Restoration Period," 220–21.

the attention of their Achaemenid Persian overlords when rebuilding recommenced in the reign of Darius. This, coupled with the fact that Darius's administrators, who could apparently find the Cyrus edict (Ezr 6:1–2), were completely unaware of the injunction, points to it being a concoction of the author of the Hebrew narrative to suit his tendentious purposes.[38]

The tendentiousness of the Hebrew narrative is further displayed by the fact that the author has little direct knowledge of the supposed restoration under Cyrus. Ezr 2, ostensibly a list of repatriates under Sheshbazzar, is widely recognized to have been borrowed from Neh 7:6–72 (Eng. vv. 6–73). The purpose of this list is debated but it appears that it is a composite piece which precludes its recounting a single event, such as a repatriation in the first year of Cyrus.[39]

---

[38] So, similarly, S. Japhet, "'History' and 'Literature' in the Persian Period: The Restoration of the Temple," in *Ah, Assyria . . . Studies in Assyrian Historiography and Ancient Near Eastern Historiography Prestented to Hayim Tadmor* (ed. M. Cogan and I. Eph'al; Scripta Hierosolymitana 33; Jerusalem: Magnes, 1991) 180–81; idem, "Temple in the Restoration Period," 204–05.

The tensions between the Hebrew and Aramaic narratives support the contention that the latter was an originally independent source which the author of the Hebrew narrative incorporated into Ezr 1–6. This material is now subsumed under the overarching concern of the narrative to show that the repatriates were devoted to the Jerusalem cult of Yahweh and that they kept themselves separate from those whom they found in the land at their return.

[39] See Williamson, *Ezra, Nehemiah*, 28–32. Perhaps the most telling factor in this regard is that some people are listed by family while others are listed by town. Other commentators understand the list to be a unity, but date it to a time long after the early years of Cyrus. C. Schultz, "The Political Tensions Reflected in Ezra-Nehemiah," in *Scripture in Context: Essays in the Comparative Method* (ed. C. D. Evans et al.; Pittsburgh Theological Monograph Series 34; Pittsburgh, The Pickwick Press, 1980), 225–26, offers a partial survey of positions on the date and purpose of this list: C. C. Torrey, *Ezra Studies* (Chicago: University of Chicago Press, 1910) 250—it is a fiction created by the Chronicler; Rudolph, *Esra und Nehemia*, 17—a genuine list of returnees, composed of different registers covering the period 539–515; W. F. Albright, *The Biblical Period from Abraham to Ezra* (New York: Harper and Row, 1965) 110—a census of Judah carried out by Nehemiah which revised that begun at the initial restoration under Cyrus; Alt, "Die Rolle Samarias," 335 n. 1—a list compiled by Zerubbabel in order to determine land rights of the repatriates; G. Hölscher, "Die Bücher Esra und Nehemia," in *Die Heilige Schrift des Alten Testaments* (2 vols.; 4th ed.; ed. E. Kautzsch and A. Bertholet; Tübingen: Mohr, 1922–23) 2. 504a—a tax roll drawn up by the Persians c. 400; Galling, *Studien*, 89–108; idem, "The 'Gola List' According to Ezra 2 // Nehemiah 7," *JBL* 70 (1951) 153–55—list of members of the golah community who could participate in the 520 temple rebuilding, given to Tattenai on his request; to which one can add, among many others, L. W. Batten, *The Books of Ezra and Nehemiah* (ICC; New York: Scribner's, 1913) 72–73—it lists all the returnees from Zerubbabel to Ezra; F. Ahlemann, "Zur

Sheshbazzar is not included among those who returned, which is perhaps to be explained by the author of the Hebrew narrative in Ezra identifying Sheshbazzar with Zerubbabel, who is mentioned in Ezr 2:2. This is possibly the author's/editor's view, even though it is apparent that they were distinct persons historically.[40] Although Neh 7:6 does not mention when, or over what period of time, this return from exile took place, the list's position in Ezr 1–6 is clearly to locate it in the reign of Cyrus.[41] The 49,897 persons (49,949 in Neh 7) all returned at the edict of Cyrus.[42] The differences between the parallel texts are best explained as attempts by the author of the Hebrew narrative to integrate this material into its present literary context.[43] Attention can be drawn to the final line of the respective passages: Ezr 3:1a // Neh 7:72b (Eng. v. 73b). Both are links to events being undertaken "when the seventh month came" but whereas the latter introduces a meeting in the time of Nehemiah, the former serves as an introduction to the erection of an altar in Jerusalem in the reign of Cyrus; that is, these verses refer to two entirely different times. The author of the Ezra narrative has taken the chronological reference from the Nehemiah passage and applied it to the restoration under Cyrus. Another example of his editorial technique is Ezr 2:68 (Eng. v. 69), where a reference in Neh 7:69 (Eng. v. 70) to funds collected for otherwise unspecified "work" is expanded to funds collected for "rebuilding the temple of God". That is, Ezr 2 portrays the collection of the funds as (i) being specifically for the reconstruction of the temple, and (ii) being available from the outset of the restoration (cf. Ezr 1:6). The purpose of

---

Esra-Quelle," *ZAW* 59 (1942–43) 81–83—a list of those who returned with Ezra; Mowinckel, *Studien zu dem Buche Ezra-Nehemia*, 1. 62–109—a list of the residents of Judah c. 400. I consider that the list should be dated relatively late in the Persian period because of the large number of persons involved and because the towns listed were perhaps not settled earlier.

[40] On the identification of Sheshbazzar with Zerubbabel, see above n. 15.

[41] Neh 7:5 entitles the list as "the book of those who went up at the beginning", but no specific date or reign is assigned to this.

[42] Clines, *Ezra, Nehemia, Esther*, 38, understands "whoever is among you of all his people" in Ezr 1:3 to mean that *all* the exiled Judeans were supposed to return to their homeland. This interpretation could explain why Ezr 2 lists such a large number of repatriates.

[43] Galling, *Studien*, 89–108, is the most extensive study of this chapter in relation to Neh 7. Williamson, *Ezra, Nehemiah*, 28–32, 271–73, gives an excellent summary of the scholarly discussion.

placing this list here is to show that the repatriation was a single, organized event. The exiles did not trickle back to Judah over a period of time but were rather sent back by Cyrus as a group for the purpose of rebuilding the Jerusalem temple which they themselves had collected funds to undertake.

Ezr 3 also displays little knowledge of the attempt at rebuilding the temple in the reign of Cyrus. As noted above, this passage patterns the preparations for reconstruction after the narrative of the building of the original temple. Beyond the names of those leading the repatriates in their rebuilding efforts, it conveys no information that can be said to reflect access to first-hand knowledge of the events. Further, the author of the Hebrew narrative neglects those Judeans who had not been exiled and who must therefore have been in Judah when the repatriates arrived. Since one would expect that those who had stayed in Judah would have attempted to participate in any temple rebuilding, having perhaps even greater interest in the project than the foreign imports (Ezr 4:2), their exclusion from Ezr 3 again points to the fabricated character of the narrative. It was known that there was an indigenous population in Judah when the repatriates returned since they are railed against in Ezr 9, for exactly the same reason as the antagonists in Ezr 3–4—they were foreigners in the eyes of the repatriates and hence the repatriates were to keep separate from them, denying them participation in the cult of Yahweh. The conspicuous absence of any reference to the indigenous population in Judah is deliberate, since the narrative is specifically directed against the Samarians whom the narrator considers as being foreigners living north of Judah who had been imported into the region (Ezr 4:2, 9–10).

Perhaps armed only with a tradition of the repatriation of exiled Judeans in the reign of Cyrus, and knowing full well that the rebuilding of the temple was undertaken in the reign of Darius, the author of the Hebrew narrative found it unacceptable that the returnees would not immediately have given their attention to re-establishing the cult and rebuilding the temple. Even if he mistakenly understood elements of the reconstruction in the reign of Darius, such as the foundation laying, to have been undertaken in the first years of the restoration, this suited his purposes well. The author wished to show how the roots of the dispute with the Samarians current at his time of writing (c. 400) extended all the way back to the initial repatriation of the exiles in the reign of Cyrus, and how the Samarians had continuously thwarted the repatriates' legitimate attempts to rebuild their temple from the outset. The apologetic motive is thus to legitimate his community and their claims over the Jerusalem temple of Yahweh against the Samarians. To accept this interpretation of events, as is often done in the "conflict" schemas outlined in chapter 1, is to be beguiled by the text's tendentious purpose. This narrative actually knows little, if anything, about the period it recounts.

What then of the claims in the Aramaic narrative that Sheshbazzar laid the foundation of the temple in the reign of Cyrus and that the rebuilding had been continuing since that time until the reign of Darius I (Ezr 5:13–16)? This conflicts with the contention of Haggai/Zechariah 1–8 that the foundation of the temple was reconstructed by Zerubbabel in the reign of Darius. These prophets are ignorant of any foundation laying before their day. Since Ezr 5, where the prophets Haggai and Zechariah are introduced in the Aramaic narrative, makes no mention of the foundation laying attested in Haggai/Zechariah 1–8, one must conclude either that the Aramaic narrative is in error here or that the author has deliberately overstated the extent of the work undertaken by Sheshbazzar, the latter perhaps reflecting the author's concern to show that in rebuilding the temple in the reign of Darius I the Judeans were simply fulfilling the original command of Cyrus and had not neglected the work.[44] This makes sense of the Aramaic narrative in its present literary setting since the reader of Ezr 1–6 knows that the rebuilding had been delayed by the intervention of "the people of the land" and that it would not serve the Judeans' interests to disclose the reasons for the delay, which would include the fact that the rebuilding had been legally halted (Ezr 4:5). If one assumes that the Aramaic narrative was originally independent of its current setting, however, then this narrative displays no knowledge of a delay in the rebuilding *caused by "the people of the land"*.[45] The references to Samarian interference in the Judeans' building activities belong to a later period and concern

---

[44] So, for example, Williamson, *Ezra, Nehemiah*, 79–80.

[45] The Aramaic narrative assumes some hiatus in the rebuilding (despite the claim of Ezr 5:16), otherwise why would the prophets need to rouse the people to rebuild or Tattenai become interested in investigating the building activity? One could interpret the narrative in the light of Haggai and Zech 1–8 and, as argued below, hold the Judeans themselves responsible for the delay due to want of a legitimate temple rebuilder.

the wall rebuilding (Ezr 4:6–23). If this latter case obtains, then the evidence of Haggai/Zechariah 1–8 is to be preferred over the Aramaic narrative since these prophets would have to have made reference to the earlier rebuilding attempt, if only to reflect upon why it had failed.

Further, unlike the Hebrew narrative, the Aramaic narrative makes no mention of a repatriation of exiled Judeans. Ezr 5:12 speaks of the deportation of Judeans by Nebuchadrezzar, but the reference to Cyrus's commands to return the temple vessels and to rebuild the temple (Ezr 5:13–16 cf. Ezr 1:7–11 on the temple vessels), both of which Sheshbazzar supposedly carried out, does not include a repatriation of exiled Judeans with Sheshbazzar. This is in keeping with the edict of Cyrus as it is known to the author of this narrative (Ezr 6:2c–5). It mentions only the return of the vessels and the rebuilding, but not the repatriation.

In summary, the Hebrew narrative of the restoration in the reign of Cyrus (Ezr 1:1–4:5) is tendentious and lacks first-hand information of this period. It cannot be used to establish that the Judean repatriates were committed to reconstructing the Jerusalem temple or that they saw themselves as constituting a separatist "cultic community". In fact, it appears likely that this portrayal of the repatriates is tendentious and anachronistic, reflecting disputes with the Samarians current when the narrative was written. The Aramaic narrative (Ezr 4:8–6:18) also has tendentious features and displays little knowledge of events in the reign of Cyrus. The reference to Sheshbazzar as the one who re-laid the temple foundation (Ezr 5:13–16) founders on the evidence of Haggai/Zechariah 1–8 who know of no temple rebuilding before their day. These narratives cannot, therefore, serve as the basis for the contention that an attempt was made to rebuild the Jerusalem temple in the reign of Cyrus.

It has been claimed that despite the questionable historical character of these narratives, the main thrust of the Hebrew narrative— sizeable repatriation of exiled Judeans in the reign of Cyrus for the purpose of rebuilding the Jerusalem temple; concerted effort at rebuilding by the repatriates which was thwarted by outsiders—is reliable since the repatriation and rebuilding attempt are supported by two edicts promulgated by Cyrus, one contained in the Hebrew narrative (Ezr 1:2–4), the other in the Aramaic narrative (Ezr 6:2c–5). This would then lend credence to the claim of Ezr 3:1–4:5 that the work on the temple was deliberately halted by a group hostile to the rebuilding and that social conflict was the context in which the rebuilding in the reign of Cyrus was undertaken. In support of the veracity of the Cyrus's edicts it is argued that they conform to a general empire-wide policy of Cyrus in repatriating exiled populations and restoring their indigenous cults. Our attention therefore now turns to the authenticity of these edicts and their value as historical sources.

THE CYRUS EDICTS

Ezr 1–6 purports to cite two authentic decrees issued by Cyrus regarding the reconstruction of the Jerusalem temple of Yahweh. The first, written in Hebrew and situated at the head of the Hebrew narrative of the restoration, is a proclamation issued throughout the kingdom (Ezr 1:1). It is recorded in Ezr 1:2–4:

> 2) Thus says Cyrus, the king of Persia: Yahweh the God of Heaven has given me all the kingdoms of the earth and has commanded me to build him a temple in Jerusalem, which is in Judah. 3) Whoever is among you of all his people, may his God be with him and let him go up to Jerusalem, which is in Judah, and rebuild the temple of Yahweh the God of Israel—he is the God who is in Jerusalem. 4) And whoever remains in any place where he sojourns, let the men of his place assist him with silver, gold, goods, and livestock, together with freewill offering(s) for the temple of God which is in Jerusalem.

The second edict, written in Aramaic, is part of the Aramaic narrative. It is recorded in Ezra 6:2c–5:

> Memorandum: 3) In the first year of King Cyrus, King Cyrus issued a decree. (Re:) The temple of God in Jerusalem. Let the temple be rebuilt on the place where they used to offer sacrifices and let its foundation be maintained.[46] Its height—sixty cubits; its width—sixty

---

[46] For this rendering of מסובלין, cf. the pael of סבל in Imperial Aramaic which means "to provide for, support", specifically in regard to the financial support given by one person to another (cf. peal: "to carry"); see B. Porten and A. Yardeni, *Textbook of Aramaic Documents from Egypt. Vol. 1: Letters* (Jerusalem: The Hebrew University Press, 1986)14, A2.3 line 5 (Hermopolis); idem, *Textbook. Vol. 2: Contracts* (Jerusalem: The Hebrew University Press, 1989) p. xxxvi s.v. סבל; J. M. Lindenberger, *The Aramaic Proverbs of Ahiqar* (Baltimore/London: The Johns Hopkins University Press, 1983) 203 line 204; J. C. Greenfield and B. Porten, *The Bisitun Inscription of Darius the Great: Aramaic Version* (Corpus Inscriptionum Iranicarum 1/5; London: Lund Humphries, 1982) 52 line 78. None of these references has an inanimate object

cubits,[47] 4) with three courses of dressed stone and one[48] course of timber. The cost will be paid from the royal treasury.[49] 5) Further, the
gold and silver vessels of the temple of God, which Nebuchadrezzar
took from the sanctuary in Jerusalem and brought to Babylon, are to
be returned; each put in the temple in Jerusalem in its place. You will
deposit (them) in the temple of God.

There are a number of obvious differences between the two texts:
First, they are written in different languages. Second, the Hebrew
edict emphasizes the repatriation of "whoever is among you of all
his [Yahweh's] people" (Ezr 1:3) who wished to return to Jerusalem
in order to rebuild the temple.[50] In comparison, the Aramaic edict
makes no mention of a repatriation of exiled Judeans. Third, the
Aramaic edict focuses on the physical aspects of the temple, such as
its dimensions, the materials of which it was to be constructed, how
the building costs were to be met, and the restoration of the sacred
vessels. The Hebrew edict makes no mention of these matters. Fourth,
the Aramaic edict has the costs of the rebuilding met by the Achaemenid Persian treasury, while the Hebrew edict notes only that the
Judeans returning to Jerusalem to undertake the rebuilding were to

---

(such as the temple foundation) as the object of the verb, however. סבל in the
Aramaic version of the Bisitun inscription is paralleled by *suddid* in the Akkadian
version. *suddudu* has a similar meaning to the pael of סבל (*CAD* S s.v. *suddudu*: "to
take care of, to care for"), but it can be used for caretaking or maintenance of
orchards in NB/LB texts (although the majority of the citations have livestock as
the object of the verb). מסובלין in Ezr 6:3 may therefore refer to maintenance work
which has to be done on the temple foundations; cf. K. Beyer, *Die aramäischen Texte
vom Toten Meer* (Göttingen: Vandenhoeck & Ruprecht, 1984) 643 s.v. סבל, who
parses מסובלין in Ezr 6:3 as a pael passive participle (for his linquistic argument
see p. 37 n. 1) and translates it as "abstützen", apparently directly transferring the
meaning from the other examples of pael סבל which have persons as the object of
the verb. Williamson, *Ezra, Nehemiah*, 71 n. 3b, also relates מסובלין to סבל but parses
it as a poel participle and translates "be retained".

[47] Reference to the length of the structure has dropped out of the text. Also, the
figures given here are corrupt. Rudolph, *Esra und Nehemia*, 54–55, suggests that the
original reading was "its height—30 cubits; its length—60 cubits; its breadth—20
cubits".

[48] Reading חד for חדת "new" with the commentaries.

[49] Literally, "the house of the king".

[50] "Let him go up to Jerusalem in Judah" (Ezr 1:3) only makes sense if it is
directed to exiles. It at least permits the return of exiled Judeans to Judah. The
verb עלה here probably means "to go up country", that is, north (from Babylonia
along the Euphrates) rather than to go up to Jerusalem as an elevated place; so
G. R. Driver, "On עלה 'went up country' and ירד 'went down country'," *ZAW* 69
(1957) 74–77; Clines, *Ezra, Nehemiah, Esther*, 38.

receive financial assistance and freewill gifts for the temple from those who remained in Babylonia. Fifth, the Aramaic edict does not mention who should undertake the rebuilding. The Hebrew edict understands "all of his [Yahweh's] people" who wished to go to Jerusalem to have responsibility for the task.

The differences between these edicts have never been fully accounted for nor has the historical veracity of the edicts been substantiated. Three positions have been argued. First, only the Aramaic edict is original, the Hebrew edict being either the free creation of the Chronicler or based on information derived from the Aramaic section (Ezr 4:8–6:18).[51] Second, that both are original, their differences explicable in terms of the purpose and genre of the respective edicts.[52] Third, that neither is original, they are both fabrications.[53]

---

[51] This is the dominant position, see Meyer, *Entstehung*, 46–54; H. H. Schaeder, *Esra der Schreiber* (Tübingen: Mohr, 1930) 28–29; Rudolph, *Esra und Nehemia*, 53; Galling, *Studien*, 63–66; Noth, *History*, 307–08; Mowinckel, *Studien zu dem Buche Ezra-Nehemiah*, 8; In der Smitten, "Historische Probleme," 171; Donner, *Geschichte*, 407–09; Blenkinsopp, *Ezra-Nehemiah*, 74; Japhet, "Temple in the Restoration Period," 210–11; J. Briend, "L'édit de Cyrus et sa valeur historique," *Transeu* 11 (1996) 33–44.

[52] J. Nikel, *Die Wiederherstellung des jüdischen Gemeinwesens nach dem babylonischen Exil* (Biblische Studientum 5/2 and 3; Freiburg im Breisgau: Herder, 1900), 33–37; Bickerman, "Edict of Cyrus," 72–108; H. Tadmor, "The Historical Background to the Decree of Cyrus," (Heb) in *Sepher Ben Gurion* (Jerusalem: Kiryat Sepher, 1964) 450–73; F. Michaeli, *Les livres des Chroniques, d'Esdras et de Néhémie* (Commentaire de l'Ancien Testament 16; Neuchâtel: Delachaux and Niestlé, 1967) 253–56, 278–79; L. V. Hensley, *The Official Persian Documents in the Book of Ezra* (Unpublished Ph.D. thesis, University of Liverpool, 1977) 211–16, 219–21; Bright, *History*, 361; Clines, *Ezra, Nehemiah, Esther*, 36; Fensham, *Ezra and Nehemiah*, 42–45, 86–88; Williamson, *Ezra, Nehemiah*, 3–15; Miller and Hayes, *History*, 444–45. R. de Vaux, "The Decrees of Cyrus and Darius on the Rebuilding of the Temple," in *The Bible and the Ancient Near East* (trans. D. McHugh; New York: Doubleday, 1971) 63–96 (reprint of article published in *RB* 46 [1937] 29–57), is ambivalent concerning the origin of the Hebrew edict but avows that it is, like the Aramaic edict, "exceptionally reliable" (p. 96); similarly R. A. Bowman, "The Book of Ezra and The Book of Nehemiah," in *The Interpreter's Bible* (12 vols.; ed. G. A. Buttrick et al.; Nashville: Abingdon, 1952–57) 3. 571.

[53] J. Wellhausen, "Die Rückkehr der Juden aus dem babylonischen Exil," *Nachrichten der königlische Gesellschaft der Wissenschaften zu Göttingen. Phil.-hist. Klasse* (1895) 166–86; C. C. Torrey, *The Composition and Historical Value of Ezra-Nehemiah* (BZAW 2; Giessen: Riker, 1896) 5–12; idem, *Ezra Studies*, 140–183, on the whole Aramaic narrative as a fiction; L. E. Browne, *Early Judaism* (Cambridge: The University Press, 1920) 37–39; Hölscher, "Esra und Nehemia," 502–3, 514; Pfeiffer, *Introduction*, 820–21, 823–24.

The Hebrew Edict

Let us first turn to the main arguments raised in the discussion of
the authenticity of the Hebrew edict.[54] First, some consider it implau-
sible that Cyrus would have issued two edicts, particularly edicts
which differ so greatly in content.[55] In response, Bickerman accounts
for the differences between the two edicts as being due to their
different genre and purpose. The Hebrew edict was actually a public
proclamation, delivered orally to the exiled Judeans in their native
tongue (cf. Ezr 1:1, where Cyrus is said to have "delivered a proclamation throughout his kingdom"—ויעבר־קול בכל־מלכותו). All the exiles
needed to know was that they were permitted to return home to
rebuild the temple. This proclamation was also written down (במכתב),
as Ezr 1:1 states, and posted. In comparison, the Aramaic edict is
an official memorandum and deals with other, bureaucratic matters.[56]

In accepting that a proclamation was issued by Cyrus to the exiled
Judeans, and that Ezr 1:2–4 is the text of it, Bickerman assumes the
veracity of the author/editor of the narrative at these points. He
does cite evidence supporting the plausibility of Cyrus issuing such
a proclamation throughout his empire. As the narrative itself makes
clear, however, no Judeans other than those living in Babylonia
responded to this proclamation. Had it in fact been issued "throughout the empire" one would expect that those Judeans in Palestine,
at least, would have claimed the right to participate in the temple
rebuilding. But the thrust of Ezr 1:1–4:5 is that there were no Judeans
in Palestine, nor, apparently, elsewhere in the empire who could take
advantage of the edict. The phrase "throughout his empire" serves
the tendentious interests of the author in displaying that the Babylonian
exiles were, in fact, the only Judeans in the empire. Williamson, recognizing a problem with this phrase, suggests that:

> what was originally intended as a moderately localized announcement,
> probably to the leaders of the Jewish community [in Babylonia, presum-

---

[54] Bickerman, "Edict," 72–108, addresses a number of points that have been
raised against this edict's authenticity. The ones discussed below are arguably the
most telling criticisms and still have not received adequate explanation.

[55] This is an argument often used by those who support the authenticity of the
Aramaic edict—only one of the edicts can be authentic.

[56] Bickerman, "Edict," 72–76, 104–06 (on proclamations); pp. 106–07 (on writing up and posting the proclamation).

ably], has been expanded into a proclamation by the new setting in which the narrator has placed it with his composition of [Ezr 1:] v1.[57]

Even if the text of the proclamation should be kept distinct from its narrative context, as Williamson avers, there still remains the problem of the veracity of the author/editor. It should be noted, for example, that the claim in Ezr 1:6 (part of the author/editor's narrative framework of the proclamation) that the Babylonians financially supported the Judeans returning to their homeland and offered gifts for the Jerusalem cult of Yahweh is recognized by all commentators as highly improbable historically. Many consider that by drawing on the "plundering the Egyptians" motif from the Exodus tradition the author/editor in this instance should be seen to be simply exercising his editorial rights.[58] Here a methodological problem arises: how can one determine that in Ezr 1:6 the author/editor is editorializing to suit his narrative purposes, but in Ezr 1:1 (the narrative introduction to the proclamation) he is giving reliable information that a proclamation was issued by Cyrus? Perhaps this too is an example of editorializing. Thus Bickerman's claim that the differences between the two edicts are explicable in terms of their respective purposes loses much of its force if it cannot be shown that the author/editor, from whom Bickerman obtained the point that the Hebrew edict was in fact a proclamation, is a reliable witness. The differences between the two edicts may instead be the reflection of editorial purpose.[59]

Second, the edict is written in Hebrew and exhibits vocabulary that reflects the hand of the author/editor.[60] Examples of the latter are: (i) "the God of Israel" (v. 3). This is an ideological appellation in this setting given that the temple in view in this edict was in the

---

[57] Williamson, *Ezra, Nehemiah*, 6–7. He distinguishes the Hebrew edict from its current literary setting so that criticism directed at the historical plausibility of the author/editor's narrative, particularly Ezr 1:6, cannot taint the edict's authenticity; see Williamson, "Composition of Ezra i–vi," 12; idem, *Ezra, Nehemiah*, 6.

[58] On this motif, see G. W. Coats, "Despoiling the Egyptians," *VT* 18 (1968) 450–57; Japhet, "Temple in the Restoration Period," 213–14. Bickerman makes no comment on the historical veracity of Ezr 1:6.

[59] This point is stressed by those who see the Aramaic narrative as an independent source. The author of the Hebrew narrative, prompted by the Aramaic edict, wrote a separate Hebrew edict which suited his own purpose.

[60] The following discussion draws on work published in P. R. Bedford, "Early Achaemenid Monarchs and Indigenous Cults: Toward the Definition of Imperial Policy," in *Religion in the Ancient World: New Themes and Approaches* (ed. M. Dillon; Amsterdam: Hakkert, 1996) 28–31, 35–39.

former capital of the kingdom of *Judah*, not Israel. Thus "Israel" in this title cannot denote a political entity but rather reflects the appropriation of this term by certain Judeans in Babylonia as a name for their group. This title for the Judean national deity appears in exilic texts such as Deutero-Isaiah (Is 45:3, 15; 52:12; cf. "Holy One of Israel" Is 47:4; 48:17) and both Deutero-Isaiah and Ezekiel use "Israel" as a name for the exiles.[61] "Israel" is commonly used in the Hebrew sections of Ezra as a name for the repatriates (Ezr 6:16, 17, 21; 8:35; 9:1, 15) and the Chronicler should be held to be responsible for the appearance of "Israel" in Ezr 1:3. That the Achaemenid Persian bureaucracy would use "Israel" as an appellation for the god of a people known as "Judeans" would be quite strange.[62] "The God of Israel" does appear once in the so-called official Aramaic documents from the Achaemenid Persian bureaucracy (Ezr 7:6), where "Judean"/"Jew" is otherwise used. This reference is also suspect, although it may be argued that by the time of Ezra the Achaemenid bureaucracy was more familiar with the terminology used by Babylonian Judeans; (ii) the use of the terms גור "to sojourn" and נדבה "freewill offering" are technical terms whose usage would be unknown to the Achaemenid Persian bureaucracy.[63]

---

[61] Zimmerli, "Israel im Buche Ezekiel," 75–90; idem, *Ezekiel*, 2. 563–65; Williamson, "The Concept of Israel in Transition," 141–61. For the use of the term "Israel" in the prophets generally, see L. Rost, *Israel bei den Propheten* (BWANT 4; Stuttgart: Kohlhammer, 1937). On its use in Ezr-Neh see Ahlström, *Who Were the Israelites?*, 101–18; Vogt, *Studie*, 47–67. "Israel" (בני ישראל) is the prevalent name for the community in the Pentateuch, which many see as a reason for dating these narratives to the post-monarchical period. The appellation "the God of Israel" is not used in the Elephantine papyri which points to its use for the Judean national deity as a construct of the Judean exiles in Babylonia. Why they would adopt this name is another question.

[62] The only texts from the NB/LB periods specifically referring to Judeans are the ration lists concerning king Jehoiachin which are partly published in Weidner, "Jojachin, König von Juda," 923–35. The term used there is ^{lú}*ia-(a-ḫu/ú-)da-a-a*; see Zadok, *Jews in Babylonia*, 38. The ^{lú}*ia-a-ḫu-da-nu* mentioned in VAS 6, 128 (not Dar. 310 as Zadok [pp. 44–45] appears to suggest) refers to "a socio-professional category" rather than to "Judeans", so F. Joannès, "Pouvoirs locaux et organisations du territoire en Babylonie achéménide," *Transeu* 3 (1990) 179 n. 25, cf. M. San Nicolò and A. Ungnad, *Neubabylonische Rechts- und Verwaltungsurkunden* (2 vols.; Leipzig: Hinrichs, 1935) 1. 622. "Judean"/"Jew" is the only term by which the Judeans in the Elephantine papyri are known; see A. E. Cowley, *Aramaic Papyri of the Fifth Century* (Oxford: Clarendon, 1923) 290 s.v. יהוד for references, and also E. G. Kraeling, *The Brooklyn Aramaic Papyri* (New Haven: Yale University Press, 1953) nos. 5:2; 11:2.

[63] On גור as denoting a legal status for non-nationals residing in a foreign country, see D. Kellermann, "גור," in *Theological Dictionary of the Old Testament* (ed. G. J. Botterweck

In response to these charges it has been argued that knowledge of the Hebrew language and specialist terminology evidenced in the edict was gained from exiled Judeans in Babylonia. For Williamson, "the decree is a response to a petition by the Jews, and . . . it follows the language of the petition quite closely in these particulars".[64] He cites AP 32 and the Xanthos trilingual inscription as other official texts behind which are thought to lie similar petitions to the Achaemenid Persian administration regarding the building of local temples.[65] The use by the Achaemenid Persian bureaucracy of native speakers of the languages of subject peoples to write texts on behalf of the new regime or at least to be involved with the interpretation and communication of state ideology and policy to the respective subject peoples may also find support in the Cyrus Cylinder, which is commonly thought to be the work of Babylonian priests who supported Cyrus's capture of Babylon, and also in hieroglyphic inscriptions from Achaemenid Egypt.[66]

---

and H. Ringgren; trans. J. T. Willis; Grand Rapids: Eerdmans, 1974–) 2. 443–49. On נדבה, see J. Conrad, "נדב," in *TWAT*, 5. 240–41.

[64] Williamson, *Ezra, Nehemiah*, 11. Bickerman finds no problem in the Persian bureaucracy using these technical Hebrew terms.

[65] AP 32 is written in response to the petition of Elephantine Jews to have the shrine of Yahweh rebuilt (AP 30). These texts are dated to the reign of Darius II; around 407. The Xanthos trilingual is arguably a petition in Greek and Lycian to establish a new cult. The satrap's favourable reply is in Aramaic; see H. Metzger et al., *Fouilles de Xanthos VI: La stèle trilingue du Létôon* (Institute français d'études anatoliennes; Paris: Klincksieck, 1979). The reply is dated to the first year of Artaxerxes III (358). There is some debate, however, as to the purpose of this trilingual inscription. Rather than a petition to the satrap together with his response, reflecting direct Persian administrative involvement in cultic affairs, it may in fact simply be acknowledging the personnel and funding arrangements the community itself had decided on. In that way the text would be informing the administration, and others, of what the community had determined, not be ordering the community to conform to an administrative edict. If the latter interpretation obtains, the Xanthos trilingual would not be comparable to AP 32 in this regard. On interpreting the Xanthos trilingual, see P. Briant, "Polythéismes et empire unitaire. Remarques sur la politique religieuse des Achéménides," in *Le grandes figures religieuses. Fonctionnement practique et symbolique dans l'antiquité* (ed. P. Lévêque and M. M. Mactoux; Centre de Recherche d'Histoire Ancienne 68; Paris: Les Belle Lettres, 1986) 434–37, and idem, "Cités et satrapes dans l'Empire achéménide: Xanthos et Pixôdaros," *CRAIBL* (1998) 305–40. For a further discussion of Achaemenid Persian treatment of the cults of subjugated peoples, see below.

[66] On the Cyrus Cylinder, see below pp. 132–40. For the Egyptian inscriptions, see G. Posener, *La premiére domination perse en Égypte* (Cairo: Institut français d'archéologie orientale, 1936), although the Udjahorresne inscription (No. 1) was not commissioned by the Achaemenids. For further examples, see J. Yoyotte, "Une statue

There are difficulties with this argument, however. It assumes that
the Hebrew "proclamation" must be based on a (written?) petition
by the Judeans in Babylonia, something for which we have no direct
evidence. Further, that the exiled Judeans initiated Cyrus's restoration of the Jerusalem temple contradicts the text itself which understands the permission to rebuild and the repatriation of the exiles as
due to the spirit of Yahweh rousing Cyrus to act on the exiled
Judeans' behalf (Ezr 1:1). The Judeans are acted upon; they are not
the instigators. No doubt this view of events is a theological interpretation and Williamson's argument offers a historical explanation
of the same events. But even accepting that the Judeans were the
instigators, which I consider to be likely, does not necessitate the
conclusion that the Hebrew edict is the outcome of their approach
to the Persian authorities, particularly when the parallels cited are
not empire-wide proclamations but rather directives to specific local
communities. Further, that Cyrus was interested in the repatriation
of previously deported populations is questionable and not a feature
of the parallels cited.

Third, and related to the above point, verse 4 contains certain
difficult linguistic features the interpretation of which has an impact
on the historical veracity of the edict. It has been contended that
the word הַנִּשְׁאָר is a technical theological term in Ezra-Nehemiah
used to denote those Judeans who had been taken into exile (and
their descendants) and should thus be translated "the Remnant".[67]
The use of a term such as "the Remnant" points to the edict being
written by the Chronicler, not the Achaemenid Persian bureaucracy.
Others have thought this explicitly theological translation unnecessary, preferring to translate כל־הנשאר "all who survive" or the like,
but still denoting the Judeans in Babylonia.[68] אנשי מקמו "the men of
his place" is thus the subject of the verb נשא with וכל־הנשאר as a
casus pendens linked to the resumptive suffix in ינשאוהו. On this read-

de Darius découverte à Suse: les inscriptions hiéroglyphiques. Darius et l'Égypte,"
JA 260 (1972) 253–66.

[67] Torrey, *Ezra Studies*, 133; Mosis, *Untersuchungen*, 210 n. 7; Gunneweg, *Esra*,
43–44. Cf. II Chrons 36:20; Ezr 3:8; 6:16; 9:8, 13–15; Neh 1:1–3; 4:8, 13; 7:71f.;
10:29; 11:1, 20.

[68] A. B. Ehrlich, *Randglossen zur Hebräischen Bibel* (7 vols.; Leipzig: Hinrichs, 1908–14)
7. 157; J. A. Bewer, *Die Text des Buches Ezra* (Göttingen: Vandenhoeck & Ruprecht,
1922) 12; Batten, *Ezra, Nehemiah*, 59; Rudolph, *Esra und Nehemiah*, 3–5; Michaeli, *Les
livres des Chroniques, d'Esdras et de Néhemie*, 252; Blenkinsopp, *Ezra-Nehemiah*, 76.

ing, אנשי מקמו "the men of his place", that is, Babylonians and others with whom the exiled Judeans had been living, were to aid financially both the Judeans who were returning to their homeland and the Jerusalem temple reconstruction, as v. 6 confirms.[69] The verse may then be understood to mean that any exiled Judean who would have had to remain behind at the repatriation order of Cyrus, presumably because he was too poor to return, was to be financially aided by "the men of his place" and thus repatriated. The unlikelihood of this having been ordered by Cyrus is very great indeed.[70]

In an attempt to defend the veracity of the edict at this point Bickerman, followed by Williamson, has translated כל־הנשאר as "those who remain behind" and read it as the subject, not the object, of the verb נשא.[71] It is resumed later in the sentence by אנשי מקמו. The suffix on ינשאוהו refers back to "whoever is among you of all his people" in v. 3. In this interpretation, "those who remain behind" are basically identified as the Judeans who did not wish to take advantage of Cyrus's edict. They, rather than the Babylonians and other non-Judeans, are the ones commanded to support financially the repatriation and temple rebuilding.[72] This position has external evidence in its support since it is known from Ezra-Nehemiah and the Murašû archives that not all Judeans returned.[73] In order to give this interpretation more credence Williamson deletes אנשי מקמו as "an explanatory gloss or 'double reading' for the whole of the earlier phrase", since taking אנשי מקמו as the subject of the verb נשא "leads to difficulties in interpretation".[74] Williamson also contends

---

[69] Galling, *Studien*, 75–76.

[70] Even Batten, who supports the authenticity of the Hebrew edict over against the Aramaic edict, admits that Ezr 1:4 is a problem in this regard (*Ezra, Nehemiah*, p. 61); Japhet, "Temple in the Restoration Period," 212.

[71] Bickerman, "Edict of Cyrus," 83–87; Williamson, *Ezra, Nehemiah*, 14–15.

[72] Similarly, Bowman, "Ezra and Nehemiah," 572. Eph'al, "On the Political and Social Organization of the Jews," 108, understands "the men of his place" as the biblical term for a group of exiles organized in *Landsmannschaften*; that is, it refers to the Judeans.

[73] Ezra and Nehemiah themselves were Judeans who lived in exile, so one may assume that their forebears had remained in exile. Ezra also brought a number of other descendants of exiled Judeans with him when he returned (Ezr 8:1–14).

[74] Williamson, *Ezra, Nehemiah*, 5 n. 4d. The "difficulty" is that Cyrus would have ordered Babylonians to support the repatriates and their cult financially. Bickerman, "Edict of Cyrus," 86–87, 89–91, understands "the men of his place" to include non-Judeans. His emphasis, however, is on the fact that Judeans must have remained in Babylonia and it is basically to them that the call for financial aid was directed.

that the authenticity of the Hebrew edict should not be judged by
the editorial framework in which it is now set, so the fact that v. 6
understands Babylonians to be giving gifts to the Judean repatriates
is irrelevant. That is the editor's interpretation of the edict.[75] However
one views the relationship between the edict and the editorial framework, the MT as it stands points toward the Judeans who would
otherwise have remained behind in Babylonia receiving aid from
those with whom they lived. Would Cyrus have commanded that in
an empire-wide edict?

Fourth, the title "king of Persia" (v. 2).[76] In Ezra-Nehemiah this
title is used of Cyrus (Ezr 1:1–2, 8; 3:7; 4:3, 5), Darius (Ezr 4:5,
24), and Artaxerxes (Ezr 4:7; 6:14; 7:1). None of these references
occurs in the supposed official Aramaic documents,[77] and only one
reference, Ezr 6:14, occurs in the Aramaic narrative (Ezr 4:8–6:18)
where it is clearly from the hand of an editor. With regard to Cyrus,
the title "king of Persia" does not appear in Cyrus's titulary in the
extant Babylonian legal, economic and administrative texts dated to
his reign,[78] although he is designated as such in Nabonidus Chronicle
ii. 15, a Babylonian literary text conventionally dated to the early
part of his reign in Babylon.[79] Darius I uses "king of Persia" as one

---

[75] Williamson, *Ezra, Nehemiah*, 14. He recognizes that the reference to "neighbours" in v. 6 must refer to non-Judeans since elsewhere in Ezr-Neh fellow Judeans
are spoken of as "brothers" (p. 16). Since Williamson accepts that the title "king
of Persia" (discussed below) comes from the hand of the editor and conforms to
the narrative context (see Ezr 1:1, 8 where the title again appears), why does he
balk at relating verses 4 and 6?

[76] Points four and five develop arguments raised in Galling, *Studien*, 68–74.

[77] That is, the letters purported to be either written to Achaemenid kings (Ezr
4:11b–16; 5:7b–17) or by Achaemenid kings (Ezr 4:17–22; 6:2c–12; 7:12–26).

[78] This amounts to some 817 texts, plus 18 from the coregency with Cambyses,
according to A. Kuhrt, "Babylonia from Cyrus to Xerxes," in *CAH*, 2d ed., 4. 116
n. 23.

[79] Grayson, *Assyrian and Babylonian Chronicles*, 107, line 15. See R. D. Wilson, "The
Title 'King of Persia' in the Scriptures," *Princeton Theological Review* 15 (1917) 122–27,
on the titles of Cyrus in Babylonian texts, to which can be added C. J. Gadd and
L Legrain, *Ur Excavation Texts. Vol. I: Royal Inscriptions* (London: British Museum,
1928) no. 194, in which Cyrus has the title "king of the world, king of Anshan"
(cf. Nabonidus Chronicle ii. 1—"Cyrus, king of Anshan"; Cyrus Cylinder lines 12
and 21—"Cyrus, king of Anshan"). On the titulary of Cyrus in Babylonian administrative and legal texts, see W. H. Shea, "An Unrecognized Vassal King of Babylon
in the Early Achaemenid Period: II," *AUSS* 9 (1971) 99–128. M. A. Dandamaev,
A Political History of the Achaemenid Empire (trans. W. J. Vogelsang; Leiden: E. J. Brill,
1989) 55 n. 9, claims that YOS VII 8 14, dated to Cyrus's first year as king of
Babylon, reads "Cyrus, king of the Persians". The text reads ᵐ*ku-raš* LUGAL

of his titles in certain Achaemenid royal inscriptions (DB I, 2; DBa, 2). "King of Persia and Media" is incorporated into the titulary of Xerxes I and Artaxerxes I in Babylonian texts (all non-literary), although commonly with the traditional Babylonian royal title "king of Babylon".[80] Two exceptions are a text dated to the fifth year of Xerxes where the title "king of Persia" occurs alone, and a text from the first year of Artaxerxes I bearing the title "king of Persia and Media".[81] "King of Persia" is also occasionally used of Achaemenid kings in Greek literary-historical texts.[82] The use of this title by Cyrus in the Hebrew edict is incongruous since all Achaemenid kings use some form of the royal titulary of the indigenous monarchy, or simply use "the king" after their name.[83] Its appearance in one text from the reign of Xerxes cannot support its possible use by Cyrus in the Hebrew edict. Bickerman's contention that since "Greek terminology shows that the Achaemenids were known in the West as 'Kings of Persia'", the use of the title "king of Persia" by the Chronicler is therefore acceptable,[84] must be rejected on the grounds

KUR.KUR *par-su*, where *parsu* is a form of the verb *parāsu*; see M. San Nicolò, "Materialien zur Viehwirtshaft in den neubabylonischen Tempeln. III," *Or* NS 20 (1951) 141. "Cyrus, (great) king, Achaemenid" appears to be Cyrus's Persian titulary, if the trilingual inscriptions (Old Persian, Elamite, Akkadian) ascribed to him are accepted as legitimate. For a discussion of these texts, see P. Lecoq, "Le problème de l'écriture cunéiforme vieux-perse," in *Commémoration Cyrus. Hommage Universel* (3 vols; AcIr 1–3; Tehran/Liège: Bibliothèque Pahlavi, 1974) 3. 52–58.

[80] On the titulary of Xerxes and Artaxerxes I in Babylonian texts, see A. Kuhrt and S. Sherwin-White, "Xerxes' Destruction of Babylonian Temples," in *Achaemenid History II: The Greek Sources* (ed. H. Sancisi-Weerdenburg and A. Kuhrt; Leiden: Nederlands Instituut voor het Nabije Osten, 1987) 72–73; F. Joannès, "La titulature de Xerxès," *Nouvelles assyriologiques brèves et utilitaires* 1989/37.

[81] For the Xerxes text, see J. Oppert, "L'inscription cunéiform la plus moderne connue," *Mélanges d'archéologie égyptienne et assyrienne* 1 (1873) 22–29. The royal name in the date formula (l. 13) is broken but is commonly restored *[Aḫ]-ḫa-ri-šú* "Xerxes", following A. Boissier, "Pacorus ou Xerxès," *ZA* 11 (1896) 83–84. For the Artaxerxes text, see J. Strassmaier, "Einige kleinere babylonische Keilschrifttexts aus dem Britischen Museum," in *Actes du 8e Congrès Internationale des Orientalistes* (Duexième Partie, Section 1; Leiden: Brill, 1893) no. 19.

[82] For the references to the titulary of the Achaemenid kings in Greek texts, see Wilson, "'King of Persia,'" 128, 131–40. This article is an exhaustive review of the titulary of Achaemenid kings in the Biblical, Akkadian, Egyptian, Old Persian, and Classical sources extant at the author's time. Wilson attempts to affirm the veracity of the use of this title in Ezra against the claim of G. B. Gray, "The Title 'King of Persia'," *Expository Times* 25 (1913–14) 245–51, that since there is no attested use by Cyrus of this title it must come from the hand of the author/editor of Ezra.

[83] See Wilson, "'King of Persia'," 120–31, for extensive references.

[84] Bickerman, "Edict of Cyrus," 78.

that (i) our concern is with official terminology, not with the titles evidenced in the local literary tradition; (ii) Judah was within the satrapy of "Babylon and Across-the-River" in which Cyrus should be expected to use the standard titulary of the king of Babylon such as "king of Babylon" or "king of lands" or both. The title "king of Persia" in Ezr 1:2 must be understood to be from the hand of the author/editor of Ezra.[85]

Fifth, "the God of Heaven" as an appellation for Yahweh is attested here and in other biblical texts of the Persian and Hellenistic periods (Ezr 5:11–12; 6:9–10; 7:12, 21, 23; Neh 1:4–5; 2:4, 20; Jonah 1:9; Dan 2:18–19, 28, 37, 44; 4:34), as well as in the Aramaic texts from Elephantine (AP 30:2, 15, 27–28; 31:26–27; 32:3–4; 38:3, 5; 40:1). A. Vincent understands the title as having had some currency in the patriarchal and monarchical periods.[86] He considers that it was used by the Achaemenid Persian chancellery as a means of connecting Yahweh with the other celestial deities in the empire, such as Ba'al Šamēm, Marduk, and Ahura Mazda.[87] While it is ques-

---

[85] Williamson, who holds that the Hebrew edict is otherwise authentic, admits that this title is editorial (*Ezra, Nehemiah*, 11).

[86] Vincent, *La religion des judéo-araméens d'Éléphantine*, 104–12.

[87] Ibid., 141–43. On pp. 100–41 he outlines the evidence for the appellation "the god of heaven" (אל שמיא ;אלה שמיא; אלהי השמים) and the related "lord of heaven" (מרא שמין ;בעל שמין ;בעל שמם). This evidence is reviewed and updated in R. A. Oden, "*Ba'al Šamēm* and *'Ēl*," *CBQ* 39 (1977) 457–73; H. Niehr, *Der höchste Gott: Alttestamentlicher JHWH-Glaube im Kontext syrisch-kanaanäischer Religion des 1. Jahrtausends v. Chr* (BZAW 190; Berlin/New York: W. de Gruyter, 1990) 17–68 (cf. the critique in K. Engelken, "BA'ALŠAMEN—Eine Auseinandersetzung mit der Monographie von H. Niehr," *ZAW* 108 (1996) 233–48, 391–407); C. Houtman, *Der Himmel im Alten Testament. Israels Weltbild und Weltanschauung* (OTS 30; London/New York/Cologne: E. J. Brill, 1993), 85–107. While "the lord of heaven" is attested in royal inscriptions of Syro-Palestinian states from the mid-second to mid-first millennium (ᵈIM *ša-me-e*—RS 17.227, 51; RS 17.237 r. 11; RS 17.340 r. 17 [cf. ᵈIM *i-na ša-me* EA 149, 7]; for ᵈIM = Ba'al see M. H. Pope and W. Röllig, "Syrien. Die Mythologie der Ugariter und Phönizier," in *Götter und Mythen im Vorderen Orient* [ed. H. W. Haussig; Wörterbuch der Mythologie 1/1; Stuttgart: Klett, 1965] 253]; בעל שמן— KAI 202 A 3, 11–12, B 23 [Aramaic]; בעל שמם—KAI 4:3; KAI 26 A III 18 [Phoenician] cf. ᵈ*ba-al—sa-me-me* in Esarhaddon's treaty with Tyre IV, 10 [R. Borger, *Die Inschriften Asarhaddons, Königs von Assyrien* (AfO Beiheft 9; Graz: Weidner, 1956) 107–09]) and its use continued throughout the Achaemenid period (as attested in AP 30:15 [מרא שמיא]; KAI 259 [בעלשמין]) and into the Hellenistic and Roman periods (on which see J. Teixidor, *The Pagan God: Popular Religion in the Greco-Roman Near East* [Princeton: Princeton University Press, 1977]), it remains unclear as to whether or not before the Greco-Roman period it was the proper name of a deity or simply an appellation. The connection between Ba'al Šamēm and Ahura Mazda under the Achaemenids is also affirmed by F. Cumont, *Les religions orientales dans la paganisme romain* (Paris: Librairie Leroux, 1929) 200.

tionable that it was ever used of Yahweh before the Persian period,[88] the contention that the appellation "the God of Heaven" was taken up by the Achaemenid Persian administration, reflecting their acceptance of Yahweh as a deity either similar to or the equivalent of Ahura Mazda, has gained wide acceptance.[89] It is at issue, however,

---

[88] Neither "the god of heaven" nor "the lord of heaven" is an appellation used of Yahweh in monarchical period texts and inscriptions. The references to Yahweh as "the god of heaven" in Ps 136:26 and Gen 23:4, 7, should be dated to the Persian period at the earliest (note the hypostatizing of wisdom in Ps 136:5 cf. Prov 3:19; 8:1, 27–29). O. Eissfeldt, "Baʿalšamēm und Jahwe," *ZAW* 57 (1939) 1–31, argues for the existence of the cult of Baʿal Šamēm in Judah and Israel in the monarchical period which explains why the appellation was not applied to Yahweh. It is unclear from the available evidence, however, that the Baʿal against whom certain of the prophets rail is in fact Baʿal Šamēm.

[89] D. K. Andrews, "Yahweh and the God of the Heavens" in *The Seed of Wisdom: Essays in Honour of T. J. Meek* (ed. W. S. McCullough; Toronto: University of Toronto Press, 1964) 45–57, who places the origin of this appellation in the Persian period, contending that it was introduced by the Achaemenid Persian bureaucracy. He does not assign a specific date to its introduction but seems to support some time early in the Achaemenid period; R. Bowman, "Ezra and Nehemiah," 572; Williamson, *Ezra, Nehemiah*, 12; Blenkinsopp, *Ezra-Nehemiah*, 75. Depending on one's view of the origin of and religious influences on the Elephantine Jewish community, it is possible that they brought the Syrian/Aramaic name "the God of Heaven" with them to Egypt, see Niehr, *Der höchste Gott*, 43–48; K. van der Toorn, "Anat-Yahu, Some Other Deities, and the Jews of Elephantine," *Numen* 39 (1992) 80–101.

G. Gnoli, "Politique religieuse et conception de la royauté sous les Achéménides," in *Commémoration Cyrus*, 2. 131, states well the representative view:

> La conception iranienne d'Auramazdā créateur du ciel et de la terre [DNa 1–3; DSf 1–2; DZc 1–2; DE 1–4; XPa 1–2; XPb 1–4; XPc 1–2; XPd 1–3; XPh 1–2; XPf 1–3; XE 3–4; XV 2–4; A²Hc 2–3; A³Pa 1–3], si clairement exprimée dans les inscriptions royales, a une forte analogie avec celle, pan-sémitique, de dieu créateur. Cette nature d'Auramazdā put certes favoriser une assimilation, même partielle, avec Marduk, avec Yahweh et avec Baʿal Šamīm. On a justement reconnu dans l'expression "le dieu du ciel," en usage dans la chancellerie achéménide, notoirement constituée de scribes araméens, la trace éloquente d'un tel syncrétisme.

Ahura Mazda is never termed "the god of heaven", however, and there is some problem in trying to equate him with Baʿal Šamēm seeing that there is no evidence that this deity was recognized as the creator in Aramean or Phoenician theology. If Baʿal Šamēm is an appellation for the chief god of the respective pantheons then he may be able to correspond to Ahura Mazda, but the available evidence is scant and admits a number of interpretations. Little is known regarding the members of the Aramean pantheon and their respective functions. In KAI 202 (Zakir) Baʿal Šamēm has close connections with the Aramean king which suggests that he was the chief god of the pantheon. For Phoenician religion Philo of Byblos's Phoenician History is a commonly used source. In this text Baʿal Šamēm is neither the head of the pantheon nor the creator deity; see A. I. Baumgarten, *The Phoenician History of Philo of Byblos: A Commentary* (EPROER 89; Leiden: Brill, 1981) 149–52; but cf. KAI 4 (Yehimilk) where Baʿal Šamēm is the head of the pantheon. Should the Ugaritic mythological texts be considered reliable evidence for Phoenician religion

whether Ahura Mazda was the principal deity worshipped by Cyrus.[90] This raises the complex and much debated question of the religion of the Achaemenids. This topic can be only touched on here. It involves not only the problem of dating when Ahura Mazda rose to prominence among the Achaemenids, but also the relationship of their worship of Ahura Mazda to Zoroastrianism, the teaching of the prophet Zoroaster regarding the nature and status of this deity.[91] For our present purposes we need only be concerned with the place of Ahura Mazda in the religion of Cyrus. The longstanding consensus that Cyrus was a Zarathustrian, or that at the very least Ahura Mazda was his principal deity, has been critically evaluated by J. Duchesne-Guillemin who contends that Mithra and not Ahura Mazda was the god of Cyrus. Ahura Mazda rose to prominence only under Darius I.[92] Certainly the first evidence for the importance of Ahura Mazda to the Achaemenids is found in the royal inscriptions of Darius I.

---

then there also Ba'al is not the supreme deity, but scholarly debate still rages over whether or not he is a creator deity. For a brief survey of Ugaritic Ba'al as a creator, see J. Day, *God's Conflict with the Dragon and the Sea. Echoes of a Canaanite Myth in the Old Testament* (Cambridge: Cambridge University Press, 1985) 7–18. Oden, "*Ba'al Šamēm* and *'Ēl*," 457–73, considers Ba'al Šamēm to be an appellation for El the creator deity, but the earliest unequivocal evidence for Ba'al Šamēm as the creator is found in the Hatran texts from the first-second century C.E. For a critique of Oden, see Olyan, *Asherah and the Cult of Yahweh*, 62–64. Yahweh is, of course, a creator deity; see N. C. Habel, "'Yahweh, Maker of Heaven and Earth': A Study in Tradition Criticism," *JBL* 91 (1972) 321–37.

[90] Among those supporting the traditional view, that Cyrus was a Zoroastrian who worshipped Ahura Mazda, are W. Hinz, *Zarathustra* (Stuttgart: Kohlhammer, 1961) 146–49; M. Boyce, *A History of Zoroastrianism. Vol. II: Under the Achaemenians* (Handbuch des Orientalistik; Leiden/Cologne: Brill, 1975) 47–69; eadem, "The Religion of Cyrus the Great," in *Achaemenid History III: Method and Theory* (ed. A. Kuhrt and H. Sancisi-Weerdenburg; Leiden: Nederlands Insituut voor het Nabije Oosten, 1988) 15–31; D. Stronach, "Notes on the Religion in Iran in the Seventh and Sixth Centuries B.C.," in *Orientalia J. Duchesne-Guillemin Emerito Oblata* (AcIr 23; Leiden: Brill, 1984) 479–90.

[91] The main issues in the debate are outlined in J. Duchesne-Guillemin, "La religion des Achéménides," in *Beiträge zur Achämenidengeschichte* (ed. G. Walser; Historia Einzelinscriften 18; Wiesbaden: Steiner, 1972) 59–82. See also the extensive discussion of G. Gnoli, "Politique religieuse," 117–90. For religious developments in the early Achaemenid period (Cyrus II—Darius I), see J. Wiesehöfer, *Der Aufstand Gaumatas und die Anfänge Dareios' I* (Bonn: Habelt, 1978) 123–55. C. Herrenschmidt, "La religion des Achéménides: État de la question," *Studia Iranica* 9 (1980) 325–39, summarizes the major literature of the 1970's on the subject.

[92] J. Duchesne-Guillemin, "Le dieu de Cyrus," in *Commémoration Cyrus*, 3. 11–21, followed by R.-A. Turcan, *Mithra et Mithriacisme* (Paris: Presses Universitaires de France, 1981) 12–16. Duchesne-Guillemin had thought that the emblem over the

If it were the case that Ahura Mazda became the principal deity of the Achaemenids only in the reign of Darius I, then the use of the title "the God of Heaven", otherwise only attested for Yahweh from the reign of Artaxerxes I, would be anachronistic in the Hebrew edict of Cyrus.[93] Since the evidence regarding the religion of Cyrus

---

door of Cyrus's tomb at Pasargadae (published in D. Stronach, "A Circular Symbol on the Tomb of Cyrus," *Iran* 9 [1971] 155–58) must represent Mithra on the basis of a comparison with a lotus motif in the Taq-i Bustan relief. He has since withdrawn this claim given that the lotus has been shown to be unrelated to Mithra in the Taq-i Bustan relief. He now identifies the emblem in Cyrus's tomb as a symbol for the Sun, another representation of Mithra; see J. Duchesne-Guillemin, "Sonnenkönigtum und Mazdareligion," in *Kunst, Kultur und Geschichte der Achämenidenzeit und ihr Fortleben* (ed. H. Koch and D. N. Mackenzie; Mitteilungen aus Iran Ergänzungsband 10; Berlin: Reimer, 1983) 136–37.

On Darius I being responsible for the rise in status of Ahura Mazda, see also I. Gershevitch, "Zoroaster's Own Contribution," *JNES* 23 (1964) 16–18; J. Duchesne-Guillemin, "Die Religion der Achämeniden," *AcAnt* 19 (1971) 25–35. This is not necessarily equivalent to the introduction of Zoroastrianism, so G. Widengren, *Die Religionen Irans* (Die Religionen der Menschheit 14; Stuttgart: Kohlhammer, 1965) 141–49, and M. A. Dandamaev, *Persien unter den ersten Achämeniden (6. Jahrhundert v. Chr)* (trans. H.-D. Pohl; Beiträge zur Iranistik 8; Wiesbaden: Reichert, 1976) 215–41, who cite practices of the Achaemenid kings which they believe to show that these kings were not Zoroastrians. This position is disputed by a number of scholars working on early Achaemenid religion, although a distinction must be made between Zoroastrianism of the Achaemenid period and that of the better known Parthian period. Elsewhere Dandamaev ("La politique religieuse des Achéménides," in *Hommages et opera minora. Monumentum H. S. Nyberg* [3 vols.; AcIr 4–6; Tehran/Liège: Bibliothèque Pahlavi, 1975] 1. 193–200) modifies his position and holds that:

> à cette époque [that is, the Achaemenid period], où le zoroastrisme n'était pas encore devenu une religion dogmatique, aux normes strictement arrêtées, diverses modifications surgirent dans la nouvelle doctrine religieuse et, en ce sens, il est possible d'estimer—moyennant des réserves précises—que la religion des Achéménides, depuis le temps de Darius Iᵉʳ, fut une forme de zoroastrisme ancien. (p. 200)

Heleen Sancisi-Weerdenburg, "Political Concepts in Old-Persian Royal Inscriptions," in *Anfänge politischen Denkens in der Antike: Die nahöstlichen Kulturen und die Griechen* (ed. K. Raaflaub; Schriften des Historischen Kollegs 24; Munich: R. Oldenbourg, 1993) 150, is much more circumspect in her views. She contends that:

> If one compares our knowledge of Zoroastrian religion with the evidence on religion at the time of the Achaemenid kings, not only do we find *no* signs of an active propagation of Zoroastrian beliefs throughout the empire, but the statements of the kings themselves show remarkable 'divergences' from the sacred texts. . . . For the moment it only distorts the discussion seriously if we attempt to explain Persian politics and political behaviour through the possibly anachronistic knowledge of Zoroastrian texts. (author's emphasis)

[93] If one accepts the official correspondence in the Aramaic narrative as authentic, then the earliest other attestation for the appellation "the God of Heaven" applied to Yahweh is from the reign of Darius I (Ezr 5:11–12; 6:9–10), otherwise the references in the Nehemiah Memoir (Neh 1:4–5; 2:4, 20), which is conventionally dated to the end of the reign of Artaxerxes I, are the earliest. Supposedly

is so scant, it is improper to rule out the possibility that Cyrus's principal deity was Ahura Mazda even while recognizing that it is questionable. The use of "the God of Heaven" in the Hebrew edict must presume not only that Ahura Mazda was Cyrus's main deity but also that Cyrus was responsible for connecting the deities of the subject peoples with Ahura Mazda. The earliest other example where a foreign deity is connected with Ahura Mazda is again in the reign of Darius I.[94] While Cyrus, Cambyses, and Darius all often show respect for the cults of subject peoples, there is no evidence that Cyrus and Cambyses connected any of the leading foreign deities with Ahura Mazda, assuming they indeed worshipped him. This too may have been an innovation of Darius. Regarding these kings' atti-

---

from around this period is the rescript given to Ezra (Ezr 7) which some date to the reign of Artaxerxes I, while most place it in the reign of Artaxerxes II, if it is indeed authentic. Yahweh is referred to as "the God of Heaven" in Ezr 7:12, 21, 23. The earliest non-Biblical example is from Elephantine (AP 30:2, 27), dated to the seventeenth year of Darius II (407). It occurs in other, non-dated texts in this corpus which are also placed in the reign of Darius II.

Both the biblical texts and the Aramaic papyri from Elephantine used the same title for Yahweh. Since it is unlikely that the respective communities arrived at the same appellation independently, and since this appellation was not current in the monarchical period, one might speculate that it was assigned to Yahweh by the Achaemenid bureaucracy, perhaps at the behest of Judeans (in Babylonia?) who sought to speak of their deity in terms that would find resonances in the theology of their Achaemenid overlords, so Houtman, *Der Himmel im Alten Testament*, 98–107; cf. Vincent, *La religion des judéo-araméens d'Éléphantine*, 109, who holds that an Israelite colony which arrived in Egypt c. 630 (that is, the forefathers of the Elephantine community) brought the terminology with them from their homeland.

Were Mithra Cyrus's main deity it is unlikely that Cyrus would have identified Yahweh or Marduk (in the Cyrus Cylinder) with him. Mithra was a celestial deity but was identified with the sun. On Mithra, see G. Gnoli, "Sol Persice Mithra," in *Mysteria Mithrae* (ed. U. Bianchi; EPROER 80; Leiden: Brill, 1979) 725–40. On Solar elements in the cult of Yahweh, see H.-P. Stähli, *Solare Elemente im Jahweglauben des Alten Testaments* (OBO 66; Freiburg: Universitätsverlag/Göttingen: Vandenhoeck & Ruprecht, 1985); M. S. Smith, "The Near Eastern Background of the Solar Language for Yahweh," *JBL* 109 (1990) 29–39.

[94] The statue of Darius found at Susa has a trilingual inscription (Old Persian, Elamite, Akkadian) and five hieroglyphic inscriptions. In both the second and third hieroglyphic inscriptions, which are thoroughly Egyptian in their literary style and outlook, the god Re appears as the preeminent deity. In the cuneiform trilingual, which conforms to the style of Darius's other Old Persian royal inscriptions, Ahura Mazda is Darius's god. See F. Vallat, "L'inscription cunéiforme trilingue (DSab)," *JA* 260 (1972) 247–51; J. Yoyotte, "Une statue de Darius," 253–66; idem, "Les inscriptions hiéroglyphiques de Darius à Suse," *Cahiers de la délégation archéologique française en Iran* 4 (1974) 181–209. The statue is dated to c. 495 on the style of the figure's Persian dress (so, D. Stronach, "Description and Comment," *JA* 260 [1972] 246) and on epigraphic grounds (Yoyotte, "Une statue de Darius," 266).

tudes toward foreign cults, there has been a tendency among some scholars to read back into the reigns of Cyrus and Cambyses the attitudes of the better-attested later Achaemenid kings, particularly those of Darius I, in order to argue for a consistent Achaemenid policy. The fact that Cyrus extols Marduk in the Cyrus Cylinder proves nothing regarding how this deity's relationship to Ahura Mazda was viewed, unless one assumes *a priori* that the two gods were "connected" or "identified". Cyrus could be simply acknowledging the local deity as a means of legitimating his kingship in Babylonia. The contention that the later Achaemenids identified foreign deities with Iranian gods is itself open to question since none of the evidence cited in its support is unambiguous. Much of the evidence comes from Asia Minor, where the introduction of Iranian gods and the syncretism between local and Iranian deities (notably Mithra and Anahita, but also Ahura Mazda) is held by some to be an imperial policy.[95] In short, it appears most likely that the appellation "the

---

[95] So, Gnoli, "Politique religieuse," 148–56; P. Briant, "Forces productives, dépendance rurale et idéologies religieuses dans l'Empire achéménide," in *Rois, tributs et paysans. Etudes sur les formations tributaires du Moyen-Orient ancien* (Centre de Recherches d'Histoire Ancienne 43. Paris: Les Belle Lettres, 1982) 456–73. The attempt to push this policy back to the reign of Cyrus is based on questionable evidence. Tacitus, *Annals*, iii. 62, recounts the tradition that Cyrus dedicated a sanctuary for "Persian Diana" (= Anahita) in Hierocaesarea (for possible background to this see Herodotus i. 158–60), but this tradition may be a late fabrication. In any case, it tells us nothing of Cyrus's understanding of the relationship between the local deity and Anahita. B. Fehr, "Zur Geschichte des Apollo-Heiligtums von Didyma," in *Marburger Winckelmann-Programm 1971/72* (Marburg: Verlag des Kunstgeschichtelichen Seminars, 1972) 51–54, suggests that the temple of Apollo at Didyma was built by Cyrus, and even if this is so it does not necessarily mean syncretism between Apollo and Mithra at this time. Note regarding this shrine that it was destroyed by Darius I in 494 (Herodotus vi. 19).

The Sardis inscription, a mid-second century C.E. copy of a text dated to the thirty-ninth year of Artaxerxes II (365), speaks of the consecration of a statue to "Zeus the lawgiver" (Gk *Baradateo* = OI **baradata-*). L. Robert, who published this inscription ("Une nouvelle inscription grecque de Sardes: Règlement de l'autorité perse relatif à un culte," *CRAIBL* [1975] 306–30), argued that Zeus must be understood to be Ahura Mazda, following the standard practice of Greek writers (from the time of Herodotus at least) who replace the name Ahura Mazda with Zeus. The significance of this Zeus—Ahura Mazda interchange is difficult to determine. Does it presume that the two deities were identified with each other? Is "Zeus" a "translation" of "Ahura Mazda" for Greek readers? If so, what would this mean in terms of the relationship between the two deities and cultures? Herodotus consistently uses the name Zeus for Ahura Mazda. Is one to deduce from this that he also is a syncretist? This inscription has been viewed as reflecting the introduction or penetration of the worship of Ahura Mazda into Asia Minor, which may be part of an imperial policy (so, P. Briant, "Polythéismes et empire unitaire," 429–30,

God of Heaven" is an anachronism in Ezr 1:2, although the available evidence stops short of offering conclusive proof on this point.

On balance there is some reason to question the authenticity of the edict. Bickerman's confidence that it is authentic is certainly overstated. To accept it would demand that: the title "king of Persia" be the only editorializing in the edict; that Cyrus issued Ezr 1:2–4 as "a proclamation throughout his empire", but that only Judeans exiled in Babylonia responded; that Cyrus commanded non-Judeans in Babylonia to support the Judean repatriates financially; that Ahura Mazda was Cyrus's principal deity; that the appellation "the God of Heaven" was current in his reign to relate other celestial deities of subjugated peoples in the empire to Ahura Mazda; and that "the God of Israel" was a phrase known to the Achaemenid Persian bureaucracy at this time, perhaps told to them by Babylonian Judeans themselves. To have recourse to the contention that the Hebrew edict is an edited version of an original issued by the Achaemenid Persian bureaucracy demands the acceptance of the existence of an original edict and assumes that the editorial work is limited to only peripheral concerns.[96] As has been noted above, the edict, although issued throughout the empire (Ezr 1:1), is really directed to the Judeans exiled in Babylonia. They are the ones who respond to it (Ezr 1:5f., 11b) since according to Ezr 3:1–4:5 there were no Judeans left in Judah, only syncretistic foreign neighbours imported into the area by an earlier Assyrian king (Ezr 4:2). This serves the author's anti-Samarian polemic. The myth of the empty land serves to undermine the claim of any non-exiled group to hold a legitimate, alternate indigenous tradition. They are "foreigners" and therefore have no claim to be listened to regarding Yahwism. Within Ezr 1–6 the purpose of the Hebrew edict is to legitimate the Jerusalem temple and to show that it was the repatriates who were commanded by

---

438). Frei, "Zentralgewalt und Localautonomie im Achämenidenreich," in *Reichsidee und Reichsorganisation im Perserriech*, 20–21, considers the cult to be local, not the product of Achaemenid policy; cf. P. Briant, "Droaphernès et la statue de Sardes," in *Studies in Persian History: Essays in Memory of David M. Lewis* (ed. M. Brosius and A. Kuhrt; Achaemenid History XI; Leiden: Nederlands Instituut voor het Nabije Oosten, 1998) 205–26, who, after re-analyzing the text, now contends against Robert that it reflects an interest by members of the Persian governing group in local deities rather than the introduction of the cult of Ahura Mazda.

[96] This is contended by Oesterley and Robinson, *History*, 2. 74–77; Williamson, *Ezra, Nehemiah*, 8–15.

Cyrus to rebuild, as they themselves explicitly claim in Ezr 4:3. The tradition that Cyrus was the Persian king who permitted the repatriation and temple rebuilding may have arisen under the influence of Deutero-Isaiah's identification of Cyrus as the anointed of Yahweh who was charged with these tasks. Ezr 1:1–11 would then be simply recounting the fulfilment of prophecy (cf. Ezr 1:1).

The Aramaic Edict

The authenticity of the Aramaic edict has enjoyed much wider acceptance among commentators, due largely to the work of Eduard Meyer and H. H. Schaeder who argued for the general reliability of the Aramaic documents in Ezra (Ezr 4:9–22; 5:7b–17; 6:2c–12; 7:12–24) and supported by R. de Vaux specifically on the edict in Ezr 6:3–5.[97] Not only does the fact that it is written in Aramaic, the language of the Achaemenid Persian bureaucracy, support its authenticity but as Meyer argues regarding the Aramaic documents generally in Ezra, the vocabulary, syntax, and historical veracity of these documents supports their authenticity. L. V. Hensley has conducted a study of the Aramaic documents showing that they conform linguistically and stylistically to other similar texts in Aramaic, Greek and Demotic generated by, or purported to be to or from, the Achaemenid bureaucracy.[98] De Vaux, like Bickerman on the Hebrew edict, has addressed many of the questions raised concerning the Aramaic edict's authenticity and has cited much of the same evidence as Bickerman to show that it would not have been uncharacteristic of Cyrus to have issued such an edict. That is, the authenticity of the Aramaic edict

[97] Meyer, *Entstehung*, 8–71, on the Aramaic source, and pp. 46–54 on the Aramaic edict of Cyrus specifically; H. H. Schaeder, *Iranische Beiträge I* (Schriften der Königsberger gelehrten Gesellschaft, 6 Jahr. Geisteswissenschaftliche Kl., Heft 5; Halle: Niemeyer, 1930); de Vaux, "Edicts," 63–96. From a study of the vocabulary and syntax of the documents Meyer thought that they were originally written in Persian and then translated into Aramaic. This view has found little acceptance.

[98] Hensley, *Official Persian Documents*. He has a review and discussion of previous scholarship on these documents on pp. 1–26. Considerable research has been conducted on the Aramaic epistolography of the Achaemenid period and later; see J. A. Fitzmyer, "Aramaic Epistolography," in *A Wandering Aramean: Collected Aramaic Essays* (Missoula, MT: Scholars Press, 1979) 183–204; P. S. Alexander, "Remarks on Aramaic Epistolography in the Persian Period," *JSS* 23 (1978) 155–70; J. D. Whitehead, "Some Distinctive Features of the Language of the Aramaic Arsames Correspondence," *JNES* 37 (1978) 119–40; P. E. Dion, "Les types épistolaires hébréo-araméens jusqu'au temps de Bar-Kokhba," *RB* 96 (1979) 544–79.

is defended by recourse to a policy of Cyrus and later Achaemenid kings towards the indigenous cults of peoples in the empire.[99] The Aramaic edict lacks the difficulties noted above regarding the Hebrew edict which have been associated with the Chronicler as its author, and the practical matters with which it is concerned are thought better to befit an official memorandum.

The tendentiousness, not only of the Hebrew edict but of the whole of Ezra, led a number of commentators, most forcefully C. C. Torrey, to the conclusion that all the documents in Ezra purportedly from the Achaemenid bureaucracy are fabrications.[100] Torrey argues, first, that ancient authors are known to compose letters, speeches and documents to enliven their narratives. The documents in Ezra are comparable to the speeches and documents in the books of Daniel, Maccabees and the Letter of Aristeas which are widely recognized to be fictitious. Other biblical books such as Kings and Chronicles also use this device. Second, the Aramaic of Ezra is late. Torrey considers it to be later than that of the Elephantine papyri, contending that it is comparable to the Aramaic in the book of Daniel which he dates to c. 165. Third, the Ezra narrative is not only vitiated by historical inaccuracies, such as the order of the Achaemenid Persian kings in the Aramaic source, but also the issues it addresses, such as the legitimation of the Jerusalem cult of Yahweh, date it to the Hellenistic period when Judaism was under threat from both Hellenism and the Samaritans.

Torrey's remarks regarding the date of the Aramaic in Ezra can now be set aside since Aramaicists agree that the Aramaic of the book of Ezra does indeed predate that of the book of Daniel, although both are categorized as being Imperial Aramaic.[101] Torrey's other

---

[99] De Vaux, "Edicts," 63–96.

[100] Torrey, *Ezra Studies*, 140–83.

[101] A late date for the Aramaic of Ezra is in Torrey's interest for although he cites biblical examples of fictitious letters his strongest evidence comes from Hellenistic Jewish texts. The linguistic arguments for the relative dating of the Aramaic of Ezra and Daniel have been much discussed and the consensus rests as much on historical interpretation as it does on linguistic features. A summary of the main issues can be found in F. Rosenthal, *Die Aramaistische Forschung seit Th. Nöldeke's Veröffentlichungen* (Leiden: Brill, 1939) 48–71. The discovery of texts such as the Genesis Apocryphon which is dated to the first century B.C.E. has not proven to add much force to the linguistic arguments that the Aramaic of Daniel belongs to the Hellenistic period. For the inclusion of Daniel in the category of Imperial Aramaic, see J. A. Fitzmyer, "The Phases of the Aramaic Language," in *A Wandering Aramean*, 61, who sees the limits on Imperial Aramaic as being "from roughly . . . 700 B.C.–200 B.C."

remarks still carry much weight and have never been satisfactorily addressed. He ridicules the likes of S. R. Driver who in his celebrated *Introduction to the Old Testament* considered the documents to be spurious but their content accurate.[102] He pays considerable attention to E. Meyer's *Entstehung*, probing the arguments presented there. Meyer's defence of the authenticity of the Aramaic documents based on there being no good reason evident for their fabrication is condemned. Torrey disparages those—Meyer is again singled out though his followers are many—who contend that the Judeans themselves may well have written documents such as Ezr 7 (Ezra's brief from Artaxerxes [II?]) and simply had them ratified by the Achaemenid Persian bureaucracy; and that the Chronicler has edited the documents into the form that we now have them. He rightly points out that such arguments cannot defend the documents' authenticity since they could just as possibly have been forged. There is a fine line between positing that Ezra wrote a document to have it ratified by the Achaemenids, or that the Chronicler edited the documents, and the position that the author simply concocted the documents. As noted above regarding the Hebrew edict, it is extremely difficult to determine where editorial activity stops and historically reliable information begins. Torrey rejects the characterization of the narrative as a tendentious reworking of a substantially historical base since, in

---

Against Torrey, those who seek to date the Aramaic of both Ezra and Daniel to the same time almost universally argue for an *early* date; that is, the Aramaic in both texts belongs to the Achaemenid Persian period; so, for example, K. A. Kitchen, "The Aramaic of Daniel," in *Notes on Some Problems in the Book of Daniel* (ed. D. J. Wiseman; London: Tyndale, 1965) 31–79; G. F. Hasel, "The Book of Daniel and Matters of Language," *AUSS* 19 (1981) 211–25. K. Beyer, *The Aramaic Language: Its Distribution and Subdivision* (trans. J. F. Healey; Göttingen: Vandenhoeck & Ruprecht, 1986), contends that the biblical texts in Aramaic

> ... were originally produced in Achaemenid Imperial Aramaic. However, since the Masoretic consonantal text of the Old Testament (Biblia Hebraica) was first definitely established along with the canon in the 1st cent. A.D., later orthographic conventions and grammatical forms (as well as a few Hebraisms) were able to penetrate the text ... (p. 19)

So while giving the Aramaic of Ezra and Daniel in the canonical text the same date, and a late one at that, Beyer still considers the late features to have been introduced into both texts and that both should be classified as having originally been Imperial Aramaic.

[102] Driver's view still finds adherents; see J. Lust, "The Identification of Zerubbabel with Sheshbazzar," 91–95, who understands the Aramaic letters as the composition of the author who "employed the form of a letter as a literary device" (p. 95), but that this does not necessarily entail that the information in the letters is untrustworthy.

his view, it has yet to be shown that this historical kernel exists.[103]

Much of the discussion regarding the authenticity of the official documents in Ezra depends on one's perspective on the character of the narrative as a whole. Torrey gives full weight to the tendentiousness of the text as a whole, which alerts him to the probability that the documents are fictitious. Others, such as de Vaux, Bickerman, and Williamson, consider the *Tendenz* of the text to have not affected its general historical veracity. In response to Torrey the position that the texts are either originals or reworked originals was re-emphasized by de Vaux and Bickerman.[104] They particularly stressed that the authenticity of both the Hebrew and Aramaic edicts of Cyrus in Ezra could be supported by extra-biblical evidence showing that Cyrus pursued a policy of repatriating exiled populations and restoring their indigenous cults. Those supporting the veracity of the Hebrew edict have sought to substantiate by this means not only the permission to rebuild, common to both the Hebrew and Aramaic edicts, but also the other major concern of the Hebrew edict, namely, the repatriation of the exiled Judeans. It is to a consideration of this supposed policy of Cyrus that we now turn.

THE POLICY OF CYRUS

Cyrus's policy of restoring indigenous cults and repatriating exiled peoples is supposedly exemplified by the Cyrus Cylinder.[105] In this Babylonian text, which is commonly dated early in the reign of Cyrus, Cyrus is called by Marduk, the chief deity of the Babylonian

---

[103] Torrey himself considers the Aramaic narrative to come from a hand other than the Chronicler since it does not exhibit the characteristic features of his writing. The Chronicler took up this narrative and incorporated it into his work. It was written around the same time that the Chronicler was at work (for Torrey, that is mid-third century) (*Ezra Studies*, 159–61).

[104] Against Torrey, Batten (*Ezra and Nehemiah*, 60) and Bickerman ("Edict," 98–99) both deal with the problem of the forgery of the Hebrew edict. They ask why the Hebrew edict is not a better forgery; that is, why is it not more closely aligned with the Aramaic edict?

[105] Text: H. C. Rawlinson, *The Cuneiform Inscriptions of Western Asia* (5 vols.; London: British Museum, 1861–91) 5. no. 35; transliteration and translation: F. H. Weissbach, *Die Keilinschriften der Achämeniden* (VAB 3; Leipzig, Hinrichs, 1911) xi, 2–9; re-edition including new fragment: P.-R. Berger, "Der Kyroszylinder mit dem Zusatzfragment BIN II, 32 und die akkadischen Personennamen im Danielbuch," *ZA* 64 (1975) 192–234.

pantheon and the god of Babylon, to redress cultic and civil abnormalities perpetrated by Nabonidus in Ur, Babylon, and other Babylonian cultic cities.[106] Nabonidus's actions had led to the divine abandonment of sanctuaries in Babylonia ("Sumer and Akkad"), and the Babylonian people had languished under his rule (lines 1–12). The text recounts how Marduk chose Cyrus as his king and gave him victory over the Gutians and the Medes, after which Marduk ordered Cyrus against Babylon, accompanying him on the trek and delivering the city into his hands without a military struggle (lines 13–17). In Babylon Cyrus was received as Marduk's legitimate king whereupon he acted as such by instituting social reforms, returning the cultic practices of the Babylonian deities to normality, and undertaking building activities in Babylon (lines 18–45).

The purpose of this text is apologetic. The sovereignty of Marduk over the affairs of Babylonia and neighbouring states, as well as Marduk's concern for the people of Babylonia, figure prominently. The "impious" Nabonidus is thrust aside by Marduk and replaced by a king who properly respects the god of Babylon.[107] In this context

---

[106] It is only assumed that the Cyrus Cylinder is to be dated early in the reign of Cyrus in Babylon, perhaps under the influence of the date formula in Ezr 1:1. There is no further evidence which would allow us to date the "reforms" undertaken by Cyrus as outlined in the Cyrus Cylinder since none of the Babylonian texts which speak of Cyrus's building activity bears a date. The "reforms" recounted in the Cyrus Cylinder may have been telescoped to give the appearance that all were undertaken immediately Cyrus gained the throne of Babylon

[107] The Cyrus Cylinder mentions a number of Nabonidus's cultic improprieties (incorrect offerings; interruption of regular offerings; taking gods from their shrines and bringing them to Babylon: on the last point, cf. M. Weinfeld, "Cult Centralization in Israel in the Light of a Neo-Babylonian Analogy," *JNES* 23 [1964] 202–12; P.-A. Beaulieu, *The Reign of Nabonidus, King of Babylon 556–539 B.C.* [Yale Near Eastern Researches 10; New Haven/London: Yale University Press, 1989] 221–24), and describes him as "the king who did not worship him [Marduk]" (line 17). Further disregard for Marduk is displayed in Nabonidus's non-attendance for many years at the *akītu* festival at which he had royal functions to fulfil (this is mentioned in the Nabonidus Chronicle ii. 5ff., 10ff., 19ff., 23ff.; see Grayson, *Assyrian and Babylonian Chronicles*, 106–08). The equally tendentious Verse Account of Nabonidus (S. Smith, *Babylonian Historical Texts Relating to the Capture and Downfall of Babylon* [London: Methuen, 1924] 110–18) reiterates many of the same complaints levelled against Nabonidus in the Cyrus Cylinder and adds to them Nabonidus's elevation of Sin to preeminence. These texts re-establish Marduk as the head of the pantheon and justify the ousting of Nabonidus by Cyrus. For a critical assessment of these sources and Nabonidus's religious activities, see W. von Soden, "Kyros und Nabonid. Propaganda und Gegenpropaganda," in *Kunst, Kultur und Geschichte*, 61–8; Beaulieu, *The Reign of Nabonidus*, 43–65, 214–19; A. Kuhrt, "Nabonidus and the Babylonian Priesthood," in *Pagan Priests: Religion and Power in the Ancient World* (ed. M. Beard and J. North; Ithaca: Cornell University Press, 1990) 119–155.

the text seeks to legitimate Cyrus's capture of Babylon and his assumption of the kingship of Babylon. Although a foreigner, he was specially selected by Marduk to liberate Babylon from the distress and disorder occasioned by Nabonidus's reign. His legitimacy is further evidenced not only in the manner in which he captured the city, where he is shown to be not a foreign despot or usurper since he enters Babylon as its liberator or as though he were already its king, but also in his treatment of the people and gods of Babylon. In contrast to Nabonidus, Cyrus reveres Marduk and complies with his will, restoring the city to cultic and social normalcy, bringing the people and gods much sought-after relief.

Interest in this text for those arguing for the authenticity of the biblical edicts ascribed to Cyrus lies in Cyrus's treatment of the Babylonian cults, which is held to display not only a tolerance of these indigenous deities but also active support for them. Thus, in lines 33–34 of the Cyrus Cylinder, Cyrus redresses Nabonidus's cultic infraction mentioned in line 10, namely, his removing the Babylonian deities from their shrines and bringing them into Babylon, by returning them to their own sanctuaries. Cyrus is not only at pains to restore to normalcy the cults of "the gods of Sumer and Akkad" (line 33) but also those of deities further afield:

> . . . from [. . .]x,[108] Assur and Susa, Agade, Eshnunna, Zamban (Zabban), Meturnu, (and) Der up to the territory of the land of Guti, the cult centres on the other side of the Tigris whose sanctuaries were abandoned long ago,[109] the gods who dwelt therein I returned to their place and installed in a permanent sanctuary. I gathered together all their people and returned (them) to their settlements. (lines 30b–32)

---

[108] "[Ninev]eh" has been the commonly suggested restoration here, but now I. Finkel, "No Nineveh in the Cyrus Cylinder," *Nouvelles assyriologiques brèves et utilitaires* 1997/23, states that the very few traces do "not fit with any of the known writings of Nineveh, and thus the proposed reading may now be safely excluded".

[109] *ša ištu panāma*(!) *nadû šubassunu* has commonly been been translated "whose sanctuaries were abandoned long ago". Other possible translations are "whose sancturaries were established long ago" (cf. *CAD* N/1 s.v. *nadû* 2 b) 1', p. 83, parsing the verb as a G stative), or "whose sanctuaries became dilapidated long ago". In favour of "whose sanctuaries were established long ago" may be the use of the N preterite in line 10 (*ša innadû šubassunu*) to denote the abandonment of shrines by the Babylonian deities (*ilū āšib libbišunu īzību atmanšun*—line 9) cf. S. Langdon, *Die neubabylonischen Königsinschriften* (VAB 4; Leipzig: Hinrichs, 1912) Nbn 8 x 13, where *ša innadû 54 šanati* apparently means "which was in ruins fifty-four years", but here the translation "was abandoned" for the N preterite of *nadû* is possible. The common way the dilapidation of shrines is spoken of in Neo-Babylonian royal inscrip-

But does this text in fact support a policy of Cyrus regarding the *general* restoration of indigenous cults and the repatriation of exiled peoples, one that would also include the Jerusalem cult of Yahweh and his devotees? Amélie Kuhrt has made a number of helpful observations regarding the Cyrus Cylinder generally and the question of Cyrus's supposed policy in particular.[110] She notes, following Harmatta, that the text is a type of Mesopotamian building inscription, bearing a close relationship to texts of this genre written in the reign of Assurbanipal.[111] It is exclusively devoted to the god Marduk and the return to cultic and civil normalcy in the region over which Marduk and the members of his pantheon presided. Affairs in the city of Babylon in particular figure prominently. In regard to the repatriation of peoples mentioned in the passage quoted above, she notes that:

> nowhere in the text are there any remarks concerning a general return or releasing of deportees or exiled communities; the passage that has frequently been taken to indicate this (with such important consequences) is in lines 30–32; but in fact what is stated there is that the 'gods' (presumably statues) of *specified* places together with their people are returned to their (sc. the gods') original dwelling-places. The places listed are interesting as the majority relate to locations which are very close to, or even in, Babylonia, and whose deities in most cases would

---

tions is *ša ištu ūm rūqūti . . . innamûma* (for references see *CAD* N/1 s.v. *namû* 4 a), p. 252). *ša ištu ūm rūqūti* is paralleled by *ša ištu panāma* in line 31 of the Cyrus Cylinder, but it may be significant that *nadû* is the verb used rather than *namû*. The translation "which were abandoned long ago" makes good sense with *ana ašrišunu utērma* "I returned to their place" in line 32.

[110] A. Kuhrt, "The Cyrus Cylinder and Achaemenid Imperial Policy," *JSOT* 25 (1983) 83–97.

[111] Kuhrt, "Cyrus Cylinder," 88, 91–92. J. Harmatta, "The Literary Pattern of the Babylonian Edict of Cyrus," *AcAnt* 19 (1971) 217–31 (French translation in *Commémoration Cyrus*, 1. 22–49), recognized certain literary connections with inscriptions of Assurbanipal, a position which is seemingly supported by the reference to Assurbanipal as "a king who preceded me" in the Yale fragment edited by Berger (line 43). It appears likely that the Cyrus Cylinder is not directly dependent on Assurbanipal texts but that it stands in the same literary tradition as a number of Nabonidus's building inscriptions (especially Langdon, *Die neubabylonischen Königsinschriften*, Nbn 8) which also exhibit formal features in common with Assurbanipal texts. That is to say, that before Cyrus arrived in Babylon there was already a Babylonian literary tradition which was influenced by Assyrian royal inscriptions and that this was not introduced by Cyrus out of respect for Assurbanipal. On the likelihood that Esarhaddon was responsible for its introduction, see B. N. Porter, *Images, Power, and Politics: Figurative Aspects of Esarhaddon's Babylonian Policy* (Memoirs of the American Philosophical Society 208; Independence Square, PA: American Philosophical Association, 1993).

actually have held a place in the Babylonian pantheon—this must certainly be true of places such as Nineveh, Akkad, Esnunna, Meturnu, and Der even if it is less clear for the others. With the re-establishment of these cults in their home cities the passage connects the returning of Babylonian deities to their own cities from Babylon; that is to say, the emphasis in lines 30–34 is on previous long neglect and the re-establishing of the *norm* in terms of cultic correctness.[112]

In regard to the rebuilding of sanctuaries, a concern of both biblical edicts, Kuhrt states:

> Whether Cyrus ever actually 'restored' any cults is quite unclear and to some extent the answer to this question depends on an evaluation of the effect of Nabonidus' religious reforms on the Babylonian cities; it is possible that some kind of restoration of normal cult-practice, disrupted by the fall of the Assyrian empire, was also envisaged . . . But such a restoration does not appear to have been carried out; the emphasis in the relevant passages of the cylinder is not on the actual restoration of cults but on the re-establishment of a *normal*, i.e. *correct*, state of affairs—a literary device used to underline the piety of Cyrus as opposed to the blasphemy of Nabonidus.[113]

While the Cyrus Cylinder does not explicitly mention the restoration of sanctuaries, other foundation deposits attest that as a pious Babylonian king Cyrus undertook restoration work on shrines at Ur and Uruk.[114] The fragment of the Cyrus Cylinder edited by Berger shows Cyrus fulfilling his royal duties by undertaking building projects in Babylon on the city and quay walls and constructing elaborate doors (lines 38–43). Whether or not Cyrus undertook restoration work at the sites named in lines 30–32 remains unknown.[115]

---

[112] Kuhrt, "Cyrus Cylinder," 87–88 (author's emphasis).

[113] Kuhrt, "Cyrus Cylinder," 93 (author's emphasis).

[114] At Ur: Gadd and Legrain, *Ur Excavation Texts I*, nos. 194 and 307 (the royal name is lost on the latter, but it is commonly ascribed to Cyrus). At Uruk: A. Schott in J. Jordan, *Erster Vorläufiger Bericht über die von der Notgemeinschaft der Deutschen Wissenschaft in Uruk-Warka unternommenen Ausgrabungen* (Abhandlung der Preussischen Akademie der Wissenschaften Jahrgang 1929. Phil.-Hist. Klasse. 7; Berlin: Akademie der Wissenschaft, 1930) Taf. 31, no. 31; Weissbach, *Die Keilinschriften der Achämeniden*, 8, b. In these texts Cyrus is cast as a Babylonian king either by stated deference to the Babylonian deities or by virtue of his titulary.

[115] Confusion over whether or not Cyrus restored these shrines centres on the translation of *ušarmâ šubat dārâti* in line 32. A. L. Oppenheim, *ANET*, 316, translates this as "established for them permanent sanctuaries" which some commentators have understood to denote the restoration (that is, rebuilding) of the shrines; so, explicitly, Clines, *Ezra, Nehemiah, Esther*, 37, although many others assume this

The Cyrus Cylinder displays a limited geographical purview and focuses on Marduk and the cults of Babylonian deities, emphasizing Cyrus's role as a legitimate Babylonian king responsible for the care and maintenance of local cultic affairs, a monarch who fulfils the will of Marduk. It is thus not a manifesto for a general policy regarding indigenous cults and their worshippers throughout the empire. Does it, however, suggest a principle with which Cyrus operated elsewhere in the empire? Kuhrt tentatively suggests that:

> Cyrus followed a policy similar to that of some earlier Assyrian rulers, whereby cities occupying a key-position in troublesome areas or areas where there was likely to be international conflict had their privileges and/or exempt status reinstated and guaranteed by the central government.[116]

---

interpretation. While *ušarmâ šubat dārâti* and analogous clauses (such as *ušarmâ šubassun zīrtim/ṣīrtim; ušarmâ šubassu/n; ušarmâ parak dārâti*) almost exclusively appear in royal inscriptions in the context of temple restoration, the clause refers to the reintroduction or installation of the deity (statue) in the temple. It occurs after the account of the rebuilding is complete; it does not itself denote the rebuilding. This meaning is borne out by clauses such as *ina parakkēšunu ušarmû šubat dārâti* "I settled (the deities) in a lasting abode on their cult stands" (Borger, *Asarhaddon*, §27 ep. 3, 26f.), which must refer to replacing the cult statue on its dais or in the cella, not the construction of such. Also, in M. Streck, *Assurbanipal und die letzten assyrischen Könige bis zum Untergange Nineveh's* (3 vols.; VAB 7/1–3; Leipzig: J. C. Hinrichs, 1916) 2. 58, col. VI, 124 // p. 220, c), 35, the clause *ušarmâ šubat dārâti* is used in speaking of the return of a cult statue of Nanai from exile in Elam. No mention is made of restoring the shrine, only the deity is reinstalled in the shrine. For examples of this and related clauses in royal inscriptions where it appears after the restoration of the shrine, see A. Ungnad, "Schenkungsurkunde des Kurigalzu mâr Kadašman-Harbe," *Archiv für Keilschriftforschung* 1 (1923) 19, lines 17f.; Borger, *Asarhaddon*, §11 ep. 32, 16f., 41; §27 ep. 3, 26f.; §47, 20f.; §48, 14; §49, 14; §50, 16; Streck, *Assurbanipal* 2. 146, col. X, 16; p. 216, K 3065; Langdon, *Die neubabylonischen Königsinschriften*, Nbk 16 i 32; Nbk 20 iii 21f.; Nbn 1 i 22; Nbn 8 x 9; CT 34 28, 61. The Cyrus Cylinder thus uses a well-attested idiom from Assyrian and Babylonian royal inscriptions to say that Cyrus reinstalled in their respective shrines certain cult statues which he found in Babylon, thus conforming to a longstanding tradition of royal responsibility to the gods.

It is also unclear whether or not the shrines in Babylonia ("Sumer and Akkad") were in need of restoration. Against the interpretation that *ša innadû šubassunu* in line 10 of the Cylinder means that the shrines were in ruins are lines 33–34 where Cyrus redresses Nabonidus's cultic infractions. There is no mention of the restoration of the Babylonian shrines. This is the place in the text where it would most naturally have been mentioned; cf. Langdon, *Die neubabylonischen Königsinschriften*, Nbn 8 x, which similarly mentions the commissioning of the king (Nabonidus) to renew shrines and the return of cult statues to shrines that are said to have been destroyed, but also includes some attention to aspects of the rebuilding work undertaken.

[116] Kuhrt, "Cyrus Cylinder," 93.

The Jerusalem cult of Yahweh, in a city strategically situated on the
land-bridge joining Mesopotamia with Egypt, may thus have also
received beneficence from Cyrus for political reasons.[117] Cyrus's normalization of cultic affairs in both Babylonia and Judah would then
be viewed not as a new initiative but rather as the adoption of an
earlier policy pursued by certain Neo-Assyrian monarchs which engen-
dered favour with devotees of the indigenous cult while simultaneously expressing the authority of the great king over local cultic
affairs.[118] Later Achaemenid kings generally continued to support

---

[117] De Vaux, "Decrees," 78. On the permission for repatriation and rebuilding
as part of a wider policy to strengthen the defence of the Levant, see M. Durand,
"La défence du front mediterranéen de l'empire achéménide," in *The Role of the
Phoenicians in the Interaction of Mediterranean Civilizations* (ed. W. A. Ward; Beirut:
American University, 1968) 43–51.

[118] Neo-Assyrian royal inscriptions not only speak of the normalization and regulation of Assyro-Babylonian cults and cult centres but also have a number of references to the repatriation of captured foreign deities (that is, deities from outside
the Assyro-Babylonian cultural sphere) and the re-establishment of regular offerings
and income for these foreign cults; see Borger, *Asarhaddon*, §11 ep. 36, 5–11; §21,
7f.; §27 ep. 3, 23–26; §27 ep. 14, 6–16; §27 ep. 17, 46b–48; §47, 22–23 (// A. Goetze,
"Esarhaddon's Inscriptions from the Inanna Temple in Nippur," *JCS* 17 [1963]
130, line 11); §53, obv. 37; §65, rev. 4–5; Streck, *Assurbanipal*, 2. 132, B vii 98; pp.
222–24, K. 3405, lines 8, 14, and 18 (transliteration and translation in Cogan,
Imperialism and Religion, 16). For a discussion of the purpose of this policy; see Cogan,
Imperialism and Religion, 15–17, 29–30, 35–41; H. Spieckermann, *Juda unter Assur in
der Sargonidenzeit* (FRLANT 129; Göttingen: Vandenhoeck & Ruprecht, 1982) 354–62;
M. Cogan, "Judah Under Assyrian Hegemony: A Re-examination of *Imperialism and
Religion*," *JBL* 112 (1993) 403–14. Only two texts speak of the restoration of the
shrines of foreign gods—Borger, *Asarhaddon*, §27, ep. 3, 24f. and L. D. Levine, *Two
Neo-Assyrian Stelae from Iran* (Royal Ontario Museum Art and Archaeology Occasional
Paper 23; Ontario: The Royal Ontario Museum, 1972) 40 line 44 (Sargon). None
of these texts mentions the repatriation of exiled peoples along with their deities.
This is a privilege for Babylonian shrines only; see G. Widengren, "Yahweh's
Gathering of the Dispersed," 234–38.
    In Neo-Babylonian texts there is only one reference to the repatriation of for-
eign gods: Grayson, *Assyrian and Babylonian Chronicles*, 88, Chronicle 2, lines 16–17
(Nabopolassar returned deities to Susa). Neo-Babylonian royal inscriptions after
Nabopolassar do not refer to the return of foreign deities. The focus of these texts
is on the the cults of Assyro-Babylonian deities. Langdon, *Die neubabylonischen
Königsinschriften*, Nbk 19, B ix 31–32 speak of the repatriation of people who lived
in the Lebanon region, but no mention is made of either local deities or cult places.
The Cyrus Cylinder, with its emphasis on Mesopotamian cult centres, bears close
similarities to many of the Neo-Assyrian royal inscriptions and to the inscriptions
of Nebuchadnezzar and Nabonidus.
    On similarities between Cyrus's and earlier Assyrian treatment of subjugated peo-
ples, see also R. J. van der Spek, "Did Cyrus the Great Introduce a New Policy
Towards Subdued Nations? Cyrus in Assyrian Perspective," *Persica* 10 (1982) 279–82;
idem, "Cyrus de Pers in Assyrisch perspectief. Een vergelijking tussen de Assyrische

indigenous cults in Babylonia, Egypt, Asia Minor and Judah as an expression of their legitimate rule over these areas. De Vaux cites the examples of Cambyses and Darius with the cult of Neith in Egypt as portrayed in the Udjahorresne biography; Darius's codification of Egyptian laws (including cultic laws); and Darius's taxation concession to the cultic officials of Apollo in the Gadatas inscription, among others.[119] He does not neglect to point out that these Achaemenid rulers also undertook actions against indigenous cults, destroying temples and withdrawing their income.[120] De Vaux de-emphasizes the latter activities, preferring to stress the positive aspects

---

en Perzische politiek ten opzichte van onderworpen volken," *Tijdschrift voor Geschiedenis* 96 (1983) 1–27. Ackroyd, "Temple Vessels," 180 n. 2, cites the suggestion of A. Gelston that "the theme of the temple vessels could be regarded as an appropriate Old Testament counterpart of the 'restoring the gods' claimed by the Cyrus Cylinder". Ezr 7:19 perhaps alludes to the return of other temple vessels with Ezra.

[119] De Vaux, "Decrees," 71–77. Darius is shown to have paid respect to the Apis bull that died in mid-518, to have had a temple to Amon-Ra constructed at Hibis in the el-Khargeh oasis, to have been active in the temple of Kasr el Ghoueita in the same area, to have had work done at Abusir, and to have granted donations to the temple of Horus at Edfu. On the adoption of Egyptian royal mythology, pharaonic titles and artistic representation, see A. B. Lloyd, "The Inscription of Udjahorresnet, a Collaborator's Testament," *JEA* 68 (1982) 173–75, who rightly understands the Udjahorresne inscription, as well as the respect shown by Cambyses and Darius for Egyptian religion in their search for the new Apis bull, to reflect the desire of these Achaemenid monarchs to be viewed as fulfilling traditional pharaonic roles. Traditional pharaonic titles are given to Cambyses and Darius in the Udjahorresne inscription and to Darius also in the Susa statue (see above n. 94). On the representation of Darius at the Hibis temple, see E. Cruz-Uribe, *Hibis Temple Project* (San Antonio: TX: Van Siclen Books, 1988). For a brief overview of the activities of Cambyses and Darius in Egypt, see E. M. Yamauchi, *Persia and the Bible* (Grand Rapids, MI: Eerdmans, 1990) 95–124, 148–54; on Darius in Egypt see also Dandamaev, *Political History of the Achaemenid Empire*, 141–46.

[120] On these activities see also Kuhrt, "Cyrus Cylinder," 94; J. Wiesehöfer, "Kyros und die unterworfenen Völker. Ein Beitrag zur Entstehung von Geschichtsbewußtsein," *Quaderni di Storia* 26 (1987) 114–118; and on the destruction of shrines after the Ionian revolt, see P. Tozzi, "Per la storia religiosa della politicà religiosa degli Achemenidi. Distruzioni persiane di templi greci agli inizi del V. secolo," *Rivista Storica Italiana* 31 (1978) 18–32. De Vaux focuses on Cambyses's alleged attack on the Apis cult at Memphis (Herodotus iii. 27–38) and other cults (AP 30:13–14), as well as his cutting back on donations to Egyptian temples (on the reverse of the Demotic Chronicle; see W. Spiegelberg, *Die sogenannte Demotische Chronik des pap. 215 der Bibliothèque Nationale zu Paris* [Demotische Studien 7; Leipzig: Hinrichs, 1914]). Much of this negative view of Cambyses is now widely considered to be tendentious and largely unhistorical, see the discussion in A. B. Lloyd, "Herodotus on Cambyses: Some thoughts on Recent Work," in *Achaemenid History III*, 55–66; Yamauchi, *Persia and the Bible*, 115–24; C. Tuplin, "Darius' Suez Canal and Persian Imperialism," in *Achaemenid History VI: Asia Minor and Egypt: Old Cultures in a New Empire* (ed. H. Sancisi-Weerdenburg and A. Kuhrt; Leiden: Nederlands Instituut

of the actions of these kings as reflecting a consistent Achaemenid Persian policy within which the order to rebuild the Jerusalem temple can be set.[121] This position has drawn wide scholarly support; indeed it is commonly supposed that all the Achaemenid Persian kings were in general sympathy with the approach towards indigenous cults instituted by Cyrus.[122]

De Vaux, combining the evidence as he does, regards all subjugated cults as comparable. In this way the treatment of the Babylonian and major Egyptian cults can inform his understanding of Achaemenid Persian attitudes towards the Jerusalem temple. This handling of the evidence is potentially misleading, however. A more nuanced reading would highlight the variegated approach adopted by the Persians

---

voor het Nabije Oosten, 1991) 259–64; cf. L. Depuydt, "Murder in Memphis: The Story of Cambyses's Mortal Wounding of the Apis Bull (*ca.* 523 B.C.E.)," *JNES* 54 (1995) 119–26, for a more positive estimate of Herodotus's narrative. As Kuhrt points out, Persian rulers also pursued a policy of deporting the population (or sections of the population) of territories either initially unwilling to submit to their rule or who proved to be recalcitrant subjects. In this they of course followed the practices of their Neo-Assyrian and Neo-Babylonian predecessors. Mazares, Cyrus's general, "enslaved the people of Priene, and overran the plain of the Meandrus, giving it up to his army to pillage, and Magnesia likewise" (Herodotus i. 161). Enslavement probably entailed deportation. This was the case for the Miletians whom Darius I resettled on the Persian Gulf (Herodotus vi. 19–20) and the Barcaeans who were deported to Bactria (Herodotus iv. 204). Darius also deported Paeonians from Thrace to Phyrigia (Herodotus v. 13–16). The Murašû texts from Babylonia (second half of the fifth century) attest the existence of communities of deportees from Phyrigia, Lydia and India in the vicinity of Nippur. Eph'al ("Western Minorities," 82–83) notes, "It is clear that few people from Western Anatolia and India would have arrived in Babylonia prior to the campaigns of the Achaemenid kings to these lands. Thus . . . [the evidence of the Murašû archive] may attest to the fact that the Achaemenid kings also deported ethnic groups and settled them in the arable region of Nippur". The establishment of these communities could have commenced under Darius I, however the evidence does not permit certainty on this point

[121] "If we . . . consider all three reigns [Cyrus, Cambyses, Darius I] together in the context of the Empire as a whole, we can safely say that this benevolence was general and continuous. There is no reason at all why the Jews should have been excluded from the benefits of this liberal policy" (De Vaux, "Decrees," 78).

[122] This view has found its way into many of the textbooks on Achaemenid Persia and Israelite/Judean history. Xerxes has been viewed as an exception due to the "daiva" inscription in which he says he destroyed the shrines of "the demons" (*daivadana-*) in order to institute the worship of Ahura Mazda there (E. Herzfeld, *Altpersische Inschriften* [Archaeologische Mitteilungen aus Iran Ergänzungsband 1; Berlin: Reimer, 1938] no. 14). This text has to do with the suppression of rebellion rather than with intolerance towards the cults of subjugated peoples per se; see Briant, "Polythéismes et empire unitaire," 425–29. Also, Kuhrt and Sherwin-White, "Xerxes' Destruction of Babylonian Temples," 69–79, have shown that Xerxes cannot be viewed as an enemy of Babylonian cults.

towards the cults of subjugated peoples, acknowledging that Cyrus and the rulers who immediately followed him were less than universal in offering beneficence to such cults. It would also recognize that the cults that were beneficiaries differed in both the types of support they received and the bases for that support. As Kuhrt outlines:

> In the realm of religion, too, the Persian kings did *not* simply let everyone do what they wished. In Egypt and Babylonia, they were careful to appear as active upholders of local cults in order to ensure control of the wealthy sanctuaries and the adherence of their staff. In smaller centres, such as Jerusalem and Magnesia-on-the-Maeander, they granted some privileges to the temples, because they acknowledged the support their gods had given the Persians. . . . Conversely, the shrines of people who had rebelled could be, and were, destroyed.[123]

This draws attention to the fact that the Achaemenid Persian rulers saw their interests as best served by differentiating between major political/cultural entities, such as Babylonia and Egypt, and minor political/cultural entities, such as Judah and Magnesia on the Meander. To the first group the Persian king was represented as a legitimate, local ruler. In Babylonia, as noted above, Cyrus became the king of Babylon who was called by Marduk to institute justice and cultic normalcy, a common theme in Babylonian literary expressions of legitimate kingship. In Egypt, Cambyses and Darius were represented both textually and artistically in traditional pharaonic terms, fulfilling traditional pharaonic duties. The Persians may have been foreigners in Egypt and Babylonia, but they stressed political legitimacy through continuity with and conformity to cultural norms. In short, they acted like native rulers and called themselves such. By comparison, in Judah, Magnesia on the Meander, and other "smaller centres" such as the Phoenician city-states, the Persian kings did not adopt the role and titulary of the indigenous monarchy. Instead, they behaved like rulers of an empire within which these smaller polities resided; in respect of Syro-Palestinian polities at least, they acted as though they were the successors to the rulers of the Neo-Assyrian and Neo-Babylonian empires, which is exactly what they were. Judah was part of the Babylonian empire that Cyrus inherited by conquering the city of Babylon. It would not have had the same standing as

---

[123] A. Kuhrt, *The Ancient Near East c. 3000–330 B.C.* (2 vols.; London/New York: Routledge, 1995) 2. 699 (author's emphasis).

Babylonia in that the latter had been the dominating centre of an empire within which Judah was a subjugated territory. Even if Cyrus construed Judah as lying within some "Greater Babylonia" of which he was now king,[124] as a sub-province within his newly won Babylonian realm Judah was on the periphery both geographically and politically, and this distinguished it from Babylonia and its cults at the centre. It bears repeating that the Cyrus Cylinder and the foundation deposits from Ur and Uruk cannot be cited as evidence for Cyrus's attitude toward the Jerusalem cult of Yahweh as these refer to Babylonian regional cults and peoples only. In these texts Cyrus was keen to be seen as a legitimate Babylonian ruler who restored dilapidated shrines said to have been neglected due to Nabonidus's impiety (whatever the historical accuracy of such claims). Not only was the Jerusalem temple positioned outside the Babylonian "centre", it differed in that it was not a shrine in need of repair out of Nabonidus's (or, more generally, Babylonian) neglect. It certainly lay in ruins, but its condition was the result of a Babylonian invasion prompted by repeated acts of Judean rebellion. As the destroyed shrine of a people who had proven rebellious to imperial rule, the Jerusalem temple of Yahweh would not have been an obvious or natural candidate for restoration under Cyrus. It certainly would not have fallen under any rubric for the restoration of Babylonian temples, and that supposed act of restoration cannot serve as a model for Cyrus's attitude towards the Jerusalem temple. Also, while Cyrus may have restored cults in Babylonia, there is no reason to think that he went to all the subjugated peoples in the former Babylonian empire enquiring after their cultic needs or ensuring that everywhere was in a state of cultic normalcy with their displaced adherents repatriated. There was no political imperative to do so, unlike in Babylonia. Arguably a similar perspective was adopted by Cambyses and Darius when Egypt was brought into the empire. Persian beneficence was politically expedient rather than the result of pious magnanimity, even accepting that the Persians believed the gods of all the subjugated peoples to have called them to rule over their territories. Beneficence towards the cults of subjugated peoples was never equally spread throughout the empire because, quite simply, some territories and the cults found there were more important to the Persians

---

[124] "Babylon and Across-the-River" formed a single satrapy.

than others. So it is improper to speak of an empire-wide or uni-
form policy.

A useful distinction, then, can be made between Babylonia and
Egypt where the Persians saw themselves as adopting the responsibilities of indigenous monarchs, and Syria-Palestine and Asia Minor
where they conducted themselves more as imperial rulers, although
all these areas were part of the Persian empire and were viewed as
subjugated territories. Kuhrt recognizes that the Persians adopted
this attitude towards Babylonia and Egypt as a strategy to facilitate
the smooth running of these important parts of the empire. Although
the evidence is patchy, this discrimination between the cults of subjugated peoples is attested in the form of beneficence received by
those of arguably less importance or in less politically sensitive places
in comparison with that offered to major (and some minor) shrines
in Babylonia and Egypt. Kuhrt categorizes the former beneficence
as the granting of "some privileges", while with the latter Persian
rulers acted as "upholders of local cults". That is to say, in the latter case they could be considered patrons of the cults, whereas in
the former case they were something less.[125] What this meant in
practice is that smaller centres received less: they were offered tax

---

[125] Categorizing the relationship between the Achaemenid Persians rulers and
these "lesser cults" remains problematic. On one level they guarded the rights of
these sanctuaries against encroachments by Persian administrative officials (witness
the Gadates inscription and Darius's response to Tattenai's inquiry in Ezr 6). Single
acts of donation to cults are also attested as an expression of good will and to win
favour (Herodotus vi. 97; cf. Ezr 7:21–22 as a grant). Rather than interfering in
how these cults were run, the Persians may have been quite "hands-off", leaving
them to their own devices under indigenous leadership. The Xanthos trilingual may
offer a case in point (see above n. 65), as may the Pherendates correspondence (see
below pp. 197–98). The so-called Passover Papyrus from Elephantine (AP 21) is
thought by some to reflect royal intervention in a religious matter, namely, when
and how the Jewish garrison should observe Passover. But as J. Wiesehöfer,
"'Reichsgesetz' oder 'Einzelfallgerechtigkeit'? Bemerkungen zu P. Freis These von
achaimenidischen 'Reichsautorisation'," *ZABR* 1 (1995) 41–42, rightly notes, the
administrative concern was with the smooth running of the garrison and the impact
the festival might have on that. He writes, "Ziel königlichen Eingreifens ist also
nicht die offizielle Verkündigung der Passahvorschriften als *religiöser* Bestimmungen,
sondern die Gewährleistung der Vereinbarkeit von Kultus und Dienst, von erwün-
schter Glaubenspraxis und angeordneter Verteidigungsbereitschaft" (p. 42; author's
emphasis). Impinging on this matter is consideration of the extent to which the
Persian administration involved itself in cultic appointments and concerned itself
with the regulation (codification) of cultic law. "Lesser cults" also existed in Egypt,
among which the temple of Yahweh at Elephantine should be included (further on
which see below).

privileges, such as that accorded the cult of Apollo at Magnesia on the Meander and the Jerusalem cult of Yahweh under Artaxerxes (Ezr 7:24), while the more important centres were the direct recipients of largesse for building and cultic offerings. Patronage did not preclude the regulation and economic exploitation of these major shrines, however.[126]

What then should be made of the claim, made in both Cyrus's Aramaic edict (Ezr 6:4) and Darius's response to Tattenai's query (Ezr 6:8–10), that the Achaemenid Persian administration was to fund the reconstruction of the Jerusalem temple of Yahweh and to meet the costs of its sacrificial cult? Here a useful comparison can be made between the rebuilding of the Jerusalem temple and the (re)establishment of three other "minor" shrines, one of them Jewish. The temple of Yaho at Elephantine had been destroyed by "Egyptian and other troops" (AP 30:4–8) in 410 and Jewish community leaders sought permission to rebuild it. The eventual support for the petition from officials in Judah and Samaria (AP 32) does not include any mention of imperial funding for the temple or offerings, it mentions only what types of offerings were to be permitted.[127] One must conclude that the costs for both the rebuilding and the regular offerings were to be met by the Jewish community itself. That the local community took financial responsibility for its cult is explicit in the second example, the Xanthos trilingual inscription (dating to the mid-fourth century) in which the "citizens" gave a land grant to the cult they were establishing, committed themselves to the annual funding of cultic personnel (and sacrifices?), and offered a tax concession

---

[126] See M. A. Dandamaev, "State and Temple in Babylonia in the First Millennium B.C.," in *State and Temple Economy in the Ancient Near East*, 2.589–98; M. A. Dandamaev and V. Lukonin, *The Culture and Social Institutions of Ancient Iran* (trans. P. L. Kohl with D. J. Dadson; Cambridge: Cambridge University Press, 1989) 362–65; Tuplin, "Darius' Suez Canal," 259–70.

[127] Why Bagohi and Delaiah, the governor of Judah and the son of the governor of Samaria respectively, were involved by the Elephantine Jewish community in their quest to gain permission to rebuild remains a point of contention. Perhaps the administration viewed Egyptian Jews as under the jurisdiction of Judah/Samaria (together?) in religious matters, or perhaps the Elephantine Jews hoped these officials could exert influence over Arsames, the satrap of Egypt; see Porten, *Archives from Elephantine*, 293 n. 29; Briant, "Poythéismes et empire unitaire," 432–33; J. Mélèze Modrzejewski, *The Jews of Egypt: From Ramses II to Emperor Hadrian* (trans. R. Cornman; Edinburgh: T&T Clark, 1995) 40–43; P. Schäfer, *Judeophobia: Attitudes towards the Jews in the Ancient World* (Princeton: Princeton University Press, 1997) 130.

to the priest.[128] No mention is made of any involvement by the Achaemenid Persian administration in the cult, neither is mention made of the costs for building the shrine. One can deduce from the texts that these costs were also assumed by the community. Something similar seems to have obtained at Teima in Arabia in the mid- to late fifth century, the third example for comparison. KAI 228 is a cult foundation stele from Teima establishing a grant of palms for the cult of a new deity in order to support its priest.[129] Whether this is a land grant or the grant of the produce from the groves need not detain us here. The donors are said to have been three deities with already existing local cults that obtained income from (their own?) estates and from "the property of the king". Although the beginning of the stele is fragmentary, it appears that it was within the power of these cults to dispose of their income from these estates and to share some of it with the newcomer. There is no evidence that they had been ordered to do so by some higher administrative authority; it is a local community-level decision. Accepting that local cults had the power to dispose of "the property of the king" (שימתא זי מלכא; KAI 228:18–19), would this not show that the king was a patron of such minor cults since his palms provided them with a regular income? The problem here is determining the referent of "king". It most probably refers to the local Arab (Lihyanite) ruler, designated "king" in another inscription, who was a client of the Persian Great King.[130] This second inscription dedicates a new shrine

---

[128] On the Xanthos trilingual see n. 65 above; A. Lemaire, "The Xanthos Trilingual Revisited," in *Solving Riddles and Untying Knots: Biblical, Epigraphic, and Semitic Studies in Honor of Jonas C. Greenfield* (ed. Z. Zevit, S. Gitin and M. Sokoloff; Winona Lake, IN: Eisenbrauns, 1995) 423–32.

[129] For this text see also J. C. L. Gibson, *Textbook of Syrian Semitic Inscriptions* (3 vols.; Oxford: Clarendon, 1971–82) 2.148–51. F. M. Cross, "A New Aramaic Stele from Tayma'," *CBQ* 48 (1986) 394, would date the stele to the early fourth century.

[130] The other inscription is a dedication stele dated to c. 400 and published in A. Livingstone et al., "Taima': Recent Soundings and New Inscribed Material," *Atlal* 7 (1983) 108–111 + pl. 96. For a discussion of this text, see Cross, "New Aramaic Stele," 387–94; K. Beyer and A. Livingstone, "Die neuesten aramäischen Inschriften aus Taima," *Zeitschrift der deutschen morgenländischen Gesellschaft* 137 (1987) 286–88. On the administration of this region, see W. J. Dumbrell, "The Tell El-Maskhuta Bowls and the 'Kingdom' of Qedar," *BASOR* 203 (1971) 33–44; Cross, "New Aramaic Stele," 387–94; E. A. Knauf, "The Persian Administration in Arabia," *Transeu* 2 (1990) 201–17; D. F. Graf, "The Origin of the Nabataeans," *ARAM Periodical* 2 (1990) 48–50; idem, "Arabia During Achaemenid Times, " in *Achaemenid History IV: Centre and Periphery* (ed. H. Sancisi-Weerdenburg and A. Kuhrt; Leiden:

in Taima that had been built by a local official and may also include
the donation of an estate for the maintenance of the cult.[131] The
funding for the cults of Taima should then be seen as a local matter and not involve the imperial administration.

It is such examples of smaller, less significant shrines, rather than
the major shrines of Babylonia and Egypt, that should inform our
understanding of Achaemenid Persian attitudes towards the Jerusalem
temple. The evidence from Elephantine, Xanthos and Teima points
to the likely conclusion that the costs for the rebuilding of the
Jerusalem temple were to be met by the Judean community, as Ezr
1–3 and Haggai presume. It may also be noteworthy that according to Ezr 5 (and Hag 1:8) the Judeans commenced work on the
temple in the reign of Darius I in advance of any funds being issued
by the Achaemenid Persian administration, which may reflect the
Judeans' understanding that they themselves were responsible for
undertaking the work and meeting its costs. Williamson considers
the imperial funding for the rebuilding spoken of in Ezr 6:4, 8 to
have actually "taken the form of an allowance against tax due",
which, while historically more likely than the Achaemenid Persian
administration making direct payments for the project, seems to go

Nederlands Instituut voor het Nabije Oosten, 1990) 140–41; Lemaire, "Populations
et territoires," 45–54.
    In line 3 of this stele Cross reads לחין {ז} מ]ל[ך [מ] "king of Lihyan", while Knauf
translates "kings of Lihyan" (apparently reading מלכי לחין, following the editio prin-
ceps). Beyer and Livingstone translate מלכי לחין as "des königlichen Beamten von
Lihyan", that is, the official representing the king of Lihyan who was serving in
Taima (similarly, K. Dijkstra, *Life and Loyalty: A Study in the Socio-Religious Culture of
Syria and Mesopotamia in the Graeco-Roman Period Based on Epigraphical Evidence* [Religions
in the Graeco-Roman World 128; Leiden/New York/Cologne: E. J. Brill, 1995]
248). Beyer and Livingstone's translation opens up the possibility of reading מלכא
in KAI 228:19 as "royal official", but I accept, following Cross and Knauf, that in
both texts (א)מלכ should be translated "king". Knauf, "Persian Administration in
Arabia," 206, considers the king in question to be the Persian king and he understands שימתא in KAI 228:18 to refer to "treasury, depository, tax collection office"
(after Palestinian Aramaic and Syriac *śimta*), not an estate.
    [131] Beyer and Livingstone, "Die neuesten aramäischen Inschriften," 286–86, trans-
late מרחבה [ה]קים...בי]ת צ[לם זי רב ומרחבה (lines 2–4) as "errichtete ... den Tempel des
Salm von Rabb und seine Weite", מרחבה referring to the temple domain. There
are other possibilities for interpretation, as they admit; and Cross, "New Aramaic
Stele," 390, 392, reads ארחבה, which he understands to be the name of a deity.
Dijkstra, *Life and Loyalty*, 248, follows the reading of Beyer and Livingstone, trans-
lating it as "its extension(?)" and acknowledges that "the exact meaning of *mrhbh* is
obscure".

against the plain sense of the text.[132] Such extensive payments for the purposes of rebuilding and maintaining the Jerusalem cult are unknown in other contemporary biblical sources, were not granted to other minor cults, and were most likely never granted. Williamson sees parallels in the Persepolis fortification tablets and the Persepolis treasury tablets for maintaining the Jerusalem cult from the imperial treasury.[133] While largely dealing with a circumscribed geographical area (a sizeable region surrounding Persepolis that constituted the heartland of Persia), and focusing almost exclusively on Iranian and Elamite cults and the *lan*-sacrifice, a ceremony which Heidemarie Koch sees as an expression of the official state religion, more telling is the rather small amounts that were generally paid.[134] There is nothing approaching Ezr 6:9—"And whatever is needed in the way of bullocks, rams, and sheep for the burnt offerings to the God of Heaven, or wheat, salt, wine, or oil as requested by the priests in Jerusalem is to be given to them daily without fail"—in these texts. While conceding that Darius may have conceivably financed the day-to-day running of the temple out of satrapal revenues (a questionable proposition to my mind), Blenkinsopp quite properly notes that:

> it is highly unlikely that the subsidy would be practically on demand. . . . We must also ask whether Darius would have absolved a subject people in advance and in perpetuity of any wrongdoing, making use of sanctions to protect them from the consequences of possible future rebellion.[135]

---

[132] Williamson, *Ezra, Nehemia*, 81; cf. Japhet, "Temple in the Restoration Period," 220–21, who suggests that the reason why Tattenai investigated the temple rebuilding was because the Judeans were withholding taxes to pay for it.

[133] H. G. M. Williamson, "Ezra and Nehemiah in the Light of the Texts from Persepolis," *Bulletin for Biblical Research* 1 (1991) 50–54.

[134] On the tablets, see C. Tuplin, "The Administration of the Achaemenid Empire," in *Coinage and Administration in the Athenian and Persian Empires* (ed. I. Carradice; BAR International Series 343; Oxford: British Archaeological Reports, 1987) 115–16, 130–31, 139; G. Aperghis, "The Persepolis Fortification Tablets—Another Look," in *Studies in Persian History* (ed. M. Brosius and A. Kuhrt) 35–62. On the donations, see also H. Koch, *Die religiösen Verhältnisse der Dareizeit: Untersuchungen an Hand der elamischen Persepolistäfelchen* (Göttinger Orientforschungen III/4; Wiesbaden: Harrassowitz, 1977); Dandamaev and Lukonin, *Culture and Social Institutions*, 339–42. Questioning the *lan*-sacrifice as an expression of state religion is M. Handley-Schachler, "The *lan* Ritual in the Persepolis Fortification Texts," in *Studies in Persian History* (ed. M. Brosius and A. Kuhrt) 195–204 (esp. pp. 201–202 commenting on Koch).

[135] Blenkinsopp, *Ezra, Nehemiah*, 127, commenting on sanctions mentioned Ezr 6:11–12. Ezr 7:22 is similar in recounting Persian generosity, on which see Blenkinsopp's comments, *Ezra, Nehemiah*, 150.

The claim in Ezr 6 to such generous beneficence is tendentious. At best it is an overstatement, perhaps made due to the writer's pro-Persian proclivity, or reflecting the myth of early Persian beneficence.[136] Perhaps it is an outcome of simple cultic aggrandizement: the conviction that the Jerusalem cult of Yahweh was not some minor cult but was recognized by the Persians as being of great importance, with the Great Kings as patrons.[137] At this point, at least, the Aramaic edict is arguably suspect. What then of Cyrus's granting permission to rebuild?

Commonly, while patronage depended on the economic and political significance of the cult, one basis for beneficence to less significant cults would seem to have been overt support for and continued fidelity to the empire and its ruler. Rebellious peoples were quashed and their cults destroyed, but submissive peoples were rewarded for their service. The Gadatas inscription, in which Darius states that by extracting taxes from the temple lands of Apollo Gadatas was "ignoring the sentiments of my ancestors toward the god who spoke the truth to the Persians",[138] offers a reason why Cyrus granted tax privileges to this cult—it was supportive of him. Reflecting on the privilege granted, Briant plausibly supposes that "lors de la conquête de l'Asie Minuere, Cyrus avait noué de bon rapports avec les prêtres qui, en échange, avaient obtenu une immunité fiscal"; a privilege upheld by Darius.[139] This form of beneficence may indeed offer a parallel to the treatment of the Jerusalem cult of Yahweh under the Achaemenid Persians. As has already been noted, Jeremiah 50–51 and Deutero-Isaiah looked forward to the demise of Babylon, and Deutero-Isaiah saw Cyrus as a legitimate king who was appointed by Yahweh for the task of restoring cultic normalcy in Jerusalem.

---

[136] See Wiesehöfer, "Kyros und die unterworfenen Völker," 107–26, on the myth of Cyrus's benevolence in ancient texts.

[137] Surely in the time of the writer/editor of Ezr 1–6 this support was not forthcoming, and Neh 10 seems to know nothing of it, otherwise there would be no need to organize financial support for the cult.

[138] F. Lochner-Hüttenbach, "Brief des Königs Darius an den Satrapen Gadatas," in *Handbuch des Altpersischen* (ed. W. Brandenstein and M. Mayrhofer; Wiesbaden: Harrasowitz, 1964) 91–98; L. Boffo, "La lettera di Dario a Gadata: I privilegi del tempio di Apolloa Magnesia sul Meandro," *Bulettino dell'Istituto di Diritto Romano, Vittorio Scialoja'* 81 (1978) 267–303; J. Wiesehöfer, "Zur Frage der Echtheit des Dareios-Briefes an Gadatas," *Rheinisches Museum für Philologie* 130 (1986) 396–98.

[139] P. Briant, *Histoire de l'empire perse de Cyrus à Alexandre* (2 vols.; Achaemenid History 10; Leiden: Nederlands Instituut voor het Nabije Oosten, 1996) 1. 508.

There is some reason then to accept the view that on Cyrus's capture of Babylon, or sometime afterwards, it was made known to him that the (Babylonian) Judeans also saw him as their liberator and welcomed him as their divinely chosen ruler.[140] Perhaps on that basis the Judeans were rewarded with permission to rebuild their temple in Jerusalem.[141] This need not have included mass repatriation and may have concerned just a small group returning with the temple vessels, as Galling supposed.

Was this granting of permission to rebuild notable in any way, to be characterized as an act of beneficence? The question is worth considering, particularly if the (re)establishment of minor cults were simply a local affair, a matter for that specific community which did not necessarily need the permission of or funding from the Achaemenid Persian administration. This decision in respect of the Jerusalem temple does seem to have been significant due to the fact that this shrine had been destroyed as a result of rebellion, and so needed special permission to be rebuilt. Judeans had not sought such permission under the Babylonians as such a request was likely to be pointless given their history of rebellion. That special permission was needed for the rebuilding of a destroyed shrine is evident also in texts concerning the temple of the Elephantine Jewish community. Noteworthy here is that the Elephantine Jews did not simply commence rebuilding their shine after it had been destroyed. It is clear that special permission from the administration was needed, but only at the satrapal level (AP 32:2–3 "Say to Arsames" [the satrap of Egypt]), in order to undertake the work. Why could they not have simply begun rebuilding their shine? Because there was a question mark over why it had been destroyed. Temples were usually destroyed as a reprisal for rebellion or some other serious crime, so rebuilding would only have attracted the attention of the satrap who would have questioned its legitimacy. This is exactly what happened in the case of Tattenai in Ezr 5, who, seeing in Jerusalem a destroyed shrine that

---

[140] Kuhrt, "Nabonidus," 144–46, considers Deutero-Isaiah to have been written after Cyrus's capture of Babylon. Like the Cyrus Cylinder and the Verse Account of Nabonidus, Deutero-Isaiah's prophecies "too might well be exhortations to loyalty to the new Persian conqueror rather than subversive propaganda predating his victory" (p. 145).

[141] It may have been an initiative of the Judeans in Babylonia, as Williamson, *Ezra, Nehemiah,* 11, suggests, but that does not mean that the Hebrew edict is the outcome. See also AP 30 as another example of a request, which is discussed below.

had for all intents and purposes lain in desuetude for seventy years, was concerned to find out why it was being rebuilt and by whose authority. At Elephantine there had been a history of strife between the Jews and the priests of Khnum, whose shrines were neighbouring. Whether it was due to the offence of animal sacrifice or competition over land, the Khnum priests obtained the support of the local governor and his troops to demolish the temple of Yahweh.[142] On one level, then, the matter looked like conflict between cults, which the Achaemenid Persian administration would have sought to avoid in all circumstances. It is noteworthy that after the destruction of the shrine in 410, no administrative officials were concerned to redress the supposed wrong done to the Elephantine Jews and there was no action to return that community to cultic normalcy. As it was, whether due to official disinterest in this minor cult, or the culpability of the Jewish community, or a concern over local community tensions, it took around three years for the Elephantine Jews to obtain permission to rebuild their shrine. There was indeed some substance to the claim of inter-cultic conflict, and the satrap would have been loath to take the initiative in possibly exacerbating the tension between the two squabbling communities. It is understandable in light of this that the Elephantine Jews took the initiative, seeking permission before rebuilding rather than trying to justify it later. The three bases for their petition were that the temple had been destroyed illegally, for no legitimate reason; that the Jewish community had been most loyal Persian subjects; and that the Khnum priesthood was the group disturbing the peace by, among other things, bribing local officials in order to get their own way.[143] The permission that was granted for the rebuilding is careful to ensure that one cause for contention between the two religious communities was not rekindled, so the shrine was to be an "altar-house"

---

[142] The destruction of this shrine was most probably not the result of a rebellion in Egypt but was rather due to inter-community conflict. On this, see Briant, "Polythéismes et empire unitaire," 432–33; idem, "Ethno-classe dominate et populations soumises dans l'Empire achéménide: le cas de l'Egypt," in *Achaemenid History III*, 144–47; J. Mélèze Modrzejewski, *The Jews of Egypt*, 40–43; Schäfer, *Judeophobia*, 121–35. I am persuaded by Briant's contention that the shrine was destroyed legally and that Jewish protestations to the contrary, as well as claims regarding the perpetrators' anti-Persian and disorderly actions, served their apologetic interests.

[143] See AP 27 and AP 30. In these petitions the Jews consistently protest their innocence. Note, however, that in AP 30:28–29 and AP 33:12–14, the leaders of the Jewish community were themselves not above offering a bribe to aid their cause.

(בית מדבחא AP 32:3) where meal-offering and incense were to be offered, not a "temple" (אגורא AP 30, passim) where animal sacrifices were also offered (cf. the request in AP 30:25–26). As at Elephantine, the original permission granted for rebuilding the Jerusalem temple may have been the result of a petition by Judeans since, otherwise, the Achaemenid Persian administration would have ignored the cult. Also, like the Elephantine Jews and the priests of Apollo at Magnesia on the Meander, promoters of the Jerusalem temple would have emphasized their support for the current regime and pledged continuing loyalty.

It bears repeating here that permission to rebuild the Jerusalem temple, the shrine of a relatively minor cult that had been destroyed due to rebellion, cannot be construed as a result of a putative empire-wide policy by the Achaemenid Persian administration to refurbish dilapidated shrines or to (re)establish cults in subjugated territories. Many local cults did not need express permission to build and would not have received financial support for their work. For the Jerusalem temple permission was specifically needed, and the granting of that permission would have been a deliberate act by the Achaemenid Persian administration. The granting of such permission should not be confused with a commitment to financial support on their part. The two are not coincident. In the case of the Jerusalem temple, as with other minor cults, the local community was substantially responsible for both undertaking the work and meeting its costs.

The Jerusalem cult of Yahweh seemingly received little beneficence from Cyrus beyond the permission to rebuild and the return of the temple vessels with Sheshbazzar, in contrast to Cyrus's support of Babylonian cults. Cyrus may have issued an edict authorizing the rebuilding of the Jerusalem temple, but the upshot of this was that little or no work was undertaken during his reign. In response to Cyrus's inactivity towards the Jerusalem cult, Bickerman contends that "to ask why [Cyrus's rebuilding] command was not fulfilled is to postulate an assured harmony between commands and their execution, a postulate contrary to established historical facts".[144] As an example of this he cites the restoration of Esagila in Babylon which Esarhaddon undertook and sought to complete but which was in fact not completed until the reign of Assurbanipal some twelve years

---

[144] Bickerman, "Edict," 100.

later.[145] This example does indeed prove Bickerman's point regarding commands and their often slow execution but it is not relevant
to the reconstruction of the Jerusalem temple. Work on the Esagila
was at least commenced during the reign of Esarhaddon, although
how long after he actually decreed the rebuilding to take place is
not known.[146] Even if it was some ten years after the decision to
rebuild, it is notable that the undertaking was considered important
enough for Esarhaddon to ensure that a start be made. This can be
compared with Cyrus's attitude towards the Jerusalem temple where
construction of the Jerusalem temple was not commenced until some
eighteen years after the original edict was supposedly issued, and
then in the reign of another king (Darius I). That is, Cyrus's edict
for rebuilding was not acted upon.[147] It is not an issue of the length
of the delay before rebuilding was begun but rather one of determining the character of Cyrus's supposed attitude towards the cults
of subjugated peoples as it affected the Jerusalem cult. If Cyrus's
"policy" extended to include the Jerusalem cult, it had little impact.

Regarding the scant benefit the Jerusalem cult of Yahweh obtained
during the reign of Cyrus the following points are noteworthy. First,
if there were a repatriation of exiled Judeans along with the return

---

[145] Ibid., 100–101.

[146] On Esarhaddon's policy towards Babylon, see J. A. Brinkman, *Prelude to Empire: Babylonian Society and Politics, 747–626 B.C.* (Occasional Publications of the Babylonian Fund 7; Philadelphia: The Babylonian Fund, University Museum, 1984) 71–76; G. Frame, *Babylonia 689–627 B.C.: A Political History* (Uitgaven van het Nederlands Historisch-Archaelogisch Instituut te Istanbul 69; Leiden: Nederlands Historisch-Archaelogisch Instituut te Istanbul, 1992) 64–101; Porter, *Images, Power, and Politics.* While Esarhaddon's commitment to the rebuilding of Esagila has been questioned (B. Landsberger, *Brief des Bischofs von Esagila an König Asarhaddon* [Amsterdam: N. V. Noord-Hollandische Uitgevers Maatschappis, 1965] 19–20), it would appear from S. Parpola, *Letters from Assyrian Scholars to Kings Esarhaddon and Assurbanipal* (2 vols.; AOAT 5/1–2; Neukirchen-Vluyn: Neukirchener Verlag, 1970–1983) nos. 29, 284, 286, that reconstruction of Esagila was sufficiently well advanced in the last year of Esarhaddon's reign that he sought to have the statue of Marduk returned to Babylon from Assur. This undertaking was unsuccessful and the statue was returned in the first year of the reign of Assurbanipal.

[147] Ezra 5:16 contends that work had been continuing on the temple through-out the reign of Cyrus, but Ezr 3–4 admits that the work had ceased and Haggai and Zechariah do not know of any construction at all before their day. Cyrus's relationship with the Jerusalem cult of Yahweh can be compared not only with that of Babylonian cults but also with the temple of Apollo at Didyma, assuming that B. Fehr, "Apollo-Heiligtums," 51–54, is correct in assigning the rebuilding of this shrine to the reign of Cyrus. However, there is no direct evidence is support of this attribution, and it has won few adherents.

of the temple vessels, following the example offered in lines 32ff. of the Cyrus Cylinder, it was of such small consequence that Haggai and Zechariah 1–8, prophetical texts contemporary with the rebuilding under Darius, display no knowledge of it. As noted above, Ezr 1:1–4:5 also lacks first-hand information on the supposed repatriation. It might be thought that Ezr 3:1–6 speaks of the establishment of cultic normalcy since the repatriates set up the altar on the site of the temple and reinstituted the proper sacrifices. The problem, however, is that this passage attributes this activity to Joshua and Zerubbabel, whose links to the time of Cyrus are tenuous indeed.[148] Further, there is no acknowledgement of the presence of the sizable Judean population who had remained in the land. These people may or may not have been worshipping at the temple site (see Jer 41:5), but their omission from the text and the placement of Zerubbabel and Joshua among the first repatriates is tendentious. The archaeological evidence for a large-scale repatriation is ambiguous since the available evidence cannot be dated very closely. The evidence of archaeological surveys points to the renewed settlement of the area south of Jerusalem in the Persian period. These small, mainly unwalled, settlements have been linked to the returning exiles, although it is impossible to determine which wave of returnees was responsible for them or, indeed, if repatriated Judeans inhabited them at all. In any case, the survey shows that the number of inhabitants in this area could not have been very large.[149]

---

[148] See the section above headed "The Ezra Narrative" on the problem of the date of the foundation-laying, erroneously placed in the reign of Cyrus by the author/editor. It is probable that the erection of the altar in Ezr 3:1–6 has been attributed to Zerubbabel and Joshua because of their connection with the foundation-laying. Note that Sheshbazzar does not appear either in the foundation laying passage (Ezr 3:8–13) or in the episode of the re-establishment of the altar (Ezr 3:1–6). It is probable that he returned to Jerusalem (with the temple vessels?) in the reign of Cyrus. Whatever work he undertook on the temple has been overstated by the author of the Aramaic narrative who attributes the foundation-laying to him (Ezr 5:14–16). Ezr 2:1–2 cannot be cited as evidence for Zerubbabel's and Joshua's return in the first years of Cyrus, as this list of repatriates has been pressed into its present chronological setting by the author/editor. On the probability that Zerubbabel and Joshua returned to Judah some time near to the temple rebuilding, see the following section of this chapter.

[149] For the survey see M. Kochavi ed., *Judea, Samaria and the Golan: Archaeological Survey, 1967–68* (Jerusalem: Carta, 1972) (Hebrew); Carter, "Social and Demographic Study," 93–165; idem, "Province of Yehud," 122–133. K. Hoglund, "The Achaemenid Context," in *Second Temple Studies: 1. Persian Period* (ed. P. R. Davies. JSOTSup 117; Sheffield: JSOT Press, 1991) 57–60, contends that "[this] settlement pattern is fixed

Second, with regard to the rebuilding of the Jerusalem temple, it is noteworthy that Haggai and Zechariah display no knowledge of any attempt to rebuild the temple before their own day. If an edict to rebuild the temple was issued in the reign of Cyrus it would appear that the reconstruction work was a low priority for the Achaemenid bureaucracy. The Jerusalem temple was not comparable in economic or political importance to the Mesopotamian shrines known to have been restored by monarchs as a means of acknowledging their patron deity or in order to legitimate their claim to the throne. Perhaps the most pertinent examples are Esarhaddon's and Assurbanipal's reconstruction of Esagila, which had been earlier destroyed by Sennacherib; Nabonidus's restoration of Eḫulḫul in Harran; Cyrus's restoration of temples in Ur and Uruk. These kings

---

within the first generation of returned exiles and does not represent a chronological dispersion over the entire period of Persian rule" (p. 58). Prompted by Pierre Briant's work on the Hellenistic period, he understands these settlements to reflect an Achaemenid policy of ruralization by which means more land could be placed under cultivation, ensuring a continual flow of tribute. It is unclear, however, that returning Judeans should be held wholly, or even largely, responsible for these settlements. It is just as likely that they reflect local settlement reorganization, without an influx of new settlers. Two pieces of evidence support this. First, the survey by Kochavi et al. shows a decline in settlements elsewhere in Benjamin, Ephraim, Manasseh and the Judean Desert. Second, the material remains in the new Judean settlements are consistent with a local population. For the fragmentary evidence for settlements in Samaria, Judea, and the Negev, see Stern, *Material Culture*, 29–46, 237–40, 245–49. The biblical texts, however, assume that the land was unoccupied and that the repatriated Judeans could thus return to their ancestral land. While the notion that the land was unoccupied is false, it is possible that the returnees sought out relatives who were already living in this territory and who had taken charge of ancestral land. A corollary of this hypothesis would be that the repatriates did not live together in a separate group. Ezr 2:21–35 // Neh 7:26–38, which register people by domicile, and Neh 11:20–36 may be evidence for this, but the date of these texts is disputed.

While the Cyrus Cylinder speaks of the return of people "to their settlements" in the Mesopotamian region, some have seen in the Neirab texts evidence for the repatriation of persons to Syria under Darius. There is some debate over whether the Neirab in these texts refers solely to the Syrian town or whether it refers to a settlement of the same name in the vicinity of Nippur inhabited by deportees from Syrian Neirab. In only the latter case would repatriation obtain. For the discussion, see F. M. Fales, "Remarks on the Neirab Texts," *Oriens Antiquus* 12 (1973) 131–42; Eph'al, "Western Minorities," 84–87, arguing the latter case; cf. L. Cagni, "Considérations sur les textes babyloniens de Neirab près d'Alep," *Transeu* 2 (1990) 169–85, arguing the former case. See also the evaluation of the positions in J. Oelsner, "Weitere Bermerkungen zu den Neirab-Urkunden," *Altorientalische Forschungen* 16 (1989) 68–77. The Neirab texts concern a single family and it is unclear how relevant they are to considering the repatriation of Judeans to their homeland.

saw that the respective restoration work was carried out.[150] The temples with which they were concerned were of prominent Assyro-Babylonian deities and restoration work was undoubtedly a major policy initiative in important political and/or economic areas. Judah and Jerusalem were not particularly important either politically or economically, despite the supposed strategic location of Judah. Rebuilding the city walls of Jerusalem, for example, had to wait until the governorship of Nehemiah in the reign of Artaxerxes I (Neh 1:1–4:17 [Eng. 1:1–4:23]; 6:1–19). Deutero-Isaiah and Ezr 1:1–4 may revere Cyrus as the restorer of the temple of Yahweh in Jerusalem, but the fact of the matter is that he did not undertake this work. Yahweh was not a particularly significant deity, certainly not important enough to ensure that his temple was rebuilt or his decimated city refurbished.[151]

In summary then, the attempt to defend the authenticity of the Cyrus edicts, and through them the veracity of the main points in Ezr 1:1–4:5 (major repatriation in the reign of Cyrus for the purpose of reconstructing the Jerusalem temple; rebuilding attempt thwarted by outsiders), by arguing that they conform to a general policy of Cyrus towards indigenous cults, must be judged unsuccessful. There is insufficient evidence to support the supposed general policy of Cyrus. This does not mean that it is impossible for

---

[150] K. Heinz, "Religion und Politik in Vorderasien im Reich der Achämeniden," *Klio* 69 (1987) 322, recognizes that the Jerusalem temple reconstruction could easily have been hastened by the Achaemenid Persian administration, comparing the relatively short time it took for the building of palaces and the Egyptian canal. He supposes, following Ezr 1–6, that rebuilding went on over a long period (538–516) due to the discord or disputes in Judah and that the Achaemenid Persian administration wished to pursue "eine Politik des Gleichgewichtes". The explanation of the Ezra narrative cannot be accepted, however, and Heinz pays no attention to Haggai's and Zechariah's ignorance of any rebuilding before their day.

[151] The Achaemenid Persian administration's disinterest in the rebuilding of the shrine of a minor cult, such as the Jerusalem temple, may find something of a parallel in Assyrian disinterest in the rebuilding of the temple in Der (Parpola, *Letters*, 1. no. 277, rev. 11–28; idem, *Letters*, 2. 265–67, with corrections to the translation given in Vol. 1. This letter is dated to the reign of Esarhaddon; September, 621). The foundations of that temple had been laid but work had come to a halt, perhaps due to lack of skilled workmen and a local dispute over who was responsible for overseeing the work. The fact that the Assyrian official Mar-Ištar wrote directly to Esarhaddon over the matter points to the fact that the rebuilding of such shrines was considered to lie within the jurisdiction of the Assyrian administration. This is further substantiated by the remainder of this letter, as well as others in the corpus edited by Parpola, which is concerned with the cults of other deities in the region.

Cyrus to have issued such edicts as those in Ezra 1–6, indeed certain elements in them are similar to actions undertaken by Cyrus elsewhere. It is only to emphasize that their authenticity cannot be defended by an appeal to a general, empire-wide policy of Cyrus. There was no general policy, yet it is true to say that minor cults, among which the Jerusalem temple should be numbered, did receive certain beneficence. In the case of the Jerusalem temple this was in the form of permission to rebuild and the return of cultic vessels, but was unlikely to have included direct financial support for the cult. Local communities were to take responsibility for the (re)establishment of minor cults, their upkeep, and the financial costs incurred.

Rather than the biblical edicts helping to substantiate the veracity of Ezra 1–6, as supporters of their authenticity had hoped they would, the narrative must be judged on its own merits. As has been argued above, the historical reliability of the Hebrew narrative and edict is very questionable. The repatriates' attitude toward the temple rebuilding and their conflict with "the people of the land" should be viewed as being a late, tendentious and anachronistic reconstruction. The veracity of the Aramaic narrative and edict have enjoyed greater acceptance among scholars, but this narrative does not know of a major repatriation under Sheshbazzar, nor of conflict between any repatriates and those whom they found in the land at their return. It does accept, however, that Sheshbazzar laid the foundation of the temple on his arrival (Ezr 5:16 cf. Ezr 3:8–13), although Haggai and Zechariah 1–8 know of no such work. A reasonable case can be made for Cyrus's granting permission for the Jerusalem temple to be rebuilt (some form of the Aramaic edict being a probable candidate), but it appears most likely that Judeans themselves had to take responsibility for the work. No direct support for or involvement in the rebuilding was offered by Cyrus and the Jerusalem cult was not restored to cultic normalcy until Zerubbabel and Joshua purified the site and re-laid the foundation in 520 (Haggai, Zechariah 1–8) in the reign of Darius I. From this arises another historical problem: assuming Cyrus gave permission for the rebuilding of the temple, why was there such a long delay before the task was undertaken? Part of the answer given above was the central administration's disinterest in the "minor" Jerusalem cult so that they did not ensure that the work was done. Given that the responsibility for the rebuilding lay with the Judeans, why did they not immediately undertake the work? It has been argued above that the account given in

Ezr 3–4 which blames the "people of the land" cannot be accepted as an explanation for the delay. The following section considers another possible explanation.

BETWEEN CYRUS AND DARIUS: EXPLAINING THE DELAY IN REBUILDING

Those who hold that one or both of the biblical edicts of Cyrus are authentic are confronted with the eighteen-year delay in the commencement of the Jerusalem temple's reconstruction. It was suggested above that this delay probably reflects the relative unimportance of the Jerusalem cult of Yahweh to the Achaemenid bureaucracy. Many commentators, perhaps influenced by the pro-Persian proclivity of Deutero-Isaiah and Ezra 1–6 with respect to the temple rebuilding, have sought to place the blame for the delay elsewhere.

For the small group of scholars who deny the authenticity of both the Hebrew and Aramaic edicts, the response to the issue of the delay in the rebuilding is, of course, that Cyrus never issued an edict either repatriating the exiled Judeans or granting permission for the Jerusalem temple to be rebuilt. Since the vast majority of scholars support the authenticity of both edicts or at least the Aramaic edict, the latter permitting rebuilding but making no mention of repatriation, this issue remains.

For defenders of the Hebrew edict the problem of the delay in the rebuilding is acute. As noted above, Ezr 3:1–4:5 has an answer to this problem. The rebuilding of the temple begun by the repatriates in the first years of the reign of Cyrus was halted by the intervention of "the people of the land" soon after its foundation was laid. This attribution should be understood as polemic directed by the author against antagonists in his own day. It has been shown that there is some reason to question the knowledge of the author of Ezr 1:1–4:5 (the Hebrew narrative) regarding the attempt to reconstruct the Jerusalem temple in the reign of Cyrus. There are questions regarding the authenticity of the Hebrew edict; it is widely accepted that Ezr 2, ostensibly a list of those who returned with Sheshbazzar, has been taken from Neh 7; and the narrative of Ezr 3 is patterned after the narrative of the building of the first temple.

This emphasis in the narrative on the legitimate right of the repatriated Judeans as the temple rebuilders and their separation from those whom they found in the land is not evidenced in Haggai and Zechariah 1–8, so the social conflict with which it is concerned must be later than these prophets. Ezr 3:1–4:5 should be considered to be a late explanation arising not only from the need to account for the delay, but also as rhetoric against the Judeans' current antagonists, the Samarians, and thus should be read as an attempt to justify the preeminence of the Jerusalem cult and its worshippers over against criticisms or counter-claims. For the author of Ezr 1:1–4:5 the Jerusalem temple had always been recognized by Judeans as being the legitimate cult; that is, since the very day of their repatriation and even throughout the exile in Babylonia. Since the author has no knowledge of the real reasons for the delay, he anachronistically places current antagonists in this setting. Ezr 1:1–4:5 thus becomes a narrative about current struggles read back into the early return; his forebears versus his antagonists' forebears.

Those who maintain the authenticity of the Hebrew edict, recognizing that the explanation for the delay in rebuilding offered in Ezr 3–4 is unacceptable, have sought other causes for the delay. Williamson, for example, contends that although the Aramaic edict has the temple reconstruction funded by the Achaemenid Persian chancellery, these funds had to be generated from within the satrapy and, moreover, due to the poor financial state of the region, these funds were not available for many years.[152] Others, basing themselves on Hag 1:2–11, which speaks of the economic plight of the Judean community in the early years of the reign of Darius I, hold that the community itself was too poor to undertake the rebuilding.[153]

Bickerman, who accepts the explanation for the delay in the rebuilding offered in Ezr 3–4 that the "people of the land" thwarted the repatriates' project, suggests a further reason for the delay which arose among the Judeans themselves.[154] This is "a reason which Jewish authors of the Persian period could not state openly", namely, that many of the exiled Judeans resented the idea that a foreigner,

---

[152] Williamson, *Ezra, Nehemiah*, 81; cf. the preceding discussion, pp. 144–49. This contention contradicts Ezr 1:6; 2:68–70, of course, which claims that the repatriates had ample funds of their own with which to undertake the rebuilding.

[153] This is suggested in a number of commentaries on Haggai and in some histories of Israel/Judah. It is explicitly cited as the reason for the delay in rebuilding by Bright, *History*, 366; Wolff, *Haggai*, 41, 44.

[154] Bickerman, "Edict," 101–103.

indeed a foreigner who purportedly worshipped numerous foreign deities, such as Cyrus, could be used by Yahweh in the restoration of Judah. Bickerman cites the complaints to this effect by some of the exiles in Is 45:9. He surmises that:

> Jewish opposition to salvation through the agency of a pagan deputy of God had something to do with the cessation of work which Sheshbazzar had begun in the beginning of Cyrus' reign (Ezra 5,61).[155] (sic; read Ezra 5,16)

With Darius's later appointment of Zerubbabel, work on the temple could recommence since Zerubbabel was of the royal house of Judah and thus acceptable as the agent of Yahweh in rebuilding the temple. All Darius sought in return for this concession was that the temple priests "pray for the life of the king and his sons" (Ezr 6:10).

This suggestion has a number of difficulties. It must have been apparent to the exiled Judeans when Cyrus issued the proclamation, assuming that Ezr 1:2–4 represents its text, that he was claiming to be acting on Yahweh's behalf in returning the exiles to their homeland and ordering the reconstruction of the Jerusalem temple. Surely the exiles would not have been repatriated only to realize thereafter that they resented Cyrus being Yahweh's agent. Had they accepted repatriation, and had Cyrus justified it in the terms stated in the Hebrew edict, then they must already have come to terms with Yahweh using Cyrus to act on their behalf. Further, if Williamson's defence of the Hebrew edict whereby Cyrus issued the proclamation in response to a Judean petition (thus explaining the proclamation's distinctive vocabulary) is accepted, it is impossible that the leadership of the exiles would not have accepted Cyrus as a legitimate divine instrument, as Deutero-Isaiah also suggests.

For those who accept the authenticity of only the Aramaic edict the problem of the delay in the rebuilding the temple is seemingly less pressing since they deny that Cyrus undertook a large-scale repatriation of the exiled Judeans for the express purpose of rebuilding (which is mentioned only in the Hebrew edict and narrative). For Galling, Sheshbazzar was sent to Jerusalem with the temple vessels by Cyrus (the return of these vessels is mentioned both in the Aramaic edict and Ezr 1:8–11), but few Judeans returned with him. Sheshbazzar did not lay the foundation of the new temple at that time (contra

---

[155] Ibid., 102.

Ezr 5:16) since Haggai and Zechariah know nothing of a foundation laying before that undertaken by Zerubbabel in the second year of Darius. Sheshbazzar was also to set the temple reconstruction in motion but the governor of Samaria, under whose jurisdiction Judah then was, resisted this.[156] The Samarian district officials are thus to be held responsible for the delay in rebuilding. The main repatriation of the exiled Judeans under the leadership of Zerubbabel, whose main role was as "Commissioner for Repatriation" rather than Governor of Judah, took place some time closer to the actual reconstruction of the temple, perhaps in the reign of Cambyses or Darius, and this helped to precipitate the temple rebuilding.[157] This being so, the problem of how the repatriates could have been delayed some eighteen years before rebuilding evaporates.

These various attempts to account for the delay in the reconstruction of the Jerusalem temple neglect the fact there was a sizeable population of Judeans who, not having been exiled by Nebuchadrezzar, had remained in Judah. Had Cyrus issued an edict permitting the temple rebuilding and sent Sheshbazzar to Jerusalem to initiate the task, would not this community have been able to take advantage of the edict and have rebuilt the temple? Why would this population not have undertaken the temple rebuilding? Galling's suggestion that the Samarian officials stalled the rebuilding only goes part way in dealing with this issue since the question arises as to why those in Judah would not have pressed their claim to rebuild based on the permission granted. Even if the Judeans suffered under severe economic constraints, why would they not have made an attempt to start the rebuilding and sustain it, however modestly, over time, as indeed Ezr 4:12–16 claims they did? Further, if, as seems likely, Sheshbazzar was the first of a series of governors of Judah who ruled independently of Samaria, then Samarian officials cannot be held responsible for the delay in rebuilding the Jerusalem temple.[158]

[156] Galling, *Studien*, 40–41, 133–34. On Sheshbazzar as a "building commisioner" see also idem, "'Gola List'," 158; Alt, "Die Rolle Samarias," 333–34; also, see above chapter 3 n. 4.

[157] On the main repatriation taking place quite close to the rebuilding in the reign of Darius, or possibly in the reign of Cambyses, see Alt, "Die Rolle Samarias," 334; Galling, *Studien*, 56–57, 126; Ackroyd, *Exile and Restoration*, 147–48; Herrmann, *History*, 299–301; Donner, *Geschichte*, 411. On Zerubbabbel as "Repatriierungskommissar", see Alt, "Die Rolle Samarias," 335; Galling, *Studien*, 126.

[158] On Sheshbazzar as governor of an autonomous Judah see, for example, Avigad, *Bullae and Seals*; Japhet, "Sheshbazzar and Zerubbabel," 80, 98; Williamson, *Ezra*,

Another perspective on why it was only in the reign of Darius that the temple was rebuilt is offered in Haggai and Zechariah 1–8. Neither of these prophets cites "external factors" such as local political machinations, social conflict or economic hardship as reasons for the temple rebuilding being undertaken only in the reign of Darius I. They are not concerned to explain why there was such an apparently long delay in rebuilding; rather they are concerned with justifying that the rebuilding be undertaken in their own day. These prophets claim that the determination of the divinely appointed time for rebuilding the temple was the integral factor in commencing the reconstruction of the temple. The divine ire directed against the people, land and city (as expressed in the divine abandonment of Jerusalem, the dissolution of the state and the concomitant exile) had only now been lifted. Up until this time Jerusalem, Judah and the people had remained under the judgement of Yahweh.

In contradistinction then to Deutero-Isaiah and Ezr 1:1–4:5, which contend that Yahweh had sanctioned both the repatriation under Cyrus and the permission to rebuild the Jerusalem temple granted by Cyrus, these prophets, by disavowing any knowledge of such and by dating to their own day Yahweh's change of heart towards Jerusalem and the people of Judah, offer a different vision of the history of this period.[159] For these prophets, even if there was a repatriation under Cyrus, it was not for the purpose of rebuilding the temple since they hold that only in their day had Yahweh granted permission to rebuild. Again, even if Cyrus had issued an edict permitting the rebuilding, these prophets deem it irrelevant since it is only now that divine permission to rebuild has been granted.

The fact that Haggai and Zechariah 1–8 do not refer to any earlier rebuilding attempt nor castigate the people for long-term neglect of the temple may be significant for interpreting the Cyrus edicts in Ezr 1–6—Galling concludes that this means that the main repatriation took place close to the rebuilding under Darius (on the basis that only the Aramaic edict is authentic); Torrey thinks that this means that Cyrus issued no edict at all. Regardless of one's position on the authenticity of the Cyrus edicts, had these prophets accepted

---

Nehemiah, 17–19; idem, "Governors of Judah," 59–82; Meyers and Meyers, *Haggai, Zechariah 1–8*, 13–16; also, see above chapter 3 n 4.
[159] Similarly, Japhet, "Temple in the Restoration Period," 212, 231–33.

the view, and indeed had the popular perception been, that the demise of the Babylonian empire and the edict(s) of Cyrus marked a new day for the Judeans, which included the return of Yahweh to Jerusalem/Zion and the rebuilding of the Jerusalem temple, it is impossible that they could have neglected to address the issue of why Yahweh's will was thwarted.[160] The fact that these prophets see no need to explain the delay must mean that there was no perception that one existed. From this perspective there is no need to speak of a "delay" in rebuilding, apart from a brief, recent one considered by Haggai. It is to a closer examination of these prophetical texts that our attention may now turn.

Zechariah in his first vision (Zech 1:7–17), dated to the end of Darius's second year (1:7),[161] sees horses that Yahweh has sent out

---

[160] There is no mention of a long delay in rebuilding attributed to the Judeans' "sin" (cf. the pre-exilic prophets who use this as the reason for the ire of Yahweh against the people). I disagree with Carroll, *When Prophecy Failed*, 157–68, that these prophecies were reactions to or reinterpretations of the "failed" expectations of blessing announced by Deutero-Isaiah. They make no attempt to interact with nor to explain why these earlier prophecies went unfulfilled. Haggai and Zechariah thus do not appear to be indebted to Deutero-Isaiah for their understanding of the timetable of the restoration. They may in fact be altogether ignorant of Deutero-Isaiah, or simply ignore it, since, as will be argued in chapter 4, they need not be dependent on Deutero-Isaiah for their temple ideology and conceptions of restoration. All three prophets are drawing on motifs from the Jerusalem cult as represented by the Zion Psalms and the *Yahweh mālak* Psalms. The relationship between Haggai, Zechariah and Ezek 40–48 is also problematic. I remain unconvinced that there is any direct influence of Ezek 40–48 on the other now, although that case cannot be argued here. The expectation of restoration that Deutero-Isaiah, Ezek 40–48, Haggai and Zech 1–8 all share can be explained by their common indebtedness to the widely-held notion of historical recurrence. While it is true that all four prophetical texts develop the idea that it is possible to have the temple in a new type of polity (not the monarchical state revisited), their understandings are sufficiently distinct to suggest that their positions were arrived at independently. The significance of Deutero-Isaiah and Ezek 40–48 for the interpretation of Haggai and Zech 1–8 lies in their common concerns about restoration, their shared cultural background, and their varied attempts to address these concerns. Deutero-Isaiah and Ezek 40–48 show how early these concerns were aired and addressed, even if they are unacknowledged by Haggai and Zech 1–8. This and the following discussion overlaps with and in part reproduces sections of Bedford, "Discerning the Time," 71–86.

[161] Zech 1:7 "On the twenty-fourth day of the eleventh month, that is the month of Shebat, in the second year of Darius . . ." This is the most extensive date formula in Haggai and Zech 1–8. The day of this vision was, accordingly, February 15, 519; see R. A. Parker and W. H. Dubberstein, *Babylonian Chronology 626 B.C.–A.D. 75* (Brown University Studies 19; Providence, RI: Brown University, 1956) 15–17. The date formulas may come from a later, editorial hand, so Beuken, *Haggai— Sacharja 1–8*, 26.

to range over the earth (1:8–10). Their riders report to the messenger of Yahweh, who in the vision was accompanying Zechariah, that "All the earth is dwelling quietly" (1:11). The fact that the earth is at rest while Jerusalem and Judah remain devastated gives rise to the following exchange (1:12–17):

12) The messenger of Yahweh then responded, "How long, O Yahweh Sebaoth, before you show compassion for Jerusalem and the cities of Judah with which you have been angry these past seventy years?" 13) Yahweh answered the messenger who spoke with me with kind, comforting words.

14) The messenger who spoke with me then said to me, "Proclaim! 'Thus says Yahweh Sebaoth: I have become very zealous on behalf of Jerusalem and Zion, 15) and I feel great anger towards the nations which rest securely[162] who, though I was only a little angry,[163] helped

---

[162] While שָׁאֲנָן can have the sense of "self-assurance" or "arrogance" (Is 37:29, and perhaps Ps 123:4; Job 12:5), it more commonly means "at rest, secure" (Is 32:9, 11, 18; Am 6:1). Arrogance is cited as a reason for Yahweh's ire against the nations (for example, Is 10:12–19; 16:6–12; 37:23–29; 47:8–11; Jer 48:28–33; 50:31–40; Ezek 28:1–10), but in light of the report delivered to Yahweh in v. 11 that כל־הָאָרֶץ יֹשֶׁבֶת וְשֹׁקָטֶת "all the earth is dwelling quietly", the translation of שָׁאֲנָן given above is to be preferred.

[163] This translation is adopted by a number of commentators; for example, Galling, Studien, 113; Beuken, Haggai—Sacharja 1–8, 242; Ackroyd, Exile and Restoration, 176; S. Amsler, Aggée, Zacharie 1–8 (Commentaire de l'Ancien Testament 11c; Neuchâtel/Paris: Delachaux and Niestlé, 1981) 60. Others translate מְעָט with a temporal sense—"a little while" so, for example, W. Ruldolph, Haggai—Sacharja 1–8, 72; C. Jeremias, Die Nachtgesichte des Sacharja. Untersuchungen zu ihrere Stellung im Zusammenhang der Visionsberichte im Alten Testament und zu ihrem Bildmaterial (FRLANT 117; Göttingen: Vandenhoeck & Ruprecht, 1977) 139–40; Petersen, Haggai and Zechariah 1–8, 137. There are, however, no other instances where מְעָט alone has this temporal sense (עוֹד מְעָט is used elsewhere for "a little while"; see Ex 17:4; Hos 1:4; Is 10:25; Jer 51:33; Ps 37:10). In support of his translation Jeremias refers to Zech 7:12 (cf. Zech 1:2) where Yahweh is said to have had "great anger" with his people. There is no text where Yahweh berates the nations because they ruled over Israel/Judah for too long, however. In fact, Yahweh is always presented as being in control of the duration of Israel and Judah's oppression; see Is 10:25; Jer 25:11; 29:10. Zech 1:15 is thus not concerned with explaining why Judah's oppression had gone on so long; that is, that Yahweh gave permission for the nations to chasten Judah for "a short time" (מְעָט) and hence the nations have incurred the deity's ire by prolonging Judah's sufferings since Yahweh's anger had in fact subsided some time ago. By asking "how long?" (v. 12) and by Yahweh responding that he is now returning to Jerusalem (v. 16) the text admits that it was unclear exactly when Yahweh's anger against Jerusalem and Judah was to be lifted.
Zech 1:15 should be interpreted in the light of other prophetical texts which exhibit a concern for the excessively harsh treatment Israel/Judah received at the hands of her oppressors, which is related to Yahweh's judgement on the nations (see Ezek 35; Jer 50:29; 51:7, 34–40, 49–52; Is 10:5–11; 47:6–9 cf. Is 40:2 where

turn it into evil.[164] 16) Therefore,' thus says Yahweh, 'I am returning to Jerusalem with compassion. My house shall be rebuilt in her'—oracle of Yahweh Sebaoth—'A measuring line shall be stretched out over Jerusalem.'

17) Proclaim again! 'Thus says Yahweh Sebaoth: My cities shall again overflow with plenty. Yahweh shall again comfort Zion; he shall again choose Jerusalem.'"

According to this passage, the reason why the temple had not been rebuilt before this time was that Yahweh had been absent from Jerusalem after the destruction of the temple in 587 and was only now returning to Jerusalem (see also Zech 2:14, 16 [Eng. 2:10, 12]; 8:3). Temple rebuilding could be undertaken only once the divine displeasure against the nation, as reflected in the dissolution of the kingdom and divine abandonment of the temple, had passed. Yahweh's return to Jerusalem precipitates the rebuilding of the temple and the renewal of the divine presence in Jerusalem will ensure prosperity for the whole land.

This outlook bears considerable similarity to Deutero-Isaiah's expectations regarding Yahweh's return to Jerusalem in the days of Cyrus,[165] but with the significant difference that the reign of Cyrus did not mark the end of Yahweh's ire with his people and city. Yahweh had not returned to Jerusalem at the fall of the kingdom of Babylon. Similarly, Ezr 1:1–3 (cf. II Chrons 36:20–23) understands the edict of Cyrus to mark the end of the "seventy years" of suffering spoken of by Jeremiah,[166] but in Zech 1:12 the divine messenger seeks

---

Jerusalem is said to have received "double punishment for all her crimes"). This is the "evil" committed by the nations, for which they incur Yahweh's ire. Another element here is that foreign nations "rest quietly" while Judah and Jerusalem still suffer deprivation and loss of Yahweh's presence. Yahweh is cajoled into action by the plight of his own people and city when compared with the state of the nations.

[164] The verb עזר has troubled commentators since the sense of "helped to evil" is not clear. Some have followed I. Eitan, *A Contribution to Hebrew Lexicography* (New York: Columbia University, 1924) 8, who suggests Arabic *ġzr* "to be copious" as a cognate and that עזר here should be read as a hiph'il (with the ה lost to haplography or to be taken from the last consonant of המה). The translation would then be "they did too much evil"; see Ackroyd, *Exile and Restoration*, 176 n. 17; Rudolph, *Haggai—Sacharja 1–8*, 73 n. 15 b.

[165] See above pp. 75–78. See also Zech 2:10–17 (Eng. vv. 6–13); 8:1–8, 20–23 for restoration motifs similar to those expressed in Deutero-Isaiah and Jer 50–51.

[166] Jer 25:11–12; 29:10. These texts refer to the duration of Babylonian hegemony over Judah, not to the length of the divine abandonment of Jerusalem. If the "seventy years" is taken literally, then this period would have started around 609, when the Babylonians were gaining power in Palestine (for this view, see

to know when the period of Yahweh's ire will elapse. Zechariah sees the end of this period as coming only in his own day.

The lament formula "How long?" (Zech 1:12) should not be construed as a complaint directed against Yahweh because earlier expectations had not been met. This would be to read the concerns of Ezr 1:1–4:5 and Deutero-Isaiah into this text. This formula is a standard address to the deity in laments, an address which functions to fasten the deity's attention on the plight of his worshippers rather than referring to unfulfilled promises of restoration.[167] The "seventy years" of Yahweh's anger against Jerusalem (Zech 1:12) should not be understood as a reference to Jeremiah's "seventy years" prophecy, as is often done. That is, it is not an attempt to reinterpret the Jeremiah prophecy by making the starting point 587 so that the period between the destruction of the Jerusalem temple and the commencement of reconstruction was approximately seventy years

---

Jeremias, *Nachtgesichte*, 130–35; but note that Jer 25:1 dates the Jer 25:11–12 prophecy to 605, so at best "seventy years" is only approximate, and not to be taken literally). II Chrons 36:20–21 sees the end of the "seventy years" arriving with the edict of Cyrus and its beginning with the exile of *all* Judeans in 587, a period in which the land could enjoy the sabbatical years the Judeans had not observed (see Lev 25:1–7; 26:32–35). On this interpretation of the "seventy years", see P. Grelot, "Soixante-dix semaines d'années," *Biblica* 50 (1969) 175–78; M. Fishbane, "Revelation and Tradition: Aspects of Inner-Biblical Exegesis," *JBL* 99 (1980) 356–57; S. J. De Vries, "The Land's Sabbath in 2 Chron 36:21," *Proceedings, Eastern Great Lakes and Midwest Biblical Societies* 6 (1986) 96–103. This may support the suggestion that "seventy years" is not literal, but formulaic; on this point see below. For an attempt to interpret the "seventy years" in the biblical texts (Jer 25:11–12; 29:10; II Chron 36:20–21; Dan 9:2) literally and to harmonize the beginning of this period in the various texts, see R. E. Winkle, "Jeremiah's Seventy Years for Babylon: A Re-Assessment. Part I: The Scriptural Data," *AUSS* 25 (1987) 201–14; idem, "Jeremiah's Seventy Years for Babylon: A Re-Assessment. Part II: The Historical Data," *AUSS* 25 (1987) 289–99. For a recent discussion of arguments and evidence pertaining to the "seventy years", see J. Applegate, "Jeremiah and the Seventy Years in the Hebrew Bible: Innerbiblical Reflections of the Prophet and his Prophecy," in *The Book of Jeremiah and its Reception—Le livre Jérémie et sa réception* (ed. A. H. W. Curtis and T. Römer; BETL 128; Leuven: Leuven University Press/Peeters, 1997) 91–110 (esp. 92–97, 102–06).

[167] Beuken, *Haggai—Sacharja 1–8*, 240–41. For the cultic use of עד־מתי "how long?" see Ps 6:4; 74:10; 80:5 (Eng. v. 4); 90:13; 94:3. It also occurs in other prophetical texts, see Is 6:11; Jer 12:4; Dan 12:6 (where it is related to discerning the duration or "time" of a prophesied event to take place). This formula also occurs in Sumerian laments; for references, see M. E. Cohen, *The Canonical Lamentations of Ancient Mesopotamia* (2 vols.; Potomac, MD: Capital Decisions Limited, 1988) 2. 766 s.v. me-ne-šè. For its use in Akkadian appeals to deities (Akk. *adi mati*), see L. King, *The Seven Tablets of Creation* (2 vols.; London: Luzac, 1902; reprint, New York: AMS, 1976) 1. Appendix 5, lines 56, 59, 93, 94; Streck, *Assurbanipal*, 2. 252, rev. 14.

(587–520).[168] Zech 1:12 does not display any expectation that Yahweh's
ire ought be coming to an end, nor is there any mention of earlier
prophecy on the basis of which the prophet might call upon Yahweh
to relent. On the contrary, the text reflects the prophet's uncertainty
regarding the will of the deity. Following a suggestion of Ackroyd,
it is likely that seventy years was understood to be a reasonable time
for the deity to punish his people since by that time all members of
the generation which had offended the deity would have died.[169]
Jeremiah's "seventy years" prophecy can be similarly understood, as
can the reference in a royal inscription of Esarhaddon which speaks
of Marduk's ire at the destruction of Babylon by Sennacherib lasting seventy years.[170] Zech 1:12 thus reflects the notion that "seventy
years" *may* be sufficient time to exhaust the deity's anger, but the
text reflects the possibility that this anger could continue.[171] At least
at the end of approximately "seventy years" (starting in 587) it is
possible to ask "How much longer?" The interpretation of the "seventy years" as a life-span appears to be supported by Zech 1:1–6.
Here the prophet speaks of the earlier prophetic judgement against
his listeners' "fathers". The judgement referred to is generally accepted
to be the divine abandonment of Jerusalem, the dissolution of the
kingdom of Judah and the exile to Babylonia. As the punishment
foretold by these prophets had been accomplished, and the generation who were cursed by these prophets were all dead (Zech 1:5–6),
the prophet Zechariah could then turn to addressing the question
of when Yahweh's anger might come to an end. This topic is taken

---

[168] Following Petersen, *Haggai and Zechariah 1–8*, 150, against the majority of commentators, including P. R. Ackroyd, "Two Old Testament Historical Problems of
the early Persian Period," *JNES* 17 (1958) 25; Fishbane, "Revelation and Tradition,"
356–57; Meyers and Meyers, *Haggai, Zechariah 1–8*, 117–18.

[169] Ackroyd, "Historical Problems," 24. See also R. Borger, "An Additional Remark
on P. R. Ackroyd, *JNES*, XVII, 23–27," *JNES* 18 (1959) 74; A. Malamat, "Longevity:
Biblical Concepts and Some Near Eastern Paralles," *28. Rencontre Assyriologique
Internationale in Wien* (ed. H. Hirsch and H. Hunger. *AfO* Beiheft 19; Horn: Berger,
1982) 217–18. Ps 90:10 and Is 23:15–18 speak of seventy years as a life-span.

[170] Borger, *Asarhaddon*, §11 ep. 10. Weinfeld, *Deuteronomic School*, 143–46, compares
Jeremiah's "seventy years" to that mentioned in the Esarhaddon inscription and
concludes that it is a conventional, not a literal, term; see also, Lipiński, "Recherches,"
38–39. For further references to the deity's appointment of a certain duration for
his ire see below n. 192.

[171] Cf. Pss 44:24 (Eng. v. 23, if post 587 in date. Perhaps it is to be dated to
after the 597 deportation); 74:10; 79:5; 85:6 (Eng. v. 5); 89:47 (Eng. v. 46); Lam
5:20, 22 which contemplate the possibility that Yahweh's ire may continue "forever".

up in the section immediately following—Zech 1:7–17. The fact that
Zechariah understands Yahweh's ire against his people to have continued unabated until his own day may indirectly support Galling's
contention that the repatriation took place some time close to the
rebuilding under Darius since if the exiles had returned earlier, under
Cyrus, why would that time have not been viewed as propitious for
the end of Yahweh's anger and the commencement of temple rebuilding as Deutero-Isaiah claimed?

The notion that Judeans were waiting for Yahweh's anger to abate
in order for the temple to be rebuilt is articulated in other texts
from this period. In Ps 74 the Psalmist, after detailing how the
Babylonian invaders destroyed the temple, asks Yahweh:

> How long (עד מתי) will the oppressor blaspheme? Is the enemy to insult
> your name forever? Why hold back your hand? Why keep your right
> hand hidden? (Ps 74:10–11)

Similarly in Ps 79, also after recounting the destruction of the temple, the Psalmist asks:

> How long (עד־מה) will you be angry, Yahweh? For ever? (Ps 79:5; sim-
> ilarly Ps 89:47 [Eng. v. 46])

The Psalmist is vexed by not knowing when Yahweh will turn and
act on behalf of his people. He says:

> We have not seen our signs; there is no longer a prophet; there is no-
> one with us who knows how long (עד מה). (Ps 74:9)[172]

Also vexed by Yahweh's absence and seeking his return to Jerusalem
is the author of Is 63:7–64:11 (Eng. 64:12), a lament which must
also be dated before the reconstruction of the Jerusalem temple.[173]
In common with Pss 74 and 79 this prophet laments the destruction of the temple (Is 63:18; 64:9–10 [Eng. vv. 10–11] cf. Ps 74:3–8)
and awaits news of Yahweh's return. The poem recounts Yahweh's
actions in the past on behalf of his people, it admits the wrongdo-
ing of the people, and calls on Yahweh to rule over them again.

---

[172] On this verse see J. J. M. Roberts, "Of Signs, Prophets, and Time Limits: A
Note on Psalm 74:9," *CBQ* 39 (1977) 474–81. Ps 80 should probably be seen as
another exilic Psalm exhibiting this characteristic of not knowing "how long" (Ps
80:5 [Eng. v. 4]).

[173] H. G. M. Williamson, "Isaiah 63,7–64,11. Exilic Lament or Post-Exilic Protest?"
ZAW 102 (1990) 48–58.

After noting the current devastation of Jerusalem and Judah the poem ends with a poignant plea:

> Yahweh, can you go unmoved by all of this, oppressing us beyond measure by your silence? (Is 64:11 [Eng. v. 12])

Similar sentiments concerning the desolation of Zion and the pain of not knowing when, or if, Yahweh's anger will abate are expressed in Lamentations 5.

All these texts exhibit a concern for the Jerusalem temple and the restoration of Jerusalem. Unlike Jeremiah (Jer 25:11–12; 29:10; 50–51), Deutero-Isaiah, and Ezr 1:1–4:5, these writers do not date the end of Yahweh's ire to the demise of the Babylonian empire. They do not know "how long" the oppression is to last. Indeed, they fear that it may go on "forever" (Pss 74:10; 79:5; 85:6 [Eng. 5]; 89:47 [Eng. 6]; Lam 5:20, 22). Zech 1:12–16 offers the answer these writers have sought. In the second year of Darius I Yahweh announces that his attitude has changed. He will now return to Jerusalem.

To be sure, the prophet's emphasis on discerning the right "time" to rebuild the Jerusalem temple is ideologically charged. There may have been a number of other reasons why the people did not want to rebuild the temple, but the prophet ties it to the divine will— Yahweh himself had not called for the rebuilding.

The prophet Haggai, Zechariah's contemporary, offers a similar perspective on the timing of the temple rebuilding. He considers, however, that the rebuilding has been briefly delayed, but places the responsibility for this on the people themselves, not on any external political or social circumstances, nor on Yahweh. Haggai 1:2–11 records two oracles on this issue:[174]

---

[174] The dates and narrative sections are part of the editorial framework of the book, not from the prophet himself; see Beuken, *Haggai—Sacharja 1–8*, 27–49, who understands the editorial framework to be from the hand of the Chronicler; cf. Mason, "'Editorial Framework'," 413–21, who holds that the work has undergone a Deuteronomistic redaction. According to Hag 1:1 the date of this oracle was "the second year of King Darius, in the sixth month, on the first day of the month"; that is, August 29, 520, see Parker and Dubberstein, *Babylonian Chronology*, 15–17. On the unity of vv. 4–11, see J. W. Whedbee, "A Question-Answer Schema in Haggai 1: The Form and Function of Haggai 1:9–11," in *Biblical and Near Eastern Studies in Honor of W. S. LaSor* (ed. G. A. Tuttle; Grand Rapids: Eerdmans, 1978) 184–94; W. S. Prinsloo, "The Cohesion of Haggai 1:4–11," "*Wünschet Jerusalem Frieden.*" *IOSOT Congress, Jerusalem 1986* (ed. M. Augustin and K.-D. Schunck; BEATAJ 13; Frankfurt am Main: Lang, 1988) 337–43, cf. O. H. Steck, "Zu Haggai 1 2–11,"

2) Thus says Yahweh Sebaoth: "This people says, 'The time has not yet come to build the house of Yahweh.'"[175]

3) Then the word of Yahweh came through Haggai the prophet, 4) "Is it time for you yourselves to dwell in your panelled[176] houses while this house remains in ruins?" 5) Now thus says Yahweh Sebaoth: "Consider how you have fared! 6) You have sown much but brought in little. You eat but are not filled up. You drink but are not satisfied. You put on clothes but no one is warm. And the hired worker puts (his) labour into a purse with holes."

7) Thus says Yahweh Sebaoth: "Consider how you have fared! 8) Go up into the hills, fetch timber and build the house! I will take pleasure in it and be glorified, says Yahweh. 9) You have expected much but there has been little. When you brought it home I blew it away. Why?"—oracle of Yahweh Sebaoth—"Because of my house which lies in ruins while you run about, each for his own house. 10) Therefore {over you}[177] the heavens have withheld their dew and the earth has withheld its produce. 11) I have summoned a drought upon the land, upon the hills and upon the grain, upon the new wine and upon the fresh oil, upon that which the ground brings forth, upon man and beast, and upon all the work of their hands."

Verse 2 is particularly interesting since it claims that the temple had not been built earlier because "this people" considered the time not right. This raises a number of issues: First, the identity of "this people." Although העם is used in the Hebrew Bible to refer to foreign nations, it is highly unlikely that Haggai would be addressing them in the context of undertaking the reconstruction of the temple of Yahweh. The audience is local since in the narrative sections (1:1, 12, 14; 2:2–3) Zerubbabel the פחה and Joshua the high priest are addressed as their leaders. In Hag 1:12, 14; 2:2–3 it is "the remnant of the people" to whom Haggai speaks, which has led a number of commentators to conclude that it is the repatriates whom Haggai has in view since "remnant" is a term used of them in other

---

ZAW 83 (1971) 355–79, who considers 1:2, 4–8 to have been directed to non-repatriates and 1:9–11 to those who had just returned with Zerubbabel.

[175] Literally, "The time has not come, the time to build the house of Yahweh". For a discussion of the attempts to make sense of MT, see Rudolph, *Haggai—Zacharja 1–8*, 29 n. 2 b); Wolff, *Haggai*, 14 n. 2 a-a.

[176] Or "roofed". In comparison with the temple, the people's houses are either finely appointed or they simply have roofs. For a discussion of ספונים, see Rudolph, *Haggai—Sacharja 1–8*, 29 n. 4 b).

[177] עליכם may be due to dittography, therefore perhaps delete; cf. LXX. The translation "because of you" would seemingly be redundant in this context; see Wolff, *Haggai*, 15 n. 10a, for a discussion of the options.

texts from the Persian period.[178] The problem is whether "the remnant of the people", which occurs only in the narrative sections should be viewed as denoting the same as "this people" in Hag 1:2, a prophetic section. The narrator, perhaps sharing the attitude of the author of Ezra, thought that only the repatriates would have participated in the rebuilding and so wrote accordingly.[179] It is notable that in Hag 2:3 the prophet addresses those "left among you who saw this house in its former glory". This group is likely to include Judeans who did not go into exile since if the repatriation took place quite close to the time of the rebuilding not many, if any, of the exiles who remembered the former temple would have returned since they would have been over seventy years old.[180] To claim that they may have returned under Cyrus and thus have been living in Judah for the past eighteen years demands an answer to the question why these same repatriates did not rebuild earlier and why, indeed, Haggai claims that they had rejected an earlier call to rebuild, as Hag 1:2 avers. All that can be affirmed is that "this people" in Hag 1:2 refers to Judeans, and that Hag 2:3 would seem to include in this Judeans who had not gone into exile.

In support of the contention that the prophet's words were directed to Judeans who had been recently repatriated, Galling has pointed out that Haggai's connection between the land's economic woes and the lack of a temple would be convincing only to those who had just returned.[181] This is possible as such a claim would have lacked force for those who had remained in Judah or who had been repatriated in the reign of Cyrus since they would have experienced good and bad harvests over the years, even without a temple.[182] But it is

---

[178] Wolff, *Haggai*, 34, 51–52; Beuken, *Haggai—Sacharja 1–8*, 30; Amsler, *Aggée, Zacharie 1–8*, 26; cf. the discussion in Hausmann, *Israels Rest*, 37–39. Also, see pp. 154–56 above.

[179] Following Beuken, *Haggai—Sacharja 1–8*, 27–31, who claims that the Chronicler is responsible for the narrative framework; Mason, "'Editorial Framework'," 420–21; Wolff, *Haggai*, 40, 51. For Petersen, *Haggai and Zechariah 1–8*, 47, "There is little reason to think that 'the people' refers to an entity different from 'the remnant of the people' in any of these texts". This "entity" includes both repatriates and those Judeans who had remained in the homeland.

[180] So, S. Japhet, "People and Land in the Restoration Period," *Das Land Israel in biblischer Zeit* (ed. G. Strecker; Göttingen: Vandenhoeck & Ruprecht, 1983) 109, 121 n. 33.

[181] Galling, *Studien*, 57.

[182] On agricultural conditions in the Judean hills, see Meyers and Meyers, *Haggai, Zechariah 1–8*, 29.

equally possible that the severity of this particular drought had brought forth a need to account for it, in which case Haggai's words would have had meaning for Judeans repatriated some time ago. Galling is correct in affirming that the bad harvest(s) referred to in Hag 1:6, 9–11 was a recent event for had the land been experiencing many years of bad harvests, surely this would have demanded prophetic interpretation and perhaps led to an earlier call for a temple. Thus had there been a repatriation of exiled Judeans under Cyrus, the prophecy of Haggai cannot be used to claim that the repatriates were delayed for so long in their rebuilding venture by poor harvests.[183] The eighteen years between the supposed repatriation and the prophesying of Haggai would have offered sufficient opportunity to garner some resources had the repatriates been committed to the rebuilding. For all the supposed poverty of the community they were still able to respond immediately to the prophet's call to get wood and start rebuilding. If they could do that in the midst of a famine why could they not have done it five or fifteen years earlier? It should also be noted that the prophet understands the drought to be the *effect* of the temple remaining in ruins, not the cause of the people's delay in rebuilding. Economic hardship was an outcome of the neglect for the temple and not an excuse for inattention to it. Yahweh had cursed the people and land as a means of drawing attention to the fact that he had been angered by the people's refusal to rebuild.[184]

Steck has rightly contended that the futility curses in Hag 1:5–11, 2:15–17 were probably understood by the Judeans as a continuation of those divinely implemented in 587 with the destruction of the state.[185] This may account for their interpretation of the drought: it

---

[183] Contra Bright, *History*, 366; Wolff, *Haggai*, 41, 44, among others, who account for the delay in the rebuilding by contending that the interest of Judeans repatriated under Cyrus in their own affairs, rather than in temple reconstruction, was occasioned by longstanding economic hardship. It is unclear, however, that Judeans had been experiencing long-term economic hardship. Japhet, "Temple in the Restoration Period," 206–207, considers economic hardship to be a major factor in the delay, but recognizes (pp. 228–29) that the prophets turn this on its head and blame the poor economic state on the failure to build the temple.

[184] See, similarly, Japhet, "Temple in the Restoration Period," 228–29.

[185] Steck, "Zu Haggai 1 2–11," 374–77; Petersen, *Haggai and Zechariah 1–8*, 54. On the significance of the drought as a curse due to some cultic or other (covenantal) infraction, see Beuken, *Haggai—Sacharja 1–8*, 190–97. Steck considers that Hag 1:2, 4–8 was directed at those Judeans who did not go into exile. These people held to the Deuteronomistic conception that Yahweh had cursed the land in 587

is not a punishment for rejecting the call to rebuild but rather further evidence that it is not yet time to rebuild, since the divine ire against the people still continued. Haggai holds a different view, however, interpreting the curses to be the direct result of the rejection of the recent call to rebuild the temple. Futility curses are not only to be found in the context of covenant breaking (as the demise of the kingdom, the exile, and the absence of Yahweh are interpreted). They are also understood to be the result of cultic or ethical infractions (for example, II Sam 21:1–14; Amos 4:4–14; Hos 4:1–3; Is 5:8–10; Joel 1–2).[186] The futility curses in Haggai arise from such a cultic infraction, namely, inattention to the temple.

Haggai, then, offers no explanation for the length of the delay had the exiles returned to Judah at the edict of Cyrus, nor does he account for the inattention to the temple by those who had remained in Judah and not gone into exile. The delay with which this prophet is concerned is in the immediate past. The corollary of this argument is that the call to rebuild the temple, the rejection of which prompted the drought, was a recent event. Again, it would make little sense for the drought to be Yahweh's response to a call to rebuild made many years ago (for example, in the reign of Cyrus), especially since the prophet makes no mention of the length of the delay in rebuilding.[187] The conclusion to be drawn from the lack of an explanation for the delay in rebuilding, the absence of any castigation of the people for the length of the delay, and the call to rebuild being a recent event is that up until the prophetic activity of Haggai and Zechariah there had been little concern among Judeans for rebuilding the temple. This is further supported in Zechariah

---

and that the drought(s) c. 520 was a further expression of this. I agree with Steck that the people saw no reason hitherto to consider that Yahweh's anger had passed, but Haggai implies that Yahweh's attitude towards the people has now changed. This latest drought is in response to the people's rejection of the recent call to rebuild. Haggai's interpretation of the drought stands in continuity with the Deuteronomistic conception of the curse on the land in that the current drought emphasises the continued lack of divine presence (tangibly represented by the ruined temple). It can be redressed only by reconstructing the temple. It is this possibility of an end to the absence of Yahweh that is new to Haggai over against the Deuteronomistic theology, and it stands in close relation to Zechariah 1–8.

[186] Further on this, see below pp. 233–34.

[187] There is no information as to exactly when this earlier call to rebuild was made or who delivered it.

1:16 by the reference to Yahweh's return to Jerusalem only in the second year of Darius I.

The following chapter will investigate the reasons why the first years of the reign of Darius were considered the opportune time to rebuild the temple. For the present discussion it is important to note the conceptual framework regarding temple rebuilding reflected in the Judeans' rejection of the recent call to rebuild. In Hag 1:2 the people are reported as stating, "It is not yet time to rebuild the temple of Yahweh". A number of commentators interpret this statement as reflecting the Judeans' self-interest as the reason why the call to rebuild was rejected. The complaint in Hag 1:4, 9 is that the people were much more concerned with their own homes than with the temple of Yahweh. In the light of the poor harvest(s) the Judeans had experienced (Hag 1:6, 10–11) a number of commentators suggest that the Judeans may have been defending their inactivity regarding the temple rebuilding by claiming lack of funds for the task, although this is not explicitly stated in the text.[188] "It is not yet time to rebuild" would thus mean "We lack sufficient resources to undertake the rebuilding"; that is, that the available resources are being channelled into the people's homes rather than into rebuilding the temple.

The import of the word "time" (עת) in this context is the important consideration. Commentators adopting the above interpretation consider "not yet time to rebuild" in Hag 1:2 to mean something like "we are not willing/prepared to rebuild". Within the context of Hag 1:4–9 where the people have houses but Yahweh does not, the term is given moral connotations. This is further reflected in the interpretation of "time" in Hag 1:4 (an oracle addressed to the people): "Is it time for you to dwell in your panelled houses while this house remains in ruins?" In this verse "time" is construed in moral terms by commentators who give it the nuance "right", "proper". The common interpretation of Hag 1:2–9 is that the people have paid insufficient attention to the worship of Yahweh, exemplified by their refusal to rebuild the temple, preferring to look after their own interests (that is, their own homes).

This reading of Hag 1:2–9 misconstrues the sense of the passage. Rather than seeing Hag 1:2 as evidence for moral turpitude on the

---

[188] See above notes 153 and 183. Ezr 5, part of the Aramaic narrative of the temple reconstruction, exhibits no knowledge of economic constraints being a reason for a delay in rebuilding.

part of the Judeans, attention should be turned to the possibility that
the community had excellent ideological reasons for not rebuilding
the temple. Lying behind the people's claim that it was "not yet
time to rebuild" is the concern evidenced in Pss 74:9; 79:5; 80:5
(Eng. v. 4); Lam 5:20–22; Is 64:8–11 (Eng. vv. 9–12) that the "time"
for abatement of the deity's anger and the return of the divine presence to Jerusalem was not known. עת in Hag 1:2 refers to the divinely
appointed, propitious time to rebuild. That עת can have this technical sense in Biblical Hebrew is shown by Ps 102:14 (Eng. v. 13),
which similarly deals with concern for Yahweh's return to Jerusalem.
The text reads:

אתה תקום תרחם ציון כי־עת לחננה כי־בא מועד—"You will arise, you
will have mercy on Zion; For it is time to be gracious to her, the
appointed time has come" (cf. Ezek 30:3; Is 49:8).

The determination of the "time" when the angry deity was to
return to the abandoned shrine he had consigned to destruction is
a recurring motif in Assyrian and Babylonian royal inscriptions.
Rebuilding of the shrine could be undertaken only when it had been
determined that the deity's ire had turned to compassion and that
he was returning to his shrine. In the light of the use of the formula
ūmū imlû ikšuda adannu "the days were fulfilled, the appointed time
arrived", and the shorter formula *ūmū imlû* "the days were fulfilled",
in Assyrian and Babylonian royal inscriptions, עת in Hag 1:2 can be
understood as a technical term denoting the divinely appointed occasion either for the end of a deity's anger with his people and land
(which can include the notion of the return of the deity to a previously abandoned shrine) or for the restoration of a shrine.

These formulae presume that there is a divine timetable determining the length of the deity's anger, and a number of texts
specifically include the change of the deity's disposition as a precursor to the rebuilding of the destroyed shrine or the return of the
deity to the shrine. The classic example is the destruction and restoration of Babylon and Esagila, Marduk's temple in Babylon, as recounted
in the inscriptions of Esarhaddon.[189] J. A. Brinkman understands
these events to be presented with a thematic structure: divine alienation—devastation: divine reconciliation—reconstruction.[190] For present

---

[189] Borger, *Asarhaddon*, 10–29, §11.
[190] Brinkman, "Through a Glass Darkly," 35–42.

purposes it need only be noted that the "divine alienation—devastation" aspect is exemplified in the anger of Marduk with his people and land (§11, ep. 5) which leads to the divine abandonment of shrines, the devastation of Babylon and Esagila, and the depopulation of the land (§11, ep. 7–9). Originally Marduk had determined the punishment to last for seventy years, the completion of this period being stated in the formula *adi ūmē im[lû]* "until the days were fulfilled", but out of compassion he changed the period to eleven years (§11, ep. 10b).[191] Shortening of the period of divine ire marks the beginning of "divine reconciliation"—*dMarduk inūḫuma ana māti ša eninu iršû salī[mu] . . . rēmu iršīma iqtabî aḫulap* "Marduk quieted down and became reconciled with the land he had punished . . . he had pity and said 'Enough!'" (§11, ep. 10b)—a theme continued by means of divinely given signs (planetary omens, extispicy) which convinced Esarhaddon that he had been commissioned to undertake the rebuilding of Babylon and Esagila ("reconstruction") (§11, ep. 12–17). This task he dutifully fulfils (§11, ep. 18–41). This pattern can been seen in other Akkadian royal inscriptions which, because they are written *ex eventu*, often cite the specific duration of the deity's absence.[192]

---

[191] That is, in reversing his decision Marduk reversed "seventy" years (the numeral written verticle [60] + Winkelhaken [10]) with it thus becoming "eleven" years (written Winkelhaken [10] + verticle [1]).

[192] There are a number of texts which speak of an appointed time being reached (*ūmū imlû ikšuda adannu* "the days were completed, the appointed time arrived"; cf. Jer 25:12; Ps 102:14 [Eng. v. 13]), at which point the angry deity returned to his shrine, giving the king permission to rebuild it. See, for example, C. J. Gadd, "Inscribed Barrel Cylinder of Marduk-Apla-Iddina II," *Iraq* 15 (1953) 123, lines 9f. (number of years broken): [MU-x]-KAM-*ma . . . [ad]i? ūmē imlû ikšû adanna [bēlu] rabû dMarduk ana kurAkkadiki ša ikmilu iršû salīma* "[x ye]ars . . . until the days were fulfilled, the appointed time arrived when the great [lord] Marduk became reconciled with the land of Akkad with which he had been angry". This is followed by the divine choice of a king, the defeat of enemies, and the restoration of Ištar's shrine Eanna; Borger, *Asarhaddon*, §11 ep. 10b (eleven years. The formula used here is *adi ūmē im[lû libbi bēlī rabî?] . . . inūḫūma* [line 19]); Langdon, *Die neubabylonischen Königsinschriften*, Nbn 8 i 23 (twenty-one years): 21 *šanāti qirib Aššuriki irtamê šubatšu [i]mlû ūmē ikšuda adannu inḫuma uzzašu ša šar ilāni* "For twenty-one years he (Marduk) established his seat in Assur. The days were fulfilled, the appointed time arrived, the anger of the king of the gods abated"; Nbn 8 x 12–21 (fifty-four years): *Eḫulḫul ša innadû 54 šanāti . . . itekpuš itti ilāni adannu salīmu 54 šanāti enūma dSin iturru ašruššu* "as to Eḫulḫul which had lain in ruins for fifty-four years, the time when the gods were to be reconciled, (that is) fifty-four years, approached, when Sin would return to his home" (the formula *ekēpu adannu* has replaced *kašādu adannu* here). The deity can also appoint the duration of the exile of others from their cities. See, for example, C. J. Gadd, "The Harran Inscriptions of Nabonidus," *AnSt* 8 (1958) 60–61 col. II, lines 11–12 (Nbn H$_2$, A and B) for the ten year period Nabonidus was sent

Other examples of the "time" formula are used to denote the return
to a shrine by a deity whose absence was not due to anger.[193] This
formula can also be used to denote the appointed time set by a non-
absent deity for the renewal of a dilapidated shrine.[194] While the
"time" formula is not always used to introduce the change in the
deity's attitude towards his people and abandoned sanctuary, a clear
sign of the deity's new mood is nevertheless signalled, usually through
the appointment of a new king (the king who has had the royal
inscription written) who is charged with fulfilling the deity's will which
includes the restoration of the shrine, return to cultic normalcy, and,
where appropriate, punishment of the previous regime.[195] A number
of these texts also speak of the use of divinely given signs, such as
dreams, extispicy and planetary omens, by which means the king is
informed of the deity's will regarding his return and/or temple
rebuilding.[196] All these examples show that the determination of the

---

away from Babylon; then: 10 *šanāti ikšudama adannu imlû ūmū ša iqbû šar ilī ᵈNannari*
"(In) ten years the appointed time arrived, the days were fulfilled which Nannar,
king of the gods, had commanded".

[193] See, for example, R. Borger, "Gott Marduk und Gott-König Šulgi als Propheten.
Zwei prophetische Texte," *BiOr* 28 (1971) 8, col. ii, 12, where the "time" formula
is also used: *ūmīja umallima šanātija umallima* (UD.MEŠ.MU SI.A-*ma* MU.1.KAM.
MEŠ.MU SI.A-*ma*) "I fulfilled my days, I fulfilled my years", but in this text the
deity has not been absent out of anger but rather has been on a series of journeys
to foreign lands (immediately following is a "prophecy" regarding the restoration
of Ekursagila). One of these excursions has the number of years cited (twenty-four
years—i, 17). The other journeys may also have given the exact number of years
the deity had determined to be away from his land, but the text is quite fragmentary.

[194] So, for example, S. Langdon, *The H. Weld-Blundell Collection in the Ashmolean
Museum Vol. 1. Sumerian and Semitic Religious and Historical Texts* (Oxford Editions of
Cuneiform Inscriptions 1; London: Oxford University Press, 1923), plates 23–25
(Cylinder of Nabonidus), and note pl. 23, lines 1–3: *inūm Anum u ᵈEnlil ša ᵘʳᵘSipparⁱᵏⁱ
iqbû edeššu adanšunu kīni ikšudam* "When Anu and Enlil commanded the restoration
of Sippar, the right time for them arrived".

[195] For example, Langdon, *Die neubabylonischen Königsinschriften*, Nbn 1 i 1–53 and
Gadd, "Harran Inscriptions," 46 cols. I, 39–II, 21 (Nbn H₁, B); p. 56 col. I, 11–14
(Nbn H₂, A and B) which do not have the "time" formula but nevertheless display
the need for the angry deity to give a sign that his countenance has changed, is
now returning to his shrine, and wants the king to rebuild the temple. The Cyrus
Cylinder (lines 11–34) similarly has a change in the angry deity's attitude followed
by the appointment of a new king and the renewal of shrines. In a message from
Aššur to Ashurbanipal, the god's anger is said to have abated as a result of the
obedient action of Assurbanipal, who had been divinely commissioned to crush
Šamaš-šuma-ukīn. Assurbanipal is then directed to renew the gods of Babylon and
their shrines; see A. Livingstone (ed. and trans.), *Court Poetry and Literary Miscellanea*
(State Archives of Assyria 3; Helsinki: Helsinki University Press, 1989) no. 44, rev.
19–23 (text partially restored).

[196] So, for example, Borger, *Asarhaddon*, §11, eps. 12–18; Langdon, *Die neubaby-*

deity's will regarding the rebuilding or refurbishment of a shrine was considered to be of paramount importance.

It is such a concern that lies behind both the Judeans' statement in Hag 1:2 and Zechariah's question in Zech 1:12. The people's lack of interest in temple rebuilding in Hag 1:2 arises not out of self-interest or any other supposed moral deficiency, rather it reflects a perspective similar to that exhibited in Zech 1:12, namely, that they were unsure of the correct time to rebuild. How was one to know that Yahweh's ire had abated and that since he was returning to his city, he wanted his shrine reconstructed?[197] Since the rebuilding of a shrine which an angry deity had consigned to destruction could not be undertaken without clear evidence that such work had divine sanction, Hag 1:2 can be interpreted as reflecting the Judeans' perception that the dissipation of Yahweh's anger was not yet evident nor was his return hitherto known to be imminent. The tension between the prophet and the people does not lie in the area of moral rectitude but in a difference of opinion as to whether the "propitious time" had in fact arrived.[198]

The reference to "time" in Hag 1:4 is to be similarly understood. Those who interpret Hag 1:2–9 in moralistic terms are forced to give a different nuance to the term "time" in Hag 1:2 as compared with Hag 1:4. It is proposed here that עת "time" has exactly the same connotation in both verses. "Is it time for you to dwell in your panelled houses while this house remains in ruins?" (Hag 1:4) is a rhetorical question satirizing the people's understanding of the current

---

lonischen Königsinschriften, Nbn 8 vi–vii; Langdon, *Weld-Blundell Collection*, pl. 25, col. II, 20ff., and see the examples cited in V. (A.) Hurowitz, *I Have Built You an Exalted House: Temple Building in Light of Mesopotamian and Northwest Semitic Writings* (JSOTSup 115; JSOT/ASOR Monograph Series 5; Sheffield: JSOT Press, 1992) 143–60.

[197] Like Zech 1–8, Haggai exhibits no knowledge of Deutero-Isaiah's expectation of divine blessing accompanying the fall of Babylon and the return of Yahweh to Jerusalem in the reign of Cyrus. In Haggai the possibility for the return of Yahweh is presented as only having arisen recently.

[198] On this technical sense of עת "time", see also Japhet, "Temple in the Restoration Period," 206; H. Tadmor, "'The Appointed Time Has Not Yet Arrived': The Historical Background of Haggai 1:2," in *Ki Baruch Hu: Ancient Near Eastern, Biblical, and Judaic Studies in Honor of Baruch A. Levine* (ed. R. Chazan, W. W. Hallo and L. H. Schiffman; Winona Lake, IN: Eisenbrauns, 1999) 401–08. J. Kessler, "'t (le temps) en Aggée I 2–4: conflit théologique ou 'sagesse mondaine'," *VT* 48 (1998) 555–59, disputes this interpretation of עת and promises (p. 559 n. 20) a detailed critique of my argument in Bedford, "Discerning the Time," 71–84 (which is substantially reproduced here).

"time". The anomaly of the people having houses and Yahweh not having a house (temple) finds a counterpart in the anomaly regarding the interpretation of the "time". Yahweh clearly considers it the "appointed time" for himself to dwell again in a house. The people, however, consider it the "appointed time" for *themselves* to dwell in houses, but not Yahweh. This is particularly pointed for those recently repatriated. It is their "time" to return to their homeland and take up residence, not Yahweh's. יֹשֵׁב "to dwell" connotes the Zion theology of Yahweh "dwelling" on Mount Zion. It is the people who "dwell", however, whereas Yahweh implicitly claims that it is he who should be taking up residence.

The idea that the people are more concerned with their own homes than with the temple certainly is a feature of Hag 1:2–11. The point of Hag 1:2–4, 9, is to stress the dual anomaly that the people have completed houses while Yahweh lacks a "house" and that the people do not view it as the "time" to rebuild the temple while Yahweh, according to Haggai, does. How can the people say that "it is not yet time to build the house of Yahweh" (Hag 1:2) when they themselves have houses (Hag 1:4)? Can they not correctly determine what "time" this is? Hence the prophet understands the drought as a sign of Yahweh's displeasure with the people's misinterpretation of the "time" given the recent call to rebuild. Clearly the reconstruction of the temple has not been a high priority for the community, but the prophet claims that if they are to receive divine blessing they must now turn their attention to this task. It is not self-interest, rather a lack of concern for this temple based on a misunderstanding of the deity's will, that has incurred Yahweh's ire.

Allied to this interpretation is the contention that the people saw no need for the temple to be rebuilt since it was considered to be a monarchical institution. The Jerusalem temple of Yahweh was the former national shrine of the kingdom of Judah. Since Judah was no longer an independent state nor had an indigenous king, why would this temple be needed? What would it signify? Who would oversee its organization and funding? Deutero-Isaiah and Ezekiel 40–48 attempted to recast the role of the temple in a non-monarchical context, but their views did not command much adherence since there is no evidence that they were ever implemented. Indeed, many of them could not be. Attention to the Jerusalem temple undoubtedly meant more to certain of the Judeans in exile than to those who had remained in Judah since a sizeable portion of those

exiled came from Jerusalem or were connected in some way with
the bureaucratic machinery of the monarchy and hence were more
likely to be devoted to the Jerusalem cult of Yahweh. Many of those
who had remained in Judah were not Jerusalemites and may have
had little interest in the monarchical Jerusalem cult of Yahweh. There
may have been little reason in their minds to restore this monarchical institution which had served as an arm of the central government administration. Once free from the taxation demands to
fund this cult they may have simply abandoned it and concentrated
on their own local cults of Yahweh and/or other deities.[199] Further,
rebuilding such a temple demanded that a legitimate temple builder,
such as a king, undertake the task. Deutero-Isaiah had hoped that
Cyrus would fill this role as Yahweh's anointed. Once he abandoned
the task, since at best he permitted exiled Judeans to return but did
not ensure that the temple be rebuilt, and certainly took no direct
part in the rebuilding, those Judeans who would have seen the temple restored lacked a legitimate temple builder. It was not until the
recent arrival of Zerubbabel, a descendant of David and hence a
member of the Judean royal house, whose presence could itself be
viewed as a divine sign, that expectations for a legitimate rebuilding could arise.[200]

The passages from Haggai and Zechariah discussed above thus
offer a radically different assessment of the attitudes of Judeans
towards the Jerusalem temple from that portrayed in Deutero-Isaiah
and Ezr 1:1–4:5. Rather than being a "cultic community" dedicated
to the re-establishment of the Jerusalem temple who were thwarted
by the intervention of hostile neighbours, as Ezr 1:1–4:5 claims, the
people (who must have included non-repatriates) are shown to be
unsure of when to rebuild the temple, and perhaps, indeed, currently uninterested in it. Neither of these prophets know of any
rebuilding attempt before their own time (contra both Ezr 3:1–4:5
and Ezr 5:13–16), nor do they view the reign of Cyrus to have
ushered in a new age of Judean renewal (contra Deutero-Isaiah and
Ezr 1:1–4:5). These texts would therefore support the argument that

---

[199] That is, with the dissolution of the monarchy the centralization of the cult of
Yahweh in Jerusalem which had been undertaken by Hezekiah and Josiah could
be abandoned. It must be admitted, however, that there is little evidence available
for the nature of the worship of Yahweh in these local communities.

[200] On Zerubbabel's arrival in Judah prompting the rebuilding, see similarly,
Japhet, "Temple in the Restoration Period," 217–18.

Ezr 1:1–4:5 is not a reliable source for the history of the Judean community in the reign of Cyrus. The contention of those who hold, following Ezr 1:1–4:5, that the conflict between the repatriates and "the people of the land" over participation in the temple rebuilding can be assigned to the first years of the reign of Cyrus also falters on the witness of Haggai and Zechariah. Temple rebuilding was not an issue before their time, since it was only in their own day that Yahweh's ire had abated and, returning to Jerusalem, he wanted his temple rebuilt. Following Galling, this conclusion may itself suggest that the main repatriation of exiled Judeans was undertaken quite close in time to the rebuilding in the second year of Darius I.

SUMMARY

There is scant evidence to support an attempted rebuilding of the Jerusalem temple in the reign of Cyrus. Ezr 1:1–4:5, the Hebrew narrative which reports the repatriation of Babylonian Judeans in order to rebuild the Jerusalem temple in the reign of Cyrus, is historically unreliable and displays no first-hand knowledge of the events. This narrative's portrayal of the repatriates as a separatist "cultic community" dedicated to the temple cult and Torah is anachronistic and reflects conflict with Samarians current at the time of the Chronicler (c. 400). Thus the contention of some that social division in Achaemenid Judah began with the repatriation of the Babylonian Judeans and their temple rebuilding project in the reign of Cyrus, and that this social division was the reason for the delay in the temple rebuilding, must be viewed as uncritically adopting the perspective of the author of this narrative. Ezr 5:13–16 agrees with the Hebrew narrative that the temple foundation was laid in the reign of Cyrus, but attributes that work to Sheshbazzar rather than to Zerubbabel; that is, the sources are confused on this point. On the basis of Haggai and Zechariah 1–8, however, whatever work was conducted on the temple in the reign of Cyrus was of very little note. The authenticity of the biblical edicts of Cyrus, upon which much historical reconstruction has been based, cannot be supported by recourse to a supposed empire-wide policy of Cyrus in which beneficence was shown to indigenous cults. The Hebrew edict in particular exhibits a number of anachronistic features which call its authenticity into question. With regard to the two main events raised in the edicts, repatriation of exiled Judeans (Hebrew edict) and permission to rebuild the Jerusalem temple (Hebrew and Aramaic edicts), both remain historically possible, but the claim made in the Hebrew edict that the repatriation was for the explicit purpose of rebuilding the Jerusalem temple must be rejected since there is no policy of Cyrus to which it conforms and the reason for the work not progressing cited in Ezr 4:1–5 is tendentious. In regard to work on the temple in this period, both the Hebrew and Aramaic narratives prove to be unreliable witnesses when compared to Haggai and Zechariah 1–8. As Ezr 2, which claims to be an account of the repatriation, was shown to be later than its current setting, we do not know exactly when the repatriation took place nor how many persons were involved. Similarly, in regard to temple rebuilding in the reign of Cyrus, Ezr 3 is not a reliable account.

It would appear that the foundation of the temple was not laid until the first years of Darius I (Haggai and Zechariah 1–8). Despite Ezr 3:1–4:5, this apparent delay in rebuilding does not demand an explanation. From the perspective of Haggai and Zechariah 1–8, there was no delay since the fall of the Babylonian empire and the edict of Cyrus did not mark the end of Yahweh's ire against his people and his land. For these prophets the abatement of the anger of Yahweh and his return to Jerusalem had come only in their day. This does not mean that Cyrus did not issue an edict for the rebuilding of the Jerusalem temple, only that if he did it appears that most Judeans (those who had remained in Judah as well as any repatriates) rejected the opportunity to rebuild since they as yet saw no confirmation that Yahweh's ire had abated and that he wanted the temple rebuilt, nor did they currently see a need for what was likely to have been perceived as a monarchical institution. Further, had Cyrus issued a rebuilding edict (a form of the edict in the Aramaic narrative), it is apparent that he himself did little to ensure that it was fulfilled. The Jerusalem temple was not a significant institution to the Achaemenid Persian administration. Rebuilding would have been considered by them to have been a responsibility of the Judeans themselves, in terms of both undertaking the work and meeting the costs. Cyrus thus did not fulfill the role of temple rebuilder that Deutero-Isaiah had expected. Without a temple builder the work could not go forward. It was only with the arrival of Zerubbabel, the Davidide, that rebuilding work was undertaken, for he could be cast in the role of a legitimate temple rebuilder.

CHAPTER FOUR

REBUILDING THE JERUSALEM TEMPLE OF YAHWEH IN
ACHAEMENID JUDAH II: THE REIGN OF DARIUS I

The previous chapter contended that while Cyrus may well have
issued a decree permitting the rebuilding of the Jerusalem temple of
Yahweh (most likely, a form of the Aramaic decree), and that while
the Babylonian Judean prophets Deutero-Isaiah and Ezekiel (Ezek
40–48) held out expectations for the renewal of Judah and the return
of the divine presence to Jerusalem (the former explicitly proclaiming its fulfilment at the fall of Babylon), there was little interest shown
by either Judeans or the Achaemenid Persian administration in the
reconstruction of the Jerusalem temple of Yahweh before the reign
of Darius I. The explanation offered in Ezra 1:1–4:5 for the delay
in rebuilding, namely, that there was conflict between the repatriates and "the people of the land", with the latter gaining an injunction against the rebuilding, has been shown to display no first-hand
knowledge of the period but rather is a late, polemical understanding of early Achaemenid Judean society reflecting tensions between
Judeans and Samarians current at the time the text was written.
Haggai and Zechariah show that the reason for the delay in the
rebuilding was that Judeans did not consider the divinely appointed
"time" for the undertaking to have yet arrived.

Attention therefore turns to determining why the first years of
Darius I were considered propitious for rebuilding the temple. What
was the impetus for rebuilding the temple at this time? This question is pressing given the discussion at the end of the previous chapter that indicated that up until this time Judeans had seen no reason
to think that Yahweh's anger against them had abated. It was suggested that the arrival in Judah of Zerubbabel, who as a descendant
of the Judean royal house ("son of Shealtiel"—Hag 1:1, 12, 14; 2:23)[1]

---

[1] Shealtiel is the son of Jehoiachin ("Jeconiah") in I Chron 3:17. According to
I Chron 3:17–19, however, Zerubbabel is the nephew of Shealtiel. For attempts to
harmonize the sources, see Meyers and Meyers, *Haggai, Zechariah 1–8*, 9–10.

was a legitimate temple rebuilder, helped precipitate the rebuilding of the Jerusalem temple. Soon after his arrival the prophets Haggai and Zechariah proclaimed that Yahweh's disposition had now changed and hence the reconstruction of the temple should commence. The presence of Zerubbabel in Judah is the departure point for previous studies on the rebuilding of the Jerusalem temple in the reign of Darius.

Although one can point to the prophetic impetus for the rebuilding of the Jerusalem temple, the social and political context in which the rebuilding was undertaken still needs to be considered. The first section of this chapter considers two views which contend that standing behind the prophets' call to rebuild the temple was an Achaemenid Persian administrative policy which sought to establish Judean semi-autonomy within the Persian empire. The first of these views, argued by Carol L. and Eric M. Meyers, understands the temple rebuilding as an outcome of the administrative reorganization of the provinces by Darius. The temple was made the economic and administrative centre of the sub-province and the high priest was given important powers beside those exercised by the governor. The second view, propounded by Joel P. Weinberg, contends that a community composed substantially of the Judeans repatriated from Babylonia was formed within the territory of Judah (which at that time still remained under the jurisdiction of Samaria). This community derived economic and political power from the temple and thus division was entrenched in the society between those who were participants in the temple community and those who were outside it. This form of socio-economic organization derived from a policy of the Achaemenid Persian provincial administration. Both these views thus understand the impetus for the rebuilding to have originally come from the Achaemenid Persians and that it was taken up by the prophets Haggai and Zechariah and by Zerubbabel in reaction to this policy initiative. These views are discussed and found wanting.

The second part of this chapter considers the temple rebuilding as a Judean initiative. Since the Jerusalem temple of Yahweh was the former national shrine of the kingdom of Judah, some have interpreted the temple rebuilding as an act of Judean rebellion. This contention is briefly investigated and dismissed, but consideration of it raises important issues regarding how Judeans could undertake the rebuilding of their former national shrine within the changed political and social context in which they found themselves. It will be argued that the Judeans undertook the rebuilding on their own initiative in that while the Aramaic edict of Cyrus had granted them permission to rebuild, it was incumbent upon them, rather than the Achaemenid Persian administration, to take responsibility for the undertaking. This occurred only when Zerubbabel arrived, the prophets Haggai and Zechariah claiming it was now the "time" to rebuild. A central concern was the development of an ideology which could legitimate the temple rebuilding for Judeans yet still pose no threat to Judah's status within the Persian empire. A review of the temple ideology of Haggai and Zechariah shows how this was accomplished and establishes these prophets' understanding of the purpose of the temple rebuilding within the context of expectations for Judean restoration. The prophets' temple ideology and expectations of restoration show that the social context of the rebuilding was not one of social division but rather one of social integration since both repatriates and non-repatriates participated in the rebuilding. Indeed, it will be argued that it was Judeans whom Zerubbabel and the repatriates found in the land when they returned, represented by Haggai, who initially promoted the temple rebuilding. This then leads to a consideration of why Zerubbabel and Joshua participated in the temple rebuilding, an activity which was not the original purpose of their return.

TEMPLE REBUILDING AS AN ACHAEMENID PERSIAN INITIATIVE

The Meyerses

Carol L. and Eric M. Meyers, in their extensive commentary on Haggai and Zechariah 1–8, have argued that the Jerusalem temple of Yahweh was rebuilt in the first years of Darius I as the result of an Achaemenid Persian administrative policy which sought to establish Judah as an independent sub-province within the Achaemenid Persian empire.[2] That is, the temple was rebuilt by the Judeans as a result of Achaemenid Persian initiative. They summarize their position so:

> Temple building, as we have asserted in our discussion of various parts of Haggai and Zechariah 1–6, was a critical beginning step, initiated through Persian policy, in the establishment of Yehudite [that is, Judean]

---

[2] Meyers and Meyers, *Haggai, Zechariah 1–8*.

self-governance within the imperial structure. It provided a physical setting and legitimization for indigenous leaders—i.e., priests—who would attend to local internal affairs in cooperation with the Persian-appointed governor, who would handle relations with the empire, mainly by providing the requisite tribute. All of Haggai reverberates with the efforts made in 520 to begin the restoration of the temple. Zechariah picks up on that theme in his set of visions and oracles and adds to it his program for the leadership associated with the temple in this postmonarchic era. The priesthood emerges as the key to Yehudite governance, although Zechariah wisely and skillfully retains the strong monarchic component that normally accompanied temple building and that was the dominant feature of Yehud's political heritage.[3]

The Meyerses contend that the establishment of the self-governance ("semiautonomy" is the preferred term elsewhere in their book) of Judah reflects Darius I's strategy to bring about political stability in the various provinces of the empire, in the aftermath of his suppression of the rebellions which attended his rise to the throne, through the reorganization of provincial administration. This reorganization encouraged the establishment of loyal indigenous leadership and administrative structures among the empire's diverse national-ethnic groups according to their traditional polities. Superintending these indigenous forms of political and social organization was the Persian satrapal administration. Darius's strategy was supposedly a continuation of that pursued by Cyrus who also favoured indigenous leadership in local affairs. According to the Meyerses:

> The need to formalize a system of self-governance was particularly acute during the early years of Darius. This emperor attended to the arrangement and administration of the vast territories and multitudinous national groups that composed the imperium, whereas his predecessors, caught up in the momentum and power of conquest, had treated lightly, if at all, the organization of the territories.[4]

The rebuilding of the Jerusalem temple played an integral part in the establishment of Judean self-governance since the reconstructed temple functioned as the administrative centre of Judah. The Meyerses contend that:

---

[3] Ibid., 390.
[4] Ibid., 220. For the temple rebuilding undertaken on Persian initiative and as part of administrative reorganization, see also ibid., xxxii, xxxviii–xl, 20, 23, 37, 44, 147, 220–21, 331, 368, 380. On Darius continuing Cyrus's policy of using local leaders, see ibid., xxxii, xxxviii–xxxix.

The apparently magnanimous gesture of Darius in allowing the ancient Judean temple to be rebuilt was in Persian eyes part of an overarching plan to restore local governance in political territories. The temple in Jerusalem was, like all temples in the ancient world, an administrative institution. It functioned in political, economic, and judicial matters as well as in strictly cultic or religious ones. Consequently, the restoration of a temple was a means of fostering local self-rule in a subunit of the Persian Empire.[5]

Important in this regard was the temple's role as the central economic institution which controlled "a significant part of the annual budget of the province" (p. 220), including the priestly revenues that were collected, and which managed the agricultural economy of Judah.[6] Although the Jerusalem temple fulfilled similar roles in the monarchical period, its roles in the Achaemenid administration of Judah were expanded in the absence of an indigenous monarchy and, as a corollary, so were the duties and authority of the priesthood.

The appointment of Zerubbabel as governor (פחה *peḥāh*) of the sub-province of Judah and Joshua as high priest of the Jerusalem temple should be understood in the light of Darius's administrative policy.[7] In monarchical Judah both religious and political authority resided in the king. Since indigenous kingship was no longer a viable option in Achaemenid Judah, this authority was shared between the Persian appointed *peḥāh*, Zerubbabel, and the high priest, Joshua. Each member of this "diarchy" was accorded specific functions; the governor was concerned with relations between Judah and the Persian government, while the high priest managed local affairs. The Meyerses summarize their respective duties so:

> Zerubbabel as governor was responsible to the king for returning tribute and tax payments from the province, and at the same time he served as official agent of imperial policy. Joshua, on the other hand, exercised expanded or new powers in managing the fiscal resources

---

[5] Ibid., 37–38.

[6] See, especially, ibid., 41–43; but see also pp. 20–23, 35, 39–41, 220–21.

[7] I accept that Zerubbabel returned to Judah as governor of this district, but the evidence is not incontrovertible. On the basis of the seals published in Avigad, *Bullae and Seals*, and the so-called Shemolith seal published by F. M. Cross in P. W. and N. L. Lapp (eds). *Discoveries in the Wadi ed-Daliyeh* (AASOR 41; Cambridge, MA: ASOR, 1974) 14, it has been argued that Judah was an independent district by the late sixth century and that this evidence points to the title פחה (used of both Sheshbazzar and Zerubbabel) as denoting their position as governors of Judah, not merely officers appointed by the Achaemenid Persian administration to undertake

brought in by the priesthood to the temple, as well as in acting as chief legal and religious authority of the land.[8]

This role for the high priest

... represents an accommodation which the traditional biblical views of the relationship between monarchy and priesthood made to the political realities of the late sixth century. The civil role of the governor was hardly as broad as that of the king had been, and the priesthood took up the slack. Those ... who contend that royal privileges had been given to the priesthood to strengthen it have not properly

---

a specific task (for example, leading a repatriation of exiled Judeans) while the territory of Judah lay under the jurisdiction of Samaria. For a discussion of the evidence, see Avigad, *Bullae and Seals*, 28–36; E. M. Meyers, "The Shemolith Seal and the Judean Restoration: Some Additional Considerations," *Eretz Israel* 18 (1985) 33*–38*; Meyers and Meyers, *Haggai, Zechariah 1–8*, 13–16; Williamson, "Governors of Judah," 59–82. On Sheshbazzar, see chapter 3 n. 4 above. פחה can be used of positions other than governor (be it governor of a satrapy, part of a satrapy, or of a sub-province; פחה is used of all of these offices), see Fensham, "*Peḥâ* in the Old Testament," 44–52; T. Petit, "L'évolution sémantique des termes hébreux et araméns *pḥḥ* et *sgn* et accadienes *pāḫatu* et *šaknu*," *JBL* 107 (1988) 53–67. The Meyerses consider Sheshbazzar to have been the first governor of Achaemenid Judah, but it is only in the reign of Darius that Judah was firmly established as an independent, semi-autonomous sub-province by means of the rebuilding of the temple, the appointment of a high priest alongside the indigenous governor, and the codification of indigenous laws. It appears from Ezr 5 that Tattenai, rather than the governor of Samaria, undertook the investigation of the Jerusalem temple rebuilding in the first years of Darius. This points, to my mind, to Zerubbabel being the governor of Judah. Had he simply been a repatriation commissioner and the territory of Judah under the jurisdiction of Samaria (so, Alt and Galling), one might have expected the governor of Samaria to investigate. It is notable, however, that in Ezr 6:7 the leader of the Judean community is termed פחת יהודיא "*peḥāh* of the Jews/Judeans" not פחת יהוד "*peḥāh* of Judah". That is, he is the head of a people, not a district.

F. Bianchi, "Le rôle de Zorobabel et de la dynastie davidique en Judée du VIᵉ siècle au IIᵉ siècle av. J.-C.," *Transeu* 7 (1994) 153–65; A. Lemaire, "Zorobabel et la Judée à la lumière de l'épigraphie (fin du VIᵉ s. av. J.-C.)," *RB* 103 (1996) 48–57, argue that Zerubbabel was installed as a vassal king by the Persians, and that the monarchical language used of Zerubbabel in Haggai and Zech 1–8 reflects this. If this were so, it would be unlikely that a "diarchy" of king and high priest would have been operating. In noting the use of פחה as a title for Zerubbabel, Lemaire, "Zorobabel et la Judée," 53–54, cites evidence in support of the contention "qu'il ne serait pas totalement impossible qu'un même personnage ait été appelé 'gouverneur' par l'administration centrale et 'roi' par la population locale." This is not too distant from the notion that Zerubbabel was chosen to be governor because of his Davidic ancestry. However, whether the Achaemenid Persians were re-establishing the Davidic dynasty is another matter. It is true that the Persians used local dynastic houses as "rulers" within the provincial administration, but these were already existing rather than defunct and in need of revivification, as was the case with the Davidic house of Judah.

[8] Meyers and Meyers, *Haggai, Zechariah 1–8*, xxxix, and see also pp. 17, 39–41, 180–82, 195–96, 220.

assessed the dynamics of the shifting configuration of civil and priestly functions under Darius's rule. The resulting theocratic form of provincial government in Yehud was as much a result of Persian interests and limitations as it was of independent local attempts to elevate priestly authority. Yet the outcome was an increase in the scope and status of the legitimate priesthood despite the retention of a combined civil and ecclesiastical governance.[9]

The reason why the internal administration of Judah fell to the temple and its priesthood appears to be historical. The administrative function of priests in monarchical Judah was carried over into the Persian period where it was further developed in the new non-state setting. The office of the high priest

> ... takes over much of the internal administration that previously resided in the royal house. The priesthood had always been important during the monarchy, even though the king had to be supreme, because the temple had to be an administrative institution along with the palace. The apparent expansion of priestly powers may have been to a certain extent the result of the removal of royal powers so that the priesthood, no longer sharing power, loomed larger.[10]

---

[9] Ibid., 196. On the diarchic form of government in Judah, see also ibid., xl–xli, 73–75, 361–62. For the Achaemenid administration as the instigator of this system, see ibid., xxxviii, 39–40, 268, 362.

[10] Ibid., 39, and see also pp. 181–82, 196, 352. Blenkinsopp, *History of Prophecy*, 196–99, offers an interpretation of the role of the Jerusalem cult and its personnel with a number of similarities to that of the Meyerses. The main elements of his position are: (i) the sub-province of Judah was a "temple community". This implies that the authority of the Jerusalem priesthood extended not only over the repatriated Judeans, but also over all who lived in Judah; (ii) the temple served as an Achaemenid Persian administrative centre. The day-to-day administration of the temple (and the sub-province?) was undertaken by the cultic personnel. The status and function of the Jerusalem cult and its personnel were established and maintained as part of Achaemenid Persian provincial policy; (iii) membership of the "cultic community", which was headed by the priests, was essential to the "legal standing" of residents of the sub-province. Title to real estate, for example, was contingent on this. (This is also the justification for the importance of the Jerusalem cult given by Smith, *Palestinian Parties*, 75, 82.) This third point bears close similarity to arguments propounded by J. P. Weinberg discussed below. Blenkinsopp does not determine when the temple and its personnel obtained these roles (for example, in the reign of Darius I or only later?). He cites no evidence in support of his understanding of the status and function of the cult and its personnel beyond passing references to supposed parallels with Ionian Greek cities in this period and to Cyrus's relationship to Esagila in Babylon, nor does he attempt to relate his understanding to the biblical texts. Blenkinsopp's book is an introduction to the history of Israelite and Judean prophecy, so one might not expect full argumentation for his view (cf. his paper "Temple and Society in Achaemenid Judah," in *Second Temple Studies*, 22–53, where he argues a modification of Weinberg's position).

In concert with the policy of granting semi-autonomy to national-ethnic groups under indigenous leadership, Darius's strategy for polit-ical stability called for the codification of local laws in order "to uphold if not strengthen traditional legal frameworks".[11] This further enhanced the authority of the Jerusalem priesthood since they were the custodians of traditional law. Thus:

> For the Yehudites, the ancient Torah laws were already authoritative in some form, but the Judean king as locus of judicial authority no longer existed. The priests thus resumed and extended the adjudica-tory powers inherent in their traditional roles. That they ruled on cul-tic matters is obvious, but they also had in the monarchical period resolved difficult cases . . . As teachers and/or custodians of pentateuchal materials, they were able to fill the gap left by the cessation of royal legislative and judicial powers.[12]

According to the Meyerses, the prophets Haggai and Zechariah sup-ported Darius's administrative reforms, giving Zerubbabel, Joshua, and the temple rebuilding prophetic legitimation. Although temple rebuilding was commonly undertaken by kings as part of the con-stitution and legitimation of the state, these prophets justified the rebuilding in the current political circumstances by reference to Zerubbabel's royal lineage and by the promise his activity held for a restoration of the monarchy. The Meyerses note that:

> By retaining the ideal of kingship to be re-established in a future time, and by simultaneously accepting the reality of its absence in the pre-sent, Zechariah resolves the anomaly of a temple's being restored with-out a monarch's direction. The prophet has been very careful in stating his case. A monarchic participant is needed for temple building, and the Davidic Zerubbabel can fill that position. It is only a symbolic participation, but one that leaves open the possibility that a descen-dant of Zerubbabel will occupy the royal throne. Zerubbabel's role in the temple refoundation ceremony gives it the necessary royal spon-sorship. The future hope is proleptically realized in that event. Zechariah is hardly provoking insurrection. Rather, he is affirming two things: first, that the ceremonial events surrounding the temple restoration have been efficacious because of Zerubbabel's involvement as well as because of Joshua's investiture; second, that Zerubbabel's present posi-

---

[11] Meyers and Meyers, *Haggai-Zechariah 1–8*, xxxix. On Darius's codification of indigenous laws, see also ibid., 20, 101–02, 220, 232, 278–79, 290–92, 380.

[12] Ibid., 220; see also pp. 198, 200; but cf. p. 354, where the high priest is said not to have civil authority.

tion and limited authority, though not ideal, have potential for becoming the legitimate kingship of an independent state.[13]

Thus this monarchical expectation has nothing to do with fomenting rebellion, rather the use of the traditional ideology of temple building was primarily a means of securing Judean support for Achaemenid administrative policy, including both the rebuilding of the temple and the sharing of powers between the governor and the high priest (that is, a diarchic form of governance) that were formerly held by the Judean king. The prophetic legitimation of the Achaemenid administrative organization therefore reflects not only political expediency, it also retains features of Judean nationalism. In Zechariah, at least, there is the expectation that the future re-establishment of the kingdom of Judah under Davidic kingship will not simply be a return to the political organization of monarchical Judah since the high priest is to retain important functions and status which he acquired as a result of the role given him in the restoration of Judah under the Achaemenids. In commenting on Zech 6:13 where the priest is said to sit on a throne beside the royal figure, the Meyerses assert that:

> The appearance here of a priest occupying a chair of office, or "throne," does not make him a royal figure equivalent to a king. Rather, it acknowledges the increase in his responsibilities in the postexilic community . . . Reading the Hebrew text as it is does not assign greater powers to the priest than to a king; it endows him, in recognition of the postexilic situation, with a larger role than during the monarchy. Consequently the future restoration of monarchy will entail a cooperative leadership between the two . . . This second "on his throne" is contextually essential for depicting the priest along with the Davidic dynast. The repetition of the phrase is thus distributive, providing the concept of important and official roles for both priest and monarch.[14]

---

[13] Ibid., 203–4; see further, pp. 22, 68–69, 122, 206, 223–24, 243, 356–57, 361–62, 370–72.

[14] Ibid., 361–62. See their comments on Zech 3:8–10, 6:9–15, particularly ibid., 223–24, 352–54, 361–63, but cf. p. 239:

> The diarchy represents a necessary stage in the scheme of Israel's contemporary history. The new Jerusalem temple, and the theocratic provincial state under Joshua's priestly leadership and Zerubbabel's governorship, is but an intermediate stage in the ongoing drama which will lead finally to the fulfillment of God's plan. Jerusalem's independence will be achieved and full Davidic rule will be restored.

This is not the only instance in the Meyerses' commentary where they appear to be offering contradictory positions.

For these prophets, the authority of the Achaemenid administration over Judean affairs and the prophets' expectation of the restoration of the indigenous kingship and independent kingdom of Judah were not too greatly in tension. The rebuilding, prompted by the Achaemenid Persian administration with their appointment of Zerubbabel and Joshua, was a legitimate undertaking due to Zerubbabel's involvement, and the temple could currently serve as "a residence for Yahweh as well as the administrative center of a semiautonomous state".[15] In line with Darius's administrative policies, the prophets' immediate concern was the establishment of Judah as an independent district, coupled with the economic benefits that would accrue to the population once a central administrative and economic institution (namely, the temple) was completed.[16]

The Meyerses offer a potentially useful analysis of the purpose of the rebuilding of the Jerusalem temple in the changed political and social circumstances of Achaemenid Judah. They address a number of important historical questions. First, they recognize the problem of legitimating the rebuilding of this former monarchical temple when Judeans currently lacked an indigenous king, interpreting Haggai and Zechariah as apologists for the rebuilding in this new political context. These prophets use old, monarchical conceptions of temple legitimation. There is a legitimate temple rebuilder, Zerubbabel, upon whom are bestowed royal designations such as "shoot", "servant", and "signet ring". While Zerubbabel may not currently be "king", temple rebuilding holds out the prospect that he will soon assume this office.

Second, the Meyerses can account for the purpose and timing of the rebuilding, as well as the function of the temple personnel, by citing Darius's provincial administrative reforms granting semi-autonomy

---

[15] Ibid., 22.
[16] Ibid., 41–43. See also G. Anderson, *Sacrifices and Offerings in Ancient Israel. Studies in their Social and Political Importance* (HSM 41; Atlanta: Scholars Press, 1987) 118–19, for the temple acting as storehouse to help the community overcome times of famine. Neh 13:10–14 notes that the temple had storerooms to hold agricultural tithes which were disbursed to the Levites. J. Schaper, "The Jerusalem Temple as an Instrument of the Achaemenid Fiscal Administration," *VT* 45 (1995) 528–39, argues for an economic and administrative role for the temple, but the evidence he adduces points to these functions being developed later in the Achaemenid Persian period, not at the time of the temple rebuilding. That is to say, that the *purpose* for rebuilding the temple was not to act as an administrative and economic centre; it later developed such roles.

to national-ethnic communities as the context in which to understand these matters. The timing of the rebuilding, in the second year of Darius, corresponds to his empire-wide reforms; the purpose of rebuilding the temple was to establish an administrative and economic centre for the sub-province, as well as being the symbolic centre of the newly restored (= incorporated?) community; the function of the temple personnel includes, alongside their traditional cultic roles, their role as administrators of the economic and day-to-day running of the sub-province, together with their role as custodians of traditional laws by which the sub-province was governed.

Third, the Meyerses elucidate the social mechanisms involved in the temple rebuilding. This rebuilding project was actually initiated by the Achaemenid Persian provincial administration, not the Judeans themselves. The administration's will—to establish Judah as a separate sub-province of the empire, semi-autonomous under its own, indigenous "diarchic" form of governance with an indigenous governor (Zerubbabel) and high priest (Joshua) with each office having particular, circumscribed duties; to rebuild the temple and have it function as the central economic and administrative centre of the sub-province—was couched by Haggai and Zechariah in acceptable ideological terms and given legitimacy but, nevertheless, the temple rebuilding was undertaken by the command of the Achaemenid authorities. Temple rebuilding and the roles of Zerubbabel and Joshua were imposed on the Judeans by the Achaemenid administration.

Fourth, the Meyerses answer the question of the nature of the polity which the temple served: it is the sub-province of Judah. Against those who understand social relations in early Achaemenid Judah to have been characterized by conflict between the repatriates and those Judeans they found in the land at their return, the Meyerses emphasize the social unity brought about by the temple rebuilding and Judah's semi-autonomy.[17] The temple is, as it was in

---

[17] The Meyerses respond only briefly to the view that there was conflict between the repatriates and the Judeans who had remained in their homeland. Hanson's thesis is, on my perusal of their commentary, the only such view mentioned; see Meyers and Meyers, *Haggai, Zechariah 1–8*, 51, 58, 66, 427. They note on p. 422, however, in commenting on "remnant of the people" in Zech 8:11, that "Presumably not all elements of Judahite society embraced the new theocratic scheme as Hanson has so forcefully argued (1975). The exclusive nature of Yahweh's 'remnant,' however, is not clear at all, and it is best to understand that term in the most inclusive way"; "inclusive" in that non-repatriated Judeans are part of the community rebuilding the temple.

the monarchical period, the constitutive institution of the polity. Social conflict still figures in the Meyerses understanding of this period, but the conflict is between the Judeans and the inhabitants of the province of Samaria (for the Meyerses, these people are Samaritans).[18]

The Meyerses' interpretation of the purpose of the rebuilding of the Jerusalem temple and the roles of Zerubbabel and Joshua in Achaemenid Judah rests on two suppositions. First, that Darius I instigated an administrative reform of the empire in the early years of his reign and, second, that the character of this reform was the establishment of semi-autonomous national-ethnic polities under indigenous leaders (p. 220 of their commentary offers a succinct summary of these two points). Both suppositions are questionable. Neither is argued at any length by the Meyerses in their commentary. They derive the idea of Darius's administrative reform from Herodotus iii. 89–94 which lists and describes the geographical extent of the twenty satrapies into which Darius supposedly organized his empire; this reorganization occurring, according to the Meyerses, soon after Darius had secured his kingship.[19] Whereas in the reigns of Cyrus and Cambyses the territory "Across-the-River" formed part of the large satrapy "Babylon and Across-the-River", in Herodotus's list Palestine is separated from "Babylonia and the rest of Assyria" (constituting the ninth satrapy) and forms, together with the rest of the territory "Across-the-River", the fifth satrapy.[20] The commencement of the Jerusalem temple reconstruction "on the twenty-fourth day of the sixth month in the second year of Darius" (Hag 1:15; that is, September 21, 520) is, according to the Meyerses, the direct result of this reorganization. They submit that this view is supported by Zechariah's pronouncement that "all the earth indeed rests quietly" (Zech 1:11b, dated to February 15, 519) which they understand as referring to Darius's successful suppression of the rebellions which attended his accession to the throne after which he turned his attention to pressing administrative matters.[21]

---

[18] Ibid., xxxiv.

[19] Ibid., xxxviii, 37, 147, 368.

[20] For the references in cuneiform sources to the satrapy "Babylon and Across-the-River" in reigns of Cyrus and Cambyses, see M. W. Stolper, "The Governor of Babylon and Across-the-River in 486 B.C.," *JNES* 48 (1989) 290–91.

[21] Meyers and Meyers, *Haggai, Zechariah 1–8*, 115. Information on these rebellions is found in Darius's Bisitun inscription. On the date of the suppression of these rebellions and its connection to the timing of the rebuilding of the Jerusalem

The Meyerses' attempt to relate the date of temple rebuilding to Herodotus's passage (iii. 89–94) regarding the reorganization of the provinces undertaken soon after Darius had established his kingship faces significant problems, however. It has been questioned that Herodotus's list reflects a general reorganization of the empire.[22] Further, the date of any administrative reform, notably the separation of the territory "Across-the-River" from the satrapy "Babylon and Across-the-River", should be dated to the reign of either Xerxes or Artaxerxes I rather than to the reign of Darius.[23] This position is now supported by an Achaemenid Babylonian receipt published by M. W. Stolper showing that "Across-the-River" was still part of the large satrapy "Babylon and Across-the-River" as late as 5 October 486.[24] Even J. M. Cook, upon whom the Meyerses so often depend for their understanding of Achaemenid Persian history and who wrote before Stolper's publication, noted that "we no longer need to assume that Darius's reorganization was carried out in the early part of his reign".[25] He considered that some time around 493, that is towards the end of Darius's reign, to be a more likely date.[26] Of those scholars writing before Stolper who accepted that the reorganization took place in the reign of Darius, the generally accepted *terminus post quem* was 516, with many preferring a later date in his reign.[27] The above

---

temple see below. The Meyerses appear to say that the Egyptian rebellion (which is not mentioned in the Bisitun inscription) had been put down by Darius by the time of Zechariah's first vision (Zech 1:7–17; dated to February 15, 519), but Darius probably did not arrive in Egypt before early 518; see R. A. Parker, "Darius and his Egyptian Campaign," *AJSL* 58 (1941) 373–77.

[22] So, for example, G. G. Cameron, "The Persian Satrapies and Related Matters," *JNES* 32 (1973) 47–56; T. C. Young, "The Consolidation of the Empire and the Limits of its Growth under Darius and Xerxes," in *CAH* 2nd ed., 4. 87–89. See the helpful overviews of P. Calmeyer, "Zur Genese altiranischer Motive, VIII: Die 'Statistische Landcharte des Perserreiches'—I," *Archaeologische Mitteilungen aus Iran* NF 15 (1982) 105–87; idem, "Die sogenannte fünfte Satrapie und die achaemenidischen Documente," *Transeu* 3 (1990) 109–29; D. F. Graf, "Greek Tyrants and Achaemenid Politics," *The Craft of the Historian. Essays in Honor of Chester G. Starr* (ed. J. W. Eadie and J. Ober; Lanham, MD: University Press of America, 1985) 79–123, although the following discussion differs from Graf's interpretation of the codification of Egyptian law and the appointment of the administrator of the temple of Khnum.

[23] For a brief outline of the arguments with the relevant bibliography, see Stolper, "The Governor of Babylon and Across-the-River," 292–93.

[24] Ibid., 284–95.

[25] J. M. Cook, *The Persian Empire* (New York: Schoken, 1983) 81.

[26] Ibid., 81, where he cites reasons for this dating.

[27] See the works cited in Stolper, "The Governor of Babylon and Across-the-River," 292 n. 9, 293 n. 12.

discussion of the date of the supposed reorganization of the empire, neglected by the Meyerses, was well advanced before they wrote their commentary. They also neglect to discuss the long-known Achaemenid Babylonian economic and administrative texts which show that at the time of the Jerusalem temple reconstruction, when Tattenai was "Governor of Across-the-River" (Ezr 5:3), Ushtanu was "Governor of Babylon and Across-the-River". The extant texts mentioning Ushtanu's governorship cover the period 21 March 521–June/July 516.[28] Tattenai's title "Governor of Across-the-River" in Ezr 5:3 is not evidence for the administrative independence of this region at the time of the temple rebuilding for he was subordinate to Ushtanu, the reorganization of the satrapy "Babylon and Across-the-River" having yet to take place.[29] This does not, of course, mean that an administrative reorganization of Judah could not have occurred early in Darius's reign, but it cannot be connected with any general reorganization of the empire at that time, and Herodotus cannot be cited as evidence for such a general reorganization.

Second, even if one were to accept, for the sake of argument, that Darius undertook an administrative reorganization of Judah (alone?), and that it was conducted very early in his reign, there is little evidence to support the Meyerses' contention that the rebuilding of the Jerusalem temple and the appointment of Zerubbabel and Joshua was for the purpose of establishing a semi-autonomous national-ethnic polity under indigenous leaders and traditional social institutions and laws. The administrative reform to which Herodotus iii. 89–94 is held to witness has been the subject of intense debate and, as noted above, this text is in any case inadmissible for the period of the Jerusalem temple reconstruction.[30] The Meyerses defend their

---

[28] See, ibid., 292–93 n. d., for the references.

[29] Attempts to see Tattenai's title as denoting that "Across-the-River" was divided from "Babylon and Across-the-River", although Tattenai was still subordinate to Ushtanu (so, for example, O. Leuze, *Die Satrapienteilung in Syrien und im Zweistromlande von 520 bis 320* [Haale: Niemeyer, 1935] 196, 226–29; Meyer, *Ezra, Nehemiah*, 44; Dandamaev, *Slavery*, 41), should be rejected; see the discussion in Stolper, "The Governor of Babylon and Across-the-River," 293–95; T. Petit, *Satrapes et satrapies dans l'empire achéménide de Cyrus le Grand à Xerxès Ier* (Bibliothèque de la Faculté de Philosophie et Lettres de l'Université de Liège 254; Liège: Bibliothèque de la Faculté de Philosophie et Lettres de l'Université de Liège, 1990) 190–92.

[30] The Meyerses cite only Cook, *Persian Empire*, 71f, 77ff., in support of their interpretation of the administrative reform, although this interpretation has a distinguished pedigree. For a brief outline of other views of the reform, see Stolper,

interpretation of the putative administrative reorganization by citing Darius's appointment of the Egyptian priest Udjahorresne to over-see the temple of Neith at Sais in order to re-establish the priests' college ("House of Life") and Darius's commission to the satrap of Egypt (commonly held to be Aryandes) to collect the Egyptian "laws".[31] For other examples of this policy the Meyerses refer the reader to J. M. Cook, *The Persian Empire*, pp. 71–2, where reference is made to Darius's interest in maintaining the cultic and legal traditions of his subject peoples, exemplified by the above examples as well as in Darius's directive maintaining the privileges of the priests of Apollo at Magnesia on the Meander (Gadates inscription; date: between 493 and 486), and his orders regarding suitable candidates for priesthood at the temple of Khnum in Egypt (Pherendates correspondence; date: 492–486).[32] From these examples the Meyerses deduce that Darius

---

"The Governor of Babylon and Across-the-River," 293 and see n. 13 there for rel-evant bibliography.

[31] Meyers and Meyers, *Haggai, Zechariah 1–8*, xxxii, xxxviii–xxxix, 101–02, 380. On Udjahorresne, see Posener, *La première domination perse*, 22–26; F. K. Kienitz, *Die politische Geschichte Ägyptens vom 7. bis zum 4. Jahrhundert vor der Zeitwende* (Berlin: Akademie, 1953) 61; A. H. Gardiner, "The House of Life," *JEA* 24 (1938) 157–79; Lloyd, "The Inscription of Udjahorresnet," 166–80.

On the codification of Egyptian laws in the reign of Darius, see Spiegelberg, *Die sogenannte Demotische Chronik*, 30–32 (transliteration and translation of the commission to codify the laws is on pp. 30–31; note, however, that Aryandes is not mentioned by name); E. Meyer, "Gesetzsammlung des Darius und Erlass des Kambyses über die Einkünfte der Tempel," in *Kleine Schriften* (2 vols.; Halle: Niemeyer, 1924) 2. 91–100; N. J. Reich, "The Codification of the Egyptian Laws by Darius and the Origin of the 'Demotic Chronicle'," *Mizraim* 1 (1937) 178–85; A. T. Olmstead, *History of the Persian Empire* (Chicago/London: University of Chicago Press, 1948) 142; Keinitz, *Die politische Geschichte Ägyptens*, 61; G. Mattha, *The Demotic Legal Code of Hermopolis West* (preface, and additional notes and glossary, by G. R. Hughes; Cairo: Institut français d'archéologie orientale du Caire, 1975) xii (who thinks that this lawcode is the one that was codified by Darius; but others disagree); E. Bresciani, "Egypt, Persian Satrapy," in *CHJ*, 1. 360–61; J. D. Ray, "Egypt 525–404 B.C.," in *CAH* 2d ed., 4. 262. Dates for the "codification": Begun in year 4 (518; although the text itself has year 3, year 4 is to be preferred; see Spiegelberg, *Die sogenannte Demotische Chronik*, 144; Parker, "Darius and his Egyptian Campaign," 373) and com-pleted in year 19 (503).

[32] On the Gadates inscription, see above chapter 3 n. 138. For its date, see Petit, *Satrapes et satrapies*, 180. On the Pherendates correspondence, see W. Spiegelberg, "Drei demotische Schreiben aus der Korrespondenz des Pherendates, des Satrapen Darius' I., mit den Chnum-Priestern von Elephantine," in *Sitzungsberichte der Preussischen Akademie der Wissenschaften Jahrgang 1928, Philosophisch-Historischen Klassen*, XXX (Berlin: Akademie der Wissenschaften, 1928) 604–22, Tafeln IV–VI; G. R. Hughes, "The So-called Pherendates Correspondence," in *Grammata Demotika. Festschrift für Erich Lüddeckens zum 15. Juni 1983* (eds. H.-J. Thissen and K.-Th. Zauzich; Würzburg: Gisela Zauzich, 1984) 75–86; K.-Th. Zauzich, "Die demotischen Papyri von der

must have also codified Judean laws at the time of the rebuilding
of the Jerusalem temple.[33]

Do these examples relate to a policy supposedly pursued by Darius
regarding the reorganization of the provinces and the character of
provincial self-governance? There is no reason to think that they do.
The Gadates and Udjahorresne inscriptions do not connect the actions
of Darius towards the cults of Apollo and Neith respectively to their
establishment as economic and/or administrative centres, or to their
priests sharing power with the governor in their respective provinces, or to the codification of indigenous laws. That is, there is no
mention of the features which the Meyerses contend were characteristic of Darius's reorganization of the provinces and which are
supposedly clearly evident in Judah at the time of the reconstruction of the Jerusalem temple. According to the Udjahorresne inscription, Udjahorresne, whose activities are commonly cited by the
Meyerses as being the closest parallel to the Judean experience, was
only empowered to normalize worship in the temple of Neith and
to recommence the teaching undertaken in the "House of Life".[34]
There is no mention in this inscription that Darius sought to have
the temple law codified or that authority in the province would be
shared between the priests and the governor. Further, the Pherendates
correspondence need not reflect an Achaemenid Persian policy regarding the appointment of temple administrators (cf. the Meyerses' claim
that Joshua was appointed due to a specific policy initiative). Hughes
notes that:

> one must wonder whether "what Darius, the Pharaoh, has commanded"
> (lines 5 and 7 [of Berlin P. 13540]) included anything more than that
> each local priesthood was free to choose its own chief administrator,
> but gave no guidelines as to the qualifications required of the one to
> be chosen by them. The objections of the two previous nominees in
> this case were probably *ad hoc* objections of the satrap himself.[35]

Insel Elephantine," in *Egypt and the Hellenistic World* (eds. E. van 't Dack, P. van
Dessel and W. van Gucht; Studia Hellenistica 27; Louven: Orientaliste, 1983) 421–35.
[33] See the references cited in n. 11 above. This codified law is thought to be the
Pentateuch.
[34] Posener, *La première domination perse*, 18–22. J. Blenkinsopp, "The Mission of
Udjahorresnet and those of Ezra and Nehemiah," 409–21, considers the activities
of Ezra and Nehemiah, rather than Zerubbabel and Joshua, regarding the Jerusalem
temple to be similar to those of Udjahorresne.
[35] Hughes, "The So-Called Pherendates Correspondence," 82.

The Meyerses appear to presume that the commission to codify Egyptian laws must reflect Darius's desire to impose these laws upon the indigenous population of the province. Even if this were the case, there is no evidence connecting the codification of laws to the administrative reorganization of Egypt. This undermines the Meyerses claim that the period of the Jerusalem temple rebuilding, as an expression of administrative reform, should be viewed as the opportune time for the codification of Judean law by the Jerusalem priesthood. Further, the codification of Egyptian law, while commonly accepted, rests on rather flimsy evidence. The text recounting Darius's establishment of a commission to codify Egyptian law is written on the back of the Demotic Chronicle, is poorly preserved with many lacunae and thus difficult to interpret, is written in Ptolemaic-period hand,[36] and may be influenced by Greek perceptions of Darius as a law giver.[37] It is thought by some Egyptologists that this codification

---

[36] My thanks to J. G. Manning for pointing this out.

[37] Diodorus Siculus I.95.4: "A sixth man to concern himself with the laws of the Egyptians, it is said, was Darius the father of Xerxes, for he was incensed at the lawlessness which his predecessor, Cambyses, had shown in his treatment of the sanctuaries of Egypt, and aspired to live a life of virtue and of piety towards the gods" (*Diodorus of Sicily I* [trans. C. H. Oldfather; The Loeb Classical Library; Cambridge, MA: Harvard University Press, 1933] 325). The quotation reflects the Herodotean tradition of the impiety of Cambyses, although the "lawlessness" may simply refer to Cambyses's taxing of Egyptian shrines and his limiting his beneficence to only a few (that is, it need not refer to the destruction of shrines; see above chapter 3 n. 120). On both the Demotic Chronicle text and Diodorus reflecting Hellenistic period legitimation of Egyptian law, see U. Rüterswörden, "Die perische Reichsautorisation der Thora: Fact or Fiction," *ZABR* 1 (1995) 52–55.

On the contention that Darius codified the laws of the indigenous peoples of the empire, see A. T. Olmstead, "Darius as Lawgiver," *AJSL* 51 (1935) 247–49; idem, *Persian Empire*, 120–28; R. N. Frye, *The History of Ancient Iran* (Handbuch der Altertumswissenschaft 3/7; Munich: C. H. Beck, 1984) 119 (Frye speaks of a "dual system of laws in the empire . . . the king's law applicable everywhere, and local laws which were codified by the king"); O. Bucci, "L'Impero achemenide come ordinamento giuridico sovrannazionale e *arta* come principo ispiratore di uno 'Jus commune persarum' (*data*)," *Modes de contacts et processus de transformation dans les sociétés anciennes* (Rome: École française de Rome, 1983) 89–122; cf. A. Kuhrt, "Babylonia from Cyrus to Xerxes," 132, regarding the supposed codification of Babylonian law by Darius, that "the evidence for this is slight and disputed" (she refers to *Reallexikon der Assyriologie* III [1957–71] s.v. Gerecht). It is held by the vast majority of biblical scholars that it was only with the arrival of Ezra (in the reign of Artaxerxes II?) that a codification of Judean law was promulgated (Ezr 7:11–26). P. Frei, "Die persische Reichautorisation. Ein Überblick," *ZABR* 1 (1995) 1–35, has argued on the basis of texts from the Hebrew Bible (Ezr-Neh, Esther), the reverse of the Demotic Chronicle, the so-called "Passover papyrus" from Elephantine (AP 21), the Udjahorresne biography, the Xanthos trilingual, the Pherendates correspondence,

of Egyptian law was an archetype for the later Hermopolis "code",
and thus "codified" a large number of property and inheritance laws,
but, importantly, no cultic law (cf. the Pentateuch).[38] But as S. Allam
correctly points out, this supposition is fragile given the absence of
any fragment of Darius's "code".[39] What laws were codified by the
commission and for what purpose remain impossible to determine,
if indeed there was such a codification of law. For Weisehöfer, Darius
sought to revoke the fiscal arrangements for temples instituted by
Cambyses which required understanding the legal relationship between
the Pharaoh and temples that obtained in the preceding period. It
was this set of arrangements that Darius wanted to reinstitute. The
collecting of these norms in a "lawbook" would thus be to the mutual
advantage of the central administration and the temples and their
priests. Darius's concern was limited to the legal-fiscal regulation of
temples, not with turning these local norms into imperial law, nor
with some general codification of Egyptian law. The reason why

and other sources, that the Persians pursued a policy of "Reichsautorisation"; that
is, they did not simply sanction or accept local legal norms but in reality "owned"
them as the imperial law. These laws thus had the authority of imperial law within
that territory and over the community, and were recognized across the empire. It
is on this basis that satraps and other administrative officials had both to revere
and enforce such laws. Commonly the Great King himself was involved in this process. This perspective overlaps somewhat with that of the Meyerses since they too
affirm the active involvement of Darius in the formation of Judean law and its recognized binding authority over Judeans. Both Wiesehöfer ("'Reichsgesetz' oder 'Einzelfallgerechtikeit'?" 36–46) and Rüterswörden ("Die perische Reichsautorisation der
Thora," 47–61) have critiqued Frei's arguments largely on the basis that he over-
states the authority and scope of the legal provisions mentioned in these texts, and
that commonly they result from the initiative of the subjugated community, not the
Great King, with only the satrap as the highest administrative official involved.

[38] See, for example, S. Grunert, "Der juristische Papyrus von Hermopolis—Kodex
oder Kommentar?" *Altorientalische Forschungen* 10 (1983) 154. The demotic text published by Spiegelberg (*Die sogenannte demotische Chronik*, 30–31) speaks of gathering
"The . . . law of Pharaoh, the temple (and) the people". Collaborating in this venture were "the learned [among?] the military, the priests and the scribes of Egypt".
To what does "the law of the temple" refer? J. Quaegebeur, "Sur la 'loi sacrée'
dans l'Egypte gréco-romaine," *Ancient Society* 11/12 (1980/81) 240, relates it to the
"lois sacrée" known from the Graeco-Roman period, but it may just as well refer
to the property and inheritance laws governing the temples and their officials.
P. W. Pestman, "L'origine et l'extension d'un manuel de droit égyptien. Quelques
réflections à propos du soi-disant Code de Hermopolis," *JESHO* 26 (1983) 14–21,
understands the Hermopolis code to have roots in the eighth century.

[39] S. Allam, "Réflections sur le 'code légal' d'Hermopolis dans l'Égypt ancienne,"
Chronique d'Égypt 61 (1986) 65–66. For a discussion of the bibliography through the
1980s on the so-called Hermopolis Code, see J. Mélèze-Modrzejewski, "Bibliographie
de papyrologie juridique (v. 1)," *Archiv für Papyrusforschung* 34 (1988) 80–83.

Darius himself was involved with this process is that traditionally it was the responsibility of the Pharaoh to regulate these particular matters, whereas lower level officials could deal with other administrative arrangements.[40]

Ezra 5–6, the Aramaic narrative of the rebuilding in the time of Darius I, raises further problems for the Meyerses' contention that the rebuilding of the Jerusalem temple was undertaken as a result of Achaemenid Persian administrative policy; that is, that it reflects an administrative reform instigated by Darius I in order to establish self-autonomous national-ethnic polities under indigenous leaders. According to this text, the Judeans' rebuilding of the Jerusalem temple under the leadership of Zerubbabel and Joshua was investigated by Tattenai, the governor of the satrapy "Across-the-River" (Ezr 5:1–17). The temple rebuilding is portrayed as having taken the Achaemenid Persian administrators of the satrapy by surprise. This is remarkable if the rebuilding was commissioned by the Achaemenid Persian administration and Zerubbabel and Joshua sent to Judah for this specific purpose, as the Meyerses claim. The Judean elders in responding to Tattenai's request for their authority to rebuild the temple (Ezr 5:9) did not refer to permission that had been granted by Darius, but only to the Cyrus edict (Ezr 5:13–16). Equally remarkable is that Darius was ignorant of his own supposed policy. Rather than reacting to the letter from Tattenai regarding the propriety of the Judeans' project (Ezr 5:7–17) by restating his policy of administrative reorganization, Darius had a search made for the edict of Cyrus (Ezr 6:1–2). Once found, it was this edict which convinced Darius that the Judeans should be permitted to complete their temple (Ezr 6:6–12). Thus Tattenai, the Judeans (including Zerubbabel and Joshua), and Darius knew nothing of the rebuilding being undertaken as the result of a specific Achaemenid Persian administrative policy. Ezra 5–6 has the Judeans taking the initiative for the temple rebuilding in the reign of Darius with this monarch only *later*

---

[40] Wiesehöfer, "'Reichsgesetz' oder 'Einzelfallgerechtikeit'?" 38–41. If the Torah was codified in Judah in the early years of the reign of Darius I, the Meyerses need to account for Ezr 7:14 where Ezra is said to have brought the Torah with him from Babylonia. How could Ezra, a Babylonian Jew, be reinforcing a law which was promulgated for Judeans living in Judah? The Meyerses do not enter into the debate regarding the extent, character and date of the Pentateuch. On these matters see chapter 1 n. 15; chapter 2 nn. 22–27.

supporting the undertaking, after it was well under way (Ezr 6:6–15). Ezra 5–6 may be historically spurious, but the Meyerses need to discuss this text rather than simply ignore it. They accept that Tattenai paid a "visit" to the temple site, which they interpret as being "surely a reflection of the Samaritans' [sic] concern about their favoured position within the empire, a privilege they had enjoyed since the fall of the kingdom of Israel" (p. xxxiv); that is, the establishment of Judah as an independent sub-province did not meet with Samarian approval. This hardly does justice to the problems raised for their theory by the character of both Tattenai's investigation and Darius's response. The emphasis in the Aramaic narrative of the temple rebuilding is on the temple as a cultic centre, not as an economic and administrative centre of an independent district. Unless the prophecies of Haggai and Zechariah 1–8 are misdated, they could not have been articulating Achaemenid Persian administrative policy by calling for the temple to be rebuilt since Ezra 5–6 and the arguments outlined above show that no such policy existed. If one admits from Ezra 5–6 only that Tattenai undertook an investigation of the legitimacy of the temple rebuilding, then the Meyerses' theory that it was sanctioned, indeed fostered, by the Achaemenid administration falls flat. It bears pointing out that Zerubbabel's appointment as governor by the Achaemenid Persian administration is not under question, only that he received a brief for the rebuilding of the Jerusalem temple.

Since there was no brief originally given to Zerubbabel regarding the rebuilding of the Jerusalem temple, the temple could not have figured in the Meyerses' putative administrative reorganization of Judah. Further, this lack of a brief raises doubts regarding the position and authority of Joshua, the high priest, who, according to the Meyerses, was supposed to undertake the daily economic and administrative running of Judah from his temple headquarters. It is only in the Hellenistic period that the preeminent authority of the priesthood, especially the high priest, in religious and civil matters is evidenced.[41]

---

[41] E. J. Bickerman, *God of the Maccabees: Studies on the Meaning and Origin of the Maccabean Revolt* (trans. H. R. Moehring; SJLA 32; Leiden: Brill, 1979) 36–38; idem, *The Jews in the Greek Age* (Cambridge, MA/London: Harvard University Press, 1988) 140–47; V. Tcherikover, *Hellenistic Civilization and the Jews* (trans. S. Applebaum; Philadelphia: Jewish Publication Society of America, 1959; reprint, New York: Atheneum, 1979) 58–59, 120–21, 124–25, 155.

The evidence regarding the status of the high priest before the Hellenistic period is very slight and cannot support the contention that the authority of the priesthood was growing throughout the Achaemenid Persian period at the expense of the Persian-appointed governor. The Meyerses contend that with the building of the Jerusalem temple a diarchy was established in Judah by the Persians.[42] The two officials were Zerubbabel, the Persian-appointed governor, and Joshua, the high priest. Under this arrangement the high priest was responsible for the administration of the temple, which was rebuilt by the Persians as the administrative centre of the sub-province of Judah. They conclude "that a priest [that is, the high priest] is now on par with a civil figure [that is, the governor] as the highest authority in the land".[43]

Haggai 1:1, 12, 2:2, 4, and Zech 3:1–10, 6:9–10, which are dated to 520–19, address the high priest as a leader in the community, often beside Zerubbabel the *peḥāh*. Nothing is mentioned of the high priest's role, however. Zech 6:11, 13 speak of the high priest in royal terms, but this may reflect a hope for the future or it may be a later insertion. Zech 6:9–15 has been much discussed. Although the MT in 6:11 speaks of the manufacture of crowns, one of which is to be placed on the head of Joshua, many commentators have emended MT to singular "crown" (in agreement with LXX Lucian, Peshitta, Targum) and view "Joshua, the son of Jehozadak" as a late interpolation for "Zerubbabel", probably made in response to the failed royal prophecies regarding Zerubbabel.[44] Resolution of the interpretation of Zech 6:11 is not necessary here since 6:13 is commonly held to refer to royal expectation focused on Zerubbabel. An exception is Rudolph, who considers "branch" to be a reference to a royal figure coming after Zerubbabel since Zerubbabel did not fulfil the prophecy regarding the temple rebuilding (Zech 6:12–13).[45] If it is original to the prophet then it appears that he held the notion of a

---

[42] Meyers and Meyers, *Haggai, Zechariah 1–8*, 17, 39–41, 203, 238–40; and in a similar vein, A. Sérandour, "Les récits bibliques de la construction du second temple: leurs enjeux," *Transeu* 11 (1996) 9–32.

[43] Meyers and Meyers, *Haggai, Zechariah 1–8*, 17.

[44] See, among others, H. Mitchell, *A Critical and Exegetical Commentary on Haggai, Zechariah, Malachi, and Jonah* (ICC; Edinburgh: Clark, 1912) 185–86; Amsler, *Aggée, Zacharie 1–8*, 105, 107–08. In support of MT, see Meyers and Meyers, *Haggai, Zechariah 1–8*, 349–53.

[45] Rudolph, *Haggai-Sacharja 1–8*, 130.

diarchic form of leadership. This is something quite different, however, than claiming that such a form of governance was actually instituted by the Achaemenid Persian administration.[46] There is no evidence to corroborate the argument that the Persians established the temple as an administrative centre or that the high priest had an important administrative function. There is also no evidence to support the contention that when Zerubbabel disappeared from the scene, the high priest assumed the sole leadership position.[47] If there were a diarchy, why did not Zerubbabel's successor as governor participate in it? Why would authority necessarily devolve upon the high priest?

One needs to beware of understanding the role of the cult and high priesthood in the early Achaemenid Persian period in terms of what is known of their role in the Hellenistic period. Nothing is heard of the high priest or the status and role of the other priests in Ezra 7–10 and Nehemiah, texts which supposedly recount episodes in the history of Judah some 80–150 years later. Had the high priest been a significant political figure one cannot help but think that Ezra and/or Nehemiah would have had dealings with him. Neither Ezra-Nehemiah nor the books of Chronicles say much about the social status or authority of the Jerusalem cultic personnel. Chronicles devotes considerable attention to the organization of the Jerusalem cultic personnel, particularly the Levites, but little information is imparted regarding the role of the priests and Levites beyond their various forms of cultic service (for example, I Chrons 23–26, II Chrons 31:2–21 cf. Hag 2:10–14).[48] Ezra-Nehemiah and Chronicles place the priests under the authority of others, be it the king (Chronicles), Ezra (Ezr 7, 9–10; Ezra is said to be a priest himself in Ezr

---

[46] Tollington, *Tradition and Innovation*, 154–81, for example, sees the diarchic form of leadership as an idea original to Zechariah, and notes that "as far as is known the diarchy never came into being" (p. 180); similarly, D. Goodblatt, *The Monarchic Principle: Studies in Jewish Self-Government in Antiquity* (Texte und Studien zum Antiken Judentum 38; Tübingen: J. C. B. Mohr [Paul Siebeck], 1994), 60: "Whether in fact a diarchic regime existed around 520 or in the time of the Chronicler is probably unknowable. At the very least, the fragmentary nature of our sources for the Persian period . . . prevents us from drawing any firm conclusions".

[47] Contra J. M. Balcer, *Sparda By the Bitter Sea. Imperial Interaction in Western Anatolia* (Brown Judaica Studies 52; Chico, CA: Scholars Press, 1984) 138; Hanson, *A People Called*, 265.

[48] Myers, *I Chronicles*, lxviii–lxxiii. The high priest is mentioned in priestly texts (Num 35:25; Lev 21:10–15 cf. II Ki 12:11, 22:4–8, 23:4), but his role is in cultic matters only. However, since these priestly texts consider Israel to be a cultic community there is really no distinction between religious and secular authority.

7:5) or Nehemiah (Neh 2:16–18; 10; 12:44–13:31; Nehemiah is not
a priest but he is the governor of Judah. The Jerusalem cult and
personnel are therefore under the authority of the governor). Perhaps
the most telling piece of information regarding the status of the upper
echelons of the Jerusalem priesthood is imparted by Neh 13:28. For
the governor of Samaria to permit his daughter to marry the son
of the Jerusalem high priest the social status of the high priest must
have been significant. Alas, no information is given regarding the
function of the high priest.

AP 30:18–19, dated to 407, mentions "Yoḥanan the high priest"
(כהנא רבא) beside the Judean governor Bagohi (= "your lordship" cf.
line 1) and "the notables of the Jews" (חרי יהודיא). The high priest
is important enough to receive an appeal from the Elephantine Jews
in their quest to gain Achaemenid Persian permission to rebuild their
temple. Clearly, it is thought that he could wield some influence on
their behalf. Nothing is learned, however, of his role in Judean society. The same can be said of the incident recounted in Josephus in
which a certain Bagoses, a Persian general (?) (Gk. *strategos*), has dealings with a high priest named Joannes (Yoḥanan).[49] It is commonly
assumed that they are the same individuals as those mentioned in
AP 30, although this is by no means certain.[50]

There is one Judean coin minted in the mid-fourth century which
bears the inscription [י]וחנן הכוהן—"Yoḥanan the Priest".[51] The title
הכוהן is otherwise unattested on Judean coins of the Persian period,
the only other title appearing on coins with a personal name being

---

[49] Josephus, *Antiquities*, xi. 297–301.

[50] See H. G. M. Williamson, "The Historical Value of Josephus' Jewish Antiquities
XI. 297–301," *JTS* NS 28 (1977) 49–66, who dates this incident to the reign of
Artaxerxes III, c. 333; cf. the critical discussion in J. C. VanderKam, "Jewish High
Priests of the Persian Period: Is the List Complete?" in *Priesthood and Cult in Ancient
Israel* (ed. G. A. Anderson and S. M. Olyan; JSOTSup 125; Sheffield: Sheffield
Academic Press, 1991) 81–87. L. L. Grabbe, "Josephus and the Reconstruction of
the Judean Restoration," *JBL* 106 (1987) 231–46, points out that it is impossible
to date this incident or to identify the persons involved with any precision; idem,
"Who was the Bagoses of Josephus (*Ant.* 11.7.1, §297–301)?" *Transeu* 5 (1992) 49–55,
admits that three possibilities for identifying Josephus's Bagoses are viable but that
preference should currently be given to identifying him with Bagohi of the Elephantine
papyri. D. R. Schwartz, "On Some Papyri and Josephus' Sources and Chronology
for the Persian Period," *JSJ* 21 (1990) 192–94, supports the view that the Bagoses
and Joannes in Josephus, *Antiquities*, xi. 297–301, are the same individuals mentioned in AP 30.

[51] D. P. Barag, "Some Notes on a Silver Coin of Johanan the High Priest," *BA*
48 (1985) 166–68.

"the governor" (הפחה). The significance of this coin is hard to assess. Dan Barag assumes that "the issue of coins by the high priest occurred at a time when he also controlled the secular government".[52] It has been proffered that if the priest were the minting authority then the Persian-appointed governor had been overthrown. The most likely occasion for this event would have been during the Tennes rebellion.[53] Following F. M. Cross's reconstruction of the Jerusalem high priestly line in the Persian Period, Barag posits that the Yoḥanan who minted the coin was "the grandson of the high priest Johanan, the addressee of the letter sent from Elephantine in 410 B.C."[54]

The identity of this Yoḥanan and the circumstances of the minting of the coin are, however, open to question. Cross's reconstruction of the high priestly line has received criticism on a number of grounds.[55] Also, it is unclear that "the priest" denotes the high priest. The priest minting the coin need not denote the expulsion of the governor since the priest may have been an official under the authority of the governor.[56] At most one can say that "the priest" was an important enough official to have minted a coin, but the nature of his authority remains unclear.[57]

---

[52] Ibid., 168.

[53] So, Barag, "Silver Coin," 168; J. W. Betlyon, "The Provincial Government of Persian Period Judea and the Yehud Coins," *JBL* 105 (1986) 639. On supposed Judean participation in the Tennes rebellion see D. P. Barag, "The Effects of the Tennes Rebellion on Palestine," *BASOR* 183 (1966) 6–12, but cf. Stern, *Material Culture*, 243, 255; and see the circumspect comments of P. Machinist, "The First Coins of Judah and Samaria: Numismatics and History in the Achaemenid and Early Hellenistic Periods," in *Achaemenid History VIII: Continuity and Change* (ed. H. Sancisi-Weerdenburg, A. Kuhrt and M. C. Root; Leiden: Nederlands Instituut voor het Nabije Osten, 1994) 375–76.

[54] Barag, "Silver Coin," 168, so also Betlyon, "Provincial Government," 639. The letter referred to is AP 30. For Cross's reconstruction of the high priestly line see his "Reconstruction of the Judean Restoration," 1–17.

[55] See Widengren, "Persian Period," 506–9; VanderKam, "Jewish High Priests," 67–91.

[56] Mildenberg, "Yᵉhud-Münzen," in Weippert, *Palästina in vorhellenistischen Zeit*, 726.

[57] Similar problems surround the use of the late fourth century coins from Tell Jemme and Beth Zur which bear the inscription "Hezekiah the governor" (Tell Jemme: הפחה יחזקיו/ה; Beth Zur: יחזכיה [ה]פחה); L. Y. Rahmani, "Silver Coins of the Fourth Century from Tel Gamma," *IEJ* 21 (1971) 158–60, who concluded that this shows that Ezekias (Hezekiah), the high priest at the time of Ptolemy I according to Josephus, *Contra Apionem*, ii. 187, could not have been responsible for the minting (as had formerly been thought when the Beth Zur coin was read *yhzkyh yhd*) because of the title (*pḥḥ*) given him. A. Kindler, "Silver Coins Bearing the Name of Judea from the Early Hellenistic Period," *IEJ* 24 (1974) 73–76, has con-

We may conclude this brief study of the Meyerses' interpretation of the purpose of the Jerusalem temple rebuilding by noting that none of their central contentions can be accepted. The temple cannot be shown to have been rebuilt as a result of an Achaemenid Persian policy of provincial administrative reorganization in the first years of the reign of Darius.

J. P. Weinberg

In a number of publications J. P. Weinberg has propounded the view that the Jerusalem temple was rebuilt as a result of Achaemenid Persian administrative policy which had as its goal the formation of a self-determining polity within Judah.[58] This polity, which for reasons

---

tended that since Judea remained a separate administrative district under Ptolemy I it is quite within reason to consider that the high priest Hezekiah was responsible for the district at the end of the Persian period and that he was also the governor of the sub-district. There is no other evidence to support this contention. Further, it faces problems with the reconstruction of the high priestly line (cf. Josephus, *Antiquites*, xi. 297–301). For a recent discussion of the Hezekiah coins, see B. Bar-Kochva, *Pseudo-Hecateus, On the Jews: Legitimating the Jewish Diaspora* (Hellenistic Culture and Society 21; Berkeley/Los Angelos/London: University of California Press, 1996) 82–91, 255–70.

On Judean coins of the Persian period see, in addition to the above works, L. Mildenberg, "Yehud: A Preliminary Study of the Provincial Coinage of Judaea," in *Greek Numismatics and Archaeology: Essays in Honor of Margaret Thompson* (ed. O. Mørkholm and N. M. Waggoner; Wetteren: NR, 1979) 183–96; U. Rappaport, "The First Judean Coinage," *JJS* 32 (1981) 1–17; Y. Meshorer, *Ancient Jewish Coinage* (Dix Hills, NY: Amphora, 1982).

[58] J. P. Weinberg, "Demographische Notizen zur Geschichte der nachexilischen Gemeinde in Juda," *Klio* 54 (1972) 45–59; idem, "Das *bēit 'ābōt* im 6.–4. Jh. v. u. Z.," *VT* 23 (1973) 400–14; idem, "Der *'am hā'āreṣ* des 6.–4. Jh. v. u. Z.," *Klio* 56 (1974) 325–35; idem, "N^{e}înîm und 'Söhne der Sklaven Salomos' im 6.–4. Jh. v. u. Z.," *ZAW* 87 (1975) 355–71; idem, "Die Agrarverhältnisse in der Bürger-Tempel-Gemeinde der Achämenidenzeit," *AcAnt* 22 (1976) 473–86; idem, "Bemerkungen zum Problem 'Der Vorhellenismus im Vorderer Orient'," *Klio* 58 (1976) 5–20; idem, "Zentral- und Partikulargewalt im achämenidischen Reich," *Klio* 59 (1977) 25–43, all of which can be found in English translation in Weinberg, *The Citizen-Temple Community* (although the translation needs to be used with caution). In preparing this study I have relied on the German originals of the above articles and cite references to the English translations where appropriate. I have also drawn on J. P. Weinberg, "Probleme der sozialökonomischen Struktur Judäas vom 6. Jahrhundert v. u. Z. bis zum 1. Jahrhundert u. Z.," *Jahrbuch für Wirtschaftgeschichte* 1 (1973) 237–51, and Weinberg, *Der Chronist in seiner Mitwelt*, his most recent synthetic statement. I have been unable to consult Weinberg's publications in Latvian and Russian. Other recent publications by Weinberg on this topic include, "Die Mentalität der jerusalemischen Bürger-Tempel-Gemeinde des 6.–4. Jh. v. u. Z.," *Transeu* 5 (1992) 133–41; idem, "Transmitter and Recipient in the Process of Acculturation: The Experience of the Judean Citizen-Temple Community," *Transeu* 13 (1997) 91–105.

outlined below Weinberg terms the Bürger-Tempel-Gemeinde ("Citizen-Temple Community"), consisted largely, though not entirely, of the Judeans repatriated from Babylonia who formed a close connection to the temple, which they themselves rebuilt. The status of the Bürger-Tempel-Gemeinde was considerable given the important administrative and economic roles given it by the Achaemenid Persian administration, and members' title to land was dependent on their connection to the temple.

In developing this understanding of the nature of Achaemenid Judean society and the place of the Jerusalem temple in Achaemenid Judah, Weinberg has drawn upon research by a number of his former Soviet colleagues from which he argues that:

> Im System des nahöstlichen Vorhellenismus fiel eine bedeutende Rolle dem eigentümlichen sozialpolitischen Organismus zu, der mit dem Terminus "Tempel-Gemeinde" oder genauer "Bürger-Tempel-Gemeinde" bezeichnet wird. Dieser Anfang des 1. Jt. v. u. Z. enstandene sozial politische Organismus verbreitete sich besonders intensiv in achämenidischer Zeit, als die Bürger-Tempel-Gemeinden in Kleinasien (Komana, Olba, Pessinus, Zela u. a.) und Armenia (Tordan, Ani u. a.), Mesopotamien (Uruk, Barsippa, Nippur u. a.) und Syrien (Bambyke, Emessa u. a.), Phönizien und Palästina vorhanden waren.[59]

Weinberg's work has attracted increased scholarly attention over the past decade, particularly by those who view social conflict as endemic to early Achaemenid Persian Judah and who see in this interpretation an excellent explanation for that conflict. A brief summary of some of the main points can be found in Schottroff, "Zur Sozialgeschichte Israels," 61–63; Grabbe, *Judaism from Cyrus to Hadrian*, 1. 116–18. Summaries, and overall positive evaluations, can be found in Blenkinsopp, "Temple and Society," 22–53; Smith, *Religion of the Landless*, 106–08; P. E. Dion, "The Civic-and-Temple Community of Persian Period Judaea: Neglected Insights from Eastern Europe," *JNES* 50 (1991) 281–87; D. L. Petersen, "Israelite Prophecy: Change versus Continuity," in *Congress Volume: Leuven, 1989* (ed. J. A. Emerton; SVT 43; Leiden/New York/Cologne: E. J. Brill, 1991) 190–203; J. E. Dyke, *The Theocratic Ideology of the Chronicler* (Biblical Interpretation Series 33; Leiden/New York/Cologne: E. J. Brill, 1998) 103–109, 203. For critical evaluations, see H. Kreissig, "Eine beachtenswerte Theorie zur Organization altvorderorientalischer Tempelgemeinden im Achämenidenreich. Zu J. P. Weinbergs 'Bürger-Tempel-Gemeinde' in Juda," *Klio* 66 (1984) 35–39; P. R. Bedford, "On Models and Texts: A Response to Blenkinsopp and Petersen," in *Second Temple Studies I*, 154–59; H. G. M. Williamson, "Judah and the Jews," in *Studies in Persian History* (ed. M. Brosius and A. Kuhrt) 145–163.

[59] Weinberg, "Vorhellenismus," 12 (*Citizen-Temple Community*, 24). For the development of this polity and its existence in the Achaemenid empire Weinberg cites the work of G. Kh. Sarkisian, I. M. Diakonoff, A. G. Perichanjan, and M. A. Dandamaev. Much of the results of their research is written in Russian.

The Bürger-Tempel-Gemeinde was developed in subjugated territories throughout Western Asia during the first millennium B.C.E. as a type of autonomous, self-governing structure within successive imperial provincial systems. It integrated economically and administratively the inhabitants of a city or territory with the local temple and its personnel giving rise to a community of free, fully enfranchised members, organized mainly in large agnatic Lay and Priestly associations who, as members, had a right to property or landed estate. The Bürger-Tempel-Gemeinde was self-governing with authority exercised by the Head Priest together with a council and the assembly of community members, having jurisdiction over such matters as the disposal of land and the right to exact taxes and services from members, among other things.[60]

Weinberg outlines the development of the Bürger-Tempel-Gemeinde so:

> Die Verbreitung dieser Gemeinde wurde vom Prozeß der sozialökonomischen Entwicklung Vorderasiens bedingt, von der Evolution der zwei Sektoren der vorderasiatischen Ökonomie—des staatlichen und gemeindlich-privaten . . . hervorgerufen. Das Wachstum der Produktivkräfte und die Entwicklung der Waren-Geldwirtsschaft, die intensifikation des Handels und der aktiv Urbanisationsprozeß haben dazu geführt, daß in den beiden erwähnten Sektoren gleichartige individuelle Wirtschaften entstanden. Dank dieser gleichartigen wirtschaftlichen Organisation begann ein Zusammenschluß der Vertreter der beiden Sektoren (hauptsächlich in den Städten) und ein Verblassen der sozialen Unterschiede zwischen ihnen. Die Absonderung der individuellen Wirtschaften von staatlichen Sektor vollzog sich, indem deren Besitzer sich dem Tempel anschlossen. Der letztere verwandelte sich jedoch schon während der zweiten Hälfte des 2. Jts. v. u. Z. zu einer autonomen und privilegierten Organisation der herrschenden Oberschicht. Durch den Zusammenschluß mit der Stadtgemeinde bildete der Tempel die wesentlich neue Struktur—die Bürger-Tempel-Gemeinde, die eine geeinte Organisation für die früheren Gemeindemitglieder und auch für die vorherigen Angehörigen des staatlichen Sektors war. Diese Bürger-Tempel-Gemeinde gab ihren Mitgliedern eine organisatorische Einheit und kollektive Selbstverwaltung, sie sorgte für politische und ökonomische Hilfeleistung.[61]

The Achaemenid Persian period saw the encouragement of the development of a "gemeindlich-privaten Sektor" of the economy alongside

---

[60] Weinberg, *Chronist*, 27.
[61] Weinberg, "Die Agrarverhältnisse in der Bürger-Tempel-Gemeinde," 473–74 (*Citizen-Temple Community*, 92–93).

the "staatlichen Sektor." The latter consisted of "[d]ie königlichen Ländereien, Güter der Spitz, Siedlungen der abhängigen Bauern und Lehen der Söldner," while the former comprised "die Länder der Stämme, der zahlreichen Dorfgemeinden und die so umfangreichen Tempelgüter,"[62] and was promoted in Babylonia, Syria, Asia Minor, Armenia, Phoenicia, and Palestine by means of the Bürger-Tempel-Gemeinde.[63] This polity formed a type of autonomous, self-governing structure within the Achaemenid Persian provincial system. To use Weinberg's term, it was a type of "Partikulargewalt" which the Achaemenid Persian administration ("Zentralgewalt") fostered.[64]

Although Weinberg offers an extended treatment of the development of the Bürger-Tempel-Gemeinde within the context of Achaemenid Persian economic and administrative policy, it is not necessary to summarize it here. Our interest lies in how Weinberg connects the Bürger-Tempel-Gemeinde polity to the rebuilding of the Jerusalem temple of Yahweh, since he views Achaemenid Judah as exhibiting an excellent example of a particular type of this polity.[65] The background to the development of the Judean Bürger-Tempel-Gemeinde was the economic policy of the earlier Babylonian administration of Judah. Weinberg contends that:

> Die babylonische Oberherrschaft rief bedeutende Wandlungen im System der Grundeigentumsverhältnisse, hauptsächlich im südlichen Judäa, hervor, die aber nicht zu einer Verstärkung des Privateigentums sondern zu einem kolossalen Zuwachs des staattlichen Sektors führten . . . [D]ie agararen Maßnahmen der Babylonier einen Teil der nichtdeportierten Bevölkerung—den *dallat ʿam hāʾāreṣ* d.h. den landlossen *ʿam*

---

[62] Weinberg, "Vorhellenismus," 12 (*Citizen-Temple Community*, 24).

[63] Weinberg, "Zentral- und Partikulargewalt," 25–26 (*Citizen-Temple Community*, 106); idem, "Vorhellenismus," 8–13 (*Citizen-Temple Community*, 20–26).

[64] Weinberg, "Zentral- und Partikulargewalt," 25 (*Citizen-Temple Community*, 106). He notes that:

> Der Terminus "Partikulargewalt" . . . nur die selbst verwaltenden, autonomen Gebilde, deren Formen im achämenidischen Weltreich sehr verschieden waren. Zu den Selbstverwaltungen gehörten die Poleis Kleinasiens und die Städte Phöniziens, die Dynasten Kariens, Paphlagoniens usw., die Stämme der Kolche, Araber und andere, aber der bedeutende und fortschrittliche Typus autonomer Selbstverwaltungen war vom 6. bis 4. Jh. v. u. Z. die Bürger-Tempel-Gemeinde in Babylonien und Syrien, Kleinasien und Armenien, Phönizen und Palästina.

[65] Weinberg, "Vorhellenismus," 13 (*Citizen-Temple Community*, 26); idem, "Zentral-und Partikulargewalt," 26 (*Citizen-Temple Community*, 106). On the develpoment of the Bürger-Tempel-Gemeinde in the Achaemenid Persian period, see Weinberg, "Vorhellenismus," 5–20 (*Citizen-Temple Community*, 17–33).

hāʾāreṣ [cf. II Ki 25:12; Jer 39:10, 52:16], mit Bodenparzellen auf den Ländereien der Davidíten und Deportierten versorgten.[66]

Upon the repatriation of the Judean exiles after the edict of Cyrus there was considerable friction between the repatriates who sought to reclaim possession of their ancestral holdings and those who were occupying this land when they returned. The repatriates gradually organized themselves into a Bürger-Tempel-Gemeinde polity in order to facilitate their claims to land and their economic development. Weinberg asserts that:

> Die vorhandenen Quellen beweisen das hartnäckige Bestreben der Repatrianten, sich 538 v. u. Z. an den Wohnplätzen ihrer Vorfahren vor der Deportation anzusiedeln. Solch ein Bestreben war bedingt durch den Wunsch der *bātēi ʾābōt* [fathers' houses] des 6. bis 4. Jahrhunderts v. u. Z., die verlorengegangene *ʾāḥuzā—naḥălā* zurckzugewinnen. Die Verwircklichung dieses Wunsches mußte unvermeidlich den Widerstand derer hervorrufen, die 586 v. u. Z. auf diesen Ländereien angesiedelt wurden oder die sich ihrer bemächtigten. Damit war der Anfang des Konfliktes gelegt, der in bedeutendem Maße die Formierung der Agrarverhältnisse in der Bürger-Tempel-Gemeinde beeinflußte.[67]

The *bêt ʾābôt* of the Achaemenid Persian period, of which there were priestly and lay examples, was

> ... ein in den eigentümlichen Verhältnisse des Exils und der Repatriierung entstandener agnatischer Verband, der eine Anzahl miteinander (real oder fingiert) verwandter Familien vereinte und genetisch mit *mišpāḥā* (Sippe) oder *bēt ʾāb* (Großfamilie) der vorexilischen Zeit verbunden war.[68]

The *bêt ʾābôt* was thus a "collective of the repatriates" and formed the basic component of the Judean Bürger-Tempel-Gemeinde. The *bāttê ʾābôt* held the land in common and parcelled it out to individual families who were members of a particular *bêt ʾābôt*. The solidarity

---

[66] Weinberg, "Die Agararverhältnisse in der Bürger-Tempel-Gemeinde," 480–81 (*Citizen-Temple Community*, 100, although the second half of this quotation, along with a few other lines in this paragraph, are missing from the English translation).

[67] Weinberg, "Probleme der sozialökonomischen Struktur Judäas," 248.

[68] Weinberg, "Vorhellenismus," 15 (quotation missing from *Citizen-Temple Community*, 28). For an extensive discussion of the Achaemenid period *bāttê ʾābōt*, see Weinberg, "Das *bēt ʾābōt*," 400–14; H. G. Kippenberg, *Religion und Klassenbildung im antiken Judäa. Eine religionssoziologische Studie zum Verhältnis von Tradition und gesellschaftlicher Entwicklung* (2nd ed.; Studien zum Umwelt des Neuen Testaments 14; Göttingen: Vandenhoeck & Ruprecht, 1981) 23–41 (particularly on the development of the *mišpāḥāh*); Dyck, *Theocratic Ideology of the Chronicler*, 188–203.

of the *bāttê ʾābôt* was based on their common ownership of land.
This "war das wirksamte Bindemittel, das eine gewisse innere Einheit
und relative Stabilität des *bēit ʾābōt* bedingte".[69] Unlike other examples of the Bürger-Tempel-Gemeinde form of socio-economic organization in the Achaemenid Persian empire in which the temple was
the *de facto* owner of the cultivatable land (which thus can be termed
"temple land")—either some of this land being leased to members
of the community while the remainder was managed by the temple
itself, or all of the land being utilized by the members of the community, the temple retaining none for itself—the Jerusalem temple
"kein Land und keine Wirtschaft besassen".[70] In the Judean Bürger-
Tempel-Gemeinde land was possessed by the *bāttê ʾābôt*.

Weinberg divides the development of the Judean Bürger-Tempel-
Gemeinde into two periods. In the first period, from the repatriation
edict of Cyrus in 539/8 to the mission of Ezra in 458/7 (Weinberg's dates; he follows the traditional order of Ezra coming to Judah
before Nehemia), "die nachexilischen Gemeinde noch keine ausgeprägte Bürger-Tempel-Gemeinde, sondern ein Organismus ist in
statu nascendi".[71] At the time of Ezra's arrival in Judah only c. 20%
of the population were members of the Bürger-Tempel-Gemeinde.[72]
The second period, after 458/7, is marked by a rapid growth of the
membership of the Bürger-Tempel-Gemeinde—to c. 70% of the population of Judah after the mission of Nehemiah due to the acceptance of numbers of the local, non-deported population of Judah

---

[69] Weinberg, "Das *bēit ʾābōt*," 409 (*Citizen-Temple Community*, 57).

[70] Weinberg, "Die Agrarverhältnisse in der Bürger-Tempel-Gemeinde," 485 (*Citizen-Temple Community*, 104); idem, "Vorhellenismus," 16 (*Citizen-Temple Community*, 29).
He classifies the first two types of Bürger-Tempel-Gemeinde noted here as Groups
A$_1$ ("umfaßt die Gemeinden, deren Tempel de facto Eigentümer von Boden waren
und den Boden teilweise an Mitglieder der Gemeinde verpachteten, teilweise aber
selbst bewirtschaften, z. B. die Gemeinden in Uruk, Sippara und anderen Städten
Mesopotamiens, in Comana, Zela, Akilisene und anderen Ortschaften Kleinasiens
und Armeniens") and A$_2$ ("gehören die Gemeinden, deren Tempel de facto Eigentümer
waren, aber keine eigene Wirtschaft führten und das gesamte Tempelland sich in
der Nutzung der Gemeindemitglieder befand, z. B. die Gemeinde in Mylasa-Olymos
u.a.") respectively, while the Judean Bürger-Tempel-Gemeinde is classified as an
example of Group B ("bilden die Bürger-Tempel-Gemeinde, deren Tempel kein
Land und keine Wirtschaft besassen. Im achämenidischen Vorderasien war die
Bürger-Tempel-Gemeinde Palästinas ausgeprägte Repräsentantin dieser Gruppe").
Weinberg classifies the first two types (A$_1$ and A$_2$) together due to their common
practice of the temple possessing the cultivatable land.

[71] Weinberg, "Zentral- und Partikulargewalt," 33 (*Citizen-Temple Community*, 115).

[72] Weinberg, "Demographische Notizen," 53 (*Citizen-Temple Community*, 43).

into the community.[73] At no time, however, was the Bürger-Tempel-Gemeinde identical, either demographically or territorially, with the district of Judah which, according to Weinberg, appears to have been separated from the district of Samaria and granted the status of an independent district only in the reign of Artaxerxes I. Both Ezra and Nehemiah were appointed by Artaxerxes I as officials over the developing Judean Bürger-Tempel-Gemeinde. Their role was to establish firmly the Bürger-Tempel-Gemeinde in Judah as an autonomous, self-governing polity within the district of Judah.[74] This reflected the willingness of the Achaemenid Persian administration ("die Zentralgewalt") to support various forms of indigenous "Partikulargewalt" in the empire.[75]

The first period in which the Judean Bürger-Tempel-Gemeinde was beginning its development (that is, from 539/8 to 458/7) is of particular interest for our present purposes as it directly relates to the rebuilding of the Jerusalem temple of Yahweh. Weinberg, who accepts the veracity of the Hebrew edict of Cyrus (Ezr 1:2–4), contends that the repatriation of Judeans by Cyrus II reflects a policy of religious and political tolerance whose underlying purpose in this case was "in Palästina einen gesicherten Aufmarschraum für die geplante Eroberung Ägyptens aufzubauen".[76] He recognizes that the

---

[73] Weinberg, "Demographische Notizen," 53 (*Citizen-Temple Community*, 43); idem, "Zentral- und Partikulargewalt," 36 (*Citizen-Temple Community*, 118).

[74] On Ezra's and Nehemiah's roles, see Weinberg, "Zentral- and Partikulargewalt," 34–38 (*Citizen-Temple Community*, 116–21). Ezra's brief from Artaxerxes I is outlined in Ezr 7. Of note here is that while Judah became an independent district in the reign of Artaxerxes I, Nehemiah was not appointed governor of Judah. For Weinberg, the title *peḥāh* which is used of Nehemiah's office designates him as "nicht Statthalter der Provinz Jehud, sondern offizieller Leiter der autonomen Bürger-Tempel-Gemeinde, d. h. der schon im westlichen ausgebildeten Partikulargewalt war" (p. 38; *Citizen-Temple Community*, 121).

[75] Weinberg, "Zentral- und Partikulargewalt," 25–43 (*Citizen-Temple Community*, 105–126); idem, "Vorhellenismus," 17–18 (*Citizen-Temple Community*, 30–31). Weinberg notes ("Vorhellenismus," p. 17; *Citizen-Temple Community*, 30):

> Die Einstellung der achämenidischen Zentralgewalt zur als Partikulargewalt organisierten Bürger-Tempel-Gemeinde war allgemein wohlwollend (was natürlich zeitliche und lokale Abweichungen nicht ausschließt), weil die Achämeniden mit Recht diese Form von Partikulargewalt als loyaler im Vergleich mit den übrigen Abarten (Poleis, Dynasten, Stämmen usw.) betrachten.

On the semi-autonomy of certain groups within the Achaemenid Persian provincial system and their relationship to the Achaemenid Persian administration, see also P. Frei, "Zentralgewalt und Lokalautonomie," 7–131. Frei does not deal with the Bürger-Tempel-Gemeinde form of socio-economic organization, however.

[76] Weinberg, "Zentral- und Partikulargewalt," 30 (*Citizen-Temple Community*, 110).

repatriation was not a single event but rather a gradual and protracted process.[77] He understands developments in the years directly
after repatriation edict as follows:

> ... die anfangs nichts sehr zahlreichen Rückkehrer, die auf den Wider-
> stand der örtlichen Bevölkerung Palästinas stießen, hätten sich ohne
> Unterstützen der Zentralgewalt in Juda nicht halten können. Ein der-
> artiger notwendiger Schutz wurde für die Rückkuhr der Jahwetempel
> benötigt, der von der Zentralgewalt ausging und auch die Teilnehmer
> des Tempelbaus umfaßte. Der auf Befehl der Zentralgewalt zu errichtende
> Tempel wurde darum Sammelpunkt und Konsolidierszentrum der *bāttê*
> *'ăḇôt* anschaulich Offenbarung der Gunst Jahwes und des Wohlwollens
> Kyros' II. Eben darum verwiesen die Führer der Samaritaner [sic]
> daraf, daß die Wiederherstellung des Tempels und der Stadt Aufruhr
> hervorrufen würde (Esr 4, 9 16 u. a.). Es ist schwer zu entscheiden,
> inwiefern solche Beschuldigen begrundet waren, aber sie entsprachen
> der Politik des Kambyses, der die Kontrolle der Zentralgewalt über
> die großen Tempel verschärfte. Die Klage der Samaritaner erreichte
> ihr Ziel, und der Tempelbau wurde zeitweilig eingestellt (Esr 4, 24).[78]

When Darius I instituted his administrative reorganization of the
empire, work recommenced on the Jerusalem temple.[79] The edict
Darius promulgated supporting the rebuilding of the temple (Ezr 6:
7–12) demonstrates

> ... daß keine westlichen Änderungen in der Palästinapolitik der
> Achämeniden eingetreten waren, aber die Vorherrschaft der Zentralgewalt
> über Tempel und werdende Gemeinde [that is, the community of the
> repatriates] sich ein wenig verstärkte, was die Position der letzerten in
> Palästina zweifelos festige. Obwohl die Mitglieder der werdenden
> Gemeinde, genau wie die übrige Bevölkerung Judas, administrative der
> Provinz Samaria und den übrigen Provinzen uberstand, besaß die Ge-
> meinde schon vor 458/7 eine wenn auch beschränkte Selbstverwaltung.[80]

Since the territory of Judah lay under the control of the Samaritans,
Weinberg understands neither Sheshbazzar nor Zerubbabel to be the
governor of an independent sub-province of Judah. Sheshbazzar was
responsible for leading a group of repatriates and returning the tem-

---

[77] Weinberg, "Demographische Notizen," 51 (*Citizen-Temple Community*, 41).
[78] Weinberg, "Zentral- und Partikulargewalt," 30–31 (*Citizen-Temple Community*,
111–12).
[79] For which Weinberg does not give a particular date, although he ties it in
with Zerubbabel's rebuilding.
[80] Weinberg, "Zentral- und Partikulargewalt," 31 (*Citizen-Temple Community*, 112–13).

ple vessels, while Zerubbabel was "nur inoffizieller Vorsteher der Gemeinde und Leiter des Tempelbaus."[81]

Weinberg's work is further concerned with outlining the development of the Judean Bürger-Tempel-Gemeinde under Ezra and Nehemiah, but this falls outside the purview of the current study. The above summary of some of the major points raised in Weinberg's research on the socio-economic and political organization of Achaemenid Judah as it pertains to the rebuilding of the Jerusalem temple of Yahweh shows that he undertakes a holistic interpretation of the character of Achaemenid Judean society and the place of the temple in it. Like the Meyerses, Weinberg is concerned to identify the polity that the temple served, contending that the Jerusalem temple was rebuilt in order to develop Judean self-autonomy. The character of this self-autonomy is radically different from that propounded by the Meyerses, however. The Meyerses view the temple rebuilding as establishing Judah as an independent sub-province within the Achaemenid Persian empire, while Weinberg considers the temple rebuilding as a step in the development of an independent polity (Bürger-Tempel-Gemeinde) within the territory of Judah (which at the time of the rebuilding lay within the sub-province of Samaria). The Meyerses and Weinberg share the contention that Darius I's reorganization of the provinces precipitated the temple rebuilding. Social conflict forms part of the context in which the rebuilding was undertaken—both the Meyerses and Weinberg agree that there was conflict between the repatriates and neighbouring peoples to the north ("Samaritans"), but they differ on social conflict with non-repatriates (Weinberg includes this conflict, while the Meyerses do not). Also, Weinberg's studies reflect the influence of the idea of the repatriates forming a "cultic community", but he emphasizes the socio-economic, rather than religious, basis of this community.

An extended critique of Weinberg's work need not be undertaken here. A more limited critique is offered, particularly as it relates to the issue of the purpose of rebuilding the Jerusalem temple. Certain of his claims fall to criticisms raised in chapter 3 above regarding the Hebrew narrative of the temple rebuilding (Ezra 1:1–4:5), others to criticisms noted above regarding the Meyerses' interpretation.

Weinberg holds that the impetus for the rebuilding of the temple

---

[81] Weinberg, "Zentral- und Partikulargewalt," 33 (*Citizen-Temple Community*, 114–115).

came from administrative reforms of the empire undertaken by Darius I in the first years of his reign. As noted above in the discussion of the Meyerses' views, the evidence in support of this position is ambiguous at best. One might care to argue that the rebuilding of the Jerusalem temple was a special act by Darius in accordance with other examples where he showed respect toward the religious cults of subject peoples (see, for example, the Udjahoressne inscription; the Gadates text; beneficence shown to Egyptian temples, including the building of the temple of Hibis in the Kharga Oasis), but as was argued above when discussing the "policy" of Cyrus, in the case of the Jerusalem temple one must think in terms of the granting of permission for the rebuilding of a minor cult, not the direct involvement of the administration in the undertaking. It cannot be shown, however, that such beneficence was in any way connected with the establishment of either Judah as an independent sub-province or a particular polity of the repatriates within the territory of Judah. The contention that the temple rebuilding was a special act of Darius falters in the light of Ezra 5–6, however, where rather than being the instigator of the rebuilding, Darius is portrayed as granting permission to continue the work only after finding Cyrus's memorandum. If it cannot be shown that Darius instigated or supported administrative reforms in the first years of his reign, and that they were, at least in some instances, for the development of Bürger-Tempel-Gemeinde polities, then it undermines Weinberg's claim that the temple rebuilding in Jerusalem and the establishment of the Judean Bürger-Tempel-Gemeinde are to be interpreted within the framework of an Achaemenid Persian policy. I do not question here that the Achaemenid Persians pursued a policy of limited self-autonomy of sub-provinces or particular groups. The questions to be faced are: when was this policy to establish limited self-autonomy instituted in Judah? Is it connected to the rebuilding of the temple? Did the policy establish a Bürger-Tempel-Gemeinde? Merely citing cases where the Achaemenid Persians showed deference to the religious cults of some of their subject peoples or established the limited self-autonomy of some groups proves nothing in the specific case of the rebuilding of the Jerusalem temple of Yahweh. Closer study of Achaemenid Persian provincial policy, particularly, where possible, the policy of specific rulers, is in order. If the policy were instituted after the temple rebuilding, and thus not tied to the rebuilding itself, then other reasons for the rebuilding must be sought. If the establishment of the Judean Bürger-Tempel-Gemeinde was not related to the temple rebuilding, then when was it instituted, how did it arise, under whose authority, and for what reasons?

The relationship of land holding to participation in the Bürger-Tempel-Gemeinde is a significant issue since for Weinberg, along with a number of other commentators, it was only as a member of the temple community that one had rights to land. Such membership marked a social and economic division centred on the temple, and thus temple rebuilding was fundamental to its development and legitimation. In the following I seek to juxtapose modes of land holding in Neo- and Achaemenid Babylonia with Weinberg's understanding of the Judean Bürger-Tempel-Gemeinde as a way of questioning the validity of his model and to place a question mark over the issue of relating land holding to temple community membership.

While written sources from Babylonia in the Neo-Babylonian and Achaemenid Persian periods are plentiful, there being perhaps as many as 100,000 legal and economic texts of which only about 10,000 are published, our picture of economic life is skewed somewhat by the provenance of these texts. A sizable proportion of them come from the main sanctuaries of Uruk (Eanna) and Sippar (Shamash temple Ebabbara), "and, thus, primarily illustrate the day-to-day activities of temple, their estates and staffs".[82] There are also family business archives, such as those belonging to Egibi (based in Babylon), Murašû (Nippur) and Ea-ilūta-bāni (Sippar), among others. These archives also offer some insight into forms of land tenure and land use. It is difficult to reconstruct the political landscape within which these major temples and business houses operated since we lack extensive archives from the central administration.

We know from texts that land (and here we are interested in arable land, not house or building plots) was owned, "in the sense of exclusive dominion", by private individuals or families, by the crown, and by temples.[83] There is no doubt that there was privately

[82] Kuhrt, *Ancient Near East*, 2.603.
[83] J. Oelsner, "Erwängungen zum Gesellschaftsaufbau Babyloniens von der neubabylonischen bis achämenidischen Zeit (7.–4. Jh. v. u. Z.)," *Altorientalische Forschungen* 4 (1976) 131–49; idem, "Die neu- und spätbabylonische Zeit," in *Circulation of Goods in Non-Palatial Context in the Ancient Near East* (ed. A. Archi; Rome: Edizioni dell'Ateneo, 1984) 221–40; idem, "Grundbesitz/Grundeigentum im achämenidischen und seleukidischen Babylonien," in *Das Grundeigentum in Mesopotamien* (ed. B. Brentjes; *Jahrbuch für Wirtschaftsgeschichte* (1987) (Berlin: Akademie Verlag, 1987) 117–34; J. Renger, "Institutional, Communal, and Individual Ownership or Possession of Arable Land in Ancient Mesopotamia From the End of the Fourth to the End of the First Millennium B.C.," *Chicago-Kent Law Review* 71/1 (1995) 308–18. The quotation is from Renger, p. 309.

held land in Babylonia in the Neo-Babylonian and Achaemenid
Persian periods apparently without any limitation on its control. This
land could be used as surety, sold, inherited, and passed on in
dowries. There are numerous field sales, but almost exclusively of
small plots, most not larger than 1.35 hectares (3.3 acres). From the
available evidence it appears that there were few large private estates,
but we must be careful in what we surmise. An important and still
unknown aspect of privately owned land is its quantity—the percentage of all cultivatable land that was privately owned remains
unclear. The documents informing us of privately held land come
mostly from large urban sites and tend to offer insight into the more
substantial and better connected families. Although it is not unusual
that mention be made of villages and small settlements, private land
holding in these locations remains to be studied, and it may not
prove possible to elucidate the situation there from the available documents in any case.

The House of Ea-ilūta-bāni, studied by Joannès, on which we have
sources spanning six generations, can be taken as an example of a
reasonably well-to-do urban family.[84] From the city of Borsippa, the
family owned several hectares of land in the immediate environs of
the city, some slaves, and a certain number of claims in silver and
gold. To best maintain and manage their land, family solidarity
needed to be reinforced and it often happened that property was
not divided among heirs in order to avoid fragmentation of land.
Another partial solution to this problem was to marry a near relative, such as a niece, in order to keep land in the family.

Royal land is the second category of land and is made mention
of more frequently in the documents from Babylonia than privately
held land, but to my knowledge no comprehensive study of the scattered references has been undertaken. Much of the royal land was
probably acquired via canal building activities that opened up or
maintained arable land, rather than by means of confiscation. It was
made available for exploitation in basically two ways:

(i) to members of the ruling elite—that is, members of the extended
    royal family, the nobility, and senior bureaucrats in the adminis-
    tration (they were commonly overlapping groups). These either

---

[84] F. Joannès, *Archives de Borsippa, la famille Ea-ilûta-bâni: étude d'un loy d'archives familiales en Babylonie du VIII* au V* siècle av. J.-C.* Geneva: Librarie Droz, 1989.

cultivated the land using slaves or other agricultural workers, or leased the land to others and received rental payments;

(ii) by leasing the land to tenants, who were obligated to undertake military service or to outfit a chariot, or to make an equivalent payment, usually in silver—these are the so-called "fiefs", such as the "bow fief", "horse fief", and "chariot fief" which are best attested in the late Achaemenid period Murašû texts. These lands "were occupied by groups of agnatic relatives . . . The properties could be leased or pawned, and shares in them were transmitted by inheritance, but they were not normally alienable".[85] There are other fiefs such as "hand land" (*bīt ritti*), which do not seem to have carried military obligations. Fiefs could be allotted to corporate groups of royal dependents, sometimes organized by profession or by ethnic group, or by place of origin—these are called *ḫaṭru*s.[86] The organization of the various types of fiefs and their modes of holding and exploiting the land have been studied by Stolper and others, and cannot detain us here. Again it remains unclear as to what percentage of cultivatable land belonged to the crown.

The temple was the third land owner and, if our sources are anything to go by, the largest. Temple lands had been acquired by means of land grants from the crown, through the development and maintenance of canals, and through the appropriation of the privately owned land of indebted small holders. These temples, in large cities such as Uruk, Sippar, Babylon, Borsippa, and Dilbat, were the centre of their respective urban communities. Much of the land owned by the temple was not exploited directly by temple agricultural workers, rather it was leased to entrepreneurs and other families who were members of the urban elite. They then leased the land on to others for rents or organized the temple land using indentured or other agricultural labour. Temples granted bow fiefs, but it is unclear that they carried obligations similar to the royal fiefs. However, the nexus of the urban elite, the temple administration, and the exploitation of *temple* land has given rise to the notion of the Bürger-Tempel-Gemeinde. It is true to say that economically

---

[85] M. W. Stolper, "Mesopotamia, 482–330 B.C.," in *CAH* (2d ed.; ed. D. M. Lewis et al.; Cambridge: Cambridge University Press, 1994) 6. 245.

[86] Stolper, *Entrepeneurs and Empire*, 70–103.

prominent urban families were in close connection with the temple
and occupied leading positions in the city and temple administration,
being integrated into the economic interests and activities of the temples.[87] They were extended families who spread the wealth and positions among their members (i.e. relatives). But not all "citizens" of
these cities were so economically advantaged, and there was not equal
access to temple holdings nor equal opportunity to exploit them.

According to Dandamaev, who has written most extensively on
this, the Bürger-Tempel-Gemeinde (although he does not use this
explicit terminology) of Babylonian cities was the highest level of a
three (sometimes described as four) tiered social structure:[88]

(i) Fully-Fledged Citizens: This group is designated by the Akkadian
    term *mār banî*, which is usually translated "free person", "citizen",
    or "nobleman", and taken to refer to persons with full citizen
    rights, including a seat on the city's governing council (Akk. *puḫru*).

(ii) Free Born Persons Deprived of Civic Rights: For example, aliens
     who lived in Babylonia for various reasons and who did not pos-
     sess land within the city's common fund. They were settled, in
     some cases, in separate and distinct communities with their own
     self-government.[89]

(iii) Various Dependent Social Groups: For example, fief holders.
      One part of this category consisted of slaves, so on occasion
      Dandamaev divides this category into two—Category 3 becomes
      Dependent Social Groups such as fief holders; Category 4: slaves

This view of the social structure of Babylonian cities is generally
accepted.[90] Weinberg also accepts that this three tiered social structure—consisting of free citizens; free persons deprived of civic status; and dependent social groups—obtained in Achaemenid Judah.

---

[87] Kümmel, *Familie, Beruf und Amt im spätbabylonischen Uruk*; G. Frame, "The 'First
Families' of Borsippa during the Early Neo-Babylonian Period," *Journal of Cuneiform
Studies* 36 (1984) 67–80; S. Zawadzki, "Great Families of Sippar during the Chaldean
and Early Persian Periods (626–482 B.C.)," *RA* 84 (1990) 17–25.

[88] M. A. Dandamaev, "Social Stratification in Babylonia (7th–4th Centuries B.C.),"
AcAnt 22 (1974) 433–44; idem, "The Neo-Babylonian Elders," 38–41; idem, "The
Neo-Babylonian Popular Assembly," in *Šulmu: Papers on the Ancient Near East Presented
at International Conference of Socialist Countries* (ed. P. Vavrousek and V. Soucek; Prague:
Charles University, 1988) 63–71.

[89] Eph'al, "Western Minorities," 74–90; Dandamaev, "Aliens and the Community,"
133–45.

[90] See, for example, Kuhrt, *Ancient Near East*, 2.618–21; M. Van De Mieroop,
The Ancient Mesopotamian City (Oxford: Clarendon, 1997) 118–41.

Since it is the highest social stratum, that is, the fully-fledged citizens, that make up the membership of the Bürger-Tempel-Gemeinde, our attention now focuses on them.

Dandamaev describes the *mār banî*s as "citizens with full rights [who] were members of the city or village assembly (*puḫru*), which had a certain judicial authority in the resolution of family and property matters" and who "possessed immovable property within the communal land district which came under the jurisdiction of the popular assembly. Many of them were holders of certain shares of income from the temple. Such citizens included persons of high rank (upper echelons of the state, and temple officials, merchants, prosperous scribes etc.) as well as craftsmen and peasants".[91]

When Dandamaev writes that citizens of Babylonian cities "possessed immovable property within the communal land district which came under the jurisdiction of the popular assembly" this "communal land district" is not land belonging to the Bürger-Tempel-Gemeinde (contra Weinberg). Rather, Dandamaev means that the citizens held private land within the legal jurisdiction of the city and that the *puḫru* (assembly) could make decisions in such matters as disputes over boundaries or inheritance (but even here one needs to review the evidence for the jurisdiction of the assembly's authority over privately held land—cf. judges making rulings over land). The lands that the Babylonian Citizen-Temple communities had authority over were temple lands, and even here the nature of that authority is complicated by the internal administrative structures of the temples. It is clear, however, that the integration of the private and the communal or temple economies in the first millennium B.C., a fundamental development in the appearance of the Bürger-Tempel-Gemeinde according to its proponents, did not mean the abolition of privately owned land in favour of community owned land.

While not economically equal, all citizens were, theoretically, legally equal. All citizens may have been entitled to a determined part of the temple revenue, but this did not necessarily mean that all were entitled to usufruct of a portion of temple land. As mentioned earlier, entrepreneurs and leading families exploited the land via leases or the temple cultivated the land directly by means of its labourers.

---

[91] Dandamaev, "Neo-Babylonian Elders," 40–41. For a compendium of the textual evidence for *mār banî*, with a brief discussion, see M. A. Dandamaev, "The Neo-Babylonian Citizens," *Klio* 63 (1981) 45–49.

There are gaps in our understanding of the *mār banî* or the citizen stratum of society. Martha Roth has collected evidence showing that some individuals were slaves or dedicated to a temple and *mār banîs* simultaneously. She notes that "there is no evidence to suggest that a person's status as *mār banî* was determined by birth; rather the status is one that can be conferred on a former slave . . . such translations as 'free-(born) person' or 'citizen' imply a social and political structure inappropriate for Neo-Babylonian society".[92] There is further evidence for the descendants of foreigners being designated as *mār banîs*.[93] This might suggest that persons could move from status level 2 "alien without civic rights" to status 1 "fully fledged citizens".

Weinberg too has a problem with the citizen stratum of his Judean Bürger-Tempel-Gemeinde, but his problem is different from that confronting Dandamaev. In Babylonia the "citizens" were connected to specific *cities*—Babylon, Sippar, Uruk, etc. They had rights to participate in the assembly and access to temple income on that basis. Being a "citizen" of a city meant membership of that specific Bürger-Tempel-Gemeinde; in Babylonia there was no Bürger-Tempel-Gemeinde apart from the city of which one was a citizen. In Judah, however, being a "citizen" was not connected to one specific city, say Jerusalem. According to Weinberg, the Judean Bürger-Tempel-Gemeinde drew on citizens of towns that were scattered throughout the territory and amalgamated them into a single, unified socio-political organization.

Not only is the composition of the citizen stratum in the Judean Bürger-Tempel-Gemeinde different from what we observe in Babylonia, amalgamating as it does citizens of *various* towns, the land exploited by the respective Citizen-Temple Communities is also quite different. Weinberg contends that the Judean Bürger-Tempel-Gemeinde was an association of free, fully enfranchised members who exploited land belonging to the community. But these "community lands" are apparently only an amalgamation of the plots belonging to the *bāttê 'ābôt*. This can be compared with Babylonian cities where "community lands" are the temple lands that had been acquired by royal grants

---

[92] M. Roth, "A Case of Contested Status," in *DUMU-E2–DUB-BA-A: Studies in Honor of Åke W. Sjöberg* (ed. H. Behrens, D. Loding, and M. T. Roth; Occasional Publications of the Samuel Noah Kramer Fund 11; Philadephia: Babylonian Section, University Museum, 1989) 487.

[93] See, van Driel, "Murašûs in Context," 206.

and other means. Members did not amalgamate their holdings to establish a common land fund, nor did they submit their private lands to the Bürger-Tempel-Gemeinde for it to superintend or redistribute, nor pool their private lands with Bürger-Tempel-Gemeinde lands. In Babylonia there is a clear distinction between private and Bürger-Tempel-Gemeinde lands, a distinction that Weinberg does not wish to observe in Judah. He sees all the land cultivated by members of the community being administered by the *bāttê 'ābôt* on behalf of the Bürger-Tempel-Gemeinde, with all this land classified as "property of the deity" (*makkūr* DN). He contends that this situation obtained in Babylonia also, following the work of Sarkisian on Hellenistic Babylonia which claimed a monopoly of ownership by temples of all, or nearly all, the land, and therefore of the economic base. Weinberg, citing Diakonoff and Dandamaev, reads this situation back into the pre-Hellenistic period. But Sarkisian's proposals have been shown (by van der Spek in particular) to oversimplify and misrepresent this aspect of Hellenistic Babylonian economic life. Given this, along with clear evidence for private land in our period, Sarkisian cannot be accepted as a reliable guide.[94]

There are, of course, biblical texts, perhaps from the Persian period, that speak of the land as being the property of the deity (Lev 25, for example). Weinberg has even suggested that Ezek 40–48 is something of a programmatic statement of the Bürger-Tempel-Gemeinde's views on land (a notion I consider to be suspect). In any case, to say that the land belongs to the deity is not to say that the land belongs to or should be administered by the Bürger-Tempel-Gemeinde. The sacredness of the land, however one is to construe that, need not be incompatible with private (i.e. family) ownership of land. Even

---

[94] To the extent that Weinberg draws on putative Hellenistic period parallels from Babylonia and Asia Minor (basing himself on the work of former Soviet colleagues, to be sure) to understand land holding in the Neo-Babylonian and Achaemenid Persian periods, his position is questionable. See the research conducted on Hellenistic Babylonia by R. J. van der Spek, and published in "The Babylonian Temple during the Macedonian and Parthian Domination," *BiOr* 42 (1985) 541–62; idem, *Grondbezit in het Seleucidische Rijk* (Amsterdam: VU Uitgeverij, 1986) (with English summary, pp. 249–56); idem, "The Babylonian City," in *Hellenism in the East: The Interaction of Greek and Non-Greek Civilizations from Syria to Central Asia after Alexander* (ed. A. Kuhrt and S. Sherwin-White; London: Duckworth, 1987) 57–74; idem, "Land Ownership in Babylonian Cuneiform Documents," in *Legal Documents of the Hellenistic World* (ed. M. J. Geller and H. Maehler; London: Warburg Institute, 1995) 173–245 (esp. 189–97); and see also S. Sherwin-White and A. Kuhrt, *From Samarkhand to Sardis: A New Approach to the Seleucid Empire* (London: Duckworth, 1993) 59–61.

the inalienability of land need point to nothing beyond the desire of the *bāttê ʾābôt* to retain land holdings within their control. Inalienability of land is not evidence for *bāttê ʾābôt* being in possession of land as agents of the Bürger-Tempel-Gemeinde.

Weinberg understands the Babylonian temples and the Judean *bāttê ʾābôt* as fulfilling the same role in the respective Citizen-Temple Communities—that of land holders who make land available to Community members. But they are not really comparable:

– In Babylonia the temple "owns" the Bürger-Tempel-Gemeinde lands which are independent of members' private land holdings. These community lands are made available to members in the form of leases and prebends; income from rents perhaps being made available to members. Land is not parcelled out to members for personal use. Membership of the Bürger-Tempel-Gemeinde does not give one rights to usufruct of a parcel of Community land.
– In Judah, on the other hand, the *bāttê ʾābôt* "own" the land and construct the notion of Community land by amalgamating their holdings. The *bāttê ʾābôt* are extended families which parcel out land for members to use. Membership of a *bêt ʾābôt* and hence membership of the Bürger-Tempel-Gemeinde does give rights to usufruct of a parcel of Community land.

In considering Weinberg's contention that forms of the Bürger-Tempel-Gemeinde are evidenced in both Babylonia and Judah, attention must be drawn to the significant differences between the two examples. Summarized here are seven differences touched on above:

1) The Jerusalem temple did not hold land, as Weinberg himself noted, but the attempt to have the Judean *bāttê ʾābôt* play a role in land holding in the Bürger-Tempel-Gemeinde equivalent to the Babylonian temples means that these two examples are fundamentally different structurally.
2) In Babylonia, Community lands were leased out to a variety of parties by the temple on behalf of the Bürger-Tempel-Gemeinde, while in Judah they were parcelled out by the *bāttê ʾabôt* to members for their own use.
3) In Babylonia, membership of the Bürger-Tempel-Gemeinde did not give one rights to usufruct of land, while in Judah it did.
4) In Babylonia, the communal land fund consisted of temple lands acquired by royal land grants, canal building, and the claiming

of sureties on bad debts. In Judah, the communal land fund consisted of the amalgamated plots held by the *bāttê 'ābôt.*

5) In Babylonia, there was a clear differentiation between private
   and Community land; citizens could hold both types of land by
   different means without the two being confused. In the Judean
   Bürger-Tempel-Gemeinde, according to Weinberg, members held
   no private land, it was all Community land.

6) Despite Weinberg's claims in 5) above, the *bêt 'ābôt* looks to be
   much more like an extended family or cluster of families owning
   its own land that it then portions out to family members to use
   (see 2) above). In Babylonia that is *private* land, not Bürger-Tempel-
   Gemeinde land.

7) Although not strictly to do with land holding, it bears repeating
   that in Babylonia "citizens" were connected to a Bürger-Tempel-
   Gemeinde of a specific city, whereas in Judah "citizens" from
   various towns were banded together to form their regional Bürger-
   Tempel-Gemeinde.

I am compelled to leave to one side the issue of the validity of the
Bürger-Tempel-Gemeinde hypothesis in explaining the other examples cited by Weinberg in its support. Since this theory has received
little direct attention from classicists, assyriologists, and ancient historians, it is premature to pronounce judgement on his use of these
examples. Further research is needed to establish the propriety of
the Bürger-Tempel-Gemeinde as a form of socio-economic and political organization in Western Asia during the first millennium. With
regard to the Achaemenid Babylonian temples, for example, much
more study needs to be undertaken on their socio-economic function, particularly as compared with earlier periods. In the meantime,
on the basis of these differences in land holding alone, I believe the
putative Judean and Babylonian Bürger-Tempel-Gemeinde as understood by Weinberg are not comparable entities, and his claim that
they are examples of the same form of socio-economic organization
should be set aside.[95]

---

[95] If the Büger-Tempel-Gemeinde was not the mechanism by which land was
held by the repatriates in Achaemenid Judah, what was? Hoglund, "The Achaemenid
Context," 57–60, followed by Ben Zvi, "Inclusion and Exclusion from Israel,"
110–13, consider land holding by both the repatriates and non-repatriates to result

Even if one were to assume that the Bürger-Tempel-Gemeinde structure was valid for certain other peoples in the Achaemenid Persian empire, the above analysis highlights the need to be wary of interpreting the socio-economic organization of Judah and the function of the Jerusalem temple in light of supposed parallels. They are not necessarily comparable entities as shown above, and as intimated by Weinberg's own admission that the Jerusalem temple differs from all other examples cited in that it held no land. Further, since it is acknowledged that the Judean literary texts are not concerned with economic matters, one has to be particularly careful of conforming the little information gleaned from these texts to the supposed parallels. This is true also regarding matters of social organization, where the biblical texts seemingly offer more information, even where certain aspects of social organization appear to be similar. In other words, there is a need to be aware of the problems commonly confronting the use of models based on the use of comparative material.

A further difference should give one caution. The Babylonian temples cited as parallels for the organization and function of the Jerusalem temple are characterized by continuity of use. They were established institutions with, in many cases, a long history of economic enterprise and long-standing socio-economic networks which either conformed to or could be adapted to the Bürger-Tempel-Gemeinde structure. In comparison, the Jerusalem temple had been destroyed in the Babylonian invasion of 588–87. Before the rebuilding of the temple the site may have been in use as a cultic site (Jer 41:5), but it would have had no economic function comparable to the parallels cited. The temple had to be rebuilt from the ground up and

---

from an Achaemenid Persian policy of "ruralization" (so, Hoglund) by which agricultural output was increased by settling people on previously unused or underutilized arable land. They make no comment on "ownership" beyond calling these lands "imperial domain", but conclude that there is thus no basis for conflict in Judah over rights to land. Even if a policy of ruralization did not obtain (and "imperial domain" is itself a debatable concept), one wonders what happened to the vacant arable land in Judah, especially if there was a rather small population there as Carter argues. There need not have been competition for land. Further, the contention of Ezr 2 // Neh 7 (admittedly a later text) that some of the repatriates returned to their own towns may well be correct (note Eph'al, "Political and Social Organization", 107–09, who considers the Babylonian exiles to have lived in *Landsmannschaften* probably named after their home towns), and even former Jerusalemites may well have had extended family holdings to which they could lay claim or with which they could connect themselves on their return.

this new form of socio-economic organization instituted from scratch. Even if one were to accept that this type of organization, unfamiliar in Palestine, was introduced by the repatriates based on knowledge of the function of Babylonian temples, a question remains: Is there any other example where a temple was constructed for the explicit purpose of constituting a Bürger-Tempel-Gemeinde polity? If not, then an argument needs to be made as to why the Jerusalem temple is the sole example. If it is the sole example, then the Judean Bürger-Tempel-Gemeinde is notable not only for this but also for being the sole example of the land of the Bürger-Tempel-Gemeinde not being held by the temple itself. One can therefore hardly agree with Weinberg that the Judean Bürger-Tempel-Gemeinde is an excellent example of this type of polity.[96]

In what sense is the rebuilding of the Jerusalem temple connected to the development of the Judean Bürger-Tempel-Gemeinde? Before the mission of Ezra Weinberg considers the Judean Bürger-Tempel-Gemeinde to be "in statu nascendi". But if after the edict of Cyrus the repatriates returned knowing that they wished to establish this type of polity in Judah, why was there a delay of some eighteen years (538–520) before work on the temple began in earnest? Why did it take almost sixty years more (515 [the completion of the temple] to 458 [the arrival of Ezra, assuming this disputed date for the sake of argument]) before the Judean Bürger-Tempel-Gemeinde was firmly established? As noted in chapter 3, Ezra 1:1–4:5 cannot be used to reconstruct events in Achaemenid Judah in the reign of Cyrus. Opposition to the temple rebuilding from the Samarians and other neighbours, particularly the notion that they informed the Achaemenid Persian administration that Judah was likely to rebel once the temple was rebuilt, cannot be accepted as the reason for the delay in rebuilding, especially when Weinberg himself accepts

---

[96] Mylasa in Asia Minor, which Weinberg cites as another example of a Bürger-Tempel-Gemeinde, seems to be comparable to Judah in that the polity consisted of a collection of villages with a religious centre (rather than consisting of one city; cf. point 7 above); see S. Hornblower, *Mausolus* (Oxford: Clarendon, 1982) 53–54 (and on Carian communities more generally, pp. 52–78). However, this form of social organization was not introduced or promoted by the Persians, rather it was already existing and was permitted to continue by them. It would be highly unlikely that the Judeans repatriated from Babylonia would have returned with a Carian conception of the Bürger-Tempel-Gemeinde and have sought to institute that in Judah.

the veracity of the Hebrew edict of Cyrus in which Cyrus himself
commands the repatriates to rebuild the temple. The Achaemenid
Persian administration would itself have been behind the temple
rebuilding project. There is no evidence outside the late, tendentious
Hebrew narrative in Ezra that the repatriates saw themselves as having to keep separate from those they found in Judah at their return.
Further, there is no evidence to support the contention either that
the land claims of the repatriates were in any way dependent on
their participation in the nascent Judean Bürger-Tempel-Gemeinde.
In any case, how would this polity have worked when the temple
itself was not constructed before 520?

Because of the paucity of sources Weinberg cannot say what the
relationship between the community and the temple was before 458,
so the Judean Bürger-Tempel-Gemeinde being "in statu nacsendi"
is a cover for the fact that the repatriates do not function according to Weinberg's model before the arrival of Ezra. If the symbiotic
relationship between temple and city is a hallmark of the Bürger-
Tempel-Gemeinde then it appears that such a relationship possibly
could not have developed in Judah before the mission of Nehemiah,
since it is with reference to this period that the first clear evidence
for the intensive population of Jerusalem is obtained. It might be
supposed on the basis of Ezr 4:12 and Neh 1:2–3 that Jerusalem
had been inhabited for a time after the temple rebuilding and that
much of the city's population had been forced to leave when the
city walls were torn down sometime later. Nothing is known of
Jerusalem in the decades directly after the temple rebuilding so one
must be circumspect in drawing conclusions as to what went on or
what role the temple had during that period.

Even if one were to assume that the Jerusalem temple rebuilding
was undertaken by the repatriates for the purpose of establishing a
Judean Bürger-Tempel-Gemeinde and that the city was populated
at that time, the fact that Nehemiah found the city depopulated
(Nehemiah 7:4; 11:1–19) means that the Bürger-Tempel-Gemeinde
structure had, to some extent at least, broken down. The period of
Nehemiah might therefore be seen as the renaissance of the structure. I leave to one side the issue of how this structure would have
survived the city's depopulation and instead question that Nehemiah
would have been responsible for reinstituting or reinvigorating the
Judean Bürger-Tempel-Gemeinde. As Kreissig points out in his critical appraisal of Weinberg's hypothesis, Nehemiah was the governor

of the whole sub-province of Judah, not just of Jerusalem or the temple community. His responsibilities were over a wider domain.[97] It would be unlikely that he, as governor, would foment division in the sub-province by establishing a community whose members had status and rights beyond other groups. Indeed, the Nehemiah Memoir suggests his aim was to suppress the power of certain interest groups in favour of the broader population and the unity of the district (Neh 5–6; 13:28–30). The rebuilding of Jerusalem's walls and the repopulating of the city should be understood as an attempt to establish a focal point for the district as a whole, rather than the resuscitation of the supposed Bürger-Tempel-Gemeinde structure. The restored city was a symbol of Judah's independence from the influence and meddling of the leaders of neighbouring districts.[98]

In summary, Weinberg's contention that the Jerusalem temple of Yahweh was rebuilt in order to develop a Judean Bürger-Tempel-Gemeinde cannot be sustained since his best evidence (which is itself open to question) comes from the period of Ezra and Nehemiah and the development of this polity is read back into the reigns of Cyrus and Darius. There is no evidence to suggest that the repatriates returned to Judah with the expectation of establishing themselves as a Bürger-Tempel-Gemeinde, and putative claims to land holding based on participation in the temple community are questionable. The development of this polity in Judah has no known parallels since Weinberg admits that the temple did not hold land and no other example is known of a temple being built to institute the Bürger-Tempel-Gemeinde or of this polity existing with a depopulated city. Further, Weinberg cannot successfully explain the delay in rebuilding or account for the timing of the rebuilding in the reign of Darius.

---

[97] Kreissig, "Eine beachtenswerte Theorie," 37.

[98] Neh 10, if it is to be dated to the governorship of Nehemiah, offers further problems for Weinberg's hypothesis. Why would this agreement to support the temple financially be needed if the temple formed an integral part of the Judean Bürger-Tempel-Gemeinde? Surely members of the community were already duty bound to support the temple. Weinberg does not discuss this text. Also, this text seems to be more inclusivist, being addressed to all the inhabitants of Judah. Only with Nehemiah, for reasons mentioned above, did the Jerusalem temple become a prominent social and economical institution in the sub-province of Judah. It was to become a focus for Judean identity to counter the influence of those outside the district. Note that those whom Nehemiah prohibits Judeans to marry and those with whom he strives for political ascendancy over Judah all come from outside the borders of Judah (Neh 1:19; 4:1; 13:23–28).

To establish the community's special status and privileges would have demanded the overt support of the Achaemenid Persian authorities. When would such support have been forthcoming? As recent studies have shown, recourse to a supposed policy of or administrative reorganization by Darius I to account for this is ill-founded.

TEMPLE REBUILDING AS A JUDEAN INITIATIVE

Seeing that the arguments outlined above cannot support the contention that the rebuilding of the Jerusalem temple in the reign of Darius was undertaken as a policy initiative of the Achaemenid Persian administration, attention now turns to investigating the view that the rebuilding was a Judean initiative, as the biblical texts Haggai, Zechariah 1–8, and Ezra 5–6 aver.

Temple Rebuilding as an Act of Judean Rebellion

One view of the purpose of the rebuilding of the Jerusalem temple is that it was an act of Judean rebellion against Achaemenid Persian control. In the monarchical period the Jerusalem temple had been the symbol of the kingship of Yahweh and had legitimated the kingdom and royal house of Judah. The rebuilding of this former monarchical shrine meant that Judeans were re-establishing their independent monarchical polity. Two factors have been cited in support of this interpretation of the purpose of the temple rebuilding.

First, the date of the rebuilding has been held to coincide with other rebellions throughout the empire which immediately followed Darius I's accession to the throne. According to Darius's Bisitun inscription, he wrested control of the empire from Gaumata on the tenth day of the seventh month (September 29, 522) but faced a series of rebellions across the empire which he quelled "in one year"— December 10, 522 to December 28, 521.[99] The claim is made that

---

[99] On the date of Darius's accession, see DB I. 35–61 (R. G. Kent, *Old Persian: Grammar, Texts, Lexicon* [2d ed., rev.; American Oriental Series 33; New Haven: American Oriental Society, 1953] 120); R. Borger, *Die Chronologie des Darius-Denkmals am Behistun-Felsen* (Göttingen: Vandenhoeck & Ruprecht, 1982) 14. Of the voluminous secondary literature on Darius's rise, see Dandamaev, *Persien unter den ersten Achämeniden*; Wiesehöfer, *Der Aufstand Gaumatas*. The precise dates of the "one year" in which Darius quelled the rebellions are still debated. The dates given above follow Borger, but cf. A. S. Shabazi, "The 'One Year' of Darius Re-examined," *BSOAS*

the second year of Darius in which the prophets Haggai and Zechariah spoke (Hag 1:1; 2:10, 20; Zech 1:1) must follow the calendar year 522–21 (March 27, 522 to April 13, 521) since, although Darius became ruler over the whole empire only in the seventh month of the year 522–521, that year should be counted as the first of his reign. Haggai's prophecies should therefore be dated in the period August to December, 521. Although the rebellion of Judah is not mentioned in the Bisitun inscription, Haggai's call to rebuild the Jerusalem temple reflects the wide-spread rebellion of which that text speaks.[100]

Second, Haggai's and Zechariah's description of Zerubbabel and the language used in support of the rebuilding of the temple bespeak the restoration of an independent monarchical state. Notable in this regard is Hag 2:20–23—

> 20) The word of Yahweh came a second time to Haggai on the twenty-fourth [day] of the month: (21) "Speak to Zerubbabel the governor of Judah: 'I shake the heavens and the earth. (22) I overthrow the throne of kingdoms and destroy the power of the kings[101] of the nations. I overturn the chariot and its riders; the horses and their riders fall, each on the sword of his brother. (23) On that day'—oracle of Yahweh Sabaoth—'I will take you, Zerubbabel, son of Shealtiel, my servant'—oracle of Yahweh—'and I will set you as my signet ring, for I have chosen you'—oracle of Yahweh Sabaoth."

This oracle: (i) speaks of the overthrow of the nations, among which the Achaemenid Persian empire must be included; (ii) uses royal terminology of Zerubbabel.[102] Examples of the royal terminology are: "my servant", a title used of the Davidic king in II Sam 7:5, 8;

---

35 (1972) 609–14, who gives the dates November 10, 522 to November 27, 521. The debate turns on whether the battle against Frada (DB III. 10–19; Kent, *Old Persian*, 127) was undertaken in Darius's accession year (Shabazi) or his first regnal year (Borger); see Borger, *Die Chronologie des Darius-Denkmals*, 23–24.

[100] So, for example, Meyer, *Entstehung*, 82–84; idem, "König Darius I," in *Meister der Politik* (3 vols.; 2d ed.; ed. E. Marcks and K. A. von Müller; Stuttgart/Berlin: Deutsche Verlags-Anhalt, 1923–24) 1. 17 n. 1; Olmstead, *History of the Persian Empire*, 135–142; J. Morgenstern, "Two Prophecies from 520–516 B.C.," *HUCA* 22 (1949) 400–14; L. Waterman, "The Camouflaged Purge of Three Messianic Conspirators," *JNES* 13 (1954) 73–78; Mowinckel, *He That Cometh*, 119–22; E. J. Bickerman, "En marge de l'écrite II. La seconde année de Darius," *RB* 88 (1981) 23–28; Balcer, *Sparda by the Bitter Sea*, 138; idem, *Herodotus & Bisitun: Problems in Ancient Persian Historiography* (Historia Einzelschriften 49; Stuttgart: Steiner, 1987) 149–51.

[101] MT "kingdoms"; LXX reads "kings". Wolff, *Haggai*, 98 n. 22b, wants to omit "kingdoms".

[102] On these titles, see also Tollington, *Tradition and Interpretation*, 135–44, 168–78.

I Ki 11:32, 34, 36; II Ki 19:34 // Is 37:35; Ps 78:70; 89:4 (Eng
v. 3), 40 (Eng 39), 51 (Eng v. 50); 132:10; Ezek 34:23; 37:24, 25;[103]
the king as "chosen" by Yahweh—I Sam 16:8–10; II Sam 6:21;
I Ki 8:16; 11:34; Ps 78:70; 89:4 [Eng v. 3]; "signet ring", a designation for the Judean king in Jer 22:24.[104]

Zechariah uses the title "branch" in Zech 3:8b; 6:12 to designate
Zerubbabel. This title is used in Jer 23:5 (// Jer 33:14–16 cf. Is 4:2;
11:10) for a Judean king expected to arise after the dissolution of
the kingdom who will restore the nation to normalcy. Monarchical
themes are also present in Zech 6:13 where in the context of an
oracle concerning the manufacture of crowns (Zech 6:9–15) it is said
of "branch" (Zerubbabel) that ". . . he will bear royal majesty (הוד)
and sit on his throne and rule". הוד also attends the king in Ps 21:6
(Eng v. 5) and 45:4 (Eng v. 3).[105] Both Haggai and Zechariah affix
the appellation "Sabaoth" to the name Yahweh. This appellation
found currency in the monarchical period Zion ideology.[106]

The purpose of rebuilding the Jerusalem temple of Yahweh is
clearly interpreted in Haggai and Zechariah 1–8 as marking an
impending change in the fortunes of the Judeans and Jerusalem, as
has been noted by all commentators—Yahweh is to return to Jerusalem
(Zech 1:16; 2:14, 16–17 [Eng vv. 10, 12–13]; 8:3; and this notion

---

[103] On "servant" as a royal designation in Psalms, see Eaton, *Kingship in the Psalms*,
149–50. "My servant" is also used of foreign kings—Nebuchadnezzar in Jer 25:9;
Cyrus in Is 45:1. Is 42:1 also refers to a "servant" whose identity is, however,
debated.

[104] On the relationship of Jer 22:24 to Hag 2:23, see K. Baltzer, "Das Ende des
Staates Juda und die Messias-Frage," *Studien zur Theologie der alttestamentlichen Überlieferungen* (ed. R. Rendtorff and K. Koch; Neukirchen-Vluyn: Neukirchener Verlag,
1961) 33–43; K. Seybold, "Die Königserwartungen bei den Propheten Haggai und
Sacharja," *Judaica* 28 (1972) 71–72.

[105] הוד also attends Yahweh as the divine king; see Ps 8:2 (Eng v. 1); 96:6; 104:1;
145:5. On the relationship of the Judean royal *hôd* to the royal *pulḫu/melammu* in
Akkadian royal inscriptions, see E. Lipiński, *La royauté de Yahwé dans la poésie et la
culte de l'ancien Israël* (2d ed.; Vlaamse Academie voor Wetenschappen, Letteren en
schone Kunsten van België. Klasse der Letteren. Verhandeligen, jaarg. 27, 1965,
55. Brussels: Palais der Academiën, 1968) 433–34; A. Petitjean, *Les Oracles du Proto-
Zacharie* (Paris: Gabala, 1969) 295–96.

[106] "Yahweh Sabaoth" occurs in Hag 1:2, 5, 7, 14; 2:4, 6–9, 11, 23; Zech 1:3,
4, 6, 12, 14, 16, 17; 2:12, 13, 15; 3:7, 9, 10; 4:6, 9; 5:4; 6:12, 15; 7:3, 4, 9, 13,
14; 8:1–4, 6, 7, 9, 11, 14, 18–23. Some of these references are from the hand of
the redactor: Hag 1:14; Zech 2:13, 15; 4:9; 6:15. For the connection of Yahweh
Sabaoth to the monarchical Jerusalem cult, see Mettinger, *Dethronement of Sabaoth*,
19–37; H.-J. Kraus, *Theology of the Psalms*, (trans. K. Crim; Minneapolis: Augsburg,
1986) 17–24.

is implicit in Haggai's temple rebuilding, see Hag 1:8); Yahweh's sovereignty over the earth will be manifest in the "shaking of the heavens and the earth . . . and kingdoms" (Hag 2:6–7, 22; Zech 2:13 [Eng v. 9]); upon the revelation of Yahweh's sovereignty some form of the Judean monarchy is to be re-established, with Zerubbabel assuming this position (Hag 2:20–23; Zech 3:9b; 6:13); the exiles will return to Jerusalem (Zech 2:10–14 [Eng vv. 6–10]; 8:7–8); the temple, land and people will be the beneficiaries of divine blessing (Hag 2:6–9, 18–19; Zech 8:4, 12–13). In short, the results of the dissolution of the kingdom of Judah in 587 will be reversed. For most commentators this use of language from the Judean monarchical ideology does not mean that the temple rebuilding denoted immediate rebellion, rather that the overthrow of the nations and the installation of Zerubbabel as king was to happen soon. Hag 2:6–7 reports Yahweh as saying: "Very soon I will shake the heavens and the earth . . . [and] the nations." It is "on that day" (Hag 2:23) that Yahweh will make Zerubbabel king.[107] For Haggai, this "day" must arrive in the lifetime of Zerubbabel since monarchical aspirations are focused on him. The re-establishment of Judean political ascendancy and kingship does not depend on Judean rebellion or military activity since Yahweh himself will bring them about—"*I* will shake the heavens and the earth . . ." (Hag 2:6, 21); "This is the word of Yahweh with regard to Zerubbabel: 'Not by might nor by power, but by my spirit, says Yahweh Sabaoth'" (Zech 4:6b). Even if the temple rebuilding were not an act of immediate rebellion, many commentators point to Zerubbabel's disappearance from the political stage as evidence that the implications of the temple rebuilding and of the preaching of Haggai and Zechariah regarding Zerubbabel were not lost on Judah's Achaemenid Persian overlords.[108]

---

[107] Petersen, *Haggai and Zechariah 1–8*, 105, rightly draws attention to the fact that Haggai does not say to the Judeans "Crown Zerubbabel king!" Similarly, see Meyers and Meyers, *Haggai, Zechariah 1–8*, xli–xlii, 68–69, 83–84, 223–24. Some commentators consider the reference to the "sons of oil" in Zech 4:14 to denote the anointing of Zerubbabel (as king?), but this is a misinterpretation; see the discussion in Petersen, *Haggai and Zechariah 1–8*, 230–31; Meyers and Meyers, *Haggai, Zechariah 1–8*, 258–59.

[108] So, for example, E. Sellin, *Serubbabel. Ein Beitrag zur Geschichte der messianischen Erwartung und der Entstehung des Judentums* (Leipzig: Deichert, 1889) 16–28; G. Sauer, "Serubbabel in der Sicht Haggais und Sacharjas," *Das ferne und nahe Wort* (ed. F. Maass; BZAW 105; Berlin: Töpelmann, 1967) 199–207; Schmidt, *Prophet und Tempel*, 192–213; Seybold, "Königserwartung," 69–78. According to Olmstead, *History*

These two arguments in favour of the Jerusalem temple rebuilding being an act of rebellion are questionable, however. The dating of the rebuilding as coincident with rebellions elsewhere in the empire founders on the general consensus that "the second year of Darius" in fact began in the spring of 520 since the period from September 29, 522 to April 13, 521 should be viewed as Darius's accession year, not as his first year.[109] That the prophecies of Haggai and Zechariah were delivered after Darius had suppressed the revolts outlined in the Bisitun inscription is further supported by Zech 1:11—"All the earth is dwelling quietly".[110] The contention that the monarchical terminology applied by the prophets to Zerubbabel implies Judean

---

of the Persian Empire, 138, Zerubbabel himself is not to be implicated with the idea of rebellion. This notion belongs to Haggai and Zechariah only, but "by their well circulated prophecies they had placed him [Zerubbabel] in so ambiguous a position that he might justifiably be accused of high treason against his royal benefactors". These studies understand the monarchical expectation centred on Zerubbabel in Messianic terms, although it must be recognized that messianism can be construed in various ways depending on the definition used (see Collins, *The Scepter and the Star*, 11–12, 24–34; G. S. Oegema, *The Anointed and His People: Messianic Expectations from the Maccabees to Bar Kochba* [Journal for the Study of the Pseudepigrapha Supplement Series 27; Sheffield: Sheffield Academic Press, 1998] 21–27, 30–34). I contend that Zerubbabel's kingship should be understood in terms of historical recurrence: having rebuilt the temple, he will be the king who returns Judah to cultic and political normalcy. A. S. van der Woude, "Serubbabel und die messianischen Erwartungen des Propheten Sacharja," *ZAW* 100 Supplement (1988) 138–56, claims that Zechariah displays no messianic expectation regarding Zerubbabel, "sondern von Anfang an seine Hoffnung auf die Dyarchie eines künftigen Fürsten und Hohenpriesters gesetz hat" (p. 156). There was no Achaemenid Persian intervention in Judean affairs at the time of the temple rebuilding as there was no threat to Achaemenid Persian authority.

[109] A. Poebel, "Chronology of Darius' First Year of Reign," *AJSL* 55 (1938) 142–65; idem, "The Duration of the Reign of Smerdis, the Magician, and the Reigns of Nebuchadnezzar III and Nebuchadnezzar IV," *AJSL* 56 (1939) 134, 143; Parker and Dubberstein, *Babylonian Chronology*, 15; Ackroyd, "Two Old Testament Problems," 15–17. For a discussion of Bickerman's arguments and a defence of the traditional date (520), see Wolff, *Haggai*, 74–76; J. Kessler, "The Second Year Of Darius and the Prophet Haggai," *Transeu* 5 (1992) 69–80 (esp. 79–80). The earliest cuneiform evidence for the reign of Darius in Babylon is 22 December, 522.

[110] The shaking of the nations in Hag 2:6–9, 20–23 is an event in the (near) future and thus is not in tension with Zech 1:11 which speaks of the current state of affairs. Since these two passages in Haggai refer to a future event, attempts to relate them to the revolts at the beginning of Darius's reign must be rejected. These prophecies may have been prompted by the expectation that another series of empire-wide rebellions, issuing in the liberation of Judah, was soon to occur. Zech 1:11–17 certainly displays dissatisfaction at the peace and stability currently enjoyed by the nations and implies that Yahweh's anger will break out against "the proud nations".

rebellion, or is at least an explicit threat to Achaemenid Persian control of Judah, is questioned by Ackroyd who outlines three points:[111] First, the Achaemenid Persian administration that appointed Zerubbabel (as governor) was not ignorant of his Davidic descent. "He was to effect some measure of re-establishment of the community centred on Jerusalem, and for this to be possible, the descendant of the Davidic line would obviously have considerable advantages over any other personage. If risk there was, it was a calculated risk". Second, Ezr 5–6 has Darius confirming the edict of Cyrus. The purpose of so doing was to show that *Darius* was a legitimate king of Judah. Third, "there is no indication of any interruption of the rebuilding of the rebuilding of the Temple subsequently". One might have expected military intervention against Judah had the Achaemenid Persians construed the temple rebuilding as an act of rebellion (so, Darius's Bisitun inscription). The temple was not torn down; indeed, Ezr 5–6 portrays Darius's active support for the enterprise.

To the above three points can be added a fourth. The rebuilding of the temple was not a political threat to Achaemenid Persian authority since these prophets' expectation of the revelation of Yahweh as divine king and the elevation of Zerubbabel to kingship was clearly dependent on the activity of Yahweh, not on the Judeans themselves. The kingship of both Yahweh and Zerubbabel is solely a matter of prophetic rhetoric. The prophets' belief that a new age for Judah was soon to be manifest, indeed within Zerubbabel's lifetime (Hag 2:20–23; Zech 6:13), need trouble the Achaemenid Persian administration only if Judean political activity was to bring about this new age. So long as the arrival of the new age remained firmly tied to divine intervention alone and did not find a reflex in Judean political activity, Judean expectations of the renaissance of Yahweh's authority over the earth, and hence their own political renaissance, could be dismissed by the Achaemenid Persians as wishful thinking.[112] As the focus of monarchical expectation Zerubbabel was in a difficult position. He had to balance his role as the Achaemenid Persian-appointed governor with Judean hopes that Yahweh would soon make him king. Yet it is clear from Haggai and Zechariah 1–8 that Zerubbabel lent his support to the rebuilding project. Had he

---

[111] Ackroyd, *Exile and Restoration*, 165, including the following quotations.
[112] Similarly, and independently, Kessler, "Second Year of Darius," 82–83.

not it would have lapsed for want of a legitimate temple builder. From this the question arises as to why Zerubbabel participated in the rebuilding rather than dismissing it as either inopportune, as his fellow Judeans had originally done (Hag 1:2), or potentially politically disastrous given that the Achaemenid Persians might interpret the undertaking as an act of rebellion. Given the monarchical rhetoric of Haggai and Zechariah, would Zerubbabel not be compromised in the eyes of the Achaemenid Persians by participating in the temple rebuilding?

There is no reason to assume, however, that the monarchical aspirations focused on Zerubbabel were known to the Achaemenid Persian administration. The prophecies of Haggai and Zechariah were directed to the Judeans and were framed in a manner so as to legitimate the temple rebuilding to this audience. It would appear from Ezr 5–6 that a rather different aspect of the temple rebuilding was presented to Tattenai and Darius by the Judeans, namely, that it was a continuation of the work sanctioned by Cyrus and commenced in his reign (Ezr 5:11–16). Although the Judeans misrepresent the work undertaken on the temple by claiming that it had been ongoing since the edict of Cyrus (Ezr 5:16), it is clear that they seek to justify the rebuilding by recourse to the edict of Cyrus; that is, the rebuilding is legitimately sanctioned by the Achaemenid Persian administration and is not a threat to order. This explanation is accepted by Darius (Ezr 6:1–18). It is notable that Tattenai both in his discussion with the Judeans (Ezr 5:1–4) and in his letter to Darius (Ezr 5:6–17) had not claimed that the rebuilding of the Jerusalem temple denoted rebellion. Rather, his concern was with the legitimacy of the undertaking.

It may be argued that Ezr 5–6 reflects a later reinterpretation of the temple rebuilding which seeks to disclaim that the temple was rebuilt as an act of rebellion or was underpinned by monarchical aspirations.[113] There may indeed be embellishment of Darius's positive response to the temple rebuilding (Ezr 6:6–12).[114] Also, after being mentioned in Ezr 5:2, Zerubbabel does not appear in the narrative, the negotiations with Tattenai being conducted by "the elders of the Jews" (Ezr 5:9) rather than by the governor, Zerubbabel. This may serve the editor's interest in elevating the role of the elders and

---

[113] So, for example, Rudolph, *Esra und Nehemia*, 49.

[114] See, for example, Blenkinsopp, *Ezra—Nehemiah*, 116, 122–23, 126–27.

community in the rebuilding over against that of leaders such as
Zerubbabel and Joshua.[115] There is, however, no reason to question
Tattenai's investigation or the desire of the Judeans to present the
temple rebuilding as a legitimate undertaking within the framework
of the Achaemenid Persian empire. As noted above, neither Haggai
nor Zechariah call for the immediate reconstitution of Judah as a
kingdom. That these prophets do not try to legitimate the temple
in terms of the Cyrus edict is not surprising since continuity with
monarchical period temple ideology (including the expectation of a
Judean king) is held to be the only valid means of legitimating the
temple rebuilding. It is to a consideration of this ideology that attention is now turned.

Ideology for Temple Rebuilding

What was the ideology underpinning the rebuilding of this former
monarchical shrine in the changed political and social circumstances
of Achaemenid Judah? Haggai and Zechariah offer related but distinct ideologies of temple rebuilding. Both are drawn from the monarchical period Zion/*Yahweh mālak* ideology which had legitimated the
building of the original temple and justified the existence of the kingdom of Israel (later, Judah). This ideology has been refracted through
the historical experience of divine abandonment and the loss of statehood. It also reflects the influence of the late-monarchical and post-
monarchical prophetic tradition of Oracles against the Nations.[116]
For both Haggai and Zechariah temple rebuilding is an expression
of the kingship of Yahweh. Yahweh is returning to Zion/Jerusalem
to rule over his people and the nations, bringing the period of divine

---

[115] So, Eskenazi, *In an Age of Prose*, 52–53, who notes that the Aramaic narrator
plays down the role of Zerubbabel and pushes "the elders of Judah" to the fore,
making the rebuilding appear to be led by them. This follows this text's emphasis
on the "community" and community participation over against the role of supposed
great leaders (like Zerubbabel), in comparison to other biblical and ancient Near
Eastern texts where the king is assigned the role of temple builder. While this is
true, she does not mention that Haggai shares this view with Ezra-Nehemiah. In
Hag 1:8 the Judean community ("this people"—Hag 1:2) is directed to undertake
the rebuilding, under the leadership of Zerubbabel and Joshua, rather than assigning the task to Zerubbabel as a king (cf. II Sam 7; I Ki 6–8; II Chron 2–7). On
this change to the standard monarchical ideology in Haggai see the following discussion on Ideology for Temple Rebuilding.

[116] For a similar understanding, arrived at independently and developed in a
somewhat different direction, see Tollington, *Tradition and Innovation*, 216–44.

ire to an end and proving Yahweh to be sovereign in the affairs of his people. A temple from where the divine king will rule is therefore needed. The construction of the temple is thus the initial step towards the expression of Yahweh's kingship.

Haggai
Hag 2:6–9:

> 6) For thus Yahweh Sabaoth has spoken: "Very soon[117] I will shake (אני מרעיש) the heavens and the earth, the sea and the dry land. (7) I will shake (הרעשתי) all the nations and all the treasures of the nations shall come. I will fill this house with glory," said Yahweh Sabaoth. (8) "To me belongs silver, to me belongs gold"—oracle of Yahweh Sabaoth. (9) "The glory of this latter house will be greater than that of the former," spoke Yahweh Sabaoth; "and in this place I will grant well-being"—oracle of Yahweh Sabaoth.

Hag 2:20–23:

> 20) The word of Yahweh came a second time to Haggai on the twenty-fourth [day] of the month: (21) "Speak to Zerubbabel the governor of Judah: 'I shake (אני מרעיש) the heavens and the earth. (22) I overthrow (הפכתי) the throne of kingdoms and destroy the power of the kings of the nations. I overturn the chariot and its riders; the horses and their riders fall, each on the sword of his brother. (23) On that day'—oracle of Yahweh Sabaoth—'I will take you, Zerubbabel, son of Shealtiel, my servant'—oracle of Yahweh—'and I will set you as my signet ring, for I have chosen you'—oracle of Yahweh Sabaoth."

These texts offer insight into the ideology which, for Haggai, underpinned the rebuilding of the Jerusalem temple of Yahweh. It is a reworking of the old monarchical ideology, adapting motifs from the monarchical period Zion psalms (Pss 46, 48, 76), the *Yahweh mālak* psalms (Pss 47, 93, 96–99), and a number of other Psalms which extol the kingship of Yahweh (Pss 24, 29).[118] These psalms, in turn,

---

[117] עוד אחת מעט היא is convoluted and not without difficulties. The translation "It is only a little while" or similar is generally adopted by commentators. For a discussion see Wolff, *Haggai*, 71 n. 6a–a; Kessler, "Second Year of Darius," 81–82.

[118] G. Wanke, *Die Zionsideologie des Korachiten in ihrem traditionsgeschichtlichen Zusammenhang* (BZAW 97; Berlin: de Gruyter, 1966), has argued for a Persian period date for the Zion psalms. Similarly, for dating both the Zion psalms and *Yahweh mālak* psalms to the Persian period, see O. Loretz, *Ugarit-Texte und Thronbesteigungspsalmen. Die Metamorphose des Regenspenders Baal-Jahwe (Ps 24, 7–10; 29; 47; 93; 95–100 sowie Ps 77, 17–20; 114)* (Ugaritische-Biblische Literatur 7; Munich: Ugarit, 1988). Very few accept this dating, however, preferring to adopt a monarchical period date.

draw on the North-West Semitic myth of the Storm God who obtains kingship by defeating the deity Yam (Sea) and who is then enthroned on his mountain after having his palace (temple) built. This myth is exemplified by the Ugaritic Baʿal cycle of texts.[119]

As noted in chapter 1, the enthronement of Yahweh, the divine king, on Zion is a monarchical construct.[120] It legitimated Jerusalem

---

J. Jeremias has attempted to plot a Deuteronomistic development of the original monarchical ideology in these Psalms, tracking this development from the early monarchical period through the Hellenistic period; see J. Jeremias, *Das Königtum Gottes in den Psalmen. Israels Begegnung mit dem kanaanäischen Mythos in den Jahweh-König-Psalem* (FRLANT 141; Göttingen: Vandenhoeck & Ruprecht, 1987). For an overview of the issues in the study the *Yahweh mālak* psalms, see B. Janowski, "Das Königtum Gottes in den Psalmen. Bemerkungen zu einem neuen Gesamtentwurf," *ZThK* 86 (1989) 389–454 (with extensive bibliography).

[119] Specifically, the Baʿal—Yam cycle of texts is the section relevant to the current discussion. The main editions of this myth are A. Herder, *Corpus des tablettes en cunéiformes alphabétiques découvertes à Ras Shamra-Ugarit de 1929 à 1939* (Mission de Ras Shamra 10; Paris: Imprimerie Nationale/Geuthner, 1963) 1–31; A. Caquot, M. Sznycer and A. Herder, *Textes Ougaritiques. Tome 1: Myths et légendes* (Litteratures anciennes du proche-orient 7; Paris: Éditions du Cerf, 1974) 101–21; M. Dietrich, O. Loretz, J. Sanmartin, *The Cuneiform Alphabetic Texts from Ugarit, Ras Ibn Hani and Other Places (KTU)* (2d enlarged ed.; Abhandlung zur Literatur Alt-Syrien-Palästinas und Mesopotamiens 8; Münster: Ugarit-Verlag, 1995); J. C. L. Gibson, *Canaanite Myths and Legends* (2d ed.; Edinburgh: Clark, 1978) 32–67; G. Del Olmo Lete, *Mitos y leyendas de Canaan. Segun la tradicion de Ugarit* (Madrid: Ediciones Cristiandad, 1981) 157–212. The ensuing discussion uses the sigla of Herder to identify the tablets. CTA 1–4 is the Baʿal—Yam cycle. For Baʿal's battle with and defeat of Yam, see CTA 2 iv. That the victor in this battle gains kingship is clear from CTA 2 iv 10, 32; 4 vii 49–50. Baʿal's kingship demands that he have a new palace (temple) constructed on his mountain, see CTA 3 E 40–50; 4 iv 43–4 v 102; 4 v 111–119; 4 vi 35–38. For Baʿal's enthronement in his palace, see CTA 4 vii; RS 24.245. On RS 24.245, see D. Pardee, *Les textes para-mythologiques de la 24ᵉ campagne (1961)* (Ras Shamra-Ougarit 4; Mémoire No. 77; Paris: Éditions recherche sur les civilisations, 1988) 75–152.

There is an extensive bibliography on the relationship between the Ugaritic mythological texts and the the conception of the kingship of Yahweh in the Hebrew Bible, particularly the *Yahweh mālak* and Zion pslams; see, for example, Schmid, "Jahweh und die Kulttraditionen von Jerusalem," 168–98; W. H. Schmidt, *Königtum Gottes in Ugarit und Israel. Zur Herkunft der Königsprädikation Jahwes* (2d ed.; BZAW 80; Berlin: de Gruyter, 1966); Stolz, *Strukturen und Figuren von Jerusalem*, passim; Steck, *Friedenvorstellung im alten Jerusalem*, 5–51; Roberts, "The Davidic Origin of the Zion Tradition," 329–44; idem, "Zion in the Theology of the Davidic-Solomonic Empire," 93–108; Cross, *Cananite Myth and Hebrew Epic*, 90–163, 196–77; J. Gray, *The Biblical Doctrine of the Reign of God* (Edinburgh: Clark, 1979) 39–85; Day, *God's Conflict*, 18–38; C. Kloos, *Yhwh's Combat with the Sea: A Canaanite Tradition in the Religion of Ancient Israel* (Amsterdam: G. A. van Oorschot/Leiden: E. J. Brill, 1986); Jeremias, *Das Königtum Gottes in den Psalmen*, passim; Loretz, *Ugarit-Texte und Thronbesteigungspsalmen*, passim; N. Wyatt, *Myths of Power: A Study of Royal Myth and Ideology in Ugaritic and Biblical Tradition* (Ugaritisch-Biblische Literatur 13; Münster: Ugarit-Verlag, 1996).

[120] See above, pp. 3–5, and the works cited in the footnotes thereto.

as the capital city of Israel (later, Judah) and concomitantly legitimated both the Davidic dynasty which built the temple of Yahweh
in Jerusalem and the existence of the kingdom itself. The connection between the above sections of Haggai and the monarchical
ideology of Yahweh's kingship and his enthronement on Zion is
seen in the shared imagery of the "shaking of the heavens and the
earth, the sea and the dry land" (אני מרעיש את־השמים ואת־הארץ
Hag—אני מרעיש את־השמים ואת־הארץ ;Hag 2:6 ואת־הים ואת־החרבה
2:21) and the "shaking of the nations" (הרעשתי את־כל־הגוים)—Hag
2:7) whose origins ultimately lie in the theophany of the enthroned
Storm God, derived from the North-West Semitic myth of the Storm
God who ascends to kingship having defeated Yam.

In the following discussion an attempt will be made not only to
draw out the connection between Haggai's prophecies and the monarchical period ideology of Yahweh's kingship but also to explore how
his ideology has been refracted through late-monarchical and post-
monarchical thought, when Judah was either under the control of
foreign powers or had been destroyed by them. As Judah lay within
the Achaemenid Persian empire when Haggai's prophecies were delivered, these late- and post-monarchical texts are particularly pertinent
and give insight into the prophetic tradition in which Haggai stood.

In the *Yahweh mālak* psalms and in Pss 24 and 29, Yahweh is portrayed as the Storm God who is the divine king now enthroned on
his holy mountain (Zion). Although in the *Yahweh mālak* psalms the
victory over Yam is explicitly mentioned only in Ps 93:3–4, it is generally accepted that this is the context in which Yahweh's kingship
and enthronement mentioned in the rest of these psalms are to be
understood.[121] Important for the present discussion is the occurrence
of the motif of the shaking (רעש ,חיל) of the earth (or parts of the

---

[121] Ps 93:3–4 alludes to Yahweh's defeat of Yam (here termed "rivers" [*nhrwt*]
cf. "Judge Nahar" [*tpt nhr*] as an apellation for or name of Yam in, for example,
CTA 2 i 7, 22, 26, 30; 2 iii 7; 2 iv 4; 3 D 36). While Ps 97 does not mention
the defeat of Yam, this psalm should be compared with, for example, Ps 18 where
many similar storm motifs occur in the context of the battle with Yam. Pss 24 and
29 directly relate the kingship of Yahweh to the defeat of Yam; the former text
making the victorious battle the precusor to creation (Ps 24:1–2). There are a number of passages in Job which speak of the absolute authority of Yahweh using the
myth of the Storm God's defeat of Yam; see Job 9:5–14, arguably a late text (post-
dating Haggai) (v. 6: "he shakes [המרגיז] the earth from its place, he makes its
pillars tremble [יתפלצון]". Perhaps relevant for Hag 2:22 is v. 5: "He moves mountains without their knowing, overturning them [הפכם] in his wrath"); Job 26:5–14

earth) and the nations before the enthroned king.[122] In Pss 29:3–10 and 97:1–5, the storm theophany prompts this "shaking" (חיל is the common verb used) either because of its ferocity or its fearsome appearance, while in Ps 96:9–10 (v. 9b "tremble [חילו] before him all the earth!"); 99:1 ("Yahweh is king, the peoples tremble [ירגזו]; enthroned on the cherubim, the earth quivers [תנוט]"),[123] where storm motifs are not used, it is a response to his being divine king. A sharp division should not be drawn between these two contexts.

Throughout the *Yahweh mālak* psalms, as well as in other psalms, there is an emphasis on the judgement and chastisement of the nations as the corollary of Yahweh being king of the earth and nations.[124]

(v. 11a: "the pillars of the heavens shake [ירופפו]"). These texts relate the defeat of Yam to Yahweh's creation of the world (similarly Ps 104:1–9 and, perhaps, Jer 5:22; 10:12–16). It is debated as to whether the *Yahweh mālak* and Zion psalms hold a similar view. This is in part related to whether "creation" is a feature of the Ugaritic Ba'al—Yam myth. On this see the discussion in Day, *God's Conflict*, 7–18.

[122] The writing (חיל) of the earth (hills, heavens, and/or nations) at the Storm God's enthronement or theophany is paralleled to their shaking (רעש) in similar texts; see A. Avishur, *Stylistic Studies of Word-Pairs in Biblical and Ancient Semitic Literatures* (AOAT 210; Neukirchen-Vluyn: Neukirchener Verlag, 1984) 661. In Jer 51:29 these two terms occur in "syndetic parataxis". There is a cluster of other synonymns— רגז, מוג, מוד, נעש, (and a number of hapaxlegomena; for example, נוט in Ps 99:1). These terms do not all have exactly the same meaning, but their appearance either in parallel to רעש or in similar contexts points to extensive semantic overlap.

In the Ugaritic Ba'al myth, after gaining kingship and having his palace (temple) built on his mountain, Ba'al ascends to take up residence in the palace. He opens a window in the building and announces his sovereignty to the world (CTA 4 vii 25–52). "Ba'al uttered his holy voice" (*qlh. qdš* [.] *b['l. y]tn*—CTA 4 vii 29), a metaphor for the thunder, with the result that the earth shook (CTA 4 vii 31–32; the verbs used are *trr* and *ntt*) and his enemies were "troubled" (CTA 4 vii 32–41).

[123] נוט is a hapaxlegomenon which is commonly taken as cognate with Ugaritic *ntt*; see H. R. Cohen, *Biblical Hapaxlegomena in the Light of Akkadian and Ugaritic* (SBLDS 37; Missoula, MT: Scholars Press, 1978) 121. Its occurence in CTA 4 vii 35 is significant for the present discussion since *ntt* denotes the reaction of the earth to the storm theophany of Ba'al, who has been enthroned on his temple mount; see R. Scoralick, *Trishagion und Gottesherrschaft. Psalm 99 als Neuinterpretation von Tora und Propheten* (Stuttgarter Bibel-Studien 138; Stuttgart: Katholisches Bibelwerk, 1989) 18–22.

[124] *Yahweh mālak* psalms: Pss 47:1–2, 7–9; 96:4, 7–10, 13; 97:6–9; 98:9; 99:2–4. Other psalms: Pss 7:7–9 (Eng vv. 6–8); 9:6–9 (Eng v. 5–8); 22:28; 67:5 (Eng v. 4); 68:33–34 (Eng vv. 32–33; this text uses the epithet "the rider on the heavens" cf. "rider on the clouds" in 68:5 [Eng v. 6] which is also an epithet of Ba'al in CTA 2 iv 8; 3 B 40); 75:3–4 (Eng vv. 2–3); 82:8; 83:18; cf. the portrayal of the enthroned Storm God in CTA 4 vii 32–51. In the monarchical period this ideology expressed imperial aspirations based on the notion that it was "proper" for all peoples to worship Yahweh since he was the highest God. See also Ps 2 where this view is promulgated.

This theme also finds expression in the Zion psalms. Yahweh, enthroned as king on Zion, his temple mount, can defend Zion from the attack of foreign nations. According to Ps 46, though the earth be threatened by the chaos waters, Zion need not fear since "God is inside the city" (v. 6; Eng v. 5). Similarly, the raging nations hold no threat for Zion. Yahweh, the divine king, will "shout" and prove himself to be these nations' master.[125] In Ps 48 Yahweh drives away from Zion, "the city of the Great King" (v. 3; Eng v. 2), an advancing cadre of kings (vv. 5–7; Eng vv. 4–6) by using "the east wind". The kings "were astounded; terrified, they fled. Shuddering (רעדה) seized them there; they writhed (חיל) like a woman in labor". Psalms 46 and 48 may display a historicization of the Storm God's battle with Yam. Zaphon, the mountain from which Baʿal reigns in the Ugaritic myth (see, for example, CTA 3 C 36; 3 D 44; 4 v 85) is, in fact, Zion (Ps 48:3; Eng v. 2). Like Yam/the waters, the nations "shuddered and writhed" at the attack of Yahweh in the storm (Ps 48:7; Eng v. 6 cf. Ps 114 translated below). The nations are cast as the threat to Yahweh's kingship in Ps 46:7 (Eng v. 6 cf. vv. 3–4 [Eng vv. 2–3] where the chaotic waters are described in similar language).[126]

The influence of the myth of the Storm God's defeat of Yam in order to gain kingship, with the attendant themes of defender or saviour of his people and the judge of the nations evident in the above texts, is seen in certain poetic texts recounting the Exodus tradition. Yahweh liberates his people Israel from Egypt and makes a passage through the sea and/or the Jordan to bring his people into the land of Canaan. The significant difference between the texts cited above and the texts relating the Exodus tradition is that in the former emphasis is placed on Yahweh as the divine king enthroned on his mountain (Zion) after the successful completion of the battle with Yam, whereas in the latter stress the travelling of Yahweh either to do battle with Yam or as the divine warrior who leads the people

---

[125] Ps 46:7b (Eng v. 6b): נתן בקולו תמוג ארץ—"he thunders, the earth shakes." The use of the storm motif (*ntn ql* = thunder) by the enthroned Storm God as an expression of his kingship also appears in CTA 4 vii 29–31. Also cf. Ex 9:23; 19:19; Am 1:2; Ps 29:3–9.

[126] On the historicization of the battle myth in these Psalms, see Day, *God's Conflict*, 120–21, 125–27. CTA 4 vii 25–52 does not portray Baʿal's enemies as a threat to his kingship, rather they are, so to speak, put in their place relative to Baʿal. The notion that Baʿal can defend his mountain and palace against potential enemies is reflected in CTA 4 vii 43–52.

whom he has rescued by winning the battle.[127] The "shaking" of the earth and/or the nations also appears in the latter texts. Ps 114 exhibits these themes related to Yahweh as the saviour of his people.

Praise Yahweh![128]
1) When Israel came out of Egypt,
   the House of Jacob from a foreign people,
2) Judah became his sanctuary,
   Israel his dominion.
3) The sea [הַיָּם] looked and fled,
   the Jordan turned back.
4) The mountains skipped like rams,
   the hills like young sheep.
5) Why do you run away, sea?
   Jordan, why do you turn back?
6) Mountains, why skip like rams?
   Hills, why like young sheep?
7) Writhe (חוּלִי), Earth, at the presence of Yahweh,
   at the presence of the God of Jacob,
   who turned the rock into a pool of water,
   flint into a fountain of water.

Is 17:12–14 displays many of the motifs evident in Pss 46 and 48. The nations coming to attack Yahweh's people (Zion is not specified) roar like the seas; they are mighty waters (מַיִם רַבִּים). Yahweh rebukes them (נער), driving them off in a storm wind (סוּפָה). For נער as a term comparable to *ntn qwl* used of the Storm God in the mythological battle with Yam, see II Sam 22:16 = Ps 18:16 (Eng v. 15); Ps 104:7; Nah 1:4.

[127] It is not necessary to discuss the relationship between the "enthroned" and "travelling" traditions here; see J. Jeremias, *Theophanie. Die Geschichte einer alttestamentlichen Gattung* (2nd. ed.; WMANT 10; Neukirchen-Vluyn: Neukirchener Verlag, 1977). Cross, *Canaanite Myth and Hebrew Epic*, 162–63, contends that the "travelling" of the victorious Storm God to his temple Mount has roots also in the North-West Semitic myth of the Storm God's victory over Yam. The Ugaritic Baʿal cycle of texts has Baʿal travelling to his temple mount in CTA 4 vii 7ff., but he is not attended by the storm theophany which appears only when he has taken up residence in his palace (CTA 4 vii; RS 24.245). The storm theophany also does not appear in the battle with Yam (CTA 2 iv), although lightning and thunderbolt appear to be used by Baʿal as weapons (cf. CTA 4 vii 40–41). The motif of the Storm God travelling to the battle site may be related to the Akkadian literary tradition; see Lipiński, *La royauté de Yahvé*, 187–209; T. W. Mann, *Divine Presence and Guidance in Israelite Traditions: The Typology of Exaltation* (The Johns Hopkins Near Eastern Studies; Baltimore: The Johns Hopkins University Press, 1977) 30–58.

Ex 15–19 can be read as Yahweh defeating Yam (Ex 15—historicized as Pharaoh and the Egyptian army) and then travelling with his people to the mountain of his enthronement (Sinai). In Ex 19 Yahweh is portrayed as the enthroned Storm God (see Ex 19:16–25). The "shaking" motif also appears here (v. 18—חרד), as does volcanic imagery (cf. Ps 18:9 [Eng v. 8]).

[128] Transposed from the end of Ps 113.

Ex 15:1–18, a poem recounting the defeat of the Egyptians who pursued the Israelites leaving Egypt, also exemplifies this tradition, conjoining the Exodus tradition and the mythological defeat of Yam by the Storm God (Ex 15:7–8, 10–11 cf. Ps 114 above). The "shaking" motif appears in vv. 14–16a (רגז, חיל, מוג) where it is the reaction of local nations (Philistia, Edom, Moab, Canaan) to Yahweh's opening a way through the sea and his destruction of the Egyptian army (= the defeat of Yam in the myth).[129] These nations' reaction and the punishment of Egypt may be connected to the judgement of the nations theme. The underlying idea in this text, at least, is these nations' fear of Yahweh induced by his liberation of his people. Another (earlier?) aspect of the Exodus tradition appears in Ps 68:8–9 (Eng vv. 7–8) // Jud 5:4, which include the storm theophany accompanying Yahweh's travelling.[130] In these texts it is not the defeat of Yam in view, but rather the coming of Yahweh from Edom (Seir) at the head of his people. Significantly for the present discussion, one of the motifs used is the "shaking" (רעש—the same root as used in the Haggai prophecies) of the heavens and earth at the divine presence (ארץ רעשה אף־שמים נטפו—Ps 68:9 [Eng v. 8] // Jud 5:4).

There are other monarchical period texts in which the mythological defeat of Yam becomes a paradigm for Yahweh's ability to save his people (or the individual supplicant) from historical, temporal enemies. The view espoused is that just as Yahweh defeated Yam, so too he is able to defeat Israel's enemies. Unlike Pss 46 and 48, however, these texts share with those relating the Exodus tradition the theme of the travelling or coming of Yahweh to the scene of battle. The motif of the "shaking" of the earth, heavens, and nations appears as a response to the storm theophany or battle.

Texts exhibiting this perspective are:

---

[129] Ex 15:1–18 is understood by a number of commentators to be another historicization of the myth of the Storm God's battle with Yam, so Day, *God's Battle*, 97–101; Kloos, *Yhwh's Combat with the Sea*, 127–212; Wyatt, *Myths of Power*, 172–86; cf. Cross, *Canaanite Myth and Hebrew Epic*, 121–44, who speaks of this narrative as mythologized history. From this "historicization" of the myth one cannot conclude that the Israelites' escape through the Sea was a historical event; see Ahlström, *Who Were the Israelites?*, 45–55. Yahweh's casting of the Egyptian chariots and their riders into the sea in order to save the fleeing Israelites may be reflected in Hag 2:22. The preservation of Israel from foreign armies may be related to the motif of Yahweh's defence of Zion in Pss 46 and 48.

[130] On these verses, see Lipiński, *La royauté de Yahweh*, 186–209; Mann, *Divine Presence*, 182–84.

Ps 18:7–18 (Eng vv. 6–17) // 2 Sam 22:7–18. At Yahweh's coming in the storm to the scene of battle with Yam—[131]

> 8) The earth quaked (תנעש) and shook (תרעש),
> the foundations of the mountains (2 Sam 22:8—heavens) trembled (ירגזו),
> they quivered (יתגעשו) because he was angry . . .
> 17) . . . he drew (?) me out of mighty waters (מים רבים).
> 18) He rescued me from my powerful enemy . . .

Ps 77:17–21 (Eng vv. 16–20). In response to the storm attending Yahweh at the battle—

> 17) . . . when the waters saw you, they writhed (יהילו),
> yea, the deep trembled (ירגזו).
> 19c) . . . the earth trembled (רגזה) and shook (רעש)

Hab 3:2–15 has the theophany of the Storm God attending Yahweh as he marches from Edom to do battle against Yam (Hab 3:8). This text also recounts the actual battle with Yam (cf. CTA 2 iv). At Yahweh's coming—

> 6) He makes the earth shake (ימדד),[132]
> the nations look and tremble (יתר root: נתר) . . .
> 10a) the mountains see you and writhe (יהילו) . . .
> 13a) You went out to save your people, to save your anointed.

In this text, "the nations" are placed alongside "the earth" as "shaking" at the coming of Yahweh (cf. Hag 2:7 and the texts relating the Exodus tradition cited above).[133]

Nahum 1:2–8 explicitly incorporates the theophany of the Storm God and the defeat of Yam with the judgement of the nations.[134] In this oracle Yahweh comes in the storm to judge the nations. This

---

[131] See also Ps 144:5–7 which shares many motifs in common with 2 Sam 22:10–18 // Ps 18:10–18 (Eng vv. 9–17).

[132] Taking the verb from the root מוד rather than from מדד—"to measure". In support of this interpretation, see A. J. Baumgartner, Le prophète Habakuk. Introduction critique et exégèse (Leipzig: Drugulin, 1885) 195; G. R. Driver, "Hebrew Notes," ZAW 52 (1934) 54–55; J. Barr, Comparative Philology and the Text of the Old Testament (Oxford: Oxford University Press, 1968) 252; J. J. M. Roberts, Nahum, Habakkuk, and Zephaniah: A Commentary (OTL; Louisville, KY: Westminster/John Knox, 1991) 136 n. 28.

[133] Hab 3:2–15 is commonly dated to c. 600. On the relationship between this text and the Ugaritic Ba'al myth, see W. F. Albright, "The Psalm of Habakkuk," in Studies in Old Testament Prophecy (Th. H. Robinson Festschrift; ed. H. H. Rowley; Edinburgh: Clark, 1950) 1–18; T. Hiebert, God of My Victory: The Ancient Hymn of Habakkuk 3 (HSM 38; Atlanta: Scholars Press, 1986) 101–09.

[134] This text is commonly dated to the mid- to late-seventh century, usually c. 630.

text reintroduces a central theme from the *Yahweh mālak* and Zion psalms, namely, that Yahweh is the victorious Storm God who, by virtue of his victory over Yam and his procurement of kingship, has authority to judge the nations. The salient sections of this poem for our purposes are—

> 2b) Yahweh takes vengeance on this foes,
>   He vents his wrath against his enemies . . .
> 3b) In whirlwind and storm he makes his way,
>   clouds are dust beneath his feet.
> 4) He rebukes the sea (נוער בים) and it dries up,
>   he makes all the rivers fail.
>   Bashan and Carmel languish,
>   the green shoots of Lebanon wilt.
> 5) The mountains shake (רעשו) before him,
>   the hills tremble (התמגגו),
>   the earth is laid waste[135] before him,
>   the world and all who live in it.
> 6) Who can stand before his wrath?
>   Who can resist his fury?
>   His anger pours out like fire,
>   and the rocks break[136] before him . . .
> 7b) he knows those who seek refuge in him,
> 8a) and he carries (them) over the flood.[137]

Other prophetical texts from the late- and post-monarchical periods speaking of Yahweh's judgement of the nations often divest themselves of the storm theophany but retain the notion of the "shaking" of the nations, heavens, and earth at Yahweh's judgement. Noteworthy here is that the "shaking" motif also occurs in certain of the *Yahweh mālak* psalms without explicit storm theophany motifs, although it is not questioned that the myth of the Storm God's suc-

---

[135] Reading חשא (from the root שאה, cf. Is 6:11) for MT חשא (from the root נשא), see J. M. Smith, W. H. Ward, J. A. Bewer, *A Critical and Exegetical Commentary on Michah, Zephaniah, Nahum, Habakkuk, Obadiah and Joel* (ICC; Edinburgh: Clark, 1911) 299. In defence of MT see Roberts, *Nahum, Habakkuk, and Zephaniah*, 44 n. 7, who translates חשא intransitively to mean "it rises up" (= heaves).

[136] In view of the reference to the fire of Yahweh's anger in the first half-line, a number of commentators have suggested reading נצתו (root: יצת—"to burn up") for MT נתצו (root: נתץ—"to break up, demolish"); see Smith et al., *A Critical and Exegetical Commentary on Michah, Zephaniah, Nahum, Habakkuk, Obadiah and Joel*, 299. This has not found wide acceptance but is reintroduced by *BHS* in its note to this word.

[137] This translation presumes עבירם; see *BHS* note and commentaries. Or, "when the flood overtakes (them)".

cessful quest for kingship is the context in which to understand this motif. It is suggested here that this is also the background for the "shaking" motif in these prophetical texts. The "shaking" motif in these texts belongs to the tradition of the kingship of Yahweh, either as the Storm God, enthroned on Zion, who is king and judge of the nations or as the Storm God who is coming to inflict defeat on the enemy. Many of these prophetical texts belong to the genre called "Oracles against the Nations" (Am 1–2; Is 13–23; Jer 25:24–38; Jer 46–51; Ezek 25–32); that is, oracles which proclaim the coming downfall of the designated nations because of Yahweh's judgement upon them. This judgement is sometimes specified as going to take place on "the Day of Yahweh".[138]

The earliest set of Oracles against Nations is Amos 1:2–2:16. Its introduction clearly places it within the context of Yahweh's enthronement on Zion and the myth of the Storm God's defeat of Yam. Amos 1:2—

---

[138] The origin of the Oracles against the Nations and their relationship to the concept of "the Day of Yahweh" have been much discussed; see, for example, G. von Rad, "The Origin of the Concept of the Day of Yahweh," *JSS* 4 (1959) 97–108, idem, *Old Testament Theology*, 2. 119–125, 199; Ahlström, *Joel*, 62–97; D. L. Christensen, *Transformation of the War Oracle in Old Testament Prophecy: Studies in the Oracles Against the Nations* (HDR 3; Missoula, MT: Scholars Press, 1975); H. D. Preuss, *Jahweglaube und Zukunftserwartung* (BWANT 87; Stuttgart: Kohlhammer, 1968) 170–97; H.-M. Lutz, *Jahwe, Jerusalem und die Völker* (WMANT 27; Neukirchen-Vluyn: Neukirchener Verlag, 1968) 130–46; M. Saebø, *Sacharja 9–14. Untersuchungen von Text und Form* (WMANT 34; Neukirchen-Vluyn: Neukirchener Verlag, 1969) 252–317. Von Rad understands the origin of "the Day of Yahweh" to lie in the pre-monarchical tribal traditions of Yahweh as a warrior who leads Israel into battle against the hostile inhabitants of Canaan. It is thus connected with traditions regarding "Holy War" and the Ark of the Covenant (see, for example, Num 10:35–36; Num 21:21–35; Jud 5 [which also includes motifs from the Storm God tradition; Jud 5:4–5]; I Sam 4:1–11; 5:1–6:19). The Oracles against the Nations developed out of this "Holy War" tradition. S. Mowinckel, *Psalmenstudien*, 2.230–44, among others, connects "the Day of Yahweh" to the annual enthronement festival which was a cultic celebration of Yahweh's kinship and the defeat of his enemies (both mythological and historical enemies). Against Von Rad, the arguments of C. H. J. de Geus, *The Tribes of Israel: An Investigation into Some of the Presuppositions of Martin Noth's Amphictiony Hypothesis* (Studia Semitica Neerlandica 18; Assen/Amsterdam: Van Gorcum, 1976); Lemche, *Ancient Israel*; Ahlström, *Who Were the Israelites?*, 11–36; I. Finkelstein, *The Archaeology of the Israelite Settlement* (Jerusalem: Israel Exploration Society, 1988), seriously call into question the biblical portrayal of the pre-monarchical period, particularly the tradition of the tribal league and the invasion of Palestine by the Israelites. Rather than resolving the issue of the origin of the Oracles against the Nations and their relationship to "the Day of Yahweh", it suffices here to affirm that a number of the Oracles against the Nations draw upon the mythological battle of the Storm God, connecting it to Yahweh's historical enemies (the nations) as is done in the Zion psalms.

Yahweh roars from Zion, and thunders (יתן קולו) from Jerusalem.
The shepherds' pastures wilt, the top of Carmel dries up.[139]

Is 13:9–13, an oracle against Babylon—

> 6) Howl! For the Day of Yahweh is near,
>   bringing devastation from Shaddai ...
> 7) ... The heart of each man fails him,
>   they are terrified, pangs and pain seize them,
>   they writhe (יחילון) like a woman in labour ...
> 9) The Day of Yahweh is coming,
>   with cruelty, wrath, and fierce anger ...
> 13) Therefore I will make the heavens tremble (ארגיז),
>   the earth will shake (תרעש) from its place,
>   before the rage of Yahweh Sebaoth,
>   the day when his fierce anger.

Jer 4:24, where one effect of Yahweh's judgement on Judah is—

> I looked at the mountains, they were shaking (רעשים),
>   and all the hills were quaking (התקלקלו).

Jer 10:10, which summarizes a comparison of Yahweh and the idols
of the nations—

> But Yahweh is the true God,
>   he is a living god, the eternal king.
> At his wrath the earth quakes (תרעש),
>   the nations cannot endure his fury.

Jer 50:34, an oracle against Babylon—

> Their redeemer is strong,
>   Yahweh Sabaoth is his name.
> He will plead their case, so as to give rest to the earth,
>   and to make the inhabitants of Babylon tremble (הרגיז).

Jer 51:29, an oracle against Babylon—

> The earth shakes (תרעש) and writhes (תחל),
>   for the plans of Yahweh against Babylon stand.[140]

---

[139] The languishing of nature at the coming or enthronement of the Storm God
does not appear in the Ugaritic Ba'al cycle of texts (contra Cross, *Canaanite Myth
and Hebrew Epic*, 150–162). It is, however, part of the Israelite tradition; see also
Joel 4:16; Nah 1:4; Is 24:4; 42:15.

[140] Similarly on the shaking of the earth as a response to the Yahweh's judgement on the nations, see Jer 49:21 (רעש); 50:46 (רעש); Ezek 26:18 (חרד).

The continuing significance of the myth of the Storm God's victory over Yam as a means of expressing post-monarchical Judean understanding of the kingship of Yahweh and hopes for Yahweh to act on their behalf against their enemies and to redress their current plight is evidenced in a number of texts. Ps 74, an exilic Psalm, holds out the hope of Yahweh's salvation of the people using the theme of the destruction of the Sea Monster[141]—

> Yet God my King is from old,
>   working salvation in the midst of the earth.
> You divided (the) sea (ם׳) by your might,
>   you smashed the heads of the dragons on the waters.
> You crushed the heads of Leviathan . . . (Ps 74:12–14)

There is no shaking of the Earth or nations, but it is clear that the myth of the successful battle with Yam expresses Yahweh's kingship and also his power to undertake another saving act on behalf of the people.

Deutero-Isaiah portrays the return of Yahweh to Jerusalem in terms of the re-establishment of Yahweh's kingship using the myth of the Storm God's battle. This is also wedded to the Exodus motif in that Yahweh saves his people from exile and brings them back to their land. Is 51:9–10 reads—

> Awake, awake! put on strength, arm of Yahweh!
>   Awake, as in days of old!
> Was it not you that cut Rahab in pieces,
>   pierced the dragon?
> Was it not you that dried up the sea (ם׳),
>   the waters of the great deep,
> that made the depths of the sea a road
>   for the redeemed to cross?[142]

The return of Yahweh to Zion with his exiled people in train is in order to display to Zion that "Your God is king" (Is 52:7; cf. Is 41:20; 43:15; 44:6; also cf. Mic 4:7; Zeph 3:15).[143]

---

[141] Cf. Ps 89:10–11 (Eng vv. 9–10), which is probably to be dated to the monarchical period. On these two passages, see Day, *God's Conflict*, 21–28.

[142] Explicit references to the second Exodus motif are found in Is 40:3–5, 10–11; 41:17–20; 42:10–17; 43:16–21; see above chapter 2 nn. 43, 70.

[143] On the connection between the battle motifs and Yahweh's kingship in Deutero-Isaiah, see Mettinger, "YHWH as King in Isaiah 40–55," 148–57. Is 24–27 exhibit a number of features drawn from the Storm God myth similar to those noted here

Is 63:7–64:11 (Eng v. 12), another exilic or early Persian period poem,[144] expresses the hope of Yahweh's saving intervention using the tradition of Yahweh's coming to do battle on behalf of his people—

> 63:19b [Eng 64:1]) Oh that you would rend the heavens and come down!
>   —the mountains would shudder (נזלו)[145] at your presence,
> 64:1) as when fire blazes in brushwood,
>   as fire makes water boil—
> To make your name known to your enemies,
>   that at your presence nations might tremble (ירגזו).

These verses are closely related to Ps 18:8–11 [Eng vv. 7–10] // 2 Sam 22:8–11 which also speak of Yahweh's coming to save and which mention the fire emanating from Yahweh's mouth and nostrils as he prepares to go into battle (against Yam). It is also mentioned that Yahweh "bent the heavens and came down" (v. 10).[146] In this psalm it is the earth and mountains that "shake" (רגז, רעש; v. 8) rather than the nations.

Joel 2:1–11 is an early Persian period text (c. 500?) exhibiting the same features. Yahweh is leading either a plague of locusts or a foreign army (that is, the theme of Yahweh's "coming"). The storm imagery of Yahweh's entry into battle is used—

> 1) Blow the horn in Zion,
>   sound the alarm on my holy mountain!
>   Let all the peoples of the earth tremble (ירגזו),
>   for the Day of Yahweh is coming,
>   indeed, it is near:

---

from Deutero- and Trito-Isaiah. They are also connected with Yahweh's salvation of his people. See Is 24:4,7 (nature languishing); 24:19 ("shaking" [מוט // פרר] of the earth cf. מוט in Ps 46:7 [Eng v. 6]); 24:23 (Yahweh as king); 26:1; 27:1, 2 ("that day" signifying "the Day of Yahweh"); 26:17–18 ("writhing" [חיל] of Yahweh's people when in his presence); 27:1 (successful battle with Leviathan//sea-dragon). The dating of Is 24–27 is problematic. Many date it to the late Persian or Hellenistic period due to its connections with apocalypticism; see, for example, Plöger, *Theocracy and Eschatology*, 77–78, for a third century date. Others, for example, W. R. Millar, *Isaiah 24–27 and the Origin of Apocalyptic* (HSM 11; Missoula, MT: Scholars Press, 1976); D. G. Johnson, *From Chaos to Restoration: An Integrative Reading of of Isaiah 24–27* (JSOTSup 61; Sheffield: Sheffield Academic, 1988), date these chapters to the sixth century. Since I accept the late dating of these chapters, they have not been included in the discussion of post-monarchical and early Persian period texts.

[144] Williamson, "Isaiah 63,7–64, 11," 48–58.
[145] The verb זלל is in parallelism with רעש in Jud 5:5.
[146] Similarly, Ps 144:5–7.

2) A day of darkness and gloom,
  a day of cloud and blackness . . .
6a) Before him the peoples writhe (יחילו) . . .
10a) Before him the earth trembles (רגזה),
    the heavens shake (רעשו) . . .
11a) Yahweh thunders (נתן קולו) before his army . . .

Joel 4:16 is related to "the Day of Yahweh", but reflects the tradition of Yahweh's enthronement on Zion (cf. Am 1:2):

Yahweh roars from Zion,
he thunders (יתן קולו) from Jerusalem;
heaven and earth shake (רעשו).

The twin notions of the kingship of Yahweh and the judgement of the nations which are evidenced in the texts cited above and which are expressed by the motif of the shaking of the heavens, earth, and nations serve as the context in which to interpret the Hag 2:6–9, 20–23. Like the late- and post-monarchical prophetic Oracles against the Nations, and also some of the *Yahweh mālak* psalms, the Haggai prophecies do not employ the theophany of the Storm God, but the "shaking" motif nevertheless has roots in the monarchical ideology of Yahweh's kingship and Zion's election as the throne of Yahweh.[147]

Another connection between the prophetical Oracles against the Nations and the Haggai prophecies is "the Day of Yahweh". This was understood to be the day when Yahweh would vindicate his people and vent his wrath against their enemies in judgement. Haggai understands "that day" (Hag 2:23) to be coming "very soon" (Hag 2:6). It is not a coincidence that this prophecy regarding "the Day of Yahweh" comes at the time of the re-laying of the temple foundation since, working with the old monarchical ideology of the enthronement of Yahweh as king and judge on Mount Zion, for Yahweh to return to Jerusalem in order to take up residence in the

---

[147] The oracle against Babylon in Is 14:3–23 is significant in the context of this discussion since it includes the representation of the king of Babylon (Is 14:13–14) as one who sought to make his throne in the heavens, specifically on Mt Zaphon (cf. Ps 48:3 [Eng v. 2]), in order to make himself "like the Most High" (עליון). For such hubris he is brought low. However, it is interesting that in reflecting on his previous high station, observers remark regarding his kingship (Is 14:16b): "Is this the man who made the earth tremble (מרגיז), who shook (מרעיש) kingdoms?" That is, his kingship, modelled after the divine king enthroned on Zaphon, is spoken of in exactly the same terms: this soveriegnty is expressed by shaking king(dom)s and the earth.

new temple is for him to exercise his kingship, to judge the nations, and to save his people. These notions have a close connection to the role of the legitimate rebuilder in Haggai since "on that day" the rebuilder will be vindicated or revealed to be Yahweh's vice-regent (Hag 2:20–23). The prophet does not reveal the precise date of "that day". One must assume that it is within Zerubbabel's life-time since the prophecy is explicitly directed to him, but it is unclear whether or not it coincides with the completion of the temple.[148]

There are three further connections to the monarchical *Yahweh mālak*/Zion ideology. The first is the employment of the concept of "glory" (כבוד; Hag 2:7, 9). While emphasis here is placed on the material wealth in the building, particularly to allay the misgivings of those who had known the monarchical period temple (Hag 2:3), "glory" is not simply a material term.[149] It is a highly charged, sym-bolic term to denote the presence of Yahweh. The material wealth which will adorn the rebuilt temple is a tangible reflection of the glory of the great divine king who dwells within it (see Hag 1:8 cf. Is 54:11–12). For a comparison with "glory" in the *Yahweh mālak* and other Psalms, see Pss 24:7–10; 26:8; 29:1–3, 9; 66:2; 96:7–8; 97:6.[150] Haggai's second connection to the monarchical *Yahweh mālak*/

---

[148] Cf. Is 60:22 which concludes a prophecy regarding the glorification of the temple and the restoration of Israel with the words: "I am Yahweh; at its time (עת) I will hasten it". None of the references to "the Day of the Lord" in the prophets give this "day" a precise date.

[149] Cf. D. J. A. Clines, "Haggai's Temple, Constructed, Deconstructed and Reconstructed," in *Second Temple Studies: 2. Temple and Community in the Persian Period* (ed. T. C. Eskenazi and K. H. Richards; JSOTSup 175; Sheffield: JSOT Press, 1994) 60–70, who understands the temple to be nothing more than a treasury in Haggai and that "glory" refers to the treasure to be stored there. He castigates those (I will now have to be included among them) who consider some notion of divine presence to attend the notion of "glory" without, on my reading, paying much attention to the arguments adduced for such an interpretation. R. P. Carroll, "So What Do We *Know* about the Temple? The Temple in the Prophets," in *Second Temple Studies: 2. Temple and Community in the Persian Period* (ed. T. C. Eskenazi and K. H. Richards) 41, also views the temple as a treasury but, unlike Clines, explic-itly connects this with an imperial administrative role.

[150] A similar understanding of the "glory" of Yahweh is to be found in Ezekiel. Yahweh's "glory" abandons the temple as a judgement on Jerusalem and Judah (Ezek 8:4; 9:3; 10:4, 18, 19; 11:22, 23) and will later return to the rebuilt temple (Ezek 43:2–5; 44:4). On the concept of the "glory of Yahweh" in Ezekiel and its connection to the monarchical ideology of the divine presence in the temple, see Mettinger, *Dethronement of Sabaoth*, 97–111. On divine presence = glory see also Is 4:5; 60:2, 7; Jer 17:12. Like Hag 2:7–9, Is 60:6–9, 11, 13, 17 also speak of the glorification of the temple by the material wealth brought to it from various places

Zion ideology is the use of the monarchical designation for Yahweh as Yahweh Sabaoth—Hag 1:2, 5, 7, 14; 2:4, 6–9, 11, 23. The third connection is that the re-establishment of Yahweh as king in Jerusalem brings about שלום (Hag 2:9). שלום is both abeyance of war and well-being or prosperity. It will be given "in this place" (Hag 2:9), which refers either to the temple itself or to Jerusalem.[151] "Peace" for Jerusalem is implicit in the Zion Psalms (Ps 46, 48, 76) where the divine king quells all attempted attacks on the city.[152] In Ps 29:11 the divine king "blesses his people with שלום". Hopes for the restoration of Jerusalem are couched in terms of a return of שלום to the city and its people (Ps 122). In Deutero-Isaiah Yahweh's return to Zion calls forth the proclamation that there will be שלום (Is 52:7; cf. 60:17; see also Jer 33:6).[153]

The combination of the above elements shows that Haggai was using the monarchical ideology of the temple to legitimate its rebuilding. Haggai displays that the rebuilding of the temple is intimately connected with the kingship of Yahweh, as the temple was in the monarchical period ideology. For Yahweh to return to Jerusalem, to his rebuilt temple, is for him to reassert his kingship over the nations. One significant difference in Haggai in comparison with the monarchical ideology, which is also evidenced in Zechariah 1–8, is that Judean kingship post-dates the construction of the temple.[154] In II Samuel 7 the idea for building the temple of Yahweh in Jerusalem

---

(cf. CTA 4 v 75–81 // 4 v 91–97 where silver, gold and gems will adorn Baʿal's palace). The date of Is 60 is difficult to ascertain. Most commentators date it, along with the rest of Trito-Isaiah (Is 56–66) to the period after the construction of the temple, but J. Scullion, *Isaiah 40–66* (Old Testament Message 12; Willmington, Delware: Michael Glazier, 1982) 148–49, 184, notes that Is 60–62 would well suit the time of the reconstruction of the temple. Is 60–62 also find many resonances in the Zech 1–8 passages cited below.

[151] On "the place" denoting the temple, see Browne, "A Jewish Sanctuary," 400–01. For "the place" denoting Jerusalem, see S. Talmon, "The Biblical Concept of Jerusalem," *Journal of Ecumenical Studies* 8 (1971): 300–16.

[152] Steck, *Friedensvorstellung im alten Jerusalem*, draws attention to the pre-Israelite (= pre-Davidic?) Jerusalemite traditions of the glorification of the city which depict it as the city of God (El; El Elyon) where there is complete happiness and prosperity (note the incorporation of the שלם element in the name Jerusalem, although this may have originally been the name of the deity Shalim). These notions were borrowed by the monarchical Zion ideology.

[153] On שלום, see S. Talmon, "The Signification of שלום and its Semantic Field in the Hebrew Bible," in *The Quest for Context and Meaning* (ed. C. A. Evans and S. Talmon) 75–115 (Hag 2:9 is mentioned on p. 108).

[154] So, similarly, Japhet, "Temple in the Restoration Period," 232.

occurs only after David had become king over Israel; that is, kingship preceded temple building. In II Samuel 5–7 David entertains
the possibility of building the original temple only after he had been
made king, captured Jerusalem, and "Yahweh had given him rest
from his enemies round about" (II Sam 7:1). The prophet Nathan
does not introduce the idea of building the temple but reacts to
David's suggestion on Yahweh's behalf (II Sam 7:4–17). Solomon
eventually undertakes the task of temple building (II Ki 5–8). It is
noteworthy that both David's and Solomon's plans to build the temple are preceded by victory over enemies (II Sam 7:1 quoted above;
I Ki 5:18 [Eng 5:4]—"Yahweh my God has given me rest on every
side; there is neither enemy nor misfortune"). This element is con-
spicuously lacking at the time of the building of the second temple.[155] Since Haggai and Zechariah do not consider the temple
rebuilding to be an act of Judean rebellion—Zerubbabel is not proclaimed king before the work commences—the ideology is reworked
so that it is only after the temple is constructed and Yahweh returns
to Jerusalem that Judean kingship will be reinstated.

Zechariah
Zechariah 1–8 also displays many features of the monarchical ideology of the temple, but emphasizes different elements from those
used by Haggai. For Haggai, the kingship of Yahweh was expressed
with motifs drawn from the mythological battle of the Storm God
with Yam, refracted through later prophetical conceptions of Yahweh,
the divine king, as the judge of the nations. Zechariah also understands Yahweh as the judge of the nations who acts to rescue and
protect his people, but he reflects the influence of another prophetic
tradition, that of the nations coming to Zion to do homage to
Yahweh, thus acknowledging Yahweh as their king. The gathering
of the exiles to Zion is the necessary prelude to this.
    Zech 2:10–17 (Eng 6–13)—

---

[155] I Ki 12:26–32 recounts how Jeroboam built two shrines in his kingdom after
he had led the northern terriory in a revolt against the government in Jerusalem.
Kings also take the initiative in temple restoration immediately (II Ki 12; 22:3–7).
Among Israel's neighbours temple building was also a royal perogative. The extant
texts commonly relate the building or restoration of shrines to victory over enemies; so, for example, KAI 181:3–4, 9–10 (Mesha stela).

10) Away! away! Flee from the land of the north—oracle of Yahweh—
For like the four winds of heaven I have scattered you—oracle of
Yahweh. (11) Away, Zion! Escape, dweller in the daughter of Babylon!
(12) For thus has Yahweh Sabaoth spoken, who after glory has sent
me to the nations who have plundered you, for whoever touches you
touches the apple of my eye: (13) "I am raising my hand against them,
and they will be plunder for their slaves." So shall you know that
Yahweh Sabaoth has sent me. (14) "Shout and rejoice, daughter of
Zion; for I am coming. I will dwell in your midst"—oracle of Yahweh.
(15) Many nations will be joined to Yahweh on that day.—"They will
be my people and I will dwell in your midst."—So shall you know
that Yahweh Sabaoth has sent me to you. (16) Yahweh will claim
Judah as his possession in the holy land, and once again choose
Jerusalem. (17) Silence, all flesh, in the presence of Yahweh! For he
bestirs himself from his holy dwelling-place.

Zech 8:1–8—

1) Then the word of the Yahweh Sabaoth came: "Thus spoke Yahweh
Sabaoth:
2)   'I am extremely zealous for Zion;
                    with great fury I am zealous for her.'
3) Thus spoke Yahweh:
                          'I am returning to Zion,
             I will dwell in the midst of Jerusalem.
             Jerusalem shall be called City of Truth;
       and the mountain of Yahweh Sabaoth, Holy Mountain.'
4) Thus spoke Yahweh Sabaoth:
'Old men and old women shall again sit in the squares of Jerusalem,
each with a staff in his hand because of great age. (5) The squares of
the city shall be filled with boys and girls playing in the squares.'
6) Thus spoke Yahweh Sabaoth:
'Even if that seems amazing in the eyes of the remnant of this people in those days, will it also seem amazing to me?'—oracle of Yahweh
Sabaoth.
7) Thus spoke Yahweh Sabaoth:
'I am delivering my people from the land of the east and the west.
(8) I will bring them back to live in the midst of Jerusalem. They will
be my people and I will be their God, in truth and righteousness.'"

There are a number of features which connect these oracles with
the monarchical ideology of the temple. As in Haggai, the appellation "Sabaoth" (Zech 1:3, 4, 6, 12, 14, 16, 17; 2:12, 13, 15; 3:7, 9,
10; 4:6, 9; 5:4; 6:12, 15; 7:3, 4, 9, 13, 14; 8:1–4, 6, 7, 9, 11, 14,
18–23) is drawn from the monarchical period ideology. The above
oracles also display features of the monarchical *Yahweh mālak*/Zion

ideology in their portrayal of Zion as the earthly dwelling-place of
Yahweh (Zech 2:14 [Eng v. 10]; 8:3),[156] which includes the notions
of Yahweh "coming" to Zion and "choosing" Zion (Zech 2:14, 16,
17 [Eng 2:10, 12, 13]; 8:2–3); the blissful conditions that pervade
Zion because of the divine king in her midst (Zech 8:4–6);[157] the
shouting for joy that attends Yahweh's and the exiles' return to Jerusalem (Zech 2:14 [Eng v. 10]);[158] and Yahweh as the judge of the
nations (Zech 2:13). In common with Haggai, Zechariah 1–8 speaks
of Yahweh's return to Jerusalem as issuing in "glory" for the city
(Zech 2:9 [Eng v. 5]—"I will be the glory within her") and שלום
for his people (Zech 8:12—"Indeed, there will be a sowing of peace").

As with Haggai, Zechariah's prophecies have been influenced by
late- and post-monarchical prophetic traditions of the Oracles Against
the Nations and the hopes for restoration. The use of the formula
"that day" (Zech 2:15, cf. 8:6, 23) relates to these traditions.[159] It is
important to note that while the Haggai prophecies discussed above
are closely related to the concept of "the Day of Yahweh" as a day
of Yahweh's judgement of the nations, Zechariah, while mentioning
the judgement (Zech 2:13), features a different prophetic tradition
which expresses Yahweh's lordship over the nations in terms of their
coming to Zion to worship him and, thus, to acknowledge his sovereignty. Although Zechariah emphasizes the coming of the nations
to Zion to worship, and indeed to be incorporated into the people
of Yahweh, rather than the destruction of the nations as in Haggai,
both these prophets are underpinned by nationalist aspirations since
they promote the kingship of their people's deity over those of all
others. This is evidenced not only in Zech 2:15 (Eng v. 11), but also
in Zech 8:20–23—

---

[156] The verb used is שכן. On its connection to the monarchical Zion ideology,
see Mettinger, *Dethronement of Sabaoth*, 93–94. For Zion as הר הקדש—"the holy mountain" cf. Ps 48:2.

[157] This motif is prevalent in the Zion psalms (Ps 46, 48, 76) and post-monarchical prophetic texts (Jer 31:13–14; 33:9–13; Is 32:15–20; 52:7; 54:1–2, 11–17;
60:1–22).

[158] For this motif in the *Yahweh mālak* psalms, see Ps 96:1–5; 97:8; 98:1, 5–6;
99:3, 5, 9. It also appears in other post-moarchical texts proclaiming the return of
Yahweh to Zion and the restoration of Jerusalem; see Jer 31:12–13; Is 52:9; 54:1.

[159] For "in those days" in Zech 8:6, 23 as the plural form of "on that day", see
Petitjean, *Oracles*, 434–35.

20) Thus spoke Yahweh Sabaoth:
"Peoples will yet come, and the inhabitants of many cities. (21) The inhabitants of one (city) will go to another saying, 'Let us go to entreat the favour of Yahweh, to seek Yahweh Sabaoth; I myself am going.' (22) Many peoples and mighty nations will come to seek Yahweh Sabaoth in Jerusalem and to entreat the favour of Yahweh."
23) Thus spoke Yahweh Sabaoth:
"In those days, ten men of nations of all languages will seize, will seize a Judahite by the hem and say, 'Let us go with you, for we have heard that God is with you.'"

The acknowledgement of Yahweh's sovereignty by the nations is of course a feature of the *Yahweh mālak* psalms, Zion psalms, and other psalms which extol Yahweh's kingship, but the only time the nations are said to come to Zion in monarchical period texts is in order to attack it (Ps 46, 48). In exilic prophecy the homage of the nations is transformed so that they will come to Zion in peace. Is 45:14 represents a transition in this regard since certain nations will be forcibly brought to Zion—

Thus spoke Yahweh:
"The produce of Egypt and the wealth of Cush,[160]
    and the Sabeans, men of stature,
will come over to you and be yours;
    they will follow you
they will come over in chains.
They will bow down before you,
    they will pray to you,
'With you alone is God, and there is no other;
    there is no other god.'"

Even more closely aligned with Zech 8:20–23 is Is 55:4–5—

4) See, I have made of you a witness to the nations,
    a leader and master of the nations.
5) See, you will summon a nation you never knew,
    a nation that does not know you will come hurrying to you,
    for the sake of Yahweh your God,
    of the Holy one of Israel who will glorify you.[161]

---

[160] A number of translations emend MT so as to permit the translation "The labourers of Egypt and the traders of Cush"; see the notes in *BHS* and the commentaries.

[161] Depending on one's interpretation of the so-called Servant Songs in Deutero-Isaiah, there may be other examples where Israel serves to bring the nations to Zion in order to worship Yahweh; see Is 42:6; 49:6. Is 45:20–25 is also relevant to the present discussion, although it is more closely related to the motif of Yahweh as the judge of the nations.

Other texts from the post-monarchical period exhibiting the theme
of the nations gathering at Jerusalem to do homage to Yahweh are
Is 2:2–4 // Mic 4:1–4; Jer 3:17; Is 11:10; 14:1–2; 25:6–8; 45:22–24;
60:1–3; 66:18–21; Ps 22:27–29; Ps 87 (cf. Is 19:16–25; Jer 12:15–16;
16:19–21; Zeph 3:9–10; Jonah; Ps 86:9–10 which speak of the nations
acknowledging Yahweh but do not mention their coming to Jerusalem).[162] Most noteworthy is Is 2:2–4 // Mic 4:1–4—

> 2) In the days to come
>   the mountain of the house of Yahweh
>   shall be established over the mountains
>   and be lifted up over the hills.
> 3) All the nations shall stream to it,
>   and many nations shall come and say:
>   "Come, let us go up to the mountain of Yahweh,
>   to the house of the God of Jacob,
>   that he may teach us his ways,
>   so that we may walk in his paths.
>   For instruction issues from Zion,
>   the word of Yahweh from Jerusalem.
> 4) He will judge between nations,
>   adjudicate between many peoples.
>   They shall beat their swords into ploughshares,
>   their spears into sickles.
>   Nation shall not lift sword against nation,
>   they shall no longer teach warfare."[163]

Zechariah's understanding of the return of Yahweh to Jerusalem and
its concomitant effects (such as the return of the exiles and the divine
blessing on the people and city/land) stands in a tradition quite similar to Deutero-Isaiah which is imbued with the myth of Yahweh's
kingship won in battle. Also drawn from this tradition is the notion
of the exiles' return from Babylonia as a flight from "the land of
the North" (Zech 2:10 [Eng v. 6]; 6:8) which appears in Is 48:20.[164]
Zechariah differs from Deutero-Isaiah in that it gives a more promi-

---

[162] The date of these passages relative to Zechariah 1–8 is impossible to determine. It is clear, however, that these passages, the texts cited from Deutero-Isaiah,
and Zech 2:15 (Eng v. 11); 8:20–23 all belong to a common post-monarchical tradition of the pilgrimage of the nations to Jerusalem; see Beuken, *Haggai—Sacharja
1–8*, 179; Rudolph, *Haggai, Sacharja 1–8*, 152.
[163] On the post-monarchical date of this text, see Sweeney, *Isaiah 1–4*, 163–74.
[164] See also Jer 16:14–15; 23:8; 31:8; 50:8; 51:6, 45. Jer 50–51 stand in a tradition similar to Deutero-Isaiah.

nent role to Davidic kingship in the restoration (in the person of Zerubbabel) and is thus more closely aligned at this point, as is Haggai, to the prophetic tradition which envisioned the reinstatement of "David" as part of the expectations of Yahweh's renewal of Judah and Jerusalem.[165] If Zech 6:13b is ascribed to the prophet then his vision of the future government includes the novel development of a role for the High Priest beside that of the king.

Zechariah concurs with Haggai in supporting the forthcoming elevation of Zerubbabel to kingship (Zech 3:9b; 6:13a) and in connecting the temple rebuilding to the presence of Zerubbabel. Zerubbabel is a legitimate rebuilder and he is called upon to commence and complete the rebuilding of the temple (Zech 4:6b–10a). The temple foundation ritual underlying Zechariah 4:6b–10a highlights the royal position and prerogatives this prophet ascribes to Zerubbabel.[166] Like Haggai, Zechariah reworks the monarchical ideology to place temple rebuilding before the elevation of Zerubbabel to kingship and he carefully words his oracles so that the temple rebuilding is not considered to be an act of Judean rebellion. A new age of blessing for Judah attends Yahweh's return to his rebuilt temple, but Judeans are not called upon to take up arms against their Achaemenid Persian overlords or to declare Zerubbabel king as a means of establishing the kingship of Yahweh. Their primary role is to rebuild the temple and to await the fulfilment of the promises of Yahweh (Zech 4:6b). Unlike Haggai, however, Zechariah does not mention the destruction of the nations preceding the elevation of Zerubbabel, rather the nations will come to Jerusalem to acknowledge Yahweh's sovereignty.

This discussion of the ideology underpinning the temple rebuilding was prompted by the contention that temple rebuilding was an act of Judean rebellion since the Jerusalem temple was originally a

---

[165] So, for example, Is 11:10; Jer 23:1–8; 30:9, 21; 33:14–18; Ezek 34:23–31; 37:24–31.

[166] On this ritual, see the bibliography cited in chapter 3 n. 19. Some commentators (for example, D. L. Petersen, "Zechariah's Visions: A Theological Perspective," *VT* 34 [1984] 195–206; P. Marinković, "What Does Zechariah 1–8 Tell us about the Second Temple," in *Second Temple Studies: 2. Temple and Community in the Persian Period* [ed. T. C. Eskenazi and K. H. Richards] 88–103) question that the renewal of the temple was the major focus of Zechariah 1–8's concerns. Although this text is not exclusively devoted to temple reconstruction, on the basis of the arguments presented in this section of the study there is good reason to conclude that it is a fundamental interest, connected to the overarching theme of restoration.

monarchical shrine which, as a symbol of the kingship of Yahweh, legitimated the kingdom of Judah. Further, the language used by Haggai and Zechariah regarding the temple and Zerubbabel has been interpreted as supporting this view. The ideology underpinning the rebuilding of the Jerusalem temple of Yahweh evidenced in Haggai and Zechariah 1–8 is indeed rooted in the monarchical period ideology which underpinned the building of the original temple. It reaffirms the kingship of Yahweh gained through his mythological battle for kingship and his subsequent enthronement on Zion (Jerusalem), the chosen place for his abode on earth; it is connected to earthly kingship by the commissioning of the Davidic house to establish the divinely constituted order on earth, the chief symbolic act being the building of the deity's temple on Zion. The kingship of Yahweh which finds expression in these prophecies, as in the monarchical period ideology, would not brook the idea that Yahweh or his king served under some foreign overlord. His people must be politically emancipated. Indeed they shall be, for a "new age" is inaugurated by the return of Zerubbabel and the rebuilding of the Jerusalem temple since now is the "time" for Yahweh's return to Jerusalem. Israel's restoration will finally be consummated, however, on that undefined "day". For the present, Judeans must rebuild the temple, reap some of the blessings attending Yahweh's return to Jerusalem, and wait for Yahweh to act to manifest his kingship.

With Deutero-Isaiah and Ezekiel 40–48, Haggai and Zechariah share the view of historical recurrence rather than eschatology. Their understanding of Israel's restoration is an idealized projection of its monarchical past. Like Deutero-Isaiah and Ezekiel 40–48, which also draw on the monarchical period ideology of the temple and Yahweh's kingship, these prophets have reworked this ideology in the light of late- and post-monarchical prophetical traditions. Their temple ideology reflects a modification of the monarchical ideology so that while affirming the kingship of Yahweh and announcing the reversal of the disaster that befell Judah in 587, the consummation of the restoration of Judah ("Israel") still lies sometime in the not-too-distant future. Other modifications to the monarchical period ideology are, for example, the coming of the nations to Zion rather than their subjugation by Israel's armies—in Zechariah; Yahweh's personal responsibility for the overthrow of the nations—in Haggai; the responsibility of the community, not just the royal figure, for temple rebuilding—in Haggai; temple building preceding the establishment of the monarchy—in Haggai and Zechariah.

The emphasis of Haggai's and Zechariah's prophecies certainly has similarities with Deutero-Isaiah: a new age is about to dawn with Yahweh's return to Jerusalem; Yahweh will prove himself to be Israel's divine king (Is 42:21; 43:15; 44:6; 52:7; cf. the use of the appellation "Sebaoth" in Haggai and Zechariah) and he will manifest his kingship over the nations (Is 41:2–4; 45:1–3, 11–13; 45:20–47:15; 48:12–16; 51:9–10; Hag 2:6–9, 20–23; Zech 2:13 [Eng v. 9]); Yahweh is to return to Jerusalem, bringing the exiles with him (Is 40:3–5, 9–11; 41:17–20; 42:10–17; 43:1–7, 16–21; 52:7–12; 54:1–3; Zech 2:10–17 [Eng vv. 6–13]; 8:7–8); Jerusalem will be repopulated and enjoy blissful conditions (Is 52:7; 54:1–3, 11–17; Hag 2:9; Zech 8:1–8). As was argued above (pp. 164–68, 178–79), these shared elements do not necessarily mean that Haggai and Zechariah were attempting to revive and reschedule the deferred hopes of Deutero-Isaiah.[167] In drawing upon ideas developed around the monarchical Zion ideology, Haggai and Zechariah need not be dependent on Deutero-Isaiah and/or Ezekiel 40–48; rather they draw independently on this monarchical tradition, as well as other traditions such as the Oracles against the Nations. Similarly, the notion of historical recurrence, which included the need for Yahweh to redress the events of 587, was sufficiently widespread to have been known by Haggai and Zechariah without the direct influence of Deutero-Isaiah or Ezek 40–48. It is noteworthy that Haggai and Zechariah draw on the tradition that looked to the re-establishment of indigenous kingship in Judah, a notion that Deutero-Isaiah and Ezek 40–48 both rejected.[168] This development highlights their independence from the earlier prophets.

---

[167] Carroll, *When Prophecy Failed*, 160–62, has contended that Haggai and Zechariah are exhibiting cognitive dissonance because they, together with the rest of the community knew of Deutero-Isaiah's prophecies which had not reached fulfilment, and so Haggai blamed the people for the delay in the promised blessing since they would not rebuild the temple (Hag 1:2–4). As Carroll himself has pointed out elsewhere (R. P. Carroll, "Second Isaiah and the Failure of Prophecy," *Studia Theologica* 32 [1978] 121–24), the background for Deutero-Isaiah's thought is the monarchical Jerusalem cult. As was shown above in discussing the use of motifs drawn from the Zion psalms and the *Yahweh mālak* psalms, the same can be said of Haggai and Zechariah.

[168] Many commentators see Zech 1–8 as dependent on Ezek 40–48, cf. Petersen, *Haggai and Zechariah 1–8*, 116–19, who notes eight significant differences which "surely suggest that Zechariah has presented an alternative to or a revision of the notions of restoration present in Ezek. 40–48" (p. 119). But one need not read Zech 1–8 over against Ezek 40–48, either as a revision or an alternative. Elements that the two share in common (vocabulary, ideas of restoration) do not necessarily denote dependence, and there is scant evidence to support the claim that Ezek 40–48 represented a viable, current option for restoration at the time of the rebuilding.

These prophets' continuity with, yet modification of, the monarchical period ideology of the temple is a result of their desire to balance two concerns, namely, the concern to legitimate the temple rebuilding in the eyes of the Judeans and the concern not to confront Judah's Achaemenid Persian overlords. There are thus two complementary faces of the legitimation of the rebuilding of the Jerusalem temple. One is directed towards the Judeans, largely in traditional Judean monarchical terms, as evidenced in Haggai and Zechariah 1–8. The initiative for the rebuilding is understood to have come from Yahweh who determined the "time" for his return to Jerusalem. He is taking action to restore Israel to normality, including reinstituting some form of indigenous kingship. These prophets are, however, cognizant of current political realities and, as their modified monarchical ideology shows, are careful not to cast temple rebuilding in terms of rebellion. The other face of the legitimation of the temple rebuilding is directed towards the Achaemenid Persian administration from which was concealed the implications of the undertaking as understood by these prophets and, one may assume given the fact that these prophets' call to rebuild was heeded, by the Judean temple rebuilders themselves. This face, presented in Ezr 5–6, casts the temple rebuilding as an activity legitimated by the Achaemenid Persian administration, specifically by the edict of Cyrus. Ezr 5–6 holds the initiative for the rebuilding to have been given originally by Cyrus (albeit at the behest of Yahweh; Ezr 1:1–4), but in the reign of Darius it is the prophets Haggai and Zechariah who prompt the Judeans to rebuild (Ezr 5:1). For the Judeans, these two faces are not in tension but reflect different purposes and audiences. In contending that the temple rebuilding was a Judean initiative this study does not commend the view that the rebuilding was an act of Judean rebellion. Rather, it points to the fact that although permission to rebuild the temple resided in and was granted by the Achaemenid Persian administration in the reign of Cyrus, it was incumbent on the Judeans themselves to undertake the work. The initiative for the temple rebuilding in the reign of Darius came not from some putative Achaemenid Persian policy (contra the Meyerses and Weinberg) but from the Judean prophets Haggai and Zechariah.

Seeing that in the monarchical period the Jerusalem temple served and legitimated the kingdom of Judah, over whom and over what territory will Yahweh reign when the new temple is built? The Meyerses, Weinberg, and those who contend that the rebuilding was in order to establish the repatriates as a separate cultic community in Judah or that it was an act of rebellion, all articulate various understandings of the polity the temple sought to serve, for as in the monarchical period this temple must have legitimated a specific polity. We have seen, however, that attempts to relate the temple either to a polity established by the Achaemenid Persian administration (for example, the sub-province of Judah; Bürger-Tempel-Gemeinde) or to a community established by the repatriates themselves (various understandings of the "cultic community"; establishment of a monarchical state) must be judged to be unsuccessful. The polity that the temple serves is, according to Haggai and Zechariah, fundamentally "Israel"/Yahweh's people. They are not yet a nation as they were in the monarchical period. Temple rebuilding is the first step along that road. It creates a nascent kingdom which will finally be constituted on "that day". It re-establishes Yahweh as the "king" of Israel enthroned in Zion and "Israel" as a people living under their god in his land.[169] Haggai focuses on those now living in Judah, but this need not be to the exclusion of those still in exile. Zechariah, however, focuses much more on the return of the exiles and has such an inclusive (albeit nationalistic) view of the polity that Yahweh is establishing that he also includes foreigners within it. This is a polity created by Yahweh himself to manifest his sovereignty. It is done by means of chastising the nations, returning the exiles to their homeland, and blessing all who reside in Jerusalem and Judah. These prophets do not define the polity that the temple served more closely than this since their interest lies in reaffirming the kingship of Yahweh in the wake of the dissolution of the kingdom and the exile, and it is in this context that the symbolic meaning of the temple is to be

---

[169] So, G. W. Ahlström, "Some Aspects of the Historical Problems of the Early Persian Period," *Proceedings, Eastern Great Lakes Biblical Society* 4 (1984) 61. He correctly notes that: "Religion and state (nationhood, peoplehood) had not yet been separated. King and temple were the only categories by which the people could conceive of themselves as a people". There are also two faces of the Judeans' view of themselves as a polity, however. One face, directed toward the Achaemenid Persians in Ezr 5–6, portrays the "king" in the above quotation as Darius. Thus Ahlström is correct when he writes (p. 61): "It was mandatory for the returnees [I would add, 'together with those who had stayed in the land'] to build a temple in order to become once more a people under the god. . . . By giving permission for the restoration of the temple, the Persian king would have been recognizing this people as a 'nation' under his rule". Haggai and Zech 1–8 present another face to the Judeans. For them the "king" will be Zerubbabel who will rule over an independent Judah in the future, after the exiles have returned and the nations been "shaken".

interpreted. What is important is that Jerusalem will again be the home of Yahweh, the great king, under whom will serve his earthly monarch of the house of David. Those now living in Judah have a fundamental role to play by rebuilding the temple. Unlike Ezekiel 40–48, therefore, but in concert with Deutero-Isaiah, these prophets do not attempt to define the territorial borders of Israel or to parcel out the land of Israel to the tribes. Since temple rebuilding was undertaken to reconstitute Israel in its land under Yahweh its deity, the reconstitution of Israel would assume that Israel can be defined, but it is notable that Haggai and Zechariah, unlike Ezra-Nehemiah, do not attempt this definition themselves. As will be argued below, these prophets do not distinguish between repatriates and non-repatriates, nor do they necessarily exclude Samarian Yahwists from participation in the temple rebuilding. Temple rebuilding was not undertaken to establish a distinct community of repatriates within Judah.

Temple Rebuilding as an Act of Political Legitimation and Social Integration

Haggai and Zechariah as "Millenarian" Prophets[170]

Haggai's and Zechariah's understanding of the purpose of the temple rebuilding and the "new age" accompanying Yahweh's return to Jerusalem can best be understood within the context of what soci-

---

[170] I have not attempted to integrate fully here the important study of S. L. Cook, *Prophecy and Apocalypticism: The Postexilic Setting* (Minneapolis: Ausburg Fortress, 1995). Cook offers a discussion of the sociology of millennial groups (pp. 19–84) and is keen to emphasize that not all such groups are socially deprived. In this way he seeks to argue against those who understand the development of Israelite apocalypticism in terms of deprivation theory (for example, Plöger, Hanson). Cook does not discuss Haggai, but Zech 1–8 receives extended treatment on pp. 123–65. He considers that Zechariah, as a member of the priestly establishment, represented a group which "held power within an endogenous environment" (p. 156); that is, the social environment of the group involved one culture alone rather than contact with another culture (which is termed exogenous condition) (see p. 57 and also the table there). Cook considers the Persian imperial context to be not strictly relevant since the administration was not threatening the group and was in fact supportive of its undertaking. However, I believe this diminishes the impact of imperialism on the formation of the ideas expressed in Haggai and Zech 1–8. While indebted to the notion of historical recurrence with the expectation that Yahweh would reverse the disasters of 587 and thus display his sovereignty, these texts recognize that the restoration is to be played out in the context of current political realities. Indeed, the current political conditions, despite the "benign" rule of the Persians, stand in need of correction: the nations have to be shaken; Yahweh's sovereignty has to be

ologists of religion term "millenarian movements". This term refers to a diverse range of groups which "expect imminent, total, ultimate, this-worldly collective salvation".[171] They are not restricted to groups which expect a literal millennium of peace on earth (cf., for example, certain Christian Adventist movements expecting the rule of Christ on earth for a millennium), rather they include "cultural phenomena as far apart as Californian communes, Melanesian cargo cults and African proto-nationalism".[172] While it is recognized that the diverse groups categorized as millenarian movements are not all of one type, there is an ongoing debate as to how to classify these groups relative to each other.[173] This debate can be left to one side for the present discussion since its purpose to note how Haggai and Zechariah exhibit the general characteristics attributed to millenarian movements, particularly indigenous millenarian movements in developing nations which are "almost invariably more politically

---

established; the nations have gone too far in punishing Judah; the nations are at rest while Judah awaits restoration. From Cook's classification of millennial groups (p. 57), I would place Zechariah in Class C—Exogenous Condition: dominated but central (pp. 59–62). Cook also sees Zech 1–8 as standing in continuity with Ezek 40–48 and the Zadokite party, which I would contest.

Deutero-Isaiah and Ezek 40–48 might be considered "millenarian prophets" since they too envisaged a change in the people's fortunes and articulated restoration hopes. As outlined earlier, I understand these texts to have been originally directed to Judeans in exile to maintain their fidelity to Yahweh. In comparison with Haggai and Zech 1–8, Deutero-Isaiah and Ezek 40–48 leave the people in a rather passive position rather than assigning them actions that will facilitate the in-breaking of the new set of conditions. On Nehemiah's mission as another expression of a nativist or revitalization movement, see K. D. Tollefson and H. G. M. Williamson, "Nehemiah as Cultural Revitalization: An Anthropological Perspective," *JSOT* 56 (1992) 41–68.

[171] Y. Talmon, "Millenarian Movements," *Archives européennes de sociologie* 7 (1966) 159. Talmon's article is an excellent study of the main lines of research into millenarian movements undertaken up to the mid-1960's. G. W. Trompf, "Introduction," in *Cargo Cults and Millenarian Movements. Transoceanic Comparisons of New Religious Movements* (ed. G. W. Trompf; Religion and Society 29; Berlin/New York: Mouton/de Gruyter, 1990) 1–10, offers an overview of recent methodological developments in the study of millenarian movements. Trompf includes in his endnotes an extensive bibliography of the major theoretical works and case studies on millenarian movements.

[172] Trompf, "Introduction," 2.

[173] Ibid., 8–9, notes:

the common feature to be found in millenarian movements of some projected or intended "counter-stroke" against cosmic evil, threat or opposition, is undeniable, thus legitimating the category sociologically and providing a key tool for comparative analysis.

For an outline of positions and a discussion of the debate, see Cook, *Prophecy and Apocalypticism*, 19–84.

defined, as restatements of cultural identity which are there to resist colonial oppression".[174] They are protest movements whose participants are experiencing oppression or political estrangement and who seek justice and political power (the latter often in terms of self-determination). Often they perceive their plight to be so dire that only divine intervention will redress the situation. In these cases, as well as in others, there is invariably some activity the group can undertake either to inaugurate the new order or to hasten its arrival. For those groups looking to divine intervention, this activity is usually cultic in nature.

The social context of Haggai's and Zechariah's prophecies bears close similarities with those common to millenarian movements. Certain Judeans felt acutely the disparity between, on the one hand, their ideology that Yahweh was not only the god of Israel and Judah but indeed of the nations of the earth[175] and, on the other hand, Judah's current political status and the plight of the exiles. The current social order, characterized by economic hardship (Hag 1:6–11; Zech 8:10), social disharmony (Zech 5:3, 6; 8:10),[176] the treatment of Judah by the nations and her subjugation to them (presumed by Hag 2:20–23; Zech 1:15), was unsatisfactory and could only be set right by the intervention of Yahweh. The first steps in this direction were the return of Yahweh to Jerusalem and the rebuilding of the temple of Yahweh. It would eventually issue in the manifestation of the sovereignty of Yahweh, the overthrow of the nations, the return

---

[174] Trompf, "Introduction," 6.

[175] See the explanation of the dissolution of the kingdoms of Israel and Judah in the canonical prophets and the Deuteronomistic History as an act of Yahweh in that he commanded the armies of foreign nations to destroy these kingdoms; see the discussion above, pp. 64–69.

[176] Zech 8:16–17 lists a number of activities—speaking the truth, correct judgements, no plotting of evil, no false oaths—that the Judeans must do to ensure that the blessings of the new age spoken of in Zech 8:1–15 eventuate. This assumes that the opposite had been occurring at that time. According to Zech 5:1–4 there was theft and false oath-taking that was going unpunished. This may reflect inadequacies in the current legal system or may be a metaphor for the powerful in society exploiting the weak, the latter seemingly having no legal redress. Justice will only be done when Yahweh intervenes to punishes the wrong-doers, eradicating such activities from the community. This expectation for a changed community is also evidenced in Zech 5:5–11 where iniquity (Zech 5:6; reading עונם with LXX and Syriac; see *BHS* note) and wickedness (Zech 5:8) are removed from the land. Cultic considerations are also part of the concern for a changed community as the purification of Joshua in Zech 3 and the *kalû* ritual evidence in Zech 4:6b–10a attest.

of the Judean exiles, the incorporation of foreigners into Israel, the reestablishment of Davidic kingship, and the eradication of theft, false oaths and iniquity. That is, to use a phrase common in studies of millenarian movements, there will be "heaven on earth".

Prophets have a central role in millenarian movements since they carry the message that the present order is wrong and that a new order is coming, if only the community will heed the message and perform the correct acts to bring it about. They present to the community the possibility that the current situation, characterized by anxiety, social disruption and lack of political power, need not continue for the deity is prepared to act on the community's behalf.[177] Commonly the prophet is a charismatic leader who is the focus for the community's hopes (for example, a "messiah"),[178] but Haggai and Zechariah do not cast themselves as leaders in this sense. Rather, they point to Zerubbabel and Joshua, particularly the former, as leaders.[179] Identification by the prophets of both the leader(s) inaugurating the

---

[177] In his study of millenarian movements in modern colonial contexts, M. Adas, *Prophets of Rebellion: Millenarian Protest Movements against European Colonial Order* (Chapel Hill: The University of North Carolina Press, 1979) 112, notes:

> Though the overall millenarian visions were characteristically vague, they conveyed a sense of supernatural concern for the sufferings and anxieties of the groups addressed and often dealt with the resolution of specific grievances. It was prophesied, for example, that all foreigners would be destroyed or driven away or that all taxes and debts would be abolished . . . Prophetic leaders and their millennial visions gave voice and hope to these discontented groups when other avenues [that is, by means of the current political system] seemed closed.

Little study has been undertaken of Achaemenid Judah and the biblical texts belonging to this period in the context of the comparative study of colonial systems. This may be a fruitful area for further investigation. Provisionally, see Gottwald, *Hebrew Bible*, 409–594; J. L. Berquist, "The Shifting Frontier: The Achaemenid Empire's Treatment of Western Colonies," *Journal of World-Systems Research* 1/17 (1995) 1–39 [on line] gopher://csf.colorado.edu/wsystems/journals/

[178] There is already an extensive literature on charismatic prophet as the leader of a millenarian movement; see the examples cited in, for example, P. Worsley, *The Trumpet Shall Sound: A Study of "Cargo" Cults in Melanesia* (New York: Schocken, 1968); K. O. L. Burridge, *New Heaven, New Earth: A Study of Millenarian Activity* (New York: Oxford University Press, 1969); N. Cohn, *The Pursuit of the Millennium: Revolutionary Millenarians and Mystical Anarchists of the Middle Ages* (Revised and Expanded Edition; New York: Oxford University Press, 1970); B. R. Wilson, *Magic and the Millennium: A Sociological Study of Religious Movements of Protest among Tribal and Third-World Peoples* (London: Heinemann, 1973).

[179] The identification of a specific individual as the "messiah" or leader by prophets of a millenarian movement is attested elsewhere; see, for example, N. Cohn, *The Pursuit of the Millennium*, 110–13, for Emperor Fredrick II as the object of eschatological expectations by German Joachites; M. Barkun, *Disaster and the Millennium* (New Haven/London: Yale University Press, 1974) 85–88.

new age and the acts that must be undertaken to bring about its
birth summons the community to instigate what Wallace terms the
"transfer culture" that will transform the "existing culture" into the
"goal culture", that is, the consummation of the new age. Wallace
summarizes this as follows:

> Contrasted with the goal culture is the *existing culture*, which is pre-
> sented as inadequate or evil in certain respects. Connecting the exist-
> ing culture and the goal culture is a *transfer culture*—a system of operations
> which, if faithfully carried out, will transform the existing culture into
> the goal culture. Failure to institute the transfer operations will . . . result
> in either the perpetuation of the present misery or the ultimate destruc-
> tion of the society (if not the whole world).[180]

As already noted, Haggai and Zechariah identify the rebuilding of
the Jerusalem temple as the most significant element of the transfer
culture. To this Zechariah adds the following:

> These are the things you must do. Speak the truth to one another;
> let the judgements at your gates be conducive to peace; do not secretly
> plot evil against one another; do not love false oaths; since all this is
> what I hate. It is Yahweh who speaks. (Zech 8:16–17)[181]

While millenarian movements are protest movements they do not
always amount to rebellions. The transfer operations, to use Wallace's
term, may reflect a willingness to work within the current political
order rather than to confront it. In any case, these transfer operations are understood to sound the death knell for the current political order since they are harbingers of the goal culture. The preaching
of Haggai and Zechariah and the rebuilding of the Jerusalem temple should be understood in this light.

---

[180] A. F. C. Wallace, *Religion: An Anthropological View* (New York: Random House,
1966) 160 (author's emphasis). Wallace's study reflect the diversity in nomenclature
and classification of millenarian movements. His general type is termed "revitalization movement" with millenarian movements forming a Christian sub-type; see
Wallace, *Religion*, 163–64. For a more extensive treatment of Wallace's revitalization movements, see A. F. C. Wallace, "Revitalization Movements: Some Theoretical
Considerations for their Comparative Study," *American Anthropologist* 58 (1956) 264–81.
On the evolution of revitalization movements, including a discussion of the work of
Wallace, see K. A. Roberts, *Religion in Sociological Perspective* (Belmont, CA: Wadsworth,
1990) 147–164.
[181] Similar notions (from an indeterminate date) regarding the character of members of the restoration community are exhibited in Is 1:17–18; 54:14; Zeph 3:13.
Zech 6:9–15 also assigns another task that must be performed: the manufacture of
crown(s) and the symbolic coronation of Zerubbabel and/or Joshua.

The societal stresses that prompted this Judean millenarian move-ment can be readily identified—the loss of indigenous kingship and political self-determination, the destruction of the Jerusalem temple and divine abandonment, the destruction of Judean cities, the exile of portions of the population, subservience to a colonial overlord, economic hardship, and social disharmony. Temple rebuilding not only promised to reverse these conditions and change the commu-nity's current plight, it also addressed the social stress of the rela-tionship between those Judeans who had been repatriated with Zerubbabel and Joshua and those who had remained in the land. One of the important points raised by Daniel Smith in his book *Religion of the Landless* was that certain sociological studies show that there is conflict between those who have experienced enforced exile and those who have not once the former return to their homeland.[182] This serves as the basis for his contention that the Judean repatri-ates were in conflict with "the people of the land" upon their repa-triation. However, temple rebuilding can be understood to be a symbolic act which binds both the community of the repatriates and those who remained in the land. As Zechariah emphasizes, the rebuilding of the temple ushers in the new age marked by the return of all the exiles to Jerusalem. Indeed, foreigners will also join in the community of Yahweh worshippers. It is an age of peace and social harmony. Far from exemplifying social division, temple rebuilding is an act of social integration. As will be argued below, both repatri-ates and non-repatriates participated in the temple rebuilding. Although Haggai does not speak of the exiles returning, he must be identified as a non-repatriate (or at least one who had not returned with Zerubbabel and Joshua) who summons both repatriates and those who remained in the land to undertake the temple rebuilding. The return of the divine presence to Jerusalem, and thus a return to "normalcy", was a concern shared by both groups. By heeding the prophetic call to rebuild both groups could participate in bringing about the new age, an age in which the catastrophe of 587 would be reversed, the people reunified in their land, and Israel restored under its sovereign deity.

Since Zechariah includes foreigners in the community of the "new age" (similarly, Is 56:3–8), it is unlikely that the Samarians, whether

---

[182] Smith, *Religion of the Landless*, 49–68.

they were perceived as the remnant of the former kingdom of Israel
or as foreign syncretists imported into the former territory of Israel,
were to be excluded from this community. It is unclear whether or
not they were to participate in the temple rebuilding but, in contradistinction to Ezr 3:1–4:5, the consequence of temple rebuilding is
not division between Judeans and Samarians. For Zechariah, as for
the Hebrew narrative of the temple rebuilding in Ezra, the rebuilding
of the Jerusalem temple is a watershed in Judean history. For the
former, however, it results in social integration not social division.

*The Timing of the Rebuilding and the Identity of the Supporters of
the Rebuilding*

As was pointed out in chapter 3, the initial ideological problem to
be addressed by Judeans who sought to rebuild the Jerusalem temple was determining that the deity did indeed wish to have his shrine
rebuilt; that it was indeed "time" to rebuild the temple. Had the
deity's anger with his people, expressed in his dissolution of the kingdom of Judah, the exile of portions of the population, and the divine
abandonment of the temple and its consignment, together with the
city, to destruction, now abated? How was one to tell that the deity's
anger was exhausted and that he now planned to return to his earthly
sanctuary? According to traditional practice, the deity "spoke" to the
king about such matters as temple rebuilding. The Judeans had no
indigenous monarch and their current king, the Achaemenid Persian
Darius, had apparently not acted to rebuild this temple. How could
Judeans now seek to rebuild it themselves?

The prophets Haggai and Zechariah, acting as intermediaries
between the deity and the community, proclaimed that in their day
the ire of Yahweh against his people had abated and that he was
now returning to Jerusalem. The deity's return demanded, of course,
the rebuilding of his sanctuary. Zerubbabel, a Davidide and hence
a legitimate rebuilder, was proclaimed as the one who was to undertake the task (Hag 1:14; Zech 4:6b–10a). How was one to determine, however, that now was in fact the "time" to rebuild? It is an
acute question given that Zerubbabel was not the king of Judah.
Why should this former monarchical shrine be rebuilt when Judah
was not an independent kingdom, and Zerubbabel not an independent king? The propriety of rebuilding the temple at this time clearly
occupied Judeans as Hag 1:2 makes clear—"This people says: 'It is
not yet time to rebuild the temple of Yahweh'".

Is it possible to account for the timing of the rebuilding, particularly in the light of the fact that according to Hag 1:2 the people had refused a recent invitation to rebuild the temple? A closely related matter is the identity of the Judeans who sought to have the temple rebuilt. Again, Hag 1:2 displays that a majority of Judeans did not consider it "time" to rebuild the temple. Who deemed it to be the correct "time" and why? This question naturally arises from the discussion of Ezr 5–6 which shows that Zerubbabel had not been sent to Judah by the Achaemenid Persian administration in order to rebuild the temple. Further, Ezr 5–6 assumes that Zerubbabel had not informed the Achaemenid Persian administration on his departure from Babylonia that he was intending to rebuild the temple. Had he done so there would have been no need for Tattenai's investigation, or at least no need for the search for the edict of Cyrus by Darius's bureaucrats (Ezr 6:1–2). Either Zerubbabel or the elders of the Judeans could simply have informed the investigators that arrangements for the rebuilding had been made before Zerubbabel's departure for Judah. Unlike Nehemiah, then, Zerubbabel had not cleared any building project with his superiors before leaving Babylonia (cf. Neh 2:1–8).

The implication of these observations should be made clear. The logical conclusion to be drawn from Ezr 5–6 and the need for Darius to have a search for the permit to rebuild the temple granted by Cyrus is that the repatriates under Zerubbabel had not returned in order to rebuild the temple. This is supported by the rejection of the earlier call to rebuild by "this people" in Hag 1:2 on the basis that it was "not yet time to rebuild the temple of Yahweh". Whatever the exact identity of "this people" is, a matter to be considered shortly, all commentators agree that the repatriates are included in (or, according to many commentators, are) this group. Had the repatriates returned to rebuild the temple they must have done so considering it to be the divinely appointed "time" for the work, just as Deutero-Isaiah, speaking of a different era (namely, immediately after the fall of Babylon and the rise of Cyrus to kingship over Babylon), obviously considered that the repatriation of the exiles denoted Yahweh's return to his city, which in turn demanded the rebuilding of the Jerusalem temple. But it is "this people" who explicitly reject the contention that it is "time" to rebuild the temple! Further evidence for the repatriation not having been undertaken for the purpose of temple rebuilding can be drawn from Zech 1:12–16. In

Zech 1:12 the messenger of Yahweh is still unsure, some years after
the repatriation under Zerubbabel, as to exactly when the divine ire
will abate and Yahweh return to his city. No mention is made of
Yahweh's return to take up residence in Jerusalem having occurred
with the repatriates. Indeed, Yahweh has only now, in the second
year of Darius, decided that he is to return to Jerusalem and have
the temple rebuilt. Had the repatriates thought that Yahweh was
returning with them, the delay in Yahweh's return would have neces-
sitated an explanation, such as we read in sections of Trito-Isaiah
(Is 56–66) after the expected blessings thought to accompany temple rebuilding were not forthcoming.

The common assumption of scholars has been that the repatriates under Zerubbabel must have returned to Judah in order to
rebuild the Jerusalem temple since Deutero-Isaiah thought such
regarding the (arguably quite limited) repatriation in his own day
and since no other reason would seem to justify the exiles' return.
Further, Joshua the high priest also returned with Zerubbabel, from
which it may be reasonably inferred that he would certainly have
sought the immediate rebuilding of the temple. Why else would
Joshua return?

The evidence of Ezr 5–6, Hag 1:2–4, and Zech 1:12–16 points
in the opposite direction, however. These texts show that whatever
the reasons for the repatriation were, one of them was not the *immediate* restoration of the Jerusalem temple. Joshua, and perhaps
Zerubbabel and others among the repatriates, may have looked forward to the temple's reconstruction some time in the future, but the
evidence shows that this was not their specific purpose for returning to Jerusalem.

Who, then, sought to have the temple rebuilt? If the repatriates
must be ruled out then we are left with certain among those Judeans
who had never gone into exile, and/or those few who had returned
with Sheshbazzar in the first years of the reign of Cyrus. If "this
people" in Hag 1:2 includes non-repatriates among its number, as
I believe it must, then clearly not all of them were devoted to temple rebuilding at Zerubbabel's return. Haggai is an important source
on this problem since his prophecies supporting the rebuilding are
the earliest extant, Hag 1:2–4 coming almost six months before
Zechariah's prophecy of Yahweh's return (Zech 1:7–17). As was
argued in chapter 3 above, the initial invitation to rebuild the temple assumed in Hag 1:2–4 must have been relatively recent at the

time of the prophet's preaching and it should, in fact, be dated to
Zerubbabel's return to Judah, the arrival of a legitimate temple
rebuilder prompting the prophet's call. Unless one cares to argue
that as a repatriate Haggai was inspired by the sight of Jerusalem
and the presence of Zerubbabel there, so that although temple rebuilding was not the purpose of the repatriates' journey the prophet immediately elevated it to the community's highest priority, Haggai should
be considered a non-repatriate. At least he did not return with Zerubbabel. Further, the fact that Zerubbabel is a Davidide, and the connection of this with temple rebuilding and the renaissance of Judean
kingship (Hag 2:20–23), could hardly have been lost on either the
repatriates or the Achaemenid Persian administration before the exiles
set out from Babylonia. That is to say, it is unlikely that the status
of Zerubbabel as a legitimate temple builder and the notion of the
arrival of Zerubbabel as marking the divinely propitious "time" to
rebuild would have dawned on Haggai only when he arrived in
Jerusalem. Surely such attitudes would have been determined and
articulated before leaving Babylonia (as with Deutero-Isaiah). But as
Hag 1:2–4, Zech 1:12–16 and Ezr 5–6 make clear, they were not;
at least not to the extent that Zerubbabel's return to Judah was
understood by the repatriates and the Achaemenid Persian administration to be for the purpose of rebuilding the Jerusalem temple.
Hence it is much more likely that Haggai was not repatriated with
Zerubbabel and that his call to rebuild and his identification of
Zerubbabel's return as denoting the "time" for rebuilding were gen-
uinely new to his hearers.[183] One could then explain Zechariah's
preaching, he being a repatriate, as being prompted by Haggai.[184]
Should one care to argue that they did in fact return to rebuild but
then put it off as they attended their own affairs, Zechariah is evidence to the contrary. Zechariah agrees in identifying his day, not
any time earlier, as the "time" for Yahweh's return and temple
rebuilding, and he is under no compulsion to explain why the repatriation was not the "time" since it was never considered to be such.

---

[183] Beuken, *Haggai—Sacharja 1–8*, 221–29, 334, offers other reasons why Haggai
should be considered resident in Judah, including his interest in agricultural matters.

[184] Zechariah is commonly assumed to be a repatriate on the basis of his genealog-
ical connection to the priestly house of Iddo which returned with Zerubbabel and
Joshua (Neh 12:4, 16). In Zech 1:1 Zechariah is "son of Berechiah, son of Iddo".
In Ezr 5:1; 6:14 he is "son of Iddo".

The Judeans supplying the impetus for the temple rebuilding cannot be more closely defined beyond saying that they were not repatriated with Zerubbabel. We do not know how extensive this group was, but it is clear from Hag 1:2 that many who were already in Judah did not consider it the "time" to rebuild the temple since the initial call to rebuild at the arrival of Zerubbabel, Joshua, and the other repatriates fell on deaf ears. Before addressing the questions of how the prophets convinced Judeans that it was indeed the "time" to rebuild the temple and why the Judeans accepted their reasons, attention is turned to an important corollary of the contention that the impetus for the rebuilding came from Judeans living in their homeland when Zerubbabel, Joshua, and the repatriates returned. As outlined in chapter 1, it is commonly assumed by scholars that the impetus for temple rebuilding came from the repatriates who excluded non-repatriates from the undertaking. That is, temple rebuilding was a focus of social division in Achaemenid Judah. If, however, the desire to rebuild the temple on Zerubbabel's arrival was voiced by those already living in Judah (exemplified by Haggai) and thereupon supported by Zerubbabel, Joshua, and the prophet Zechariah, the basis for the claim that in rebuilding the temple the repatriates rejected the participation of the non-repatriates is seriously weakened.

The books of Haggai and Zechariah 1–8 support this conclusion. Rather than exemplifying social division in Achaemenid Judah between the repatriates and non-repatriates, the temple rebuilding was undertaken by both groups. Hag 2:2–4 confirms this point.[185]

> 2) "Speak to Zerubbabel, son of Shaltiel, the governor of Judah, and to Joshua, son of Jehozadak, the high priest, and to all the remnant of the people:
> 3) 'Who is left among you who saw this house in its former glory? And how do you see it now? Is it not in your eyes as nothing? (4) Yet be strong, Zerubbabel!'—oracle of Yahweh. 'Be strong, Joshua, son of Jehozadak, high priest! Be strong, all you people of the land!'— oracle of Yahweh. 'Work! For I am with you'—oracle of Yahweh."

Hag 2:3 may include non-repatriates, or at least people repatriated before the arrival of Zerubbabel, since those "left among you who saw this house in its former glory" would be over seventy years old (given that the temple was destroyed in 587 and this oracle is dated

---

[185] See also the discussion of Hag 2:2–4 above, pp. 55, 169–71.

to October, 521 [Hag 1:15b–2:1]) and hence would have been unlikely to have made the journey from Babylonia with Zerubbabel. A clearer indication that non-repatriates are in view here is the use of the term "people of the land" (Hag 2:4). In Ezra-Nehemiah the terms "the people of the land" and "the peoples of the land(s)" refer to non-repatriates, both to Judeans who had not gone into exile and to foreigners living in neighbouring territories. It is a derogatory term used of people who must be excluded from the community of the repatriates and their work on the temple. "The people of the land" in Hag 2:4 does not carry such negative connotations since these people are called upon to participate in the rebuilding. In the light of its use in Ezra-Nehemiah, however, it is unlikely that "the people of the land" in Hag 2:4 refers to the repatriates as a discrete group.[186] Haggai may be using "the people of the land" with the sense it had in the monarchical period rather than with the nuance it was later given by the author(s)/editor(s) of Ezra-Nehemiah, in which case it refers to the established land holders in Judah.[187] Alternatively, "the people of the land" may refer to all the inhabitants of Judah, without distinction between repatriates and non-repatriates.[188] In Hag 1:2 "this people", which includes those working for wages (Hag 1:6) as well as farmers, is addressed by the prophet as the prospective temple rebuilders, so it is possible that that they are one and the same as "all the people of the land" in Hag 2:4. Similarly, Zech 7:5 introduces an oracle addressed to "all the people of the land and the priests". This is not an oracle of judgement to exclude "the people of the land"; rather it is a response to a query regarding cultic fasts (Zech 7:4–14; 8:18–19). In the light of references to

---

[186] Weinberg, "Der 'am hā'āreṣ," 325–35 (Citizen-Temple Community, 62–74), argues that "the people of the land" in Haggai and Zechariah refers to the developing Judean Bürger-Tempel-Gemeinde, largely consisting of repatriates at this time. Later, the book of Ezra, written after the Judean Bürger-Tempel-Gemeinde was fully developed, adopted new terminology for this polity (קהל, עדה) and used "the people(s) of the land(s)" to refer to the rejected Samarians. I agree that there is a different meaning attributed to "the people of the land" in Haggai and Zechariah compared with Ezra, but do not accept Weinberg's contention regarding the development of a Judean Bürger-Tempel-Gemeinde for reasons outlined earlier.

[187] So, Rudolph, Haggai-Sacharja 1–8, 42; Gunneweg, "עם הארץ," 439; Meyers and Meyers, Haggai, Zechariah 1–8, 50–51; Wolff, Haggai, 78–79.

[188] Ackroyd, Exile and Restoration, 162; May, "'This People' and 'This Nation,'" 192; Schultz, "Political Tensions Reflected in Ezra-Nehemiah," 229; Petersen, Haggai and Zechariah 1–8, 47; Japhet, "People and Land," 110; Hausmann, Israels Rest, 40–41.

"the remnant of this people" in Zech 8:6, 11, 12 referring to the community which will experience divine blessing and restoration (this includes Judeans still to be repatriated—Zech 8:7; this community is called "House of Judah" in 8:13 ["and House of Israel" may be a later interpolation]), it would appear that "all the people of the land" (Zech 7:5) refers to those already inhabiting Judah.[189] That "the people of the land" refers either to non-repatriates or to the non-repatriates and repatriates together as a single group is shown by the fact that in Zech 6:10 a group of repatriates bear the title גולה (gôlāh "exile"). Further support for "the people of the land" being, or at least including, non-repatriates may come from the reference to the fasts of the fifth and seventh months (Zech 7:5). The fast of the fifth month was undertaken for the destruction of the temple while the fast of the seventh month is commonly taken to refer to the fast undertaken in remembrance of the assassination of Gedaliah (Jer 41:1–3; II Ki 25:25).[190] While Judean exiles, particularly those who were deported after the death of Gedaliah, may have fasted in remembrance of his death, it is also likely that Judeans who had remained in the land undertook this fast.

The contention that the temple rebuilding was not a centre of conflict between repatriates and non-repatriates is further supported by a comparison of the temple ideology of Haggai and Zechariah. Haggai and Zechariah share the same symbolic universe as evidenced in their indebtedness to the monarchical Zion ideology, the expectation of the return of Yahweh to Jerusalem as the fundamental element in restoring "Israel" to normality after the catastrophe of 587, the kingship of Yahweh expressed in the return of Yahweh to Jerusalem and to his rebuilt temple, the role of Zerubbabel as legitimate temple rebuilder, and the subjection of the nations before the sovereignty of Yahweh. Although these prophets do not hold exactly the same views on all matters (Zechariah may find an important role for Joshua beside Zerubbabel and he emphasizes the return of the exiles and the coming of the nations to Zion; Haggai emphasizes

---

[189] Hausmann, *Israels Rest*, 44. On p. 47, Hausmann, following Amsler, accepts "and House of Israel" as original and interprets these references to "the remnant of the people" to include the inhabitants of the former northern kingdom.

[190] Rudolph, *Haggai—Sacharja 1–8*, 144; Petersen, *Haggai and Zechariah 1–8*, 285; Meyers and Meyers, *Haggai, Zechariah 1–8*, 388.

the shaking of the heavens and the earth), the views held in common are notable. These views are shared by both a prophet repatriated with Zerubbabel (Zechariah) and a prophet who is either a non-repatriate, or who was repatriated considerably earlier, perhaps with Sheshbazzar (Haggai). This points to an underlying ideological unity between the repatriates under Zerubbabel and those they found in the land at their return regarding the renewal and reconstitution of Judah. It is notable, against those who contend that the repatriates were a cultic community focused on the Torah under the leadership of the priests, that these prophets do not feature such concerns. In response it has been argued that these prophets represent the views of one party which was heir to the monarchical Zion/*Yahweh mālak* ideology whereas there was a second party which understood themselves as constituting a cultic community and which eschewed the monarchical ideology. This argument can be dismissed for the following reasons.

First, as noted in chapter 2, there is scant evidence to support the contention that the exiles in Babylonia before the repatriation under Zerubbabel maintained their Judean identity by forming a cultic community. Further, it was shown in chapter 3 that Ezr 1:1–4:5, the Hebrew narrative of the repatriation and temple rebuilding, is a late, polemical text which has no first-hand knowledge of the period it recounts. It anachronistically imports from a later period social tensions between the repatriates and "the people(s) of the land(s)" and an understanding of the repatriates as forming a cultic community.

Second, it is evident from Haggai and Zechariah that Joshua, who is the high priest at the time of the temple rebuilding and who is a repatriate (Ezr 2:1–2 // Neh 7:6–7; Neh 12:1), supports the temple rebuilding. Ezr 1:1–4:5 also maintains this view. According to proponents of the view that the Judean exiles in Babylonia formed a cultic community before the repatriation under Zerubbabel, this community eschewed monarchical ideology in favour of constituting the community's identity by devotion to the Torah under the leadership of the priests. Torah and priesthood had replaced temple and kingship as the central symbols of the community. As high priest Joshua was surely the leader of this community. How is it then that he participated in the temple rebuilding rather than rejecting it in favour of upholding the Torah as the central symbol of the community? One must assume from Haggai, Zechariah and Ezr 1:1–4:5 that repatriated priests wanted to officiate at the temple, as indeed Joshua

is ritually cleansed to undertake (Zech 3). The high priest, as leader
of the cultic community, does not say that a temple is unnecessary.
Further, in supporting the temple rebuilding he accepts the adapted
monarchical period ideology which legitimated the undertaking. Could
he simultaneously be the leader of the cultic community with its new
central symbols of Torah and priesthood and support the rebuilding of the Jerusalem temple which was legitimated by the monarchical period ideology, including the royal role in which Zerubbabel
is cast? Some may choose to introduce the idea of a diarchy which
ostensibly appears in Zech 6 as a means of addressing these questions, but it is clear that if the diarchy is accepted, the scholarly
notion of the character of the cultic community needs to be radically reformed. Since Joshua appears to be a willing participant in
the temple rebuilding which was legitimated by the adapted monarchical ideology, the contention that there was a division at the time
of the temple rebuilding between the members of the repatriated
cultic community and those who held to the monarchical period ideology must be abandoned.

Third, and related to the above point, it is impossible to see how
the cultic community, led by Joshua, could have legitimated the temple rebuilding in terms other than the monarchical period ideology.
The priestly redaction of the Pentateuch, the main contours of which
were supposedly formulated before the repatriation under Zerubbabel
and which supposedly reflects the exilic community's self-under-
standing, could not underpin the rebuilding of the temple since this
text disassociates the kingship of Yahweh from Judean kingship and
the Jerusalem temple. Yet Joshua accepts the modified monarchical
ideology as legitimating the temple rebuilding. That is, he accepts
the linking of the kingship of Yahweh with the Jerusalem temple
and Judean kingship (the latter in the form of Zerubbabel's royal
prerogative as temple rebuilder). Monarchical ideology could not
therefore have been anathema to the putative cultic community.
Hence, it would seem that the idea of the Judean community portrayed in the supposed priestly recension of the Pentateuch post-
dates the repatriation under Zerubbabel. This then explains in part
why Ezr 1:1–4:5 has a different understanding of the character of
the community of the repatriates. It is written at a later time when
views of the Judean community and restoration were considerably
different from that which we read in Haggai and Zechariah. How
and why these changes came about deserve study, but are outside

the scope of the present work (they are broached in chapter 5). It
is notable, however, that Ezr 1:1–4:5, which supports temple rebuilding, does not deal with the issue of the ideology legitimating the
undertaking. It appears that this narrative relies on the kingship of
Cyrus to legitimate the rebuilding (Ezr 1:1–4; cf. 5:1–6:15 relying
also on Darius). But as Haggai and Zechariah make clear, it is
Zerubbabel's royal lineage which makes *him* the legitimate rebuilder.
No reference is made in these prophets to Cyrus or Darius as the
one who legitimates the rebuilding, and Joshua appears to accept
that Zerubbabel's role in the undertaking is central to its legitimation. It bears repeating that Zerubbabel, Joshua and Zechariah as
repatriates make no mention of the concerns that supposedly defined
the repatriates as a cultic community. All subscribe to a modified
monarchical ideology as the blueprint for the restoration of Judah.

As was argued in chapter 3, the attempt of the account of the
rebuilding in Ezr 3:1–4:5 to make a division between the repatriates from the non-repatriates and to blame the latter for the delay
in the temple rebuilding is a late anti-Samarian polemic which claims
that the repatriates alone were commissioned by Cyrus to rebuild
the Jerusalem temple and that non-repatriates (both Samarians and
other "peoples of the lands" [Ezr 3:3]) were not legitimate worshippers of Yahweh. For these reasons they were forbidden by
Zerubbabel and the elders of Judah to participate in the temple
rebuilding (Ezr 4:1–5). The placement of Zerubbabel in this narrative is an anachronism since it appears that he arrived in Judah not
in the reign of Cyrus but some time quite close to the rebuilding
undertaken early in the reign of Darius. It is notable that Haggai
and Zechariah do not mention the repudiation of the Samarians or
"the people of the land". The prophets lack the invective directed
against non-repatriates which pervades the Hebrew narrative of the
rebuilding in Ezra. Had these prophets shared the perspective of the
Hebrew narrative of Ezra surely some mention of the rejected peoples would appear in their texts. The Hebrew narrative in Ezra
recounting the rebuilding attempt in the reign of Cyrus can be compared with the Aramaic narrative of the rebuilding in the reign of
Darius (Ezr 5:1–6:18) which also makes no mention of conflict
between the repatriates and other groups.

There have been attempts to read such conflict into Haggai, most
notably in Hag 2:10–14. The prophet seeks a ruling from the priests
regarding the transference of impurity. Of particular note is verse 14:

> Then Haggai replied and said: "So it is with this people and so is this
> nation before me"—oracle of Yahweh—"and so it is all the work of
> their hands. Whatever they offer there is defiled."

This oracle refers to the work on the temple and the sacrifices that
are offered on its altar. Rothstein, followed by a number of commentators, contended that "this people" and "this nation" refer to
the group of non-repatriated foreigners who sought to participate in
the temple rebuilding as recounted in Ezr 4:1–5 (for Rothstein these
people are "Samaritans"). The prophet thus warns the repatriates to
keep separate from these syncretistic foreigners lest they be ritually
contaminated by them.[191] The division between the Samaritans and
the Judeans must, however, be dated to the Hellenistic period at the
earliest.[192] There is no evidence outside of Ezr 4:1–5 that there was
conflict between the Judeans and those living in and around Samaria.
Daniel Smith, recognizing that the Samaritans cannot be in view
in Hag 2:14 but still wanting to see the text as referring to social
division, submits there are a number of other sources of potential
contamination for the repatriated temple rebuilders. He rehearses
the main conflict theories such as worshippers of "Yahweh alone"
versus "syncretists" (M. Smith, Lang), Zadokite "hierocrats" versus
Levitical "visionaries" (Hanson), repatriates devoted to the Torah
verses priestly temple religion (Mantel), class conflict (Kreissig).[193] The
concern with purity is, according to Smith, a peculiar concern of
the repatriates since it gained considerable currency in the Babylonian
exile where the priestly portions of the Pentateuch were finalized
and where, by virtue of their authority in the exilic community, the
priests inculcated the view that in order to maintain a distinct identity the exiles must separate themselves from all things "foreign".[194]
It was argued in chapter 2, however, that the evidence in support

---

[191] Rothstein, *Juden und Samaritaner*, 5–41; Beuken, *Haggai—Sacharja 1–8*, 67–68;
Rudolph, *Haggai—Sacharja 1–8*, 49–50; Wolff, *Haggai*, 92–94. In order to juxtapose
Hag 2:10–14 with Ezr 4:1–5, the latter would thus refer to the rebuilding in the
reign of Darius, not to a putative rebuilding in the reign of Cyrus. Meyers and
Meyers, *Haggai, Zechariah 1–8*, xxxiv, 57, hold that there was division between the
Samaritans (sic) and the Judeans but do not consider Hag 2:10–14 to refer to this.
For the Meyerses "Judeans" means both the repatriates and the Judeans who did
not go into exile. They do not posit a division between these two groups of Judeans.
[192] See above Chapter 1 n. 23.
[193] Smith, *Religion of the Landless*, 188–96. On various understandings of the social
conflict in Achaemenid Judah, see chapter 1 above.
[194] Ibid., 139–51, 186–88.

of this view of the role of the priests in the community of the exiles and of the place of purity concerns is quite scant. It is certainly insufficient to claim that the repatriates would have rejected the non-repatriates as "foreigners" or "unclean".[195]

Koch and May, followed by others, have made a cogent case for identifying "this people" and "this nation" in Hag 2:14 with the Judeans undertaking the rebuilding, not with some supposed opposition.[196] Koch notes that Haggai refers to "this house" (Hag 1:4; 2:3, 9) and "this day" (Hag 2:15, 18) without any pejorative sense, and the prophet had already spoken of the prospective temple rebuilders as "this people" (Hag 1:2). There are a substantial number of references in Isaiah and Jeremiah where the people of Yahweh are called "this people".[197] גוי (gôy "nation") can also be used of Israel.[198] Against the contention that social division is in view in Hag 2:10–14 it can further be noted that it is not the people/nation that is unclean but rather what they offer on the altar. Petersen submits that this is due to the fact that the altar had not been properly ritually purified, while Hildebrand argues that the impurity is due to moral failings on the part of the community rebuilding the temple.[199]

If the contention that the rebuilding of the Jerusalem temple was undertaken in the context of division between the repatriates and those whom they found in the land at their return is to be rejected, what of the argument of Paul Hanson that the temple rebuilding marked a division among the repatriates themselves? Hanson claims that there was division between, on the one hand, "hierocrats", that

---

[195] See above pp. 48–62.

[196] Koch, "Haggais unreines Volk," 52–66; May, "'This People' and 'This Nation,'" 190–97; T. Townsend, "Additional Comments on Haggai 2:10–19," *VT* 18 (1968) 359–60; Ackroyd, *Exile and Restoration*, 167–68; Petersen, *Haggai and Zechariah 1–8*, 80–82; Meyers and Meyers, *Haggai, Zechariah 1–8*, p. 57; D. R. Hildebrand, "Temple Ritual: A Paradigm for Moral Holiness in Haggai II 10–19," *VT* 39 (1989) 161–63; cf. T. Unger, "Noch Einmal: Haggais unreines Volk," *ZAW* 103 (1991) 210–25, who views these references as coming from the hand of the later Chronist redactor.

[197] See Hildebrand, "Temple Ritual," 161–62 nn. 23 and 24.

[198] A. Cody, "When is the Chosen People called a *gôy*?" *VT* 14 (1964) 1–6.

[199] Petersen, *Haggai and Zechariah 1–8*, 82–85; Hildebrand, "Temple Ritual," 16–68, who both follow the form critical study of Koch ("Haggais unreines Volk," 52–66) which reads Hag 2:10–19 as a unit. Hildebrand develops his interpretation of Hag 2:14 from the study of Hag 2:15–19, while Petersen sees Hag 2:15–19 as addressing a second, related issue. Clines, "Haggai's Temple," 71–76, also reads Hag 2:10–19 as a unit and considers the text to be duplicitous since the people are called to rebuild the holy temple yet they are deemed to be "unclean". The response to this uncleanness is not purification but "blessing" (2:19), which is arguably inappropriate.

is, the official Jerusalem Zadokite priesthood who sought to establish the rule of Yahweh through their mediation, with the rebuilt temple returning them to a position of privilege, and, on the other hand, the "visionaries" who were Levites disenfranchised by the Zadokites and who saw the rule of Yahweh as being introduced not by human activity (such as temple rebuilding) but through the suprahistorical action of Yahweh. The former group were sympathetic to Achaemenid Persian rule of Judah and received support from the administration in the form of the appointment of the Zadokite priesthood over the Jerusalem cult. It was the "hierocrats", therefore, who rebuilt the Jerusalem temple, while the "visionaries" excluded themselves from participating in the venture. Hanson argues that the division between these two "parties" goes back to the Babylonian exilic period where Deutero-Isaiah represents the "visionary" viewpoint, Ezekiel 40–48 the "hierocratic". At the time of the temple rebuilding the "visionaries" are represented by Trito-Isaiah (Is 56–66), while the "hierocrats" are represented by Haggai and Zechariah 1–8.[200]

Hanson has been criticized from a number of angles, but for present purposes the following points can be made.[201] First, Hanson stresses the differences between Deutero-Isaiah and Ezekiel 40–48 so that each prophet is made the representative of a "party" which holds competing views of the nature of the Judean restoration. He does this because he wishes to have forerunners to the social division he sees at the time of the temple rebuilding. As noted in chapter 2 of the present study, these texts do exhibit differences regarding the restoration, but Ezekiel 40–48 is not simply "hierocratic" since it also makes use of the monarchical Zion ideology which is the basis for Deutero-Isaiah's conception of the restoration. Haggai and Zechariah 1–8 similarly use the Zion ideology. Indeed, their focus on it would lead one to believe that they have much more in com-

---

[200] Hanson, *Dawn of Apocalyptic*. On Hanson's argument see also above pp. 17–19, 81–82.

[201] For critiques of Hanson, see R. P. Carroll, "Twilight of Prophecy or Dawn of Apocalyptic?" *JSOT* 14 (1979) 3–35; M. A. Knibb, "Prophecy and the Emergence of the Jewish Apocalypse," in *Israel's Prophetic Heritage: Essays in Honour of Peter R. Ackroyd* (ed. R. Coggins, A. Phillips and M. Knibb; Cambridge: Cambridge University Press, 1982) 169–76; R. Mason, "The Prophets of the Restoration," in *Israel's Prophetic Heritage*, 137–54; R. Coggins, *Haggai, Zechariah, Malachi* (Old Testament Guides; Sheffield: JSOT Press, 1987) 52–59; Williamson, "Concept of Israel in Transition," 149–53; B. Schramm, *The Opponents of Third Isaiah: Reconstructing the Cultic History of the Restoration* (JSOTSup 193; Sheffield: Sheffield Academic Press, 1995); Cook, *Prophecy and Apocalypticism*.

mon with Deutero-Isaiah than with Ezekiel 40–48. It is notable that
while Hanson makes much of the differences between Deutero-Isaiah
and Ezekiel 40–48, he does not conclude from the different emphasizes in Haggai and Zechariah regarding the restoration that they
represent different parties.[202]

Second, Haggai and Zechariah clearly express the view that the
temple rebuilding marks the beginning of the "new age" rather than
the consummation of it. Although the term "eschatology" is inappropriate to describe this view it is, nevertheless, forward-looking—
Zerubbabel is yet to be made king, the nations are yet to be overthrown
or punished, all the exiles are yet to return. Hanson claims that the
"hierocrats" eschewed such a view, believing that the re-establishment of the Jerusalem cult and Zadokite priesthood fulfilled all restoration hopes. Further, since Haggai and Zechariah placed great store
in the re-establishment of the Judean monarchy in some form, they
can hardly be said to be simply legitimating the Zadokite priesthood
and serving their political interests.

Third, Is 66:1–4, which is considered by Hanson to be the sig-
nal Trito-Isaianic text for the rejection of the rebuilding of the temple, may be dated to the time after the temple was rebuilt and reflect
a criticism of the then current cult and the activities of the priesthood rather than being interpreted as being anti-temple rebuilding.[203]
Even if one accepts a dating around the time of the rebuilding, as
P. A. Smith also does, it is not necessary to construe the text as an
attack on the undertaking or as reflecting "parties".[204] Smith views
Is 66:1–4 not as a renunciation of the temple per se but as "opposed . . .

---

[202] See the comments above, pp. 79–81, that the different views of the restoration expressed in Deutero-Isaiah and Ezekiel 40–48 need not be hardened into
"parties".

[203] So, A. Rofé, "Isaiah 66:1–4: Judean Sects in the Persian Period as Viewed
by Trito-Isaiah," in *Biblical and Related Studies Presented to Samuel Iwry* (ed. A. Kort
and S. Morschauser; Winona Lake, IN: Eisenbrauns, 1985) 205–17.

[204] P. A. Smith, *Rhetoric and Redaction in Trito-Isaiah: The Structure, Growth, and
Authorship of Isaiah 56–66* (VTSup 62; Leiden/New York/Cologne: E. J. Brill, 1995)
153–59; similarly, Williamson, "Concept of Israel in Transition," 152. Smith considers most of Is 56–66 to have been written in the period 538–515. He sees the
texts Is 56:1–8; 56:9–57:21; 58:1–59:20; 65:1–66:17, which for him constitutes
"Trito-Isaiah2", as coming from the latter end of this period (p. 188). While acknowledging that Is 66:1–4 might date from the time of the temple rebuilding, I would
consider much of Trito-Isaiah to be later than this and most likely to be the product of diverse hands; see, for example, S. Sekine, *Die Tritojesajanische Sammlung (Jes
56–66) redaktionsgeschichtlich untersucht* (BZAW 175; Berlin: W. de Gruyter, 1989).

only to the present cult and plans to build the temple, given the
social injustice and religious apostasy current among leaders, priests
and the people".[205] That is to say, the community should not adopt
the view that the temple rebuilding legitimates current social and
religious practices, nor that such are somehow irrelevant given the
return of Yahweh and the promise of the fulfilment of restoration
hopes; on the contrary, the temple can be re-established only in a
community that is fit for the divine presence. Elements of this attitude
appear in Haggai and Zechariah also. While these prophets are not
opposed to the rebuilding, as noted above Hag 2:10–14 recognizes
the impurity of the current cult (although it does not mention syncretistic practices), and Zech 3 recognizes the impurity of Joshua the high
priest. For these prophets, however, such matters were being addressed
at the time of the rebuilding. Further, Zech 8:16–17 emphasizes the
ethical demands on the community concomitant with Yahweh's return
to Jerusalem; demands that may not have been met at the time of
writing (cf. Zech 8:10).[206] For Smith, "the difference between Haggai
and T[rito-] I[saiah]2 is one of emphasis and not of kind".[207] On
his reading, Trito-Isaiah is a critic of the cult and community in the
tradition of the pre-exilic prophets.[208] The differences within the
Judean community reflected in Trito-Isaiah, Haggai, and Zechariah
are not markers of party division, and Smith criticizes those commentators who have interpreted them as such. He submits that:

> rather than regarding this group [represented by Trito-Isaiah] as a sect
> which has once and for all set itself apart from the rest of the Jewish
> community, we should perhaps think in terms of a strict, pious ele-
> ment within the community, which stood in varying relations with the
> leaders of the community and the majority of the people.[209]

---

[205] Smith, *Rhetoric and Redaction*, 197; similarly, 158–59.

[206] Also, Zech 1:2–6 calls upon the community to "return from your evil ways
and from your evil deeds" (1:4). On the connection between morality and the return
of the divine presence, as exemplified particularly in Zech 1:2–6, see E. J. C.
Tigchelaar, *Prophets of Old and the Day of the End: Zechariah, the Book of Watchers and
Apocalyptic* (OTS 35; Leiden/New York/Cologne: E. J. Brill, 1996) 71–87.

[207] Smith, *Rhetoric and Redaction*, 198, where he also notes a connection between
TI2 and Hag 2:10–14.

[208] Ibid., 202–03.

[209] Ibid., 201. In this way Smith's position can be distinguished from Blenkinsopp,
"Jewish Sect," 5–20, who concurs that Is 66:1–4 does not reject the rebuilding project (p. 9), but differs in viewing the text as representing a group "whose relations
with the parent body had been at least temporarily severed" (p. 10). While Blenkinsopp

While differing from his analysis of Trito-Isaiah, Smith's insightful study nevertheless shows how diversity of attitude or religious proclivities within the community is not tantamount to social division.

Since it cannot be shown that Deutero-Isaiah and Ezekiel 40–48 represent exilic "parties" and since there is no unequivocal evidence for parties among the repatriates struggling for ideological and political control at the time of the temple rebuilding, Hanson's portrayal of the social context of the Jerusalem temple rebuilding should be set aside.

Having rejected the claim that the rebuilding of the Jerusalem temple of Yahweh was undertaken in the context of social division in favour of the view of Haggai and Zechariah that Judeans, both repatriates and non-repatriates, participated in the rebuilding, our attention now returns to the problem of why the Judeans considered the early years of the reign of Darius I to be the "time" to rebuild the temple.

As was outlined in chapter 3, there was a concern after the dissolution of the kingdom of Judah to determine the time of Yahweh's return, but, apparently, to no avail. The return of Yahweh was universally understood in post-monarchical texts to be an expression of the kingship of Yahweh which would issue in blessing for Yahweh's people and the destruction of their enemies (for example, Pss 44; 74; 79; Ezek 28:24–26; Jer 50–51; Is 40–55; Is 63–64), or it

---

views this as nascent sectarianism, Smith, *Rhetoric and Redaction*, 203, concludes that "it would appear that we can speak of the birth of so-called sectarianism in Isa. 56–66 only in the most guarded and qualified way".

Clines, "Haggai's Temple," 81–85, sees lying behind Haggai unresolved social conflicts between leaders, such as Haggai, Zerubbabel and Joshua (supported by prophets, administrators and priests) and the people (consisting of farmers and householders; for Clines, the people are Judeans, not Samarians [p. 71 n. 43]). The two groups differ over whether the temple should be built (leaders: yes; people: not yet time); over class distinctions (the people are despised by the leaders who as an élite view them as "unclean", but the leaders are nevertheless dependent on the people for the temple reconstruction); over the status of the governor (the leaders view Zerubbabel as soon to be world dictator, after the shaking of the heavens and the earth, but "shopkeepers and farmers are not going to welcome cosmic upheaval" [p. 84]). In summary, "the gulf between the governors and the governed is intolerably wide" (p. 85). I argue that while the rebuilding of the temple serves the political interests of leaders such as Zerubbabel and Joshua, neither of them instigated the rebuilding, and that Haggai should be considered as one of "the people" rather than one of the leaders. I agree that there is social tension over determining "the time" for the rebuilding, but I place the leaders and the people in the same group needing to be convinced by Haggai that "the time" had in fact arrived.

would mean the re-establishment of the kingship of David and the reunification of Judah and Israel (for example, Ezek 34:23–31; 37:15–31; Jer 30–31). Zerubbabel's arrival in Judah was not marked by any of these. Zerubbabel was not the king of Judah, many of the Judeans were still in exile, Judah and Israel were not reunited, the enemies of Judah were not crushed, the people were not blessed. In short, there was no sign that Yahweh's anger had abated and that he had indeed returned to Jerusalem. This, coupled with the fact that the repatriates themselves had not returned in order to rebuild immediately, made the initial call to rebuild (presumed in Hag 1:2) appear premature. A prophetical call to rebuild the temple may not have been deemed sufficient reason to begin the work. Prophets had previously proclaimed the return of Yahweh to Jerusalem (Jer 28:1–4—Hananiah; Jer 50–51; Deutero-Isaiah) with no result. Prophecy on this matter may therefore have fallen into disrepute.[210] Further, temple (re)building had always been undertaken by a king who had been so directed by the deity; even Deutero-Isaiah had Cyrus, a king, cast in the role of temple rebuilder. A king was needed *before* rebuilding could commence and although Zerubbabel was of the royal house of Judah, the temple could not to be built by a would-be king.

In the second year of Darius none of the prerequisites for rebuilding the Jerusalem temple had been met beyond the appearance of a legitimate rebuilder (Zerubbabel) who, while being of the Judean royal house, was not a king. Clearly, his presence was not considered a sufficient reason in itself to commence rebuilding. Nevertheless, Haggai managed to convince the Judeans to start work on the temple. How did he achieve this? It should be noted at the outset that he does not attempt to address any of the matters that had led to the rejection of the initial call to rebuild. The legitimacy of that call is held to be proven by a drought that had descended on the land. This was interpreted by Haggai to be a sign of divine displeasure at the community's inattention to the task of temple rebuilding (Hag 1:2–11). It was the people's unwillingness to heed the prophetical call to rebuild that had precipitated the drought. According to Hag 1:4, it is the anomaly of the people having "panelled houses" in which to live while Yahweh has no "house" which is held out as a

---

[210] Roberts, "Of Signs and Prophets," 479–80.

self-evident reason why work on the temple should have already commenced. Haggai castigates the people for misappropriating the "time"—that is, that the people consider it time for them to "dwell" but not Yahweh. Neglect of the temple is viewed as willful disobedience to the prophetical call to rebuild. The prophet considers that the people had no legitimate reason to have rejected the initial call to rebuild—the prophetic call of itself was sufficient reason to commence the work.[211] The attitude that there is never any excuse to reject the prophetic word is one that is evidenced time and again in the canonical prophetical texts and shows no awareness that there might be legitimate reasons for rejecting, or at least questioning, the prophetic word.[212] From the prophet's point of view he is the mouthpiece of Yahweh whose word must be heeded else the community come under the deity's judgement. From the community's point of view it was often difficult to divine the word of Yahweh in the prophet's voice, especially after there had been earlier, inaccurate prophetic claims regarding the return of Yahweh and, indeed, in monarchical times, conflicting prophetic voices as to what the will of Yahweh was in particular situations.[213] Haggai shows no sympathy for the community's dilemma.

It is the drought, therefore, which prompted the Judeans to accept Haggai's call to undertake the rebuilding of the temple. Droughts were acknowledged to be a sign of divine judgement, the cause of

---

[211] On the interpretation of Hag 1:2–11, see above pp. 169–78.

[212] That the people should heed the prophetic word is the underlying assumption of all the prophets and need not be referenced here. On possible reasons for rejecting the prophetic word see, for example, Amos 7:10–17 where Amos is instructed to return to Judah and to cease prophesying against Israel. One would consider there to be quite legitimate reasons for the Israelite establishment to reject the prophetic utterances of a foreign prophet. In Jer 7 and 26 there are arguably good reasons for the people to reject Jeremiah's critique of the Zion ideology and sacrificial system since both are supported by the state and tradition. Similarly, Jeremiah's prophecies that Zedekiah should surrender peacefully to the Babylonian army (for example, Jer 27) are rejected on the basis that Yahweh will defend his city and land.

[213] On the problem of determining the authentic prophet see, for example, I Ki 22; Jer 14:13–16; 28:1–17; Ezek 13. In addition to the commentaries on these texts, see also J. Crenshaw, *Prophetic Conflict: Its Effect upon Israelite Religion* (BZAW 124; Berlin: W. de Gruyter, 1971); S. De Vries, *Prophet Against Prophet* (Grand Rapids: Eerdmans, 1978); Carroll, *From Chaos to Covenant*, 161–65. Carroll sees Jer 14:13–16 as a Deuteronomistic interpolation, but it reflects an issue with which the editor and his readers were familiar. In Haggai's day we know of no conflicting prophetic voices regarding the temple rebuilding (cf. Is 66:1–4), but the problem of determining whether Haggai was actually proclaiming the divine will remained real.

which needed to be discovered and remedied. There are a number of examples of this in biblical narratives. In II Sam 21 a three-year famine prompts David to discover its cause: "David consulted Yahweh and Yahweh said, 'There is blood on Saul and his family because he put the Gibeonites to death'" (II Sam 21:1).[214] David responds by having the male descendants of Saul (with the exception of Meribbaal) ritually slaughtered, after which the drought is broken (II Sam 21:5–11). In I Ki 17:1 the prophet Elijah invokes a drought on the northern kingdom of Israel apparently due to the rise of the cult of Tyrian Baʿal in the Israelite court and the subsequent persecution of the court prophets of Yahweh (II Ki 18–19). The drought is lifted when, after the confrontation between Elijah and the prophets of Baʿal on Mount Carmel, the prophets of Baʿal are ritually slaughtered (II Ki 19; esp. II Ki 19:40–46). Prophetical texts also speak of drought as a divine punishment for disobedience to divine injunctions or cultic infraction; see Amos 4:6–9; Hos 4:1–3; Is 5:8–10; Jer 5:20–25 (as commonly interpreted in the commentaries); 8:18–23; 12:4; 14:1–9; Joel 1:11–12, 16–20. Judeans at the time of Haggai would therefore have been seeking the reasons for the drought they were currently experiencing. In this context prophecy would have been an acceptable means of determining the cause of the divine punishment. Haggai thus differs from those prophets who had earlier spoken of the return of Yahweh and the restoration of Jerusalem, and who, due to the non-fulfilment of their prophecies, brought oracles of restoration into disrepute. Haggai is initially a prophet explicating the reasons for the drought. It is out of this context that he then turns to oracles of restoration.

According to Haggai, Zerubbabel and Joshua accepted the connection between the drought and the lack of a temple and this spurred them to lead the community to rebuild the temple. The prophet cannot neglect, however, the ideological concerns that attend temple rebuilding such as the temple as a symbol of the kingship of Yahweh and the need for a king as the legitimate rebuilder. The former is a particularly troubling concern for the Judeans since the

---

[214] The text does not inform the reader how David received this divine answer. It may be via a prophet; cf. II Sam 7:1–17; 12:1–15. From the Elijah-Elisha narratives (I Ki 17–II Ki 9) it is known that prophets (both court prophets and socially peripheral prophets) gave the king advice on military and other matters when in a prophetic trance. II Sam 21:1 may be similar.

return of Yahweh to his temple in Jerusalem, the throne of his kingship, was thought to be attended by tangible expressions of his kingship such as the punishment of enemies and the elevation of Zion
as the centre of the earth. As was noted in chapter 2 these notions
fell within the prophetical view of historical recurrence. Haggai
reworks the traditional understanding of the relationship between
kingship, temple, blessing, and destruction of enemies by arguing
that temple reconstruction must *precede* the establishment of kingship,
agricultural blessing, and the destruction of enemies.[215] To rebuild
the temple is not only to have Yahweh redress the current drought,
it is also to re-establish the kingship of Yahweh and commence the
restoration of Israel.

Haggai's preaching is effective because it interrelates traditional
temple ideology with conditions current in Judah. He draws on the
expectation of the return of Yahweh to Jerusalem, regarding which
the people claim ignorance as to the "time" of Yahweh's return (Pss
74:9; 79:5; 80:5 [Eng v. 4]; Lam 5:20–22; Is 64:8–11 [Eng vv.
9–12]),[216] by explaining the drought as Yahweh's punishment for not
heeding the earlier call to rebuild. This interpretation of the drought
is coupled with the presence of the legitimate temple rebuilder
(Zerubbabel) and legitimate high priest (Joshua) to prove that it is
indeed the "time" for Yahweh's return to Jerusalem. He draws upon
the traditional temple ideology, reworking it so that temple rebuilding can precede the establishment of Judean kingship.

With temple rebuilding underway Haggai's prophesying ceases,
being replaced by Zechariah.[217] One purpose of Zechariah's prophesying is to maintain the impetus for work on the temple. He does
this not by drawing attention to the drought but by addressing themes
that were of concern to exilic prophets and to the current community,

---

[215] Regarding kingship, see Hag 2:20–23, the final prophecy of Haggai which is
delivered on the day of the foundation laying (cf. Hag 2:18). Regarding agricultural prosperity, see Hag 2:15–19, also delivered on the day of the foundational
laying. Regarding the destruction of enemies, see Hag 1:15b–2:9, dated one month
after rebuilding work began.

[216] See the discussion above, pp. 131–45.

[217] Haggai's last dated prophecy is the twenty-fourth day of the ninth month in
Darius's second year (December 18, 520; Hag 2:18, 26). Although Zechariah's first
prophecy is dated to the eighth month of Darius's second year (Zech 1:1), his visions
of the restoration (Zech 1:7–6:8) are dated to the twenty-fourth day of the eleventh
month in Darius's second year (February 15, 519; Zech 1:7), two months after the
foundation of the temple was laid (Hag 2:18).

notably, the reversal of divine abandonment, the return of the exiles,
the purity of the cult and land, and social harmony. Haggai legitimated his prophecies by being able to identify the "time" of Yahweh's
return to Jerusalem, as noted above, but one should not thereby
conclude that Haggai had totally rehabilitated prophecy.[218] As a repatriate Zerubbabel lends a significant voice in support of the temple
rebuilding and its importance for the restoration of Israel. Why, however, should Zechariah's prophecies command attention when he
offers no "sign" to legitimate himself?

It appears that Zechariah deals with the problem of prophetic
authority by recourse to a new form of prophecy. He prophesies in
a manner traditional among Judean and Israelite prophets, relating
"the word of Yahweh" he had received (Zech 1:1–6; 6:9–15; 7:4–14;
8:1–17; 8:18–23), but allied to this is a new form of visionary experience. These are the night visions of Zech 1:7–6:8. They differ from
visionary experiences recounted in pre-exilic and exilic prophecy in
two ways. First, whereas in earlier prophecy the prophet received
the divine word or a dialogue took place between the prophet and
Yahweh, in Zech 1–8 this is no longer commonly the case. Zechariah
has an *angelus interpres* (מלאך; מלאך יהוה) to aid him in understanding what he sees (Zech 1:9, 11–14; 2:1 [Eng 1:18]; 2:7 [Eng 2:3];
4:1, 3–4; 5:2–5, 10; 6:4–5) and with whom he speaks. The authority for the interpretation of the vision does not, therefore, rest with
the prophet himself; it resides with the interpreting angel. Second,
Zechariah is a participant observer in the visions, he is not simply
recounting a vision which is external to him. They may thus be better termed "dreams" rather than "visions", since not only do they
occur at night, but like dreams, the one dreaming can often see him
or herself within the scene.[219] This point is made explicitly by Zechariah
and his interpreting angel conversing with one of the participants in

---

[218] It is perhaps notable in considering how Haggai and Zechariah legitimated
their prophetic role that neither of them cites a call by Yahweh. This had been
the means by which certain earlier prophets legitimated themselves (Is 6; Jer 1;
Ezek 1:1–2:15). This may point to the fact that such divine calls were no longer
considered as legitimate in the Persian period. Note, similarly, the lack of the divine
call in Joel and Malachi. On the prophetic call narratives, see N. C. Habel, "The
Form and Significance of the Call Narratives," *ZAW* 77 (1965) 305–16.

[219] Cf., for example, the visions of Micaiah in I Ki 22:13–28. Micaiah sees "all
Israel scattered on the mountains like sheep without a shepherd" (I Ki 22:17) and
observes the deliberations in the divine council (I Ki 22:19–22), but there is no
notion that he himself is actually involved in the scenes he beholds. See, similarly,
Jer 1:11–13.

the dream (Zechariah—Zech 2:6 [Eng v. 2]; Angel—Zech 1:11–12; 2:8–9 [Eng vv. 4–5]). In his dreams Zechariah is thus removed to another realm (the heavenly realm?) from where he gains information regarding the events that are soon to come to pass.[220]

The appearance of the *angelus interpres* and the participation of the prophet in the visionary scene are elements common in later apocalyptic literature. While it would be incorrect to contend that the night visions of Zechariah (Zech 1:7–6:8) form an apocalypse, this text does represent a transition from prophecy to apocalyptic.[221] It cannot be viewed as apocalyptic since it does not share sufficient of the elements commonly considered to be central to this world-view; for example, it does not speak of the eschaton, rather it is concerned with the immediate future of Israel. With Jeremias it can be affirmed that Zech 1:7–6:8 forms an inchoate apocalypse which exhibits features later developed in apocalyptic texts.[222] This new development

---

[220] Earlier prophets do not have this experience of travelling to another realm to obtain their visions. All remain located on "earth". Even visionary experiences of Yahweh (Is 6; Ezek 1) take place in this world, usually in the temple. In Ezekiel the prophet is portrayed as travelling back on forth from the Babylonian exile to Jerusalem, but this again takes place in this world. On Zechariah's visions as dreams, see Petersen, *Haggai and Zechariah 1–8*, 111.

[221] Contra H. Gese, "Anfänge und Ende der Apokalyptik dargestellt am Sacharjabuch," *ZThK* 70 (1973): 20–48 (reprinted in H. Gese, *Vom Sinai zum Zion. Alttestamentlische Beiträge zur biblische Theologie* [Beiträge zur evangelischen Theologie 64; Munich: Kaiser, 1974] 202–230), who considers Zech 1:1–6:8 to be the earliest example of the genre apocalypse; cf. R. North, "Prophecy to Apocalyptic via Zechariah," in *Congress Volume: Uppsala, 1971* (VTSup 22; Leiden: Brill, 1972) 47–74; S. Amsler, "Zacharie et l'origine de l'apocalyptique," in *Congress Volume: Uppsala, 1971*, 227–31; Cook, *Prophecy and Apocalyptic*, 124–32. One problem here is the definition of the genre apocalypse and its relationship to apocalyptic as an intellectual or social movement. The latter produced texts other than apocalypses and the study of apocalyptic has focused on the world-view exhibited in the texts and the social context in which they were produced. If apocalyptic is to be defined as a social movement it may be possible to classify Zechariah's night visions as apocalyptic, but this simply shifts the problem of definition to the determination of the social location of apocalyptic communities and/or individuals, a matter on which there is no scholarly agreement. For an overview of the debate concerning the definition of apocalypse and apocalyptic, see E. W. Nicholson, "Apocalyptic," in *Tradition and Interpretation*, 189–213; Knibb, "Prophecy and the Emergence of Jewish Apocalypses," 155–80; P. R. Davies, "The Social World of Apocalyptic Writings," in *The World of Ancient Israel*, 251–71; J. J. Collins, "Genre, Ideology and Social Movements," in *Seers, Sibyls and Sages in Hellenistic-Roman Judaism* (ed. J. J. Collins; SJSJ 54; Leiden/New York: E. J. Brill, 1997) 25–38; idem, *The Apocalyptic Imagination: An Introduction to Jewish Apocalyptic Literature* (2d ed.; Grand Rapids, MI: Eerdmans, 1998) 1–42.

[222] Jeremias, *Die Nachtgesichte des Sacharja*, 39–108, 226–33.

in prophecy reflects, to my mind, Zechariah's need to establish an authority for his prophecies in the changed social and political context of Achaemenid Judah. It can thus also be related to Zechariah as a millenarian prophet in this context. Such observations are in no way a complete explanation for Zechariah's night visions, but they may point the way to fruitful further research on nascent apocalypticism.[223]

The Participation of Zerubbabel and Joshua in the Temple Rebuilding
Since Zerubbabel and Joshua did not return to Judah for the explicit purpose of rebuilding the Jerusalem temple of Yahweh, the question arises as to why they supported the undertaking. Their participation in the project was of paramount importance as they were considered to be the legitimate temple rebuilder and legitimate high priest respectively. The temple rebuilding would have faltered without their support.

Our attention initially turns to Zerubbabel's role in the temple rebuilding. If his participation was not at the behest of the Achaemenid Persian administration (that is, it was not the result of an Achaemenid Persian policy, hence Zerubbabel's participation was not an expression of his role as *pehāh*), and if the rebuilding was not an act of Judean rebellion (that is, Zerubbabel's participation was not because he saw himself as the king of Judah), then other possible explanations for his support for the temple rebuilding must be explored.

As was argued above, the impetus for the rebuilding of the Jerusalem temple came not from Zerubbabel, or those who returned with him c. 522, but from certain Judeans who were living in the land when he returned. They, exemplified by Haggai, saw the arrival of the Davidide Zerubbabel as marking the propitious "time" to rebuild. This was believed to be confirmed when the Judeans' rejection of the call to rebuild the temple resulted in a drought; a sign of divine

---

[223] The roots of this new form of prophecy are difficult to ascertain. I Enoch (probably dated to the third century) has been shown to have close connections with Mesopotamian traditions (see J. C. VanderKam, *Enoch and the Growth of an Apocalyptic Tradition* [CBQ Monograph Series 16; Washington: Catholic Biblical Association of America, 1984]; H. S. Kvanvig, *Roots of Apocalyptic: The Mesopotamian Background of the Enoch Figure and the Son of Man* [WMANT 61; Neukirchen-Vluyn: Neukirchener Verlag, 1988]), and it is possible that the impetus for Zechariah's night visions arises from his experience of Mesopotamian culture while in exile (cf. J. J. Collins, "The Place of Apocalypticism in the Religion of Israel," in *Ancient Israelite Religion*, 544).

punishment (Hag 1:2–11). Zechariah, who was repatriated with Zerubbabel, may offer some insight into what motivated Zerubbabel to support the rebuilding. He did so not only in order to avert divine displeasure (the drought) but also as a means of integrating the repatriates with those Judeans who had remained in the land through the symbolic activity of temple rebuilding. Rather than being a threat to Judeans living in the land, the return of the exiles marked the initial stage of the revivification of Judah. Both communities participated in the restoration of the shrine of their god. If Zerubbabel were the governor of Judah he would have had authority over not only those repatriated with him but also those repatriated earlier and those who had never undergone exile. His interests would have been well served by integrating all groups in society and by offering hope for the renewal of a reunited community. The social disharmony evidenced in Zech 5:3, 6; 8:10 needed to be overcome and the proclamation of the return of Yahweh and the rebuilding of the Jerusalem temple with its attendant promises of a coming "new age" would have been one means of achieving this. Zerubbabel supports Haggai and Zechariah's attempt to reinvigorate Judean identity in the aftermath of the loss of kingship and statehood and the experience of exile while maintaining Judah's political status within the Achaemenid Persian empire.

In addition to social integration and the re-establishment of Judean identity being reasons for Zerubbabel's support for the temple rebuilding, one can also add that this project would have served to legitimate him as the leader of the reunified Judean community. Monarchs typically portrayed temple building as a sign of divine favour and legitimation.[224] Zerubbabel, as an appointee of the Achaemenid Persian administration, may have been viewed suspiciously by segments of the Judean population since he represented the Achaemenid Persian authority over them and reinforced Judah's current political position. By exploiting his royal lineage and giving support to the temple rebuilding Zerubbabel's status becomes something more than that of Achaemenid Persian *peḥāh*. His leadership resided not simply in the administrative position to which he was appointed by the Persians, but is now sanctioned by Yahweh himself in traditional terms. In

---

[224] Lundquist, "Legitimating Role of the Temple," 271–97; Ahlström, *Royal Administration*, 1–9.

accepting the prophets' interpretation of him as the divinely commissioned harbinger of the renewal of Israel, Zerubbabel could enhance the basis of his authority over the community. As the legitimate temple rebuilder he may have been able to extend his influence over Yahwists living outside his immediate jurisdiction.

The monarchical terminology surrounding Zerubbabel was necessary, not because Zerubbabel necessarily saw himself as a potential king, but rather because it was an intrinsic part of the monarchical ideology which had to legitimate the temple rebuilding. The extent to which Zerubbabel shared Haggai's and Zechariah's millenarian views, notably, that he was soon to become the ruler of Israel, is difficult to establish. My view, similar to that of the Meyerses, which has to be put tentatively as the available evidence is scant, is that in his dual role as Davidic descendant and Achaemenid Persian *peḥāh* he saw himself as mediating between prophetic hopes and the Achaemenid Persian administration. He straddled both worlds and in so doing could mediate between Judean and Achaemenid Persian conceptions of the significance of rebuilding the temple. He sought to exploit community expectations for his own political ends and for what he considered to be the good of the community (that is, social integration and identity formation, yet still living within the political realities of the Achaemenid Persian empire). To the Judeans he could be viewed as the divinely legitimate temple rebuilder whose activity inaugurated the new age of renewal, while to the Achaemenid Persians he could portray the temple rebuilding as something other than an act of rebellion since it could be shown to comply with imperial interests for the minor cults of subjugated peoples and to have been sanctioned by the Achaemenid Persian central administration. Indeed, if Ezr 5–6 is any guide, he deftly distanced himself from the rebuilding, preferring to allow the Judean elders to speak on its behalf. His success in balancing his two roles may be reflected both in the prophets' unwillingness to view the temple rebuilding as an act of Judean rebellion and in the Achaemenid Persians' permitting the work on the temple to continue.

Joshua's participation in the temple rebuilding is readily understandable given the fact that, as high priest, he would have perceived his central function as serving in the Jerusalem temple cult. For Joshua, temple rebuilding served to establish him as the leading priest in the community and, concomitantly, to establish his authority within the community. Joshua also faced problems of legitimation, however. To serve as high priest in the Jerusalem temple cult, a cult that would serve an integrated Judean community, he needed to find acceptance among those who were living in Judah when he was repatriated.[225] This was accomplished by Zechariah who, in one of his night visions (Zech 3), addresses the question of Joshua's legitimacy as high priest which had arisen from the fact that he had been in exile and was therefore of suspect purity.[226] The prophet, a fellow repatriate of Joshua's who would have accepted his high priesthood as legitimate, beholds the divine council in which Joshua stands accused as impure by Satan (הַשָּׂטָן).[227] Yahweh dismisses the accusations of Satan, removing Joshua's filthy garments (which symbolized his impurity) and replacing them with pure garments. He is then given a divine commission to serve in the temple.

Joshua's legitimacy is confirmed not only by his divine investiture but also by the place given him in Zechariah's conception of the renewal of Israel. Since the purification of Joshua and his divine commissioning are set within the context of Zechariah's night visions, the implicit contention is that Joshua's role is an integral part of the activity of renewal which Yahweh is introducing by his return to Jerusalem. To accept Zechariah's claims regarding the return of Yahweh, the rebuilding of the temple, the eradication of social ills, the repatriation of the exiles, and the coming of foreigners to worship Yahweh, demands that his hearers also accept Joshua as high priest and leader of the Jerusalem temple cult. The eradication of Joshua's impurity affects not only him but is representative of the eradication of impurity from the temple and the community. Yahweh's

---

[225] הכהן הגדול, literally, "great priest" is the title given to Joshua in Hag 1:1, 12, 14; 2:2, 4; Zech 3:1, 8; 6:11. It appears to replace the title כהן הראש "head priest" used of the leading priest in the monarchical Jerusalem cult (II Ki 25:18; Jer 52:24); cf. Tollington, *Tradition and Innovation*, 126–31, who contends for a monarchical period use of the title. The significance of this title, if new in the Persian period, is unknown. The suggestion in Meyers and Meyers, *Haggai, Zechariah 1–8*, 181, that it was revived from the monarchical period to the reflect the supposed new duties given to Joshua as priestly administrator of the temple and sub-province of Judah, is to be rejected.

[226] On Zech 3, see Petersen, *Haggai and Zechariah 1–8*, 186–214; Meyers and Meyers, *Haggai, Zechariah 1–8*, 178–227; P. Day, *An Adversary in Heaven: śāṭān in the Hebrew Bible* (HSM 43; Atlanta: Scholars, 1988) 107–26; J. C. VanderKam, "Joshua the High Priest and the Interpretation of Zechariah 3," *CBQ* 53 (1991) 553–70.

[227] The figure of הַשָּׂטָן who acts in the divine council as a prosecutor (always with negative connotations) makes it first appearance in post-exilic biblical texts; see also Job 1–2; I Chron 21:1. This role should not be confused with later New Testament and medieval conceptions of Satan.

return demands a purified cult, temple personnel and community.
Zechariah's night visions touch on each of these matters. Joshua,
representing the temple personnel, is purified in Zech 3, leading to
the promise from Yahweh that "I intend to put aside the iniquity
of this land in a single day" (Zech 3:9). The eradication of impurity from the land is supported by the visions in Zech 5. Zech 4:6b–10a
sees the community undertaking the correct cultic procedures for the
temple foundation laying. Zechariah's vision of Joshua before the
divine council thus allayed fears, held by both repatriates and non-
repatriates, regarding the purity of the restored cult and legitimated
him as the head priest of this cult.[228] Zechariah may have had a
different understanding of the political relationship between Joshua
and Zerubbabel, if one accepts that Zech 6:9–13 refers to a diarchy.
But there is no reason to think that this diarchy was to be established at the time of rebuilding, and there is no evidence to support
that it was; not the least because there is no precedent for the
Achaemenid Persian administration permitting such an arrangement.
If Zechariah held the notion of a diarchy, it was a form of political leadership that was to be instituted in the future, the crowning
of Joshua being its symbolic representation.

While the participation of Zerubbabel and Joshua ensured the
legitimacy of the temple rebuilding, there are important issues regarding the undertaking about which we are given little information.
First, how was the temple rebuilding funded? One might assume
from Ezr 2:68–69 (cf. Neh 7:70–71) and Zech 6:9–10 that a certain portion of the funds needed came from the Judean community
and, perhaps, donations from those still in exile. Ezr 6:5, 8 makes
the dubious claim that the expenses were to be met from the tax
revenues of the satrapy "Across-the-River". These conflicting claims

---

[228] Joshua plays a much less prominent role in Haggai's prophecies. For Beuken
(*Haggai—Sacharja 1–8*, 29–31, 50–52) and Mason ("'Editorial Framework'," 416) all
the references to him occur in the editorial passages—Hag 1:1, 12, 14, 2:2, 4.
Mason notes that "the framework places much greater emphasis on the role of the
two leaders than the oracles themselves do" (p. 416). Haggai did not address any
oracle solely to Joshua and only one to Zerubbabel (Hag 2:20–23), the rest being
directed also to the community. Note that in Hag 2:14 the prophet seeks a decision on a matter of ritual purity from "the priests", not from the high priest. One
need not deduce from this that Haggai thought Joshua to be unimportant, but it
is clear from Zech 3 that Zechariah needed to deal with questions that had been
raised about the propriety of Joshua's high priesthood.

need not be fully resolved here, but it is worthwhile to note that the rebuilding of the temple would have put considerable stress on the Judean economy. We are not informed as to where the many artisans needed for the project would have come from or who served as the labour force. Hag 1:8 and Ezr 5 suggests that the Judeans themselves served as the labour force, rather than the traditional slave or corvée labour used in monumental building projects. This would have meant, one assumes, that in an agrarian community the rebuilding could have been undertaken only during slack periods of the agricultural year. Even so, it must mean that Judeans were pressed into service by the local officials. This further points to the need for a strong centralized control of the rebuilding project and enhances the need for an official of Zerubbabel's position to organize the undertaking. The social impact of this labour intensive building project and the reaction of the Judeans to their participation in it over a period of some five years is not recorded.

Second, although the preaching of Haggai and Zechariah and the support of Zerubbabel and Joshua for the temple rebuilding apparently galvanized support for the undertaking, we obtain no information from them regarding any diversity of perspective towards the temple rebuilding. Hanson attempts to read Trito-Isaiah (Is 56–66) as a reflecting a "party" which rejected the call to rebuild the temple, but his argument falters on the dating of this text and the identification of the social location of those who produced it. P. A. Smith offers a nuanced reading of differences in attitude, again based on a dating of Trito-Isaiah to around the time of the temple rebuilding. Daniel Smith, David Clines, and others, see social tension lying behind Haggai, although as argued above, such tensions are not at all clear. Nevertheless, all our main sources represent the "pro-temple" position as this was the one that won out. While the present study has argued that the rebuilding of the Jerusalem temple was not undertaken to entrench social division, indeed its purpose was just the opposite, this should not blind us to the fact that Haggai, Zechariah 1–8, Ezra 1–6 are apologia for temple rebuilding and that there may have been people who objected to it. They may have done so for ideological or economic reasons, although Haggai and Zechariah struggle to meet any objections on these grounds. That there were people against the temple rebuilding (even though they did not form "parties") remains suppositional since, if they existed, they have been silenced in our sources.

SUMMARY

This chapter has attempted to ascertain why the Jerusalem temple of Yahweh was rebuilt in the early years of the reign of Darius I and in what social context it was undertaken. The various responses to these issues reviewed here—for example, that the temple was rebuilt in response to an Achaemenid Persian policy initiative in the reign of Darius; that it was an act of Judean rebellion; that it was in order to grant political self-autonomy to the sub-province of Judah; that it was in order to establish a Judean Bürger-Tempel-Gemeinde; that it entrenched division between repatriates and non-repatriates or between Zadokite "hierocrats" and Levitical "visionaries"—were all shown to have inadequacies. They all agree that the temple rebuilding denoted the restoration of Judah in the aftermath of the dissolution of that kingdom in 587. They differ widely, however, as to the character of that restoration and the identity of the participants.

Since the major views all have weaknesses, an attempt has been made to offer another interpretation of the evidence. From the rejection of the call to rebuild the temple by the Judeans (who must have included those repatriated with Zerubbabel and Joshua) not long before Haggai began preaching (Hag 1:1–4), as well as from the ignorance of the Achaemenid Persian bureaucracy of the undertaking (exemplified by Tattenai's investigation of the temple rebuilding and the need for Darius's bureaucrats to make a search for the Cyrus edict) and the recourse of the Judean rebuilders to the Cyrus edict, rather than an edict of Darius, to legitimate the rebuilding (Ezr 5–6), it appears that Zerubbabel and Joshua were not repatriated to Judah in order to rebuild the Jerusalem temple of Yahweh. Rather the impetus for rebuilding came from Judeans who were in the land when they returned (represented by Haggai). While the rebuilding was not commissioned by Darius, it was not an act of Judean rebellion since the prophets Haggai and Zechariah were careful not to cast the undertaking in such terms. To the Achaemenid Persians the temple reconstruction was portrayed as being undertaken under the auspices of the Cyrus edict, and hence of the Achaemenid Persian administration (Ezr 5–6). To legitimate the rebuilding to the Judeans when they lacked indigenous kingship and independence, Haggai and Zechariah developed modified versions of the monarchical period temple ideology. They portrayed the temple rebuilding as an act of Judean renewal predicated on the return of Yahweh to his city which redressed the dissolution of the kingdom of Judah, the exile and divine abandonment. It represented the revelation of the kingship of Yahweh which would soon issue in agricultural prosperity, social harmony, the subjugation of the nations before Yahweh, the return of all the exiles, and the re-establishment of Judean kingship. Some of these, such as agricultural prosperity, would be forthcoming immediately if only the Judeans would rebuild the temple. The preaching of these prophets was careful to stop short of calling for rebellion and it need not have been considered rebellious by the Achaemenid Persian administration, not only because they remained unaware of the implications of the temple rebuilding as understood by these prophets but also because the prophets saw the coming "new age" as an act of Yahweh himself, not dependent on the force of Judean arms.

Far from being an act which caused division in Achaemenid Judean society, the reconstruction of the temple was construed as an act of social integration bringing both repatriates and non-repatriates together in this significant symbolic project. The affirmation of the re-establishment of the kingship of Yahweh, the expectation of political emancipation, and the attendant blessings display that Haggai and Zechariah were prophets of a millenarian movement. Zerubbabel and Joshua acceded to the temple rebuilding not only because it encouraged social integration and social harmony but also because it gave divine legitimation to their position as leaders of the renewed and reunited Judean community.

CHAPTER FIVE

CONCLUSION

Two, often related, contentions have dominated accounts of the purpose for rebuilding the Jerusalem temple of Yahweh in the early
Achaemenid Persian period and the social context in which it was
undertaken. First, that there was conflict between Judeans who were
repatriated from Babylonia by the Achaemenid Persian administration and those whom they found living in the territory at their return
(both those Judeans who had never gone into exile and Samarians)
and/or there was conflict among the repatriates themselves over the
character of the Judean restoration. Second, that the repatriation
and temple rebuilding reflect an Achaemenid Persian administrative
policy effected throughout the empire for the purpose of re-establishing indigenous polities in their homelands. The temple served as
an economic and administrative centre of Judah and gave political
power to cultic officials and others connected with this shrine. The
repatriates were politically, economically and socially advantaged by
the rebuilding of the temple to the exclusion of non-repatriates (and/or
repatriates who were not sympathetic to Achaemenid Persian rule)
who were not considered to be Judeans and who therefore had to
be excluded from the community connected to the temple. Temple
rebuilding thus entrenched social division in Achaemenid Judah.

This study offers an extended critique of these contentions and
seeks to offer an alternative understanding of the purpose of the temple rebuilding and the social context in which it was undertaken.
There is no compelling evidence for the view that the roots of the
putative social division in Judah in the early Persian period lie in
the Babylonian Judeans' reformulation of their identity. The contention that the dissolution of the kingdom of Judah and the exile
led to the reformulation of Babylonian Judean identity as a "cultic
community", the rejection of non-exiles, and social division over the
nature of Judean restoration, is dismissed. Since the repatriates cannot be considered to be "theocrats", living under the authority of
the Torah and priests, excluding all "foreigners" from their number
and rejecting those Judeans who had not gone into exile, claims

regarding putative social division between them and any other group
in early Achaemenid Judah over the temple rebuilding founder. The
temple was not rebuilt to legitimate and entrench social division.
While it is true that Babylonian Judean literary texts display different
conceptions of the restoration of Judah (Deutero-Isaiah; Ezekiel 40–48;
texts expecting the renewal of the Davidic monarchy), there is no
reason to suppose that these represent "parties" whose differences
hardened into social conflict upon their arrival in Judah.

As a late, tendentious text which has little first-hand knowledge
the period it recounts, Ezr 1:1–4:5 places into the early period of
the restoration anachronistic concerns which reflect the author's
understanding of the character of Achaemenid Judean society current in his own day. Since this narrative is not a reliable historical
source for the supposed attempted temple rebuilding in the reign of
Cyrus, its claim that there was conflict between the repatriates and
"the people of the land" (both Judeans who never went into exile
and Samarians) must be discounted. The notion of conflict between
Judeans and Samarians belongs to the fourth century at the earliest
and has been read back into the early Persian period by this text.
Neither Haggai and Zechariah 1–8 nor Ezr 5–6, the latter being
the narrative of the temple rebuilding in the reign of Darius, know
of conflict between the repatriates and either the Samarians or non-
repatriated Judeans. Attempts to buttress the historical veracity of
Ezr 1:1–4:5 through the contention that the rebuilding attempt reflects
an Achaemenid Persian administrative policy were investigated and
found wanting, although it is reasonable to argue that the temple
rebuilding was sanctioned by the administration as the Aramaic version of the Cyrus edict (Ezr 6:2–5) and the Aramaic narrative of
the temple rebuilding in Ezra (Ezr 5–6) claim. Permission to rebuild
would not have been limited to Judeans in Babylonian exile, yet it
is unlikely that any work was done on the temple under Sheshbazzar
with whom some Judeans, together with the temple vessels, were
repatriated in the reign of Cyrus. The delay in the rebuilding was
not due to putative social division or the interference of Samarian
officials, but was rather due in part to lack of interest in the project by the Achaemenid Persian administration. Further, Haggai
1:2–11 and Zechariah 1:12–17 display a view of the Judeans' commitment to the temple rebuilding rather different from Ezr 1–3 with
the reasons for it not being built in the reign of Cyrus based on
ideological concerns regarding the need for both a legitimate tem-

ple rebuilder and the determination of the divinely propitious "time" to rebuild the temple.

The view that the temple was rebuilt as a result of an Achaemenid Persian administrative policy pertaining to subjugated peoples and their cults is at best only partly correct. Cyrus and Darius did not pursue a consistent, empire-wide policy in respect of these cults and temple rebuilding did not form part of any administrative reform by either of them. The rebuilding of the Jerusalem temple would have needed administrative permission, but as a minor shrine the Achaemenid Persian bureaucracy was neither interested to ensure that it was rebuilt nor funded its rebuilding, particularly since such activities were held to be the responsibility of the local community. The proposition of the Meyerses and J. P. Weinberg that the temple was rebuilt on the initiative of the Achaemenid Persian administration as a means of establishing the temple as the economic or administrative centre of Achaemenid Judah, confirming as a result the separation between the repatriates and "the people of the land", should be set aside. Similarly to be set aside is the claim of others that the temple was rebuilt without the permission of the Achaemenid Persian administration as an act of Judean rebellion. Temptations to read into the period of the rebuilding the roles of the temple attested in the late Persian and Hellenistic periods should be resisted. One cannot speak of a consistent Achaemenid Persian policy either towards the cults of subjugated peoples or regarding the roles those shrines played in the imperial administration. The development of the Jerusalem temple as an administrative and economic centre should be understood within the context of the administrative (re)organization of later Achaemenid Persian kings, not as part of the early Achaemenid's granting of permission to rebuild. The Jerusalem temple was not only a "minor" shrine in the eyes of the early Achaemenid monarchs, it also played no immediate role in the administration of the sub-province.

The temple was a centre, but of a symbolic kind. Its rebuilding represented for Judeans the end of the divine ire that brought about the dissolution of the kingdom of Judah, the exile of sections of the Judean population, and the divine abandonment of Jerusalem. It reestablished Judeans as a people living in their homeland under the direction of their national god who was enthroned once again as the sovereign divine king. Under the notions of historical recurrence there was a common expectation that the deity's anger would abate

and he would turn again to his people. Deutero-Isaiah and Ezekiel
40–48 clearly thought this, as did Haggai and Zechariah 1–8, although
they differed on their understanding of the divine timetable. The
return of Yahweh to his temple residence in Jerusalem, the concomitant repatriation of (eventually all) exiles, and the reinstatement
of cultic, political and social normalcy, was an ideological necessity.
Yahweh's sovereignty was under question unless he was able to
accomplish this. But since rebuilding needed a legitimate overseer,
the lack of such coupled with no other tangible signs that Yahweh's
ire had abated, meant that in the reign of Cyrus those in Judah,
repatriates and non-repatriates alike, would not take advantage the
permission to rebuild. In contradistinction to Ezr 1:1–4:5, it was the
Judean people themselves who let the rebuilding project lapse.

The reign of Darius saw a renewed impetus for the work, not due
to an administrative policy per se, but as an outcome of the administration's decision to send Zerubbabel, a Davidide, to Judah as its
governor. The prophets Haggai and Zechariah convinced their fellow Judeans (who included both repatriates and non-repatriates) that
the second year of Darius I was in fact the divinely propitious "time"
to rebuild and that it was marked by the arrival of Zerubbabel in
Jerusalem, his membership of the Judean royal house marking him
as a legitimate temple rebuilder. The impetus for the temple rebuilding did not come from those who returned with Zerubbabel and
Joshua c. 520 nor from an Achaemenid Persian administrative policy, since Zerubbabel and Joshua were not repatriated in order to
rebuild the temple. Rather, it came from Judeans already living in
their homeland when Zerubbabel, Joshua and others returned, the
Achaemenid Persian bureaucracy having established a favourable
context for Judeans to undertake the work themselves. Temple rebuilding was thus undertaken by both repatriates and non-repatriates,
which belies the claim that division between these two groups was
the social context of the rebuilding.

The relationship of the Achaemenid Persian administration to the
temple rebuilding and its impact on temple ideology must also be
considered. While Judah appears to have been a separate sub-province
of the Achaemenid Persian empire at the time of the temple rebuilding in the reign of Darius, the temple was not rebuilt in order to
establish either a semi-autonomous national-ethnic polity under indigenous leaders and traditional institutions and laws or a new separatist,
socio-economically privileged polity within the sub-province (for exam-

ple, a Bürger-Tempel-Gemeinde). The prophets Haggai and Zechariah understand the temple rebuilding to be the first step to the re-establishment of an independent kingdom of Judah. This is the polity that the temple will eventually serve, although for now the kingdom is only nascent. As the building of temples in the ancient Near East was a significant act symbolically, socially, and politically, the problem of developing an ideology to justify and legitimate the rebuilding of this former monarchical shrine in Achaemenid Judah was one that had to have been addressed by Judeans. The temple ideology in Haggai and Zechariah 1–8 can be understood as an attempt to remain in continuity with monarchical period ideas of the temple while reworking these traditions for a changed political context. Temple rebuilding, while extolling the sovereignty of Yahweh, was not an act of rebellion; rather, it was the first episode in the restoration of Judah. Temple rebuilding would precede indigenous kingship and Yahweh himself would bring about the renewal of the kingdom of Judah. Judeans would not have to do it by force of their own arms. These prophets thus share restoration hopes with post-monarchical texts expecting the renewal of indigenous kingship, but they also share with Deutero-Isaiah and Ezekiel 40–48 the possibility of reworking the monarchical royal-state ideology. The role of Zerubbabel both as the legitimate temple rebuilder in the eyes of the Judeans and as the Judean governor appointed by the Achaemenid Persian administration is central in understanding how the rebuilding could proceed in a manner which was ideologically acceptable to Judeans and politically acceptable to the Achaemenid Persians. He could present the rebuilding to the administration as being conducted under their auspices and control. Temple rebuilding served both his and Joshua the high priest's political goals as it legitimated their position in the community as Yahweh's chosen leaders. Further, both recognized that temple rebuilding was a socially symbolic activity which would integrate the recent repatriates and those who were already in the land. The symbolic significance of the temple and the ideology underpinning the temple rebuilding are particularly pertinent in this regard since they were drawn from traditions common to both groups. The social and political reasons why Zerubbabel and Joshua decided to participate in the rebuilding are thus related to social integration and also to political legitimation.

Haggai and Zechariah 1–8 exhibit many features in continuity with the monarchical period conceptions of Judean identity and frame

restoration hopes in terms of a reworked monarchical period royal-
state ideology. While these texts are unlikely to be directly dependent on either Deutero-Isaiah or Ezekiel 40–48, their common concern
to articulate a return to cultic, social, political "normalcy"—variously
construed to be sure, but all dependent on monarchical period ideologies—in the aftermath of the destruction of the kingdom of Judah
emphasizes continuity between monarchical, post-monarchical and
early Achaemenid period conceptions of Judean identity. Notions of
social division and separatism do not feature in these texts. The
return to normalcy was necessary, not only because divine anger had
to be followed by restoration, but also because Yahweh had to prove
his sovereignty over the affairs of his people. Notions of historical
recurrence, drawing on ideological concerns regarding the return of
Yahweh to Jerusalem and the re-establishment of his divine sovereignty, emphasize continuity between monarchical and post-monarchical (early Achaemenid) Judah in conceptions of Judean identity
that reach into the late Achaemenid Persian, Hellenistic and Roman
periods. Many of those arguing for various forms of conflict surrounding the temple rebuilding contend that the end of the kingdom of Judah and the exile marked a radical disjuncture in the
history and conception of "Israel". A completely new "Israel", characterized by the authority of the priesthood and the Torah—that is,
"Israel" as a cultic community—arose from the ashes of the kingdom of Judah among the Babylonian exiles. Social organization,
authority structures and the definition of Judean identity were all
recast. The historiographic reconstruction of the Persian period set
forth in Ezra-Nehemiah is one of the well-springs for this understanding. However, these notions have been anachronistically read
back into the community of the Babylonian exiles in order to establish the background to the understanding of early Achaemenid society propagated in Ezr 1:1–4:5. It may well be the case that new
constructions of Judean identity, which issued in social division, were
introduced into Judah from the Babylonian Judean community with
the arrival of Nehemiah and/or Ezra. This topic was not touched
upon in the present work and it also demands further study. Given
that Ezra-Nehemiah is undoubtedly a late text in the form we now
have it (probably to be dated to the end of the Achaemenid Persian
period or the Hellenistic period), it may well be that the concerns
it reflects at the time of the missions of Ezra and Nehemiah are
anachronistic also. In any case, the present study has argued that

the immediate post-monarchical period and the early Achaemenid Persian period should be marked off as a distinct historical period, the interpretation of which should not be undertaken in the light of concerns, such as social conflict, evident in later texts.

The emphasis of the present work on the continuity of ideological concerns for restoration should not be construed as reflecting a commitment on my part to idealist historiography. On the one hand, the argument has attempted to reflect what I believe to be the emphases in the contemporary sources themselves against modern historiographic constructs developed from the late source Ezra-Nehemiah. On the other hand, an attempt was made to ground the temple ideology of Haggai and Zechariah in contemporary social and political realities. It was argued, for example, that these prophets take cognizance of the fact that although the temple rebuilding ushered in a new age for Israel, it was not an act of Judean rebellion. Further, since the two main theories of temple rebuilding were rejected, namely that it was undertaken as the result of an Achaemenid Persian administrative policy initiative or as an act of Judean rebellion, an alternative understanding of the social context of the rebuilding was offered which explained Haggai's and Zechariah's call to rebuild in the context of their roles as prophets of a millenarian or revitalization movement, the former prophet having temporal priority and being prompted by the arrival of Zerubbabel, a legitimate temple rebuilder. In concert with the rejection of social division as the context of the rebuilding, this argument was related to the fact that those already living in Judah at the repatriation of Zerubbabel, Joshua and others gave impetus to the temple rebuilding, leading to the conclusion that the temple rebuilding was undertaken as a means of integrating repatriates and those Judeans already in the homeland. This interpretation of the purpose of the temple rebuilding would seem to gain further credence from the fact that Haggai, a text from a prophet who was already living in Judah, and Deutero-Isaiah, Ezekiel 40–48, and Zechariah 1–8, texts by Babylonian Judeans, all share a common temple ideology. Further, it also highlights the importance of ideology, specifically temple ideology and the ideology of the kingship of Yahweh, in understanding this period. Since Zerubbabel did not return in order to rebuild the temple, his and Joshua's participation in the rebuilding project was interpreted as being politically and socially advantageous to them, not the least because it legitimated their positions of leadership in the Judean community. It was also argued that Zerubbabel had an important role in mediating between Judean expectations and the Achaemenid Persian administration. While Haggai and Zechariah are millenarian prophets, Zerubbabel's dual role as legitimate temple rebuilder and the Achaemenid Persian appointed *peḥāh* brings the temple rebuilding under the control of the Achaemenid Persian administration. It is, to use Weberian terms, a classic example of the routinization of charisma. How successful this attempt at social integration was may be impossible to determine since for the generations after the temple rebuilding our only source is Ezra-Nehemiah.

The historiographic reconstruction of the present work thus gives a much greater role both to those Judeans who had remained in the land and to Zerubbabel than has hitherto been done. In this reconstruction the Achaemenid Persian administration, in regard to the temple rebuilding at least, are cast in a more passive role. They sanction the rebuilding rather than initiate it, leaving the Judeans to determine when and how to undertake the project. As noted above, these issues are presented in Haggai and Zechariah as being fundamentally ideological concerns—how to determine that the deity's ire has passed and that he wishes to return to a rebuilt shrine in his city. This study has also given priority to those texts which date to the period of the temple rebuilding (namely, Haggai and Zechariah 1–8), rather than to later, tendentious accounts of the period (such as Ezr 1:1–4:5). Texts generated before the period of the temple rebuilding (such as prophetical texts from the Babylonian Judean community) are, however, helpful in identifying issues and concerns upon which the Judean community reflected arising from the dissolution of the kingdom of Judah. These texts can be used to inform the interpretation of Haggai and Zechariah 1–8. Haggai and Zechariah are also tendentious texts. It should not be assumed that their understanding of the purpose and social context of the Jerusalem temple rebuilding exhausts historical explanation. Their importance lies in the fact that as sources contemporary with the temple rebuilding they can be used to correct interpretations derived from later texts, such as Ezra, and they heighten our awareness of ideological issues which Judeans had to address in order to undertake the rebuilding of the temple.

Haggai and Zechariah 1–8 hold out expectations for the renewal of Israel that were not fully realized. Kingdoms were not overturned, nor was Yahweh's sovereignty universally recognized. Zerubbabel did not become king (or on one reading of Zechariah, Zerubbabel and Joshua share the rule), all the exiles did not come home. The Jerusalem cult was reinstituted and one assumes it was accepted that Yahweh had returned to Jerusalem. The divine ire had abated, but the new age had not fully dawned. What was the reaction to this? While much has been made by some of the centrality of the Jerusalem temple in Achaemenid Judean society, there is some evidence to suggest that once it was recognized that expectations for renewal were not going to be met, the temple may have become a socially marginalized institution—Malachi attests a level of unconcern for the temple cult; in Neh 10 the temple has a funding crisis; in Neh 13 Nehemiah complains "Why is the house of God forsaken" (Neh 13:11), in part referring to lack of payment of tithes; Chronicles, if it is to be read as a work separate from Ezra-Nehemiah, has been interpreted as a plea for renewed community commitment to the temple.[1] The failure of expectations undoubtedly gave rise to the recriminations of Trito-Isaiah.

It is improper to attempt to judge the rebuilding of the Jerusalem temple in the reign of Darius a "success" or a "failure". It is true to say, however, that the existence of the rebuilt temple gave rise to a further set of ideological problems rather than answering those posed by the dissolution of the kingdom, as was hoped it would have. One of these problems is expressed by Daniel Schwartz:

> The central problem of the Second Temple period was the contradiction between the existence of the Temple in Jerusalem, which seemed to be the palace of a sovereign in the capital of his state, and the fact of foreign sovereignty.[2]

As the ancient sources attest, this problem generated much discussion in the later Persian, Hellenistic and Roman periods. There is a second, related matter. Why was the exile continuing? Why had so few exiled Judeans availed themselves of opportunities afforded by the Achaemenid Persian administration to return to their homeland? I believe that it is in defence of the continuing eastern diaspora that Ezra-Nehemiah came to be written. The Jerusalem temple

---

[1] Braun, "The Message of Chronicles: Rally 'Round the Temple," 502–14.

[2] D. R. Schwartz, *Studies in the Jewish Background of Christianity* (Wissenschaftliche Untersuchungen zum Neuen Testament 60; Tübingen: J. C. B. Mohr [Paul Siebeck], 1992) 9–10; this quotation is in italics in the original.

is still their temple, even though most of them live outside the homeland, and their representatives, the repatriates, manage it on their
behalf. It is for this reason that the repatriates were called upon to
keep themselves separate from those they found in the land, for their
larger community resides in the Babylonian diaspora not among
those found living in the homeland on their return. Those in the
diaspora need a continuing community of their own in the homeland to legitimate their identity and thus they attempt to manipu-
late the triangular nexus between the repatriates, the peoples of the
land, and those still in exile. Haggai and Zechariah, like Deutero-
Isaiah and Ezekiel 40–48 before them, could not have adopted such
views since they considered the divine ire to be abating, marked in
their day by the temple's reconstruction. It was only when the
expected "new age" did not eventuate that there proved to be a
need to articulate new forms of post-monarchical Judean identity.
Attaining the goals envisaged in rebuilding the Jerusalem temple of
Yahweh thus proved to be much more problematic than these prophets
of restoration were able to recognize.

BIBLIOGRAPHY

Abadie, P. "Ancien Testament III. Où en est aujourd'hui la recherche sur l'historiographie du Chroniste?" *Transeu* 1 (1989): 170–76.

Ackroyd, P. R. "Two Old Testament Historical Problems of the Early Persian Period." *JNES* 17 (1958): 23–27.

———. *Exile and Restoration: A Study of Hebrew Thought of the Sixth Century B.C.* London: SCM, 1968.

———. "Historians and Prophets." *SEÅ* 33 (1968): 37–54.

———. *Israel under Babylon and Persia.* New Clarendon Bible. Oxford: Oxford University Press, 1970.

———. "The Temple Vessels: A Continuity Theme." In *Studies in the Religion of Ancient Israel*, 166–81. VTSup 23. Leiden: E. J. Brill, 1972.

———. "The Theology of the Chronicler." *Lexington Theological Quarterly* 8 (1973): 110–16.

———. "Historical Problems of the Early Achaemenian Period." *Orient* 20 (1984): 1–15.

Adas, M. *Prophets of Rebellion: Millenarian Protest Movements against European Colonial Order.* Chapel Hill: The University of North Carolina Press, 1979.

Ahlemann, F. "Zur Esra-Quelle." *ZAW* 59 (1942–43): 77–98.

Ahlström, G. W. *Aspects of Syncretism in Israelite Religion.* Horae Soederblomianae V. Lund: Gleerup, 1963.

———. *Joel and the Temple Cult of Jerusalem.* VTSup 21. Leiden: E. J. Brill, 1971.

———. "Heaven on Earth—at Hazor and Arad." In *Religious Syncretism in Antiquity*, 67–83. Edited by B. A. Pierson. Missoula, MT: Scholars Press, 1975.

———. *Royal Administration and National Religion in Ancient Palestine.* Studies in the History of the Ancient Near East 1. Leiden: E. J. Brill, 1982.

———. *An Archaeological Picture of Iron Age Religions in Palestine.* Studia orientalia 55.3. Helsinki: Societas Orientalis Fennica, 1984.

———. "Some Aspects of the Historical Problems of the Early Persian Period." *Proceedings, Eastern Great Lakes Biblical Society* 4 (1984): 54–65.

———. *Who were the Israelites?* Winona Lake, IN: Eisenbrauns, 1986.

———. *The History of Ancient Palestine from the Palaeolithic Period to Alexander's Conquest.* With a contribution by G. O. Rollefson. Edited by D. Edelman. JSOTSup 146; Sheffield: JSOT Press, 1993.

Albertz, R. *A History of Israelite Religion in the Old Testament Period.* 2 vols. Translated by J. Bowdon. London: Scm Press, 1994.

Albrektson, B. *History and the Gods: An Essay on the Idea of Historical Events as Divine Manifestations in the Ancient Near East and in Israel.* ConBOT 1. Lund: Gleerup, 1967.

Albright, W. F. "The Psalm of Habakkuk." In *Studies in Old Testament Prophecy*, 1–18. Th. H. Robinson Festschrift. Edited by H. H. Rowley. Edinburgh: T&T Clark, 1950.

———. *The Biblical Period from Abraham to Ezra.* New York: Harper and Row, 1965.

Alexander, P. S. "Remarks on Aramaic Epistolography in the Persian Period." *JSS* 23 (1978): 155–70.

Allam, S. "Réflections sur le 'code légal' d'Hermopolis dans l'Égypt ancienne." *Chronique d'Égypt* 61 (1986): 50–75.

Allen, N. "The Identity of the Jerusalem Priesthood during the Exile." *Heythrop Journal* 23 (1982): 259–69.

Alt, A. "Die Rolle Samarias bei der Entstehung des Judentums." In *Kleine Schriften zur Geschichte des Volkes Israel*. 3 vols. Munich: C. H. Beck, 1953–59, 2 (1953): 316–37.

———. "Judas Gaue unter Josiah." In *Kleine Schriften zur Geschicte des Volkes Israels*. 3 vols. Munich: C. H. Beck, 1953–59, 2 (1953): 276–88.

Alter, R. *The Art of Biblical Narrative*. New York: Basic Books, 1981.

Amir, Y. "θεωκρατία as a Concept of Political Philosophy: Josephus' Presentation of Moses' *Politeia*." *Scripta Classica Israelica* 8–9 (1985–88): 83–105.

Amsler, S. "Zacharie et l'origine de l'apocalyptique." In *Congress Volume: Uppsala, 1971*, 227–31. VTSup 22; Leiden: E. J. Brill, 1972.

———. *Aggée, Zacharie 1–8*. Commentaire de l'Ancien Testament 11c. Neuchâtel/Paris: Delachaux and Niestlé, 1981.

Anderson, B. W. "Exodus Typology in Second Isaiah." In *Israel's Prophetic Heritage: Studies in Honor of James Muilenburg*, 177–95. Edited by B. W. Anderson and W. Harrelson. New York: Harper, 1962.

———. *Understanding the Old Testament*. 4th ed. Englewood Cliffs, NJ: Prentice-Hall, 1986.

Andersen, F. I. "Who Built the Second Temple?" *ABR* 6 (1958): 1–35.

Anderson, G. *Sacrifices and Offerings in Ancient Israel: Studies in their Social and Political Importance*. HSM 41. Atlanta: Scholars Press, 1987.

Andreasen, N.-E. A. *The Old Testament Sabbath: A Tradition Historical Investigation*. SBLDS 7; Missoula, MT: Society for Biblical Literature, 1972.

Andrews, D. K. "Yahweh the God of the Heavens." In *The Seed of Wisdom: Essays in Honour of T. J. Meek*, 45–57. Edited by W. S. McCullough. Toronto: University of Toronto Press, 1964.

Aperghis, G. "The Persepolis Fortification Tablets—Another Look." In *Studies in Persian History: Essays in Memory of David M. Lewis*, 35–62. Edited by M. Brosius and A. Kuhrt. Achaemenid History XI. Leiden: Nederlands Instituut voor het Nabije Oosten, 1998.

Applegate, J. "Jeremiah and the Seventy Years in the Hebrew Bible: Innerbiblical Reflections of the Prophet and his Prophecy." In *The Book of Jeremiah and its Reception—Le livre Jérémie et sa réception*, 91–110. Edited by A. H. W. Curtis and T. Römer. BETL 128. Leuven: Leuven University Press/Peeters, 1997.

Auerbach, E. "Der Aufsteig der Priesterschaft zur Macht im Alten Israel." In *Congress Volume: Bonn 1960*, 236–49. VTSup 9. Leiden: E. J. Brill, 1962.

Avigad, N. "Two Hebrew Inscriptions on Wine Jars." *IEJ* 22 (1972): 1–9.

———. *Bullae and Seals from a Post-Exilic Judean Archive*. Qedem 4. Jerusalem: Hebrew University Press.

Avishur, A. *Stylistic Studies of Word-Pairs in Biblical and Ancient Semitic Literatures*. AOAT 210. Neukirchen-Vluyn: Neukirchener Verlag, 1984.

Avi-Yonah, M. *The Holy Land. From the Persian to Arab Conquest (536 B.C.–A.D. 640): A Historical Geography*. Text Revisions and Toponymic Index by Anson F. Rainey. Grand Rapids: Baker, 1977.

Balcer, J. M. *Sparda By the Bitter Sea: Imperial Interaction in Western Anatolia*. Brown Judaica Studies 52. Chico, CA: Scholars Press, 1984.

———. *Herodotus & Bisitun: Problems in Ancient Persian Historiography*. Historia Einzelschriften 49. Stuttgart: Steiner, 1987.

Baltzer, D. *Ezechiel und Deuterojesaja. Berührungen in der Heilswartungen der beiden großen Exilspropheten*. BZAW 121. Berlin/New York: W. de Gruyter, 1971.

Baltzer, K. "Das Ende des Staates Juda und die Messias-Frage." *Studien zur Theologie der alttestamentlichen Überlieferungen*, 33–43. Edited by R. Rendtorff and K. Koch. Neukirchen-Vluyn: Neukirchener Verlag, 1961.

Barag, D. P. "The Effects of the Tennes Rebellion on Palestine." *BASOR* 183 (1966): 6–12.

———. "Some Notes on a Silver Coin of Johanan the High Priest." *BA* 48 (1985): 166–68.

Barker, M. *The Older Testament: The Survival of Themes from the Ancient Royal Cult in Sectarian Judaism and Early Christianity.* London: SPCK, 1987.

Bar-Kochva, B. *Pseudo-Hecateus, On the Jews: Legitimating the Jewish Diaspora.* Hellenistic Culture and Society 21. Berkeley/Los Angelos/London: University of California Press, 1996.

Barkun, M. *Disaster and the Millennium.* New Haven/London: Yale University Press, 1974.

Barr, J. *Comparative Philology and the Text of the Old Testament.* Oxford: Oxford University Press, 1968.

Barstad, H. M. "On the History and Archaeology of Judah during the Exilic Period. A Reminder." *OLP* 19 (1988): 25–36.

——. *A Way in the Wilderness: The "Second Exodus" in the Message of Second Isaiah.* JSS Monograph 12. Manchester: University of Manchester, 1989.

——. *The Myth of the Empty Land: A Study of the History and Archaeology of Judah During the "Exilic" Period.* Symbolae Osloenses Fasciculi suppletorri 28. Oslo: Scandinavian University Press, 1996.

——. *The Babylonian Captivity of the Book of Isaiah: "Exilic" Judah and the Provenance of Isaiah 40–55.* Oslo: Novus: Instituttet for sammenlignende kulturforskining, 1997.

Bartlett, J. R. "Edom and the Fall of Jerusalem, 587 B.C." *PEQ* 114 (1982): 13–24.

Batten, L. W. *The Books of Ezra and Nehemiah.* ICC. New York: Scribner's, 1913.

Baumgarten, A. I. *The Phoenician History of Philo of Byblos: A Commentary.* EPROER 89. Leiden, E. J. Brill, 1981.

Baumgartner, A. J. *Le prophète Habakuk. Introduction critique et exégèse.* Leipzig: Drugulin, 1885.

Beaulieu, P. A. *The Reign of Nabonidus, King of Babylon 556–539 B.C.* Yale Near Eastern Researches 10. New Haven/London: Yale University Press, 1989.

Becker, J. *Messianic Expectation in the Old Testament.* Translated by D. E. Green. Philadelphia: Fortress, 1980.

Bedford, P. R. "On Models and Texts: A Response to Blenkinsopp and Petersen." In *Second Temple Studies: 1. Persian Period,* 154–62. Edited by P. R. Davies. JSOTSup 117; Sheffield: JSOT, 1991.

——. "Discerning the Time: Haggai, Zechariah and the 'Delay' in the Rebuilding of the Jerusalem Temple." In *The Pitcher is Broken: Memorial Essays for Gösta W. Ahlström,* 71–94. Edited by S. W. Holloway and L. K. Handy. JSOTSup 190. Sheffield: Sheffield Academic Press, 1995.

——. "Early Achaemenid Monarchs and Indigenous Cults: Toward the Definition of Imperial Policy." In *Religion in the Ancient World: New Themes and Approaches,* 17–39. Edited by M. Dillon. Amsterdam: Hakkert, 1996.

——. "Jews at Elephantine." *Australian Journal of Jewish Studies* 13 (1999): 6–23.

Beit-Arieh, I. "New Data on the Relationship between Judah and Edom toward the End of the Iron Age." In *Recent Excavations in Israel: Studies in Iron Age Archaeology,* 125–31. Edited by S. Gitin and W. G. Dever. Annual of ASOR 49. Winona Lake, IN: Eisenbrauns for ASOR, 1989.

Ben Zvi, E. "Inclusion and Exclusion from Israel as Conveyed by the use of the Term 'Israel' in Post-Monarchical Bublical Texts." In *The Pitcher is Broken: Memorial Essays for Gösta W. Ahlström,* 95–149. Edited by S. W. Holloway and L. K. Handy. JSOTSup 190. Sheffield: Sheffield Academic Press, 1995.

——. "The Urban Centre of Jerusalem and the Development of the Literature of the Hebrew Bible." In *Urbanism in Antiquity: From Mesopotamia to Crete,* 194–207. Edited by W. E. Aufrecht, N. A. Mirau, and S. W. Guley. JSOTSup 244. Sheffield: Sheffield Academic Press, 1997.

Berger, P.-R. "Zu den Namen ששבצר und שנאצר." *ZAW* 83 (1971): 98–100.

——. "Der Kyroszylinder mit dem Zusatzfragment BIN II, 32 und die akkadischen Personnenamen im Danielbuch." *ZA* 64 (1975): 192–234.

Berquist, J. L. *Judaism in Persia's Shadow: A Social and Historical Approach.* Minneapolis: Fortress Press, 1995.

——. "The Shifting Frontier: The Achaemenid Empire's Treatment of Western Colonies." *Journal of World-Systems Research* 1/17 (1995): 1–39. [on line] gopher:// csf.colorado.edu/wsystems/journals/

Betlyon, J. W. "The Provincial Government of Persian Period Judea and the Yehud Coins." *JBL* 105 (1986): 633–42.

Bewer, J. A. *Die Text des Buches Ezra.* Göttingen: Vandenhoeck & Ruprecht, 1922.

Beuken, W. A. M. *Haggai—Sacharja 1–8. Studien zur Überlieferungsgeschichte der frühnachexilischen Prophetie.* Studia Semitica Neerlandica 10. Assen: Van Gorcum, 1967.

Beyer, K. *Die aramäischen Texte vom Toten Meer.* Göttingen: Vandenhoeck & Ruprecht, 1984.

——. *The Aramaic Language: Its Distribution and Subdivision.* Translated by J. F. Healey. Göttingen: Vandenhoeck & Ruprecht, 1986.

Beyer, K. and Livingstone, A. "Die neuesten aramäischen Inschriften aus Taima." *Zeitschrift der deutschen morgenländischen Gesellschaft* 137 (1987): 286–88.

Beyse, K.-M. *Serubbabel und die Königserwartungen der Propheten Haggai und Zechariah. Eine historische und traditionsgeschichtliche Untersuchung.* Arbeiten zur Theologie 1/48. Stuttgart: Calwer, 1972.

Bianchi, F. "Le rôle de Zorobabel et de la dynastie davidique en Judée du VIe siècle au IIe siècle av. J.-C." *Transeu* 7 (1994): 153–65.

Bickerman, E. J. "The Edict of Cyrus in Ezra 1." In *Studies in Jewish and Christian History.* 3 vols. AGAJU 9. Leiden: E. J. Brill, 1976–86, 1 (1976): 72–108.

——. *God of the Maccabees: Studies in the Meaning and Origin of the Maccabean Revolts.* Translated by H. R. Moehring. SJLA 32. Leiden: E. J. Brill, 1979.

——. "En marge de l'écrite II. La seconde année de Darius." *RB* 88 (1981): 23–28.

——. "The Diaspora: The Babylonian Captivity." In *CHJ.* 3 vols. Edited by W. D. Davies, L. Finkelstein et al. Cambridge: Cambridge University Press, 1984–99, 1 (1984): 342–58.

——. "The Generation of Ezra and Nehemiah." In *Studies in Jewish and Christian History.* 3 vols. AGAJU 9. Leiden: E. J. Brill, 1976–86, 3 (1986): 299–326.

——. *The Jews in the Greek Age.* Cambridge, MA/London: Harvard University Press, 1988.

Black, J. "The New Year Ceremonies in Ancient Babylon: 'Taking Bel by the Hand' and a Cultic Picnic." *Religion* 11 (1981): 39–54.

Blenkinsopp, J. *Prophecy and Canon: A Contribution to the Study of Jewish Origins.* University of Notre Dame Center for the Study of Judaism and Christianity in Antiquity. Notre Dame/London: University of Notre Dame Press, 1977.

——. "Interpretation and the Tendency to Sectarianism: An Aspect of Second Temple History." In *Jewish and Christian Self-Definition.* 3 vols. Edited by E. P. Sanders with A. I. Baumgarten and A. Mendelson. Philadelphia: Fortress, 1980–83, 2 (1981): 1–26.

——. "The Mission of Udjahorresnet and those of Ezra and Nehemiah." *JBL* 106 (1987): 409–21.

——. *Ezra-Nehemiah.* OTL. Philadelphia: Westminster Press, 1988.

——. "Second Isaiah—Prophet of Universalism." *JSOT* 41 (1988): 83–103.

——. "A Jewish Sect of the Persian Period." *CBQ* 52 (1990): 5–20.

——. "Temple and Society in Achaemenid Judah." In *Second Temple Studies: 1. Persian Period,* 22–53. Edited by P. R. Davies. JSOTSup 117; Sheffield: JSOT Press, 1991.

——. "The Nehemiah Autobiographical Memoir." In *Language, Theology and the Bible: Essays in Honour of James Barr,* 199–212. Edited by S. E. Balentine and J. Barton. Oxford: Clarendon, 1994.

——. *A History of Prophecy in Israel.* Revised ed. Louisville: Westminster John Knox Press, 1996.

——. "An Assessment of the Alleged Pre-Exilic Date of the Priestly Material in the Pentateuch." *ZAW* 108 (1996): 495–518.

——. "The Judean Priesthood during the Neo-Babylonian and Achaemenid Periods: A Hypothetical Reconstruction." *CBQ* 60 (1998): 25–43.

Bloch, H. *Die Quellen des Flavius Josephus in seiner Archäologie.* Leipzig: Teubner, 1879.

Bloch-Smith, E. "'Who is the King of Glory?' Solomon's Temple and its Symbolism." In *Scripture and Other Artifacts: Essays on the Bible and Archaeology in Honor of Philip J. King*, 18–33. Edited by M. D. Coogan, J. C. Exum and L. E. Stager; Louisville: Westminster/John Knox Press, 1994.

Böhler, D. *Die heilige Stadt in Esdras A und Esra-Nehemia. Zwei Konzeptionen der Wiederherstellung Israels.* OBO 158. Freiburg: Universitätsverlag. Göttingen: Vandenhoeck & Ruprecht, 1997.

Boissier, A. "Pacorus ou Xerxès." *ZA* 11 (1896): 83–84.

Boffo, L. "La lettera di Dario a Gadata: I privilegi del tempio di Apolloa Magnesia sul Meandro." *Bulettino dell'Istituto di Diritto Romano, Vittorio Scialoja'* 81 (1978): 267–303.

Bolin, T. M. "When the End is the Beginning: The Persian Period and the Origins of the Biblical Tradition." *SJOT* 10 (1996): 3–15.

Bongenaar, A. C. V. M. *The Neo-Babylonian Ebabbar Temple at Sippar: Its Administration and its Prosopography.* Uitgaven van het Nederlands Historisch-Archaelogisch Instituut te Istanbul 80. Leiden: Nederlands Historisch-Archaelogisch Instituut te Istanbul, 1997.

Borger, R. *Die Inschriften Asarhaddons, Königs von Assyrien. AfO* Beiheft 9. Graz: Weidner, 1956.

——. "An Additional Remark on P. R. Ackroyd, *JNES*, XVII, 23–27." *JNES* 18 (1959): 74.

——. "Gott Marduk und Gott-König Šulgi als Propheten. Zwei prophetische Texte." *BiOr* 28 (1971): 3–24.

——. *Die Chronologie des Darius-Denkmals am Behistun-Felsen.* Göttingen: Vandenhoeck & Ruprecht, 1982.

Bottéro, J. *Mythes et rites de Babylone.* Preface by M. Fleury. Bibothèque de l'École des Hautes Études IVe Section: Sciences Historiques et Philologiques 328. Geneva: Slatkine/Paris: Champion, 1985.

Bowman, R. A. "The Book of Ezra and The Book of Nehemiah." In *The Interpreter's Bible.* 12 vols. Edited by G. A. Buttrick, W. R. Bowie, P. Scherer, J. Knox, S. Terrien, N. B. Harmon. Nashville: Abingdon, 1952–57, 3 (1954): 549–819.

Boyce, M. *A History of Zoroastrianism. Vol. II. Under the Achaemenians.* Handbuch des Orientalistik. Leiden/Cologne: E. J. Brill, 1975.

——. "The Religion of Cyrus the Great." In *Achaemenid History III: Method and Theory*, 15–31. Edited by A. Kuhrt and H. Sancisi-Weerdenburg. Leiden: Nederlands Insituut voor het Nabije Oosten, 1988.

Braun, R. L. "The Message of Chronicles: Rally 'Round the Temple." *Concordia Theological Monthly* 42 (1971): 502–14.

——. "A Reconsideration of the Chronicler's Attitude toward the North." *JBL* 96 (1977): 59–62.

——. "Chronicles, Ezra and Nehemiah: Theology and Literary History." In *Studies in the Historical Books of the Old Testament*, 52–64. Edited by J. A. Emerton. VTSup 30. Leiden: E. J. Brill, 1979.

Bresciani, E. "La satrapia d'Egitto." *Studi classici ed orientali* 7 (1958): 132–88.

——. "Egypt, Persian Satrapy." In *CHJ.* 3 vols. Edited by W. D. Davies, L. Finkelstein et al. Cambridge: Cambridge University Press, 1984–99, 1 (1984): 358–72.

Briant, P. "Forces productives, dépendance rurale et idéologies religieuses dans l'Empire achéménide." In *Rois, tributs et paysans. Etudes sur les formations tributaires du Moyen-Orient ancien*, 456–73. Centre de Recherches d'Histoire Ancienne 43. Paris: Les Belle Lettres, 1982.

——. "Polythéismes et empire unitaire. Remarques sur la politique religieuse des Achéménides." In *Le grandes figures religieuses. Fonctionnement practique et symbolique dans l'antiquité*, 425–43. Edited by P. Lévêque and M. M. Mactoux. Centre de Recherche d'Histoire Ancienne 68. Paris: Les Belle Lettres, 1986.

——. "Ethno-classe dominate et populations soumises dans l'Empire achéménide: le cas de l'Egypt." in *Achaemenid History III: Method and Theory*, 137–73. Edited by H. Sancisi-Weerdenburg and A. Kuhrt. Leiden: Nederlands Instituut voor het Nabije Osten, 1988.

——. *Histoire de l'empire perse de Cyrus à Alexandre*. 2 vols. Achaemenid History 10; Leiden: Nederlands Instituut voor het Nabije Oosten, 1996.

——. "Cités et satrapes dans l'Empire achéménide: Xanthos et Pixôdaros." *CRAIBL* (1998): 305–40.

——. "Droaphernès et la statue de Sardes." In *Studies in Persian History: Essays in Memory of David M. Lewis*, 205–226. Edited by M. Brosius and A. Kuhrt. Achaemenid History XI. Leiden: Nederlands Instituut voor het Nabije Oosten, 1998.

Briend, J. "L'édit de Cyrus et sa valeur historique." *Transeu* 11 (1996): 33–44.

Bright, J. *Covenant and Promise: The Prophetic Understanding of the Future in Pre-Exilic Israel*. Philadelphia: Westminster, 1976.

——. *A History of Israel*. 3rd ed. OTL. Philadelphia: Westminster, 1981.

Brinkman, J. A. "Through a Glass Darkly: Esarhaddon's Retrospects on the Downfall of Babylon." *JAOS* 103 (1983): 35–42.

——. *Prelude to Empire: Babylonian Society and Politics, 747–626 B.C.* Occasional Publications of the Babylonian Fund 7. Philadelphia: The Babylonian Fund, University Museum, 1984.

Broshi, M., and Finkelstein, I. "The Population of Palestine in Iron Azge II." *BASOR* 287 (1992): 47–60.

Browne, L. E. "A Jewish Sanctuary in Babylonia." *JTS* OS 17 (1916): 400–1.

——. *Early Judaism*. Cambridge: The University Press, 1920.

Bucci, O. "L'Impero achemenide come ordinamento giuridico sovrannazionale e *arta* come principo ispiratore di uno 'Jus commune persarum' (*data*)." *Modes de contacts et processus de transformation dans les sociétés anciennes*, 89–122. Rome: École française de Rome, 1983.

Burridge, K. O. L. *New Heaven, New Earth: A Study of Millenarian Activity*. New York: Oxford University Press, 1969.

Busink, Th. A. *Der Tempel von Jerusalem von Salomo bis Herodes. Eine archälogisch-historisch Studie unter Berücksichtigung des westsemitischen Tempelbaus*. 2 vols. Nederlands Instituut voor het Nabije Oosten/Studia Francisci Scholton memoriae dicta 3. Leiden: E. J. Brill, 1970–80.

Cagni, L. "Considérations sur les textes babyloniens de Neirab près d'Alep." *Transeu* 2 (1990): 169–85.

Calmeyer, P. "Zur Genese altiranischer Motive, VIII: Die 'Statistische Landcharte des Perserreiches'—I." *Archaeologische Mitteilungen aus Iran* NF 15 (1982): 105–87.

——. "Die sogenannte fünfte Satrapie und die achaemenidischen Documente." *Transeu* 3 (1990): 109–29.

Cameron, G. G. "The Persian Satrapies and Related Matters." *JNES* 32 (1973): 47–56.

Camp, C. V. *Wisdom and the Feminine in the Book of Proverbs*. Bible and Literature Series 11. Sheffield: Almond, 1985.

Caquot, A., M. Sznycer and A. Herder. *Textes Ougaritiques. Tome 1: Myths et légendes*. Litteratures anciennes du proche-orient 7. Paris: Éditions du Cerf., 1974.

Carroll, R. P. "Twilight of Prophecy or Dawn of Apocalyptic?" *JSOT* 14 (1979): 3–35.

——. "Second Isaiah and the Failure of Prophecy." *Studia Theologica* 32 (1978): 121–24.

——. *When Prophecy Failed: Cognitive Dissonance in the Prophetic Traditions of the Old Testament.* New York: Seabury, 1979.

——. *From Chaos to Covenant: Prophecy in the Book of Jeremiah.* New York: Crossroad, 1981.

——. *Jeremiah: A Commentary.* OTL. London: SCM, 1986.

——. "Prophecy and Society." In *The World of Ancient Israel: Sociological, Anthropological and Political Perspectives*, 203–25. Edited by R. E. Clements. Cambridge: Cambridge University Press, 1989.

——. "Israel, History of (Post-Monarchic Period)." In *The Anchor Bible Dictionary.* 6 vols. Edited by D. N. Freedman. New York: Doubleday, 1992, 3. 567–76.

——. "The Myth of the Empty Land." *Semeia* 59 (1992): 79–93.

——. "So What Do We *Know* about the Temple? The Temple in the Prophets," in *Second Temple Studies: 2. Temple and Community in the Persian Period*, 34–51. Edited by T. C. Eskenazi and K. H. Richards. JSOTSup 175. Sheffield: JSOT Press, 1994.

Carter, C. E. "A Social and Demographic Study of Post-Exilic Judah." Ph.D. Dissertation, Duke University, 1992. Ph.D. Ann Arbor: Univerity Microfilms International.

——. "The Province of Yehud in the Post-Exilic Period: Soundings in Site Distribution and Demography." In *Second Temple Studies: 2. Temple and Community in the Persian Period*, 106–46. Edited by T. C. Eskenazi and K. H. Richards. JSOTSup 175. Sheffield: JSOT Press, 1994.

Cazelles, H. "587 ou 586." In *The Word of the Lord Shall Go Forth*, 427–35. Edited by C. L. Meyers and M. O'Connor. Winona Lake, IN: Eisenbrauns/ASOR, 1983.

Chong, J. H. "Were there Yahwistic Sanctuaries in Babylon?" *Asia Journal of Theology* 10 (1996): 198–217.

Christensen, D. L. *Transformation of the War Oracle in Old Testament Prophecy: Studies in the Oracles Against the Nations.* HDR 3. Missoula, MT: Scholars Press, 1975.

Clements, R. E. *God and Temple.* Oxford: Blackwell, 1965.

Clifford, R. J. *The Cosmic Mountain in Canaan and the Old Testament.* HSM 4. Cambridge, MA: Harvard University Press, 1972.

——. "The Function of Idol Passages in Second Isaiah." *CBQ* 42 (1980): 450–64.

Clines, D. J. A. *I, He, We, and They: A Literary Approach to Isaiah 53.* JSOTSup 1. Sheffield: JSOT Press, 1976.

——. *Ezra, Nehemiah, Esther.* NCB. Grand Rapids: Eerdmans, 1984.

——. "The Nehemiah Memoir: The Perils of Autobiography." In *What Does Eve Do to Help? and Other Readerly Questions to the Old Testament*, 124–64. JSOTSup 44. Sheffield: Sheffield Academic, 1990.

——. "Haggai's Temple, Constructed, Deconstructed and Reconstructed." In *Second Temple Studies: 2. Temple and Community in the Persian Period*, 60–87. Edited by T. C. Eskenazi and K. H. Richards. JSOTSup 175. Sheffield: JSOT Press, 1994.

Coats, G. W. "Despoiling the Egyptians." *VT* 18 (1968): 450–57.

Cocquerillat, D. *Palmeraies et cultures de l'Eanna d'Uruk (559–520).* Ausgrabungen der Deutschen Forschungsgemeinschaft in Uruk-Warka 8. Berlin: Mann, 1968.

——. "Recherches sur le verger du temple campagnard de l'Akitu (KIRI$_6$ ḫallat)." *WdO* 7 (1973): 96–134.

——. "Compléments aux 'Palmeraies et cultures de l'Eanna d'Uruk.'" (I–III) *RA* 75 (1981): 151–69; *RA* 78 (1984): 49–70, 143–67.

Cody, A. "When is the Chosen People called a *gôy*?" *VT* 14 (1964): 1–6.

——. *A History of Old Testament Priesthood.* AnBi 35. Rome: Pontifical Biblical Institute, 1969.

Cogan, M. *Imperialism and Religion: Assyria, Judah and Israel in the Eighth and Seventh Centuries B.C.E.* SBLMS 19. Missoula, MT: Scholars Press, 1974.

———. "Judah Under Assyrian Hegemony: A Re-examination of *Imperialism and Religion.*" *JBL* 112 (1993): 403–14.

Coggins, R.J. *Samaritans and Jews: The Origins of Samaritanism Reconsidered.* Growing Points in Theology. Atlanta: John Knox, 1975.

———. *Haggai, Zechariah, Malachi.* Old Testament Guides. Sheffield: JSOT Press, 1987.

Cohen, H. R. *Biblical Hapaxlegomena in the Light of Akkadian and Ugaritic.* SBLDS 37. Missoula, MT: Scholars Press, 1978.

Cohen, M. E. *The Canonical Lamentations of Ancient Mesopotamia.* 2 vols. Potomac, MD: Capital Decisions Limited, 1988.

Cohen, S. J. D. *Josephus in Galilee and Rome: His Vita and Development as a Historian.* Columbia Studies in the Classical Tradition. Leiden: E. J. Brill, 1979.

Cohn, N. *The Pursuit of the Millennium: Revolutionary Millenarians and Mystical Anarchists of the Middle Ages.* Revised and expanded ed. New York: Oxford University Press, 1970.

Collins, J. J. "The Place of Apocalypticism in the Religion of Israel." In *Ancient Israelite Religion: Essays in Honor of Frank Moore Cross*, 539–58. Edited by P. D. Miller, P. D. Hanson and S. D. McBride. Philadelphia: Fortress, 1987.

———. *The Scepter and the Star: The Messiahs of the Dead Sea Scrolls and Other Ancient Literature.* The Anchor Bible Reference Library. New York: Doubleday, 1995.

———. "Genre, Ideology and Social Movements." In *Seers, Sibyls and Sages in Hellenistic-Roman Judaism*, 25–38. Edited by J. J. Collins. Supplements to *JSJ* 54. Leiden/New York: E. J. Brill, 1997.

———. *The Apocalyptic Imagination: An Introduction to Jewish Apocalyptic Literature.* 2d ed. Grand Rapids, MI: Eerdmans, 1998.

Coogan, M. D. "Life in the Diaspora: Jews at Nippur in the Fifth Century B.C." *BA* 37 (1974): 6–12.

———. *West Semitic Personal Names in the Murašû Documents.* HSM 7. Missoula, MT: Scholars Press, 1976.

Conrad, J. "נדב." In *TWAT.* 5 (1986): 237–45.

Cook, J. M. *The Persian Empire.* New York: Schoken, 1983.

Cook, S. L. *Prophecy and Apocalypticism: The Postexilic Setting.* Minneapolis: Ausburg Fortress, 1995.

Cooper, J. S. *The Curse of Agade.* The Johns Hopkins Near Esatern Studies. Baltimore/London: The Johns Hopkins University Press, 1983.

Coppens, J *Le messianisme royal.* LeDiv 54; Paris: Editions du Cerf, 1968.

Cowley, A. E. *Aramaic Papyri of the Fifth Century.* Oxford: Clarendon, 1923.

Crenshaw, J. *Prophetic Conflict: Its Effect upon Israelite Religion.* BZAW 124. Berlin: W. de Gruyter, 1971.

Cross, F. M. *Cannanite Myth and Hebrew Epic.* Cambridge, MA: Harvard University Press, 1974.

———. "A Reconstruction of the Judean Restoration." *JBL* 94 (1975): 4–18.

———. "A New Aramaic Stele from Tayma'." *CBQ* 48 (1986): 387–94.

Crown, A. D. "Redating the Schism between Judeans and the Samaritans." *Jewish Quarterly Review* 82 (1991): 17–50.

Crüsemann, F. *Der Widerstand gegen das Königtum. Die antiköniglichen Texte des Alten Testamentes und der Kampf um den frühen israelitischen Staat.* WMANT 49. Neukirchen-Vluyn: Neukirchener Verlag, 1978.

Cruz-Uribe, E. *Hibis Temple Project.* San Antonio: TX: Van Siclen Books, 1988.

Cumont, F. *Les religions orientales dans la paganisme romain.* Paris: Librairie Leroux, 1929.

Damrosch, D. *The Narrative Covenant: Transformations of Genre in the Growth of Biblical Literature.* San Francisco: Harper and Row, 1987.

Dandamaev, M. A. "Social Stratification in Babylonia (7th–4th Centuries B.C.),"
    AcAnt 22 (1974): 433–44.
——. "La politique religieuse des Achéménides." In *Hommages et opera minora. Monu-
    mentum H. S. Nyberg*. 3 vols. AcIr 4–6. Tehran/Liège: Bibliothèque Pahlavi, 1975,
    1. 193–200.
——. *Persien unter den ersten Achaemeniden (6. Jahrhundert v. Chr.)*. Translated by H.-D.
    Pohl. Beiträge zur Iranistik 8. Wiesbaden: Reichert, 1976.
——. "State and Temple in Babylonia in the First Millennium B.C." In *State and
    Temple Economy in the Ancient Near East*. 2 vols. Edited by E. Lipiński. OLA 6.
    Leuven: Departement Oriëntalistiek, 1979, 2. 589–98.
——. "The Neo-Babylonian Citizens." *Klio* 63 (1981): 45–49.
——. "The Neo-Babylonian Elders." In *Societies and Languages of the Ancient Near
    East. Studies in Honour of I. M. Diakonoff*, 38–41. Warminster: Aris and Phillips,
    1982.
——. "Aliens and the Community in Babylonia in the 6th–5th Centuries B.C."
    Recueils de la Société Jean Bodin 41 (1983): 133–45.
——. *Slavery in Babylonia: From Nabopolassar to Alexander the Great (626–331 B.C.)*.
    Revised ed. Translated by V. A. Powell. Edited by M. A. Powell with D. B.
    Weisberg co-editor. De Kalb, IL: Northern Illinios Univerity Press, 1984.
——. "The Neo-Babylonian Popular Assembly." In *Šulmu: Papers on the Ancient Near
    East Presented at International Conference of Socialist Countries*, 63–71. Edited by P. Vav-
    rousek and V. Soucek. Prague: Charles University, 1988.
——. *A Political History of the Achaemenid Empire*. Translated by W. J. Vogelsang.
    Leiden: E. J. Brill, 1989.
Dandamaev M. A. and V. Lukonin, *The Culture and Social Institutions of Ancient Iran*.
    Translated by P. L. Kohl with D. J. Dadson. Cambridge: Cambridge University
    Press, 1989.
Davies, P. R. "The Social World of Apocalyptic Writings." In *The World of Ancient
    Israel: Sociological, Anthropological and Political Perspectives*, 251–71. Edited by R. E.
    Clements. Cambridge: Cambridge University Press, 1989.
——. *In Search of Ancient Israel*. JSOTSup 148. Sheffield: JSOT Press, 1992.
Day, J. *God's Conflict with the Dragon and the Sea: Echoes of a Canaanite Myth in the Old
    Testament*. Cambridge: Cambridge University Press, 1985.
Day, P. *An Adversary in Heaven: śāṭān in the Hebrew Bible*. HSM 43. Atlanta: Scholars, 1988.
Del Olmo Lete, G. *Mitos y leyendas de Canaan. Segun la tradicion de Ugarit*. Madrid:
    Ediciones Cristiandad, 1981.
Depuydt, L. "Murder in Memphis: The Story of Cambyses's Mortal Wounding of
    the Apis Bull (*ca.* 523 B.C.E.)." *JNES* 54 (1995): 119–26.
Dequeker, L. "Darius the Persian and the Reconstruction of the Jewish Temple in
    Jerusalem (Ezra 4, 23)." In *Ritual and Sacrifice in the Ancient Near East*, 67–92. Edited
    by J. Quaegebeur. OLA 55. Leuven: Peeters, 1993.
——. "Nehemiah and the Restoration of the Temple after Exile." In *Deuteronomy
    and Deuteronomic Literature: Festschrift C. H. W. Brekelmans*, 547–67. BETL 133.
    Leuven: Peeters/Leuven University Press, 1997.
De Vries, S. *Prophet Against Prophet*. Grand Rapids: Eerdmans, 1978.
——. "The Land's Sabbath in 2 Chron 36:21." *Proceedings, Eastern Great Lakes and
    Midwest Biblical Societies* 6 (1986): 96–103.
Dexinger, F. "Limits of Tolerance in Judaism: The Samaritan Example." In *Jewish
    and Christian Self-Definition*. 3 vols. Edited by E. P. Sanders with A. I. Baumgarten
    and A. Mendelson. Philadelphia: Fortress, 1980–83, 2 (1981): 88–114.
Dietrich, M.; Loretz, O.; and Sanmartin, J. *The Cuneiform Alphabetic Texts from Ugarit,
    Ras Ibn Hani and Other Places (KTU)*. 2d enlarged ed. Abhandlung zur Literatur
    Alt-Syrien-Palästinas und Mesopotamiens 8. Münster: Ugarit-Verlag, 1995.

Dijkstra, K. *Life and Loyalty: A Study in the Socio-Religious Culture of Syria and Mesopotamia in the Graeco-Roman Period Based on Epigraphical Evidence.* Religions in the Graeco-Roman World 128. Leiden/New York/Cologne: E. J. Brill, 1995.

Diodorus. *Diodorus of Sicily I.* Translated by C. H. Oldfather. The Loeb Classical Library. Cambridge, MA: Harvard University Press, 1933.

Dion, P. E. "Les types épistolaires hébréo-araméens jusqu'au temps de Bar-Kokhba." *RB* 96 (1979): 544–79.

———. "ששבצר and שנאצר." *ZAW* 95 (1983): 111–12.

———. "The Civic-and-Temple Community of Persian Period Judaea: Neglected Insights from Eastern Europe." *JNES* 50 (1991): 281–87.

Donner, H. *Geschichte des Volkes Israel und seiner Nachbarn in Grundzügen.* 2 vols. ATD Ergänzungsreihe Band 4/1–2. Göttingen: Vandenhoeck & Ruprecht, 1985–6.

van Driel, G. "The Murašûs in Context." *JESHO* 32 (1989): 203–29.

Driver, G. R. "Hebrew Notes." *ZAW* 52 (1934): 51–56.

———. "On עלה 'went up country' and ירד 'went down country.'" *ZAW* 69 (1957): 74–77.

Driver, S. R. *An Introduction to the Literature of the Old Testament.* rev. ed. New York: Scribner's, 1913.

Duchesne-Guillemin, J. "Die Religion der Achämeniden." *AcAnt* 19 (1971): 25–35.

———. "La religion des Achéménides." In *Beiträge zur Achämenidengeschichte,* 59–82. Edited by G. Walser. Historia Einzelinscriften 18. Wiesbaden: Steiner, 1972.

———. "Le dieu de Cyrus." In *Commémoration Cyrus. Hommage Universel.* 3 vols. AcIr 1–3. Tehran/Liège: Bibliothèque Pahlavi, 1974, 3. 11–21.

———. "Sonnenkönigtum und Mazdareligion." In *Kunst, Kultur und Geschichte der Achämenidenzeit und ihr Fortleben,* 135–39. Edited by H. Koch and D. N. Mackenzie. Mitteilungen aus Iran Ergänzungsband 10. Berlin: Reimer, 1983.

Duguid, I. M. *Ezekiel and the Leaders of Israel.* SVT 56. Leiden: E. J. Brill, 1994.

Duke, R. K. "Punishment or Restoration? Another Look at the Levites in Ezekiel 44.6–16." *JSOT* 40 (1988): 61–81.

Dumbrell, W. J. "The Tell El-Maskhuta Bowls and the 'Kingdom' of Qedar." *BASOR* 203 (1971): 33–44.

Durand, M. "La défence du front mediterranéen de l'empire achéménide." *The Role of the Phoenicians in the Interaction of Mediterranean Civilizations,* 43–51. Edited by W. A. Ward. Beirut: American University, 1968.

Dyke, J. E. *The Theocratic Ideology of the Chronicler.* Biblical Interpretation Series 33. Leiden: E. J. Brill, 1998.

Eaton, J. H. "The Psalms and Israelite Worship." In *Tradition and Interpretation: Essays by the Members of the Society for Old Testament Study,* 238–73. Edited by G. W. Anderson. Oxford: Clarendon, 1979.

———. *Festal Drama in Deutero-Isaiah.* London: SPCK, 1979.

———. *Kingship in the Psalms.* 2d ed. The Biblical Seminar. Sheffield: JSOT, 1986.

Ehrlich, A. B. *Randglossen zur Hebräischen Bibel.* 7 vols. Leipzig: Hinrichs, 1908–14.

Eissfeldt, O. "Ba'alšemēm und Jahwe." *ZAW* 57 (1939): 1–31.

———. "The Promises of Grace to David In Isaiah 55:1–5." *Israel's Prophetic Heritage: Studies in Honor of James Muilenburg,* 196–207. Edited by B. W. Anderson and W. Harrelson. New York: Harper, 1962.

———. *The Old Testament: An Introduction.* Translated by P. R. Ackroyd. Oxford: Blackwell, 1965.

Eitan, I. *A Contribution to Hebrew Lexicography.* New York: Columbia University, 1924.

Elayi, J. "Studies in Phoenician Geography during the Persian Period." *JNES* 41 (1983): 83–110.

Engelken, K. "BA'ALŠAMEN—Eine Auseinandersetzung mit der Monographie von H. Niehr." *ZAW* 108 (1996): 233–48, 391–407.

Engnell, I. *Studies in Divine Kingship in the Ancient Near East.* 2d ed. Oxford: Blackwell, 1967.

Eph'al, I. "The Western Minorities in Babylonia in the 6th–5th Centuries B.C.: Maintenance and Cohesion." *Or* NS 47 (1978): 74–90.

——. "On the Political and Social Organization of the Jews in Babylonian Exile." In *XXI. Deutscher Orientalistentag. Vorträge*, 106–12. Edited by F. Steppat. Zeitschrift der Deutschen Morgenländischen Gesellschaft Supplement 5. Wiesbaden: Steiner, 1983.

——. "Syria-Palestine under Achaemenid Rule." In *CAH.* 2d ed. Edited by J. Boardman, N. G. L. Hammond, D. M. Lewis, M. Ostwald. Cambridge: Cambridge University Press, 1970–, 4 (1988): 139–64.

Eskenazi, T. C. *In an Age of Prose: A Literary Approach to Ezra-Nehemiah.* SBLMS 36. Atlanta: Scholars Press, 1988.

——. "The Structure of Ezra-Nehemiah and the Integrity of the Book." *JBL* 107 (1988): 641–56.

Fales, F. M. "Remarks on the Neirab Texts." *Oriens Antiquus* 12 (1973): 131–42.

——. "The Enemy in Assyrian Royal Inscriptions: 'The Moral Judgement.'" In *Mesopotamien und seine Nachbarn. Politische und kulturelle Wechselbeziehungen im Alten Vorderasien vom 4. bis 1. Jahrtausand v. Chr.* 2 vols. Edited by H.-J. Nissen and J. Renger. Berliner Beiträge zum Vorderen Orient 1/1–2; Berlin: Reimer, 1982, 2. 425–35.

Fehr, B. "Zur Geschichte des Apollo-Heiligtums von Didyma." *Marburger Winckelmann-Programm 1971/72*, 14–59. Marburg: Verlag des Kunstgeschichtelichen Seminars, 1972.

Fensham, F. C. "*Peḥâ* in the Old Testament and the Ancient Near East." *Die Oud Testamentiese Werkgemeenskap in Suid-Afrika* 19 (1976): 44–52.

——. *The Books of Ezra and Nehemiah.* NICOT. Grad Rapids: Eerdmans, 1982.

Finkel, I. "No Nineveh in the Cyrus Cylinder," *Nouvelles assyriologiques brèves et utilitaires* 1997/23.

Finkelstein, I. *The Archaeology of the Israelite Settlement.* Jerusalem: Israel Exploration Society, 1988.

Fishbane, M. "Revelation and Tradition: Aspects of Inner-Biblical Exegesis." *JBL* 99 (1980): 343–61.

——. *Biblical Interpretation in Ancient Israel.* Oxford: Clarendon, 1985.

Fitzmyer, J. A. "Aramaic Epistolography." In *A Wandering Aramean: Collected Aramaic Essays*, 183–204. Missoula, MT: Scholars Press, 1979.

——. "The Phases of the Aramaic Language." In *A Wandering Aramean: Collected Aramaic Essays*, 57–84. Missoula, MT: Scholars Press, 1979.

Floyd, M. H. "The Nature of Narrative and the Evidence for Redaction in Haggai." *VT* 45 (1995): 470–90.

Fohrer, G. *Die Hauptprobleme des Buches Ezechiel.* BZAW 72. Berlin: Töpelmann, 1952.

——. *Introduction to the Old Testament.* Translated by D. E. Green. Nashville/New York: Abingdon, 1968.

Foster, R. S. *The Restoration of Israel.* London: Darton, Longman and Todd, 1970.

Frame, G. "The 'First Families' of Borsippa during the Early Neo-Babylonian Period." *Journal of Cuneiform Studies* 36 (1984): 67–80.

——. *Babylonia 689–627 B.C.: A Political History.* Uitgaven van het Nederlands Historisch-Archaelogisch Instituut te Istanbul 69. Leiden: Nederlands Historisch-Archaelogisch Instituut te Istanbul, 1992.

Freedman, D. N. "The Chronicler's Purpose." *CBQ* 23 (1961): 436–42.

——. "The Earliest Bible." *Michigan Quarterly Review* 22 (1983): 167–75.

Frei, P. "Die persische Reichautorisation. Ein Überblick." *ZABR* 1 (1995): 1–35.

——. "Zentralgewalt und Localautonomie im Achämenidenreich." In *Reichsidee und*

Reichsorganisation im Perserriech, 7–131. 2d ed. Edited by P. Frei and K. Koch. OBO 55. Göttingen: Vandenhoeck & Ruprecht, 1996.

Fretheim, T. E. "The Priestly Document: Anti-Temple?" *VT* 18 (1968): 313–29.

Frye, R. N. *The History of Ancient Iran*. Handbuch der Altertumswissenschaft 3/7. Munich: Beck, 1984.

Gadd, C. J. "Inscribed Barrel Cylinder of Marduk-Apla-Iddina II." *Iraq* 15 (1953): 123–34.

———. "The Harran Inscriptions of Nabonidus." *AnSt* 8 (1958): 35–92.

Gadd, C. J. and L Legrain. *Ur Excavation Texts. Vol. I: Royal Inscriptions*. London: British Museum, 1928.

Galil, G. The Babylonian Calendar and the Chronology of the Last Kings of Judah." *Biblica* 72 (1991): 367–78

Galling, K. "The 'Gola List' According to Ezra 2 // Nehemia 7." *JBL* 70 (1951): 149–58.

———. *Studien zur Geschichte Israels im persischen Zeitalter*. Tübingen: Mohr-Siebeck, 1964.

Garbini, G. *History and Ideology in Ancient Israel*. Translated by J. Bowden. New York: Crossroad, 1988.

Gardiner, A. H. "The House of Life." *JEA* 24 (1938): 157–79.

Gaster, M. *The Samaritans: Their History, Doctrines and Literature*. London: Oxford University Press, 1925.

Gelston, A. "The Foundations of the Second Temple." *VT* 16 (1966): 232–35.

Gerbrandt, G. E. *Kingship According to the Deuteronomistic History*. SBLDS 87. Atlanta: Scholars Press, 1986.

Gershevitch, I. "Zoroaster's Own Contribution." *JNES* 23 (1964): 12–38.

Gese, H. *Der Verfassungsentwurf des Ezechiel Kap. 40–48: traditionsgeschichtlich untersucht*. Beiträge zur Historischen Theologie 25. Tübingen: Mohr-Siebeck, 1957.

———. "Anfange und Ende der Apocalyptik dargestellt am Sacharjabuch." *ZThK* 70 (1973): 20–48.

———. *Vom Sinai zum Zion. Alttestamentliche Beiträge zur biblische Theologie*. Beiträge zur evangelischen Theologie 64. Munich: Kaiser, 1974.

———. "Wisdom Literature in the Persian Period." In *CHJ*. 3 vols. Edited by W. D. Davies, L. Finkelstein et al. Cambridge: Cambridge University Press, 1984–99, 1 (1984): 189–218.

de Geus, C. H. J. *The Tribes of Israel: An Investigation into Some of the Presuppositions of Martin Noth's Amphictiony Hypothesis*. Studia Semitica Neerlandica 18. Assen/Amsterdam: Van Gorcum, 1976.

Gibson, J. C. L. *Textbook of Syrian Semitic Inscriptions*. 3 vols. Oxford: Clarendon, 1971–82.

———. *Canaanite Myths and Legends*. 2d ed. Edinburgh: T&T Clark, 1978.

Gnoli, G. "Politique religieuse et conception de la royauté sous les Achéménides." In *Commémoration Cyrus. Hommage Universel*. 3 vols. AcIr 1–3. Tehran/Liège: Bibliothèque Pahlavi, 1974, 2. 117–90.

———. "Sol Persice Mithra." In *Mysteria Mithrae*, 725–40. Edited by U. Bianchi. EPROER 80. Leiden: E. J. Brill, 1979.

Goetze, A. "Esarhaddon's Inscriptions from the Inanna Temple in Nippur." *JCS* 17 (1963): 119–131.

Goldman, M. D. "Misunderstood Polaric Meaning of a Word." *ABR* (1951): 61–63.

Goodblatt, D. *The Monarchic Principle: Studies in Jewish Self-Government in Antiquity*. Texte und Studien zum Antiken Judentum 38; Tübingen: J. C. B. Mohr (Paul Siebeck), 1994.

Gordis, R. "Religion, Wisdom and History in the Book of Esther—A New Solution to an ancient Crux." *JBL* 100 (1981): 359–88.

Gosse, B. *Isaïe 13, 1–14, 23 dans la tradition littéraire du livre d'Isaïe et dans la tradition des oracles contre les nations.* OBO 78. Fribourg: Universitätsverlag/Göttingen: Vandenhoeck & Ruprecht, 1988.

Gottwald, N. K. *The Hebrew Bible: A Socio-Literary Introduction.* Philadelphia: Fortress, 1985.

Gowan, D. E. *Eschatology in the Old Textament.* Philadelphia: Fortress, 1986.

Grabbe, L. L. "Josephus and the Reconstruction of the Judean Restoration." *JBL* 106 (1987): 231–46.

——. "Synagogues in Pre-70 Palestine." *JTS* NS 39 (1988): 401–10.

——. *Judaism from Cyrus to Hadrian, Vol. 1: The Persian and Greek Periods.* Minneapolis: Fortress, 1992.

——. "Who was the Bagoses of Josephus (*Ant.* 11.7.1, §297–301)?" *Transeu* 5 (1992): 49–55.

——. "What was Ezra's Mission?" In *Second Temple Studies: 2. Temple and Community in the Persian Period*, 286–99. Edited by T. C. Eskenazi and K. H. Richards. JSOTSup 175. Sheffield: JSOT Press, 1994.

Graf, D. F. "Greek Tyrants and Achaemenid Politics." *The Craft of the Historian. Essays in Honor of Chester G. Starr*, 79–123. Edited by J. W. Eadie and J. Ober. Lanham, MD: University Press of America, 1985.

——. "Arabia During Achaemenid Times." In *Achaemenid History IV: Centre and Periphery*, 131–48. Edited by H. Sancisi-Weerdenburg and A. Kuhrt. Leiden: Nederlands Instituut voor het Nabije Oosten, 1990.

——. "The Origin of the Nabataeans." *ARAM Periodical* 2 (1990): 45–75.

Graham, J. N. "Vinedressers and Ploughmen." *BA* 47 (1984): 55–58.

Gray, J. *The Biblical Doctrine of the Reign of God.* Edinburgh: T&T Clark, 1979.

Gray, G. B. "The Title 'King of Persia.'" *Expository Times* 25 (1913–14): 245–51.

Grayson, A. K. *Assyrian and Babylonian Chronicles.* Texts from Cuneiform Sources 5. Locust Valley, NY: Augustin, 1975.

Green, M. W. "Eridu in Sumerian Literature." Ph.D. dissertation, University of Chicago, 1975.

Greenberg, M. "The Design and Themes of Ezekiel's Program of Restoration." *Interpretation* 38 (1984): 181–208.

Greenfield, J. C., and Porten, B. *The Bisitun Inscription of Darius the Great: Aramaic Version.* Corpus Inscriptionum Iranicarum 1/5. London: Lund Humphries, 1982.

Greenwood, D. C. "On the Jewish Hope for a Restored Northern Kingdom." *ZAW* 88 (1976): 376–85.

Grelot, P. "Soixante-dix semaines d'années." *Biblica* 50 (1969): 169–86.

Griffiths, J. G. "Egypt and the Rise of the Synagogue." *JTS* NS 38 (1987): 1–15.

Gross, W. "Israel's Hope for the Renewal of the State." *JNSL* 14 (1988): 101–33.

Grunert, S. "Der juristische Papyrus von Hermopolis—Kodex oder Kommentar?" *Altorientalische Forschungen* 10 (1983): 151–90.

Grünwaldt, K. *Exil und Identität. Beschneidung, Passa und Sabbat in der Priesterschrift.* Bonner Biblische Beiträge 85. Frankfurt am Main: Anton Hain, 1992.

Gunneweg, A. H. J. *Leviten und Priester. Hauptlinien der Traditionsbildung und Geschichte des israelitische-jüdischen Kultpersonels.* FRLANT 89. Göttingen: Vandenhoeck and Ruprecht, 1965.

——. "Die aramäische und die hebräische Erzählung über die nachexilische Restauration—ein Vergleich." *ZAW* 94 (1982): 299–302.

——. "הארץ עם—A Semantic Revolution." *ZAW* 95 (1983): 437–40.

——. *Esra.* KAT 19/1. Gütersloh: Mohn, 1985.

Güterbock, H. G. "Die historische Tradition und ihre literische Gestaltung bei Babylonieren und Hethitern bis 1200 (pt. 1)." *ZA* 42 (NS 8) (1934): 1–91.

Habel, N. C. "The Form and Significance of the Call Narratives." *ZAW* 77 (1965): 297–323.

——. "'Yahweh, Maker of Heaven and Earth.' A Study in Criticism." *JBL* (1972): 321–37.

Handley-Schachler, M. "The *lan* Ritual in the Persepolis Fortification Texts." In *Studies in Persian History: Essays in Memory of David M. Lewis*, 195–204. Edited by M. Brosius and A. Kuhrt. Achaemenid History XI. Leiden: Nederlands Instituut voor het Nabije Oosten, 1998.

Halpern, B. "The Ritual Background of Zechariah's Temple Song." *CBQ* 40 (1978): 167–90.

———. "A Historiographic Commentary on Ezra 1–6: Achronological Narrative and Dual Chronology in Israelite Historiography." In *The Hebrew Bible and Its Interpreters*, 81–142. Edited by W. H. Propp, B. Halpern, and D. N. Freedman. Winona Lake, IN: Eisenbrauns, 1990.

Hanhart, R. "Zu Text und Textgeschichte des ersten Esrabuches." In *Proceedings of the Sixth World Congress of Jewish Studies*, 201–12. Edited by A. Shinan. Jerusalem: World Union of Jewish Studies, 1977.

Hanson. P. D. *The Dawn of Apocalyptic: The Historical and Sociological Roots of Jewish Apocalyptic Eschatology*. Revised ed. Philadelphia: Fortress, 1979.

———. *A People Called: The Growth of Community in the Bible*. San Francisco: Harper and Row, 1987.

———. "Israelite Religion in the Early Postexilic Period." In *Ancient Israelite Religion: Essays in Honor of Frank Moore Cross*, 485–508. Edited by P. D. Miller, P. D. Hanson and S. D. McBride. Philadelphia: Fortress, 1987.

Haran, M. "Priests and Priesthood." In *Encyclopaedia Judaica*. 16 vols. Jerusalem: Keter, 1971, 13. 1069–86.

———. *Temple and Temple Service in Ancient Israel: An Inquiry into the Character of Cult Phenomena and the Historical Setting of the Priestly School*. Oxford: Clarendon, 1978.

———. "The Law-Code of Ezekiel xl–xlviii and Its Relation to the Priestly School." *HUCA* 50 (1979): 45–71.

———. "Behind the Scenes of History: Determining the Date of the Priestly Source." *JBL* 100 (1981): 321–33.

Harmatta, J. "The Literary Pattern of the Babylonian Edict of Cyrus." *AcAnt* 19 (1971): 217–49.

Hasel, G. F. *The Remnant: The History and Theology of the Remnant Idea from Genesis to Isaiah*. 2d ed. Andrews University Monograph Studies in Religion 5. Berrien Springs, MI: Andrews University, 1974.

———. "The Book of Daniel and Matters of Language." *AUSS* 19 (1981): 211–25.

Hausmann, J. *Israels Rest. Studien zum Selbstverstandnis der nachexilischen Gemeinde*. BWANT 124. Stuttgart: Kohlhammer, 1987.

Hawkins, J. D. "The Neo-Hittite States in Syria and Anatolia." In *CAH*. 2d ed. Edited by J. Boardman, I. E. S. Edwards, N. G. L. Hammond, E. Sollberger. Cambridge: Cambridge University Press, 1970–, 3/1 (1982): 388–435.

Hayes, J. H. "The Tradition of Zion's Inviolability." *JBL* 82 (1963): 419–26.

Heinz, K. "Religion und Politik in Vorderasien im Reich der Achämeniden." *Klio* 69 (1987): 317–25.

Heltzer, M. "The Story of Suzanna and the Self-Government of the Jewish Community in Achaemenid Babylonia." *Annali dell'Institute Orientale di Napoli* 41 (1981): 35–39.

Hensley, L. V. *The Official Persian Documents in the Book of Ezra*. Unpublished Ph.D. thesis, University of Liverpool, 1977.

Hentschke, R. *Die Stellung der vorexilischen Schriftpropheten zum Kultus*. BZAW 75. Berlin: Töpelmann, 1957.

Herder, A. *Corpus des tablettes en cunéiformes alphabétiques découvertes à Ras Shamra-Ugarit de 1929 à 1939*. Mission de Ras Shamra 10. Paris: Imprimerie Nationale/Geuthner, 1963.

Herodotus, *Herodotus*. 4 vols. Translated by A. D. Godley. The Loeb Classical Library. Cambridge, MA: Harvard University Press, 1920–25/London: Heinemann, 1920–25.

Herrenschmidt, C. "La religion des Achéménides: État de la question." *Studia Iranica* 9 (1980): 325–39.

Herrmann, S. *Die prophetischen Heilserwartungen im Alten Testament. Ursprung und Gestaltwandel.* BWANT 85. Stuttgart: Kohlhammer, 1965.

———. *A History of Israel in Old Testament Times.* 2d ed. Revised and enlarged. Translated by J. Bowden. Philadelphia: Fortress, 1981.

Herzfeld, E. *Altpersische Inschriften.* Archaeologische Mitteilungen aus Iran Ergänzungsband 1. Berlin: Reimer, 1938.

Hiebert, T. *God of My Victory: The Ancient Hymn of Habakkuk 3.* HSM 38. Atlanta: Scholars Press, 1986.

Hildebrand, D. R. "Temple Ritual: A Paradigm for Moral Holiness in Haggai II 10–19." *VT* 39 (1989): 154–68.

Hilprecht H. V. and A. T. Clay, *Business Documents of Murashû Sons of Nippur.* The Babylonian Expedition of the University of Pennsylvania, Series A: Cuneiform Texts 9. Philadelphia: Department of Archaeology and Palaeontology of the University of Pennsylvania, 1898.

Hinz, W. *Zarathustra.* Stuttgart: Kohlhammer, 1961.

Hölscher, G. "Die Bücher Esra und Nehemia." In *Die Heilige Schrift des Alten Testaments.* 2 vols. 4th ed. Edited by E. Kautzsch and A. Bertholet. Tübingen: J. C. B. Mohr (Paul Siebeck), 1922–23, 2 (1923): 491–562.

Hoffmann, H.-D. *Reform und Reformen. Untersuchungen zu einen Grundthema der deuteronomistischen Geschichtsschreibung.* Abhandlung zur Theologie des Alten und Neuen Testaments 66. Zurich: Theologischer, 1980.

Hoglund, K. "The Achaemenid Context." In *Second Temple Studies: 1. Persian Period,* 54–72. Edited by P. R. Davies. JSOTSup 117; Sheffield: JSOT, 1991.

Holladay, W. L. *Jeremiah.* 2 vols. Hermeneia. Philadelphia: Fortress, 1986–89.

van Hoonacker, A. *Zorobabel et la second temple.* Gent/Leipzig: Engelcke, 1892.

———. "Notes sur l'histoire de la restauration juive." *RB* 10 (1901): 7–10.

Hornblower, S. *Mausolus.* Oxford: Clarendon, 1982.

Houtman, C. "Ezra and the Law: Observations on the Supposed Relationship between Ezra and the Pentateuch." *OTS* 21 (1981) 91–115.

———. *Der Himmel im Alten Testament: Israels Weltbild und Weltanschauung.* OTS 30. London/New York/Cologne: E. J. Brill, 1993.

Hughes, G. R. "The So-called Pherendates Correspondence." In *Grammata Demotika. Festschrift für Erich Lüddeckens zum 15. Juni 1983,* 75–86. Edited by H.-J. Thissen and K.-Th. Zauzich. Würzburg: Gisela Zauzich, 1984.

Hughes, J. *Secrets of the Times: Myth and History in Biblical Chronology.* JSOTSup 66; Sheffield: Sheffield Academic, 1990.

Hurowitz, V. "Another Fiscal Practice in the Ancient Near East: 2 Kings 12:5–17 and a Letter to Esarhaddon (LAS 277)." *JNES* 45 (1986): 289–94.

———. *I Have Built You an Exalted House: Temple Building in Light of Mesopotamian and Northwest Semitic Writings.* JSOTSup 115. JSOT/ASOR Monograph Series 5. Sheffield: JSOT Press, 1992.

Hurvitz, A. *A Linguistic Study of the Relationship between the Priestly Source and the Book of Ezekiel: A New Approach to an Old Problem.* Cahiers de la Revue Biblique 20. Paris: Gabalda, 1982.

———. "Dating the Priestly Source in Light of the Historical Study of Biblical Hebrew. A Century after Wellhausen." *ZAW* 100 (1988): 88–100.

In der Smitten, W. Th. "Nehemias Parteigänger." *BiOr* 29 (1972): 155–57.

———. "Historische Probleme zum Kyrosedikt und zum Jerusalemer Tempelbau von 515." *Persica* 6 (1972–74): 167–75.

———. "Erwängungen zu Nehemias Davidszität." *JSJ* (1975): 41–48.

———. *Gottesherrschaft und Gemeinde. Beobachtungen an Frühformen eines jüdischen Nationalismus in der Spätzeit des Alten Testaments.* Europäische Hochschulschriften 23/42. Frankfurt am Main: Lang, 1974.

Janowski, B. "Das Königtum Gottes in den Psalmen. Bemerkungen zu einem neuen Gesamtentwurf." *ZThK* 86 (1989): 389–454.

Janssen, E. *Juda in der Exilzeit. Ein Beitrag zur Frage der Entstehung des Judentums.* FRLANT 69. Göttingen: Vandenhoeck & Ruprecht, 1956.

Japhet, S. "The Supposed Common Authorship of Chronicles and Ezra-Nehemiah Investigated Anew." *VT* 18 (1968): 330–71.

——. "Sheshbazzar and Zerubbabel. Against the Background the Historical and Religious Tendencies of Ezra-Nehemiah." *ZAW* 94 (1982): 66–98.

——. "People and Land in the Restoration Period." *Das Land Israel in biblischer Zeit,* 103–25. Edited by G. Strecker. Göttingen: Vandenhoeck & Ruprecht, 1983.

——. "Sheshbazzar and Zerubbabel. Against the Background the Historical and Religious Tendencies of Ezra-Nehemiah II." *ZAW* 95 (1983): 218–29.

——. *The Ideology of the Books of Chronicles and Its Place in Biblical Thought.* Translated by A. Barber. BEATAJ 9. Frankfort am Main: Lang, 1989.

——. "'History' and 'Literature' in the Persian Period: The Restoration of the Temple." In *Ah, Assyria . . . Studies in Assyrian Historiography and Ancient Near Eastern Historiography Prestented to Hayim Tadmor,* 174–88. Edited by M. Cogan and I. Eph'al. Scripta Hierosolymitana 33. Jerusalem: Magnes, 1991.

——. "The Temple in the Restoration Period: Reality and Ideology." *Union Seminary Quarterly Review* 44 (1991): 195–251.

Jeremias, C. *Die Nachtgesichte des Sacharja. Untersuchungen zu ihrere Stellung im Zusammenhang der Visionsberichte im Alten Testament und zu ihrem Bildmaterial.* FRLANT 117. Göttingen: Vandenhoeck & Ruprecht, 1977.

Jeremias, J. *Theophanie. Die Geschichte einer alttestamentlichen Gattung.* 2nd. ed. WMANT 10. Neukirchen-Vluyn: Neukirchener Verlag, 1977.

——. *Das Königtum Gottes in den Psalmen. Israels Begegnung mit dem kanaanäischen Mythos in den Jahweh-König-Psalem.* FRLANT 141. Göttingen: Vandenhoeck & Ruprecht, 1987.

Joannès, F. *Textes économiques de la Babylonie récente.* Recherche sur les Civilisations 5. Paris: Éditions Recherche sur les Civilisations, 1982.

——. *Archives de Borsippa, la famille Ea-ilûta-bâni: étude d'un loy d'archives familiales en Babylonie du VIIIe au Ve siècle av. J.-C.* Geneva: Libraire Droz, 1989.

——. "La titulature de Xerxès." *Nouvelles assyriologiques brèves et utilitaires* 37 (1989): 29.

——. "Pouvoirs locaux et organisations du territoire en Babylonie achéménide." *Transeu* 3 (1990): 173–89.

Joannès, F., and Lemaire, A. "Trois tablettes cunéiformes à onomastique ouest-sémitique." *Transeu* 17 (1999): 17–33.

Johnson, A. R. *Sacral Kingship in Ancient Israel.* 2d ed. Cardiff: University of Wales Press, 1967.

Johnson, D. G. *From Chaos to Restoration: An Integrative Reading of of Isaiah 24–27.* JSOTSup 61. Sheffield: Sheffield Academic, 1988.

Jones, D. R. "The Cessation of Sacrifice after the Destruction of the Temple in 586 B.C." *JTS* NS 14 (1963): 12–31.

Joosten, J. *People and Land in the Holiness Code: An Exegetical Study of the Ideational Framework of the Law in Leviticus 17–26.* VTSup 67. Leiden/New York/Cologne: E. J. Brill, 1996.

Jordan, J. *Erster Vorläufiger Bericht über die von der Notgemeinschaft der Deutschen Wissenschaft in Uruk-Warka unternommenen Ausgrabungen.* Abhandlung der Preussischen Akademie der Wissenschaften Jahrgang 1929. Phil.-Hist. Klasse. 7. Berlin: Akademie der Wissenschaft, 1930.

Josephus, *Against Apion.* In *The Life; Against Apion.* Translated by H. St. J. Thackeray. The Loeb Classical Library. Cambridge, MA: Harvard University Press, 1926/ London: Heinemann, 1926.

——. *Jewish Antiquities.* 5 vols. Translated by H. St. J. Thackeray, R. Marcus,

A. Wilkgren, L. H. Feldman. The Loeb Classical Library. Cambridge, MA: Harvard University Press, 1930–65/London: Heinemann, 1930–65.

Jursa, M. *Die Landwirtschaft in Sippar in neubabylonischer Zeit.* AfO Beiheft 25. Vienna: Institut für Orientalistik der Universität Wien, 1995.

———. *Der Tempelzehnt in Babylonien: vom siebenten bis zum dritten Jahrhundert v. Chr.* AOAT 254. Münster: Ugarit-Verlag, 1998.

Kaiser, O. *Introduction to the Old Testament.* Translated by J. Sturdy. Minneapolis: Augsburg, 1975.

Kalimi, I. "Die Abfassungszeit der Chronik—Forschungsstand und Perspektiven." *ZAW* 105 (1993): 222–33.

Kalugila, L. *The Wise King: Studies in Royal Wisdom as a Divine Revelation in the Old Testament and Its Environment.* ConBOT 15. Lund: Gleerup, 1980.

Kapelrud, A. S. "Temple Building, A Task for Gods and Kings." *Or* NS 32 (1963): 56–62.

———. "The Date of the Priestly Code." *Annual of the Swedish Theological Institute* 3 (1964): 58–64.

Katzenstein, H. J. *The History of Tyre: From the Beginning of the Second Millennium B.C.E. until the Fall of the Neo-Babylonian Empire.* 2d ed. Beer Sheva: University of the Negev, 1997.

Kaufmann, Y. *The Religion of Israel from Its Beginnings to the Babylonian Exile.* Translated and abridged by M. Greenberg. Chicago: University of Chicago Press, 1960.

———. *History of the Religion of Israel IV: From the Babylonian Captivity to the End of Prophecy.* Translated by C. W. Efroymson. New York: Ktav, 1977.

Keel, O. *The Symbolism of the Biblical World: Ancient Near Eastern Iconography and the Book of Psalms.* Translated by T. J. Hallett. New York: Crossroad, 1985.

Keel, O., and Uehlinger, C. *Gods, Goddesses and Images of God in Ancient Israel.* Translated by T. H. Trapp. Minneapolis: Fortress, 1998.

Keller, M. *Untersuchungen zur deuteronomisch-deuteronomischen Namenstheologie.* BBB 105. Weinheim: Beltz Athenäum, 1996.

Kellermann, D. "נור." In *Theological Dictionary of the Old Testament.* Edited by G. J. Botterweck and H. Ringgren. Translated by J. T. Willis. Grand Rapids: Eerdmans, 1974–, 2 (1975): 439–49.

Kellermann, U. *Nehemiah. Quellen, Überlieferung und Geschichte.* BZAW 102. Berlin: Töpelmann, 1967.

———. "Erwägungen zum Ezragesetz." *ZAW* 80 (1968): 373–85.

———. *Messias und Gesetz. Grundlinien einer alttestamentlicher Heilerwartung. Einer traditionsgeschichtliche Einführung.* Biblische Studien 61. Neukirchen-Vluyn: Neukirchener Verlag, 1971.

Kent, R. G. *Old Persian: Grammar, Texts, Lexicon.* 2d ed., revised. American Oriental Series 33. New Haven: American Oriental Society, 1953.

Kessler, J. "The Second Year Of Darius and the Prophet Haggai." *Transeu* 5 (1992): 63–84.

———. "*'t* (le temps) en Aggée I 2–4: conflit théologique ou 'sagesse mondaine'." *VT* 48 (1998): 555–59.

Kienitz, F. K. *Die politische Geschichte Ägyptens vom 7. bis zum 4. Jahrhundert vor der Zeitwende.* Berlin: Akademie, 1953.

Kindler, A. "Silver Coins Bearing the Name of Judea from the Early Hellenistic Period." *IEJ* 24 (1974): 73–76.

King, L. *The Seven Tablets of Creation.* 2 vols. London: Luzac, 1902; reprint, New York: AMS, 1976.

Kippenberg, H. G. *Garizim und Synagogue. Traditionsgeschichtliche Untersuchungen zur samaritanische Religion der aramäische Period.* Religionsgeschichtliche Versuche und Vorarbeiten 30. Berlin/New York: W. de Gruyter, 1971.

———. *Religion und Klassenbildung im antiken Judäa. Eine religionssoziologische Studie zum*

Verhältnis von Tradition und gesellschaftlicher Entwicklung. 2nd ed. Studien zum Umwelt des Neuen Testaments 14. Göttingen: Vandenhoeck & Ruprecht, 1981.

Kitchen, K. A. "The Aramaic of Daniel." In *Notes on Some Problems in the Book of Daniel,* 31–79. Edited by D. J. Wiseman. London: Tyndale, 1965.

Klein, R. W. *Israel in Exile. A Theological Interpretation.* Overtures to Biblical Theology. Philadelphia: Fortress, 1979.

——. *Ezekiel: The Prophet and His Message.* Studies on Personalities in the Old Testament. Columbia, South Carolina: University of South Carolina, 1988.

Kleinig, J. W. "Recent Research in Chronicles." *CR:BS* 2 (1994): 43–76.

Kloos, C. *Yhwh's Combat with the Sea: A Canaanite Tradition in the Religion of Ancient Israel.* Amsterdam: G. A. van Oorschot/Leiden: E. J. Brill, 1986.

Knauf, E. A. "The Persian Administration in Arabia." *Transeu* 2 (1990): 201–17.

Knibb, M. A. "Prophecy and the Emergence of the Jewish Apocalypse." In *Israel's Prophetic Heritage: Essays in Honour of Peter R. Ackroyd,* 169–76. Edited by R. Coggins, A. Phillips and M. Knibb. Cambridge: Cambridge University Press, 1982.

Knohl, I. "The Priestly Torah versus the Holiness School: Sabbath and Festivals." *HUCA* 58 (1987): 65–117.

——. *The Sanctuary of Silence: The Priestly Torah and the Holiness School.* Minneapolis: Fortress Press, 1995.

Koch, H. *Die religösen Verhältnisse der Dareizeit: Untersuchungen an Hand der elamischen Persepolistäfelchen.* Göttinger Orientforschungen III/4. Wiesbaden: Harrassowitz, 1977.

Koch, K. *Die Priesterschrift von Exod. xxv bis Lev. xvi.* FRLANT 71. Göttingen: Vandenhoeck & Ruprecht, 1959.

——. "Haggais unreines Volk." *ZAW* 79 (1967): 52–66.

Kochavi, M., ed. *Judea, Samaria and the Golan: Archaeological Survey, 1967–68.* Jerusalem: Carta, 1972. (Hebrew)

Kraeling, E. G. *The Brooklyn Aramaic Papyri.* New Haven: Yale University Press, 1953.

Kraemer, D. "On the Relationship of the Books of Ezra and Nehemiah." *JSOT* 59 (1993): 73–92.

Kraus, H.-J. *Klagelieder (Threni).* BKAT 20. Neukirchen: Kries Moers, 1956.

——. *Worship in Israel: A Cultic History of the Old Testament.* Translated by G. Buswell. Richmond: John Knox, 1966.

——. *Theology of the Psalms.* Translated by K. Crim. Minneapolis: Augsburg, 1986.

Kreissig, H. *Die sozialökonomische Situation in Juda zur Achämenidenzeit.* Schriften zur Geschichte und Kultur des Alten Orients 7. Berlin: Akademie, 1973.

——. "Eine beachtenswerte Theorie zur Organization altvorderorientalischer Tempelgemeinden im Achämenidenreich. Zu J. P. Weinbergs 'Bürger-Tempel-Gemeinde' in Juda." *Klio* 66 (1984): 35–39.

Kümmel, H. M. *Familie, Beruf und Amt in spätbabylonischen Uruk: Prosopographische Untersuchungen zu Berufsgruppen des 6. Jahrhunderts v. Chr. in Uruk.* Abhandlung der Deutschen Orient-Geschellschaft 20. Berlin: Mann, 1979.

Kuenen, A. *The History of Israel to the Fall of the Jewish State.* 3 vols. Translated by A. H. May. London/Edinburgh: Williams and Norgate, 1874–75.

Kuhrt, A. "The Cyrus Cylinder and Achaemenid Imperial Policy." *JSOT* 25 (1983): 83–97.

——. "Babylonia from Cyrus to Xerxes." In *CAH.* 2d ed. Edited by J. Boardman, N. G. L. Hammond, D. M. Lewis, M. Ostwald. Cambridge: Cambridge University Press, 1970–, 4 (1988): 112–38.

——. "Nabonidus and the Babylonian Preisthood." In *Pagan Priests: Religion and Power in the Ancient World,* 119–55. Edited by M. Beard and J. North. Ithaca: Cornell University Press, 1990.

——. *The Ancient Near East c. 3000–330 B.C.* 2 vols. London/New York: Routledge, 1995.

Kuhrt A., and Sherwin-White, S. "Xerxes' Destruction of Babylonian Temples." In *Achaemenid History II: The Greek Sources*, 69–78. Edited by H. Sancisi-Weerdenburg and A. Kuhrt. Leiden: Nederlands Instituut voor het Nabije Osten, 1987.

Kümmel, H. M. *Familie, Beruf und Amt im spätbabylonischen Uruk: prosopographische Untersuchungen zu Berufsgruppen des 6. Jh. v. Chr. in Uruk.* Abhandlungen der Deutschen Orient-Gesellschaft 20. Berlin: Mann, 1979.

Kvanvig, H. S. *Roots of Apocalyptic: The Mesopotamian Background of the Enoch Figure and the Son of Man.* WMANT 61. Neukirchen: Neukirchener, 1988.

Laato, A. *Josiah and David Redivivus: The Historical Josiah and the Messianic Expectations of Exilic and Postexilic Times.* ConBOT 33. Stockholm: Almqvist & Wiksell, 1992

——. *The Servant of YHWH and Cyrus: A Reinterpretation of the Exilic Messianic Programme in Isaiah 40–55.* ConBOT 35. Stockholm: Almqvist and Wiksell, 1992.

——. "Zachariah 4,6b–10a and the Akkadian Royal Building Inscriptions." *ZAW* 106 (1994): 53–69.

——. *A Star is Rising: The Historical Development of the Old Testament Royal Ideology and the Rise of the Jewish Messianic Expectations.* University of South Florida International Studies in Formative Christianity and Judaism 5. Atlanta: Scholars Press, 1997.

Landsberger, B. *Brief des Bischofs von Esagila an König Asarhaddon.* Amsterdam: N. V. Noord-Hollandische Uitgevers Maatschappis, 1965.

Lang, B *Monotheism and the Prophetic Minority: An Essay in Biblical History and Sociology.* The Social World of Biblical Antiquity 1. Sheffield: Almond, 1983.

Langdon, S. *Die neubabylonischen Königsinschriften.* Translated by R. Zehnpfund. VAB 4. Leipzig: Hinrichs, 1912.

——. *The H. Weld-Blundell Collection in the Ashmolean Museum Vol. 1. Sumerian and Semitic Religious and Historical Texts.* Oxford Editions of Cuneiform Inscriptions 1. London: Oxford University Press, 1923.

Lapp, P. W. and N. L. Lapp eds. *Discoveries in the Wadi ed-Daliyeh.* Annual of ASOR 41. Cambridge, MA: ASOR, 1974.

Lemaire, A. "Le sabbat à l'époque royale israélite." *RB* 80 (1983): 161–85.

——. "Les inscriptions palestiniennes d'époque perse: un bilan provisoire." *Transeu* 1 (1989): 87–105.

——. "Les transformations politiques et culturelles de la Transjordanie au VIᵉ siècle av. J.-C." *Transeu* 8 (1994): 9–27.

——. "The Xanthos Trilingual Revisited." In *Solving Riddles and Untying Knots: Biblical, Epigraphic, and Semitic Studies in Honor of Jonas C. Greenfield*, 423–32. Edited by Z. Zevit, S. Gitin and M. Sokoloff. Winona Lake, IN: Eisenbrauns, 1995.

——. "Zorobabel et la Judée à la lumière de l'épigraphie (fin du VIᵉ s. av. J.-C.)." *RB* 103 (1996): 48–57.

Lemche, N. P. *Early Israel: Anthropological and Historical Studies on the Israelite Society before the Monarchy.* VTSup 37. Leiden: E. J. Brill, 1985.

——. "The Old Testament—a Hellenistic Book." *SJOT* 7 (1997): 163–93.

Lecoq, P. "Le problème de l'écriture cunéiforme vieux-perse." In *Commémoration Cyrus. Hommage Universel.* 3 vols. AcIr 1–3. Tehran/Liège: Bibliothèque Pahlavi, 1974, 3. 52–58.

Leuze, O. *Die Satrapieneinteilung in Syrien und im Zweistromlande von 520 bis 320.* Haale: Niemeyer, 1935.

Levenson, J. D. *Theology of the Programme of Restoration of Ezekiel 40–48.* HSM 10. Missoula, MT: Scholars Press, 1976.

——. "From Temple to Synagogue: 1 Kings 8." In *Traditions in Transformation. Turning Points in Biblical Faith*, 143–66. Edited by B. Halpern and J. D. Levenson. Winona Lake, IN: Eisenbrauns, 1981.

——. *Sinai and Zion: An Entry into the Jewish Bible.* New Voices in Biblical Studies. Minneapolis: Winston Press, 1985.

Levin, C. *Der Jahwist.* FRLANT 157. Göttingen: Vandenhoeck & Ruprecht, 1993.
Levine, L. D. *Two Neo-Assyrian Stelae from Iran.* Royal Ontario Museum Art and Archaeology Occasional Paper 23. Ontario: The Royal Ontario Museum, 1972.
Lindenberger, J. M. *The Aramaic Proverbs of Ahiqar.* Baltimore/London: The Johns Hopkins University Press, 1983.
Lindsay, J. "The Babylonian Kings and Edom, 605–550 B.C." *PEQ* 108 (1976): 23–39.
Lipiński, E. *La royauté de Yahwé dans la poésie et la culte de l'ancien Israël.* 2d ed. Vlaamse Academie voor Wetenschappen, Letteren en schone Kunsten van België. Klasse der Letteren. Verhandeligen, jaarg. 27, 1965, 55. Brussels: Palais der Academiën, 1968.
———. "Recherches sur le livre de Zacharie." *VT* 20 (1970): 25–55.
Liverani, M. "Memorandum on the Approach to Historiographic Texts." *Or* NS 42 (1973): 178–94.
Livingstone, A. *Court Poetry and Literary Miscellanea.* State Archives of Assyria 3. Helsinki: Helsinki University Press, 1989.
Livingstone, A.; Spaie, B.; Ibrahim, M.; Kamal, K.; and Taimaini, S. "Taima': Recent Soundings and New Inscribed Material." *Atlal* 7 (1983): 102–16.
Lloyd, A. B. "The Inscription of Udjahorresnet, a Collaborator's Testament." *JEA* 68 (1982): 166–80.
Lochner-Hüttenbach, F. "Brief des Königs Darius an den Satrapen Gadatas." In *Handbuch des Altpersischen*, 91–98. Edited by W. Brandenstein and M. Mayrhofer. Wiesbaden: Harrassowitz, 1964.
Lods, A. *The Prophets and the Rise of Judaism.* Translated by S. H. Hooke. New York: Dutton, 1937.
Loretz, O. *Ugarit-Texte und Thronbesteigungspsalmen. Die Metamorphose des Regenspenders Baal-Jahwe (Ps 24, 7–10; 29; 47; 93; 95–100 sowie Ps 77, 17–20; 114).* Ugaritische-Biblische Literatur 7. Munich: Ugarit, 1988.
Lust, J. "'Gathering and Return' in Jeremiah and Ezekiel." In *Le livre de Jérémie: le prophète et son milieu, les oracles et le transmission*, 119–42. Edited by P.-M. Bogaert. BETL 54. Leuven: Leuven University Press/Peeters, 1981.
———. "The Identification of Zerubbabel with Sheshbazzar." *EThL* 63 (1987): 91–95.
Lundquist, J. M. "The Legitimating Role of the Temple in the Origin of the State." In *Society of Biblical Literature 1982 Seminar Papers*, 271–91. Edited by K. H. Richards. Scholars Press/The Society of Biblical Literature, 1982.
———. "The Common Temple Ideology of the Ancient Near East." In *The Temple in Antiquity: Ancient Records and Modern Perspectives*, 53–76. Edited by T. G. Madsen. Religious Studies Center Monograph Series 9. Provo: Brigham Young University Press, 1984.
Lutz, H.-M. *Jahwe, Jerusalem und die Völker.* WMANT 27. Neukirchen-Vluyn: Neukirchener Verlag, 1968.
McEvenue, S. "The Political Structure in Judah from Cyrus to Nehemiah." *CBQ* 43 (1981): 353–64.
Machinist, P. B. "Literature as Politics: The Tukulti-Ninurta Epic and the Bible." *CBQ* 38 (1976): 455–82.
———. "The Epic of Tukulti-Ninurta: A Study in Middle Assyrian Literature." Ph.D. Dissertation, Yale University, 1978. Ann Arbor: Univerity Microfilms International.
———. "The First Coins of Judah and Samaria: Numismatics and History in the Achaemenid and Early Hellenistic Periods." In *Achaemenid History VIII: Continuity and Change*, 365–79. Edited by H. Sancisi-Weerdenburg, A. Kuhrt and M. C. Root. Leiden: Nederlands Instituut voor het Nabije Osten, 1994.
Malamat, A. "The Last Wars of the Kingdom of Judah." *JNES* 9 (1950): 218–227.
———. "The Twilight of Judah: In the Egyptian-Babylonian Maelstrom." In *Congress Volume: Edinburgh 1974*, 123–45. Edited by J. A. Emerton. VTSup 28. Leiden: E. J. Brill, 1975.

———. "The Last Years of the Kingdom of Judah." In *The Age of the Monarchies: Political History*, 205–22. Edited by A. Malamat. World History of the Jewish People First Series: Ancient Times 4/1. Jerusalem: Massada, 1979.

———. "Longevity: Biblical Concepts and Some Near Eastern Paralles." *28. Rencontre Assyriologique Internationale in Wien*, 215–24. Edited by H. Hirsch and H. Hunger. *AfO* Beiheft 19. Horn: Berger, 1982.

Mann, T. W. *Divine Presence and Guidance in Israelite Traditions: The Typology of Exaltation.* The Johns Hopkins Near Eastern Studies. Baltimore: The Johns Hopkins University Press, 1977.

Mantel, H. "The Dichotomy of Judaism during the Second Temple." *HUCA* 44 (1973): 55–87.

Margalith, O. "The Political Background of Zerubbabel's Mission and the Samaritan Schism." *VT* 41 (1991): 312–23.

Marinković, P. "What Does Zechariah 1–8 Tell us about the Second Temple," in *Second Temple Studies: 2. Temple and Community in the Persian Period*, 88–103. Edited by T. C. Eskenazi and K. H. Richards. JSOTSup 175. Sheffield: JSOT Press, 1994.

Mason, R. A. "The 'Editorial Framework' of the Book of Haggai." *VT* 27 (1977): 413–21.

———. "The Prophets of the Restoration." In *Israel's Prophetic Heritage: Essays in Honour of Peter R. Ackroyd*, 137–54. Edited by R. Coggins, A. Phillips and M. Knibb. Cambridge: Cambridge University Press, 1982.

Mattha, G. *The Demotic Legal Code of Hermopolis West.* Preface, and additional notes and glossary, by G. R. Hughes. Cairo: Institut français d'archéologie orientale du Caire, 1975.

May, H. G. "'This people' and 'this nation' in Haggai." *VT* 18 (1965): 190–97.

Mayes, A. D. H. *The Story of Israel between Settlement and Exile: A Redactional Study of the Deuteronomistic History.* London: SCM: 1983.

McCullough, W. S. *The History and Literature of the Palestinian Jews from Cyrus to Herod, 550BC to 4BC.* Toronto/Buffalo: University of Toronto Press, 1975.

Meeks, D. "Les donations aux temples dans l'Egypte du Ier millénaire avant J.-C." In *State and Temple Economy in the Ancient Near East.* 2 vols. Edited by E. Lipiński. OLA 6. Leuven: Departement Oriëntalistiek, 1979, 2. 605–87.

Mélèze-Modrzejewski, J. "Bibliographie de papyrologie juridique (v. 1)." *Archiv für Papyrusforschung* 34 (1988): 79–136.

———. *The Jews of Egypt: From Ramses II to Emperor Hadrian.* Translated by R. Cornman. Edinburgh: T&T Clark, 1995.

Meshorer, Y. *Ancient Jewish Coinage.* Dix Hills, NY: Amphora, 1982.

Mettinger, T. N. D. *King and Messiah: The Civil and Sacral Legitimation of the Israelite Kings.* ConBOT 8. Lund: Gleerup, 1976.

———. "YHWH Sabaoth—The Heavenly King on the Cherubim Throne." In *Studies in the Period of David and Solomon and Other Studies*, 109–38. Edited by T. Ishida. Winona Lake, IN: Eisenbrauns, 1982.

———. *The Dethronement of Sabaoth: Studies in the Shem and Kabod Theologies.* ConBOT 18. Lund: Gleerup, 1982.

———. *A Farewell to the Servant Songs: A Critical Examination of an Exegetical Axiom.* Lund: Gleerup, 1983.

———. "In Search of the Hidden Structure: YHWH as King in Isaiah 40–55." *SEÅ* 51–52 (1986–87): 148–57. Revised edition in *Writing and Reading the Scroll of Isaiah: Studies of an Interpretive Tradition*, 1. 143–54. 2 vols. Edited by C. C. Broyles and C. A. Evans. VTSup 70, 71. Leiden: E. J. Brill, 1997.

———. "The Name and the Glory: The Zion-Sabaoth Theology and its Exilic Successors." *JNSL* 24 (1998): 1–24.

Metzger, H. et al. *La stèle trilingue du Létôon.* Fouilles de Xanthos 6. Institute français d'études anatoliennes. Paris: Klincksieck, 1979.

Metzger, M. "Himmlische und irdische Wohnstatt Jahwehs." *Ugarit-Forschungen* 2 (1970): 139–58.

Meyer, E. *Die Entstehung des Judentums. Eine historische Untersuchung.* Halle: Niemeyer, 1896.

——. "König Darius I." In *Meister der Politik.* 3 vols. 2 ed. Edited by E. Marcks and K. A. von Müller. Stuttgart/Berlin: Deutsche Verlags-Anhalt, 1923–24, 1 (1923): 1–35.

——. "Gesetzsammlung des Darius und Erlass des Kambyses über die Einkünfte der Tempel." In *Kleine Schriften.* 2 vols. Halle: Niemeyer, 1924, 2. 91–100.

Meyers C. L. and E. M. Meyers, *Haggai, Zechariah 1–8.* AB 25B. Garden City, NY: Doubleday, 1987.

——. *Zechariah 9–14.* AB 25C. New York: Doubleday, 1993.

Meyers, E. M. "The Shemolith Seal and the Judean Restoration: Some Additional Considerations." *Eretz Israel* 18 (1985): 33*–38*.

Michaeli, F. *Les livres des Chroniques, d'Esdras et de Néhémie.* Commentaire de l'Ancien Testament 16. Neuchâtel: Delachaux and Niestlé, 1967.

Michalowski, P. *The Lamentation over the Destruction of Sumer and Ur.* Mesopotamian Civilizations 1. Winona Lake, IN: Eisenbrauns, 1989.

Mildenberg, L. "Yehud: A Preliminary Study of the Provincial Coinage of Judaea." In *Greek Numismatics and Archaeology: Essays in Honor of Margaret Thompson*, 183–96. Edited by O. Mørkholm and N. M. Waggoner. Wetteren: NR, 1979.

Millar, W. R. *Isaiah 24–27 and the Origin of Apocalyptic.* HSM 11. Missoula, MT: Scholars Press, 1976.

Miller, J. M., and J. H. Hayes. *A History of Israel and Judah.* Philadelphia: Westminster Press, 1986.

Mitchell, H. *A Critical and Exegetical Commentary on Haggai, Zechariah, Malachi, and Jonah.* ICC. Edinburgh: T&T Clark, 1912.

Mittmann, S. "Die Küste Palastinas bei Herodot." *ZDPV* 99 (1983): 130–140.

de Moor, J. C. "Lexical Remarks Concerning YAḤAD and YAḤDAW." *VT* 7 (1957): 350–55.

——. *New Year with Canaanites and Israelites.* 2 vols. Kamper Cahiers 21–22. Kampen: Kok, 1972.

Moore, C. A. "Archaeology and the Book of Esther." *BA* 38 (1975): 62–79.

Morgenstern, J. "Two Prophecies from 520–516 B.C." *HUCA* 22 (1949): 365–431.

Mosis, R. *Untersuchungen zur Theologie des chronistischen Geschichtswerkes.* Freiburger Theologische Studien 92: Freiburg: Herder, 1973.

Mowinckel, S. *Psalmenstudien.* 6 vols. Videnskapsselskapets skrifter II. Hist.-filosof. Klasse 1921, 4, 6; 1922, 1–2; 1923, 3; 1924, 1. Kristiania: Dybwad, 1921–24.

——. *He That Cometh.* Translated by G. W. Anderson. Nashville: Abingdon, 1955.

——. *Studien zu dem Buche Ezra-Nehemia.* 3 vols. Skrifter utgitt av det Norske videnskaps-akademi i Oslo. II. Hist.-filos. klasse. Ny serie 3, 5, 7. Oslo: Universitetsforlaget, 1964–5.

Müller, H.-P. "Phönizien und Juda in exilisch-nachexilischer Zeit." *WdO* 6 (1971): 189–204.

Myers, J. M. *I Chronicles.* AB 12. Garden City, NY: Doubleday, 1965.

——. *Ezra-Nehemiah.* AB 14. New York: Doubleday, 1965.

——. *The World of the Restoration.* Background to the Bible Series. Englewood Cliffs, NJ: Prentice-Hall, 1968.

——. "Edom and Judah in the Sixth–Fifth Centuries B.C." In *Near Eastern Studies in Honor of William Foxwell Albright*, 377–92. Edited by H. Goedicke. Baltimore: The Johns Hopkins University Press, 1971.

——. *I and II Esdras.* AB 42. Garden City, NY: Doubleday, 1974.

Newsome, J. D. "Toward a New Understanding of the Chronicler and His Purpose." *JBL* 94 (1975): 201–17.

Nicholson, E. W. "Apocalyptic." In *Tradition and Interpretation: Essays by the Members of the Society for Old Testament Study*, 189–213. Edited by G. W. Anderson. Oxford: Clarendon, 1979.

———. *God and His People: Covenant and Theology in the Old Testament*. Oxford: Clarendon, 1986.

———. *The Pentateuch in the Twentieth Century: The Legacy of Julius Wellhausen*. Oxford: Clarendon, 1998

Niditch, S. "Ezekiel 40–48 in a Visionary Context." *CBQ* 48 (1986): 208–24.

Niehr, H. *Der höchste Gott: Alttestamentlicher JHWH-Glaube im Kontext syrisch-kanaanäischer Religion des 1. Jahrtausends v. Chr.* BZAW 190. Berlin/New York: W. de Gruyter, 1990.

Nikel, J. *Die Wiederherstellung des jüdischen Gemeinwesens nach dem babylonishen Exil.* Biblische Studientum 5/2–3. Freiburg im Breisgau: Herder, 1900.

Nodet, E. *A Search for the Origins of Judaism: From Joshua to the Mishnah.* Translated by E. Crowley. JSOTSup 248. Sheffield: Sheffield Academic Press, 1997.

North, R. "Prophecy to Apocalyptic via Zechariah." In *Congress Volume: Uppsala, 1971,* 47–74. VTSup 22; Leiden: E. J. Brill, 1972.

Noth, M. *The History of Israel.* 2d ed. Translated by P. R. Ackroyd. Edinburgh: Black, 1960.

———. *Exodus: A Commentary.* Translated by J. Bowden. OTL. Philadelphia: Westminster, 1962.

———. *A History of Pentateuchal Traditions.* Translated by B. W. Anderson. Englewood Cliffs, NJ: Prentice-Hall, 1972.

O'Brien, M. A. *The Deuteronomy History Hypothesis: A Reassessment.* OBO 92. Freiburg: Universitätsverlag/Göttingen: Vanderhoeck & Ruprecht, 1989.

Oded, B. "Judah and the Exile. §5. The last days of Judah and the destruction of Jerusalem (609–586 B.C.E.)." In *Israelite and Judean History*, 469–76. Edited by J. H. Hayes and J. M. Miller. OTL. London: SCM, 1977.

———. *Mass Deportation and Deportees in the Neo-Assyrian Empire.* Wiesbaden: Reichert, 1979.

Oden, R. A. "*Ba'al Šamēn* and *'Ēl.*" *CBQ* 39 (1977): 457–73.

Oegema, G. S. *The Anointed and His People: Messianic Expectations from the Maccabees to Bar Kochba.* Journal for the Study of the Pseudepigrapha Supplement Series 27. Sheffield: Sheffield Acadmeic Press, 1998.

Oelsner, J. "Erwängungen zum Gesellschaftsaufbau Babyloniens von der neubabylonischen bis achämenidischen Zeit (7.–4. Jh. v. u. Z.)." *Altorientalische Forschungen* 4 (1976) 131–49.

———. "Die neu- und spätbabylonische Zeit." In *Circulation of Goods in Non-Palatial Context in the Ancient Near East*, 221–40. Edited by A. Archi. Rome: Edizioni dell'Ateneo, 1984.

———. "Grundbesitz/Grundeigentum im achämenidischen und seleukidischen Babylonien." *Jahrbuch für Wirtschaftsgeschichte* (1987): 117–34.

———. "Weitere Bermerkungen zu den Neirab-Urkunden." *Altorientalische Forschungen* 16 (1989): 68–77.

Oesterley, W. E. O. and T. H. Robinson. *Hebrew Religion: Its Origin and Development.* 2d ed. Revised and enlarged. New York: Macmillan, 1937.

———. *A History of Israel.* 2 vols. Oxford: Clarendon, 1932.

Ollenburger, B. C. *Zion. City of the Great King: A Theological Symbol of the Jerusalem Cult.* JSOTSup 41. Sheffield: Sheffield Academic, 1987.

Olmstead, A. T. "Darius as Lawgiver." *AJSL* 51 (1935): 247–49.

———. *History of the Persian Empire.* Chicago/London: University of Chicago Press, 1948.

Olyan, S. M. *Asherah and the Cult of Yahweh in Israel.* SBLMS 34. Atlanta: Scholars Press, 1988.

Oppert, J. "L'inscription cunéiform la plus moderne connue." *Mélanges d'archéologie égyptienne et assyrienne* 1 (1873): 22–29.

Otto, E. "צִיּוֹן." *TWAT*. Edited by G. J. Botterweck, H. Ringgren and H.-J. Fabry. Stuttgart: Kohlhammer, 1970–, 6 (1989): 994–1020.

Pardee, D. *Les textes para-mythologiques de la 24ᵉ campagne (1961)*. Ras Shamra-Ougarit 4, Mémoire 77. Paris: Éditions recherche sur les civilisations, 1988.

Parker, R. A. "Darius and his Egyptian Campaign." *AJSL* 58 (1941): 373–77.

Parker, R. A. and W. H. Dubberstein. *Babylonian Chronology 626 B.C.–A.D. 75*. Brown University Studies 19. Providence, RI: Brown University, 1956.

Parpola, S. *Letters from Assyrian Scholars to Kings Esarhaddon and Assurbanipal*. 2 vols. AOAT 5/1–2. Neukirchen-Vluyn: Neukirchener Verlag, 1970–1983.

Pestman, P. W. "L'origine et l'extension d'un manuel de droit égyptien. Quelques réflections à propos du soi-disant Code de Hermopolis." *JESHO* 26 (1983): 14–21.

Petersen, D. L. "Zerubbabel and Jerusalem Temple Reconstruction." *CBQ* 36 (1974): 366–72.

——. *Late Israelite Prophecy: Studies in Deutero-Canonical Literature and in Chronicles*. SBLMS 23. Missoula, MT: Scholars Press, 1977.

——. *Haggai and Zechariah 1–8: A Commentary*. OTL. Philadelphia: Westminster, 1984.

——. "Zechariah's Visions: A theological Perspective." *VT* 34 (1984): 195–206.

——. "Israelite Prophecy: Change versus Continuity." In *Congress Volume: Leuven, 1989*, 190–203. Edited by J. A. Emerton. SVT 43. Leiden/New York/Cologne, 1991.

——. *Zechariah 9–14 and Malachi: A Commentary*. OTL. Louisville: Westminster/John Knox, 1995.

Petit, T. "L'évolution sémantique des termes hébreux et araméns *pḥh* et *sgn* et accadienes *paḫātu* et *šaknu*." *JBL* 107 (1988): 53–67.

——. *Satrapes et satrapies dans l'empire achéménide de Cyrus le Grand à Xerxès Iᵉʳ*. Bibliothèque de la Faculté de Philosophie et Lettres de l'Université de Liège 254. Liège: Bibliothèque de la Faculté de Philosophie et Lettres de l'Université de Liège, 1990.

Petitjean, A. "La mission de Zorubabel et la reconstruction du temple." *EThL* 42 (1966): 40–71.

——. *Les oracles du proto-Zacharie; un programme de restauration pour la communaute juive apres l'exil*. Paris: Gabala, 1969.

Pfeiffer, R. H. *Introduction to the Old Testament*. Revised edition. New York: Harper, 1948.

——. *Religion in the Old Testament: The History of a Spiritual Triumph*. New York: Harper and Brothers, 1961.

van der Ploeg, J. P. M. "Eschatology in the Old Testament." *OTS* 17 (1972): 89–99.

Plöger, O. *Theocracy and Eschatology*. 2d ed. Translated by S. Rudman. Oxford: Blackwell, 1968.

Poebel, A. "Chronology of Darius' First Year of Reign." *AJSL* 55 (1938): 142–65.

——. "The Duration of the Reign of Smerdis, the Magician, and the Reigns of Nebuchadnezzar III and Nebuchadnezzar IV." *AJSL* 56 (1939): 121–45.

Pohlmann, K. F. *Studien zum dritten Esra. Ein Beitrag zur Frage nach dem ursprünglichen Schluß des chronistischen Geschichtswerkes*. FRLANT 104. Göttingen: Vandenhoeck & Ruprecht, 1970.

——. *Studien zum Jeremiabuch. Ein Beitrag zur Frage nach der Entstehung des Jeremiabuches*. FRLANT 118. Göttingen: Vandenhoeck & Ruprecht, 1978.

——. "Zur Frage von Korrespondenzen und Divergenzen zwischen den Chronikbüchern und dem Esra/Nehemia-Buch." In *Congress Volume: Leuven, 1989*, 314–30. Edited by J. A. Emerton. VTSup 43. Leiden/New York/Cologne: E. J. Brill, 1991.

Polzin, R. *Late Biblical Hebrew: Toward a Typology of Biblical Hebrew Prose*. HSM 12. Missoula, MT: Scholars Press, 1976.

——. *Samuel and the Deuteronomist: a Literary Study of the Deuteronomistic History*. San Francisco: Harper and Row, 1989.

Pongratz-Leisten, B. *ina šulmi īrub. Die kulttopographische und ideologische Programmatik der akītu-Prozession in Babylonien und Assyrien im 1. Jahrtausend v. Chr.* Baghdader Forschungen 16. Mainz am Rhein: P. von Zabern, 1994.

Pope, M. H. and W. Röllig. "Syrien. Die Mythologie der Ugariter und Phönizier." In *Götter und Mythen im Vorderen Orient,* 217–312. Edited by H. W. Haussig. Wörterbuch der Mythologie 1/1. Stuttgart: Klett, 1965.

Porten, B. *Archives from Elephantine: The Life of an Ancient Jewish Military Colony.* Berkeley/ Los Angeles: University of California Press, 1968.

——. "The Jews in Egypt." In *CHJ.* 3 vols. Edited by W. D. Davies, L. Finkelstein et al. Cambridge: Cambridge University Press, 1984–99, 1 (1984): 372–400.

Porten, B. and A. Yardeni, *Textbook of Aramaic Documents from Egypt.* 4 vols. Jerusalem: The Hebrew University Press, 1986–.

Porter, B. N. *Images, Power, and Politics: Figurative Aspects of Esarhaddon's Babylonian Policy.* Memoirs of the American Philosophical Society 208. Independence Square, PA: American Philosophical Association, 1993.

Posener, G. *La premiére domination perse en Égypte.* Cairo: Institut français d'archéologie orientale, 1936.

Poulsson, N. *König und Tempel im Glaubenzeugnis des Alten Testaments.* Stuttgarter Biblische Monographien 3. Stuttgart: Katholisches Bibelwerk, 1967.

Preuss, H.-D. *Jahweglaube und Zukunftserwartung.* BWANT 87; Stuttgart: Kohlhammer, 1968.

Prinsloo, W. S. "The Cohesion of Haggai 1:4–11." In *"Wünschet Jerusalem Frieden." IOSOT Congress, Jerusalem 1986,* 337–43. Edited by M. Augustin and K.-D. Schunck. BEATAJ 13. Frankfurt am Main: Lang, 1988.

Purvis, J. D. *The Samaritan Pentateuch and the Origin of the Samaritan Sect.* HSM 2. Cambridge, MA: Harvard University Press, 1968.

Quaegebeur, J. "Sur la 'loi sacrée' dans l'Egypte gréco-romaine." *Ancient Society* 11/12 (1980/81): 227–40.

von Rad, G. *Das Geschichtsbild des chronistischen Werkes.* Stuttgart: Kohlhammer, 1930.

——. "The Origin of the Concept of the Day of Yahweh." *JSS* 4 (1959): 97–108.

——. *Old Testament Theology.* 2 vols. Translated by D. M. G. Stalker. New York: Harper and Row, 1962–65.

Rahmani, L. Y. "Silver Coins of the Fourth Century from Tel Gamma." *IEJ* 21 (1971): 158–60.

Raitt, T. M. *A Theology of Exile: Judgment/Deliverance in Jeremiah and Ezekiel.* Philadelphia: Fortress, 1977.

Rappaport, U. "The First Judean Coinage." *JJS* 32 (1981): 1–17.

Rawlinson, H. C. *The Cuneiform Inscriptions of Western Asia.* 5 vols. London: British Museum, 1861–91, 5 (1884): no. 35.

Ray, J. D. "Egypt 525–404 B.C." In *CAH.* 2d ed. Edited by J. Boardman, N. G. L. Hammond, D. M. Lewis, M. Ostwald. Cambridge: Cambridge University Press, 1970–, 4 (1988): 254–86.

Rehm, M. *Der könglishe Messias im Licht der Immanuel-Weissagungen des Buches Jesaja.* Kevelaer: Butzon and Berker, 1968.

Reich, N. J. "The Codification of the Egyptian Laws by Darius and the Origin of the 'Demotic Chronicle'." *Mizraim* 1 (1937): 178–85.

Rendsburg, G. "Late Biblical Hebrew and the Date of P." *JANES* 12 (1980): 65–80.

Renger, J. "Institutional, Communal, and Individual Ownership or Possession of Arable Land in Ancient Mesopotamia From the End of the Fourth to the End of the First Millennium B.C." *Chicago-Kent Law Review* 71/1 (1995): 269–319.

Rendtorff, R. *Das überlieferungsgeschichtliche Problem des Pentateuch.* BZAW 147. Berlin: W. de Gruyter, 1977.

Ries, G. *Prolog und Epilog in Gesetzen des Altertums.* Münchener Beiträge zur Papyrusforschung und Antiken Rechtsgeschichte 76. Munich: C. H. Beck, 1983.

Ringgren, H. *Word and Wisdom: Studies in the Hypostatization of Divine Qualities and Functions in the Ancient Near East.* Lund: Gleerup, 1947.
Ringgren, H. *The Messiah in the Old Testament.* Studies in Biblical Theology 18. London: SCM, 1956.
Rivkin, E. *The Shaping of Jewish History: A Radical New Interpretation.* New York: Scribner's, 1971.
——. "Aaron." In *The Interpreter's Dictionary of the Bible: Supplementary Volume,* 1–3. Edited by K. Crim et al. Nashville: Abingdon, 1976.
Robert, L. "Une nouvelle inscription grecque de Sardes: Règlement de l'autorité perse relatif à un culte." *CRAIBL* (1975): 306–30.
Roberts, J. J. M. "The Davidic Origin of the Zion Tradition." *JBL* 92 (1973): 329–44.
——. "Of Signs, Prophets and Time Limits: A Note on Psalm 74:9." *CBQ* 39 (1977): 474–81.
——. "Zion in the Theology of the Davidic-Solomonic Empire." In *Studies in the Period of David and Solomon and Other Studies,* 93–108. Edited by T. Ishida. Winona Lake, IN: Eisenbrauns, 1982.
——. *Nahum, Habakkuk, and Zephaniah: A Commentary.* OTL. Louisville, KY: Westminster/John Knox, 1991.
Roberts, K. A. *Religion in Sociological Perspective.* Belmont, CA: Wadsworth, 1990.
Robinson, G. *The Origin and Development of the Old Testament Sabbath: A Comprehensive Exegetical Approach.* Beiträge zur biblischen Exegeses und Theologie 21. Frankfort am Main: Lang, 1988.
Rofé, A. "Isaiah 66:1–4: Judean Sects in the Persian Period as Viewed by Trito-Isaiah." In *Biblical and Related Studies Presented to Samuel Iwry,* 205–17. Edited by A. Kort and S. Morschauser. Winona Lake, IN: Eisenbrauns, 1985.
Römer, T., and de Pury, A. "L'historiographie deutéronomiste (HD). Histoire de la recherche et enjeux du débat." In *Israël construit son histoire: L'historiographie deutéronomiste à la lumière de recherches récentes,* 9–120. Edited by A. de Pury, T. Römer and J.-D. Macchi. Le Monde de la Bible 34. Geneva: Labor et Fides, 1996.
Rosenthal, F. *Die Aramaistische Forschung seit Th. Nöldeke's Veröffentlichungen.* Leiden: E. J. Brill, 1939.
Rost, L. *Israel bei den Propheten.* BWANT 4. Stuttgart: Kohlhammer, 1937.
——. "Sinaibund und Davidsbund." *TLZ* 72 (1947): 129–34.
Roth, M. "A Case of Contested Status." In *DUMU-E2–DUB-BA-A: Studies in Honor of Åke W. Sjöberg,* 481–89. Edited by H. Behrens, D. Loding, and M. T. Roth. Occasional Publications of the Samuel Noah Kramer Fund 11. Philadephia: Babylonian Section, University Museum, 1989.
Rothstein, J. W. *Judean und Samaritaner.* BWANT 3. Leipzig: Hinrichs, 1908.
Rowley, H. H. "The Samaritan Schism in Legend and History." In *Israel's Prophetic Heritage: Studies in Honor of James Muilenburg,* 208–22. Edited by B. W. Anderson and W. Harrelson. New York: Harper, 1962.
Rudolph, W. *Esra und Nehemiah samt 3. Esra.* HAT 20. Tübingen: J. C. B. Mohr (Paul Siebeck), 1949.
——. "Problems of the Books of Chronicles." *VT* 4 (1954): 401–9.
——. *Chronikbücher.* HAT 21. Tübingen: J. C. B. Mohr (Paul Siebeck), 1955.
——. *Haggai—Sacharja 1–8—Sacharja 9–14—Maleachi.* KAT 13/4; Gütersloh: Mohn, 1976.
Rüterswörden, U. *Von der politischen Gemeindschaft zur Gemeinde. Studien zu Dt 16,18–18,22.* BBB 65. Frankfurt am Main: Athenäum, 1987.
——. "Die perische Reichsautorisation der Thora: Fact or Fiction." *ZABR* 1 (1995): 47–61.
Sæbø, M. *Sacharja 9–14. Untersuchungen von Text und Form.* WMANT 34. Neukirchen-Vluyn: Neukirchener Verlag, 1969.

———. "The Relation of Sheshbazzar to Zerubbabel—Reconsidered." *SEÅ* 54 (1989): 168–77.

Sancisi-Weerdenburg, H. "Political Concepts in Old-Persian Royal Inscriptions." In *Anfänge politischen Denkens in der Antike. Die nahöstlichen Kulturen und die Griechen*, 145–63. Edited by K. Raaflaub. Schriften des Historischen Kollegs 24. Munich: R. Oldenbourg, 1993.

San Nicolò, M. "Materialien zur Viehwirtshaft in den neubabylonischen Tempeln. III." *Or* NS 20 (1951): 129–50.

San Nicolò, M. and A. Ungnad. *Neubabylonische Rechts- und Verwaltungsurkunden*. 2 vols. Leipzig: Hinrichs, 1935.

Sasson, J. M. *Jonah*. AB 24B. New York: Doubleday, 1990.

Sauer, G. "Serubbabel in der Sicht Haggais und Sacharjas." *Das ferne und nahe Wort*, 199–207. Edited by F. Maass. BZAW 105. Berlin: Töpelmann, 1967.

Schaeder, H. H. *Esra der Schreiber*. Tübingen: J. C. B. Mohr, 1930.

———. *Iranische Beiträge I*. Schriften der Königsberger gelehrten Gesellschaft, 6 Jahr. Geisteswissenschaftliche Kl., Heft 5. Halle: Niemeyer, 1930.

Schäfer, P. *Judeophobia: Attitudes towards the Jews in the Ancient World*. Princeton: Princeton University Press, 1997.

Schaper, J. "The Jerusalem Temple as an Instrument of the Achaemenid Fiscal Administration." *VT* 45 (1995): 528–39.

Schenker, A. "La rélation d'Esdras A au texte massorétique d'Esdras-Néhémie." In *Tradition of the Text: Studies Offered to Dominique Barthélemy in Celebration of his 70th Birthday*, 218–48. Edited by G. J. Nelson and S. Pisano. OBO 109 Freiburg: Universitätsverlag. Göttingen: Vandenhoeck & Ruprecht, 1991.

Schmid, H. "Jahweh und die Kulttradition von Jerusalem." *ZAW* 26 (1955): 168–98.

Schmidt, M. *Prophet und Tempel: eine Studie zum Problem der Gottesnähe im Alten Testament*. Zürich: Evangelischer, 1948.

Schmidt, W. H. *Königtum Gottes in Ugarit und Israel. Zur Herkunft der Königsprädikation Jahwes*. 2d ed. BZAW 80. Berlin: W. de Gruyter, 1966.

Schottroff, W. "Zur Sozialgeschichte Israels in der Perserzeit." *Verkündigung und Forschung* 27 (1982): 46–68.

Schramm, B. *The Opponents of Third Isaiah: Reconstructing the Cultic History of the Restoration*. JSOTSup 193. Sheffield: Sheffield Academic Press, 1995.

Schultz, C. "The Political Tensions Reflected in Ezra-Nehemiah." In *Scripture in Context: Essays in the Comparative Method*, 221–44. Edited by C. D. Evans, W. W. Hallo, J. B. White. Pittsburg Theological Monograph Series 34. Pittsburg: Pickwick, 1980.

Schwartz, D. R. "On Some Papyri and Josephus' Sources and Chronology for the Persian Period." *JSJ* 21 (1990): 175–99.

———. *Studies in the Jewish Background of Christianity*. Wissenschaftliche Untersuchungen zum Neuen Testament 60. Tübingen: J. C. B. Mohr (Paul Siebeck), 1992.

Scoralick, R. *Trishagion und Gottesherrschaft. Psalm 99 als Neuinterpretation von Tora und Propheten*. Stuttgarter Bibel-Studien 138. Stuttgart: Katholisches Bibelwerk, 1989.

Scullion, J. *Isaiah 40–66*. Old Testament Message 12. Willmington, Delware: Glazier, 1982.

Seitz, C. R. "The Crisis of Interpretation over the Meaning and Purpose of the Exile. A Redactional Study of Jeremiah xxi–xliii." *VT* 35 (1985): 78–98.

Sekine, M. "Davidsbund und Sinaibund bei Jeremiah." *VT* 9 (1959): 47–57.

Sekine, S. *Die Tritojesajanische Sammlung (Jes 56–66) redakionsgeschichtlich untersucht*. BZAW 175. Berlin: W. de Gruyter, 1989.

Sellin, E. *Serubbabel. Ein Beitrag zur Geschichte der messianischen Erwartung und der Entstehung des Judentums*. Leipzig: Deichert, 1889.

Sérandour, A. "Les récits bibliques de la consctruction du second temple: leurs enjeux." *Transeu* 11 (1996): 9–32.

Seybold, K. *Das davidischen Königtum im Zeugnis der Propheten.* FRLANT 107. Göttingen: Vandenhoeck & Ruprecht, 1972.
——. "Die Königserwartungen bei den Propheten Haggai und Sacharja." *Judaica* 28 (1972): 69–78.
——. "מלך." *TWAT.* Edited by G. J. Botterweck, H. Ringgren and H.-J. Fabry. Stuttgart: Kohlhammer, 1970–, 4 (1984): 947–56.
Shabazi, A. S. "The 'One Year' of Darius Re-examined." *BSOAS* 35 (1972): 609–14.
Shea, W. H. "An Unrecognized Vassal King of Babylon in the Early Achaemenid Period: II." *AUSS* 9 (1971): 99–128.
——. "Esther and History." *AUSS* 14 (1976): 227–46.
Sherwin-White, S. and Kuhrt, A. *From Samarkhand to Sardis: A New Approach to the Seleucid Empire.* London: Duckworth, 1993.
Smith, D. *Religion of the Landless: The Social Context of the Babylonian Exile.* Bloomington, IN: Meyer-Stone, 1989.
Smith, J. M.; Ward, W.H.; and Bewer, J. A. *A Critical and Exegetical Commentary on Michah, Zephaniah, Nahum, Habakkuk, Obadiah and Joel.* ICC. Edinburgh: T&T Clark, 1911.
Smith. J. Z. "The Influence of Symbols on Social Change: A Place on Which to Stand." In *Map is not Territory: Studies in the History of Religion*, 129–46. SJLA 23. Leiden: E. J. Brill, 1978.
Smith, M. "Palestinian Judaism in the Persian Period." In *The Greeks and the Persians from the 6th to 4th Centuries*, 381–401. Edited by H. Bengston. Delacorte World History 5. New York: Delacorte,1968.
——. *Palestinian Parties and Politics that Shaped the Old Testament* (New York: Columbia University Press, 1971; reprint, with minor corrections, London: SCM, 1987).
——. "Jewish Religious Life in the Persian Period." *CHJ.* 3 vols. Edited by W. D. Davies, L. Finkelstein et al. Cambridge: Cambridge University Press, 1984–99, 1 (1984): 243–76.
Smith, M. S. "The Near Eastern Background of the Solar Language for Yahweh." *JBL* 109 (1990): 29–39.
Smith, P. A. *Rhetoric and Redaction in Trito-Isaiah: The Structure, Growth, and Authorship of Isaiah 56–66.* VTSup 62. Leiden/New York/Cologne: E. J. Brill, 1995.
Smith, S. *Babylonian Historical Texts Relating to the Capture and Downfall of Babylon.* London: Methuen, 1924.
Snaith, N. H. "Isaiah 40–55. A Study of the Teaching of the Second Isaiah and its Consequences." In *Studies on the Second Part of the Book of Isaiah*, 139–264. VTSup 14. Leiden: E. J. Brill, 1967.
von Soden, W. "Kyros und Nabonid. Propaganda und Gegenpropaganda." In *Kunst, Kultur und Geschichte der Achämenidenzeit und ihr Fortleben*, 61–8. Edited by H. Koch and D. N. MacKenzie. Archäologische Mitteilungen aus Iran Ergänzungsband 10. Berlin: D. Reimer, 1983.
Soggin, J. A. *Introduction to the Old Testament.* 3rd ed. Translated by J. Bowden. London: SCM, 1989.
Speiser, E. A. "Ancient Mesopotamia." In *The Idea of History in the Ancient Near East*, 35–76. Edited by R. C. Dentan. New Haven: Yale University Press, 1955.
van der Spek, R. J. "Did Cyrus the Great Introduce a New Policy Towards Subdued Nations? Cyrus in Assyrian Perspective." *Persica* 10 (1982): 279–82.
——. "Cyrus de Pers in Assyrisch perspectief. Een verjelijking tussen de Assyrische en Perzische politiek ten opzichte van onderwerpen volken." *Tijdschrift voor Geschiedenis* 96 (1983): 1–27.
——. "The Babylonian Temple during the Macedonian and Parthian Domination." *BiOr* 42 (1985): 541–62.
——. *Grondbezit in het Seleucidische Rijk.* Amsterdam: VU Uitgeverij, 1986.
——. "The Babylonian City." In *Hellenism in the East: The Interaction of Greek and*

Non-Greek Civilizations from Syria to Central Asia after Alexander, 57–74. Edited by A. Kuhrt and S. Sherwin-White. London: Duckworth, 1987.

———. "Land Ownership in Babylonian Cuneiform Documents." In *Legal Documents of the Hellenistic World*, 173–245. Edited by M. J. Geller and H. Maehler. London: Warburg Institute, 1995.

Spieckermann, H. *Juda unter Assur in der Sargonidenzeit*. FRLANT 129. Göttingen: Vandenhoeck & Ruprecht, 1982.

Spiegelberg, W. *Die sogenannte Demotische Chronik des pap. 215 der Bibliothèque Nationale zu Paris*. Demotische Studien 7. Leipzig: Hinrichs, 1914.

———. "Drei demotische Schreiben aus der Korrespondenz des Pherendates, des Satrapen Darius' I., mit den Chnum-Priestern von Elephantine." In *Sitzungsberichte der Preussischen Akademie der Wissenschaften Jahrgang 1928, Philosophische-Historischen Klasse, XXX*, 604–22. Berlin: Akademie der Wissenschaften, 1928.

Stähli, H.-P. *Solare Elemente im Jahweglauben des Alten Testaments*. OBO 66. Freiburg: Universitätsverlag/Göttingen: Vandenhoeck and Ruprecht, 1985.

Steck, O. H. "Das Problem theologischer Strömungen in nachexilischer Zeit." *Evangelische Theologie* 28 (1968): 445–58.

———. "Zu Haggai 1 2–11." *ZAW* 83 (1971): 355–79.

———. *Friedenvorstellung im alten Jerusalem: Psalmen, Jesaja, Deuterojesaja*. Theologischen Studien 111. Zurich: Theologischer, 1972.

———. "Beobachtungen zu Jesaja 56–59," *BZ* 31 (1987): 228–46.

Stern, E. "The Province of Yehud: the Vision and the Reality." *The Jerusalem Cathedra* 1 (1981) 9–21.

———. *The Material Culture of the Land of the Bible in the Persian Period 538–332 B.C.E.* Warminster: Aris and Phillips/Jerusalem: Israel Exploration Society, 1982.

Sternberg, M. *The Poetics of Biblical Narrative: Ideological Literature and the Drama of Reading*. Bloomington: Indiana University Press, 1985.

Stevenson, K. R. *Vision of Transformation: The Territorial Rhetoric of Ezekiel 40–48*. SBLDS 154. Atlanta: Scholars Press, 1996.

Stiegler, S. *Die nachexilische JHWH-Gemeinde in Jerusalem. Ein Beitrag zu einer alttestamentlichen Ekklesiologie*. BEATAJ 34. Franfurt am Main: Lang, 1994.

Stolper, M. W. *Entrepreneurs and Empire. The Murašû Archive, the Murašû Firm, and Persian Rule in Babylonia*. Uitgaven van het Nederlands Historisch-Archaelogisch Instituut te Istanbul 54. Leiden: Nederlands Historisch-Archaelogisch Instituut te Istanbul, 1985.

———. "The Governor of Babylon and Across-the-River in 486 B.C." *JNES* 48 (1989): 283–305.

———. "Mesopotamia, 482–330 B.C." In *CAH*. 2d ed. Edited by D. M. Lewis et al. Cambridge: Cambridge University Press, 1970–, 6 (1994): 234–60.

Stoltz, F. *Struckturen und Figuren von Jerusalem: Studien zur altorientalischen, vor- und frühisraelitischen Religion*. BZAW 118. Berlin: W. de Gruyter, 1970.

Strassmaier, J. "Einige kleinere babylonische Keilschrifttexts aus dem Britischen Museum." In *Actes du 8e Congrès Internationale des Orientalistes*, 279–83 (mit autographirte Beilage, 35 ss). Duexième Partie, Section 1. Leiden: E. J. Brill, 1893.

Streck, M. *Assurbanipal und die letzten assyrischen Könige bis zum Untergange Nineveh's*. 3 vols. VAB 7/1–3. Leipzig: J. C. Hinrichs, 1916.

Stronach, D. "A Circular Symbol on the Tomb of Cyrus." *Iran* 9 (1971): 155–58.

———. "Description and Comment." *JA* 260 (1972): 241–46.

———. "Notes on the Religion in Iran in the Seventh and Sixth Centuries B.C." *Orientalia J. Duchesne-Guillemin Emerito Oblata*, 479–90. AcIr 23. Leiden: E. J. Brill, 1984.

Stuhlmueller, C. *Creative Redemption in Deutero-Isaiah*. AnBi 43. Rome: Biblical Institute Press, 1970.

———. "Yahweh-King and Deutero-Isaiah." *Biblical Research* 15 (1970): 32–45.

Sweeny, M. A. *Isaiah 1–4 and the Post-Exilic Understanding of the Isaianic Tradition.* BZAW 171. Berlin/New York: W. de Gruyter, 1988.

Tadmor, H. "The Historical Background to the Decree of Cyrus." In *Sepher Ben Gurion*, 450–73. Jerusalem: Kiryat Sepher, 1964. (Hebrew)

——. "'The Appointed Time Has Not Yet Arrived': The Historical Background of Haggai 1:2." In *Ki Baruch Hu: Ancient Near Esatern, Biblical, and Judaic Studies in Honor of Baruch A. Levine*, 401–08. Edited by R. Chazan, W. W. Hallo and L. H. Schiffman. Winona Lake, IN: Eisenbrauns, 1999.

Talmon, S. "The Biblical Concept of Jerusalem." *Journal of Ecumenical Studies* 8 (1971) 300–16.

——. "Ezra and Nehemiah (Books and Men)." In *The Interpreter's Dictionary of the Bible: Supplementary Volume*, 317–28. Edited by K. Crim et al. Nashville: Abingdon, 1976.

——. "Polemics and Apology in Biblical Historiography—2 Kings 17:24–41." In *The Creation of Sacred Literature: Composition and Redaction of the Biblical Text*, 57–68. Edited by R. E. Friedman. Berkeley: University of California Press, 1981.

——. *King, Cult and Calendar in Ancient Israel.* Jerusalem: Magnus, 1986.

——. "The Emergence of Jewish Sectarianism in the Early Second Temple Period." In *Ancient Israelite Religion. Essays in Honor of Frank Moore Cross*, 587–616. Edited by P. D. Miller, P. D. Hanson and S. D. McBride. Philadelphia: Fortress, 1987.

——. "Esra und Nehemiah: Historiographie oder Theologie?" In *Ernten, was man sät. Festschrift für Klaus Koch zu seinem 65. Geburtstag*, 329–56. Edited by D. R. Daniels, U. Glessmer, and M. Rösel. Neukirchen-Vluyn: Neukirchener Verlag, 1991.

——. "The Signification of שלום and its Semantic Field in the Hebrew Bible." in *The Quest for Context and Meaning: Studies in Biblical Intertextuality in Honor of James A. Sanders*, 75–115. Edited by C. A. Evans and S. Talmon. Biblical Interpretation Series 28. Leiden/New York/Cologne: E. J. Brill, 1997.

Talmon, Y. "Millenarian Movements." *Archives européennes de sociologie* 7 (1966): 157–78.

Talshir, D. "A Reinterpretation of the Linguistic Relationship between Chronicles and Ezra-Nehemiah." *VT* 38 (1988): 165–93.

Tcherikover, V. *Hellenistic Civilization and the Jews.* Translated by S. Applebaum. Philadelphia: Jewish Publication Society of America, 1959; reprint, New York: Atheneum, 1979.

Teixidor, J. *The Pagan God: Popular Religion in the Greco-Roman Near East.* Princeton: Princeton University Press, 1977.

Terrien, S. *The Elusive Presence: Toward a New Biblical Theology.* Religious Studies Perspectives 26. New York: Harper and Row, 1978.

Thompson, R. J. *Moses and the Law in a Century of Criticism since Graf.* VTSup 19. Leiden: E. J. Brill, 1970.

Thompson, T. L. *The History of the Patriarchal Narratives: The Quest for the Historical Abraham.* BZAW 133. Berlin: W. de Gruyter, 1974.

——. *The Origin and Tradition of Ancient Israel: I. The Literary Formation of Genesis and Exodus 1–23.* JSOTSup 55; Sheffield: JSOT Press, 1987.

Thronveit, M. A. "Linguistic Analysis and the Question of Authorship in Chronicles, Ezra and Nehemiah." *VT* 32 (1982): 201–16.

Tigchelaar, E. J. C. *Prophets of Old and the Day of the End: Zechariah, the Book of Watchers and Apocalyptic.* OTS 35. Leiden/New York/Cologne: E. J. Brill, 1996.

Tollefson, K. D., and Williamson H. G. M. "Nehemiah as Cultural Revitalization: An Anthropological Perspective." *JSOT* 56 (1992): 41–68.

Tollington, J. E. *Tradition and Innovation in Haggai and Zechariah 1–8.* JSOTSup 150. Sheffield: Sheffield Academic Press, 1993.

van der Toorn, K. "The Babylonian New Year Festival: New Insights from the Cuneiform Texts and their Bearing on Old Testament Study." In *Congress Volume: Leuven, 1989,* 331–44. Edited by J. A. Emerton. VTSup 43. Leiden/New York/Cologne: E. J. Brill, 1991.

——. "Anat-Yahu, Some Other Deities, and the Jews of Elephantine." *Numen* 39 (1992): 80–101.

Torrey, C. C. *The Composition and Historical Value of Ezra-Nehemiah*. BZAW 2. Giessen: Riker, 1896.

——. *Ezra Studies*. Chicago: University of Chicago Press, 1910.

Tournay, R. J. *Voir et entendre dieu avec les Psaumes ou la liturgie prophétique du second temple à Jerusalem*. Cahiers de la Revue Biblique 24. Paris: Gabalda, 1988.

Townsend, T. "Additional Comments on Haggai 2:10–19." *VT* 18 (1968): 359–60.

Tozzi, P. "Per la storia religiosa della politicà religiosa degli Achemenidi. Distruzioni persiane di templi greci agli inizi del V. secolo." *Rivista Storica Italiana* 31 (1978): 18–32.

Trompf, G. W. "Notions of Historical Recurrence in Classical Hebrew Historiography." In *Studies in the Historical Books of the Old Testament*, 213–29. Edited by J. A. Emerton. VTSup 30. Leiden: E. J. Brill, 1979.

——. *The Idea of Historical Recurrence in Western Thought: From Antiquity to the Reformation*. Berkeley: University of California Press, 1979.

——. "Introduction." In *Cargo Cults and Millenarian Movements: Transoceanic Comparisons of New Religious Movements*, 1–10. Edited by G. W. Trompf. Religion and Society 29. Berlin/New York: Mouton/W. de Gruyter, 1990.

Tuell, S. S. *The Law of the Temple in Ezekiel 40–48*. HSM 49. Atlanta: Scholars Press, 1992.

Tuland, C. G. "'uššayyā' and 'uššarnâ. A Clarification of Terms, Date, and Text." *JNES* 17 (1958): 269–75.

Tuplin, C. "The Administration of the Achaemenid Empire." In *Coinage and Administration in the Athenian and Persian Empires*, 109–66. Edited by I. Carradice. BAR International Series 343. Oxford: British Archaeological Reports, 1987.

——. "Darius' Suez Canal and Persian Imperialism." In *Achaemenid History VI: Asia Minor and Egypt: Old Cultures in a New Empire*, 237–83. Edited by H. Sancisi-Weerdenburg and A. Kuhrt; Leiden: Nederlands Instituut voor het Nabije Osten, 1991.

Turcan, R.-A. *Mithra et Mithriacisme*. Paris: Presses Universitaires de France, 1981.

Unger, T. "Noch Einmal: Haggais unreines Volk." *ZAW* 103 (1991): 210–25.

Ungnad, A. "Schenkungsurkunde des Kurigalzu mâr Kadašman-Harbe." *Archiv für Keilschriftforschung* 1 (1923): 19–23.

Vallat, F. "L'inscription cunéiforme trilingue (DSab)." *JA* 260 (1972): 247–51.

Van De Mieroop, M. *The Ancient Mesopotamian City*. Oxford: Clarendon, 1997.

VanderKam, J. C. *Enoch and the Growth of an Apocaylptic Tradition*. CBQ Monograph Series 16. Washington: Catholic Biblical Association of America, 1984.

——. "Jewish High Priests of the Persian Period: Is the List Complete?" In *Priesthood and Cult in Ancient Israel*, 67–91. Edited by G. A. Anderson and S. M. Olyan. JSOTSup 125; Sheffield: Sheffield Academic Press, 1991.

——. "Joshua the High Priest and the Interpretation of Zechariah 3." *CBQ* 53 (1991): 553–70.

——. "Ezra-Nehemiah or Ezra and Nehemiah?" In *Priests, Prophets and Scribes: Essays on the Formation and Heritage of Second Temple Judaism in Honour of Joseph Blenkinsopp*, 55–75. Edited by E. Ulrich, J. W. Wright, R. P. Carroll, and P. R. Davies. JSOTSup 149. Sheffield: JSOT Press, 1992.

van Seters, J. *Abraham in History and Tradition*. New Haven/London: Yale University Press, 1975.

van Winkle, D. W. "The Relationship of the Nations to Yahweh and to Israel in Isaiah xl–lv." *VT* 35 (1985): 446–58.

de Vaux, R. *Ancient Israel: Its Life and Institutions*. Translated by J. McHugh. London: Darton, Longman and Todd, 1961.

——. "The Decrees of Cyrus and Darius on the Rebuilding of the Temple." In

The Bible and the Ancient Near East, 63–96. Translated by D. McHugh. New York: Doubleday, 1971.

Vincent, A. *La religion des judéo-araméens d'Elephantine*. Paris: Geuthner, 1937.

Vink, J. G. "The Date and Origin of the Priestly Code in the Old Testament." *OTS* 16 (1969): 1–144.

Vörlander, H. *Die Entstehungszeit des jehowistischen Geschichtswerkes*. Europäischen Hochschulschriften 109. Frankfurt am Main: Lang, 1978.

Vogt, H. C. M. *Studie zur nachexilischen Gemeinde in Esra-Nehemia*. Werl: Dietrich-Coelde, 1966.

Vriesen, T. C. "Prophecy and Eschatology." In *Congress Volume: Copenhagen 1953*, 199–229. VTSup 1. Leiden: E. J. Brill, 1953.

Wainwright, G. A. "Studies in the Petition of Peteêsi" *Bulletin of the John Rylands Library* 28 (1944): 228–71.

Wallace, A. F. C. "Revitalization Movements: Some Theoretical Considerations for their Comparative Study." *American Anthropologist* 58 (1956): 264–81.

——. *Religion: An Anthropological View*. New York: Random House, 1966.

Wallis, G. "Jüdische Bürger in Babylonien während der Achämeniden-Zeit." *Persica* 9 (1980): 129–86.

Wanke, G. *Die Zionsideologie des Korachiten in ihrem traditionsgeschichtlichen Zusammenhang*. BZAW 97. Berlin: W. de Gruyter,1966.

——. *Untersuchungen zur sogenannten Baruchschrift*. BZAW 122. Berlin: W. de Gruyter, 1971.

——. "Prophecy and Psalms in the Persian Period." *CHJ*. 3 vols. Edited by W. D. Davies, L. Finkelstein et al. Cambridge: Cambridge University Press, 1984–99, 1 (1984): 162–88.

Waterman, L. "The Camouflaged Purge of Three Messianic Conspirators." *JNES* 13 (1954): 73–78.

Weidner, E. F. "Jojachin, König von Juda, in babylonischen Keilschrifttexten." In *Mélanges syriens offerts à M. Rene Dussaud*. 2 vols. Paris: Guethner, 1939, 1 (1939): 932–35.

Weinberg, J. P. "Demographische Notizen zur Geschichte der nachexilischen Gemeinde in Juda." *Klio* 54 (1972): 45–59.

——. "Probleme der sozialökonomischen Struktur Judäas vom 6. Jahrhundert v. u. Z. bis zum 1. Jahrhundert u. Z." *Jahrbuch für Wirtschaftsgeschichte* 1 (1973): 237–51.

——. "Das *bēit 'ābōt* im 6.–4. Jh. v. u. Z." *VT* 23 (1973): 400–14.

——. "Der *'am hā'āreṣ* des 6.–4. Jh. v. u. Z.," *Klio* 56 (1974): 325–35.

——. "Nᵊtînîm und 'Söhne der Sklaven Salomos' im 6.–4. Jh. v. u. Z." *ZAW* 87 (1975): 355–71.

——. "Die Agrarverhältnisse in der Bürger-Tempel-Gemeinde der Achämenidenzeit." *AcAnt* 22 (1976): 473–86.

——. "Bemerkungen zum Problem 'Der Vorhellenismus im Vorderer Orient'." *Klio* 58 (1976): 5–20.

——. "Zentral- und Partikulargewalt im achämenidischen Reich." *Klio* 59 (1977): 25–43.

——. *The Citizen-Temple Community*. Translated by D. L. Smith Christopher. JSOTSup 151; Sheffield: Sheffield Academic Press, 1992.

——. "Die Mentalität der jerusalemischen Bürger-Tempel-Gemeinde des 6.–4. Jh. v. u. Z." *Transeu* 5 (1992): 133–41.

——. *Der Chronist in seiner Mitwelt* (BZAW 239; Berlin/New York: W. de Gruyter, 1996.

——. "Transmitter and Recipient in the Process of Acculturation: The Experience of the Judean Citizen-Temple Community." *Transeu* 13 (1997): 91–105.

Weinberg, S. S. "Post-Exilic Palestine. An Archaeological Report." *Proceedings of the Israel Academy of Sciences and Humanities* 4/5 (1969): 78–97.

Weinfeld, M. "Cult Centralization in Israel in the Light of a Neo-Babylonian Analogy." *JNES* 23 (1964): 202–12.

———. "The Covenant of Grant in the Old Testament and the Ancient Near East." *JAOS* 90 (1970): 184–96.

———. *Deuteronomy and the Deuteronomistic School.* Oxford: Clarendon, 1972.

Weippert, H. *Palästina in vorhellenistische Zeit.* Handbuch der Archäologie, Vorderasien 2/1. Munich: Beck, 1988.

Weissbach, F. H. *Die Keilinschriften der Achämeniden.* VAB 3. Leipzig, Hinrichs, 1911.

Welch, A. C. *Post-Exilic Judaism.* Edinburgh/London: Blackwood, 1935.

Wellhausen, J. "Die Rückkehr der Juden aus dem babylonischen Exil." In *Nachrichten der königlischen Gesellschaft der Wissenschaften zu Göttingen. Phil.-hist. Klasse,* 166–86. Göttingen: n.p., 1895.

———. *Prolegomena to the History of Israel. With a Reprint of the Article, Israel, from the Encyclopaedia Britannica.* With a preface by W. Robertson Smith. Translated by J. S. Black and A. Menzies. Edinburgh: Black, 1885; reprint, New York: Meridian, 1957.

Welten, P. *Geschichte und Geschichtsdarstellung in der Chronikbüchen.* WMANT 42. Neukirchen-Vluyn: Neukirchener Verlag, 1973.

Whedbee, J. W. "A Question-Answer Schema in Haggai 1: The Form and Function of Haggai 1:9–11." In *Biblical and Near Eastern Studies in Honor of W. S. LaSor,* 184–94. Edited by G. A. Tuttle. Grand Rapids: Eerdmans, 1978.

Whitehead, J. D. "Some Distinctive Features of the Language of the Aramaic Arsames Correspondence." *JNES* 37 (1978): 119–40.

Whitelam, K. *The Just King: Monarchical Judicial Authority in Ancient Israel.* JSOTSup 12. Sheffield: JSOT, 1979.

———. "Israel's Traditions of Origin: Reclaiming the Land." *JSOT* 44 (1989): 19–42.

Whybray, R. N. *The Making of the Pentateuch: A Methodological Study.* JSOTSup 53. Sheffield: Sheffield Academic, 1987.

Widengren, G. *Die Religionen Irans.* Die Religionen der Menschheit 14. Stuttgart: Kohlhammer, 1965.

———. "Yahweh's Gathering of the Dispersed." In *In the Shelter of Elyon: Essays on Ancient Palestinian Life and Literature in Honor of G. W. Ahlström,* 227–45. Edited by W. B. Barrick and J. R. Spencer. JSOTSup 31. Sheffield: JSOT, 1984.

Wiesehöfer, J. *Der Aufstand Gaumatas und die Anfänge Dareios' I.* Bonn: Habelt, 1978.

———. "Zur Frage der Echtheit des Dareios-Briefes an Gadatas." *Rheinisches Museum für Philologie* 130 (1986): 396–98.

———. "Kyros und die unterworfenen Völker. Ein Beitrag zur Entstehung von Geschichtsbewurßtsein." *Quaderni di Storia* 26 (1987): 107–26.

———. ",Reichgesetz' oder ,Einzelfallgerechtigkeit'? Bemerkungen zu P. Freis These von achaimenidischen ,Reichsautorisation'." *ZABR* 1 (1995): 36–46.

Wildberger, H. *Jesaja.* BKAT 10/1–3. 3 vols. Neukirchen-Vluyn: Neukirchener Verlag, 1972–82.

Willi, T. *Die Chronik als Auslegung.* FRLANT 106. Göttingen: Vandenhoeck and Ruprecht, 1972.

Williamson, H. G. M. *Israel in the Books of Chronicles.* Cambridge: Cambridge University Press, 1977.

———. "The Historical Value of Josephus' Jewish Antiquities XI. 297–301." *JTS* NS 28 (1977): 49–66.

———. "Eschatology in Chronicles." *TynB* 29 (1979): 120–33.

———. "The Composition of Ezra i–vi." *JTS* NS 34 (1983): 1–30.

———. *Ezra, Nehemiah.* Word Biblical Commentary 16. Waco, TX: Word, 1985.

———. "The Governors of Judah Under the Persians." *TynB* 39 (1988): 59–82.

———. "The Concept of Israel in Transition." In *The World of Ancient Israel: Sociological, Anthropological and Political Perspectives,* 141–61. Edited by R. E. Clements. Cambridge: Cambridge University Press, 1989.

——. "Isaiah 63,7–64,11: Exilic Lament or Post-Exilic Protest?" *ZAW* 102 (1990): 48–58.

——. "Ezra and Nehemiah in the Light of the Texts from Persepolis." *Bulletin for Biblical Research* 1 (1991): 41–61.

——. "The Problem with 1 Esdras." In *After the Exile: Essays in Honour of Rex Mason*, 201–16. Edited by J. Barton and D. J. Reimer; Macon, GA: Mercer University Press, 1996.

——. "Judah and the Jews." In *Studies in Persian History: Essays in Memory of David M. Lewis*, 145–163. Edited by M. Brosius and A. Kuhrt. Achaemenid History XI. Leiden: Nederlands Instituut voor het Nabije Oosten, 1998.

Wilson, A. *The Nations in Deutero-Isaiah: A Study on Composition and Structure*. Ancient Near Eastern Texts and Studies 1. Lewiston/Queenston: Mellen, 1986.

Wilson, B. R. *Magic and the Millennium: A Sociological Study of Religious Movements of Protest among Tribal and Third-World Peoples*. London: Heinemann, 1973.

Wilson, R. D. "The Title 'King of Persia' in the Scriptures." *Princeton Theological Review* 15 (1917): 90–145.

Wilson, R. R. *Prophecy and Society in Ancient Israel*. Philadelphia: Fortress, 1980.

Winkle, R. E. "Jeremiah's Seventy Years for Babylon: A Re-Assessment. Part I: The Scriptural Data." *AUSS* 25 (1987): 201–14.

——. "Jeremiah's Seventy Years for Babylon: A Re-Assessment. Part II: The Historical Data." *AUSS* 25 (1987): 289–99.

Wolff, H. W. *Haggai: A Commentary*. Translated by M. Kohl. Minneapolis: Ausburg, 1988.

Worsley, P. *The Trumpet Shall Sound: A Study of "Cargo" Cults in Melanesia*. New York: Schocken, 1968.

van der Woude, A. S. "Serubbabel und die messianischen Erwartungen des Propheten Sacharja." *ZAW* 100 Supplement (1988): 138–56.

Wright, J. S. *The Building of the Second Temple*. London: Tyndale, 1958.

Wyatt, N. "Symbols of Exile." *SEÅ* 55 (1990): 39–58.

——. *Myths of Power: A Study of Royal Myth and Ideology in Ugaritic and Biblical Tradition*. Ugaritisch-Biblische Literatur 13. Münster: Ugarit-Verlag, 1996.

Würthwein, E. *Der 'amm ha'arez im Alten Testament*. Stuttgart: Kohlhammer, 1936.

Yamauchi, E. M. *Persia and the Bible*. Grand Rapids: Baker, 1990.

Young, T. C. "The Consolidation of the Empire and the Limits of its Growth under Darius and Xerxes." In *CAH*. 2d ed. Edited by J. Boardman, N. G. L. Hammond, D. M. Lewis, M. Ostwald. Cambridge: Cambridge University Press, 1970–, 4 (1988): 53–111.

Yoyotte, J. "Une statue de Darius découverte à Suse: les inscriptions hiéroglyphiques. Darius et l'Égypte." *JA* 260 (1972): 247–66.

——. "Les inscriptions hiéroglyphiques de Darius à Suse." *Cahiers de la délégation archéologique française en Iran* 4 (1974): 181–209.

Zadok, R. *On West Semites in Babylonia during the Chaldean and Achaemenian Periods*. Jerusalem: Wanaarta, 1977.

——. "Phoenicians, Philistines, and Moabites in Mesopotamia." *BASOR* 230 (1978): 57–65.

——. "The Nippur Region during the Late Assyrian, Chaldean and Achaemenid Periods, chiefly according to written sources." *Israel Oriental Studies* 8 (1978): 266–332.

Zadok, R. *The Jews in Babylonia during the Chaldean and Achaemenian Periods*. Haifa: University of Haifa, 1979.

——. *Répertoire géographie des textes cunéiformes. Band 8: Geographical Names according to New- and Late-Babylonian Texts*. Beihefte zum Tübinger Atlas des vorderen Orients Reihe B 7/8. Wiesbaden: Reichert, 1985.

Zauzich, K.-Th. "Die demotischen Papyri von der Insel Elephantine." In *Egypt and the Hellenistic World*, 421–35. Edited by E. van 't Dack, P. van Dessel and W. van Gucht. Studia Hellenistica 27. Leuven: Orientaliste, 1983.

Zawadzki, S. "Great Families of Sippar during the Chaldean and Early Persian Periods (626–482 B.C.)." *RA* 84 (1990): 17–25.

Zenger, E. *Gottes Bogen in den Wolken. Untersuchungen zu Komposition und Theologie der priesterschriftlichen Urgeschichte*. Stuttgarter Bibelstudien 112. Stuttgart: Katholisches Bibelwerk, 1983.

Zevit, Z. "Converging Lines of Evidence Bearing on the Date of P." *ZAW* 94 (1982): 481–511.

———. "The Gerizim-Samarian Community in and between Texts and Times: An Experimental Study." In *The Quest for Context and Meaning: Studies in Biblical Intertextuality in Honor of James A. Sanders*, 547–72. Edited by C. A. Evans and S. Talmon. Biblical Interpretation Series 28. Leiden/New York/Cologne: E. J. Brill, 1997.

Zimmerli, W. "Israel im Buch Ezechiel." VT 8 (1958): 75–90.

———. "Le nouvel 'exode' dans le message des deux grands prophètes de l'exil," *Maqqél Shâqédh, la branche d'amandier. Hommage à Wilhelm Fischer*, 216–27. Montpellier: Causse, Graille, Castelnau, 1960.

———. "Plannungen für Wiederaufbau nach der Katastrophe von 587." *VT* 18 (1968): 229–55.

———. *Ezekiel*. 2 vols. Translated by J. D. Martin. Hermeneia. Philadelphia: Fortress, 1979–83.

Zorn, J.; Yellin, J.; and Hayes, J. "The *m(w)ṣh* Stamp Impressions and the Neo-Babylonian Period." *IEJ* 44 (1994): 161–83.

INDEX OF MODERN AUTHORS

Abadie, P.   104
Ackroyd, P. R.   43–44, 46, 50, 56–57,
   63, 89, 103, 139, 160, 164, 166,
   234–35, 275, 281
Adas, M.   267
Ahlemann, F.   106
Ahlström, G. W.   1–3, 6, 11, 13–15,
   58, 66, 92, 116, 244, 247, 263, 293
Albertz, R.   48, 80
Albrektson, B.   65
Albright, W. F.   106, 245
Alexander, P. S.   129
Allam, S.   200
Allen, N.   46
Alt, A.   45–46, 90–91, 106, 160
Alter, R.   29
Amir, Y.   11
Amsler, S.   163, 170, 203, 291
Andersen, F. I.   97–98
Anderson, B. W.   22, 50, 60
Anderson, G.   192
Andreasen, N.-E. A.   48
Andrews, D. K.   123
Aperghis, G.   147
Applegate, J.   165
Auerbach, E.   22
Avigad, N.   43, 90, 160, 187–88
Avishur, A.   241
Avi-Yonah, M.   45

Balcer, J. M.   204, 231
Baltzer, D.   60
Baltzer, K.   232
Barag, D.   205–206
Barker, M.   12, 68
Bar-Kochva, B.   207
Barkun, M.   267
Barr, J.   245
Barstad, H. M.   43–44
Bartlett, J. R.   45
Batten, L. W.   106, 118–19, 132
Baumgarten, A. I.   123
Baumgartner, A. J.   245
Beaulieu, P.-A.   133
Becker, J.   15–18, 77
Bedford, P. R.   42, 96, 115, 162, 177,
   208

Beit-Arieh, I.   45
Ben Zvi, E.   8, 11, 225
Berger, P.-R.   89, 132, 136
Berquist, J. L.   12, 14, 25, 267
Betlyon, J. W.   206
Beuken, W. A. M.   55, 162–63, 165,
   168, 170–71, 258, 273, 280, 296
Bewer, J. A.   118, 246
Beyer, K.   112, 131, 145–46
Beyse, K.-M.   32
Bianchi, F.   188
Bickerman, E. J.   13, 46–48, 114–15,
   119, 121, 128–29, 132, 151–52,
   158–59, 202, 231, 234
Black, J.   6
Blenkinsopp, J.   9, 12, 16, 19, 22, 25,
   46, 50, 52, 81, 91, 103, 113, 118,
   123, 147, 189, 198, 208, 236,
   284–85
Bloch, H.   88
Bloch-Smith, E.   3
Böhler, D.   88
Boffo, L.   148
Boissier, A.   121
Bolin, T.M.   8
Bongenaar, A. C. V. M.   24
Borger, R.   65, 122, 137–38, 166,
   174–76, 230–31
Bottéro, J.   65
Bowman, R. A.   113, 119, 123
Boyce, M.   124
Braun, R.   104, 309
Bresciani, E.   25, 197
Briant, P.   117, 127–28, 140, 144,
   148, 150, 154
Briend, J.   113
Bright, J.   4, 13–15, 23, 67, 89, 113,
   158, 171
Brinkman, J. A.   65, 152, 174
Broshi, M.   44
Browne, L. E.   49, 113, 253
Bucci, O.   199
Burridge, K. O. L.   267
Busink, T. A.   3, 6, 10

Cagni, L.   154
Calmeyer, P.   195

Cameron, G. G.   195
Camp, C. V.   9
Caquot, A.   239
Carroll, R. P.   10, 12, 20–21, 29, 57, 69, 162, 252, 261, 282, 287
Carter, C. E.   10, 43–45, 153
Cazelles, H.   1–2
Chong, J. H.   49
Christensen, D. L.   247
Clay, A. T.   47
Clements, R. E.   51, 64, 68
Clifford, R. J.   3, 66
Clines, D. J. A.   29, 61, 91, 97, 107, 112–13, 136, 252, 281, 285
Coates, G. W.   115
Cocquerillat, D.   24
Cody, A.   22–23, 281
Coggins, R. J.   13, 102, 282
Cohen, H. R.   241
Cohen, S. J. D.   88
Cohn, N.   267
Collins, J. J.   73, 234, 291–92
Conrad, J.   117
Coogan, M. D.   47–48
Cook, J. M.   195–97
Cook, S. L.   264–65, 282, 291
Cooper, J. S.   65
Coppens, J.   15
Cowley, A. E.   116
Crenshaw, J.   287
Cross, F. M.   15, 52, 68, 89, 103, 145–46, 187, 206, 239, 244, 248
Crown, A. D.   13
Crüsemann, F.   66
Cruz-Uribe, E.   139
Cumont, F.   122

Damrosch, D.   30
Dandamaev, M. A.   24, 46, 48, 120, 125, 139, 144, 147, 196, 208, 220–22, 230
Davies, P. R.   8, 291
Day, J.   124, 239, 241–42, 244, 249
Day, P.   298
Del Olmo Lete, G.   239
Depuydt, L.   140
Dequeker, L.   34
De Vries, S. J.   165, 287
Dexinger, F.   13
Dietrich, M.   239
Dijkstra, K.   146
Dion, P. E.   90, 129, 208
Donner, H.   13–14, 23, 113, 160
van Driel, G.   47, 222

Driver, G. R.   112, 245
Driver, S. R.   102, 131
Dubberstein, W. H.   162, 168, 234
Duchesne-Guillemin, J.   124–25
Duguid, I. M.   74, 80
Duke, R. K.   80
Dumbrell, W. J.   145
Durand, M.   138
Dyke, J. E.   208, 211

Eaton, J. H.   4–5, 74, 232
Ehrlich, A. B.   118
Eissfeldt, O.   7, 9, 51, 74, 88, 102, 104, 123
Eitan, I.   164
Elayi, J.   45
Engelken, K.   122
Engnell, I.   4
Eph'al, I.   46, 48, 119, 140, 154, 220, 226
Eskenazi, T. C.   30, 88–89, 237

Fales, F. M.   65, 164
Fehr, B.   127, 152
Fensham, F. C.   90, 96, 113, 188
Finkel, I.   134
Finkelstein, I.   44, 247
Fishbane, M.   97, 165–66
Fitzmyer, J. A.   129–30
Floyd, M. H.   55
Fohrer, G.   7, 50, 102
Foster, R. S.   13, 23
Frame, G.   152, 220
Freedman, D. N.   15, 51, 103–104
Frei, P.   25, 128, 199–200, 213
Fretheim, T. E.   64
Frye, R. N.   199

Gadd, C. J.   120, 136, 175
Galil, G.   2
Galling, K.   44, 90, 106–107, 113, 119–20, 160, 163, 170
Garbini, G.   29, 52
Gardiner, A. H.   197
Gaster, M.   13
Gelston, A.   97, 139
Gerbrandt, G. E.   68
Gershevitch, I.   125
Gese, H.   9, 22, 80, 291
de Geus, C. H. J.   247
Gibson, J. C. L.   145, 239
Gnoli, G.   123–24, 126–27
Goetze, A.   138
Goldman, M. D.   93

Goodblatt, D.   204
Gordis, R.   42
Gosse, B.   10
Gottwald, N. K.   8, 267
Gowan, D. E.   15
Grabbe, L. L.   11, 25, 49, 52, 205, 208
Graf, D. F.   145, 195
Graham, J. N.   45
Gray, G. B.   121
Gray, J.   239
Grayson, A. K.   65, 133, 138
Grelot, P.   165
Green, M. W.   65
Greenberg, M.   74, 80–81
Greenfield, J. C.   111
Greenwood, D. C.   60
Griffiths, J. G.   49
Gross, W.   64
Grunert, S.   200
Grünwaldt, K.   48
Gunneweg, A. H. J.   22, 89, 91, 105, 118
Güterbock, H. G.   71

Habel, N. C.   124, 290
Halpern, B.   89, 98, 100–101, 105
Handley-Schachler, M.   147
Hanhart, R.   88
Hanson, P. D.   17–19, 21–23, 28, 81–82, 193, 204, 264, 280, 282
Haran, M.   8, 53, 74
Harmatta, J.   135
Hasel, G. F.   54, 131
Hausmann, J.   54–56, 102, 170, 275–76
Hawkins, J. D.   2
Hayes, J. H.   2, 12, 14, 43, 67, 113
Heinz, K.   155
Hensley, L. V.   113, 129
Hentschke, R.   66
Herder, A.   239
Herrenschmidt, C.   124
Herrmann, S.   15, 23, 60, 160
Herzfeld, E.   140
Hiebert, T.   245
Hildebrand, D. R.   281
Hilprecht, H. V.   47
Hinz, W.   124
Hoglund, K.   153, 225–26
Hölscher, G.   106, 113
Hoffmann, H.-D.   69
Holladay, W. L.   56
van Hoonacker, A.   96

Hornblower, S.   227
Houtman, C.   52, 122, 126
Hughes, G. R.   197–98
Hughes, J.   1–2
Hurvitz, A.   8–9
Hurowitz, V.(A.)   6, 177

In der Smitten, W. T.   12, 14–15, 17, 19, 21, 113
Ishida, T.   4

Janowski, B.   239
Janssen, E.   43–44
Japhet, S.   32, 90, 96, 101–106, 113, 115, 119, 160–61, 170–71, 177, 179, 253, 275
Jeremias, C.   163, 165, 291
Jeremias, J.   239, 243
Joannès, F.   24, 47, 116, 121, 218
Johnson, A. R.   4
Johnson, D. G.   250
Jones, D. R.   46
Joosten, J.   50
Jordan, J.   136
Jursa, M.   24

Kaiser, O.   8
Kalimi, I.   103
Kalugila, L.   4
Kapelrud, A. S.   5, 9, 51
Katzenstein, H. J.   2
Kaufmann, Y.   8, 96
Keel, O.   3, 66
Keller, M.   68
Kellermann, D.   116
Kellermann, U.   15, 18, 52, 91
Kent, R.   230–31
Kessler, J.   177, 234–35, 238
Kienitz, F. K.   197
Kindler, A.   206
King, L.   165
Kippenberg, H. G.   14, 211
Kitchen, K. A.   131
Klein, R. W.   8, 50, 63, 74
Kleinig, J. W.   104
Kloos, C.   239, 244
Knauf, E. A.   145–46
Knibb, M. A.   282, 291
Knohl, I.   50–51
Koch, H.   147
Koch, K.   25, 52, 101–102, 281
Kochavi, M.   153
Kraeling, E. G.   116
Kraemer, D.   104

Kraus, H.-J.   46, 48, 232
Kreissig, H.   43, 228–29, 280
Kuenen, A.   23, 51
Kümmel, H. M.   24, 220
Kuhrt, A.   120–21, 133, 135–37,
    139–41, 149, 199, 217, 220, 223
Kvanig, H. S.   292

Laato, A.   15, 61, 73, 98
Landsberger, B.   152
Lang, B.   20, 280
Langdon, S.   134–35, 137–38, 175–76
Lapp, N. L.   187
Lapp, P. W.   187
Lecoq, P.   121
Legrain, L.   120, 136
Lemaire, A.   2, 10, 45, 47, 49, 145,
    188
Lemche, N. P.   8, 30, 247
Leuze, O.   196
Levenson, J. D.   49, 67, 74
Levin, C.   8
Levine, L. D.   138
Lindenberger, J. M.   111
Lindsay, J.   2
Lipiński, E.   98, 166, 232, 243–44
Liverani, M.   30
Livingston, A.   145, 176
Lloyd, A. B.   139, 197
Lochner-Hüttenbach, F.   148
Lods, A.   50–51
Loretz, O.   238–39
Lukonin, V.   144, 147
Lundquist, J. M.   3, 293
Lust, J.   72, 96, 131
Lutz, H. M.   247

McCullough, W. S.   23
McEvenue, S.   46, 90
Machinist, P.   65, 206
Malamat, A.   1, 43–44, 166
Mann, T. W.   243–44
Mantel, H.   21, 24, 280
Margarlith, O.   13
Marinković, P.   259
Mason, R. A.   55, 168, 170, 282, 296
Matta, G.   197
May, H. G.   101–102, 281
Mayes, A. D. H.   70
Meeks, D.   24
Meshorer, Y.   207
Mettinger, T. N. D.   3–5, 61, 68–69,
    73, 232, 249, 252, 256
Metzger, H.   117

Metzger, M.   3
Meyer, E.   23, 52, 89, 113, 129, 131,
    197, 231
Meyers, C. L. & E. M.   10, 13, 25, 32,
    44, 51, 90, 161, 166, 170, 183,
    185–203, 215–16, 233, 275–76,
    280–81, 295
Meyers, E. M.   188
Michaeli, F.   113, 118
Michalowski, P.   65
Mildenberg, L.   10, 207
Millar, W. R.   250
Miller, J. M.   2, 12, 14, 113
Mitchell, H.   203
Mittmann, S.   45
Modrzejewski, J. M.   144, 150, 200
de Moor, J. C.   5, 93
Moore, C. A.   42
Morgenstern, J.   231
Mosis, R.   17, 103, 118
Mowinckel, S.   5, 14–15, 52, 88, 91,
    107, 113, 231, 247
Müller, H.-P.   45
Myers, J. M.   45, 50, 52, 88, 103,
    196, 204

Newsome, J. D.   16, 104
Nicholson, E. W.   9, 67, 91, 291
Niditch, S.   74
Niehr, H.   122–23
Nikel, J.   113
Nodet, E.   49
North, R.   291
Noth, M.   23, 45, 51, 90, 113

O'Brien, M. A.   69
Oded, B.   1, 2
Oegema, G. S.   234
Oelsner, J.   154, 217
Oesterley, W. O. E.   13, 44, 48, 128
Ollenburger, B. C.   4, 5
Olmstead, A. T.   197, 199, 231, 233
Olyan, S. M.   66, 124
Oppenheim, A. L.   136
Oppert, J.   121
Otto, E.   4

Pardee, D.   239
Parker, R. A.   162, 168, 195, 197,
    234
Parpola, S.   152, 155
Perlitt, L.   4, 67
Pestman, P. W.   200
Petersen, D. L.   10, 19, 32, 98, 163,

166, 170–71, 208, 233, 259, 261,
    275–76, 281, 291, 295
Petit, T.   188, 196–97
Petitjean, A.   98, 232, 256
Pfeiffer, R. H.   7, 50, 102, 104, 113
van der Ploeg, J.   14
Plöger, O.   11, 16–18, 21, 264
Pohlmann, K.-F.   57, 88, 103
Polzin, R.   9, 29, 103
Pongratz-Leisten, B.   6
Pope, M. H.   122
Porten, B.   42, 111, 144
Porter, B. N.   135, 152
Posener, G.   117, 197–98
Poulssen, N.   5, 68
Preuss, H. D.   247
Prinsloo, W. S.   168
Purvis, J. D.   13
de Pury, A.   69

Quaegebeur, J.   200

von Rad, G.   67, 103, 247
Rahmani, L. Y.   206
Raitt, T. M.   60
Rappaport, U.   207
Rawlinson, H. C.   132
Ray, J. D.   197
Rehm, M.   15
Reich, N. J.   197
Rendsburg, G.   9
Rendtorff, R.   9
Renger, J.   217
Ries, G.   9
Ringgren, H.   4, 15
Rivkin, E.   22–23
Robert, L.   127
Roberts, J. J. M.   4–5, 167, 239,
    245–46, 286
Roberts, K. A.   268
Robinson, G.   49
Robinson, T. H.   13, 44, 48, 128
Römer, T.   69
Rofé, A.   283
Rosenthal, F.   130
Rost, L.   67, 116
Roth, M.   222
Rothstein, J. W.   13, 280
Rowley, H. H.   13
Rudolph, W.   11, 16, 32, 88, 96,
    102, 105–106, 112–13, 118,
    163–64, 169, 203, 236, 258,
    275–76, 280
Rüterswörden, U.   68, 199–200

Sæbø, M.   96, 247
Sancisi-Weerdenburg, H.   125
Sanmartin, J.   239
San Nicolò, M.   116, 121
Sasson, J. M.   10
Sauer, G.   233
Schaper, J.   192
Schaeder, H. H.   113, 129
Schäfer, P.   144, 150
Schenker, A.   88
Schmid, H.   4?/239
Schmidt, M.   67, 233
Schmidt, W. H.   239
Schott, A.   136
Schottroff, W.   11, 208
Schramm, B.   282
Schultz, C.   106, 275
Schwartz, D. R.   205, 309
Scoralick, R.   241
Scullion, J.   253
Seitz, C. R.   20, 58
Sekine, M.   67
Seline, S.   283
Sellin, E.   233
Sérandour, A.   203
Seybold, K.   4, 67, 232–33
Shabazi, A. S.   230
Shea, W. H.   42, 120
Sherwin-White, S.   121, 140, 223
Smith, D. L.   12, 22, 48, 50–51,
    53–54, 102, 208, 269, 280
Smith, J. Z.   33
Smith, M.   9, 12, 19–21, 23, 42, 45,
    90, 189, 280
Smith, M. S.   126
Smith, N. H.   76
Smith, P. A.   29, 283–84
Smith, S.   133
von Soden, W.   133
Soggin, J. A.   8
Speiser, E. A.   71
van der Spek, R. J.   138, 223
Spiegelberg, W.   139, 197, 200
Spiekermann, H.   138
Stähli, H.-P.   126
Steck, O. H.   4, 11, 16, 168, 171–72,
    253
Stern, E.   10, 43, 46, 154
Sternberg, M.   29
Stevenson, K. R.   74, 81
Stiegler, S.   11
Stolper, M. W.   47, 194–96, 219
Stoltz, F.   4, 239
Strassmaier, J.   121

Streck, M. 137–38, 165
Stronach, D. 124–26
Stuhlmueller, C. 73, 75
Sweeney, M. A. 10, 258

Tadmor, H. 113, 177
Talmon, S. 13, 21, 98–101, 103, 105, 253
Tcherikover, V. 202
Teixidor, J. 122
Terrien, S. 69
Thompson, R. J. 9, 52
Thompson, T. L. 8
Thronveit, M. A. 103
Tigchelaar, E. J. C. 284
Tollefson, K. D. 265
Tollington, J. E. 32, 204, 231, 237, 295
van der Toorn, K. 5, 123
Torrey, C. C. 106, 113, 118, 130–32, 161
Tournay, R. J. 9
Townsend, T. 281
Tozzi, P. 139
Trompf, G. W. 71, 265–66
Tuell, S. S. 25, 74, 80
Tuland, C. G. 96–97
Tuplin, C. 139, 144, 147
Turcan, R.-A. 124

Uehlinger, C. 66
Unger, T. 281
Ungnad, A. 116, 137

Vallat, F. 126
Van De Mieroop, M. 220
VanderKam, J. C. 104, 205–206, 292, 295
van Seters, J. 8
Van Winkle, D. W. 76
de Vaux, R. 48, 113, 129–30, 132, 138–40
Vincent, A. 42, 122
Vink, J. G. 9
Vörlander, H. 8
Vogt, H. C. M. 11–12, 91–92, 116
Vriesen, T. C. 15

Wainwright, G. A. 24
Wallace, A. F. C. 268
Wallis, G. 47
Wanke, G. 9, 57, 238

Ward, W. H. 246
Waterman, L. 231
Weidner, E. F. 2, 46, 116
Weinberg, J. P. 25, 43, 189, 207–17, 220–29, 275
Weinberg, S. S. 43
Weinfeld, M. 4, 68, 133, 166
Weippert, H. 10
Weissbach, F. H. 132, 136
Welch, A. C. 90
Wellhausen, J. 22–23, 52, 113
Welten, P. 103
Whedbee, J. W. 168
Whitehead, J. D. 129
Whitelam, K. 5, 8
Whybray, R. N. 9
Widengren, G. 72, 125, 138, 206
Wieshöfer, J. 124, 139, 143, 148, 200–201, 230
Wildberger, H. 67
Willi, T. 103
Williamson, H. G. M. 16, 29, 52, 55, 60, 88–90, 93, 96, 98–101, 103–107, 109, 112–17, 119–20, 122–23, 128, 132, 147, 149, 158, 160–61, 167, 188, 205, 208, 250, 265, 282–83
Wilson, A. 66, 73, 76
Wilson, B. R. 267
Wilson, R. D. 120–21
Wilson, R. R. 29, 70
Winkle, R. E. 165
Wolff, H. W. 13, 32, 158, 169–71, 231, 234, 238, 275, 280
Worsley, P. 267
van der Woude, A. S. 234
Wright, J. S. 96
Würthwein, E. 91
Wyatt, N. 48, 239, 244

Yamauchi, E. M. 139
Yardeni, A. 111
Yellin, J. 43
Young, T. C. 195
Yoyotte, J. 117, 126

Zadok, R. 16, 47–48
Zauzich, K.-T. 197
Zawadzki, S. 220
Zenger, E. 64
Zevit, Z. 9, 13
Zimmerli, W. 10, 60, 74, 116
Zorn, J. 43

INDEX OF BIBLICAL REFERENCES

HEBREW BIBLE

Genesis
23:4 — 123
23:7 — 123
27–45 — 53

Exodus
9:3 — 242
29 — 243
15:1–18 — 244
15:7–8 — 244
15:10–11 — 244
15:14–16 — 244
15–19 — 243
17:4 — 163
25–31 — 64
29 — 243
19:16–25 — 243
19:18 — 243
19:19 — 242
35–40 — 64

Leviticus
17–26 — 50
21:10–15 — 204
29 — 223
25:1–7 — 165
26:32–35 — 165

Numbers
10:35–36 — 247
21:21–35 — 247
35:25 — 204

Judges
5 — 247
5:4 — 244
5:4–5 — 247
6-9 — 67

I Samuel
4:1–11 — 247
5:1–6:19 — 247
8 — 67
8–10 — 4
10:17–24 — 67

16 — 4
16:8–10 — 232
26:19 — 49

II Samuel
5–7 — 4, 254
6 — 5
6:13 — 5
6:17–18 — 5
6:21 — 232
7 — 237, 253
7:1 — 254
7:1–14 — 288
7:4–17 — 254
7:5 — 231
7:8 — 231
8:17–18 — 6
12:1–15 — 288
21 — 288
21:1 — 288
21:5–11 — 288
22:1 — 288
24 — 4
20:25 — 6
21:1–14 — 172
22:7–18 — 245
22:8 — 245
22:8–11 — 250
22:10–18 — 245
22:16 — 243
24:25 — 5

I Kings
2:26–27 — 6
2:35 — 6
3:4 — 5
3:15 — 5
5:1 — 78
5:15 — 90
5:15–32 — 6
6 — 2
6–8 — 237
7:13–22 — 3
7:51 — 6
8:5 — 5

354 INDEX OF BIBLICAL REFERENCES

8:16	232	25:8–12	44
8:62–64	5	25:8–17	42
9:10–14	6	25:8–21	42
9:25	5, 6	25:8–27	44
11:32	232	25:12	44, 45, 211
11:34	232	25:18	295
11:36	232	25:25	44, 276
12:26–32	254	25:25–26	57
16:1–7	59	25:26	42
17:1	288		
17–18	59	*Isaiah*	
18–19	288	1:17–18	268
19	288	2:2–4	14, 60, 258
19:40–46	288	4:2	232
20:35–43	59	4:2–3	54
22	287	4:5	252
22:1–38	59	5:8–10	172, 288
		5:26–30	64
II Kings		6	67, 290, 291
1–2	4	6:1	4
5–8	254	6:5	4
5:17	49	6:13	54
5:18	254	7:3	54
9–10	59	8:23–9:6	72
12	254	9:5–6	14
12:1–17	6	10:5–11	163
12:5–9	6	10:12–19	163
12:11	204	10:20–21	54
16:10–18	6	10:25	163
16:12–15	5	11:1–5	14
17	58	11:1–9	72
17:5–23	59	11:10	60, 232, 258, 259
17:24–41	105	11:10–16	59
18:1–8	68	11:11	54
19:4	55	11:12	72
19:34	232	13–23	247
21	66	13:6–7	248
21:1–18	59	13:9	248
21:10–15	58, 59	13:9–13	248
22:1–23:27	68	13:13	248
22:3	90	14:1–2	60, 258
22:3–7	6, 90, 245	14:3–23	251
22:4–8	204	14:13–14	251
22:13–28	290	14:16	251
22:19–22	290	16:6–12	163
22:23	6, 90	17:12–14	232
23:4	204	19:16–25	60, 258
23:31–25:20	59	21	44
24:1–4	64	24–27	10, 249, 250
24:8–16	44	24:4	248, 250
24:12–16	44	24:7	250
24:14	44	24:19	250
24:16	44	24:23	4, 250
24:20–25:24	1	25:6–8	60, 258

26:1	250	43:15	77, 249, 261
27:1	250	43:47	54
27:2	250	44:6	60, 77, 249, 261
29:1–10	67	44:6–8	61
32:1–8	72	44:6–23	66
32:9	163	44:24	60
32:11	163	44:24–28	61, 75
32:15–20	256	44:24–45:13	75
32:18	163	44:25	54
33:22	4	44:26–28	77
37:4	54	44:28	76, 77, 79, 89
37:23–29	163	45:1	77, 232
37:29	163	45:1–3	75, 77, 261
37:32	54	45:1–6	76, 89
37:35	232	45:3	116
38	67	45:4–6	75, 77
40:1–2	75	45:5–6	75
40:1–11	76	45:9	159
40:2	163	45:9–13	61, 77
40:3–5	20, 60, 72, 75, 249, 261	45:11–13	75, 261
40:9	75	45:13	77, 93
40:9–11	20, 60, 75, 261	45:14	60, 257
40:10–11	60, 249	45:14–15	76
40:12–26	61	45:15	60, 116
40:12–31	66	45:20	55
40:15–26	76	45:20–25	61, 76, 257
40:25	60	45:20–47:15	261
41:1–7	61, 75, 89	45:22–24	60, 258
41:2	77	46:1–13	66
41:2–4	75, 261	46:1–47:15	61
41:2–5	77	46:3	54
41:8–16	20	46:8–10	75
41:11–12	75	46:8–13	75
41:14	60	46:10–13	75
41:16	60	46:11	77
41:17–20	20, 60, 72, 75, 249, 261	47:1–15	75
41:20	60, 249	47:4	116
41:21–29	61	47:6–9	163
41:25	77, 93	47:8–11	163
41:25–27	75	48:11	60
41:25–29	75	48:12–16	75, 261
41:27	75	48:14	75, 77
42:1	232	48:15	77
42:6	257	48:16	75
42:10–17	60, 75, 249, 261	48:17	116
42:15	248	48:20	258
42:21	77, 261	49:6	76, 257
43:1–2	76	49:7	60
43:1–7	60, 261	49:7–26	75
43:8–13	61	49:8	174
43:11	60	49:12–13	54, 59
43:14	60	49:23	60
		49:36	60
		51:3	75

51:9–10	75, 249, 261	3:18	59
51:17–52:2	75	4–6	58
52:1	75	4:5–5:17	64
52:7	77, 249, 253, 256, 261	4:24	248
		5:15–17	64
52:7–12	75, 261	5:20–25	288
52:11	76	5:22	241
52:12	116	6:1	64
52:13–53:12	61	6:22–30	64
54:1–2	256	7	69, 287
54:1–3	75, 261	7:1–15	67
54:11–12	252	7:16–20	66
54:11–17	75, 256, 261	7:29–8:3	66
54:14	75, 268	8:8–23	288
55–66	18, 29, 253, 272, 282, 297	8:19	4
		9	58
55:1–5	14, 17, 18, 74	9:9–21	64
55:3	72	10:10	248
55:4–5	60, 76, 257	10:12–16	241
56:1–8	283	12:4	288
56:3–8	269	12:15–16	60–258
56:9–57:21	283	13:18–19	44
58:1–59:20	283	14:1–9	288
60	253	14:13–16	287
60–62	28, 253	15:1–9	58
60:1–3	60, 258	15:4	58
60:1–22	256	16:14–15	20, 60, 72, 258
60:2	252	16:19–21	60, 258
60:6–9	252	17:12	4, 252
60:7	252	22:24	232
60:11	252	23:1–8	20, 72, 259
60:13	252	23:3	72
60:17	252, 253	23:3–8	59
60:22	252	23:5	232
63–64	285	23:5–6	14
63:7–64:11	167, 250	23:7–8	20, 60, 72, 258
63:18	167	24	56
63:19	250	24:1	44
64:1	250	24:1–10	20
64:8–11	174, 289	24:8	55
64:9–10	42, 167	25:1	165
64:11	168	25:1–13	58
65:1–66:17	283	25:9	232
66:1–4	28, 283, 284	25:11	20, 163
66:18–21	60, 258	25:11–12	71, 93, 164, 165, 168
		25:12	175
Jeremiah		25:24–38	247
1	290	26	69, 287
1:11–13	290	26:1–19	67
1:13–19	64	27	287
2	58	27–29	53
2:14–25	66	27:1–22	64
3:17	60, 258		

27:20	44	49:21	248
28:1–4	286	50–51	72, 75, 94, 148,
28:1–17	287		164, 168, 258,
29:1	22, 47, 54		285, 286
29:1–2	44	50:8	258
29:10	20, 71, 93, 163,	50:19	72
	164, 165, 168	50:29	163
29:11–14	20	50:31–40	163
29:16–20	56	50:34	248
30–31	59, 286	50:46	248
30:8–9	14	51:1	94
30:9	259	51:6	258
30:11	72	51:7	163
30:21	74, 259	51:11	94
31:8	258	51:29	241, 248
31:13–14	256	51:33	163
31:23–34	72	51:34–40	163
32	57	51:45	258
32:27–41	20	51:49–52	163
33	60	52:12–30	42
33:6	253	52:15	55
33:9–13	256	52:15–16	44
33:14–16	232	52:16	45, 211
33:14–18	259	52:24	295
33:14–26	14, 72	52:28	44
34:7	43	52:28–30	44
39:8–10	42	52:30	44
39:10	44, 45, 211		
40–44	57, 58, 59	*Ezekiel*	
40:11	55	1	291
40:15	55	1:1–2:15	290
41:1–3	44, 276	3:15	46
41:5	46, 153, 226	5:7–17	58
42–44	57	5:10	55
42:2	55	6–11	58
42:7–13	58	6:1–7:14	64
42:7–22	57	8	66
42:8	44	8–11	78
42:15	55	8:1	22, 47
42:19	55	8:4	252
43:4–7	42	8:17	46
43:5	55, 57	9–11	56
44	66	9–23	58
44:1	42	9:3	252
44:2	43, 57	9:8	55
44:12	55	9:8–11	58
44:14	55	10:1–22	20
44:16–19	66	10:4	252
44:18	55	10:18	252
44:22	57	10:19	252
44:28	55, 59	11:1–13	58
46–51	247	11:13	55
48:28–33	163	11:14–21	20, 56

11:15	20, 45, 54	37:28	61
11:16	49	39:27	72
11:16–21	60	40–42	78
11:17	72	40:48–41:15	3
11:22	252	43:1–6	78
11:23	252	43:7–12	78
12:15	60	43:13–17	78
12:20	60	45:1–8	79
13	287	45:13–46:24	78
13:14	60	47:1–12	78
13:21	60	47:13–23	79
13:23	60	47:13–48:29	78, 79
14:1	22, 47, 54	47:14	80
16	58, 66	48:35	78
16:62	60		
17:21	55	*Hosea*	
17:22–24	72	1:4	163
18	61	2:2	60
20	66	3:5	72
20:1	22, 47, 54	4–13	58–288
20:3	22, 47	4:1–3	172
20:9	60		
20:14	60	*Joel*	
20:22	60	1–2	172
20:33–44	20, 60	1:11–12	288
20:44	60	1:16–20	288
22	66	2:1	250
22:16	60	2:1–11	250
25–32	247	2:2	251
25:16	55	2:6	251
26:18	248	2:10	251
28:1–10	163	2:11	251
28:24–26	59, 285	4:16	248, 251
28:26	60		
29:21	14	*Amos*	
30:3	174	1–2	247
33:10–20	61	1:2	242, 247–48, 251
33:23–29	20	1:2–2:16	247
33:24	57	2–6	58
33:25–29	57	3:12	54
34:23	232	4:4–14	172
34:23–24	14	4:6–9	288
34:23–31	72, 259, 286	5:15	54
34:24	74	6:1	163
35	163	7:10–17	287
36:22	60	9:8–10	54
36:23	61	9:11–12	14
37:15–28	59	9:11–15	72
37:15–31	286		
37:21–28	72	*Jonah*	
37:24–25	14, 232	1:9	122
37:24–31	259		
37:25	72	*Micah*	
37:26	72	2:12	60, 72
		3:9–12	67

4:1–4	14, 60, 258	1:8	146, 233, 252, 297
4:6	72	1:9	98, 173, 178
4:7	4, 54, 249	1:9–11	171
5:1–3	14	1:10–11	173
5:1–5	72	1:12	55, 169, 183, 203,
5:2	54		295, 296
5:5–7	54	1:14	55, 169, 183, 232,
			253, 270, 295, 296
Nahum		1:15	194
1:2–8	245–46	1:15–2:1	86, 275
1:4	243, 248	2:2	55, 203, 295, 296
		2:2–3	169
Habakkuk		2:2–4	274
3:2–15	245	2:3	98, 170, 252, 274,
3:6	245		281
3:8	245	2:4	203, 232, 253,
3:10	245		275, 295, 296
3:13	245	2:6	233, 240, 251
		2:6–7	233
Zephaniah		2:6–9	232, 233, 234,
2:7	54		238, 251, 253, 261
2:9	54	2:7	240, 245, 252
3:9–10	60, 258	2:7–9	252
3:12	54	2:9	252, 253, 261, 281
3:13	268	2:10	231
3:14–15	4	2:10–14	204, 279, 280,
3:15	4, 249		281, 284
3:18–20	60	2:10–19	99, 102, 281
		2:11	232, 253
Haggai		2:14	279–80, 281, 296
1:1	86, 168, 169, 183,	2:15	98, 281
	203, 231, 295, 296	2:15–17	171
1:1–4	298	2:15–19	97, 287, 289
1:2	98, 169, 170, 171,	2:18	95, 98, 281, 289
	173, 174, 177,	2:18–19	233
	232, 236, 237,	2:19	281
	253, 270, 271,	2:20	231
	272, 274, 275,	2:20–23	231, 233, 234,
	281, 286, 296		235, 238, 251,
1:2–4	178, 272, 273		252, 261, 266,
1:2–9	173, 177		273, 289
1:2–11	87, 158, 168–69,	2:21	233, 240
	178, 286, 287,	2:22	233, 240, 244
	293, 302	2:23	183, 232, 233,
1:4	98, 173, 177, 178,		251, 253
	281, 286	2:26	289
1:4–8	171		
1:4–9	173	*Zechariah*	
1:4–11	168	1:1	86, 231, 273, 289
1:5	232, 253	1:1–6	166, 290
1:5–11	171	1:1–6:8	291
1:6	171, 173, 275	1:2	163
1:6–11	266	1:2–6	284
1:7	232, 253	1:3	232, 255

1:4	232, 255, 284	5:2–5	290
1:5–6	166	5:3	266, 293
1:6	232, 255	5:4	232, 255
1:7	86, 162	5:5–11	266
1:7–17	162, 167, 195, 272	5:6	266, 293
1:7–6:8	289, 290, 291	5:8	266
1:8–10	162	5:10	290
1:9	290	6	278
1:11	162, 194, 234	6:4–5	290
1:11–12	291	6:8	258
1:11–14	290	6:9–10	203, 296
1:12	164, 165, 166, 177, 232, 272	6:9–13	296
		6:9–15	203, 232, 268, 290
1:12–16	168, 271, 272, 273	6:10	276
1:12–17	87, 162, 163–64, 302	6:11	203, 295
		6:12	232, 255
1:14	232, 255	6:12–13	203
1:15	163, 266	6:13	191, 203, 232, 233, 235, 259
1:16	163, 173, 232, 255		
1:17	232, 255	6:15	232, 255
2:6	291	7:3	232, 255
2:7	290	7:4	232, 255
2:8–9	291	7:4–14	275, 290
2:9	256	7:5	275, 276
2:10	258	7:9	232, 255
2:10–14	233	7:12	163
2:10–17	164, 254–55, 261	7:13	232, 255
2:12	232, 255	7:14	232, 255
2:13	232, 233, 255, 256, 261	8:1–4	232, 255
		8:1–8	164, 255, 261
2:14	164, 256	8:1–15	266
2:15	232, 255, 256	8:1–17	290
2:16	164, 256	8:2–3	256
2:16–17	232, 256	8:3	164, 232, 256
3	266, 278, 284, 295, 296	8:4	233
		8:4–6	256
3:1	295	8:6	55, 232, 255–56, 276
3:1–10	203		
3:7	232, 255	8:7	232, 255, 276
3:8	232, 295	8:7–8	233, 261
3:9	232, 233, 255, 259, 296	8:9	232, 255
		8:10	266, 284, 293
3:10	232, 255	8:11	232, 255, 276
4:1	290	8:11–12	55
4:3–4	290	8:12	256, 276
4:6	232, 233, 255, 259	8:12–13	233
4:6–10	98, 259, 266, 270, 296	8:13	276
		8:14	232, 255
4:8–9	95	8:16–17	266, 268, 284
4:9	98, 232, 255	8:18–19	275
4:14	233	8:18–23	232, 255, 290
5	296	8:20–23	60, 164, 256–57
5:1–4	266	8:23	256

Psalms

2	4, 241
6:4	165
7:7–9	241
8:2	232
9:6–9	241
10:16	3
18	4, 140
18:7–18	245
18:8	245
18:8–11	250
18:9	243
18:10–18	245
18:16	243
18:17–18	245
20	4
21	4
21:6	232
22:27–29	60, 258
22:28	241
24	238, 240
24:1–2	240
24:7–10	252
26:8	252
29	3, 238, 240
29:1–3	252
29:3–9	242
29:3–10	241
29:9	252
29:11	253
37:10	163
44	44, 285
44:18–20	66
44:24	166
45	4
45:4	232
46	3, 238, 242, 243, 244, 253, 256
46:6	242
46:7	242, 250
47	3, 238
47:1–2	241
47:7–9	241
48	3, 238, 242, 243, 244, 253, 256
48:2	256
48:3	242, 251
48:5–7	242
48:7	242
50:2	4
65:2	4
66:2	252
67:5	241
68:5	241
68:9	244
68:17	4
68:25	3
68:33–34	241
72	4
74	44, 167, 249, 285
74:1–7	42
74:3–8	167
74:9	167, 174, 289
74:9–11	71
74:10	165, 166, 168
74:10–11	167
74:12–14	249
74:12–17	3
75:3–4	241
76	3, 238, 253, 256
77:17	245
77:17–21	245
77:19	245
78:70	232
79	167, 285
79:1	42
79:5	71, 167, 168, 174, 289
80:5	71, 165, 167, 174, 289
82:8	241
83:18	241
84:8	4
84:9–12	3
84:19	3
85:6	166, 168
86:9–10	60, 258
87	60, 258
89	4, 44, 68
89:4	232
89:10–11	249
89:29–38	68
89:39–53	68
89:40	232
89:51	232
90:13	165
93	3, 238
93:3–4	240
94:3	165
96–99	3, 238
96:1–5	256
96:4	241
96:6	232
96:7–8	252
96:7–10	241
96:9	241

96:9–10	241
96:13	241
97	240
97:1–5	241
97:6	252
97:6–9	241
97:8	256
98:1	256
98:5–6	256
98:9	241
99:1	241
99:2–4	241
99:3	256
99:5	256
99:9	256
101	4
102	44
102:14	174, 175
104:1	232
104:1–9	3, 241
104:7	243
110	4
114	242, 243, 244
122	253
123:4	163
132	4
132:10	232
132:13–14	4
133:3	4
136:5	123
136:26	123
137	49
144	4
144:4–7	245, 250
146:10	3, 4
149:2	4

Job
1–2	295
9:5	240
9:5–14	240
9:11	241
12:5	163
26:5–14	240

Proverbs
3:19	123
8:1	123
8:27–29	123

Lamentations
1:18–20	64
2	42
2:1–8	62

2:17	62
3:42	62
5	168
5:20	71, 166, 168
5:20–22	174, 289
5:22	71, 166, 168

Esther
| 2:5 | 42 |
| 4:16 | 42 |

Daniel
2:18–19	122
2:28	122
2:37	122
2:44	122
4:34	122
9:2	165

Ezra
1	17, 89, 91
1–2	101
1–3	13, 146
1–4	91
1:1–3	164
1:1–4	155, 261, 279
1:1–11	89, 129
1:1–20	120
1:1–3:13	88
1:1–4:5	32, 36, 62, 86, 87, 95, 99, 101, 102, 105, 110, 114, 153, 155, 157, 158, 161, 165, 168, 179, 180, 181, 215, 227, 277, 278, 279, 302, 204, 306, 308
1:1–4:7	88
1:1–4:24	93
1:2	120, 122, 128
1:2–3	90
1:2–4	87, 89, 110, 111, 114, 128, 159, 213
1:3	112, 115, 116, 119
1:4	117, 120
1:5	90, 128
1:5–6	95
1:6	91, 107, 115, 119, 120, 158
1:7–8	89
1:7–11	110
1:8	90, 96 120
1:8–11	88, 159

Reference	Pages
1:11	89, 128
2	88, 90, 106, 107, 157, 181, 226
2:1	90
2:1–2	153, 277
2:2	107
2:21–35	154
2:36	90
2:59	46
2:60–63	90
2:68	90, 95, 100, 101, 107
2:68–69	91, 296
2:68–70	100, 101, 158
2:68–4:5	100, 101
2:70	90, 100
3	90, 95, 96, 98, 102, 108, 157, 181
3–4	11, 104, 105, 108, 157, 158
3:1	90, 91, 107
3:1–6	94, 95, 99, 100, 153
3:1–7	100
3:1–4:5	98, 99, 102, 103, 110, 128, 157, 158, 179, 270, 279
3:2–13	89
3:3	12, 90, 91, 92, 99, 101, 279
3:4–6	90
3:6	91, 100, 101
3:7	90, 91, 95, 100, 120
3:7–10	98
3:7–13	96, 97
3:7–4:3	99, 100
3:8	91, 100, 101, 118
3:8–9	94, 95, 99
3:8–13	95, 100, 153, 156
3:8–4:5	95
3:10	96, 97
3:10–12	95, 97, 98
3:11	97
3:12	97–98
4	12, 93, 105
4:1	93
4:1–3	12, 92, 99, 102
4:1–5	12, 19, 91–92, 94, 99, 100, 105, 181, 279, 280
4:1–24	88
4:2	92, 108, 128
4:3	12. 120, 129
4:4	12, 13, 91, 92
4:4–5	99
4:5	103, 105, 109, 120
4:6–24	95, 99, 105
4:6–6:18	95
4:7	120
4:8–23	105, 110
4:8–6:18	88, 89, 105, 110, 113, 120
4:9–10	13, 92, 108
4:9–16	214
4:11–22	129
4:12	228
4:12–16	160
4:17–22	120
4:24	86, 99, 105, 120, 214
5	95, 105, 109, 146, 149, 173, 297
5–6	89, 93, 95, 99, 102, 105, 201, 202, 216, 230, 235, 236, 262, 271, 273, 294, 298, 302
5:1	95, 99, 262, 273
5:1–2	99
5:1–4	236
5:1–17	201
5:1–6:15	279
5:1–6:18	93, 279
5:1–6:22	88
5:2	236
5:3	196
5:6–17	236
5:7–17	129, 201
5:9	201
5:11–12	122, 125
5:11–16	236
5:12	110
5:13–16	87, 95, 96, 97, 109, 110, 179, 180, 201
5:14	90
5:14–16	94, 153
5:16	95, 97, 102, 109, 152, 156, 159, 160, 236
6	148
6:1–2	106, 201, 271
6:1–18	236
6:2–5	87, 97, 110, 111–12, 302
6:2–12	120, 129

6:3	112	1:1–4:17	155
6:4	144, 146	1:2–3	228
6:5	95, 296	1:4–5	12, 125
6:6–12	201, 236	1:19	229
6:6–15	202	1:19–20	12
6:7–12	214	2:1–8	271
6:8	146, 296	2:4	122, 125
6:8–9	95	2:16–18	205
6:8–10	144	2:20	122, 125
6:9	147	3:33–4:17	12
6:9–10	122, 125	4:1	229
6:10	159	4:8	118
6:14	105, 120, 273	4:13	118
6:15	88	6:1–19	12, 155
6:16	116, 118	7	88, 107, 157, 226
6:16–18	105	7:4	228
6:17	116	7:6	107
6:19–22	88	7:6–7	277
6:21	12, 91, 92, 116	7:6–72	106
7	17, 126, 131, 204, 213	7:26–38	154
		7:61	46
7:1	120	7:69	107
7:5	205	7:69–72	101
7:6	116	7:70–71	296
7:10	51	7:71	118
7:12	122, 126	7:72	91, 107
7:12–26	120, 129	8:7	62
7:14	201	8:13	62
7:21	122, 126	9:24	91, 92
7:21–22	143	9:30	91
7:23	122, 126	10	148, 205, 229, 309
7:24	144		
7:25	51	10:29	12, 91, 92, 118
8:1–14	119	11:1	118
8:35	116	11:1–19	228
9	12, 55, 108	11:20	118
9–10	204	11:20–36	154
9:1	62, 92, 116	12:1	277
9:1–2	91	12:4	273
9:1–3	12	12:16	273
9:2	12	12:27–43	91
9:7	91	12:44–13:31	205
9:8	118	13	309
9:11–15	12	13:4–9	12
9:13–15	118	13:4–31	91
9:15	116	13:11	309
10:2	91, 92	13:13–27	12
10:10–11	92	13:23–27	63
10:14	92	13:23–28	229
10:17–18	92	13:28	14, 62, 205
Nehemiah		*I Chronicles*	
1–7	91	3:17	183
1:1	42	3:17–19	183
1:1–3	118	3:18	89

21:1	295	3–5	97
22:2	90	3:3	97
22:15	90	3:3–8	97
23–26	204	5:11–14	97
23:31	90	24:27	97
		31:2–21	204
II Chronicles		34:8	90
1:18	90	36:20	118
2–7	237	36:20–21	165
2:4	90	36:20–23	164
3	3	36:21	21, 93

INDEX OF OTHER ANCIENT SOURCES

CUNEIFORM TEXTS

Sumerian Literary Texts
Laments 65, 165

Akkadian Literary Texts and Chronicles
Tukulti-Ninurta Epic 65
Erra Epic 65
Marduk Prophecy 176
Assur to Assurbanipal 176
Weidner Chron. 65
Nabopolassar Chron. 138
Nabonius Chron. 120, 133
Verse Account of Nabonidus 133, 149

Assyrian Royal Inscriptions (by reign)
Sargon 138
Esarhaddon 65, 122, 137–38, 166, 174–76
Assurbanipal 137–38, 165

Babylonian Royal Inscriptions (by reign)
Kurigalzu 137
Marduk-apla-iddina 175
Nebuchadrezzar 137, 138
Nabonidus 135, 137, 175–77

Achaemenid Persian Royal Inscriptions (by reign)
Cyrus II

Cylinder 117, 126–27, 132–37, 142, 149, 153–54, 176
Other 120, 136

Darius I
DB I, 2 121
DB I, 35–61 230
DB III. 10–19 231
DBa, 2 121
Susa Trilig. Statue 126, 139

Xerxes I
'Daiva' Inscription 140

NB/LB Legal, Economic and Administrative texts (by reign)
Nebuchadrezzar 116
Cyrus II 47, 120–21
Darius I 47, 116, 154
Xerxes I 121
Artaxerxes I 121

(by archive)
Ea-ilūta-bāni 217–18
Egibi 217
Murašu 47–48, 62, 119, 140, 217, 219

Other Cuneiform texts
EA 149, 7 122
NA Letters 152, 155

UGARITIC TEXTS

CTA			
1–4	239	2 iv 32	239
2 i 7	240	3 B 40	241
2 i 22	240	3 C 36	242
2 i 26	240	3 D 36	240
2 i 30	240	3 D 44	242
2 iii 7	240	3 E 40–50	239
2 iv	239, 243, 245	4 iv 43–4 v 102	239
2 iv 4	240	4 v 75–81	253
2 iv 8	241	4 v 91–97	253
2 iv 10	239	4 v 111–199	239
		4 vi 35–38	239

4 vii 7ff.	243	4 vii 40–41	243
4 vii	239, 243	4 vii 43–52	242
4 vii 25–52	241–42	4 vii 49–50	239
4 vii 29	241		
4 vii 29–31	242	*Other Ugaritic texts*	
4 vii 31–32	241	RS 17.227, 51	122
4 vii 32–41	241	RS 17.237 r. 11	122
4 vii 32–51	241	RS 17.340 r. 17	122
4 vii 35	241	RS 24.245	239, 243

PAPYRI AND INSCRIPTIONS

Aramaic Papyri
Cowley, *Aramaic Papyri* (AP)

21	143, 199
27	150
30	117, 149–51, 205–206
30:2	122, 126
30:2–3	149
30:4–8	144
30:13	42
30:13–14	139
30:15	122
30:18–19	205
30:21	42
30:25	42
30:25–26	151
30:27	126
30:27–28	122
30:28–29	150
31:26–27	122
32	117, 144
32:3	151
32:3–4	122
32:9	42
33:10–11	42
33:12–14	150
38:3	122
38:5	122
40:1	122

Other Aramic papyri
Ahiqar   111
Behistun   111

Brooklyn (BMAP)   116
Contracts   111
Hermopolis   111

Semitic Inscriptions

KAI 4	123
KAI 4:3	122
KAI 26 A III 18	122
KAI 181	65
KAI 181:3–4	254
KAI 181:9–10	254
KAI 202 A 3:11–12	122
KAI 202 B 23	122
KAI 228	145
KAI 228:18–19	145–46
KAI 259	122
New Taima	145–146

Egyptian Texts
Udjahorresne Autobiog.   51, 139, 197–99, 216
Demotic Chron. (Rev.)   139, 197, 199–200
Pherendates Corresp.   197–99

Inscriptions from Asia Minor
Xanthos Trilingual   117, 143–45, 199
Gadatas   139, 148, 197, 199–200
Sardis   127

JOSEPHUS

Antiquities, x. 181ff.   44
Antiquities, xi. 8   14
Antiquities, xi. 11–13   96

Antiquities, xi. 1–119   88
Antiquities, xi. 297–301   205, 207
Contra Apionem, ii. 165   11